Inside
INTERVIEWING

International Advisory Board

Inside
INTERVIEWING
New Lenses,
New Concerns

James A. Holstein
Marquette University

Editors ## Jaber F. Gubrium
University of Missouri

SAGE Publications
International Educational and Professional Publisher
Thousand Oaks ■ London ■ New Delhi

For information:

Sage Publications, Inc.
2455 Teller Road
Thousand Oaks, California 91320
E-mail: order@sagepub.com

Sage Publications Ltd.
6 Bonhill Street
London EC2A 4PU
United Kingdom

Sage Publications India Pvt. Ltd.
B-42 Panchsheel Enclave
New Delhi 110 017 India

Printed in the United States of America

Library of Congress Cataloging-in-Publication Data

Inside interviewing: New lenses, new concerns / edited by James A. Holstein, Jaber F. Gubrium.
   p. cm.
  Includes bibliographical references and index.
  ISBN 0-7619-2851-0 (Paper)
  1. Interviewing. I. Holstein, James A. II. Gubrium, Jaber F.
H61.28.I57 2003
658.3'1124—dc21   2003000661

This book is printed on acid-free paper.

03 04 05 06 07 08 09 9 8 7 6 5 4 3 2 1

Acquisition Editor:	C. Deborah Laughton
Editorial Assistant:	Veronica Novak
Production Editor:	Sanford Robinson
Typesetter:	Christina Hill
Indexer:	Jean Casalegno
Cover Designer:	Michelle Lee

CONTENTS

PART II. TECHNICAL CONCERNS

PART III. ANALYTIC OPTIONS

INTRODUCTION

1

INSIDE INTERVIEWING: NEW LENSES, NEW CONCERNS

◆ James A. Holstein
Jaber F. Gubrium

As we move into the 21st century, interviewing is more common-place than ever. The number of television news programs, daytime talk shows, and newspaper articles that provide us with the results of interviews is incalculable. Internet polls beckon for our responses at every turn of the information superhighway. Considering more systematic and methodical efforts at information gathering, some estimate that interviews are involved in up to 90 percent of social science investigations (Briggs 1986). Few would dispute that interviewing is the most widely used technique for conducting systematic social inquiry; sociologists, psy-

chologists, anthropologists, psychiatrists, clinicians, administrators, politicians, and pollsters all use interviews as their "windows on the world" (Hyman et al. 1975).

Put simply, interviewing provides a way of generating empirical data about the social world by asking people to talk about their lives. In these terms, interviews are special conversations. While these conversations vary from highly structured, standardized, survey interviews, to semiformal guided conversations, to free-flowing informational exchanges, all interviews are interactional. The narratives that emerge may be as truncated as forced-choice survey responses or as elaborate as oral life histo-

AUTHORS' NOTE: Parts of this chapter are adapted from "From the Individual Interview to the Interview Society," originally published as the introduction to the *Handbook of Interview Research* (2002) edited by J. Gubrium and J. Holstein, Thousand Oaks, CA: Sage.

ries, but they're all constructed in situ, as a product of talk between interview participants.

The interview process itself has often been portrayed as straightforward and self-evident, even as it requires close attention to its technical execution. The interviewer coordinates a conversation designed to elicit desired information. He or she makes the initial contact, schedules the interview, designates its location, sets out the ground rules, and then questions the interviewee or "respondent." Questions extract answers in more-or-less anticipatable format until the interviewer's agenda is complete and the interview ends.

The respondent supplies the answers. She or he is generally aware of the routine and waits until questions are posed before answering. The respondent isn't obliged to raise questions or run the show; that's the interviewer's job. The respondent simply offers information from his or her personal cache of experiential knowledge. This is a relatively passive role, one defined and delimited by the interviewer's coordinating activity and the available repository of answers.

This scenario provides us with a familiar model of the asymmetric relationship that we recognize as interviewing. Except for technical nuances, most people are generally well-acquainted with either role in the encounter. Most of us, for example, would know what it means to interview someone and would be able to adequately manage the activity in its broad details, from start to finish. Likewise, most of us readily respond to demographic questionnaires, product-use surveys, public opinion polls, and health inventories without discernible difficulty; we're willing and able to "dish out" all sorts of information to virtual strangers about some of the most intimate aspects of our lives. Interviews are carried out time and again with little hesitation and hardly an afterthought. The individual interview has become a ubiquitous feature of everyday life.

But as familiar as it is, interviewing is also being revolutionized. While its form and application retain many of their familiar contours, growing sensitivities to agency, authority, reflexivity, and representation are transforming the way researchers are thinking about and using interviews and their data (see, for example, Denzin and Lincoln 2000). Indeed, these heightened sensitivities have raised questions about the very possibility of assembling knowledge in heretofore conventional ways. The growing influence of poststructuralist, postmodernist, constructionist, and ethnomethodological sensibilities has intensified our awareness that meaning is socially constituted. We're more cognizant than ever before that knowledge is created from the actions undertaken to obtain it (see, for example, Cicourel 1964, 1974; Garfinkel 1967). Treating interviewing as a social encounter in which knowledge is constructed means that the interview is more than a simple information-gathering operation; it's a site of, and occasion for, producing knowledge itself.

Charles Briggs (1986), for example, argues that interviews, like all other speech events, fundamentally, not incidentally, shape the form and content of what is said. Aaron Cicourel (1974) goes farther, maintaining that interviews virtually impose particular ways of understanding reality upon subjects' responses. The upshot is that interviewers are deeply and unavoidably implicated in creating meanings that ostensibly reside within respondents (also see Holstein and Gubrium 1995; Mishler 1986; Silverman 1993). Both parties to the interview are necessarily and unavoidably involved in this process. Meaning is not merely elicited by apt questioning, nor simply transported through respondent replies; it is actively and socially assembled in the interview encounter.

A heightened awareness of the constructedness of meaning is leading interview researchers to see their data gathering techniques in new light. A conspicuous self-consciousness in relation to the research process is providing social scientists with new lenses for viewing their own enterprise as well as the social world. While they present researchers with new realms of possibility and inquiry, these new lenses also bring new and more nuanced conceptual and methodological challenges into focus. The challenges present concerns related to virtually every aspect of the interview process.

Some of the challenges are epistemological. For example, the new lenses are focusing interview researchers on the various selves that are engaged in the interview exchange. Researchers are increasingly sensitive to the *subjects* who lurk behind the interview participants, and the varied roles they play in the production of knowledge. This, of course, prompts researchers to carefully theorize just who these subjects are, and how they affect the interview process. In turn, this provokes technical challenges as researchers deal with the nuances of information collection in relation to newly conceived subjects and subject positions concerning the research topics in question. Analytic challenges emerge simultaneously, as interview researchers contemplate just what their data might possibly mean and what they might make of them. Finally, concerns with how lives are represented—by interviewees as well as interview researchers—present new challenges to the ways in which knowledge might be conveyed.

The new lenses for viewing the interview process thus raise a host of new concerns, from the conceptual to the technical. They provide us with new visions of what goes on *inside* interviewing. But along with this new vision come complications; inside interviewing is a complex conceptual and technical environment. Gazing critically and self-consciously within, researchers have begun to tackle the seemingly endless array of new issues posed by contemporary research sensibilities. *Inside Interviewing* explores these complications and emerging challenges—those relating to research subjects, technical concerns, analytic options, and representational issues—by examining

the complexities that new lenses have revealed. We begin this chapter with a look back at the development of contemporary perspectives on the interview, then proceed through some important ramifications of a renewed look inside the contemporary interview.

◆ Developing Sensibilities

As familiar as it seems today, the interview, as a procedure for securing knowledge, is relatively new historically. Indeed, individuals have not always been viewed as important sources of knowledge about their own experience. Of course, we can imagine that particular forms of questioning and answering have been with us since the beginning of talk. As long as parental authority has existed, for example, fathers and mothers have undoubtedly questioned their children regarding their whereabouts; children have been expected to provide answers, not questions, in response. Similarly, suspects and prisoners have been interrogated for as long as suspicion and incarceration have been a part of human affairs. Healers, priests, employers, journalists, and many others seeking immediate, practical knowledge about everyday life have all undertaken interviewlike activity.

Nevertheless, not so long ago it would have seemed rather peculiar for an individual to approach a complete stranger and ask for permission to discuss personal matters. Daily life was more intimate; everyday business was conducted on a face-to-face basis between persons who were well acquainted with one another. According to Mark Benney and Everett Hughes (1956), there was a time when the interview simply didn't exist as a social form; they noted more than 40 years ago that "the interview [as we now refer to it] is a relatively new kind of encounter in the history of human relations" (p. 139). Benney and Hughes were not saying that the activity of asking and answering questions was new, but rather that information gathering did not always rely upon the interview encounter. Although centuries ago a father might have interrogated his children concerning their whereabouts, this was not interviewing as we have come to know it today. The interview emerged only when specific information-gathering roles were formalized. This encounter would hardly be recognizable in a world of close relationships where the stranger was more likely to signify danger and the unknown than to be understood as a neutral conduit for the transmission of personal knowledge (Benney and Hughes 1956).

MODERN INTERVIEWING

The modern interview changed all of this. Especially after World War II, with the emergence of the standardized survey interview, individuals became accustomed to offering information and opinions that had no immediate bearing on their lives and social relations. Individuals could forthrightly add their thoughts and feelings to the mix of "public opinion." Indeed, it became feasible for the first time for individuals to speak with strangers about all manner of thoughts concerning their lives, because these new strangers (that is, interviewers) didn't tell, at least in personally recognizable terms. Individuals—no matter how insignificant they might seem in the everyday scheme of things—came to be viewed as important elements of populations. Each person had a voice and it was imperative that each voice be heard, at least in principle. Seeking everyone's opinions, the interview has increasingly democratized experiential information.

David Riesman and Benney (1956) considered the interview format to be the product of a changing world of relationships, one that developed rapidly following the war years. The new era gradually accepted routine conversational exchanges between strangers; when people encountered interview situations, they were not immediately defensive about being asked for information about their lives, their associates, or their deepest sentiments, even though, in certain quarters, defensiveness was understandable because of perceived linkages between interviewing and oppression. Within this world, we have come to recognize easily two new roles associated with talking about oneself and one's life with strangers: the role of the interviewer and the role of the respondent—the centerpieces of the familiar interview.

This is an outgrowth of what Riesman and Benney called "the modern temper," a term that we take to have both cultural and interpersonal resonances. Culturally, it denotes a shared understanding that the individual has the wherewithal to offer a meaningful description of, or set of opinions about, his or her life. Individuals, in their own right, are accepted as significant commentators on their own experience; it is not just the "chief" community commentator who speaks for one and all, in other words, or the local representative of the commonwealth whose opinions are taken to express the thoughts and feelings of every mind and heart in the vicinity.

This modern temper is also interpersonal, in that it democratizes the interpretation of experience by providing a working space and means for expressing public opinion. Everyone—each individual—is taken to have significant views and feelings about life that are accessible to others who undertake to ask about them. As William James ([1892] 1961) noted at the end of the 19th century, this assumes that each and every individual has a sense of self that is owned and controlled by him- or herself, even if the self is socially formulated and interpersonally responsive. This self makes it possible for everyone to reflect meaningfully on individual experience and to enter into socially relevant dialogue about it. The modern temper has made it reasonable and acceptable to turn to a world of individuals, most of whom are likely to be strangers, as a way of understanding the social organization of experience.

Just as the interview itself is a recent development, the selection of ordinary individuals as sources of information and opinions is also relatively new (see Kent 1981; Oberschall 1965; Selvin 1985). As Pertti Alasuutari (1998) explains, it was not so long ago that when one wanted to know something important about society or social life, one invariably asked those considered to be "in the know." In contrast to what seems self-evident today—that is, questioning those individuals whose experiences are under consideration—the obvious and efficient choice for very early interviewers was to ask *informed* citizens to provide answers to their questions. Alasuutari provides an example from Anthony Oberschall's work:

> It was natural that the questions were posed to knowledgeable citizens, such as state officials or church ministers. In other words, they were informants in expert interviews. For instance, in a survey of agricultural laborers conducted in 1874-1875 in Germany (Oberschall 1965: 19-20), question No. 25 read: "Is there a tendency among laborers to save money in order to be able to buy their own plot of land later on? Does this tendency appear already among the unmarried workers or only after marriage?" . . . The modern survey would of course approach such questions quite differently. Instead of asking an informed person whether married or unmarried workers have a tendency to save money to buy their own plot of land, a sample of workers would be asked about their marital status, savings, and plans about how to use them. (Pp. 135-36)

Those considered to be knowledgeable in the subject matter under consideration, Alasuutari notes, were viewed as informants, not respondents, the latter being superfluous under the circumstances.

INDIVIDUALIZING KNOWLEDGE

The research consequence of the subsequent democratization of opinion was part of a trend toward increased surveillance in everyday life. The growing discourse of individuality combined with an increasingly widespread and efficient apparatus for information processing. Although interviewing and the resulting production of public opinion developed rapidly after World War II, the widespread surveillance of daily life and the deployment of the category of the individual had begun centuries earlier.

Michel Foucault's (1973, 1975, 1977, 1978) iconoclastic studies of the discursive organization of subjectivity shed fascinating light on the development of the concepts of the personal self and individuality. Time and again, in institutional contexts ranging from the medical clinic and the asylum to the prison, Foucault shows us how what he calls "technologies of the self" have transformed the way we view the sources and structure of our subjectivity (see Dreyfus and Rabinow 1982; Foucault 1988).

We use the term *subjectivity* here to indicate the type(s) of subject(s) that individuals and cultures might comprehend and embody. With respect to the interview, we are referring to the putative agent who stands behind the "facades" of interview participants, so to speak, the agent who is held practically and morally responsible for the participants' words and actions. Most of us are so familiar with the contemporary Western image of the individualized self as this agent that we find it difficult to comprehend alternative subjectivities. Clifford Geertz (1984), however, points out that this is "a rather peculiar idea within the context of the world's cultures" (p. 126). In other societies and historical periods, agency and responsibility have been articulated in relation to a variety of other social structures, such as the tribe, the clan, the lineage, the family, the community, and the monarch. The notion of the bounded, unique self, more or less integrated as the center of awareness, emotion, judgment, and action, is a very recent version of the subject.

Foucault offers us new insights into how this sense of subjectivity evolved. Technologies of the self, in Foucault's terms, are the concrete, socially and historically located institutional practices through which a relatively new sense of who and what we are as human beings was constructed. These practices advanced the notion that each and every one of us has an ordinary self—the idea being that each one could acceptably reflect on his or her individual experience, personally describe it, and communicate opinions about it and its surrounding world in his or her own terms. This transformed our sense of human beings as subjects. The now self-evident view that each of us has opinions of public significance became intelligible only within a discourse of individuality.

Foucault argues that the newly formed technologies of surveillance of the 18th and 19th centuries, the quintessential manifestation of which was Jeremy Bentham's all-seeing panopticon, did not just incorporate and accommodate the experiences of individual subjects who populated the contemporary social landscape, but, instead, entered into the construction of individual subjects in their own right. Foucault poignantly exemplifies this transformation in the opening pages of *Discipline and Punish* (1977), a book that is as much about the individuation of society as it is about "the birth of the prison" (its subtitle). In the opening pages, we cringe at a vivid account of the torture of a man condemned to death for attempting to assassinate King Louis XV of France. We despair as the man's body is flayed, burned, and drawn and quartered in public view. From contemporary commentary, Foucault (1977) describes the events:

> On 2 March 1757 Damiens the regicide was condemned "to make the *amende honorable* before the main door of the Church of Paris," where he was to be "taken and conveyed in a cart wearing nothing but a shirt, holding a torch of burning wax weighing two pounds"; then, "in the said cart, to the Place de Grève, where, on a scaffold that will be erected there, the flesh will be torn from his breasts, arms, thighs and calves with red-hot pincers, his right hand, holding the knife with which he committed the said parricide, burnt with sulphur, and, on those places where the flesh will be torn away, poured molten lead, boiling oil, burning resin, wax and sulphur melted together and then his body drawn and quartered by four horses and his limbs and body consumed by fire, reduced to ashes and his ashes thrown to the winds." (P. 3)

Foucault asks why criminals were subjected to such horrible bodily torture. Why were they made to beg for forgiveness in public spectacles? His answer is that the spectacle of torture was an event whose political culture was informed by a sense of the seamless relations among the body of the king (the crown), social control, and subjectivity. As all people were, Damiens was conceived literally and legally as a subject of the king; his body and soul were inseparable extensions of the crown. An assault on the body of the king had to be attacked in turn, as a red-hot iron might be used to cauterize a festering wound. The spectacle of torture did not revolve around an autonomous agent who was regarded as an independent subject with a self, feelings, opinions, and experiential reality uniquely his own. This might have caused others sympathetically to consider Damiens's treatment to be cruel and unusual punishment, to put it in today's terms.

The disposition of the times, however, offered no sympathy for what Damiens might have been "going through." In the eyes of others, Damiens's feelings and opinions had no standing apart from the man's station in relation to the sovereign. The spectacle of punishment rested on a discourse of knowledge and power that lodged all experiential truth in the sovereign's shared embodiment. As Hubert Dreyfus and Paul Rabinow (1982) explain: "The figure of torture brings together a complex of power, truth, and bodies. The atrocity of torture was an enactment of power that also revealed truth. Its application on the body of the criminal was an act of revenge and an art" (p. 146). The idea that a thinking, feeling, consequential subject occupied the body of the criminal was simply beyond the pale of contemporary understanding. Individuality, as we know it today, did not exist as a recognizable social form.

A few pages later in *Discipline and Punish,* Foucault presents the new subject who comes into being as part of a discourse that is more in tune with the modern temper. Discussing the evolution of penal reform, he describes the emergence of the "house of young prisoners" in Paris a mere 80 years after Damiens's death. Torture as a public spectacle has gradually disappeared. The "gloomy festival of punishment" is dying out, along with the accused's agonizing plea for pardon. It has been replaced by a humanizing regime, informed by a discourse of the independent, thinking subject whose criminality is correctable. Rehabilitation is replacing retribution. Scientific methods of scrutiny and courses of instruction are viewed as the means for returning the criminal to right reason and back to the proper fold of society. The subject is no longer a selfless appendage of a larger entity; this is a new agent, one with a mind and sentiments of his or her own. With the proper regimen, this new agent is incited to individual self-scrutiny and responds to corrective action.

In time, this same subject would duly offer his or her opinions and sentiments within the self-scrutinizing regimens of what Foucault calls "governmentality," the archipelago of surveillance practices suffusing modern life. As James Miller (1993: 299) points out, governmentality extends well beyond the political and penal to include pedagogical, spiritual, and religious dimensions (see also Garland 1997). If Bentham's original panopticon was an efficient form of prison observation, panopticism in the modern temper becomes the widespread self-scrutiny that "governs" all aspects of everyday life in the very commonplace questions and answers posed about ourselves in both our inner thoughts and our public expressions. These are seemingly daily inquiries about what we personally think and feel about every conceivable topic, including our deepest sentiments and most secret actions.

We can readily view the individual interview as part of modern governmentality, impressed upon us by myriad inquiries into our lives. Indeed, the interview may be seen as one of the 20th century's most distinctive technologies of the self. In particular, it gives an "objective," "scientific" cast to the notion of the individual self, terms of reference that resolutely echo modern times. As Nikolas Rose (1990, 1997) has shown in the context of the psychological sciences, the private self, along with its descriptive data, was invented right along with the technologies we now associate with measurement.

"Scientific surveillance" such as psychological testing, case assessments, and, of course, individual interviews of all kinds have created the experiencing and informing respondent we now take for granted. The category of "the person" now identifies the self-reflective constituents of society (see Carrithers, Collins, and Lukes 1985; Lidz 1976); if we want to know what the social world is like, we now ask its individual inhabitants. The individual interview on a personal scale and the social survey on the societal level serve as democratizing agents, giving voice to individuals and, in the process, formulating public knowledge and opinion.

LEARNING FROM STRANGERS

The title of Robert Weiss's (1994) book on interviewing, *Learning from Strangers,* points to the shared expectations that surround the face-to-face experience of interviewing, as the book lays out "the art and method of qualitative interview studies." Although qualitative interviews especially are sometimes conducted with acquaintances, much of Weiss's advice on how an interviewer should proceed is based on the premise that the interviewer does not know the respondent. Behind each bit of advice about how to interview effectively is the understanding that each and every stranger-respondent is someone worth listening to. The respondent is someone who can provide detailed descriptions of his or her thoughts, feelings, and activities, if the interviewer asks and listens carefully enough. The trick, in Weiss's judgment, is for the interviewer to present a caring and concerned attitude, expressed within a well-planned and encouraging format. The aim of the interviewer is to derive, as objectively as possible, the respondent's *own* opinions of the subject matter in question, information that the respondent will readily offer and elaborate when the circumstances are conducive to his or her doing so and the proper methods are applied.

The full range of individual knowledge is potentially accessible, according to Weiss; the interview is a virtual window on experience, a kind of universal panopticon. In answering the question of why we interview, Weiss offers a compelling portrayal of the acquisition of knowledge:

Interviewing gives us access to the observations of others. Through interviewing we can learn about places we have not been and could not go and about settings in which we have not lived. If we have the right informants, we can learn about the quality of neighborhoods or what happens in families or how organizations set their goals. Interviewing can inform us about the nature of social life. We can learn about the work of occupations and how people fashion careers, about cultures and the values they sponsor, and about the

challenges people confront as they lead their lives.

We can learn also, through interviewing, about people's interior experiences. We can learn what people perceived and how they interpreted their perceptions. We can learn how events affect their thoughts and feelings. We can learn the meanings to them of their relationships, their families, their work, and their selves. We can learn about all the experiences, from joy through grief, that together constitute the human condition. (P. 1)

The opportunities for knowing even strangers by way of their opinions are now ubiquitous. We find interviews virtually everywhere. We have come a very long way from the days when individuals' experiences and voices simply didn't matter, a long way from Damiens's "unheard" cries. The interview itself has created, as well as tapped into, the vast world of individual experience and knowledge that now constitutes the substance of everyday life.

◆ The Mediation of Contemporary Life

Interviewing of all kinds mediates contemporary life. Think of how much we learn about today's world by way of interviews conducted across a broad spectrum of venues, well beyond research practice. Interviews, for example, are a source of popular celebrity and notoriety. Television interview host Larry King introduces us to politicians and power brokers who not only share their thoughts, feelings, and opinions with a mass audience but cultivate their celebrity status in the process. This combines with programming devoted to exposing the deepest personal, not just political or social, sentiments of high-profile figures. Celebrity news commentators/interviewers like Barbara Walters plumb the emotional depths of stars and pundits from across the media spectrum. To this, add the likes of talk-show hosts Oprah Winfrey, Montel Williams, Jenny Jones, and Jerry Springer, who daily invite ordinary men and women, the emotionally tortured, and the behaviorally bizarre to "spill their guts" in front of millions of television viewers. Referring to all of these, the interview is becoming the experiential conduit par excellence of the electronic age. And this is only the tip of the iceberg, as questions and answers fly back and forth on the Internet, where chat rooms are now as intimate as back porches and bedrooms.

The ubiquity and significance of the interview in our daily lives has prompted David Silverman (1997) to suggest that "perhaps we all live in what might be called an 'interview society,' in which interviews seem central to making sense of our lives" (p. 248; see also Silverman 1993). Silverman (1997) identifies three conditions required by an interview society. First, an interview society requires a particular informing subjectivity, "the emergence of the self as a proper object of narration." Societies with forms of collective or cosmic subjectivity, for example, do not provide the practical basis for learning from strangers. This is possible only in societies where there is a prevalent and shared sense that any individual has the potential to be a respondent and, as such, has something meaningful to offer when asked to do so.

Second, Silverman points to the need for an information-gathering apparatus he calls the "technology of the confessional." In other words, an interview society needs a practical means for securing the communicative by-product of "confession." This, Silverman (1997) points out, should commonly extend to friendship not only "with the policeman, but with the priest, the teacher, and the 'psy' professional" (p. 248).

Third, and perhaps most important, an interview society requires that a mass technology be readily available. An interview society is not the product of the age-old

medical interview, or of the long-standing practice of police interrogation; rather, it requires that an interviewing establishment be recognizably in place throughout society. Virtually everyone should be familiar with the goals of interviewing as well as what it takes to conduct an interview.

Silverman argues that many contemporary societies have met these conditions, some more than others. The mass media, human service professionals, and researchers all rely extensively on interviews. Internet surveys now provide instant questions and answers about every imaginable subject; we are asked to state our inclinations and opinions regarding everything from presidential candidates to which characters on TV serials should be retained or ousted. The interview society, it seems, has firmly arrived, is well, and is flourishing as a leading context for addressing the subjective contours of daily living.

It would therefore be a mistake to treat the interview as simply a research procedure. The interview is part and parcel of our society and culture. It is not just a way of obtaining information about who and what we are; it is now an integral, constitutive feature of our everyday lives. Indeed, it is at the very heart of what we have become and could possibly be as individuals.

◆ The Subjects Behind Interview Participants

In a society replete with interviews, increasing concern with individual experience has prompted a corresponding awareness of the various subjects who populate the interview encounter (see Holstein and Gubrium 1995). Recently, researchers have begun to explore inside the interview, seeking answers to myriad new questions: What does it mean to be an interviewer? What does it mean to be a respondent? What do participants presume about one another, and the interview process itself? From where does knowledge emerge, and whose knowledge is it anyway? These are but a few of the challenges and complexities that new lenses on interviewing have revealed.

Let's begin to unpack some of these complications by examining competing visions of the subjects who are imagined to stand behind interview participants. Regardless of the type of interview, there is always a working model of the subject lurking behind the persons assigned the roles of interviewer and respondent (Holstein and Gubrium 1995). By virtue of the kinds of subjects we project, we confer varying senses of epistemological agency upon interviewers and respondents. These, in turn, influence the ways we proceed technically, as well as our understanding of the relative validity of the information that is produced.

As we noted at the outset, interviewing typically has been viewed as an asymmetrical encounter in which an interviewer solicits information from an interviewee, who relatively passively responds to the interviewer's inquiries. This commonsensical, if somewhat oversimplified, view suggests that those who want to find out about another person's feelings, thoughts, or activities merely have to ask the right questions and the other's "reality" will be revealed. Studs Terkel, the legendary journalistic and sociological interviewer, makes the process sound elementary; he claims that he merely turns on his tape recorder and asks people to talk. Using his classic study *Working* (1972) as an example, Terkel claims that his questions merely evoke responses that interviewees are all too ready to share:

> There were questions, of course. But they were casual in nature . . . the kind you would ask while having a drink with someone; the kind he would ask you. . . . In short, it was a conversation. In time, the sluice gates of damned up hurts and dreams were open. (P. xxv)

As unsophisticated and guileless as it sounds, this image is common in interviewing practice. The image is one of "mining" or "prospecting" for the facts and feelings residing within the respondent. Of course, a highly sophisticated technology tells researcher/prospectors how to ask questions, what sorts of questions not to ask, the order in which to ask them, and ways to avoid saying things that might spoil, contaminate, or bias the data. The basic model, however, locates valued information inside the respondent and assigns the interviewer the task of somehow extracting it.

THE PASSIVE SUBJECT BEHIND THE RESPONDENT

In this rather conventional view, the subjects behind respondents are basically conceived as passive *vessels of answers* for experiential questions put to them by interviewers. Subjects are repositories of facts, feelings, and the related particulars of experience. They hold the answers to demographic questions, such as age, gender, race, occupation, and socioeconomic status. They contain information about social networks, including household composition, friendship groups, circles of care, and other relationships. These repositories also hold a treasure trove of experiential data pertinent to beliefs, feelings, and activities.

The vessel-like subject behind the respondent passively possesses information the interviewer wants to know; the respondent merely conveys, for better or worse, what the subject already possesses. Occasionally, such as with sensitive interview topics or with recalcitrant respondents, interviewers acknowledge that the task may be especially difficult. Nonetheless, the information is viewed, in principle, as the uncontaminated contents of the subject's vessel of answers. The knack is to formulate questions and provide an atmosphere conducive to open and undistorted communication between interviewer and respondent.

Much of the methodological literature on interviewing deals with the facets of these intricate matters. The vessel-of-answers view leads interviewers to be careful in how they ask questions, lest their method of inquiry bias what lies within the subject. This perspective has prompted the development of myriad procedures for obtaining unadulterated facts and details, most of which rely upon interviewer and question neutrality. Successful implementation of disinterested practices elicits objective truths from the vessel of answers. Validity results from the successful application of these techniques.

In the vessel-of-answers model, the image of the subject is not of an agent engaged in the production of knowledge. If the interviewing process goes "by the book" and is nondirectional and unbiased, respondents can validly proffer information that subjects presumably merely store within. Contamination emanates from the interview setting, its participants, and their interaction, not from the subject, who, under ideal conditions, is capable of providing accurate, authentic reports.

THE PASSIVE SUBJECT BEHIND THE INTERVIEWER

This model of the respondent evokes a complementary model of the subject behind the interviewer. Although not totally passive, the interviewer/subject nonetheless stands apart from the actual "data" of the field; he or she merely collects what is already there. To be sure, the collection process can be arduous, but the objective typically is to tap into information without unduly disturbing—and, therefore, biasing or contaminating—the respondent's vessel of answers. If it is not quite like Terkel's "sluice gates" metaphor, it still resembles turning on a spigot; the interviewer's role is limited to releasing what is already in place.

The interviewer, for example, is expected to keep the respondent's vessel of answers in plain view but to avoid shaping the information that is extracted. Put simply, this involves the interviewer's control-

ling him- or herself so as not to influence what the passive interview subject will communicate. The interviewer must discard serious self-consciousness; the interviewer must avoid any action that would imprint his or her presence onto the respondent's reported experience. The interviewer must resist supplying particular frames of reference for the respondent's answers. To the extent such frameworks appropriately exist, they are viewed as embedded in the subject's world behind the respondent, not behind the researcher. If the interviewer is to be at all self-conscious, this is technically limited to his or her being alert to the possibility that he or she may be contaminating or otherwise unduly influencing the research process.

Interviewers are generally expected to keep their "selves" out of the interview process. *Neutrality* is the byword. Ideally, the interviewer uses his or her interpersonal skills merely to encourage the expression of, but not to help construct, the attitudes, sentiments, and information in question. In effect, the image of the passive subject behind the interviewer is one of a facilitator. As skilled as the interviewer might be in practice, all that he or she appropriately does in principle is to promote the expression of the actual attitudes and information that lie in waiting in the respondent's vessel of answers.

In exerting control in this way, the interviewer limits his or her involvement in the interview to a specific preordained role—which can be quite scripted—that is constant from one interview to another. Should the interviewer go out of control, so to speak, and introduce anything but variations on specified questions into the interview, the passive subject behind the interviewer is methodologically violated and neutrality is compromised. It is not this passive subject who is the problem, but rather the interviewer who has not adequately regulated his or her conduct so as to facilitate the expression of respondent information.

ACTIVATING
INTERVIEW SUBJECTS

As researchers have become more aware of the interview as a site for the production of meaning, they have increasingly come to appreciate the activity of the subjects projected behind both the respondent and the interviewer. The interview is being reconceptualized as an occasion for purposefully animated participants to *construct* versions of reality interactionally rather than merely purvey data (see Holstein and Gubrium 1995). This trend reflects an increasingly pervasive appreciation for the constitutive character of social interaction and of the constructive role played by active subjects in authoring their experiences.

Sentiments along these lines have been building for some time across diverse disciplines. Nearly a half century ago, for example, Ithiel de Sola Pool (1957), a prominent critic of public opinion polling, argued presciently that the dynamic, communicative contingencies of the interview literally activated respondents' opinions. Every interview, Pool suggested, is an "interpersonal drama with a developing plot" (p. 193). The metaphor conveys a far more active sense of interview participation than the "prospector for meaning" suggests. As Pool indicated:

> The social milieu in which communication takes place [during interviews] modifies not only what a person dares to say but even what he thinks he chooses to say. And these variations in expression cannot be viewed as mere deviations from some underlying "true" opinion, for there is no neutral, non-social, uninfluenced situation to provide that baseline. (P. 192)

Conceiving of the interview in this fashion casts interview participants as virtual *practitioners* of everyday life who work constantly to discern and designate the recognizable and orderly features of the experience under consideration. It transforms the subject behind the respondent from a repository of information and opinions or a wellspring of emotions into a productive source of knowledge. From the time a researcher identifies a research topic, through respondent selection, questioning and answering, and, finally, the interpretation of responses, interviewing is a concerted interactional project. Indeed, the subject behind the respondent now, more or less, becomes an imagined product of the project. Working within the interview itself, subjects are fleshed out, rationally and emotionally, in relation to the give-and-take of the interview process, the interview's research purposes, and its surrounding social contexts.

Construed as active, the subject behind the respondent not only holds the details of a life's experience but, in the very process of offering them up to the interviewer, constructively shapes the information. The active respondent can hardly "spoil" what he or she is, in effect, subjectively constructing in the interview process. Rather, the activated subject pieces experiences together before, during, and after occupying the respondent role. This subject is always making meaning, regardless of whether he or she is actually being interviewed.

An active subject behind the interviewer is also implicated in the production of knowledge. His or her participation in the process is not viewed in terms of standardization or constraint; neutrality is not figured to be necessary or achievable. One cannot very well taint knowledge if that knowledge is not conceived as existing in some pure form apart from the circumstances of its production. The active subject behind the interviewer thus becomes a necessary, practical counterpart to the active subject behind the respondent. Interviewer and, ultimately, researcher contributions to the information produced in interviews are not viewed as incidental or immaterial. Nor is interviewer participation considered in terms of contamination. Rather, the subject behind the interviewer is seen as actively and unavoidably engaged in the interactional co-construction of the interview's content.

Interactional contingencies influence the construction of the active subjectivities of the interview. Especially important here are the varied subject positions articulated in the interview process, which need to be taken into account in the interpretation of interview material. For example, an interview project might center on the quality of care and quality of life of nursing home residents (see Gubrium 1993). This might be part of a study relating to the national debate about the organization and value of home versus institutional care. Careful attention to the way participants link substantive matters with biographical ones can vividly reveal a highly active subject. For instance, a nursing home resident might speak animatedly during an interview about the quality of care in her facility, asserting that, "for a woman, it ultimately gets down to feelings," invoking an emotional subject. Another resident might coolly and methodically list specifics about her facility's quality of care, never once mentioning her gender or her feelings about the care she receives. Offering her own take on the matter, this respondent might state that "getting emotional" over "these things" clouds clear judgment, implicating a rationalized subject. When researchers take this active subject into account, what is otherwise a contradictory and inconclusive data set is transformed into the meaningful, intentionally crafted responses of quite active respondents.

The standpoint from which information is offered continually unfolds in relation to ongoing interview interaction. In speaking of the quality of care, for example, nursing home residents, as interview respondents, not only offer substantive thoughts and feelings pertinent to the topic under consideration but simultaneously and continuously monitor who they are in relation to themselves and to the person questioning them. For example, prefacing her remarks about the quality of life in her facility with the statement "Speaking as a woman," a nursing home resident actively informs the interviewer that she is to be heard as a woman, not as someone else—not a mere resident, cancer patient, or abandoned mother. If and when she subsequently comments, "If I were a man in this place," the resident frames her thoughts and feelings about the quality of life differently, producing an alternative subject: the point of view of a man as spoken by a female respondent. The respondent is clearly working up experiential identities as the interview progresses.

Because the respondent's subjectivity and related experience are continually being assembled and modified, the "truth" value of interview responses cannot be judged simply in terms of whether those responses match what lies in an ostensibly objective vessel of answers. Rather, the value of interview data lies both in their meanings and in how meanings are constructed. These *what* and *how* matters go hand in hand, as two components of practical meaning-making action (see Gubrium and Holstein 1997). The entire process is fueled by the reality-constituting contributions of all participants; interviewers, too, are similarly implicated in the co-construction of the subject positions from which they ask the questions at hand (see in this volume Schaeffer and Maynard, Chapter 11; Briggs, Chapter 24).

The multiple subjects that could possibly stand behind interview participants add several layers of complication to the interview process as well as to the analysis of interview data. Decidedly different procedural strictures are required to accommodate and account for alternating subjects. Indeed, the very question of what constitutes or serves as data critically relates to these issues of subjectivity. What researchers choose to highlight when they analyze interview responses flows directly from how the issues are addressed (see Gubrium and Holstein 1997; see also Baker, Chapter 19, this volume).

◆ Empowering Respondents

New lenses on what it means to interview and to analyze interview material have led to far-reaching innovations in research (see Riessman, Chapter 16; Cándida Smith, Chapter 17; Ellis and Berger, Chapter 23). They have also promoted the view that the interview society is not only the by-product of statistically summarized survey data, but is constituted by all manner of alternative interview encounters and information, the diverse agendas of which variably enter into "data" production. In the process, the political dimensions of the interview process have been critically underscored (see Briggs, Chapter 24, this volume).

The respondent's voice has taken on particular urgency, as we can hear in Eliot Mishler's (1986) poignant discussion of the empowerment of interview respondents. Uncomfortable with the evolution of the interview into a highly controlled, asymmetrical conversation dominated by the researcher (see Kahn and Cannell 1957; Maccoby and Maccoby 1954), Mishler challenges the assumptions and implications behind the "standardized" interview. His aim is to bring the respondent more fully and actively into the picture, to make the respondent more of an equal partner in the interview conversation.

Following a critique of standardized interviewing, Mishler (1986) offers a lengthy discussion of his alternative perspective, one that questions the need for strict control of the interview encounter. The approach, in part, echoes our discussion of the activation of interview participants. Mishler suggests that rather than conceiving of the interview as a form of stimulus and response, we might better view it as an interactional accomplishment. Noting that interview participants not only ask and answer questions in interviews but simultaneously engage in other speech activities, Mishler turns our attention to what the participants, in effect, are doing with words

when they engage each other. He makes the point this way:

> Defining interviews as speech events or speech activities, as I do, marks the fundamental contrast between the standard antilinguistic, stimulus-response model and an alternative approach to interviewing as discourse between speakers. Different definitions in and of themselves do not constitute different practices. Nonetheless, this new definition alerts us to the features of interviews that hitherto have been neglected. (Pp. 35-36)

The key phrase here is "discourse between speakers." Mishler directs us to the integral and inexorable speech activities in which even survey interview participants engage as they ask and answer questions (see Schaeffer and Maynard, Chapter 11, this volume). Informed by a conversation-analytic perspective (see Sacks 1992; Sacks, Schegloff, and Jefferson 1974), he points to the discursive machinery apparent in interview transcripts. Highlighting evidence of the ways the interviewer and the respondent *mutually* monitor each other's speech exchanges, Mishler shows how the participants ongoingly and jointly construct in words their senses of the developing interview agenda. He notes, for example, that even token responses by the interviewer, such as "Hm hm," can serve as confirmatory markers that the respondent is on the "right" track for interview purposes. But, interestingly enough, not much can be done to eliminate token responses, given that a fundamental rule of conversational exchange is that turns must be taken in the unfolding interview process. To eliminate tokens or to refuse to take one's turn, however minimally, is, in effect, to stop the conversation, hence the interview. The dilemma here is striking in that it points to the practical need for interview participants to be linguistically animated, not just standardized and passive, in order to complete the interview conversation.

It goes without saying that this introduces us to a pair of subjects behind the interviewer and the respondent who are more conversationally active than standardization would imply, let alone tolerate. Following a number of conversation-analytic and linguistic arguments (Cicourel 1967, 1982; Gumperz 1982; Hymes 1967; Sacks et al. 1974), Mishler (1986) explains that each and every point in the series of speech exchanges that constitute an interview is, in effect, open to interactional work, activity that constructs communicative sense out of the participants as well as the subject matter under consideration. Thus, in contrast to the modeled asymmetry of the standardized interview, there is considerable communicative equality and interdependence in the speech activities of all interviewing, where participants invariably engage in the "joint construction of meaning," no matter how asymmetrical the informing model might seem:

> The discourse of the interview is jointly constructed by interviewer and respondent. . . . Both questions and responses are formulated in, developed through, and shaped by the discourse between interviewers and respondents. . . . An adequate understanding of interviews depends on recognizing how interviewers reformulate questions and how respondents frame answers in terms of their reciprocal understanding as meanings emerge during the course of an interview. (P. 52)

THE ISSUE OF "OWNING" NARRATIVE

Mishler's entry into the linguistic and conversation-analytic fray was fundamentally motivated by his desire to valorize the respondent's perspective and experience. This was, to some extent, a product of Mishler's long-standing professional interest in humanizing the doctor-patient encounter. His earlier book *The Discourse of*

Medicine: Dialectics of Medical Interviews (1984) is important in that it shows how medical interviews can unwittingly but systematically abrogate the patient's sense of his or her own illness even in the sincerest doctor's search for medical knowledge. As an alternative, Mishler advocates more open-ended questions, minimal interruptions of patient accounts, and the use of patients' own linguistic formulations to encourage their own articulations of illness. Similarly, in the context of the research interview, Mishler urges us to consider ways that interviewing might be designed so that the respondent's voice comes through in greater detail, as a way of paying greater attention to respondent relevancies.

According to Mishler, this turns us forthrightly to respondents' stories. His view is that experience comes to us in the form of narratives. When we communicate our experiences to each other, we do so by storying them. When, in turn, we encourage elaboration, we commonly use such narrative devices as "Go on" and "Then what happened?" to prompt further story-like communication. It would be difficult to imagine how an experience of any kind could be conveyed except in narrative format, in terms that structure events into distinct plots, themes, and forms of characterization. Consequently, according to this view, we must leave our research efforts open to respondents' stories if we are to understand respondents' experiences in, and on, their own terms, leading to less formal control in the interview process.

Applied to the research interview, the "radical transformation of the traditional approach to interviewing" (Mishler 1986: 117) serves to empower respondents. This resonates with a broadening concern with what is increasingly referred to as the respondent's *own* voice or authentic story. Although *story, narrative,* and the respondent's *voice* are the leading terms of reference, an equally key, yet unexplicated, usage is the term *own.* It appears throughout Mishler's discussion of empowerment, yet he gives it hardly any attention.

Consider several applications of the term *own* in Mishler's (1986) research interviewing text. In introducing a chapter titled "The Empowerment of Respondents," he writes, "I will be concerned primarily with the impact of different forms of practice on respondents' modes of understanding themselves and the world, on the possibility of their acting in terms of their *own* interests, on social scientists' ways of working and theorizing, and the social functions of scientific knowledge" (pp. 117-18; emphasis added). Further along, Mishler explains, "Various attempts to restructure the interviewee-interviewer relationship so as to empower respondents are designed to encourage them to find and speak in their *own* 'voices' " (p. 118; emphasis added). Finally, in pointing to the political potential of narrative, Mishler boldly flags the ownership in question: "To be empowered is not only to speak in one's *own* voice and to tell one's *own* story, but to apply the understanding arrived at to action in accord with one's *own* interests" (p. 119; emphasis added).

Mishler is admittedly being persuasive. Just as in his earlier book on medical interviews he encourages what Michael Balint (1964) and others (see Silverman 1987) have come to call *patient-centered medicine,* in his research interview book he advocates what might be called *respondent-centered research.* Mishler constructs a preferred version of the subject behind the respondent, one that allegedly gives voice to the respondent's own story. The image is one of a respondent who owns his or her experience, who, on his or her own, can narrate the story if given the opportunity. It is a story that is uniquely the respondent's in that only his or her own voice can articulate it authentically; any other voice or format would apparently detract from what this subject behind the respondent more genuinely and competently does on his or her own. Procedurally, the point is to provide the narrative opportunity for this ownership to be expressed, to reveal what presumably lies within.

But valorizing the individual's ownership of his or her story is a mere step away from seeing the subject as a vessel of answers. As we discussed earlier, this subject is passive and, wittingly or not, taken to be a mere repository of information, opinion, and sentiment. More subtly, perhaps, the subject behind the respondent who "owns" his or her story is viewed as virtually possessing what we seek to know about. Mishler's advice is that we provide respondents with the opportunity to convey these stories to us on their own terms rather than deploy predesignated categories or other structured formats for doing so. This, Mishler claims, empowers respondents.

Nevertheless, the passive vessel of answers is still there in its essential detail. It is now more deeply embedded in the subject, perhaps, but it is as passively secured in the inner reaches of the respondent as the vessel informing the survey respondent's subjectivity. We might say that the subject behind the standardized interview respondent is a highly rationalized version of the romanticized subject envisioned by Mishler, one who harbors his or her own story. Both visions are rhetorics of subjectivity that have historically been used to account for the "truths" of experience. Indeed, we might say that the standardized interview produces a different narrative of experience than does the empowered interviewing style that Mishler and others advocate. This is not meant to disparage, but only to point out that when the question of subjectivity is raised, the resulting complications of the interview are as epistemological as they are invidious.

It is important to emphasize that the ownership in question results from a preferred subjectivity, not from an experiential subject that is more essential than all other subjects. It is, as Silverman and his associates remind us, a romanticized discourse of its own and, although it has contributed immensely to our understanding of the variety of "others" we can be, it does not empower absolutely (see Silverman 1987, 1993; Atkinson and Silverman 1997). Rather, it empowers in relation to the kinds of stories that one can ostensibly own, that would seem to be genuine, or that are otherwise accountably recognized as fitting or authentic to oneself in the particular times and places they are conveyed.

A DISCOURSE OF EMPOWERMENT

Invoking a discourse of empowerment is a way of giving both rhetorical and practical spin to how we conduct interviews. Like all discourses, the discourse of individual empowerment deploys preferred terms of reference. For example, in the discourse of the standardized survey interview, the interview encounter is asymmetrical and the operating principle is control. Participants have different functions: one side asks questions and records information, and the other side provides answers to the questions asked. Procedurally, the matter of control is centered on keeping these functions and their roles separate. Accordingly, an important operating rule is that the interviewer does not provide answers or offer opinions. Conversely, the respondent is encouraged to answer questions, not ask them. Above all, the language of the enterprise locates knowledge within the respondent, but control rests with the interviewer.

The terms of reference change significantly when the interview is more symmetrical or, as Mishler puts it, when the respondent is empowered. The interviewer and respondent are referred to jointly as interview *participants,* highlighting their collective contribution to the enterprise. This works against asymmetry, emphasizing a more fundamental sense of the shared task at hand, which now becomes a form of "collaboration" in the production of meaning. One procedure for setting this tone is to make it clear that all participants in the interview can effectively raise questions related to the topics under consideration. Equally important, everyone should understand that answers are not meant to be con-

clusive but instead serve to further the agenda for discussion. The result, then, is more of a team effort, rather than a division of labor, even though the discourse of empowerment still aims to put the narrative ball in the respondent's court, so to speak.

Assiduously concerned with the need to "redistribute power" in the interview encounter, Mishler (1986) argues compellingly for the more equalized relationship he envisions. Seeking a redefinition of roles, he describes what he has in mind:

> These types of role redefinitions may be characterized briefly by the following terms referring respectively to the relationship between interviewee and interviewer as informant and reporter, as research collaborators, and as learner/actor and advocate. Taking on the roles of each successive pair in this series involves a more comprehensive and more radical transformation of the power relationship inherent in traditional roles, and each succeeding pair of roles relies on and absorbs the earlier one. (Pp. 122-23)

The use of the prefix *co-* is commonplace in such discussions, further signaling symmetry. Participants often become "coparticipants" and, of course, the word *collaboration* speaks for itself in this context. Some authors even refer to the interview encounter as a "conversational partnership" (Rubin and Rubin 1995).

Mishler's discourse of collaboration and empowerment extends to the representation of interview material, taking *co-* into new territory. In discussing the role of the advocate, for instance, Mishler describes Kai Erikson's (1976) activity as a researcher hired by attorneys representing the residents affected by the 1972 dam collapse in the Buffalo Creek valley of West Virginia. Erikson was advocating for the surviving residents, several of whom he interviewed, but not the local coal company from which they were seeking damages. The researcher and the sponsor clearly collaborated with each other in representing interview materials.

Others are not as forthrightly political in their corepresentations. Laurel Richardson (2002), for example, discusses alternative textual choices in relation to the presentation of the respondent's "own" story. Research interviews, she reminds us, are usually conducted for research audiences. Whether they are closed- or open-ended, the questions and answers are formulated with the analytic interests of researchers in mind. Sociologists, for example, may wish to consider how gender, race, or class background shapes respondents' opinions, so they will tailor questions and interpret answers in these terms. Ultimately, researchers will represent interview material in the frameworks and languages of their research concerns and in disciplinary terms. But, as Richardson points out, respondents might not figure that their experiences or opinions are best understood that way. Additionally, Richardson asks us whether the process of coding interview responses for research purposes itself disenfranchises respondents, transforming their narratives into terms foreign to what their original sensibilities might have been (see also Briggs, Chapter 24, this volume).

Richardson suggests that a radically different textual form can help us to represent the respondent's experience more inventively, and authentically. Using poetry rather than prose, for example, capitalizes on poetry's culturally understood role of evoking and making meaning, not just conveying it. This extends to poetry's alleged capacity to communicate meaning where prose is said to be inadequate, in the way that folk poetry is used in some quarters to represent the ineffable (see Gubrium 1988). It is not uncommon, for instance, for individuals to say that plain words can't convey what they mean or that they simply cannot put certain experiences into words, something that, ironically, poetry might accomplish in poetic terms.

How, then, are such experiences and their opinions to be communicated in interviews? Must some respondents literally sing the blues, for example, as folks traditionally have done in the rural South of the United States? Should some experiences be "performed," rather than simply translated into text? Do mere retellings of others' experiences compromise the ability of those who experience them to convey the "scenic presence" of the actual experiences in their lives? A number of researchers take such issues to heart and have been experimenting, for several years now, with alternative representational forms that they believe can convey respondents' experience more on, if not in, their own terms (see Clifford and Marcus 1986; Ellis and Flaherty 1992; Ellis and Bochner 1996; Reed-Danahay 1997; see also in this volume Ellis and Berger, Chapter 23). The border between fact and fiction itself is being explored for its empowering capacity, taking empowerment's informing discourse firmly into the realm of literature.

◆ Voice and Ownership

When we empower the respondent (or the informing coparticipant) in the interview encounter, we establish a space for the respondent's *own* story to be heard—at least this is the reasoning behind Mishler's and others' aims in this regard. But questions do arise in relation to the voices we listen to when we provide respondents the opportunity to convey their own stories. Whose voices do we hear? From where do respondents obtain the material they communicate to us in interviews? Is there always only one story for a given respondent to tell, or can there be several to choose from? If the latter, the question can become, Which among these is most tellable under the circumstances? And, as if these questions weren't challenging enough, do the queries themselves presume that they are answerable in straightforward terms, or do answers to them turn in different directions and get worked out in the very course of the interview in narrative practice?

SUBJECT POSITIONS AND RELATED VOICES

An anecdote from Jaber Gubrium's doctoral supervision duties speaks to the heart of these issues. Gubrium was serving on the dissertation committee of a graduate student who was researching substance abuse among pharmacists. The student was especially keen to allow the pharmacists being interviewed to convey in their own words their experiences of illicitly using drugs, seeking help for their habits, and going through rehabilitation. He hoped to understand how those who "should know better" would account for what happened to them.

When the interviews were completed, the student analyzed the interview data thematically and presented the themes in the dissertation along with individual accounts of experience. Interestingly, several of the themes identified in the pharmacists' stories closely paralleled the familiar recovery rubrics of self-help groups such as Alcoholics Anonymous (A.A.) and Narcotics Anonymous (N.A.). Gubrium noted this, and it turned out that many, if not all, of the pharmacists had participated in these recovery groups and evidently had incorporated the groups' ways of narrating the substance abuse experience into their "own" stories. For example, respondents spoke of the experience of "hitting bottom" and organized the trajectory of the recovery process in relation to that very important low point in their lives. Gubrium raised the issue of the extent to which the interview material could be analyzed as the pharmacists' "own" stories as opposed to the stories of these recovery programs. At a doctoral committee meeting, he asked, "Whose voice do we hear when these pharmacists tell their stories? Their own or N.A.'s?" He asked, in effect, whether the stories belonged to these individuals or to the organizations that promulgated their discourse.

The issue of voice is important because it points to the subject who is assumed to be responding in interviews (Gubrium 1993; Holstein and Gubrium 2000). Voice references the subject position that is taken for granted behind speech. Voice works at the level of everyday life, whereas subject positions are what we imagine to be their operating standpoints. This is the working side of our earlier discussion of the subjects behind interview participants. The possibility of alternative voicings and varied subject positions turned researchers' attention to concerns such as how interview participants collaborate to construct the interview's shifting subjectivities in relation to the topics under consideration.

Empirically, the concept of voice leads us to the question of who—or what subject—speaks over the course of an interview and from what standpoint. For example, does a 50-year-old man offer the opinions of a "professional" at the apex of his successful career, or might his voice be that of a husband and father reflecting on what he has missed as a result in the way of family life? Or will he speak as a church elder, a novice airplane pilot, or the "enabling" brother of an alcoholic as the interview unfolds? All of these are possible, given the range of contemporary experiences that he could call upon to account for his opinions. At the same time, it is important to entertain the possibility that the respondent's subjectivity and variable voices emerge out of the immediate interview's interaction and are not necessarily preformed in the respondent's ostensible vessel of answers. Indeed, topics raised in the interview may incite respondents to voice subjectivities never contemplated before.

As noted earlier, at times one can actually hear interview participants indicate subject positions. Verbal prefaces, for example, can provide clues to subject position and voice, but they are often ignored in interview research. Phrases such as "to put myself in someone else's shoes" and "to put on a different hat" are signals that respondents employ to voice shifts in position.

Acknowledging this, in an interview study of nurses on the qualities of good infant care, we probably would not be surprised to hear a respondent say something like, "That's when I have my RN cap on, but as a mother, I might tell you a different story." Sometimes respondents are quite forthright in giving voice to alternative points of view in precisely those terms, as when a respondent prefaces remarks with, say, "Well, from the point of view of a . . . ." Such phrases are not interview debris; they convey the important and persistent subjective work of the interview encounter.

In the actual practice of asking interview questions and giving answers, things are seldom so straightforward, however. An interview, for example, might start under the assumption that a father or a mother is being interviewed, which the interview's introductions might appear to confirm. But there is no guarantee that particular subjectivities will prevail throughout. There's the matter of the *ongoing* construction of subjectivity, which unfolds with the give-and-take of the interview encounter. Something said later in the interview, for example, might prompt the respondent to figure, not necessarily audibly, that he really had, "all along," been responding from a quite different point of view than was evident at the start. Unfortunately, shifts in subjectivity are not always evident in so many words or comments. Indeed, the possibility of an unforeseen change in subjectivity might not be evident until the very end of an interview, if at all, when a respondent remarks for the first time, "Yeah, that's the way all of us who were raised down South do with our children," making it unclear which subject had been providing responses to the interviewer's questions—the voice of this individual parent or her regional membership and its associated experiential sensibilities.

Adding to these complications, subject position and voice must also be considered in relation to the perceived voice of the interviewer. Who, after all, is the interviewer in the eyes of the respondent? How will the interviewer role be positioned into the conversational matrix? For example, respondents in debriefings might comment that an interviewer sounded more like a company man than a human being, or that a particular interviewer made the respondent feel that the interviewer was "just an ordinary person, like myself." Indeed, even issues of social justice might creep in and position the interviewer, say, as a worthless hack, as the respondent takes the interviewer to be "just one more token of the establishment," choosing to silence her own voice in the process (see Dunbar, Rodriguez, and Parker, Chapter 7, this volume). This raises the possibility that the respondent's working subjectivity is constructed out of the unfolding interpersonal reflections of the interview participants' attendant historical experiences. It opens to consideration, for example, an important question: If the interviewee had not been figured to be just an "ordinary" respondent, who (which subject) might the respondent have been in giving voice to his or her opinions?

As if this doesn't muddy the interview waters enough, imagine what the acknowledgment of multiple subjectivities does to the concept of sample size, another dimension figured to be under considerable control in traditional interview research. To decompose the designated respondent into his or her (multiple) working subjects is to raise the possibility that any single element of a sample can expand or contract in size in the course of the interview, increasing or decreasing the sample *n* accordingly. Treating subject positions and their associated voices seriously, we might find that an ostensibly single interview could actually be, in practice, an interview with several subjects, whose particular identities may be only partially clear. Under the circumstances, to be satisfied that one has completed an interview with a single respondent and to code it as such because it was formally conducted with a single embodied individual is to be rather cavalier about the complications of subjectivity and of the narrative organization of sample size.

As Mishler (1986) has pointed out, such matters have traditionally been treated as technical issues in interview research. Still, they have long been informally recognized, and an astute positivistic version of the complexities entailed has been theorized and researched with great care and insight (see, for example, Fishbein 1967). Jean Converse and Howard Schuman's (1974) delightful book on survey research as interviewers see it, for instance, illuminates this recognition with intriguing case material.

There is ample reason, then, for some researchers to approach the interview as a set of activities that are ongoingly accomplished, not just completed. In standardized interviewing, one would need to settle conclusively on matters of who the subject behind the respondent is, lest it be impossible to know to which population generalizations can be made. Indeed, a respondent who shifts the subject to whom she is giving voice would pose dramatic technical difficulties for survey researchers, such that, for example, varied parts of a single completed interview would have to be coded as the responses of different subjects and be generalizable to different populations. This takes us well beyond the possibility of coding in the traditional sense of the term, a point that, of course, Harold Garfinkel (1967) and Aaron Cicourel (1964), among others, made years ago and that, oddly enough, inspired the approach Mishler advocates.

OWNERSHIP AND EMPOWERMENT

Having raised these vexing issues, can we ever effectively address the question of who owns the opinions and stories expressed in interviews, including both the standardized interview and the more open-ended, narrative form? Whose "own" story do we obtain in the process of interviewing? Can we ever discern ownership in individual terms? And how does this relate to respondent empowerment?

Recall that ownership implies that the respondent has, or has title to, a story and that the interview can be designed to bring this forth. But the concept of voice suggests that this is not as straightforward as it might seem. The very activity of opening the interview to extended discussion among the participants indicates that ownership can be a joint or collaborative matter, if not rather fleeting in designation. In practice, the idea of "own story" is not just a commendable research goal but something participants themselves seek to resolve as they move through the interview conversation. Each participant tentatively engages the interactive problems of ownership as a way of sorting out the assumed subjectivities in question and proceeds on that basis, for the practical communicative purposes of completing the interview.

When a respondent such as a substance-abusing pharmacist responds to a question about the future, "I've learned [from N.A.] that it's best to take it one day at a time; I really believe that," it is clear that the pharmacist's narrative is more than an individual's story. What he owns would seem to have wended its way through the informing voices of other subjectivities: Narcotics Anonymous's recovery ideology, this particular respondent's articulation of that ideology, the communicative twists on both discourses that emerge in the give-and-take of the interview exchange, the project's own framing of the issues and resulting agenda of questions, the interviewer's ongoing articulation of that agenda, and the reflexively collaborative flow of unforeseen voiced and unvoiced subjectivities operating in the unfolding exchange. What's more, all of these together can raise metacommunicative concerns about "what this [the interview] is all about, anyway," which the respondent might ask at any time. Under the circumstances, it would seem that ownership is something rather diffusely spread about the topical and processual landscape of speech activities entailed in the interview.

Respondent empowerment would appear to be a working, rather than definitive, feature of these speech activities. It is not clear in practice how one could distinguish any one respondent's own story from the tellable stories available to this and other respondents, which they might more or less share. Putting it in terms of "tellable stories" further complicates voice, subjectivity, and empowerment. And, at the other end of the spectrum of what is tellable, there are those perplexing responses that, in the respondent's search for help in formulating an answer, can return "power" to the very source that would hold it in the first place. It is not uncommon to hear respondents remark that they are not sure how they feel or what they think, or that they haven't really thought about the question or topic before, or to hear them actually think out loud about what it might mean personally to convey particular sentiments or answer in a specific way—and ask the interviewer for assistance in doing so.

Philosophically, the central issue here is a version of Ludwig Wittgenstein's (1953) "private language" problem. Wittgenstein argues that because language—and, by implication, stories and other interview responses—is a shared "form of life," the idea that one could have available exclusively to oneself an unshared, private language would not make much sense. Given the reflexive duality of self-consciousness, one could not even share an ostensible private language with oneself. In more practical terms, this means that whatever is conveyed by the respondent to the interviewer is always subject to the question of what it means, in which case we're back to square one with shared knowledge and the various "language games" that can be collaboratively engaged by interview participants to assign meaning to these questions and responses. Empowerment in this context is not so much a matter of providing the communicative means for the respondent to tell his or her "own" story as it is a matter of

recognizing, first, that responses or stories, as the case might be, are collaborative accomplishments and, second, that there are as many individual responses or stories to tell as there are recognizable forms of response. This, of course, ultimately brings us full circle to the analytically hoary problem of whose interests are being served when the individually "empowered" respondent speaks, implicating power in relation to the broader social horizons of speech and discourse.

◆ Investigating New Concerns

In the following chapters, *Inside Interviewing* investigates an array of concerns that arise when we begin to look at the interview through new lenses. Ranging from the conceptual to the technical, these issues have emerged from researchers' burgeoning self-consciousness and willingness to see past conventional understandings and commonsense notions to uncover the complexities inside interviewing.

SUBJECTS AND RESPONDENTS

Part I explores the implications of a more nuanced appreciation for subjectivity—for the variety of subjects and subject positions that stand behind interview participants. The assumption of a single, stable subject behind the interview participant is now less an operating assumption for interviewing than it is a significant procedural and analytic issue. The subjective embodiments of the respondent and the interviewer are no longer merely taken for granted. While the selected respondent might be female, for the purposes of the research encounter, can we be sure that the voice that comes through in the interview represents the beliefs and sentiments of a woman, as opposed to, say, a business executive, a marathon runner, or an alcoholic?

The female respondent, like most respondents, holds many roles; she might also be African American and working class. How do these standpoints figure in what she says in the interview? Indeed, this combination of identities is located at the intersection of myriad subject positions, each with specific social, historical, and cultural resonances. Simply moving along in the interview, in technically correct form, as if subject position didn't matter—eliciting answers from, encouraging, acknowledging, and probing the respondent with an image of a constant subject behind the respondent—tends to homogenize the reports and experiences of even the most diverse set of respondents. To then analyze the data as if they also were the responses of constant subjects only exaggerates the problem.

The authors of the chapters in Part I argue against the homogenization of the interview with respect to distinctive respondents. Taken together, they convey the message that interviewers can no longer rely upon singular categories and identities as the basis for seeking and analyzing respondent standpoints. Each of the chapters also suggests that, when it comes to "distinctive" respondents, researchers would do well to combine interviewing with more ethnographic approaches. The aim is to better understand the "distinctive"—as opposed to the ostensibly more "familiar"—respondent's experience in its often hidden or overlooked social contexts.

TECHNICAL CONCERNS

New lenses on the interview also sharpen researchers' technical focus on what's happening inside the interview. This is center stage in Part II. One challenge that frequently comes to the fore as researchers approach diverse subjects/respondents is overcoming a reluctance to participate. Our complex and pluralistic society is composed of myriad subgroups and subcultures, each having its own loyalties and interests. As these diverse respondents are increasingly subjected to the demands of interviews, cooperation may be elusive. Gaining access to the lives of others now demands a technology of its own (see Adler and Adler, Chapter 8, this volume).

At one time, face-to-face interviewing was the only practical means of "learning from strangers." The rapid deployment of telephones to individual households following World War II gradually turned the matter of asking and answering, especially research interview questions, to the issue of whether the face-to-face interview was necessary to obtain useful responses. Researchers also began to ask if a more economical telephone technology would do the trick. Researchers have investigated the relative adequacy of face-to-face and telephone interviewing and continue to explore the nuances of their differences (see Shuy, Chapter 9, this volume).

Telephone interviewing may have been the first major technological leap forward for survey interviewing. It was accompanied, at the data management and analytic stages, by the rapid expansion of electronic information processing. Today, the industry standard is the telephone survey tied to computerized data-monitoring and data management technology (see Couper and Hansen, Chapter 10, and Schaeffer and Maynard, Chapter 11, this volume).

Researchers' heightened appreciation for just what their data might be has provoked closer examination of just how those data are treated. No longer do interviewers merely jot down a few notes about what was said as a way of capturing the essence of an open-ended interview. Instead, most interviewers conscientiously develop strategies for recording and transcribing interview data to suit their analytic questions and needs (see Poland, Chapter 13, this volume). And of course data analysis has now moved into the computer age, with its attendant advantages, challenges, and complexities (see Seale, Chapter 14, this volume).

ANALYTIC OPTIONS

New lenses even change the nature of what interview data can be taken to mean. They provide different ways of apprehending and understanding experience as it is conveyed through the interview process. This, in turn, implicates a set of procedures or ways of organizing, categorizing, and interpreting data. There is no single correct approach to data analysis. Even though it might appear that a naturalistic field worker, say, takes careful notes and interprets those notes in relation to a conceptual framework in much the same way as a constructionist field worker might do, the alternative perspectives present different analytic strategies. The naturalistic field worker is likely to orient to the data as the facts of experience, whereas the constructionist field worker emphasizes and aims to describe *how* those facts come into being in the first place (see Gubrium and Holstein 1997). The methods themselves—observing, recording field notes, coding, categorizing, extrapolating, interpreting—belie what those methods are considered to be doing in relation to empirical material. In the case of the naturalist, for instance, method is seen as a matter of "gathering" data; constructionist methods orient more to the goal of revealing how social actions and interactions become data. This is a distinction that Kathy Charmaz makes in Chapter 15 in relation to forms of grounded theory analysis.

Of course, these perspectives are not completely distinct from one another, either; there can be considerable overlap in analytic sensibilities. Studies of narrative, for example, center on stories in some form or other; they might be informed by interpersonal approaches at one end of a continuum (see Riessman, Chapter 16, this volume) and cultural or historical perspectives at the other (see Cándida Smith, Chapter 17, this volume). Yet they all typically attempt to identify narrative themes or narrative structures. How they interpret themes

and structures distinguishes them from one another.

While the chapters in Part III don't cover the strategic waterfront of data analysis, they do represent well-established options. One very popular strategy stems from Barney Glaser and Anselm Strauss's development in the 1960s of what has come to be called "grounded theory methodology" (see Charmaz, Chapter 15, this volume). Reacting to the post-World War II emphasis in social research on formal theory construction and hypothesis formation separate from the data, Glaser and Strauss developed an analytic strategy that viewed theoretical formulation as best conducted from the ground up, meaning in close and continuous relation to empirical material. Charmaz's chapter presents this approach, which has grown immensely popular. Charmaz adds a constructionist twist to Glaser and Strauss, drawing inspiration from the many perspectives in social research that now view social life as continuously created and not simply as empirically available.

Chapters by Catherine Riessman and Richard Cándida Smith present alternative analytic strategies for narrative materials. These perspectives approach empirical material in terms of their story-like qualities. Taking for granted that experience comes to us in the form of stories, the authors show what can be done with interview data from different points of view. Riessman focuses on *personal* stories, narratives that give shape to individual experience. Typically, she searches for the narrative strategies that storytellers use to formulate their experiences, such as compartmentalizing them by narrating them differently. Borrowing from literary analysis, Riessman points out the narrative importance of a variety of story elements, such as scene-setting, characterization, emplotment, and thematization.

Not all narrative approaches address personal stories. Cándida Smith brings other disciplinary and theoretical sensibilities to bear on alternative kinds of narrative material. As he explains, there are a number of perspectives available, ranging from naturalistic efforts to represent historical events through personal stories, to constructionist views that take concerted account of the ways respondents make meaning by appropriating historical material for their own uses. Elaborating the latter view, Cándida Smith's analysis is not concerned with the "mistakes" made in the narrative process, but rather with documenting the ways interviewees communicatively build their worlds out of the *historical* material available to them.

Marjorie DeVault and Liza McCoy's chapter offers an analytic strategy for interview material originally formulated by Dorothy Smith, a Canadian feminist working at the intersection of institutions and everyday life. While the strategy has come to be called "institutional ethnography," the approach is not immediately recognizable as either institutional or ethnographic. As the subtitle of the authors' chapter indicates, the approach orients to the use of "interviews to investigate ruling relations." According to DeVault, McCoy, and their colleagues, institutional discourses and their lived normative preferences can be made visible by approaching interviewee's responses as they are mediated by the relations of ruling in which their experiences are embedded. Distinct traces of institutional relations of ruling can be uncovered in institutionally mediated interview material. The result is that interviews can be used to study institutional processes, revealing in individual testaments what the traditional ethnographer might otherwise document from observational material.

The last chapter in Part III, by Carolyn Baker, is less focused on the substance of interview material than it is on strategies for analyzing how respondents' *use* of categories gives meaning to what they say about their lives and experiences. Presenting various forms of what ethnomethodologists call "categorization analysis," Baker shows how member categorization (not the researcher's categories or codes for interview

material) serves to make meaning. Here again, we are presented with respondents who actively construct their experiences, not merely report them in varied detail.

REPRESENTATIONAL ISSUES

In Part IV, the concluding section of *Inside Interviewing,* the authors try on new lenses to look both backward and forward at the question of how to construe and represent interview material. Postmodern sensibilities now keep us from weighing alternatives simply in terms of truth and clarity. What might be considered a truly representative depiction of interview material now must wend its way through the varied social and cultural contingencies of truth.

The representational challenges from this standpoint are manifold and complex. When respondents speak of their experiences, do we hear their "own" voices or the expressions of the social and cultural discourses that have influenced them? How might this be conveyed in writing? Do the sentiments of the popular culture industry mediate the "heartfelt" expressions of interviewees? How is this taken into account in conveying interview material? How does the sense of narrative ownership—which varies by institutional setting, generation, and culture, among other mediating conditions of speech—affect narrative expression? And how does power, as it percolates across the social statuses of interviewer and respondent, relate to what is and isn't said in interviews? In what ways does this affect representation?

Paul Atkinson and Amanda Coffey begin the discussion in Chapter 20 by revisiting a classic article published by Howard Becker and Blanche Geer in the 1950s, about the relative value of participant observation versus interviewing. Becker and Geer focus their comparison on the question of which method for obtaining data represents social life most accurately. Ultimately, they come down on the side of participant observation. For Becker and Geer, participant observation or "being there" is an ostensibly more direct or pure way of discerning the contours of social life. What the researcher sees and hears is not mediated by the invariably biased retrospections of interview respondents.

Both Becker and Geer's presentation, and the debate following the publication of the article, took for granted the essential distinction between empirical material and its representation. It is this assumption, not the methods' comparative accuracy, that becomes Atkinson and Coffey's point of departure. According to Atkinson and Coffey, in the context of postmodern epistemological sensibilities, the debate needs to be viewed in a much different light, embedded as it now must be in foundational issues of truthfulness and centering on a dialectic of reflection and representation.

Focusing more explicitly on cultural representations, the next two chapters address complex issues relating to moving outside our familiar cultural milieus. In Chapter 21, Anne Ryen examines the conceptual and methodological difficulties of transporting experiential data across cultures. Chapter 22, by Kirin Narayan and Kenneth George, takes up several of the social and cultural contingencies of truth that become topical as we begin to look inside the interview. Based mainly on interviews conducted in South Asia, Narayan and George discuss the representational difficulties of simply assigning interview material to individual respondents. Interview responses, the authors argue, are always about both individual biography and culture; researchers would be best served by articulating the interplay of biography and culture, documenting this in both individual and cultural terms. As Narayan and George point out, the idea of the "individual" interview cannot be taken for granted; individuality, as it bears on narrative relevance, is a representational issue.

Representing empirical material clearly is no longer just a matter of good, accessible writing. There's a new leading question: Is it enough to be clear about the *data,* or do the many ways interview data are mediated by their social and cultural contingencies need to be given their due in representing the data in writing? The related question of whether standard scientific writing is adequate to the challenges of postmodern interview sensibilities is now itself at the forefront.

Carolyn Ellis and Leigh Berger (Chapter 23) address this issue by extending the representation of interview material to researchers' deliberations about what the material means. Ellis and Berger offer us a view of the way ongoing reflections on the interviews in relation to interviewers' own experiences play into question formation and the interview process itself. The authors choose to represent their material in a layered account, dividing their writing between their own deliberations as co-researchers and interviewers on the one hand, and their interviewees' responses on the other. As we read the chapter, we find that this also may be too distinct a representational division, as each layer of text serves to inform the reader of the developing personal and conceptual relevance of the interview material "itself."

Finally, Charles Briggs in Chapter 24 turns us directly to the issue of power. Briggs describes the differential social and cultural statuses of interview participants as these relate to both narrative expression and narrative representation. Differences in social status between the interviewee and interviewer, for example, play into the question of whether, and how, the proverbial passive "vessel of answers" that interviewees are often assumed to be, will activate their subjectivity in the interview context. Power also bears on how interview material will be represented. This may relate to whether analytic writing, say, will display truths defined in terms of criteria such as procedural adequacy and sample representativeness, or will take into account the representational acumen and preferences of respondents themselves.

Taken together, the four parts of *Inside Interviewing* provide an array of penetrating glances through different lenses. They reveal the myriad fascinating challenges confronting us when we look inside the contemporary research interview. Our concern with the practice of interviewing is no longer just procedural. Rather, it now ranges across both technical developments and conceptual challenges to open to view not only what interview practice is, but also what it might be.

■ *References*

Alasuutari, P. 1998. *An Invitation to Social Research.* London: Sage.

Atkinson, P. and D. Silverman. 1997. "Kundera's *Immortality*: The Interview Society and the Invention of Self." *Qualitative Inquiry* 3:304-25.

Balint, M. 1964. *The Doctor, His Patient, and the Illness.* London: Pitman.

Benney, M. and E. C. Hughes. 1956. "Of Sociology and the Interview." *American Journal of Sociology* 62:137-42.

Briggs, C. L. 1986. *Learning How to Ask: A Sociolinguistic Appraisal of the Role of the Interview in Social Science Research.* Cambridge: Cambridge University Press.

Carrithers, M., S. Collins, and S. Lukes, eds. 1985. *The Category of the Person.* Cambridge: Cambridge University Press.

Cicourel, A. V. 1964. *Method and Measurement in Sociology.* New York: Free Press.

———. 1974. *Theory and Method in a Study of Argentine Fertility.* New York: John Wiley.

———. 1967. "Fertility, Family Planning, and the Social Organization of Family Life: Some Methodological Issues." *Journal of Social Issues* 23:57-81.

———. 1982. "Interviews, Surveys, and the Problem of Ecological Validity." *American Sociologist* 17:11-20.

Clifford, J. and G. E. Marcus, eds. 1986. *Writing Culture: The Poetics and Politics of Ethnography.* Berkeley: University of California Press.

Converse, J. M. and H. Schuman. 1974. *Conversations at Random: Survey Research as Interviewers See It.* New York: John Wiley.

Denzin, N. K. and Y. S. Lincoln, eds.. 2000. *Handbook of Qualitative Research,* 2nd ed. Thousand Oaks, CA: Sage.

Dreyfus, H. L. and P. Rabinow. 1982. *Michel Foucault: Beyond Structuralism and Hermeneutics.* Chicago: University of Chicago Press.

Ellis, C. and A. P. Bochner, eds. 1996. *Composing Ethnography: Alternative Forms of Qualitative Writing.* Walnut Creek, CA: AltaMira.

Ellis, C. and M. G. Flaherty, eds. 1992. *Investigating Subjectivity: Research on Lived Experience.* Newbury Park, CA: Sage.

Erikson, K. T. 1976. *Everything in Its Path: Destruction of Community in the Buffalo Creek Flood.* New York: Simon & Schuster.

Fishbein, M., ed. 1967. *Readings in Attitude Theory and Measurement.* New York: John Wiley.

Foucault, M. 1973. *Madness and Civilization: A History of Insanity in the Age of Reason.* New York: Vintage.

———. 1975. *The Birth of the Clinic: An Archeology of Medical Perception.* New York: Vintage.

———. 1977. *Discipline and Punish: The Birth of the Prison.* Translated by A. M. Sheridan. New York: Vintage.

———. 1978. *The History of Sexuality,* Vol. 1, *An Introduction.* Translated by R. Hurley. New York: Vintage.

———. 1988. *Technologies of the Self.* Edited by L. H. Martin, H. Gutman, and P. H. Hutton. Amherst: University of Massachusetts Press.

Garfinkel, H. 1967. *Studies in Ethnomethodology.* Englewood Cliffs, NJ: Prentice Hall.

Garland, D. 1997. " 'Governmentality' and the Problem of Crime." *Theoretical Criminology* 1:173-214.

Geertz, C. 1984. " 'From the Native's Point of View': On the Nature of Anthropological Understanding." Pp. 123-37 in *Culture Theory,* edited by R. A. Shweder and R. LeVine. Cambridge: Cambridge University Press.

Gubrium, J. F. 1988. "Incommunicables and Poetic Documentation in the Alzheimer's Disease Experience." *Semiotica* 72:235-53.

———. 1993. "Voice and Context in a New Gerontology." Pp. 46-63 in *Voices and Visions of Aging: Toward a Critical Gerontology,* edited by T. R. Cole, W. A. Achenbaum, P. L. Jakobi, and R. Kastenbaum. New York: Springer.

———. 1997. *The New Language of Qualitative Method.* New York: Oxford University Press.

Gumperz, J. J. 1982. *Discourse Strategies.* Cambridge: Cambridge University Press.

Holstein, J. A. and J. F. Gubrium. 1995. *The Active Interview.* Thousand Oaks, CA: Sage.

———. 2000. *The Self We Live By: Narrative Identity in a Postmodern World.* New York: Oxford University Press.

Hyman, H. H., W. J. Cobb, J. J. Feldman, C. W. Hart, C. H. Stember. 1975. *Interviewing in Social Research.* Chicago: University of Chicago Press.

Hymes, D. 1967. "Models of the Interaction of Language and Social Setting." *Journal of Social Issues* 33:8-28.

James, W. [1892] 1961. *Psychology: The Briefer Course.* New York: Harper & Brothers.

Kahn, R. L. and C. F. Cannell. 1957. *The Dynamics of Interviewing: Theory, Technique, and Cases.* New York: John Wiley.

Kent, R. 1981. *A History of British Empirical Sociology.* Farnborough, England: Gower.

Lidz, T. 1976. *The Person.* New York: Basic.

Maccoby, E. E. and N. Maccoby. 1954. "The Interview: A Tool of Social Science." Pp. 449-87 in *Handbook of Social Psychology,* Vol. 1, edited by G. Lindzey. Reading, MA: Addison-Wesley.

Miller, J. 1993. *The Passion of Michel Foucault.* Garden City, NY: Doubleday.

Mishler, E. G. 1984. *The Discourse of Medicine: Dialectics of Medical Interviews.* Norwood, NJ: Ablex.

———. 1986. *Research Interviewing: Context and Narrative.* Cambridge, MA: Harvard University Press.

Oberschall, A. 1965. *Empirical Social Research in Germany.* Paris: Mouton.

Pool, I. de S. 1957. "A Critique of the Twentieth Anniversary Issue." *Public Opinion Quarterly* 21:190-98.

Reed-Danahay, D. E., ed. 1997. *Auto/Ethnography: Rewriting the Self and the Social.* New York: Berg.

Richardson, L. 2002. "Poetic Representation of Interviews." Pp. 877-892 in *Handbook of Interview Research,* edited by J. Gubrium and J. Holstein. Thousand Oaks, CA: Sage.

Riesman, D. and M. Benney. 1956. "Asking and Answering." *Journal of Business of the University of Chicago* 29:225-36.

Rose, N. 1990. *Governing the Soul: The Shaping of the Private Self.* London: Routledge.

———. 1997. *Inventing Ourselves: Psychology, Power, and Personhood.* Cambridge: Cambridge University Press.

Rubin, H. J. and I. S. Rubin. 1995. *Qualitative Interviewing: The Art of Hearing Data.* Thousand Oaks, CA: Sage.

Sacks, H. 1992. *Lectures on Conversation,* Vols. 1 and 2. Edited by G. Jefferson. Oxford: Blackwell.

Sacks, H., E. A. Schegloff, and G. Jefferson. 1974. "A Simplest Systematics for the Organization of Turn-Taking for Conversation." *Language* 50:696-735.

Selvin, H. C. 1985. "Durkheim, Booth and Yule: The Non-Diffusion of an Intellectual Innovation." Pp. 70-82 in *Essays on the History of British Sociological Research,* edited by M. Bulmer. Cambridge: Cambridge University Press.

Silverman, D. 1987. *Communication and Medical Practice.* London: Sage.

———. 1993. *Interpreting Qualitative Data: Methods for Analysing Talk, Text and Interaction.* London: Sage.

———. 1997. *Qualitative Research: Theory, Method and Practice.* London: Sage.

Terkel, S. 1972. *Working: People Talk about What They Do All Day and How They Feel about It.* New York: Pantheon.

Weiss, R. S. 1994. *Learning from Strangers: The Art and Method of Qualitative Interview Studies.* New York: Free Press.

Wittgenstein, L. 1953. *Philosophical Investigations.* New York: Macmillan.

Part I

SUBJECTS AND RESPONDENTS

2

INTERVIEWING CHILDREN AND ADOLESCENTS

◆ **Donna Eder**
Laura Fingerson

The task of interviewing children and adolescents presents researchers with unique opportunities and dilemmas. Although some researchers advocate participant observation and ethnography rather than interviewing in the study of children (Corsaro 1997; Prout and James 1997; Weisner 1996), we believe there is a place for the interview approach in such research. We have found that interviewing can be used successfully with children from preschool age (e.g., Davies 1989) through high school age (e.g., Eckert 1989). Although very young children may not be as comfortable as adolescents in one-on-one interviews with adults, most of the issues we present in this chapter are applicable to a range of age groups.

One clear reason for interviewing youthful respondents is to allow them to give voice to their own interpretations and thoughts rather than rely solely on our adult interpretations of their lives. For example, rather than forming our own views on the content of the media that children use, it is important that we find out how they are interpreting the messages they receive through books, television, movies, and magazines. Another reason for interviewing young people is to study those topics that are salient in their lives but do not occur in daily conversations or interactions. For example, although family relationships are very salient to many adolescents, they seldom discuss these relationships in their daily conversations with peers. Likewise, adolescents discuss topics such as sexuality and menstruation in joking or playful terms, if they discuss them at all, in public settings. Thus researchers interested in these topics have relied more extensively on interviews than on observations (Lees 1993; Tolman 1994). Finally, some topics that do occur naturally in young people's daily conversations do not occur on a regular enough basis to warrant the time it would take to study them through participant observation. For example, although some boys regularly discuss media events in their daily conversations, girls are much less likely to do so on a regular basis (Eder 1995; Milkie 1994). Thus for collecting girls' interpretations of media, conducting interviews with groups of girls is a much more efficient method than observation (see Fingerson 1999).

When interviewing children, it is essential that researchers begin by examining the power dynamics between adults and youth. Researchers do not always recognize that, in general, children have lower status than adults and lack power in Western societies. Berry Mayall (1999) advocates seeing children as their own minority group compared to the adults who order and control their lives, viewing them as lacking essential abilities and characteristics of adulthood. For Mayall, "child" is a relational category defining children as subordinate to the superordinate "adult." Ivar Frønes (1994) also argues that children are primarily seen as an "age group," which positions them low in the overall age-graded power structure, rather than as a group with its own culture and unique abilities. According to Suzanne Hood, Berry Mayall, and Sandy Oliver (1999), children are a socially disadvantaged and disempowered group, not only because of their age but because of their position in society as the "researched" and never the "researchers."

Interviewers need to be sensitive to this power imbalance. Gary Alan Fine and Kent Sandstrom (1988) argue that in any participation event with children, the adults cannot have equal status because "the social roles of the participants have been influenced by age, cognitive development, physical maturity, and acquisition of social responsibility" (p. 14). Children are taught

all their lives to listen to, respect, and obey adults. They are surrounded by teachers, parents, relatives, and adult friends who all have the power to command children's actions (Caputo 1995; see also in this volume Adler and Adler, Chapter 8; Briggs, Chapter 24).

Throughout this chapter, we will explore various ways in which researchers can address this power dynamic, our first theme, when interviewing children and adolescents. In the first section below, we argue that the adult researcher's power can be reduced while making the interviewing context more natural if children are interviewed as a group rather than as individuals. Thus, unlike in most other chapters in this text, the reader should assume that we are referring to group interviews unless otherwise specified. In the next section, we emphasize reciprocity as a central means for responding to the potential power inequality between adult researchers and youthful respondents. We argue that the concept of reciprocity can be applied at several levels, from directly empowering respondents to using research findings to enrich and improve the lives of children through an action-oriented research focus. Finally, we return to the theme of power dynamics as we discuss how to represent youth in their own terms.

A second theme of this chapter is the importance of using multiple methods. Although some interviewers may seek only to collect interview data, we argue that a brief period of observation should precede the interviewing process, so that interviewers can identify natural contexts for interviewing and children's own speech routines (see in this volume Dunbar, Rodriguez, and Parker, Chapter 7; Atkinson and Coffey, Chapter 20). We also believe that a sociolinguistic approach can strengthen the validity of interviews as well as complement other modes of data analysis by showing *how* certain beliefs are acquired and communicated. Finally, we discuss how researchers can combine group interviews with single interviews and with content analysis of media to enhance our understanding of children and adolescents.

◆ Creating a Natural Context

One of the most important considerations in interview research with young people is the creation of a natural context for the interview. This can mean different things depending on the ages of the children being interviewed. Studies of peer culture among youth have emphasized the importance of social learning in the context of groups (Corsaro and Eder 1995; Eder 1995; Corsaro 1997). Children, especially young children, acquire social knowledge through interaction with others as they construct meanings through a shared process. This is also the most natural way for them to communicate social knowledge to others. Some researchers have found that African American children are more comfortable in group settings (Holmes 1998), and we have found that European American children are also relaxed and engage in typical peer routines when interviewed in groups (Simon, Eder, and Evans 1992; Eder 1995; Fingerson 1999).

The group setting is also important for minimizing the power differential between the researcher and those being studied. Power dynamics occur in all interview studies, in that the researcher has control over the research process as well as over much of the interview by virtue of being the one posing the questions. As noted previously, in studies of youth the researcher also has the added power associated with age. Both of these aspects can be minimized to some degree when interviewing takes place in group settings, as children are more relaxed in the company of their peers and are more comfortable knowing that they outnumber the adults in the setting. Also, there is less chance for a researcher to impose adult interpretations and language on the young people if they are interviewed collectively

and have the opportunity to develop and convey aspects of peer culture in their talk.

Group interviews grow directly out of peer culture, as children construct their meanings collectively with their peers. In group interviews (also referred to as focus groups), participants build on each other's talk and discuss a wider range of experiences and opinions than may develop in individual interviews (Morgan 1993). Also, the interaction in focus groups can elicit more accurate accounts, as participants must defend their statements to their peers, especially if the group is made up of individuals who interact on a daily basis. Although participants in focus groups are sometimes taken out of their natural settings, if an interview is conducted with an existing group of friends or peers, the conversations in the focus group are more indicative of those occurring in a natural setting (Albrecht, Johnson, and Walther 1993). As an alternative approach, some researchers have conducted whole-class interviews with elementary school students (Adler and Adler 1998). This technique allows interviewers to ask children from a variety of peer groups to discuss their different perspectives on issues of social power among peers.

The naturalness of the interview context can be furthered developed if the interview is placed within a larger activity with which the respondents are already familiar. According to Julie Tammivaara and D. Scott Enright (1986), researchers can reduce the artificiality of interviews by embedding them into everyday activities such as recess, "show and tell," "circle time," or sessions of ongoing small instructional groups. In some cases, interviewers might create new games that are similar to the types of games children naturally engage in, such as "Let's Pretend" or "Telling Stories," and embed their interviews in these meaningful activities. Robyn Holmes (1998) notes that she avoids formal interviews with children and instead conducts informal individual and group interviews during free-play time, while children take part in drawing activities, or on the playground. In addition, she has developed journalistic role-play scenarios in which she and the children take turns interviewing each other. Brenda Bryant (1985) conducted individual interviews with children while taking them on "neighborhood walks." The walks are intended to make the setting more inviting as well as to elicit cues and reminders to promote more accurate reporting of neighborhood experiences. In all of these cases, by avoiding decontextualized interview situations, researchers have been able to elicit more natural and valid responses from young respondents.

Another aspect of creating a natural context in the interview involves gaining an understanding of the communicative rules used by the youth being studied. Charles Briggs (1986) has argued that interview studies should be grounded in the discourse of those being interviewed. This is especially true in studies of youth, who often have their own discourse styles and peer culture. According to Briggs, the design, implementation, and analysis of interviews should emerge from an awareness of the nature of the respondents' communicative competence. The researcher can learn the communicative norms of the youth being studied through a combination of observation and informal interviewing prior to the formal interviewing process. In this observation period, the researcher should pay careful attention to the young people's sense of questions and the appropriateness of their timing and use in different contexts. Briggs also recommends that the researcher perform a microanalysis of a selected interview as a way to develop a clearer understanding of the respondents' discourse patterns. (We consider the topic of sociolinguistic analysis of interview data later in this chapter.)

One innovative approach to interview research with children is the use of children as interviewers. Tobias Hecht (1998), in a study of street children in Brazil, found success having kids take the tape recorder and interview other kids on their own. Through this method, Hecht discovered many modes of discourse and ways of referring to the home, family, and the street that were invaluable in his own interviewing and observations.

Another way in which a researcher can help respondents' norms to emerge is through the careful structuring of the interview itself. The best interview emerges from a state of egalitarian cooperation in which both the researcher and respondents form the discourse (Briggs 1986). Shulamit Reinharz (1992) advocates beginning the interview with very unstructured questions, to allow the respondents' concerns to emerge. She notes that the interviewer should be less concerned with getting his or her questions answered than with understanding the people being interviewed. In studies of youth, it is especially important for interviewers to emphasize nondirected, open, and inclusive questions (Tammivaara and Enright 1986). If the questions are open-ended, the children will have more opportunity to bring in the topics and modes of discourse that are familiar to them. Also, nondirected questions provide more opportunity for children in group interviews to collaborate in their answers and to expand on the responses of others. This type of interaction is typical of the discourse styles in many peer cultures and is reflective of children's natural way of developing shared meanings (Eder 1988, 1995).

In attempting to create a natural context for the interview, the researcher must also take care to avoid creating situations that remind youth of classroom lessons based on "known-answer" questions. Because many students are exposed to the type of lessons in which questions are asked for the purpose of getting correct answers (Tammivaara and Enright 1986), respondents in a research setting who are asked similar types of questions may seek to provide the answers they feel are expected of them rather than stating what they actually think or feel. In addition, Tammivaara and Enright (1986) suggest that interviewers should avoid certain controlling behaviors that might associate them with teachers, such as asking respondents to stop fidgeting or to stop being silly. Instead, they recommend that some of the interview time be taken up with playing with items or figuratively playing with questions; they observe that this will lead to more valid information in the end.

Another way the interviewer can avoid being associated with the classroom teacher is by resisting being the one to initiate all activities during the interview (Corsaro 1981; Tammivaara and Enright 1986). Lessons in which right answers are sought seldom include the opportunity for children to develop and ask their own questions. By inviting the children's questions and comments throughout the interview, the interviewer conveys a different context of developing knowledge. By encouraging respondents to initiate questions and comments, the interviewer breaks down the basic power dimension of the interview context by personalizing and humanizing him- or herself and empowering the respondents. In addition, when the interviewer gives respondents opportunities to introduce their own topics and concerns into the discussion, the knowledge shared and gained reflects the interests of the youth being studied as well as the interests of the researcher. Judith Cook and Mary Fonow (1986) note that feminist researchers who want to avoid treating their subjects as "objects of knowledge" use an interactive interviewing approach that allows their respondents to have a voice during the production of the data. In interview research with children, researchers can also report their findings back to the children to check the accuracy of the adults' interpretations (Mayall 1999). This allows the children to hear what the researchers think and to respond directly to researchers' interpretations of their lives.

One of the key aspects of the interview approach recommended here is flexibility. Although the researcher will have certain questions in mind to start, he or she must be willing to let the interview develop by allowing opportunities for new questions to emerge based on what is shared during the interview. These questions may arise from anyone, not just the researcher. Also, flexibility allows for changes in setting and procedure as the needs and interests of the youth being studied are revealed. It may become clear only as the interview process progresses that certain questions are inappropriate due either to ethical or substantive considerations, and these should then be omitted. On the other hand, new questions may emerge that better capture the experiences of the youth, and these might become the focus of an added stage of the research.

◆ Reciprocity as a Response to Power Dynamics

Current discussions of ethics regarding research on youth are too often limited to debates regarding the protection of children's rights. Although we support these concerns, we believe that this focus has limited the perception of ethical responsibility to that of guarding individual rights. We believe that in order to respond to the power dynamics in research with children, researchers must expand this ethical discussion to include a greater emphasis on reciprocity. The researcher's desire to gain information from child participants without giving something in return reflects an underlying sense of the adult researcher's privilege. However, by giving something in return for receiving this information, researchers can reduce the potential power inequality.

Reciprocity can take place on several levels. One important level is within the interview itself. Researchers can treat respondents in such a way that they receive something from participating in the study, whether it be a greater sense of empowerment, a greater understanding of their own life experiences, or both. Feminist researchers have discussed some general ways in which respondents may be empowered through interviews (Lather 1988; Reinharz 1992). For example, researchers can promote interactive interviews in which the researchers self-disclose along with participants. Researchers can also conduct multiple interviews with the same individuals, promoting a greater level of depth. Some feminist researchers also advocate the use of group interviews and the collective negotiation of interpretations. All of these strategies are designed to promote respondents' empowerment by encouraging respondents' self-reflection as well as researchers' deeper understanding of the respondents' situation in their worlds.

Some researchers who have interviewed adolescents have commented on the potential for adolescents to gain from the research experience. In a study of girls from different ethnic and social backgrounds, Jill Taylor, Carol Gilligan, and Amy Sullivan (1995) found that the individual interviews conducted by adult females provided these girls with opportunities to think through issues of importance to them by talking about them with interested adults. During these interviews the girls were less afraid of judgment, betrayal, misunderstanding, and anger than is generally the case when adolescents talk with adults. One respondent told the interviewer that she was able to speak freely because the interviewer was clearly interested in her. This led her to discuss things that she did not feel she could share with family members or even with friends. Some of the girls also said they were able to gain new insights about themselves during the course of their interviews. As one said: "But since the question came up, it let me know how I felt. I think that's good. I can do this forever you know . . . keep on going. I'll bring a lot up with just easy questions that you would ask anybody, you know. It lets you know about yourself" (p. 129).

Similarly, Penelope Eckert (1989) found that many participants thanked her for the opportunity to think and talk in a struc-

tured way about themselves and their high school issues. When she began her study, she was not prepared for the number of students who needed an interested adult to talk with about themselves. As the interview setting was both nonjudgmental and confidential, her respondents found their interviews to be safer than most conversations with adults.

Taylor et al. (1995) found that the adolescent girls they interviewed felt close to their mothers but did not feel they could talk to them about anything "important." White and Hispanic girls in particular have been found to have difficulty discussing issues of sexuality with their mothers (Ward and Taylor 1991). James Youniss and Jacqueline Smollar (1985) have reported that in discussions with their parents, compared to conversations with their friends, adolescents are more likely to be careful about what they say, are more likely to hide their true feelings, and are less likely to talk about doubts and fear. Given the difficulty adolescents have in talking with the adults to whom they are closest, it is not surprising that some interviewers have found their young respondents eager to be listened to in a nonjudgmental and accepting manner.

Reciprocity can also take the form of giving something back to the community in which the study takes place and/or including some form of social action or social change as part of the project. People of color have written about the importance of service in their respective ethnic communities. For example, Rayna Green (1990) says that what she does with her scholarship needs to work for people, to bring about change in some way. Patricia Hill Collins (1990) believes that thought and action should be tied closely together. For example, the struggle for self-definition among African American women includes a merging of thought and action to eliminate oppression. Creating safe communities is an important form of activism, but, Collins argues, it is not enough; broader forms of change are also needed, such as transformations in social institutions.

An interest in action-oriented research is growing among qualitative researchers. As they move away from the view that qualitative research is a detached science, researchers are realizing that they influence the participants in their studies and are in turn influenced by them (Lincoln and Denzin 1994). As researchers accept that such impacts are inevitable, many have begun to consider ways to make their influences more positive. This has led to the consideration of a new measure of validity, one that reflects the degree to which a given research project empowers and emancipates a research community (Lather 1988).

Researchers who interview youth are also calling for more action-oriented research as well as for more discussion on ethics, praxis, and qualitative work. Angela Valenzuela (1999) found a unique opportunity to assist one of the English teachers in the high school in which she was conducting research. The seasoned teacher was having difficulty controlling the classroom and asked Valenzuela to speak to his class. During her visit, she not only gathered valuable data, but was able to speak with the kids openly and honestly, diffuse the situation, and explain to the teacher the roots of the difficult classroom dynamics.

In her work with high school dropouts, Michelle Fine (1994) sought to represent the voices of African American and Hispanic adolescents in courts and public policy debates as well as in academic scholarship. She raises several dilemmas associated with this action-oriented work, including whether or not others resent her speaking on their behalf and whether she might be colluding with structures of domination when her white, middle-class translation of her respondents' words is given more authority than their own narratives. She advises that those who do such work need to create communities of friendly critical informants who can help determine whose voices and analyses are foregrounded.

Fine's experience highlights the fact that differences in culture and power make researchers' attempts at reciprocity especially challenging. What may be culturally appropriate in one context may not be in another. Also, any attempt to affect change by researchers who hold greater power due to their ethnicity and/or social class may be viewed negatively by others. In such cases it is crucial that researchers consult informants about the cultural norms of reciprocity and be willing to work collaboratively for change rather than as independent agents.

In our own research projects with young people, we have sought to include some aspect of service to the communities in which the research took place. In Laura Fingerson's case, she volunteered at "Girls Inc.," the organization in which she collected her data, both before interviewing the girls for her study and then for the following two years. During that time she brought many of her academic skills, such as knowledge of computing, into the environment to enrich the lives of the girls who had participated in her study as well as other girls in this setting. After completing her study of gender, status, and peer culture, Donna Eder applied much of what she and others have learned about peer culture in developing a conflict intervention program for the schools in the community she studied. KACTIS (Kids Against Cruel Treatment in Schools) relied primarily on speech routines that were natural aspects of children's own cultures, such as role-play and collaborative performances. During these familiar routines, children developed alternative approaches for dealing with conflict and abuse that they had witnessed in their school.

We believe that researchers should consider how they can best benefit the communities in which their research takes place by considering from the start possible applications of their research for action as well as for theory. Those involved in action-oriented research have, like Fine (1994), faced political issues and dilemmas related to their attempts to benefit others. For example, Christopher Goodey's (1999) research on assessing the needs of students with learning disabilities reveals the importance of using the concept of "difficulty" rather than "need":

> In qualitative work difficulties must be critically probed rather than just ticked off, whereas research methods based on a concept of need tend to forestall reflexivity or mutual understanding. The notion of difficulty thus has a clear interactive character. It enables us to see something not purely as a consequence of specific characteristics of the child, but of the encounter between the child and [context] and thus to question the supposed division between "special" (pathological) and normal needs. (P. 4)

In her discussion of research involving community intervention, Joan Sieber (1992) notes that researchers may be restricted as to what they can do by members of the community who seek to protect the rights of youth. She warns that researchers involved in community intervention should decide ahead of time who will have access to their data. They should also consider how they can avoid using certain terms in their studies that could potentially stigmatize children, such as *sexually promiscuous* and *at risk,* so that their participants do not face any additional labeling when their data are employed to benefit others in the community.

◆ Combining Interviews with Other Methods

A combination of methods is often useful in research because it is difficult for any single method to capture fully the richness of human experience (Denzin and Lincoln 1994). Because children's experiences are grounded in their own peer cultures and life experiences, it is especially important that researchers use interviews in combination with other methods, both to obtain

more valid responses and to strengthen the analysis of interview data. In this section we look at research that has combined group interviews with field observation, content analysis of media, and individual interviews.

COMBINING INTERVIEWS WITH FIELD OBSERVATION

Field observation has often been combined with interviewing in studies of youth. In some cases, observation sets the ground for the interviews, which are the primary mode of data collection. In other cases, participant observation is the main methodology and interviews are used to complement the collection of field notes based on extensive observation. Finally, some studies draw equally on both methods or combine them with additional methods, such as the use of diaries, surveys, or recorded observations.

We believe that it is essential to begin an interview study with at least some type of field observation. This could take place over a few days or a much longer period, depending on the setting and the research agenda. Without such initial observation, the researcher will find it difficult to assess how to introduce the interviews into the setting in a natural manner. Through observation, the researcher can identify naturally occurring events during which interviews could take place as well as typical language routines in the setting. Observation also helps the researcher to assess some of the basic communicative norms and patterns that children of given ages and backgrounds are using, so that he or she can modify the interview format to include them. Finally, observation can increase the researcher's general understanding of the children's local culture and social structure.

Whether or not interviewing is the main methodology in a study, a period of field observation can enable the researcher to gain rapport with the children prior to interviewing them. Fingerson spent a month volunteering in the setting prior to interviewing girls in groups about their reactions to family television programs. Eder and her colleagues spent several months observing adolescent lunchtime and after-school activities before formulating certain questions that they then asked in interviews with groups of students during lunchtime. In both cases, the initial periods of observation allowed us to establish a high degree of rapport with respondents, so that we could join in their conversations during the interviews, making them seem extensions of their naturally occurring talk.

Just as observations are a useful supplement to an interview-based study, interviews can add important information to studies based primarily on participant or field observation. Although interviews have played an important role in many ethnographic studies of children and youth, only some ethnographers have taken the time to write directly about their interviewing decisions. Penelope Eckert (1989), who studied social categories and identities in high school, notes that she purposely allowed her group interviews to be highly unstructured. She formed her groups by asking a student she knew to gather a group of friends to talk about "stuff." When the group met, she let them talk about whatever topics they considered interesting or important, asking questions only to get the discussion under way.

Likewise, in his study of suburban youth, Ralph Larkin (1979) emphasized the importance of unstructured group interviews. Rather than asking predetermined questions in his interviews, he developed his role as that of a discussion facilitator to a student-based conversation. Larkin purposely avoided the use of more structured questions that would place the definitions of concepts and reality in the hands of the researcher. He wanted his interviews to tap into the students' own reality rather than force their experiences and ideas to fit predetermined categories.

In Eder's study of adolescent peer cultures, the researchers used group interviews to collect more information on concepts and processes that were clearly salient based on observations, but were not fully explained by them (Eder 1995; Simon et al. 1992). For example, although popularity and status hierarchy were obvious concepts, the researchers needed to ask students specifically: "What makes certain students more popular than others?" and "What does it mean to be popular?" These questions arose in part because the researchers associated popularity with being well liked, but the students' comments during natural conversations and during the interviews suggested that they did not. In addition, because romantic feelings toward boys were such a major preoccupation for some groups of girls, the researchers asked them several questions regarding their views on the importance of boys in their lives and the difference between concepts of "liking" and "going with" someone. These interviews ended up revealing a set of norms that girls more or less agreed upon regarding romantic feelings at their age. In both cases, the researchers used interviews primarily to help them understand the adolescents' perceptions and views of these concepts and processes, rather than relying solely on their own interpretations.

Although interviewing can add important information to participant observation studies, researchers should also be aware of the limitations of interviews. There are aspects of children's cultures that are difficult to put into words, and these aspects need to be captured through direct observation rather than interviews. For example, Bronwyn Davies (1989), who studied preschool children, says this about her experience observing their play:

Sometimes the children would provide an explanation if they came to talk to me. But there was often no immediate answer, for neither they nor I could *say* what it was that was going on because we did not know how to find the words or concepts that would encapsulate the event. To this extent the children's world was as yet only partially shaped by language, by linguistic symbolic forms. And for this reason learning to interact with them on their own terms was of central importance. (P. 39)

INTERVIEWS AS
PART OF MEDIA
INTERPRETATION STUDIES

Group interviewing of children is a particularly good method for gathering data for use in media reception analysis. Many studies examining media have focused only on media content rather than on how audiences interpret the media themselves (Greenberg 1980; Cantor 1991; Cantor and Cantor 1992). How audiences perceive and understand television, for example, is not determined solely by programmed content (Granello 1997); rather, viewers select from and assign significance to specific televised messages through social interaction and experience. Janice Radway (1984) terms the social groups in which viewers collectively interpret media texts "interpretive communities." These are the groups with which viewers discuss, evaluate, and interpret television programs. They include children's peer groups. Because watching television consumes such large amounts of their time, children discuss television meanings as a social activity, and through this interaction they create meanings out of the programs' messages and content (Peterson and Peters 1983; Milkie 1994; Gillespie 1995).

It is important that researchers examine the perceptions and interpretations that youth have of media rather than relying solely on their own adult interpretations, such as is done in content analysis studies. For example, Robert Hodge and David Tripp (1986) combined semiotic content analysis with audience reception analysis in a study of 8- to 12-year-old Australian children's responses to the cartoon *Fangface.* They specifically argue for the importance of language: "For these children it is as

though their own thoughts and feelings do not really exist unless they become public and visible through language: the language of others requiring attention and consciousness, their own language reinforcing or sometimes deforming their fluid, inchoate structures of meaning" (p. 66). We agree with this formulation, which emphasizes how important group processes and language are in enabling us to understand children's worlds.

In Fingerson's (1999) research, she used individual interviews combined with focus groups to uncover how middle school girls individually and collectively interpreted family television programs. In particular, she found it interesting to see what the girls focused on in their group discussions. For example, the individual interviews brought up a variety of different issues, but in the focus groups, the girls particularly enjoyed discussing issues of the body brought up in the television programs viewed.

In one group, the girls discussed how Tim, a character on the television program *Home Improvement,* slipped and fell into a portable toilet from the top of a high steel structure at a construction site. The girls expanded and elaborated on this scene in a sequence of collaborative talk dealing with issues of body control and bodily functions. One girl noted that Tim's falling into the portable toilet was realistic because "I can't even balance on a curb!" Body control was uncovered as a salient theme in their culture, possibly because growing limbs and changing centers of gravity leave many girls in their age group feeling unusually clumsy, like Tim. According to the culturalist approach (McRobbie 1991), one cannot summarily determine the effects and meanings of media programs through their content; rather, these effects and meanings are shaped by the individual viewer's attachment of salience to particular events and experiences. The use of group interviews in combination with individual interviews is an excellent way for researchers to access children's and adolescents' understanding of media.

Other studies of children's interpretations of media indicate that children sometimes interpret stories very differently than do adults. In her study of feminist stories, Davies (1989) was surprised to find that some of the preschool children she interviewed expressed viewpoints that did not initially make sense to her, as in the following example:[1]

B.D.: If you were Oliver and you hated all the boy's things and you wanted to do girl's things, would you want to go to dancing school?

Robbie: No.

B.D.: (reads about boys teasing Oliver) So what sort of boys are they?

Robbie: Big, they//

B.D.: Big boys, and should they say that to Oliver Button?

Robbie: Yes.

B.D.: They should? (surprised) . . . (reads about boys writing "Oliver Button is a Sissy" on the school wall) How does Oliver feel?

Robbie: Sad.

B.D.: He's very sad isn't he? So should the boys have written that on the wall?

Robbie: (nods)

B.D.: They should? (surprised) Why should they have written that on the wall?

Robbie: Because he, because he's a sissy doing tap dancing.

B.D.: (reads about Oliver practicing his dancing) So why do you suppose he keeps going though everybody gives him a hard time there?

Robbie: Because he just wants to.

B.D.: He just wants to and should you keep doing what you want to do even though everybody keeps giving you a hard time?

Robbie: (nods) (Pp. 27-28)

Davies notes several contradictions in Robbie's responses as viewed from an adult perspective. Robbie states that it is both right to tease someone who is deviating and right to keep doing what you want to do. Also, even though he knows the teasing makes Oliver sad, he believes that the teasing is okay. It is important to realize that what might be contradictory viewpoints for an adult might not be contradictory for a child. It is only through interviewing children about media that researchers can reveal these different perspectives.

COMBINING SINGLE AND GROUP INTERVIEWS

In this chapter we have advocated using group interviews with children, as these can nicely capture group interactive processes in an efficient way (Morgan 1993). Also, guided interviewing techniques used in focus groups can uncover specific concepts and feelings in the peer culture of interest to the researcher that are not always spoken about regularly in everyday settings. Finally, group interviews readily allow children's own conversational styles to appear.

Some researchers have also found success with individual interviews, such as Carol Gilligan in her studies of girls' self-esteem, confidence, and communication styles (Gilligan 1982; Gilligan, Lyons, and Hanmer 1990; Brown and Gilligan 1992; Taylor et al. 1995) and Youniss and Smollar (1985) in their research on adolescents' relations with their mothers, fathers, and friends. Although Lyn Mikel Brown and Gilligan (1992) note their concern about their respondents' possibly tailoring their answers to seek approval from the researchers, we find mixed evidence of this. As the example from Davies's (1989) study presented above shows, Davies found that children frequently gave answers that were different from those she expected or approved of, even when being interviewed alone. She notes that the children simply saw her as another person who needed to have the way the world really is explained to her.

Individual interviews are especially common in studies of sexuality and body issues. For example, Deborah Tolman (1994) interviewed girls about their experiences and feelings of sexual desire; Sue Lees (1993) interviewed mostly girls and some boys about their sexuality and how they experience their worlds; Michelle Fine and Pat Macpherson (1994) interviewed teenage girls on adolescent feminism, including femininity and sexuality; and Roberta Simmons and Dale Blyth (1987) interviewed both boys and girls on the combined impacts of pubertal change and changing school contexts on self-esteem and self-image.

Sharon Thompson (1995) interviewed girls individually about sexuality, love, and romance and found great success in assessing these girls' narratives of their experience through long, open-ended interviews. Most of these interviews were individual, although she interviewed some respondents in pairs or occasionally in groups. Thompson states: "Their accounts sometimes had a polished quality that made them seem rehearsed, and in a way they were. These were the stories that teenage girls spend hundreds of hours telling each other, going over and over detail and possibility, reporting, strategizing, problem solving, constructing sexual and existential meaning for themselves" (p. 4). Thompson was able to tap into an existing mode of talk for these girls—one-on-one conversations about their romantic and sexual experiences that they already do in their everyday lives with friends.

Using both single and group interviews in conjunction can be an effective method for uncovering social phenomena among older children and adolescents. Older children and adolescents have the developmental capacity to reflect upon their experiences in the manner needed to complete individual interviews successfully. By including single interviews in research, the investigator can examine the participants' individual attitudes, opinions, and contexts and use this information to understand more fully the discussion occurring in the group interviews. Peggy Orenstein (1994) conducted group interviews first in her study of eighth-grade girls in school and then selected individuals from those groups to interview alone in further depth to understand more about their individual contexts, feelings, and experiences.

In addition, some themes may be discussed in individual interviews that may not appear in group discussions but are still important and relevant to the participants and their individual understandings of their social worlds. In this way, the researcher can explore social interaction dimensions. For example, in Hecht's (1998) research with Brazilian street children, the children interviewed in group settings would often defend their mothers to others even though they were not living at home with them. In private conversations, however, they would often reveal feelings of rejection and abandonment by their mothers.

Fingerson (1999) used a combination of individual interviews and focus groups in her research on girls' interpretations of family television programs. Background questions asked in one-on-one settings are particularly necessary in reception analysis; in Fingerson's research, the answers to such questions were essential to her understanding of the unique context of each girl's television viewing and interpretation. For example, one of the girls in the study did not participate fully during the discussions of television programs other than the program viewed for the study and appeared to be quite frustrated about this. Fingerson knew that this was based in part on the strict television-watching rules in the girl's home, which meant that she had less experience with popular television shows than did the other girls.

Also, by conducting individual interviews first, Fingerson was able to see peer power influences in the group interviews. She found that girls reflected on their own opinions and beliefs in the individual interviews but would change those beliefs in the group interviews to be more congruent with their peers. In one of the focus groups, the girls agreed that the family shown in the television program was not realistic, even though they had said the opposite in the individual interviews. The instigator, however, was Alice, who was more popular at the girls' club and more socially powerful than the other girls in this particular group. Fingerson argues that the other two girls were deferring to Alice's higher status by changing their views without introducing the contrasting views they had expressed earlier individually.

In this incident, Alice's greater status allowed her response to carry more weight in the group discussions. This points to a potential problem with group interviews— that is, the power dynamics among peers may influence the nature of their responses. Although we see this as a possible bias in group interview data, the many advantages of group interviews generally outweigh this disadvantage. In fact, many studies based on field observation data in which children are observed interacting in peer groups would have a similar disadvantage in that socially constructed knowledge often is biased in favor of more powerful peers (Adler and Adler 1998). Thus, in seeking to create the most natural contexts possible, interviewers will often need to confront naturally occurring peer power dynamics.

However, in those interview situations where researchers have a particular interest in obtaining individual, unbiased perspectives, they have the option, as Fingerson did, of including individual interviews as part of the research design. Also, researchers can interview children in groups with other classmates or schoolmates who are not part of their smaller peer groups, as long as it is possible to create such group contexts. Finally, keeping groups small in size (three or four members) further helps

to minimize the influence of peer power dynamics.

It is important to reflect on the order in which individual and group interviews are conducted. In Fingerson's (1999) research, she was interested in comparing individual responses with changes emerging in group discussion. In this context, it was important that she ask the girls their individual opinions first. In other research, it may be more appropriate to conduct group interviews first. For example, in dealing with sensitive topics, such as sexuality, the body, and intimate relationships, children and adolescents may feel more comfortable in a group. This places the respondents in a position of power as they outnumber the researcher and are among their own friends and peers. Then, after a comfort level has been reached in the group and the topics have been discussed in the open, they may feel more comfortable, confident, and relaxed in a one-on-one setting with the researcher.

◆ Issues in Data Analysis

We now turn from issues of data collection to issues of data analysis. We begin by examining the many uses of sociolinguistic analysis in interviewing studies. We then follow this examination with a discussion of the importance of representing youth in their own terms.

SOCIOLINGUISTIC ANALYSIS OF INTERVIEW DATA

Sociolinguistic analysis can help to uncover the discourse and conversational norms of the participants in a research project. This is all the more important when the focus of the study is on children, because children's conversational norms and patterns can differ substantially from those of adult respondents. Sociolinguistic analysis of interview data is also an important way to address the power dynamics between the researcher and participants so that the discourse styles of both are incorporated within the interview format (see Shuy, Chapter 9, this volume).

There are a number of ways in which a researcher can bring sociolinguistic analysis into an interview study. Briggs (1986) advocates the microanalysis of an interactional event (either a natural conversation or an initial informal interview) as a way to learn the communicative norms of the participants. Eder has conducted such an analysis in her current research on children's interpretations of animal teaching stories. In analyzing the first informal interview, Eder discovered that certain questions were picked up more often than others by the group of fourth- and fifth-grade students. Not only did they have many answers to these questions when first asked, but they continued to give answers to them at various points throughout the interview, suggesting that these questions were highly salient and fit into children's own modes of discourse as well.

Eder also noted that certain of her respondents could tell from changes in her pitch and pacing that a section of interviewing was about to end and she was ready to move on to the next story. They made a point of bringing up additional ideas before it was too late. Realizing that the interviewer has the power to end sequences prematurely, Eder modified her interviewing technique, asking the children for their comments and questions or telling them directly that she was about to finish a particular section, so that they would have the opportunity to express their viewpoints completely before moving on.

Another way of bringing sociolinguistic analysis into an interview study is to begin the analysis by looking at the interview itself as a communicative event (Briggs 1986; see also in this volume Schaeffer and Maynard, Chapter 11; Baker, Chapter 19). This involves first examining the communicative structure of the interview as a whole, so that the meanings of specific responses are considered in regard to the whole

event. It is clear from Eder's analysis that children drew upon questions asked early in the interview to provide responses throughout the interview. They also referred back to earlier humorous or salient remarks. Thus if an interviewer wants to set a tone of informality, interest in hearing from all respondents, and interest in how they see the questions as applying to their lives, it is important that he or she introduce these discourse styles and strategies early in the interview.

Analyzing the discourse styles of respondents is also an important way of assessing the degree of rapport and validity achieved during the interview. If the dialect codes and styles of talking that respondents use during the interview are those they use with people they know well and with whom they are comfortable, the researcher can be assured that a high level of validity has been achieved. For example, in her research on Puerto Rican children, Ana Celia Zentella (1998) combined discourse analysis with individual interviews, observation, and analysis of letters. When she asked one respondent about her use of mixed languages, the girl explained:

> Depends who you're talkin' to. If you're talkin' to—if you're talkin' to someone that really understands it, it's not [incorrect], not if you know the differences. . . . Because I can speak to you mixed up because I know you [ACZ: Yeah] so I got that confidence. Now if someone I don't know, I will impress them. I'll talk the language of intelligence. [ACZ: Okay] 'Cause I know you I'll talk to you how I WANNA speak to you, 'cause I know you. Like, for example, right now I'm talkin to you how I WANNA speak to you. [ACZ: Right] But if I don't know you, I'll give you that RESPECT. (P. 107)

Here the respondent feels free to switch dialectical codes during the interview because she knows the interviewer well and it is the mode of speaking with which she is most comfortable. She further acknowledges her ability to use a more standard code with people she does not know as well, as a way to convey respect. By discussing this topic directly, the interviewer gains further evidence that this young woman feels comfortable using her preferred mode of speech during the interview.

A researcher can also gain a sense of whether the language respondents use during an interview reflects the typical norms of their group by looking at the modes of talk they use while answering other questions in the interview. For example, in Fingerson's (1999) research, she found numerous examples of collaborative talk and many examples of playful discourse. Both modes are typical of the ways in which girls of that age develop shared knowledge and strengthen the cohesion of their groups (Eder 1988, 1995). The following is an illustration from the group members' answers to a question on how television shows compare to real family life:

Annette: Well, I think the difference between TV families and real life families if they're like TV families seem to get along really well.

Carolyn: Yeah.

Annette: Like on *Full House* or something well they always have a problem but they talk it out and then everyone goes back to being one big happy family. Heh heh.

Carolyn: Heh heh.

Annette: Real life doesn't work that way.

Carolyn: Sort of like a fairy tale, always like a happy ending, heh.

Shauna: Yeah, that's not the way it happens in my family.

Carolyn: No, heh heh.

Annette: Heh heh.

In this collaborative talk sequence, the girls build upon each other's ideas in the "cooperative overlap style" (Eder 1988).

Carolyn gives supporting comments to Annette, such as "yeah," and laughs along with the previous speaker. Often in collaboration, the speakers will start with minimal comments such as "yeah" and then expand on the topic later. Carolyn's first expansion is when she talks about the television program being "like a fairy tale." Shauna then enters the discussion by agreeing and expanding. Then the other two girls laugh in shared humor about how their families do not get along as well as the TV family does. The existence of this collaborative talk suggests that the girls naturally talk about television among their peers and supports the validity of using focus groups to investigate collective interpretations of media content.

So far, we have discussed sociolinguistic analysis primarily as a way to strengthen and assess the degree of validity in interview data. However, more and more research of children's experiences is addressing *how* children develop their social knowledge as well as the content of that knowledge. This indicates that sociolinguistic analysis can be an important part of the ongoing analysis of interview data, in that it can offer insights concerning how meanings are developed and shared.

Several approaches have been suggested for how to incorporate this type of analysis into more typical interview analysis of *what* people think and believe. Jaber Gubrium and James Holstein (1997) note that one way to deal with the tension of two different analytic focuses is through "analytic bracketing." Here, one employs one type of analysis at a time, looking either at what is being said or at how it is being accomplished.

Another approach is to examine both aspects of the analysis organized around the content of the material. In Eder's collaborative research on romantic norms among adolescent girls, the researchers examined both the content of each norm and the processes by which the norm was constructed and shared (Simon et al. 1992). In a group interview, girls discussed the norm of having romantic feelings for only one boy at a time. Although this was an emerging norm in this group of girls, it was not yet shared by all. Thus when this topic came up, their playful challenges became more serious, as can be seen in the following example:

Ellen: We were sittin' there starin' at guys at church last night, me and Hanna were, and—

Hanna: And she saw one that looked just like Craig.

Natalie: But// I was—

Ellen: I wasn't starin' at him.

Hanna: That was groaty.

Natalie: You're going with Craig.

Ellen: I know. I stared at Steve. Heh, heh.

Hanna: I know, but he looks like him in the face,

Natalie: But, um, he just—

Peg: You// go to church for a different reason than that, Ellen!

Natalie: I// get stuck on one guy.

Peg: Then you shouldn't of been there.

In this episode, the girls begin by providing mild challenges regarding Ellen's action of staring at one boy while going with another. Hanna comments, "That was groaty" (gross), and Natalie reminds Ellen that she is going with Craig. Ellen treats these challenges in a humorous manner, showing that she is not taking this violation seriously, and Hanna collaborates with Ellen by saying again that the boys look alike. Peg then offers another reason for the inappropriateness of Ellen's behavior—that it occurred in church. This is a more serious challenge to Ellen. It is immediately followed by Natalie stating the normative rule as she follows it: "I get stuck on one guy." In this episode we see how mild and strong challenges can be mixed together as girls

deliberate their views on the norms of romantic love. It also shows that girls' informal discourse includes both confrontations and collaborations, often side by side. In general, this interview extract demonstrates not only the content of the girls' peer culture, but some of the communicative styles used to develop and express the norms of this culture.

REPRESENTING YOUTH IN THEIR OWN TERMS

In research on children and adolescents, there are several strategies investigators can use to give their respondents a voice. For example, Barrie Thorne (1994) uses the term *kids* to describe the participants in her research rather than *children*, which is a term only adults use. They refer to themselves as kids, so she maintains their own language and terminology in her research presentation. It is important to represent youth in their own terms in data analysis and presentation. Not only does this help maintain their power in the research interaction, but it preserves their conceptions and meanings in the analysis and text.

Another way in which a researcher can represent children in their own terms is by actively bringing children's voices into the research project itself and any presentations of the research. This can be done through liberal use of direct quotes from interviews. Sara Shandler (1999) takes direct issue with adult representation of adolescent voices; she criticizes in particular the work of Mary Pipher (1994), who, in her best-selling book *Reviving Ophelia*, discusses adolescent girls and their difficulties with depression, eating disorders, addictions, and suicide attempts. Shandler, who wrote her book *Ophelia Speaks* while she was a high school student, argues that Pipher accurately uncovers issues of importance to Shandler and her friends, but notes her disappointment that the voices of the girls studied are not represented in Pipher's research. In response, Shandler solicited letters and essays from adolescent girls all over the United States; *Ophelia Speaks* is composed mostly of these unedited essays.

Other researchers have made conscious efforts to include participants' voices in their research presentations. Lees (1993) demonstrates her awareness of the importance of the language and discourse structures of the girls she studied through her open-ended and nondirective interview techniques as well as her liberal use of direct quotes in her book. She argues that "by focusing on the terms girls used to describe their world, and by looking across at the transcripts, light was thrown on the commonalities of the girls' lives and how individual experiences were socially structured" (p. 11). In a more direct approach, Hecht (1998) developed "radio workshops" in which the participants handled the audio recorder and asked each other questions. Then, in his analysis, he relied heavily on the children's questions as analytic categories. In general, researchers can use participants' own voices, which accurately express their views, and give them some power over the presentation of their voices as yet another way to combat the power differential inherent in the researcher-researched relationship.

◆ Conclusion

A theme throughout this chapter has been the importance of finding multiple ways of responding to the power differential between adult researchers and young participants. Some feminist researchers have come to the conclusion that regardless of any efforts a researcher makes, the researcher has the ultimate power in the interaction because he or she is the final distributor of the data and findings drawn from that data (Fonow and Cook 1991; Acker, Barry, and Esseveld 1991; Reinharz

1992). As Pamela Cotterill (1992) argues, the researcher and the researched both have power that fluctuates and shifts between the two during the interview; however, the researcher holds the final power because it is he or she who does the interpretation and presents the data to the wider world, and these data will most likely never reach the respondents or their everyday lives. The respondents are vulnerable because they have no control over the production or distribution of the research. In spite of this, we have argued that researchers can and should attempt to empower their respondents, particularly in research involving children, where there are inherent power differences between adult and child in addition to those between researcher and participant.

As Reinharz (1992) states, interviewing allows people access to the participants' ideas, thoughts, and memories using their own words, terminology, and language structure (see also Reinharz and Chase, Chapter 4, this volume). As interviewers, our goal is to learn about the participants' worlds in their own terms (Taylor and Rupp 1991). Rather than translating these words into our own language for data presentation, we should sustain the participants' language use, as it adds new perspectives and greater depth to the data and analyses. In particular, we need to let children and adolescents speak for themselves in the data, as their language and speech are often marginalized in adult culture.

By representing our research participants in their own language and in their own terms, we can avoid viewing them as a separate "Other" (Fine 1994; Lincoln and Denzin 1994). Yvonna Lincoln and Norman Denzin (1994) argue that social science is now in a crisis of representation, with researchers asking: "Who is the Other? Can we ever hope to speak authentically of the experience of the Other, or an Other? And if not, how do we create a social science that includes the Other?" (p. 577). They argue that the answer to these questions is that, as researchers, we must include the Other in our research processes and research presentations.

Michelle Fine (1994) believes that in order to resist Othering, we need to "work the hyphen." By this she means that we must actively understand and probe our relationships with those we study. We should bring the researcher into the text and interpret the negotiated relations between the researcher and the researched to avoid seeing the researched as a distant and separate Other. Fine asserts that we must acknowledge the researcher's context, including his or her race, class, gender, and voice. Understanding these relations and placing the researcher in the data, Fine argues, will give us better data, help us to be more true to the data and the participants, and engage us in an intimacy with our research participants that will help us to be more honest in our analyses, interpretations, and data presentation.

Hood et al. (1999) ask several questions that we as researchers must think about in our endeavors: "Whose interests are served by research? For whom is it undertaken? What research methods are appropriate? How can those researched find a voice in the research process?" It is particularly important that we ask the questions of research "for what and for whom" when we are conducting research on children, as they are among the least powerful of all research participants.

In interviewing with children and adolescents, the power imbalance between interviewer and interviewee is highlighted so that it is impossible to ignore. However, much of what we have discussed in this chapter is relevant to other interview contexts as well. Although children are perhaps the least powerful Others, women, people of color, lower-class people, and those with disabilities also lack power in our society. We have drawn on the writings of feminists and people of color for insights into how to deal with the power differential of age. In turn, we believe that many of the insights gained by those who have examined age as a power factor can be applied to other situations in which there are additional power differences between researchers and participants. Indeed, all interviewers could benefit from considering these issues, because interviewers, by virtue of their role in data collection and analysis, have a power advantage over their respondents. As we have stated throughout, this advantage is most problematic when interviewers fail to recognize it and fail to adopt strategies to minimize the power imbalance. By increasing awareness of this important issue, we hope in general to promote better interview data as well as better relationships between researchers and those they study.

■ Note

1. In the examples of discourse data, double slashes indicate where an interruption has occurred and material in parentheses describes nonverbal and paralinguistic behaviors. All names used in the examples are pseudonyms.

■ References

Acker, J., K. Barry, and J. Esseveld. 1991. "Objectivity and Truth: Problems in Doing Feminist Research." Pp. 133-53 in *Beyond Methodology: Feminist Scholarship as Lived Research,* edited by M. M. Fonow and J. A. Cook. Bloomington: Indiana University Press.

Adler, P. A. and P. Adler. 1998. *Peer Power: Preadolescent Culture and Identity.* New Brunswick, NJ: Rutgers University Press.

Albrecht, T. L., G. M. Johnson, and J. B. Walther. 1993. "Understanding Communication Processes in Focus Groups." Pp. 51-64 in *Successful Focus Groups: Advancing the State of the Art,* edited by D. L. Morgan. Newbury Park, CA: Sage.

Briggs, C. L. 1986. *Learning How to Ask: A Sociolinguistic Appraisal of the Role of the Interview in Social Science Research.* Cambridge: Cambridge University Press.

Brown, L. M. and C. Gilligan. 1992. *Meeting at the Crossroads: Women's Psychology and Girls' Development.* New York: Ballantine.

Bryant, B. K. 1985. "The Neighborhood Walk: Sources of Support in Middle Childhood." *Monographs of the Society for Research in Child Development* 50(3, Serial No. 210).

Cantor, M. G. 1991. "The American Family on Television: From Molly Goldberg to Bill Cosby." *Journal of Comparative Family Studies* 22:205-16.

Cantor, M. G. and J. M. Cantor. 1992. *Prime-Time Television: Content and Control.* Newbury Park, CA: Sage.

Caputo, V. 1995. "Anthropology's Silent 'Others': A Consideration of Some Conceptual and Methodological Issues for the Study of Youth and Children's Cultures," in *Youth Cultures: A Cross-Cultural Perspective,* edited by V. Amit-Talai and H. Wulff. London: Routledge.

Collins, P. H. 1990. *Black Feminist Thought: Knowledge, Consciousness, and the Politics of Empowerment.* New York: Routledge, Chapman & Hall.

Cook, J. A. and M. M. Fonow. 1986. "Knowledge and Women's Interests: Issues of Epistemology and Methodology in Feminist Sociological Research." *Sociological Inquiry* 56:2-27.

Corsaro, W. A. 1981. "Entering the Child's World: Research Strategies for Field Entry and Data Collection in a Preschool Setting." Pp. 117-46 in *Ethnography and Language in Educational Settings,* edited by J. Green and C. Wallet. Norwood, NJ: Ablex.

———. 1997. *The Sociology of Childhood.* Thousand Oaks, CA: Pine Forge.

Corsaro, W. A. and D. Eder. 1995. "The Development and Socialization of Children and Adolescents." Pp. 421-51 in *Sociological Perspectives on Social Psychology,* edited by K. S. Cook, G. A. Fine, and J. S. House. Boston: Allyn & Bacon.

Cotterill, P. 1992. "Interviewing Women: Issues of Friendship, Vulnerability, and Power." *Women's Studies International Forum* 15:5-6.

Davies, B. 1989. *Frogs and Snails and Feminist Tales: Preschool Children and Gender.* Boston: Allen & Unwin.

Denzin, N. K. and Y. S. Lincoln. 1994. "Introduction: Entering the Field of Qualitative Research." Pp. 1-17 in *Handbook of Qualitative Research,* edited by N. K. Denzin and Y. S. Lincoln. Thousand Oaks, CA: Sage.

Eckert, P. 1989. *Jocks and Burnouts: Social Categories and Identity in the High School.* New York: Teachers College Press.

Eder, D. 1988. "Building Cohesion through Collaborative Narration." *Social Psychology Quarterly* 51:225-35.

———. 1995. *School Talk: Gender and Adolescent Culture.* New Brunswick, NJ: Rutgers University Press.

Fine, G. A. and K. L. Sandstrom. 1988. *Knowing Children: Participant Observation with Minors.* Newbury Park, CA: Sage.

Fine, M. 1994. "Working the Hyphens: Reinventing Self and Other in Qualitative Research." Pp. 70-82 in *Handbook of Qualitative Research,* edited by N. K. Denzin and Y. S. Lincoln. Thousand Oaks, CA: Sage.

Fine, M. and P. Macpherson. 1994. "Over Dinner: Feminism and Adolescent Female Bodies." Pp. 219-46 in *Power/Gender: Social Relations in Theory and Practice,* edited by H. L. Radtke and H. J. Stam III. London: Sage.

Fingerson, L. 1999. "Active Viewing: Girls' Interpretations of Family Television Programs." *Journal of Contemporary Ethnography* 28:389-418.

Fonow, M. M. and J. A. Cook. 1991. "Back to the Future: A Look at the Second Wave of Feminist Epistemology and Methodology." Pp. 1-15 in *Beyond Methodology: Feminist Scholarship as Lived Research,* edited by M. M. Fonow and J. A. Cook. Bloomington: Indiana University Press.

Frønes, I. 1994. "Dimensions of Childhood." Pp. 145-64 in *Childhood Matters: Social Theory, Practice and Politics,* edited by J. Qvortrup, M. Bardy, G. Sgritta, and H. Wintersberger. Aldershot, England: Avebury.

Gillespie, M. 1995. *Television, Ethnicity and Cultural Change.* London: Routledge.

Gilligan, C. 1982. *In a Different Voice: Psychological Theory and Women's Development.* Cambridge, MA: Harvard University Press.

Gilligan, C., N. P. Lyons, and T. J. Hanmer, eds. 1990. *Making Connections: The Relational Worlds of Adolescent Girls at Emma Willard School.* Cambridge, MA: Harvard University Press.

Goodey, C. 1999. "Learning Disabilities: The Researcher's Voyage to Planet Earth." In *Critical Issues in Social Research: Power and Prejudice,* edited by S. Hood, B. Mayall, and S. Oliver. Philadelphia: Open University Press.

Granello, D. H. 1997. "Using *Beverly Hills, 90210* to Explore Developmental Issues in Female Adolescents." *Youth & Society* 29:24-53.

Green, R. 1990. "American Indian Women: Diverse Leadership for Social Change." Pp. 61-73 in *Bridges of Power: Women's Multicultural Alliances,* edited by L. Albrecht and R. M. Brewer. Philadelphia: New Society.

Greenberg, B. S. 1980. *Life on Television: Content Analyses of U.S. TV Drama.* Norwood, NJ: Ablex.

Gubrium, J. F. and J. A. Holstein. 1997. *The New Language of Qualitative Method.* New York: Oxford University Press.

Hecht, T. 1998. *At Home in the Street: Street Children of Northeast Brazil.* Cambridge: Cambridge University Press.

Hodge, R. and D. Tripp. 1986. *Children and Television: A Semiotic Approach.* Cambridge: Polity.

Holmes, R. M. 1998. *Fieldwork with Children.* Thousand Oaks, CA: Sage.

Hood, S., B. Mayall, and S. Oliver. 1999. "Introduction." In *Critical Issues in Social Research: Power and Prejudice,* edited by S. Hood, B. Mayall, and S. Oliver. Philadelphia: Open University Press.

Larkin, R. 1979. *Suburban Youth in Cultural Crisis.* New York: Oxford University Press.

Lather, P. 1988. "Feminist Perspectives on Empowering Research Methodologies." *Women's Studies International Forum* 11:569-81.

Lees, S. 1993. *Sugar and Spice: Sexuality and Adolescent Girls.* London: Penguin.

Lincoln, Y. S. and N. K. Denzin. 1994. "The Fifth Moment." Pp. 575-86 in *Handbook of Qualitative Research,* edited by N. K. Denzin and Y. S. Lincoln. Thousand Oaks, CA: Sage.

Mayall, B. 1999. "Children and Childhood." In *Critical Issues in Social Research: Power and Prejudice,* edited by S. Hood, B. Mayall, and S. Oliver. Philadelphia: Open University Press.

McRobbie, A. 1991. *Feminism and Youth Culture: From "Jackie" to "Just Seventeen."* Boston: Unwin Hyman.

Milkie, M. 1994. "Social World Approach to Cultural Studies: Mass Media and Gender in the Adolescent Peer Group." *Journal of Contemporary Ethnography* 23:354-80.

Morgan, D. L. 1993. "Future Directions for Focus Groups." In *Successful Focus Groups: Advancing the State of the Art,* edited by D. L. Morgan. Newbury Park, CA: Sage.

Orenstein, P. 1994. *School Girls: Young Women, Self-Esteem, and the Confidence Gap.* New York: Doubleday.

Peterson, G. W. and D. F. Peters. 1983. "Adolescents' Construction of Social Reality: The Impact of Television and Peers." *Youth & Society* 15:67-85.

Pipher, M. 1994. *Reviving Ophelia: Saving the Selves of Adolescent Girls.* New York: Ballantine.

Prout, A. and A. James. 1997. "A New Paradigm for the Sociology of Childhood? Provenance, Promise, and Problems." Pp. 7-33 in *Constructing and Reconstructing Childhood: Contemporary Issues in the Sociological Study of Childhood,* edited by A. James and A. Prout. London: Falmer.

Radway, J. 1984. "Interpretive Communities and Variable Literacies." *Daedalus* 113:49-73.

Reinharz, S. 1992. *Feminist Methods in Social Research.* New York: Oxford University Press.

Shandler, S. 1999. *Ophelia Speaks: Adolescent Girls Write about Their Search for Self.* New York: Harper Perennial.

Sieber, J. E. 1992. "Community Intervention Research on Minors." In *Social Research on Children and Adolescents: Ethical Issues,* edited by B. Stanley and J. E. Sieber. Newbury Park, CA: Sage.

Simmons, R. G. and D. A. Blyth. 1987. *Moving into Adolescence: The Impact of Pubertal Change and School Context*. New York: Aldine de Gruyter.

Simon, R., D. Eder, and C. Evans. 1992. "The Development of Feeling Norms Underlying Romantic Love among Adolescent Females." *Social Psychology Quarterly* 55:29-46.

Tammivaara, J. and D. S. Enright. 1986. "On Eliciting Information: Dialogues with Child Informants." *Anthropology and Education Quarterly* 17:218-38.

Taylor, J. M., C. Gilligan, and A. M. Sullivan. 1995. *Between Voice and Silence: Women and Girls, Race and Relationship*. Cambridge, MA: Harvard University Press.

Taylor, V. and L. J. Rupp. 1991. "Researching the Women's Movement: We Make Our Own History, but Not Just as We Please." Pp. 119-32 in *Beyond Methodology: Feminist Scholarship as Lived Research*, edited by M. M. Fonow and J. A. Cook. Bloomington: Indiana University Press.

Thompson, S. 1995. *Going All the Way: Teenage Girls' Tales of Sex, Romance, and Pregnancy*. New York: Hill & Wang.

Thorne, B. 1994. *Gender Play: Girls and Boys in School*. New Brunswick, NJ: Rutgers University Press.

Tolman, D. 1994. "Daring to Desire: Culture and Bodies of Adolescent Girls." In *Sexual Cultures and the Construction of Adolescent Identities*, edited by J. M. Irvine. Philadelphia: Temple University Press.

Valenzuela, A. 1999. *Subtractive Schooling: U.S.-Mexican Youth and the Politics of Caring*. Albany: State University of New York Press.

Ward, J. and J. Taylor. 1991. "Sex Education for Immigrant and Minority Students: Developing a Culturally Appropriate Curriculum." In *Sexuality and the Curriculum: The Politics and Practices of Sexuality Education*, edited by J. T. Sears. New York: Teachers College Press.

Weisner, T. S. 1996. "Why Ethnography Should Be the Most Important Method in the Study of Human Development." In *Ethnography and Human Development: Context and Meaning in Social Inquiry*, edited by R. Jessor, A. Colby, and R. A. Shweder. Chicago: University of Chicago Press.

Youniss, J. and J. Smollar. 1985. *Adolescent Relations with Mothers, Fathers, and Friends*. Chicago: University of Chicago Press.

Zentella, A. C. 1998. "Multiple Codes, Multiple Identities: Puerto Rican Children in New York City." Pp. 95-112 in *Kids Talk: Strategic Language Use in Later Childhood*, edited by S. M. Hoyle and C. T. Adger. New York: Oxford University Press.

3

INTERVIEWING MEN

♦ Michael L. Schwalbe
Michelle Wolkomir

For most of the history of social science, men were considered the standard, normal, unmarked category of human beings, and so it would have seemed odd, not that long ago, to write about interviewing *men,* as if doing so required special strategies or techniques. Some readers might be skeptical even now. Why, after all, isn't good technique enough? What is it about interviewing men that calls for anything more? Our answer is that good technique—as might befit the imaginary generic interview subject—does not adequately equip us to recognize and respond to problems that arise specifically from how men "do gender" in an interview. Working around these problems, and perhaps even turning them into useful data, requires seeing how they arise from men's efforts to signify, in culturally prescribed ways, a creditable masculine self.

Of course we are generalizing. All men, obviously, do not behave the same way in interviews. Much depends on who is inter-

viewing whom, how, about what, when, and where. To the extent, however, that men attempt to signify elements of what has come to be called *hegemonic masculinity,* and do so in conventional ways, their behavior will be patterned (Connell 1995). We might even say that although the category "men" is internally diverse in many ways, what gives it coherence at all is its members' recognizably similar patterns of self-presentation. Which is to say that if the creatures we call "men" did not do gender in roughly similar ways, we would not even know them as men. But, again, our claim is not that all men behave alike; rather, it is that a particular *cultural* prescription for self-presentation—when men feel compelled to abide by it—will generate a predictable set of problems in interviews.

The advice we offer for dealing with these problems applies mainly to intensive, flexible interviewing. This is the kind of interviewing that is most likely to evoke the masculinity displays that block communication and call for interviewer skill in drawing out unarticulated meanings. Our advice may thus be of less use to researchers doing survey-style interviews that do not probe sensitive territory. We are also addressing mainly those who do inductive or quasi-inductive research, because our advice presumes that interviews are open to change over the course of a study. If the aim of strict hypothesis testing dictates no evolution in interview content and strategy, then our advice will apply mostly to the phase in which an interview protocol is devised.

If one's research has to do with gender, then there is another good reason to pay attention to masculinity displays: Such displays are not simply obstacles to obtaining the data one wants, they may in fact constitute part of the data one needs (see also Reinharz and Chase, Chapter 4, this volume). *How* men answer questions and *how they behave in an interview* are potentially valuable sources of data when the research has to do with gender or topics related to gender (e.g., division of household labor). To see these data, we have to recognize the kinds of verbal and physical behaviors that can be interpreted as signifying masculinity. Knowing what to look for, as we will show, makes it possible for us to see not only problems but more information and new paths for inquiry.

In the section below we lay out our perspective on gender enactments as problems and as resources in interviewing men. In the next section of the chapter, we examine specific problems and offer potential solutions. We then consider strategies for informal interviewing—the practice of interviewing by casual question. Finally, we offer several general suggestions for doing better interviews in field studies focusing on men. Our advice grows primarily out of our experiences as field-workers studying men, usually in an inductive or quasi-inductive fashion. We hope that readers whose research styles differ will find ways to adapt our suggestions to suit their purposes.

◆ The Masculine Self and the Interview Situation

Gender is socially constructed, in part, through the identity work we do that marks us as members of the category "men" or the category "women" (Kessler and McKenna 1978; West and Zimmerman 1987). As adults, our bodies do much of this identity work for us, although we also use speech, dress, and movement to corroborate the body's silent claims (Schwalbe and Mason-Schrock 1996). But it is not merely category membership, as if this were a matter of casual choice, that we must signify. The prevailing gender order requires that we also signify possession of an essentially gendered self that makes our placement in a particular category right and proper. This self is not a psychic entity that exists inside individuals; rather, it is a dramatic effect created by performance and interpretation.[1]

For men, the dramaturgical task is to signify possession of an essentially masculine self, a self with the desires and capacities that warrant membership in the dominant group (Brittan 1989). Precisely what must be signified, and how it must be done, will vary by age, ethnicity, social class, sexual orientation, local culture, and immediate circumstance. A masculine self is thus always the product of a performance tailored to the situation and audience at hand. Despite variations in the details of performance, we can see commonalities that arise from a pervasive cultural notion of the qualities and capacities men must signify to be fully creditable as men.

In Western culture, men who wish to claim the full privileges of manhood must distinguish themselves from women by signifying greater desires and capacities for control of people and the world, autonomous thought and action, rational thought and action, risk and excitement, and (hetero)sexual pleasure and prowess (Connell 1995). Obviously, we have put things in general and abbreviated terms. Each element could be unpacked, and arguments could be made about which is most important. Our purpose, however, is only to sketch the self that men's expressive behavior is often aimed, sometimes strategically and perhaps more often as a matter of unconscious habit, at creating. We can, with this sketch in mind, get a better understanding of what goes wrong in interviews with men.

THE INTERVIEW AS
THREAT AND OPPORTUNITY

Every encounter, as Erving Goffman (1967:97-112) notes, is fraught with risk. The selves we try to create, the selves to which are attached some of our strongest feelings, can be sabotaged by our own gaffes or by the antagonistic acts of others. All selves are thus provisional; none is safe from the threat of discrepant information or disbelieving audiences. The harder it is to control the leakage of discrepant information, or the more incredulous the audience, the harder it will be to sustain a particular kind of self. A masculine self can be a tenuous construct for both reasons.

To sustain such a self requires, as noted previously, signifying desires and/or capacities for control, autonomy, rationality, risk taking, and heterosexual conquest. Acts that signify these qualities must be integrated into a performance recognizable as "being a man." The problem, however, is that reality often contradicts the performance. Most men have little control over their worlds; no man exists without ties to others; men's alleged rationality is usually a matter of post hoc rationalizing to mask the emotional basis of action; most men are conformists who take few significant risks of any kind; and most men do more sexual fantasizing than "conquesting." The manhood act, we might say, is performed rather worriedly in a field of discrepant information.

Audience cooperation is often problematic because the masculine self is crafted to evoke deference and compliance in members of the validating audience. This gives others incentive to be alert for flaws in the performance, for evidence that a particular masculine self warrants less deference. The others who are likely to be most alert in this regard are other men, whose success at crafting a masculine self depends, in part, on the lesser success of other men's efforts. Women, too, are a dangerous audience, although usually for different reasons. Even while they may help to sustain the masculine self, women, as witnesses to men's weaknesses and failures, know just how much of an illusion it is. Women thus often possess a great deal of potentially discrediting information. Heterosexual women may also have incentive to disrupt the performance of manhood because of the obstacle it presents to achieving intimacy.

It is understandable, then, that men can be insecure, anxious, and afraid even while striving to construct a self that is supposedly the antithesis of these emotions. Some situations, of course, will be more problematic than others, depending on the performance called for and the cooperativeness of the audience. In general terms, however, we can say that situations that make it difficult to signify control, autonomy, rationality, and sexual desirability may be especially anxiety provoking for men wedded to displaying hegemonic masculinity.[2] In such situations we might expect to see behaviors aimed at countering, or symbolically compensating for, the real or implied threat to the masculine self.

An interview situation is both an opportunity for signifying masculinity and a peculiar type of encounter in which masculinity is threatened. It is an opportunity to signify masculinity inasmuch as men are allowed to portray themselves as in control, autonomous, rational, and so on. It is a threat inasmuch as an interviewer controls the interaction, asks questions that put these elements of manly self-portrayal into doubt, and does not simply affirm a man's masculinity displays. We propose distinguishing between the *baseline threat* to masculinity posed by the interview situation and the *surplus threat* that arises because of who is asking whom about what.

The baseline threat is built into any intensive interview. The situation is usually defined as one in which a stranger sets the agenda, asks the questions, controls the flow of talk, and probes for information about internal or backstage realities. To agree to sit for an interview, no matter how friendly and conversational, is to give up some control and to risk having one's public persona stripped away. For these reasons, many people, men and women, find interviews discomfiting. But because male privilege is staked on signifying a masculine self, men may perceive a greater threat and may act in ways that give rise to predictable sorts of problems—even if the topics being explored are not in themselves terribly sensitive.

Surplus threat can arise from at least two sources. One is a line of questioning that might expose the masculine self as illusory. Questions calling for answers that put control, autonomy, or rationality into doubt, if only implicitly, may be experienced as threatening. The threat may be heightened if it seems that the interviewer is interested in gender, broadly construed, because this makes the subject's identity as a man more salient to the interaction. Surplus threat can also arise because of the interviewer's identity. The threat potential is likely to be different if, for example, a gay man interviews other gay men about sexual behavior, as opposed to a straight man asking the same questions. Other kinds of difference—most obviously along lines of race, class, and age—in combination with certain topics, can also heighten the threat potential of an interview (see also in this volume Kong, Mahoney, and Plummer, Chapter 5; Dunbar, Rodriguez, and Parker, Chapter 7).

We do not suppose that the threat potential of a line of questioning, a specific topic, or an interviewer's identity is always consciously perceived. More likely, it is perceived only vaguely. Reactions to such threat are also more likely to be matters of self-presentational habit than of conscious strategy. Most men, after all, are well practiced in adapting their signifying behavior to the situation at hand. A subject's conscious awareness of the threat to the masculine self is, however, beside the point. What matters is the *interviewer's* awareness of the threat potential, alertness for problems arising because of this threat, and ability to respond in a way that makes the interview successful.

Again, the category "men" is internally diverse, and therefore all generalizations about how men will perceive and respond to the threat potential of an interview are empirically suspect. But so too are generalizations about men in categories defined by sexual orientation, race, ethnicity, and class. These categories are not unitary, either. Not all men who identify as gay, or as black, or as working-class will experience the threat potential of an interview in the same way, even if all else is constant. Multiple category memberships, plus an interviewer's possible ignorance of the categories to which a subject belongs, can also complicate things. We thus propose that the best way for an interviewer to deal with diversity among men is also the best way to discover patterns among men: Avoid presuming very much based on membership in *any* categories and rely instead on the interview itself to reveal the individual.

In considering specific problems and possible responses, we assume that the interviewer's goal is to obtain accurate and complete information about whatever matters the research is concerned with. The problems we discuss in the next section are ones that impede communication and thus make it hard for the interviewer to get good data. In most cases, the interviewer can overcome these problems by using strategies that minimize threat to the masculine self. But it would be a loss, we think, to treat the identity work men do in interviews as noise that one must filter out in order to get at the "real" data. Instead, we suggest that this identity work be treated as data—the first step being to see it, in the form of how and when men try to signify masculinity in interviews. The opportunity here for researchers is not merely to get more data, but to get a kind of data that can help us develop more insightful analyses of men's lives as gendered beings.

◆ Problems and Strategies

The problems examined here have come up in our work or the work of colleagues. The strategies we suggest are, in most cases, ones we have used ourselves. Their effectiveness will depend, of course, on context and on who is interviewing whom about what. A strategy that works for a male interviewer might not work for a female interviewer, and vice versa. The keys to finding a strategy that works are, first, recognizing the nature of the masculinity threat that is evoking defensiveness and, second, careful review of tapes or transcripts yielded by alternative strategies. Without some analysis, *early in a study,* of what is going wrong in interviews, it is hard to see how to make things go right.[3]

THE STRUGGLE FOR CONTROL

The interview situation itself, as we noted earlier, is potentially threatening to the masculine self because the interviewee relinquishes control, the exercise of which is a basic way in which masculinity is signified. To open oneself to interrogation is to put oneself in a vulnerable position, and thus to put one's masculinity further at risk. It is not uncommon, then, in our experience, for men being interviewed to try to exert a sort of compensatory control over the interview situation. This behavior can take various forms, which can be more or less problematic. Three forms that can disrupt the interview process are what we call testing, sexualizing, and minimizing.

Testing is an attempt to expose a researcher's agenda and/or inferiority when it comes to grasping the matters being inquired about. Terry Arendell (1997), for example, describes how some of the divorced fathers she interviewed made a point of saying that, as a woman, she would be unable to understand men's experiences and to give them fair consideration. Michelle Wolkomir (1999) describes how, in a study of gay religious men, she was told that, as a heterosexual woman, she would not be able to face the indelicate facts of gay male sex. In these cases, subjects sought to test both the interviewer's legitimacy as an interrogator and the interviewer's ability to maintain control of the situation (see Dunbar et al., Chapter 7, this volume). If the interviewer is flustered, or concedes being in unfathomable waters, control shifts to the interviewee.

How the interviewer handles such testing will have consequences for how the interview unfolds. Losing poise or concentration because of a subject's efforts to reassert control can obviously be detrimental to the quality of an interview. Expecting and being prepared for these assertions of compensatory control—and understanding their meaning—can render them manageable and, in fact, useful as data. To manage, or perhaps even preempt them, an interviewer might employ a number of strategies:

◆ Allow *symbolic* expressions of control. For example, explain what kind of arrangement is needed for a good interview to occur, and then let the subject choose the time and place. If the subject proposes an unsatisfactory arrangement, ask, "I wonder if you could find us a place that is [quieter/more private/more accessible]?" This strategy allows the subject to feel in control even while this "control" serves the purpose of creating a good interview situation.[4]

◆ Let the subject ask the first question. We presume that the interviewer will offer some sort of preamble before launching into questions. A way to do this that lowers the threat to control is to say, "I appreciate your willingness to help me with my research. Before I ask any questions, I wonder if you'd like to know more about what it is I'm interested in." This lets men feel less like they are relinquishing control to a stranger with an unknown agenda and provides a chance for the them to test the researcher in a way that can generate useful data.

◆ Challenge the subject to take charge as an *expert*. The idea is to allow men to feel in control and powerful in a particular way: by providing useful information. This can be done with probes that altercast the subject as expert or teacher: Can you explain to me how . . . ? Can you help me understand how . . . ? What does that entail? In light of your experience, can you tell me more about _____? What's the most important thing to understand about _____?

◆ A variation on the preceding strategy is to preface a question with "I'm not sure how to ask this, but . . . ." This preface, which should be used sparingly, reduces threat by taking the interviewer out of the role of grand inquisitor. It also allows the subject to assume a triple expert role: as one whose experiences are not easily grasped by outsiders, as one who knows how questions ought to be asked to get at the heart of things, and as one who knows the answers.

◆ In the face of overt testing, adopt the stance of an investigator who is firmly and fearlessly determined to learn whatever is important to know about the subject's experience. For example, Wolkomir, in seeking access to an ex-gay men's Bible study group, was initially tested by the group leader, who told her that the men's frank talk of "fisting" and other sexual practices would be more than she could handle. She replied, "It's only sex, and it seems to bother you more than

me." This response effectively stopped the leader's testing behavior and gained Wolkomir access to the group.

◆ When the opportunity presents itself, probe sensitive topics by saying, "Since you brought it up, I was wondering if you could tell me more about _____." This allows the subject to feel more in control of the flow of talk and also invokes the conversational norm that obligates the subject to say more about a topic he has brought up.

In metaphorical terms, we are suggesting a kind of research aikido—the martial art of turning the other's movement and energy to one's own advantage. This is not to say that we see all interviews as contests or struggles. We prefer, in fact, the metaphor of conversation (Briggs 1986; Mishler 1986). Be that as it may, in interviews with men the subtle threat to control, hence to masculinity, can generate a kind of struggle —of which men themselves may be only dimly aware. It is the interviewer's job, however, to possess this awareness and to use it to keep things from going awry.

Inappropriate *sexualizing* is a way that some heterosexual men try to reassert control when being interviewed by women. This can take the forms of flirting, sexual innuendo, touching, and remarks on appearance (Arendell 1997; Gurney 1985; Lee 1997; McKee and O'Brien 1983). Although some of this behavior might be construed as innocent and harmless, it can also be seen as aimed at diminishing a woman's legitimacy and power as an interrogator, thus preserving a man's control of the situation. It is as if to say, "You might be asking the questions here, but I won't let you forget that you're a woman and I'm a man, and therefore I have the status advantage."

Given the normality of sexualized interaction between women and men, it might be hard to see sexualizing as a problem. Some interviewers might even see "flirting" as a way to establish rapport. Although this might work in some cases, it has the distinct disadvantage of encouraging a subject to try to create an impression of himself as sexually desirable—and therefore to conceal unflattering information. Sexualized rapport can thus turn out to be counterproductive for maximizing information gained from an interview. With that caveat made, all we can say is that researchers must decide for themselves, all things considered in the context of a given study, the degree to which sexualizing is a problem and needs to be discouraged.

Unfortunately, with men who habitually and aggressively use a sexualizing strategy to disempower women, there might be little that a researcher can do about it. But keeping in mind that sexualizing is often about control suggests some possible ways to preempt or reduce it. Allowing symbolic control, in the ways proposed earlier, might help reduce a subject's "need" to sexualize an interview situation. Researchers might also try the following:

◆ Dress in a style—befitting local culture and circumstance—that conveys a businesslike seriousness of purpose, without crossing into off-putting formality.

◆ Reward, with close attention, an interviewee's "on-task" answers while showing cool disinterest, perhaps even disappointment, in "off-task" remarks. This behavioral modification strategy may lead men to realize, or intuit, that they will be seen as desirable interactants only by performing well as sources of pertinent and original information, not tired come-ons. In general, keep turning the interview back to the subject's experience and reporting thereof.

◆ Hold interviews in businesslike or quiet public settings. Library or workplace conference rooms are possibilities, if they can be reserved. Clearly there are times and topics that demand special provisions for privacy and psychic comfort, and thus the subject's home may be the best venue. If so, the kitchen table— "because that's where I'll be more comfortable writing notes"—might be preferable to the living room. Where an interview is held conveys a message about what the interaction is about.

Sexualizing probably occurs more often to female researchers than straight male researchers realize. But again, the likelihood that it will occur depends on who is interviewing whom about what and on the threat potential of the interview. So it is quite possible that some female researchers will rarely have to deal with it. In any event, being ready for it increases the interviewer's chances of responding in a way that will keep the interview on track. We would also note that sexualizing, like any other kind of masculinity-signifying behavior in an interview, is data. See, for example, Deborah Lee (1997), who discusses how men's efforts to sexualize interviews gave her some insight into how they engaged in sexual harassment at work.

A subject who *minimizes* fails to take normal conversational cues to give expansive answers, instead offering terse answers that tell little. This kind of response pattern is typically seen as constituting a "bad interview" because a subject is simply not articulate. Although sheer inarticulateness can indeed be the problem, minimizing can also arise from a desire to protect a masculine self by maintaining control or by revealing no vulnerabilities and uncertainties. Male interviewers may thus be more likely to encounter minimizing, because they are the potential status competitors to whom revealing vulnerabilities and uncertainties is risky.

When minimizing becomes apparent— when none of one's questions are being answered in the kind of depth one had hoped for—it is tempting to write the interview off as a loss and hope that the next one goes better. It may be possible, however, for an interviewer to draw out a great deal more information through the use of strategies that are sensitive to the fear felt by the minimizer.

◆ If a subject persists in giving terse answers, despite cues and probes, let the interview proceed in exactly this way. This allows the minimizer to feel in control. But instead of ending the interview after the last question, *circle back*. Try saying, "I think that what you've said gives me a good overall picture, but I'm still unsure about a few of the more complicated issues you brought up. For instance, when you said ____." The interviewer thus admits uncertainty, affirms the subject's experience as complex, and puts the subject in the driver's seat. Often the subject will then feel comfortable enough to elaborate in a useful way.

◆ Invoke what other men have said. For example, "What you said about ____ was interesting. Other men have brought this up, but your experience seems to be somewhat different. I wonder if you could tell me a bit more about what that's been like for you." This kind of probe can make the revelation of further information seem less risky to the minimizer. After all, if other men have talked about these issues, then perhaps it is safe for him to do so. The hint of competition may also nudge the minimizer to try to outdo those other men who said more about their experience.

◆ Notepads and tape recorders are signs of an interviewer's power and can be intimidating. Minimizers will sometimes open up if these tools are set aside and the conversation is carried on in a more casual way. If a tape recorder is running, leave the notepad alone as long as possible. If a minimizer begins to speak more freely after the "official" interview is over and the tape recorder is put away, keep asking questions. Later, capture as much as possible in the form of field notes.

Our use of the term *minimizer* implies the possibility of a subject who uses a maximizing strategy—expounding vastly—to take control in an interview. It happens, we suppose. But maximizing is rarely a problem, because information is flowing freely, in which case the interviewer need only keep the interview on track. In our experience, it is much easier to steer a loquacious subject than to draw out a taciturn one.

NONDISCLOSURE OF EMOTIONS

In a classic article, Jack Sattel (1976) examines the problem of the "inexpressive male," concluding that in intimate relationships men's emotional reticence is a control strategy. According to Sattel, men conceal emotions to mask vulnerabilities and to maintain a negotiating advantage by implying readiness to leave a relationship if a partner demands too much. As suggested in our discussion of minimizing, inexpressivity may indeed be about control. But beyond control, the nondisclosure, or very limited disclosure, of emotions is a key part of signifying a (hegemonic) masculine self. This creates a problem when interviewers want to find out not only what it is that men think and do, but what they feel.

With a subject who seems unabashed, it may work to ask directly, "How did you feel about ____?" Sometimes a direct question will get one the data one hopes for. Often, however, the answer to such a question, in keeping with the strictures of masculine self-presentation, takes the form of "I guess I felt okay about it," with no further elaboration. And so it may be better, if it is crucial to obtain data about men's emotions, for the interviewer to try an indirect approach. Once again the idea is to lower the threat to the masculine self. An interviewer might accomplish this in several ways:

◆ Don't immediately try to probe emotionally loaded topics if a subject is hesitant to say more. Circle back to the topic later. Once trust has been established in an interview, a man may be more willing to share feelings. Return to a topic by saying, for example, "It seemed to me that when you talked about ____ you had some stronger feelings than you let on. I'd like to try to understand that, if it's something you can talk about."

◆ Instead of asking direct questions about emotionally loaded topics, ask for stories. For example, instead of asking, "How do you feel when you and your son argue about his performance in school?" ask for a story about a specific argument, and then, at the right time, ask, "How did you feel when your son said/did ____?" It may be easier for many men to report emotion that arose in the past than to give a report that implies an "emotional self" in the present.

◆ Invoke what other men have said. Again, this can help make the reporting of emotions seem safe and acceptable. If, for example, a man talks with no affect about an experience that seems likely to have evoked strong feelings, an interviewer might say, "Another man told me about a similar experience. For him it stirred up feelings of ____. I wonder if you felt anything like that?" This strategy can also help to get at emotional complexity. Often men will readily express anger or pride, but not admit fear or sadness. A useful probe for complexity might thus be, "Another man told of a similar experience. It made him angry too, but he said he also felt sad about it. Did anything like sadness come up for you?"

◆ Use elicitation devices. Reporting emotions in the absence of some concrete stimulus can seem to imply an unmanly degree of emotionality. An interviewer can often dispel this impression by focusing the subject's attention on an object that is seen as legitimately evocative of strong feelings. For instance, many men are more willing to describe—and to show—emotions when looking at photographs than when merely conversing. Maps, too, can be evocative, if they call up memories of places to which strong feelings are attached. But any object, if it is connected in a significant way to a sub-

ject's life, can be used to elicit reports of feelings.

◆ Ask about thoughts, not feelings, then work back to feelings. Asking, "How do you feel about ____?" can pose a threat to the masculine self. Asking, "What do you think about ____?" can, in contrast, seem to offer an opportunity to signify masculinity. But then, as the subject expounds, the interviewer must be ready to probe: "It sounds like ____ makes you feel a bit [sad/angry/embarrassed/ happy/ etc.]." Once men feel that they have justified themselves—by saying what they think—they may be more willing to talk about what they feel.

Researchers interested in men's emotions must pay attention not only to what men say in interviews, but to *how* they say it and what they *do*. Tears do not show up on transcripts, but they ought to be noted. Our point is that emotions are expressed in all kinds of ways, and that these emotional expressions are data. Men's most assiduous efforts to conceal their emotions are data, too. To reveal or report no emotion when talking about what seem likely to be powerfully affecting experiences is an act of gender signification that cries out for analysis.

EXAGGERATING RATIONALITY, AUTONOMY, AND CONTROL

Researchers want accurate and thorough accounts of events and experiences in men's lives. In addition to every other problem that stands in the way of getting such accounts is the problem of men's tendencies to exaggerate rationality, autonomy, and control as part of signifying a masculine self. These tendencies often can be countered by sensitive questioning and probing. In some cases, however, interviewers may need first to allow the exaggerations before trying to get behind them.

Previously, we suggested a circling-back strategy, which is, in general, a good way to work around many of the problems presented by masculinity displays. Once men have been allowed to signify a creditable masculine self—in the course of initially answering a set of questions—they may be willing to return to topics and reveal more uncertainty, confusion, vulnerability, and weakness. That is, they may be more willing to give accurate accounts of their experiences. We suggest, therefore, that an interviewer employ the circling-back strategy whenever his or her intuition suggests that there is a deeper level of experience to be tapped, but the subject does not seem ready to talk forthrightly about it (see Arendell 1997:352).

There are other strategies that interviewers can use, at any point in an interview, to lower threats to the masculine self and elicit more revealing accounts of men's experiences. Suppose, for purposes of illustration, that we are interviewing men to find out how they make certain kinds of career-related decisions. We might expect, owing to a desire to signify a masculine self, some exaggeration of control, autonomy, and rationality in our subjects' accounts. The following strategies might help counter this tendency:

◆ If we want to know who the men talked to in trying to make their decisions, and we ask about this directly, we might hear, "I didn't talk to anyone; I just decided." Although this might be true, it might also be an account that exaggerates autonomy. Anticipating this, we might approach the matter indirectly, by asking, "Did a friend ever talk to you when he was trying to make a decision about his career?" If yes, probe for details. Then ask, "Did *you* talk to anyone when you were trying to make that kind of decision?" This strategy lowers the threat value of the line of questioning by implying that it is okay if men talk to others when trying to make difficult decisions.

◆ Asking directly about fears and worries a man had when making his decision might elicit accounts of the hyperrational "I knew what I wanted and went after it" variety. We might get more accurate accounts by focusing attention on process and by giving a man the opportunity to speak about a younger self. For example, "Back then, you obviously didn't know what you know now. So what was going through your mind when you were trying to decide about _____?" This can open the door for probing about fears, worries, and uncertainties.

◆ A variation on the above strategy is to emphasize risk, the taking of which is consistent with signifying a masculine self. For example, "No one could have been sure how things were going to turn out. So you were taking a chance back then. How did you decide to do it?" Again, this can open the door to probing about the feelings that underlay a risky decision, feelings that might otherwise be masked by an overly rationalized account.

◆ Another variation is to ask the subject to imagine advising his younger self. For example, "Looking back, if you could step into the past and give yourself advice about making that decision, what would you say?" The answer is likely to reveal what the subject, at the time of the decision, was most unsure about. So if a subject replies, "I would tell myself to think about how time is more important than money," a probe might be, "Is that something you wrestled with back then?"

◆ Shift the focus to the environment. As long as the focus is on the subject and his choices and actions, the tendency to exaggerate control will be strong. Shifting the focus to the *context* of the subject's action can turn this tendency to the interviewer's advantage. For example, asking, "What was going on around you at that time? What kinds of problems were you facing?" poses the environment as a source of challenges that had to be met—success in doing so being to a man's credit as a man. This strategy may make a subject feel more comfortable about elaborating on the problems and struggles that were part of his experience.

- ◆ Use the conversational norm of reciprocity. That is, offer an equivalent piece of information about yourself, thus obligating the subject to share a bit more about himself. This is a risky strategy, however, in that it opens the door for a subject who truly wishes not to disclose to "turn the interview around" and begin interviewing the interviewer. We suggest that this strategy is best used by male interviewers in cases where a subject seems likely to benefit from reassurance that it is acceptable for men to express doubts, fears, and vulnerabilities. (See also in this volume Eder and Fingerson, Chapter 2; Reinharz and Chase, Chapter 4; Kong et al., Chapter 5; Dunbar et al., Chapter 7.)

Interviews that do not explore men's decision making may not give rise to the problems of exaggerated rationality, autonomy, and control in the ways we have suggested here. We think it unlikely, however, that any in-depth interviews in which men are asked to give accounts of their lives, experiences, actions, and so on will be free from problems of exaggeration. The important thing is for the interviewer to see where these problems are likely to arise and to devise questioning and probing strategies to get around them. Each of the strategies proposed above follows a logic of trying to lower the masculinity threat through indirect questioning, by affirming a masculine self-presentation and then circumventing it, or both. Researchers can use this logic to devise more effective questioning and probing strategies regardless of the research topic.

To recognize that men often exaggerate rationality, autonomy, and control is not to say that men's actions never genuinely reflect these qualities. Certainly they do; it is the degree to which they do that is often ex-

aggerated. Nor is this recognition tantamount to saying that men never give truthful accounts. In fact, all of us, women and men, give selective, strategically crafted accounts of our lives and actions. The key for researchers is to realize how gender enactments bias these accounts and to know how to work around this bias so as to get at the experiential complexity behind the identity work.

BONDING PLOYS; OR, "YOU KNOW WHAT I MEAN"

At times in intensive interviews, subjects may be hesitant to say, or even to try to say, what they mean. The job of the researcher, of course, is to get at these meanings, perhaps even helping subjects to articulate them. But researchers often fail to do this because of their own desire to be accepted and maintain rapport. It is tempting for interviewers to nod or say, "Yeah, I know what you mean," especially when they know that by saying, "No, I *don't* know what you mean," they might disrupt the comfortable flow of talk. What ends up happening, then, is that crucial meanings are glossed over and lost. And it may turn out later that the interviewer really didn't know what a subject meant.

Obviously, this problem does not arise only in interviews with men. It can arise whenever an interviewer gets into territory that is difficult for a subject to talk about explicitly, for fear of making a discrediting statement. For example, a white subject speaking to a white interviewer might try to avoid appearing overtly racist by referring to "those women who have one baby after another so they can collect bigger welfare checks—you know what I mean" (see Blee 1998). In this case, it is pretty clear what the subject means, although a good interviewer will draw it out. This example also suggests that the subject may be trying to engage in some bonding around a common identity.

It seems that this kind of bonding, the kind that can allow crucial meanings to go unarticulated, is most likely to arise when men are interviewing men (Williams and Heikes 1993). Subjects, as we have said, may have a moral identity at stake, and may for that reason wish to avoid stating some things explicitly. But it may also be that a male interviewer does not want to say that he does not know what another man means, because to do so would put the interviewer's identity as a man into question. By using the bonding ploy, the subject communicates, in effect, "If you are man, you must know what I mean." By falling for this ploy, the interviewer gains acceptance and loses information.

Not every instance of "you know what I mean" is going to demand a strategic response. Sometimes, in the course of an extensive field study, a researcher might indeed know what the subject means and not feel a need to probe. Or it might be that, at the outset of a study, the researcher deems acceptance and rapport to be more important than the information he or she might gain from probing. Researchers must make their own judgments in these matters. Presuming, however, that at some point a researcher wishes to explore the meanings hidden by bonding ploys, the following strategies might be helpful:

◆ Circle back to what a subject presumed you understood. For example, "Earlier you said _____. I just want to make sure I understood you. Did you mean _____?" Again, the circling-back strategy allows a subject to feel as if his self-presentation has been seen and appreciated, and thus he may be more willing to reveal information that he was hesitant to reveal initially. Asking, "Did you mean _____?" also allows the subject to take the masculinity-signifying role of corrector if the interviewer gets it wrong.

◆ Take a newcomer's license not to understand. If a subject says, "You know what I mean," a researcher can say, "I think I do, but I'd rather not presume anything before I've got a handle on what's going on here. So maybe you could clue me in."

Often this is enough to induce a subject to elaborate. Again, it allows the subject to play the mentor who is showing the greenhorn the ropes.

◆ Try to articulate what the subject presumably means, then ask for corroboration, qualification, or correction. On the one hand, this can be as simple as saying, "Do you mean _____?" and having a subject say "Yes." On the other hand, getting such a yes might be too easy and may lead nowhere. Thus a better strategy is to say, "Do you mean _____, or do you mean _____?" This presumes that it is possible to articulate plausible alternative meanings. If a researcher can do this, it invites the subject to say more about which meaning he intends.

◆ Try indirect approaches to matters that evoke bonding ploys. Suppose, for example, a man is apparently hesitant to admit that he believes women do not belong in what he construes as his properly all-male workplace, because of "well, because of how women are—you know what I mean." To crack this open, a researcher might come at the matter indirectly by asking, "What kind of jobs do women tend to be good at?" The subject's answer, whatever it might be, is likely to offer the researcher a chance to ask, "So how do you think women do/would do in your kind of job?" This indirect route gives the subject a chance to justify himself and may lead to an enthusiastic unpacking of "you know what I mean."

These strategies are best seen as ways to "crack open" an interview. Merely coming at something indirectly, if it is a transparently strategic maneuver on the interviewer's part, is unlikely to work, and may even backfire. The purpose of these moves of indirection is not to trick a subject into self-disclosure, but to lead a subject to a place where he will be comfortable enough to unpack his thoughts and feelings. This "place" is arrived at when a subject feels he has created a sufficiently durable image of himself—as a man and/or as a good person—that it will not be discredited by his saying more about some matter that was previously glossed, evaded, or unarticulated. In interviews as in life, we all want to make sure that some things about us are known first, so that others can put less flattering information into context. Interviewers who appreciate this will learn much more than those who do not.

The skill required of an interviewer is that of employing these strategies in a smooth, natural way to structure a conversation in which a subject can construct what he feels is a creditable masculine self and, against this background, share the information and articulate the meanings that will allow the researcher to see more deeply into his life. Paying attention to what is glossed, evaded, or reluctantly articulated is, of course, an important part of this. Every instance of "you know what I mean" is a piece of data.

Although the strategies suggested above are intended for use in intensive, flexible interviews, they can, to a lesser extent, be used to improve survey-style interviews. Even in such interviews, researchers may have to deal with obstructive testing, inappropriate sexualizing, and minimal responses to open-ended questions. Being able to respond effectively to this kind of behavior increases the interviewer's chances of getting thoughtful, accurate, and complete information, and of making the interview a congenial encounter. Skilled interviewers are those who have turned what we call strategies into a set of habits that they can call upon as the need arises, whether doing surveys or life histories.[5]

◆ Informal Interviewing

The stereotypical image of an interview is actually that of a *formal* interview, a peculiar occasion on which researcher and sub-

ject meet, by mutual agreement, for the express purpose of asking and answering questions. Whereas some studies rely almost entirely on this kind of data gathering procedure, field studies often involve more informal than formal interviews (see Atkinson and Coffey, Chapter 20, this volume). By an informal interview we mean any occasion, brief as it might be, when a researcher casually asks a question or two of someone in a field setting and gets an answer that constitutes usable data (see, e.g., Zurcher 1982, 1985). In studies of men, informal interviews may be especially revealing because, if they are handled properly, they may pose very little threat to the masculine self.

The formal, sit-down interview has the virtue of giving the researcher considerable control over the interaction. In interviewing men, however, this virtue is also a potential weakness, because the control that shifts to the researcher can threaten the masculine self and give rise to problems that impede communication. Although it has been our purpose to suggest how researchers can overcome these problems in formal interviews, we want also to suggest how researchers can get around many of these problems through informal interviewing. But "informal" does not mean haphazard; some strategizing is necessary here, too.

In most settings there are occasions when there is a break in the action and casual talk is appropriate. Good field researchers learn to use these occasions to obtain data they might not have gotten otherwise. A researcher can obtain a great deal of information by using only a few informal interviewing strategies:[6]

◆ Interview by comment. The proverbial example is the remark "Things sure have changed around here," which invites the other to expound on how he thinks things have changed. If this remark doesn't fit the situation, there are other possibilities: "I haven't seen anything quite like this before"; "It's interesting to think about how this all got started"; "There's more to this than a lot of people realize." Such a remark, in a well-chosen moment with a well-chosen informant, might yield more data than a pointed question in a formal interview.

◆ Preface a question with a statement that yields status to the informant. For example, "You seem to know what's going on here" cedes authority to the informant and invites help rather than competition. A good informal interview question might thus be, "You seem to know what's going on here. Have things always been like this/done like this?" This simple questioning strategy puts the subject in the superior position and safely invites a flow of informative talk.

◆ Link a question to a man's earlier talk or action (presuming it is not embarrassing). For example, in a field setting where the researcher is in a participant observer role, it is often possible for the researcher to ask, during a break in the action, "I heard you say/saw you do _____, and I wasn't sure I understood what that was about. Could you fill that in for me?" This can work because it invites a man to give a fuller account of himself and underscores the significance of what he said or did. A request for help is also less threatening than transparent grubbing for information.

The trick to informal interviewing, if indeed there is one, is not so much a matter of knowing what to ask as it is knowing *whom* to ask and *when* to ask. As for *how* to ask, a few simple strategies, as suggested above, will often suffice. In the context of a field study, informal and formal interviews should also inform each other. What we learn in informal interviewing can help us to refine the questions we ask and the approaches we take in formal interviews. What we learn in the latter can also alert us to what we need to explore informally in the field. As a general rule, we ought to pay special attention to discrepancies between

what we see and what we are told. Behind such discrepancies are often the doorways through which we must pass to figure out what is going on in a setting.

◆ General Practice

We began by saying that good interviewing technique does not fully equip us to deal with problems that can arise because of how men "do gender." As we have tried to show, it is also necessary to be aware of how men try to signify a masculine self in interviews, and to use questioning and probing strategies that reduce the threat to this virtual self. Most of the strategies we have suggested can be seen as conversational ploys that interviewers can use to elicit more information from subjects. There is, however, more to conducting good interview research than skilled questioning and probing. And so here, by way of conclusion, we would like to offer suggestions about the kind of research practice that can increase the payoff from applying our advice about interviewing men.

First, to underscore a point made earlier, interviews must evolve. If we are looking at an unfamiliar group, setting, or activity, it is unlikely that we are going to know precisely what to ask and how to ask it at the outset of a study (Becker 1970; Douglas 1985). More likely, we will have to learn, as we go along, what the right questions are and how to ask them effectively. We also have to learn when to ask, and what not to ask of whom. All of this may come to us as we gain an understanding of the setting and people under study. But we are likely to do a better job of developing this understanding if we allow our interviews to evolve systematically.

As we also suggested earlier, this requires early evaluation of what is happening in interviews. This means more than just looking for trouble spots. It means looking to see what kinds of patterns of responses are elicited by certain kinds of questions. In effect, this means beginning the analysis simultaneously with data collection. To delay analysis until "all the data are in" is to miss the chance to make midcourse adjustments and go after precisely the data needed to strengthen an emerging analysis (Kleinman and Copp 1993). We thus propose the *Twenty Percent Rule*: After 20 percent of the anticipated total number of interviews are completed, pause and develop a provisional analysis. After another 20 percent are done, pause again and revise the analysis. In this way, not only is the interview increasingly refined, but the analysis itself gains strength and focus as the study proceeds.

Second, just as field researchers are astutely advised to write analytic memos and "notes on notes" (Kleinman, Copp, and Henderson 1997), interviewers should do the same. Notes on notes constitute a running analytic commentary on the content of field notes. Writing such notes is a way to capture one's thoughts, insights, and analytic leads as a study proceeds. Every interview, just like every venture into the field, should lead to the writing of similar notes. The data may be captured on tape and, later, in a transcript for more detailed analysis. But a mix of potential data and protoanalysis can exist in the form of "head notes" that the researcher needs to get onto paper immediately after an interview. Again, as we see it, this is an essential part of refining the focus of an inductive or quasi-inductive study, so that an analysis will come together not merely sooner, but stronger.

What should an interviewer reflect on in writing notes on interviews? In general terms, we advise writing down anything and everything that one's intuition even hints might be significant. More specifically, notes on interviews can be focused with a few self-posed questions:

◆ What did I feel and when did I feel it as the interview was unfolding?

◆ What kind of impression did the subject seem to be trying to create?

◆ What was said or not said that surprised me, and why was I surprised?

◆ About what did the subject seem to have mixed feelings?

◆ About what did the subject seem to be overly glib?

◆ What did the subject seem to have trouble articulating?

◆ What would I want to ask if I could do the interview over?

There is no guarantee that answers to these questions will, on any given occasion, contain gems of insight. It is a good bet, however, that without this kind of systematic reflection and written record, those gems will be harder to generate and harder to find later. Writing notes on interviews is a way to create resources for analysis before it is too late to put them to best use.

Third, interviews—even in pure interview studies—should be seen as occasions of fieldwork; that is, interviews can be opportunities to gather data through observation as well as through talk. What does a subject say and do before the interview begins? What does he wear? How does he move, stand, and sit? What does he say and do after the interview ends? All of these are potentially data and should be captured either in field notes or in interview notes. Although this might seem rather obvious advice to experienced field researchers, it is not uncommon for beginners to treat only the formal interview—the dialogue recorded on tape—as data and to ignore other pertinent information about the subject and the setting.

The suggestion that interviews be treated as occasions of fieldwork harks back to an earlier point about the signifying of masculinity as part of what is going on when we interview men. These acts of signification, whatever form they take—before, during, or after an interview—are potentially important data that can help us to understand who and what men are and how they experience their lives. If that kind of understanding is part of what a research project aims for, then the researcher needs to develop an awareness of what men do, and how they do it, to signify their identities as men. To put it another way, we cannot understand men's lives and experiences without paying attention to what men do to ensure that others perceive and treat them as men.

These matters of general practice, as well as the specific strategies discussed earlier, are not simply ways to wring more data out of research subjects. They are also ways to see, make sense of, and then see past the gender enactments we typically take for granted. Interviewers can thus be better equipped to carry on probing conversations with the men they study. A further prospect is that researchers will be equipped to learn more about how the reproduction of the gender order is a joint accomplishment—in interviews and everywhere else. Whenever we are studying men, there is the possibility, in other words, that we will learn not only about men, but about the processes through which we create them.

■ Notes

1. From the dramaturgical perspective that we use here (Brissett and Edgley 1990:1-46; Goffman 1959), the self is an *imputed character* brought into being by expressive behavior and an audience's interpretation thereof. In this view, gendered selves are *virtual* realities created collaboratively in interaction. Such selves are thus fictions in one sense, yet are nonetheless enormously consequential because of the responses they evoke in actors and audiences.

2. Most men cannot construct a fully creditable *hegemonic* masculine self because, by definition, creating such a self requires expressive resources available only to members of the ruling group. But even if most men cannot create a hegemonic masculine self in its ideal form, they are still compelled, in a heterosexist society dominated by men, to seek privilege and avoid oppression by constructing some kind of masculine self (see, for example, Robert Connell's 1992 analysis of gay men doing "straight" masculinity). Thus any man—in fact, any person—who seeks, for whatever reason, to construct a masculine self in accord with the prevailing gender order will create for interviewers some of the problems discussed in this chapter.

3. If an interviewer never establishes rapport, if an interview feels tense and awkward from start to finish, or if a subject never opens up, then it is usually clear that something has gone wrong and a change of style or protocol is called for. It is also possible, however, for an interview to go smoothly and feel fine yet not yield much useful data. This is why we urge early review of transcripts (or at least of tapes). Often it is possible to look at a transcript and see that, although an interview did not seem to go at all wrong, it did not go as far or deep as it might have.

4. Although it should perhaps go without saying, we urge that researchers consider the safety of both parties to the interview when choosing a location.

5. Interviewing skills are developed not only in methods classes or in the course of research projects. The interviewing and probing strategies we recommend can be practiced at parties, on airplanes, during academic conferences, and so on. A roomful of strangers is a fine place to work on forming conversational habits that are effective for getting to know people.

6. David Snow, Lou Zurcher, and Gideon Sjoberg (1982) provide a discussion of additional strategies for interviewing by comment.

■ References

Arendell, T. 1997. "Reflections on the Researcher-Researched Relationship: A Woman Interviewing Men." *Qualitative Sociology* 20:341-68.

Becker, H. S. 1970. "Interviewing Medical Students." Pp. 103-6 in *Qualitative Methodology,* edited by W. J. Filstead. Chicago: Rand McNally.

Blee, K. M. 1998. "White-Knuckle Research: Emotional Dynamics in Fieldwork with Racist Activists." *Qualitative Sociology* 21:381-99.

Briggs, C. L. 1986. *Learning How to Ask: A Sociolinguistic Appraisal of the Role of the Interview in Social Science Research.* Cambridge: Cambridge University Press.

Brissett, D. and C. Edgley. 1991. *Life as Theater: A Dramaturgical Sourcebook.* 2d ed. Hawthorne, NY: Aldine de Gruyter.

Brittan, A. 1989. *Masculinity and Power.* New York: Basil Blackwell.

Connell, R. W. 1992. "A Very Straight Gay: Masculinity, Homosexual Experience, and the Dynamics of Gender." *American Sociological Review* 57:735-51.

———. 1995. *Masculinities.* Berkeley: University of California Press.

Douglas, J. D. 1985. *Creative Interviewing.* Beverly Hills, CA: Sage.

Goffman, E. 1959. *The Presentation of Self in Everyday Life.* Garden City, NY: Doubleday.

———. 1967. *Interaction Ritual: Essays on Face-to-Face Behavior.* New York: Pantheon.

Gurney, J. N. 1985. "Not One of the Guys: The Female Researcher in the Male-Dominated Setting." *Qualitative Sociology* 8:42-62.

Kessler, S. J. and W. McKenna. 1978. *Gender: An Ethnomethodological Approach.* Chicago: University of Chicago Press.

Kleinman, S. and M. A. Copp. 1993. *Emotions and Fieldwork.* Newbury Park, CA: Sage.

Kleinman, S., M. A. Copp, and K. Henderson. 1997. "Qualitatively Different: Teaching Fieldwork to Graduate Students." *Journal of Contemporary Ethnography* 25:469-99.

Lee, D. 1997. "Interviewing Men: Vulnerabilities and Dilemmas." *Women's Studies International Forum* 20:553-64.

McKee, L. and M. O'Brien. 1983. "Interviewing Men: Taking Gender Seriously." Pp. 147-59 in *The Public and the Private,* edited by E. Garmarknikow, D. Morgan, J. Purvis, and D. Taylorson. London: Heinemann.

Mishler, E. G. 1986. *Research Interviewing: Context and Narrative.* Cambridge, MA: Harvard University Press.

Sattel, J. 1976. "The Inexpressive Male: Tragedy or Sexual Politics?" *Social Problems* 23:469-77.

Schwalbe, M. L. and D. Mason-Schrock. 1996. "Identity Work as Group Process." Pp. 113-47 in *Advances in Group Processes,* Vol. 13, edited by B. Markovsky, M. J. Lovaglia, and R. Simon. Greenwich, CT: JAI.

Snow, D. A., L. Zurcher, and G. Sjoberg. 1982. "Interviewing by Comment." *Qualitative Sociology* 5:285-311.

West, C. and D. Zimmerman. 1987. "Doing Gender." *Gender & Society* 1:125-51.

Williams, C. L. and J. E. Heikes. 1993. "The Importance of Researcher's Gender in the In-Depth Interview: Evidence from Two Case Studies of Male Nurses." *Gender & Society* 7:280-91.

Wolkomir, M. 1999. "Redeeming Identities: Ideology, Emotion, and the Creation of Moral Selves." Ph.D. dissertation, Department of Sociology, North Carolina State University, Raleigh.

Zurcher, L. 1982. "The Staging of Emotion: A Dramaturgical Analysis." *Symbolic Interaction* 5:1-22.

———. 1985. "The War Game: Organizational Scripting and the Expression of Emotion." *Symbolic Interaction* 8:191-206.

4

INTERVIEWING WOMEN

◆ Shulamit Reinharz and Susan E. Chase

The interdisciplinary field of women's studies has devoted much attention to defining the word *woman* (Lorber 1993, 1998; Oyěwùmí 1997; Butler 1990). On the one hand, feminist scholars resist an essentialist definition that implies that all women are the same. On the other hand, feminists agree that denying any shared properties among women is as absurd as ignoring the vast differences among us. As Mary Rogers (1988) states, "Women do face some odds that put us in the same big boat (if not on the same deck, let alone in the same cabin)" (p. 1). For example, most women, at least in Western societies, are likely to grow up with some negative notions about female bodies; to fear rape; to be treated as "mother confessors," at work or elsewhere; to earn less than equally educated men in the labor force; if partnered with a man, to do more than half of the domestic and nurturing work at home; and to need the services of men in positions of power and authority, such as doctors, religious leaders, and school or university ad-

ministrators (Rogers 1998:1-2). Women, in general, also share characteristics that many women experience as positive, most notably the potential for bearing children.

In short, gender shapes institutions, ideologies, interactions, and identities. At the same time, race, class, and other social dimensions intersect with the gendered contours of our worlds. We assume, then, that although all women's experiences are gendered, no two women's experiences are identical. Thus in this chapter we treat "women" as encompassing the greatest possible variety of people who self-define as women, including people of many ages (approximately 18 and older), cultures, nationalities, sexual orientations, classes, races, abilities, and physical conditions.

How does interview research in the social sciences deal with women? In this chapter, we look briefly at how traditional social science has rendered women invisible, and we explore a range of issues that arise when interview research focuses on women. Drawing on the rich methodological literature that feminists have developed since the early 1970s, we concentrate on the situations of women interviewing women and, to a lesser extent, men interviewing women.[1] All the while, we keep in mind that the interviewing of women is not a "one-size-fits-all" type of activity. Researchers need to attend not only to the intersections of race, class, and gender in women's lives, but also to the ideas that different groups of women may have about "the way we talk to strangers" or "the way we think about research" (see Marin and Marin 1991; Samovar and Porter 1991; Tixier y Vigil and Elsasser 1978). Finally, throughout this chapter, we are guided by our fundamental assumption that

> interviewing offers researchers access to people's ideas, thoughts, and memories in their own words, rather than in the words of the researcher. This asset is particularly important for the study of women because this way of learning from women is an antidote to centuries of ignoring women's ideas altogether or having men speak for women. (Reinharz 1992b:19)

◆ The Missing Tradition

Throughout the 19th century and for much of the 20th century, most male social researchers did not consider women worthy of study. One of the most blatant examples of the disregard of women as interview subjects is found in the work of Alexis de Tocqueville, who traveled throughout the United States in the early 1830s without interviewing women at all. Michael Hill (1990) describes a travel journal entry in which Tocqueville assumes he understands the thoughts of a woman he observed from afar. On the basis of such observations, Tocqueville ([1835] 1994) proclaimed that "morals are the work of woman," that American women are taught to think for themselves and to speak freely, and that

they display no "timidity or ignorance" (p. 198).

Concurrent with Tocqueville's study of the fledgling United States, Harriet Martineau (one of many underrecognized women social scientists of the 19th century) undertook her own inquiry and came to quite different conclusions (see Martineau [1837] 1962; Reinharz 1992a). Perhaps because she understood the importance of women's as well as men's lives, she included both women and men in her interviews. Martineau's contact with women led her to draw an analogy between the status of women and slaves, and to predict that women would eventually win the right to vote. By contrast, Tocqueville ([1835] 1994:201-3) believed that women were satisfied with their domestic lot. Yet only 15 years after his visit, a women's rights convention in Seneca Falls, New York, initiated the first wave of the women's movement in the United States.

Well into the 20th century, most major social science studies continued to be based primarily on men's experiences. This is true of many studies now considered classics: William Foote Whyte's *Street Corner Society* (1943), Peter Blau and Otis Dudley Duncan's *The American Occupational Structure* (1967), and Lawrence Kohlberg's *The Psychology of Moral Development* (1984), to name just a few. This exclusion of women, of course, was not unique to social science. Medicine, too, was oriented toward men; studies of diseases were done on male subjects and the results then generalized to women.

During the 1970s, feminist social scientists began to analyze the "gynopia" (Reinharz 1985)—the inability to see women—in both traditional social science and conventional social arrangements. For example, in 1975, Lyn Lofland wrote:

> Despite, or perhaps in part because of, their omni-presence, [women] remain, by and large, merely part of the scene. They are continually perceived, but rarely perceivers. They are part of the

furniture of the setting through which the plot moves. Essential to the set but largely irrelevant to the action. They are simply, there. (Pp. 144-45)

Exposing and redressing women's invisibility as social actors has been one of feminist researchers' important accomplishments. Interview studies have played a central role. In *Men and Women of the Corporation,* for example, Rosabeth Moss Kanter (1977) broke through the gynopia of earlier organizational sociology by investigating the situation of women as well as men who are pivotal in corporate life, including secretaries and the wives of high-ranking male executives. Arlene Kaplan Daniels's *Invisible Careers: Women Civic Leaders from the Volunteer World* (1988) brought to light the unremunerated but significant community work of upper-class women. In *Between Women: Domestics and Their Employers,* Judith Rollins (1985) demonstrated that gynopia is not only gendered but also race and class based. She found that middle- and upper-class white women frequently treat as invisible the working-class women of color who clean their homes.

Despite the explosion of feminist interview research over the past three decades, many groups of women continue to be unrecognized as competent social actors. For example, in her study of homeless women, Meredith Ralston (1996) writes:

The women I interviewed were people whom Maria Lugones and Elizabeth Spelman define as the most silenced; women who are not "white, middle-class, heterosexual, Christian women." The value of listening to these women's voices is the value of their testimony and experiences, which have been ignored and dismissed. The women know why they are homeless. They know why they are addicts. No one has thought to ask them about what they need or what would help them, either because people assume that they do not know what

their needs are; or because people assume that they are stupid and lazy and have no potential anyway; or because people think that welfare recipients do not deserve any choices or special treatment because it is their own fault they are on welfare in the first place. The words of the women refute all of the above beliefs and demonstrate the consequences for society of not listening to the needs of the recipients of welfare services. (P. xii)

Thus the "missing tradition" in the interviewing of women includes both gynopia and the holding of untested and unexamined assumptions about women's lives.

◆ Recovering Research on Women

Despite the lack of attention to women in the foundation of male-defined social science, some women researchers did study women using the interview method even before the advent of second-wave feminism. Many of these researchers are not remembered, but some, like Martineau, produced works that feminist scholars today are recovering (Reinharz 1992a).

In the 1930s, for example, Margaret Jarman Hagood, author of *Mothers of the South: Portraiture of the White Tenant Farm Woman* ([1939] 1977), carried out studies by using the role of "visitor":

The actual first-hand gathering of data consisted of repeated visits made by the writer to the tenant farm mothers during a sixteen months' period of field work. . . . [I] stated that [I] was interested in women who live in the country and their problems of bringing up children, and asked if [I] might visit for a little while. . . . in general, questioning was avoided. Topics on which an expression of attitudes was desired were approached obliquely, and the inter-

> view was kept as much as possible to a friendly, conversational, "just visiting." No notes were taken during the first visits to the North Carolina group, but the visit was written up as quickly as possible after the interview and much of the conversation was recorded practically verbatim. (P. 227)

Not only did Hagood produce a searing indictment of the effect of tenant farming practices on women, she also explained very carefully how such studies can be done.

In the 1950s, Mirra Komarovsky (1961), the second woman to become president of the American Sociological Association, conducted a study of working-class marriages that included interviews of men and women. She wrote:

> We were struck with the openness of the women. Obviously not all were equally candid with us, but the great majority—usually during the second interview—were open enough to confide intimate feelings. Although 58 husbands did grant us interviews, more husbands than wives refused to cooperate. In fact, the initial response of many wives to our request for an interview with the husbands was "Oh, he won't be interested," or "I don't think he will talk to you," or "He's tongue-tied, he'll just say yes or no." . . .
>
> The husbands talked easily enough about their jobs, but when the interviewer turned to the marriage relationship, many became noticeably uncomfortable. . . . We do not know whether the husbands would have spoken more freely to a male interviewer. But, in any event, we shall show that the reticence of the men cannot wholly be explained by the sex of the interviewer. (Pp. 13-14)

In the 1970s, Lillian Rubin (1976) continued the study of working-class marriages, interviewing both women and men without appearing more friendly to one group than the other. Because "women tend to discuss their feelings about their lives, their roles, and their marriages more freely when men are not present" (p. 11), she interviewed women and men separately.

These few examples show that women researchers have been concerned not only with including women in their studies, but also with addressing the impact of gender on the interview process itself. By contrast, "the traditional interview paradigm does not account for gendered differences" even though social scientists have always known that "gender filters knowledge" (Fontana and Frey 1994:369). Indeed, the classic text on interviewing, Robert Merton, Marjorie Fiske, and Patricia Kendall's *The Focused Interview: A Manual of Problems and Procedures* (1956), makes no reference to gender differences among interviewers or interviewees.

◆ Feminist Methodological Issues

Since the 1970s, feminist researchers have become avid students of women's experiences and have made good use of the interview method for collecting data. At the same time, they have developed a remarkable literature on feminist methodological issues.[2] In this section we draw on that literature as we consider the effects of interviewing on both interviewees and interviewers, the issues of interviewer self-disclosure and sisterly bonds in the research relationship, and the significance of interviewers' and interviewees' complex social locations and subjectivities.

THE IMPACT OF INTERVIEWING ON WOMEN INTERVIEWEES

An interview is typically a conversation between two people in which one asks questions and the other answers. In the case of open-ended interviewing, there may be a more spontaneous exchange between interviewer and interviewee. Although on the face of it this is not a remarkable activity, it may turn out to be an extraordinary experience for some women interviewees. This is so because some women still feel powerless, without much to say. In many societies girls are still raised to be pretty objects who should be seen but not heard or fecund reproducers whose intellect is devalued. In some religious traditions, women's voices must not be heard in public because they are defined as erotic and dangerous. Even well-educated women in managerial or professional occupations are not immune from self-censoring or silencing. For example, in her study of how parental leave is used in a major U.S. corporation, Mindy Fried (1998) remarks that "even the most forceful upper-level female manager I met was relatively soft-spoken when we met together with a group of upper-level male managers" (p. 12). Nadya Aisenberg (1994) helps to make sense of this situation: "For women there have been thousands of years of silencing. The speech-act itself is a rebellion against stifling social norms which call for women's silence" (p. 99).

Interpreting any particular woman's silence or speech is a complex task that requires a strong understanding of her social location, including her place within her community and society, the cultural constraints and resources shaping her everyday life, and her particular circumstances (Gal 1991; Collins 1990:92; Tannen 1993). Yet when an interviewer approaches a woman whose culture, religion, community, family, or work situation prescribes her silence in one way or another, and says, "I want to hear what you have to say," the interviewer may be creating a relatively new social situation for that woman. When the interviewer implies that what the woman has to say is important and that she will not be interrupted, the interviewee may have an epiphany, dramatic as this may sound. The reason is quite straightforward: "The si-

lence of women, whether self-imposed as a strategy of resistance or societally imposed as a tool of subordination, is a classic clinical symptom of depressive illness" (Aisenberg 1994:102).

Researchers who interview women should thus understand the possibly radical impact of the interview on the woman herself. She may discover her thoughts, learn who she is, and "find her voice." At the same time, researchers need to be aware that women who have never had an opportunity to express themselves may not know what to do when given that opportunity, as Mary Field Belenky and her colleagues (1986, 1997) discovered when they interviewed women who grew up in violent families and who had no external sources of support. Furthermore, under some circumstances, an interview may be traumatic. In studies about women's experiences of violence, for instance, both interviewer and interviewee need to be prepared for the distress, anxiety, and flashbacks participants may experience. The interviewer needs to be able to offer referrals to support resources in case the participant finds the interview overwhelming. Otherwise, the interview may be harmful (Brzuzy, Ault, and Segal, 1997).

Although there have been no systematic studies conducted to examine the impact of interview research on participants (Maynard and Purvis 1994:5), Ruthellen Josselson's (1996) description of what interviewees said about their experience of talking to her is not unusual (see also Rothman 1993:19-20; Phoenix 1994: 60-61; Reay 1995:211). Focusing on women's self-development over time, Josselson interviewed 30 women when they were in their early 20s, early 30s, and early 40s:

> Many said they told me things they have never divulged to anyone. In that sense, I am for them a kind of private diary. Others remarked that the interview was like therapy, where "I say things out loud that I've never said before." Some told me that our conversations have

often been painful, especially when they reawakened buried loss, anger, or confusion. But there is something about our interaction that led these women to strive for naked truthfulness, and that has felt liberating—for both of us. (P. 13)

Interestingly, research on elite women may involve a completely different set of issues. Powerful women are much more likely than less powerful women to be accustomed to speaking and being heard, and so they may not find the interview experience psychologically empowering or therapeutic, as Josselson's interviewees did. In fact, they may have difficulty finding time to schedule an interview. Women with power may have less discretionary time than their male counterparts because such women usually have the additional responsibilities of "representing women" in various venues and managing (if not doing) domestic and nurturing work at home.

It is no surprise, then, that Nirmal Puwar (1997) found many women members of the British Parliament agreeing only grudgingly to be interviewed, treating the request as an imposition and a favor to the researcher (also see Adler and Adler, Chapter 8, this volume). Nonetheless, some elite women may consent to interviews because of their unique position and their ability to provide a fresh perspective. In her study of upper-class women, Susan Ostrander (1984) gained access to her respondents in part by appealing to them specifically as women. "I suggested that, while we know a good deal about the men from old and influential families, we know little about the women. This approach proved successful. I know of only two women who were unwilling to talk with me, pleading busy schedules" (p. 10; see also Ostrander 1995). In addition, high-achieving women in traditionally white- and male-dominated professions may feel that participating in research is part of their responsibility to women who aspire to follow in their footsteps (Chase 1995, 1996:46).

THE IMPACT OF INTERVIEWING ON WOMEN INTERVIEWERS

Mirroring the personal impact that interviewees sometimes mention, many researchers have discussed how the interviewing process has affected them personally (Luttrell 1997; Shostak 1989; Thompson 1990). For example, in her book about how men and women experience divorce, Catherine Riessman (1990) writes:

Not only did the interviewing process have an effect on them [interviewees], it also strongly affected me. I was divorced, as my mother and grandmother had been before me, and though I was aware that this personal history had stimulated my choice of the topic, I was not entirely prepared for my response. Listening to people's painful accounts of their marriages and trying to probe sensitively for their understandings of what had happened was sometimes difficult. It was difficult, too, when a few male interviewees asked for dates (this happened to both women interviewers) and when one threatened me when I refused. During the coding and analysis process, I had more trouble empathically interpreting men's experience than I did women's. (P. 225)

Sometimes researchers find that their interviews with women have reverberations long after their projects are done. After completing her study of identity and self-transformation in mothers' lives, Martha McMahon (1998) began rethinking her own life, especially when her mother died: "Learning to live with her death forced me to revisit my sociological story and to shift the focus from the meaning of motherhood in other women's lives to its meaning to me, a childless woman" (p. 187).

Some researchers intentionally use their personal reactions to the interview process as a source of knowledge about the topic under study. Alison Griffith and Dorothy Smith (1987) used this strategy in their project on mothers' work in relation to their children's schooling (how mothers help children with homework and how they interact with teachers). In the course of their interviews, Griffith and Smith sometimes found themselves reexperiencing the guilt and inadequacy they had felt while raising their children as single mothers and comparing themselves unfavorably to middle-class mothers who have more resources and time to help their children. They analyze these feelings—which they trace in many mothers' talk—as pointing to "a strongly moral dimension governing the relationship of mothers to the school, capable of generating an almost theological sense of guilt and anxiety" (p. 95; see also DeVault and McCoy, Chapter 18, this volume).

Daniels (1988) identifies another kind of personal and intellectual effect on herself as researcher. In an unusual preface to her study of upper-class women leaders in the volunteer world, she explains the negative bias she had toward participants while writing her book about them: "I accepted the somewhat negative stereotypes of women volunteers" (p. xii). The details she gives make us wonder why she includes the word "somewhat." Daniels was strongly influenced, however, by her participants' responses to her early analyses. "My informants helped me see the error of my ways. . . . I rewrote the study, adding new material that showed their work in a more serious and respectful light" (pp. xiv-xv). At this point, Daniels struggled with the tension between listening carefully to participants and analyzing their position sociologically.

Daniels concludes her discussion with a story about male colleagues and their wives whom she invited to dinner along with a prominent volunteer leader and her husband. The male colleagues were uninterested in, and unimpressed by, the volunteer; the colleagues' wives, however, felt privileged to meet "a woman of such spirit who had made so remarkable a career for herself" (p. xvi). Although she began with stereotypical perceptions like those of her male colleagues, Daniels ended up with a view closer to that of her colleagues' wives.

INTERVIEWER SELF-DISCLOSURE

Interviewer self-disclosure takes place when the interviewer shares ideas, attitudes, and/or experiences concerning matters that might relate to the interview topic in order to encourage respondents to be more forthcoming (see also in this volume Eder and Fingerson, Chapter 2; Dunbar, Rodriguez, and Parker, Chapter 7). In a study of sexual harassment, for instance, the interviewer might disclose her own experience of having been harassed. Conventionally, qualitative research students are instructed not to disclose their experiences, feelings, or opinions about the research topic because "the interview is about the respondent, not about the interviewer. . . . It is usually enough for the interviewer to give business card information . . . along with the study's aims and sponsorship" (Weiss 1994:79).

Some feminists reject this stance because it assumes a distant and hierarchical relationship between the interviewer and participants. Moreover, many feminists choose research topics that are deeply personal, which tends to make the interview process emotionally intense for both interviewer and participant. These conditions can lead easily to the researcher's self-disclosure. In addition to humanizing and equalizing the research relationship, some argue, interviewer self-disclosure can put the interviewee at ease, thus helping the participant to tell her story (Oakley 1981; Reinharz 1992b:32-34).

In practice, however, it is difficult to know how much and what kind of disclosure is appropriate (Blum 1999:214). Indeed, there is very little literature about the impact of interviewer self-disclosure on the interview process or on the interviewee. One report by three social work researchers suggests that in some cases interviewees may feel constrained when interviewers talk about themselves. Marilyn Wedenoja, who was at first an interviewee and later a collaborator in the project, notes that

> personal sharing on [the interviewer's part] . . . was triggering off in me a self-censoring process. I began to second [guess] what she would want to hear and not want to hear based on my perception of the information about herself. . . . She was giving me . . . personal information as a way of equalizing the relationship . . . yet it seemed more out of her need to self-disclose rather than my need . . . to know about her. (quoted in Reinharz 1992b:33)

Rather than adopting an abstract commitment to self-disclosure, interviewers need to think carefully about whether, when, and how much disclosure makes sense in the context of particular research projects and with specific participants. If the research arises in part from the researcher's personal experiences or needs, to what extent—and why—should that personal connection play a role in the research relationship itself? Under what conditions might self-disclosure put the interviewee at ease or pressure her to adopt a particular point of view? When does self-disclosure indicate openness to the other's experience or a sharing of power within the interview relationship, and when does it indicate that the researcher prefers to speak rather than listen?

The issue of self-disclosure arises for researchers when they assume that their experiences or points of view are similar to those of participants. But when researchers interview women whose perspectives are clearly different from their own, they may find a tight-lipped approach to be essential to gaining trust. For example, in *Women of the New Right,* Rebecca Klatch (1987) writes:

> I built trust by adopting a non-argumentative approach in the interviews. While I would push to clarify ideas and beliefs, I did not assert my own opinions, judgments or values nor did I try to debate ideas. If asked, of course, I would state my own doubts or disagreements, but generally I defined my own role entirely in terms of listening and absorbing the other world view. I believe this approach, more than anything else, bridged the gap between me and the women I interviewed. Because many activists on the right have been met with hostility and constant rebuttal by liberals and the media . . . , the fact that I conveyed an honest attempt to understand the opinions and values of the women I met in a non-aggressive manner was met with a welcome and open response. (P. 17)

SISTERLY BONDS

In 1981, Ann Oakley argued dramatically that interviewing women is a contradiction in terms. She claimed that women who interview women have an obligation to assist, remain in touch with, and otherwise revise the more passive, distant interviewing stance recommended by conventional research methodology.

When the researcher already knows participants, or when the study requires contact with participants over a long period, interviewers sometimes do develop connections with, and responsibilities toward, participants that extend beyond the research itself (Shostak 1989; Ellis, Kiesinger, and Tillman-Healy 1997). For example, Laurel Richardson's (1985) study of single women involved with married men included several women whom she interviewed over the course of their affairs. Richardson invited the women to contact her if they wanted or needed to (p. 162), and some did:

> Interviews took place in private settings—the respondent's home or mine, a hotel room, or occasionally a private office. They lasted between two and five hours and were tape-recorded and transcribed. . . . Many of the women cried at some point in the interview. Nearly all of them thanked me for the "therapy" the interview provided, and several still phone me. (Pp. x-xi)

Because feminists seek to create nonexploitative research relationships, it might seem that developing sisterly bonds with participants should be a feminist goal. Indeed, some of the early feminist methodological literature gave the impression that women who interview women automatically like their interviewees and will easily form bonds of mutual understanding with them (Oakley 1981; Finch 1984). Problems encountered during research, however, led many feminists to reject this romanticization of the woman-to-woman interview and to explore the complexities of research relationships (Reay 1995, 1996; Cotterill 1992; Phoenix 1994).

A major drawback to treating sisterly bonds as the ideal research relationship is that this standard precludes studies of groups of women in which such bonds are unlikely to develop. Interview-based studies of women should not be limited to women who seek such bonds, to women who need help, or to women whom researchers perceive as like themselves or as potential friends. Indeed, even if researcher and interviewee share life experiences and ideological perspectives, there is no guarantee that they will like each other and want or need to continue a relationship after the research is complete. Furthermore, to assume that interviewees want or need

an extended relationship is condescending and "maternalistic" (Reinharz 1993).

We can begin to sort out the confusion surrounding this issue by distinguishing "rapport" from "intense bonding." Rapport is a necessary ingredient for interviewing, and many women may establish rapport easily, given that women typically are socialized to connect with others. However, rapport is more likely to be established by strong listening skills than by promises of future support or friendship. In many cases, it may be the very fact that the researcher is not regularly involved in the participant's life that allows the participant the freedom to express herself in ways she might not otherwise, even with a close friend (Cotterill 1992). This is especially true if the topic is highly personal or if the interviewee has rarely or never discussed the matter before. Under these circumstances, the bond of the intimate stranger may emerge (Simmel 1971:145).

Researchers have a responsibility to express as clearly as possible to participants their expectations and the boundaries of the research relationship. The process of securing informed consent can facilitate this. And yet, as in all relationships, what may transpire during interview relationships cannot always be predicted. When a participant seeks further contact that the researcher does not welcome, the researcher needs to reflect carefully on what is going on: Does the interviewee feel exploited or abandoned? If so, why? Did the interviewer lead her, directly or indirectly, to have certain expectations regarding the relationship? Has the interviewer fulfilled whatever promises she made for follow-up? Even if she has, are there other forms of gratitude or reciprocity that would satisfy the participant and resolve the problem (Daniels 1983; Lindsey 1997; Altork 1998)?

At the other end of the relationship spectrum, if an intense bond forms between interviewer and interviewee, that should be considered a serendipitous event. In most cases, the interviewer's purpose in conducting the interview is not to create such a bond but to elicit and listen closely to the interviewee's life experiences. The feminist methodological literature cogently criticizes the overdone and self-deceiving value-neutral stance of social science, but this critique should not lead to an unexamined assumption that a feminist research project is successful only if it creates sisterly bonds between researchers and participants (Reinharz 1992b:chap. 2).

COMPLEX SOCIAL LOCATIONS AND SUBJECTIVITIES

Social scientists generally agree that a person's social location shapes his or her identity, experiences, and perspectives. What difference, then, do the similar or different social locations of researcher and participant make to interview research? How, for example, should interviewers take into account their own and their interviewees' races, ethnicities, classes, sexual orientations, ages, and disabilities or abilities?

These questions arise even in the matter of constructing a sample of research participants. In criticizing the overrepresentation of white, middle-class women as subjects in feminist research, Lynn Weber Cannon, Elizabeth Higginbotham, and Marianne Leung (1988) argue that women of color and working-class women may be less able and less willing than more privileged women to volunteer for research because of their heavy responsibilities and their well-founded skepticism about the value of social research (see also Edwards 1990:483-85; Phoenix 1994:50-55). In order to make feminist research more inclusive, Cannon and her colleagues recommend that researchers recruit participants through face-to-face contact, and they encourage researchers to be flexible and persistent in arranging and rescheduling interviews. They also recommend the use of multiracial research teams. Similarly, Kath Weston (1991) discusses her flexibility and persistence in scheduling interviews with lesbians

and gay men, some of whom are reluctant to become research subjects because they construct very private lives and often fear that researchers will disrespect their identities or experiences (pp. 10-11; see also Kong, Mahoney, and Plummer, Chapter 5, this volume).

Conventional wisdom suggests that when interviewer and interviewee share similar social locations (such as sexual orientation and racial, ethnic, and class backgrounds), access, rapport, and understanding are relatively easy to achieve. Yet in recent years feminists have been most interested in exploring the instability of "insider" and "outsider" statuses (Reay 1995; Naples 1997). For instance, in her study of the ethnic identity of Chicanas in New Mexico, Patricia Zavella (1996) found that even though she and her interviewees had much in common (like them, she was an employed Chicana mother who faced family-work tensions; she also had New Mexican kin), many of the women were reluctant to talk about their ethnicity. Because Zavella was unfamiliar with their hesitancy as well as their use of the term *Spanish* (as opposed to *Chicana*), she had to struggle to understand the meanings the women imputed to their ethnicity (see in this volume Dunbar et al., Chapter 7; Ryen, Chapter 21; Narayan and George, Chapter 22).

Feminists also address the situation of researchers whose social locations clearly differ from those of their interviewees. Ann Phoenix (1994:55-56) notes that in several of her research projects some white interviewees were surprised to discover that she, the interviewer, is black. She suggests that this racial difference may have been both inhibitory and liberating for interviewees.

Similarly, in her study of working-class women returning to school as adults, Wendy Luttrell (1997) reflects on her social location and subjectivity in relation to two groups of participants: white working-class women in Philadelphia and African American working-class women in North Carolina. In both settings, she got to know the women as their teacher before she began her study; thus the research relationship was shaped by the participants' prior teacher-student contact as well as by their educational, class, and (with one group) racial differences. Luttrell carefully sorts through the emotions that the women's stories aroused in her—guilt, envy, shame—as a way of developing "a clearer picture of what it means to define one's womanhood against controlling gender-, race-, and class-based images, including images that I projected onto the women and they projected onto me" (p. 21).

The methodological lesson that Phoenix, Luttrell, and others offer is that uncertainty and discomfort are likely to arise for interviewers and interviewees whose social locations differ dramatically, and those aspects of the relationship need to be explored rather than ignored. Along these lines, Linda Blum (1999) states that during her interviews with African American women about their experiences of breastfeeding, "I learned most from those facets of African-American women's stories which I had the most trouble hearing" (p. 213; see also Rubin 1976, 1995; DeVault 1999:chap. 5; Pierce 1995; Reay 1996; Villenas 1998; Fordham 1996; Fine 1998; Riessman 1987).

In addition to race, ethnicity, and class, and to a lesser extent sexual orientation, age, and disability, feminist researchers discuss other significant aspects of their social locations and subjectivities. Several recent studies of women's experiences of motherhood, for instance, have been conducted by women who are not mothers (Hays 1996; McMahon 1995; Lewin 1993; Taylor 1996).

In her study of the self-help movement surrounding postpartum depression, Verta Taylor (1996) presents herself as both like and unlike her interviewees. Although she is not a mother, she has suffered a period of debilitating depression:

If over the course of this research I have come to understand depression in a more personal way, I have also come to terms with my own decision not to bear and raise children. I have never been sure exactly how or when I came to the conclusion that I did not want to be a mother. But perhaps as a sign of how women's self-definitions revolve less around motherhood than they once did, the women I got to know while doing this study never questioned my decision. Nor did they challenge my ability to understand and write about their lives because I never have mothered a child. (P. xvi)

Ellen Lewin (1998) comes to a somewhat different conclusion about the effect of her nonmotherhood on her interviews. Five years after publishing her study of lesbian mothers, Lewin, herself a lesbian, remarks:

By the time I unraveled the narratives mothers offered me, I began to understand that among other dynamics they had formulated their stories for a nonmother. The mothers tended to emphasize the moral attributes of motherhood and the central part motherhood played in the way they constructed and conceptualized their identities, highlighting the ways that they saw themselves as fundamentally different from women who did not have children. How their narratives would have been shaped had I also been a mother I cannot know, but I feel sure that they would have been different, if not in substance, then in emphasis. (Pp. 40-41)

By contrast, in her study of gay and lesbian commitment ceremonies, Lewin describes herself as the " 'insider' par excellence." Like her interviewees, she and her lesbian partner had a commitment ceremony. Lewin points out that this closeness to her topic raises its own issues of subjectivity: "I have tried earnestly to avoid the pitfalls of cheerleading or polemics, but the astute reader will no doubt detect my enthusiasm for and engagement with the phenomena I report on in these pages" (p. xix).

What feminist researchers share, regardless of their status as insider or outsider in relation to interviewees, is a commitment to reflecting on the complexities of their own and participants' social locations and subjectivities.

◆ Men Interviewing Women

The situation of men studying women raises particular issues concerning interviewers' and interviewees' social locations and subjectivities. Maureen Padfield and Ian Procter (1996) looked carefully at this situation in their joint study of 39 young women's work and family experiences and aspirations. From the outset, they attempted to minimize the differences their genders made by maximizing their commonalities: Both are middle-aged, experienced field-workers who are knowledgeable about feminist critiques of research methodology. They also had a common objective—encouraging women to talk freely in response to their questions.

In comparing their interviews (each interviewed half of the women), Padfield and Procter found no significant differences in their length or the women's attitudes, even on controversial topics such as feminism and abortion. However, women who had had abortions were much more likely to reveal that information to the woman (Padfield) than to the man (Procter). (The interviewer did not ask directly whether the woman had ever aborted a pregnancy; six women volunteered this information to Padfield, none to Procter.) In follow-up interviews, two of Procter's interviewees revealed that they had had abortions before the first interview, which suggests that the interviewer's gender did affect this voluntary sharing of personal experience.

During the follow-up interviews, Padfield and Procter also asked about the

difference the interviewer's gender had made in the first interviews. The women's responses show that the salience of gender is not fixed, but shifts along with other dynamics:

> If the interviewee perceives herself as skilled in dealing with men then that can counter the implied influence of "maleness." If the interviewer puts aside "maleness" ["inappropriate features of masculinity (arrogance, not listening)" (Padfield and Procter 1996: 363)] then women could respond. (P. 362)

Along the same lines, Javier Treviño (1992) found that he had trouble getting interviews with women members of Alcoholics Anonymous until he made efforts to downplay his gender and desexualize the research encounter. For example, although he initially thought of his office as a neutral space, he discovered that some women were reluctant to meet with him there out of concern for their safety.

Because gender regulates access to space, gender can affect where interviews take place in another sense. When he studied the Ladies Professional Golf Association, for example, Todd Crosset (1992) was not allowed into the women's locker room, which "serve[s] as a private space for golfers and thus an excellent setting to collect data" (p. 44). Despite his limited access to interviewees, Crosset's rapport with them was enhanced by his ability to play golf, his general helpfulness and dedication to their work, and his status as a professional athlete.

In cases where research revolves around extremely sensitive gendered experiences, a man may decide not to do the interviews himself. For example, for his study of courtroom negotiations between judges and women who seek restraining orders, James Ptacek (1999) needed information from the women themselves. He was concerned, however, that he might cause the women harm by contacting them:

> Three types of potential harm exist. First, the conversation—even a brief conversation in which a woman declines to participate—can be upsetting. This is a very sensitive issue to discuss with anyone, let alone a stranger. Women may fear phone calls from strangers, particularly if they are no longer living with their abusive partners; abusive men often harass women by telephone and through myriad other means. . . .
>
> Second, if an interviewer telephones a woman but reaches an abusive man, there is the potential that the man may become suspicious and angry toward the woman. . . .
>
> A third type of danger concerns women who have children and fear losing their children either to their estranged abusive partner or to child-protection authorities. . . . Care must therefore be taken to establish trust in the telephone interview. . . .
>
> To protect against these risks, I had the interviews conducted by women who have experience as advocates on the issues of violence against women. (Pp. 189-90)

When men study women, then, the same general methodological principle applies as when women study women: It is crucial that the researcher take account of his or her own and the interviewee's social locations and how they might affect the research relationship.

◆ Concluding Thoughts: Interpreting Women's Words

The salience and meanings of gender, race, class, and other aspects of our social locations shift not only from study to study and across contexts, but also over time. Thus we need to continue our reflexivity even when we leave the field and turn our attention to interpretation. As social scientists, we spend years examining theory and conducting research. We assume we understand society, social structures, and a vast array of topics about everyday life, with an eye to the ways in which structures and cultures typically disadvantage most women. We also assume that people will benefit from our interpretations of these phenomena. Thus we approach our interpretive work with background, with conviction, and, yes, often with biases or "agendas" of our own (Anderson and Jack 1991).

Feminist researchers face a particular challenge when we interpret the words of women who reject feminism or other progressive movements. In such cases, it is tempting to attribute an interviewee's ideas to "false consciousness" and to discount what she says. The idea of false consciousness suggests that a person misunderstands his or her own situation, particularly with regard to self-interest (Bartky 1998). Feminists need to exercise self-control and reflexive thinking, for example, when we interview women who espouse a "pro-life" position or a submissive attitude toward men, or who embrace an apparently assimilationist ethnic identity (Andersen 1987; Zavella 1996). How are such women making reasonable decisions within the context of their particular circumstances?

Conflicts surface between researchers' and interviewees' perspectives in part because of the feminist commitment to reducing the hierarchy and inequality inherent in the conventional research relationship. Such conflicts come to light, for instance, when researchers share their analyses with interviewees before publication. In some cases, participants respond angrily (Krieger 1991:154), even requesting that they be taken out of the study (Sacks 1988:viii-ix). As we have seen, some researchers resolve such problems by altering their interpretations (Daniels 1988) or by making room within their publications for participants' autonomous responses to and critiques of researchers' interpretations (Andersen 1987; Stacey 1990; Borland 1991; Jackson 1999).

In addition to the question of what it means to listen well to perspectives different from our own, what is at stake in conflicts of this sort is "interpretive authority": To whom does it belong? How should it be negotiated? When is it appropriate for researchers to claim it for themselves (Chase 1996)? Although instances of conflict between researchers' and interviewees' perspectives may jolt researchers to reconsider their interpretations, researchers often find that they are more invested in their analyses than are their participants. Participants sometimes claim that the analysis is "your story, not mine" (Zavella 1996:154; Shostak 1989:233; Stacey 1990:273).

Rather than being seen as a failure of communication, this disjunction can be viewed in terms of the difference between individuals' interpretive work in narrating their lives and social scientists' interpretive work in articulating the social processes, ideologies, and structures embedded in interviewees' stories (Chase 1996; Cotterill 1992; Reay 1996; Holland and Ramazanoglu 1994). Thus interpreting women's words and stories requires a delicate and reflexive balancing act. We need to work at understanding and respecting participants' interpretations of their lives, particularly if those interpretations are different from our own. We need to identify how our acts of knowing—our interpretations of women's words—are socially situated, which includes reflecting on our complex social locations and subjectivities as well as our personal, political, and intellectual agendas. We need to embrace the value of feminist social scientific perspectives, the value of locating women's words within, among other things, gendered, racial, and class-based structures and cultures. Finally, we need to be open to the ways in which our interpretations, as well as those of research participants, may change over time.

■ *Notes*

1. A full discussion of the impact of gender on interview research would include the situations of men interviewing men (which much of social science is based on) and women interviewing men (see Arendell 1997; Williams 1995). It would also explore mixed-gender groups of interviewers and mixed-gender groups of interviewees. See Michael Schwalbe and Michelle Wolkomir's contribution to this volume (Chapter 3).

2. Recent contributors to this literature include Rebecca Campbell (1995), Marjorie DeVault (1999), Mary Maynard and June Purvis (1994), Virginia Olesen (1998), Shulamit Reinharz (1992b), Dorothy Smith (1987), and Diane Wolf (1996).

■ *References*

Aisenberg, N. 1994. *Ordinary Heroines: Transforming the Male Myth.* New York: Continuum.

Altork, K. 1998. "You Never Know When You Might Want to Be a Redhead in Belize." Pp. 111-25 in *Inside Stories: Qualitative Research Reflections,* edited by K. B. deMarrais. Mahwah, NJ: Lawrence Erlbaum.

Andersen, M. L. 1987. "Corporate Wives: Longing for Liberation or Satisfied with the Status Quo?" Pp. 179-90 in *Women and Symbolic Interaction,* edited by M. J. Deegan and M. Hill. Boston: Allen & Unwin.

Anderson, K. and D. C. Jack. 1991. "Learning to Listen: Interview Techniques and Analyses." Pp. 11-26 in *Women's Words: The Feminist Practice of Oral History,* edited by S. B. Gluck and D. Patai. New York: Routledge.

Arendell, T. 1997. "Reflections on the Researcher-Researched Relationship: A Woman Interviewing Men." *Qualitative Sociology* 20:341-68.

Bartky, S. L. 1998. "On Psychological Oppression." Pp. 43-52 in *Contemporary Feminist Theory: A Text/Reader,* edited by M. F. Rogers. New York: McGraw-Hill.

Belenky, M. F., B. M. Clinchy, N. R. Goldberger, and J. M. Tarule. 1986. *Women's Ways of Knowing: The Development of Self, Voice, and Mind.* New York: Basic Books.

———. 1997. *Women's Ways of Knowing: The Development of Self, Voice, and Mind.* 10th anniversary ed. New York: Basic Books.

Blau, P. and Duncan, O. D. 1967. *The American Occupational Structure.* New York: John Wiley.

Blum, L. M. 1999. *At the Breast: Ideologies of Breastfeeding and Motherhood in the Contemporary United States.* Boston: Beacon.

Borland, K. 1991. " 'That's Not What I Said': Interpretive Conflict in Oral Narrative Research." Pp. 63-76 in *Women's Words: The Feminist Practice of Oral History,* edited by S. B. Gluck and D. Patai. New York: Routledge.

Brzuzy, S., A. Ault, and E. A. Segal. 1997. "Conducting Qualitative Interviews with Women Survivors of Trauma." *Affilia* 12(1):76-83.

Butler, J. 1990. *Gender Trouble: Feminism and the Subversion of Identity.* New York: Routledge.

Campbell, R. 1995. "Weaving a New Tapestry of Research: A Bibliography of Selected Readings on Feminist Research Methods." *Women's Studies International Forum* 18:215-22.

Cannon, L. W., E. Higginbotham, and M. L. A. Leung. 1988. "Race and Class Bias in Qualitative Research on Women." *Gender & Society* 2:449-62.

Chase, S. 1995. *Ambiguous Empowerment: The Work Narratives of Women School Superintendents.* Amherst: University of Massachusetts Press.

———. 1996. "Personal Vulnerability and Interpretive Authority in Narrative Research." Pp. 45-59 in *The Narrative Study of Lives,* Vol. 4, *Ethics and Process in the Narrative Study of Lives,* edited by R. Josselson. Thousand Oaks, CA: Sage.

Collins, P. H. 1990. *Black Feminist Thought: Knowledge, Consciousness, and the Politics of Empowerment.* New York: Routledge, Chapman & Hall.

Cotterill, P. 1992. "Interviewing Women: Issues of Friendship, Vulnerability, and Power." *Women's Studies International Forum* 15:593-606.

Crosset, T. 1992. "Out Here: Sport and Gender on the Women's Professional Golf Tour." Ph.D. dissertation, Brandeis University.

Daniels, A. K. 1983. "Self-Deception and Self-Discovery in Fieldwork." *Qualitative Sociology* 6:195-214.

———. 1988. *Invisible Careers: Women Civic Leaders from the Volunteer World.* Chicago: University of Chicago Press.

DeVault, M. L. 1999. *Liberating Method: Feminism and Social Research.* Philadelphia: Temple University Press.

Edwards, R. 1990. "Connecting Method and Epistemology: A White Woman Interviewing Black Women." *Women's Studies International Forum* 13:477-90.

Ellis, C., C. E. Kiesinger, and L. M. Tillman-Healy. 1997. "Interactive Interviewing: Talking about Emotional Experience." Pp. 119-49 in *Reflexivity and Voice,* edited by R. Hertz. Thousand Oaks, CA: Sage.

Finch, J. 1984. " 'It's Great to Have Someone to Talk To': The Ethics and Politics of Interviewing Women." Pp. 70-87 in *Social Researching: Politics, Problems, Practice,* edited by C. Bell and H. Roberts. New York: Routledge.

Fine, M. 1998. "Working the Hyphens: Reinventing Self and Other in Qualitative Research." Pp. 130-55 in *The Landscape of Qualitative Research: Theories and Issues,* edited by N. K. Denzin and Y. S. Lincoln. Thousand Oaks, CA: Sage.

Fontana, A. and Frey, J. H. 1994. "Interviewing: The Art of Science." Pp. 361-76 in *Handbook of Qualitative Research,* edited by N. K. Denzin and Y. S. Lincoln. Thousand Oaks, CA: Sage.

Fordham, S. 1996. *Blacked Out: Dilemmas of Race, Identity, and Success at Capital High.* Chicago: University of Chicago Press.

Fried, M. 1998. *Taking Time: Parental Leave Policy and Corporate Culture.* Philadelphia: Temple University Press.

Gal, S. 1991. "Between Speech and Silence: The Problematics of Research on Language and Gender." Pp. 175-203 in *Gender at the Crossroads of Knowledge: Feminist Anthropology in the Postmodern Era,* edited by M. di Leonardo. Berkeley: University of California Press.

Griffith, A. I. and D. E. Smith. 1987. "Constructing Cultural Knowledge: Mothering as Discourse." Pp. 87-103 in *Women and Education: A Canadian Perspective,* edited by J. S. Gaskell and A. T. McLaren. Calgary, Alberta: Detselig.

Hagood, M. J. [1939] 1977. *Mothers of the South: Portraiture of the White Tenant Farm Woman.* New York: Norton.

Hays, S. 1996. *The Cultural Contradictions of Motherhood.* New Haven, CT: Yale University Press.

Hill, M. 1990. "The Methodological Framework of Harriet Martineau's Feminist Analyses of American Society." Presented at the annual meeting of the American Studies Association, New Orleans.

Holland, J. and C. Ramazanoglu. 1994. "Coming to Conclusions: Power and Interpretation in Researching Young Women's Sexuality." Pp. 125-48 in *Researching Women's Lives from a Feminist Perspective,* edited by M. Maynard and J. Purvis. London: Taylor & Francis.

Jackson, D. 1999. "Thoughtful Practice: Responding with Questions from the Superintendency." Pp. 217-19 in *Sacred Dreams: Women and the Superintendency,* edited by C. C. Brunner. Albany: State University of New York Press.

Josselson, R. 1996. *Revising Herself: The Story of Women's Identity from College to Midlife.* New York: Oxford University Press.

Kanter, R. M. 1977. *Men and Women of the Corporation.* New York: Basic Books.

Kohlberg, L. 1984. *The Psychology of Moral Development.* New York: Harper & Row.

Klatch, R. E. 1987. *Women of the New Right.* Philadelphia: Temple University Press.

Komarovsky, M. 1961. *Blue-Collar Marriage.* New York: Random House.

Krieger, S. 1991. *Social Science and the Self: Personal Essays on an Art Form.* New Brunswick, NJ: Rutgers University Press.

Lewin, E. 1993. *Lesbian Mothers: Accounts of Gender in American Culture.* Ithaca, NY: Cornell University Press.

———. 1998. *Recognizing Ourselves: Ceremonies of Lesbian and Gay Commitment.* New York: Columbia University Press.

Lindsey, E. W. 1997. "Feminist Issues in Qualitative Research with Formerly Homeless Mothers." *Affilia* 12(1):57-75.

Lofland, L. H. 1975. "The 'Thereness' of Women: A Selective Review of Urban Sociology." Pp. 144-70 in *Another Voice: Feminist Perspectives on Social Life and Social Science,* edited by M. M. Millman and R. M. Kanter. Garden City, NY: Anchor/Doubleday.

Lorber, J. 1993. "Believing Is Seeing: Biology as Ideology." *Gender & Society* 7:568-81.

———. 1998. *Gender Inequality: Feminist Theories and Politics.* Los Angeles: Roxbury.

Luttrell, W. 1997. *Schoolsmart and Motherwise: Working-Class Women's Identity and Schooling.* New York: Routledge.

Marin, G. and B. V. Marin. 1991. *Research with Hispanic Populations.* Newbury Park, CA: Sage.

Martineau, H. [1837] 1962. *Society in America.* Edited by S. M. Lipset. Garden City, NY: Anchor.

Maynard, M. and J. Purvis. 1994. "Doing Feminist Research." Pp. 1-9 in *Researching Women's Lives from a Feminist Perspective,* edited by M. Maynard and J. Purvis. London: Taylor & Francis.

McMahon, M. 1995. *Engendering Motherhood: Identity and Self-Transformation in Women's Lives.* New York: Guilford.

———. 1998. "Between Exile and Home." Pp. 187-200 in *Redefining Motherhood: Changing Identities and Patterns,* edited by S. Abbey and A. O'Reilly. Toronto: Second Story.

Merton, R. K., M. Fiske, and P. L. Kendall. 1956. *The Focused Interview: A Manual of Problems and Procedures.* New York: Free Press.

Naples, N. 1997. "A Feminist Revisiting of the Insider/Outsider Debate: The 'Outsider Phenomenon' in Rural Iowa." Pp. 70-94 in *Reflexivity and Voice,* edited by R. Hertz. Thousand Oaks, CA: Sage.

Oakley, A. 1981. "Interviewing Women: A Contradiction in Terms?" Pp. 30-61 in *Doing Feminist Research,* edited by H. Roberts. London: Routledge & Kegan Paul.

Olesen, V. L. 1998. "Feminisms and Models of Qualitative Research." Pp. 300-332 in *The Landscape of Qualitative Research: Theories and Issues,* edited by N. K. Denzin and Y. S. Lincoln. Thousand Oaks, CA: Sage.

Ostrander, S. A. 1984. *Women of the Upper Class.* Philadelphia: Temple University Press.

———. 1995. " 'Surely You're Not in This Just to Be Helpful': Access, Rapport, and Interviews in Three Studies of Elites." Pp. 133-50 in *Studying Elites Using Qualitative Methods,* edited by R. Hertz and J. B. Imber. Thousand Oaks, CA: Sage.

Oyewùmí, O. 1997. *The Invention of Women: Making an African Sense of Western Gender Discourses.* Minneapolis: University of Minnesota Press.

Padfield, M. and I. Procter. 1996. "The Effect of Interviewer's Gender on the Interviewing Process: A Comparative Enquiry." *Sociology* 30:355-66.

Phoenix, A. 1994. "Practicing Feminist Research: The Intersection of Gender and 'Race' in the Research Process." Pp. 49-71 in *Researching Women's Lives from a Feminist Perspective,* edited by M. Maynard and J. Purvis. London: Taylor & Francis.

Pierce, J. L. 1995. *Gender Trials: Emotional Lives in Contemporary Law Firms.* Berkeley: University of California Press.

Ptacek, J. 1999. *Battered Women in the Courtroom: The Power of Judicial Responses.* Boston: Northeastern University Press.

Puwar, N. 1997. "Reflections on Interviewing Women MPs." *Sociological Research Online* 2(1). Available Internet: http://www.socresonline.org.uk/socresonline/2/1/4.html

Ralston, M. L. 1996. *"Nobody Wants to Hear Our Truth": Homeless Women and Theories of the Welfare State.* Westport, CT: Greenwood.

Reay, D. 1995. "The Fallacy of Easy Access." *Women's Studies International Forum* 18:205-13.

———. 1996. "Insider Perspectives or Stealing the Words Out of Women's Mouths: Interpretation in the Research Process." *Feminist Review* 53:57-73.

Reinharz, S. 1985. "Feminist Distrust: Problems of Content and Context in Sociological Work." Pp. 153-72 in *The Self in Social Inquiry: Researching Methods,* edited by D. N. Berg and K. K. Smith. Beverly Hills, CA: Sage.

———. 1992a. "A Contextualized Chronology of Women's Sociological Work." Working Paper No. 1, Brandeis University Women's Studies Program.

———. 1992b. *Feminist Methods in Social Research.* New York: Oxford University Press.

———. 1993. "Neglected Voices and Excessive Demands in Feminist Research." *Qualitative Sociology* 16:69-75.

Richardson, L. 1985. *The New Other Woman: Contemporary Single Women in Affairs with Married Men.* New York: Free Press.

Riessman, C. K. 1987. "When Gender Is Not Enough: Women Interviewing Women." *Gender & Society* 1:172-207.

———. 1990. *Divorce Talk: Women and Men Make Sense of Personal Relationships.* New Brunswick, NJ: Rutgers University Press.

Rogers, M. F., ed. 1998. *Contemporary Feminist Theory: A Text/Reader.* New York: McGraw-Hill.

Rollins, J. 1985. *Between Women: Domestics and Their Employers.* Philadelphia: Temple University Press.

Rothman, B. K. 1993. *The Tentative Pregnancy: How Amniocentesis Changes the Experience of Motherhood.* New York: Norton.

Rubin, L. B. 1976. *Worlds of Pain: Life in the Working-Class Family.* New York: Basic Books.

———. 1995. *Families on the Faultline: America's Working Class Speaks about the Family, the Economy, Race, and Ethnicity.* New York: Harper Perennial.

Sacks, K. B. 1988. *Caring by the Hour: Women, Work, and Organizing at Duke Medical Center.* Urbana: University of Illinois Press.

Samovar, L. A. and R. E. Porter, eds. 1991. *Intercultural Communication: A Reader.* 6th ed. Belmont, CA: Wadsworth.

Shostak, M. 1989. " 'What the Wind Won't Take Away': The Genesis of *Nisa—The Life and Words of a !Kung Woman.*" Pp. 228-40 in *Interpreting Women's Lives: Feminist Theory and Personal Narratives,* edited by Personal Narratives Group. Bloomington: Indiana University Press.

Simmel, G. 1971. "The Stranger." Pp. 143-49 in G. Simmel, *On Individuality and Social Forms: Selected Writings,* edited by D. N. Levine. Chicago: University of Chicago Press.

Smith, D. E. 1987. *The Everyday World as Problematic: A Feminist Sociology.* Boston: Northeastern University Press.

Stacey, J. 1990. *Brave New Families: Stories of Domestic Upheaval in Late Twentieth Century America.* New York: Basic Books.

Tannen, D., ed. 1993. *Gender and Conversational Interaction.* New York: Oxford University Press.

Taylor, V. 1996. *Rock-a-By Baby: Feminism, Self-Help, and Postpartum Depression.* New York: Routledge.

Thompson, B. 1990. "Raisins and Smiles for Me and My Sister: A Feminist Theory of Eating Problems, Trauma, and Recovery in Women's Lives." Ph.D. dissertation, Brandeis University.

Tixier y Vigil, Y. and N. Elsasser. 1978. "The Effects of the Ethnicity of the Interviewer on Conversation: A Study of Chicana Women." Pp. 161-70 in *Sociology of the Languages of American Women,* edited by B. L. Dubois and I. Crouch. San Antonio, TX: Trinity University.

Tocqueville, A. de. [1835] 1994. *Democracy in America,* Vol. 2. New York: Alfred A. Knopf.

Treviño, A. J. 1992. "Interviewing Women: Researcher Sensitivity and the Male Interviewer." *Humanity and Society* 16:504-23.

Villenas, S. 1998. "The Colonizer/Colonized Chicana Ethnographer: Identity, Marginalization, and Co-optation in the Field." Pp. 172-88 in *Contemporary Feminist Theory: A Text/Reader,* edited by M. F. Rogers. New York: McGraw-Hill.

Weiss, R. S. 1994. *Learning from Strangers: The Art and Method of Qualitative Interview Studies.* New York: Free Press.

Weston, K. 1991. *Families We Choose: Lesbians, Gays, Kinship.* New York: Columbia University Press.

Whyte, W. F. 1943. *Street Corner Society: The Social Structure of an Italian Slum.* Chicago: University of Chicago Press.

Williams, C. L. 1995. *Still a Man's World: Men Who Do Women's Work.* Berkeley: University of California Press.

Wolf, D. L., ed. 1996. *Feminist Dilemmas in Fieldwork.* Boulder, CO: Westview.

Zavella, P. 1996. "Feminist Insider Dilemmas: Constructing Ethnic Identity with Chicana Informants." Pp. 138-59 in *Feminist Dilemmas in Fieldwork,* edited by D. L. Wolf. Boulder, CO: Westview.

5

QUEERING THE INTERVIEW

◆ **Travis S. K. Kong**
Dan Mahoney
Ken Plummer

The challenge lies in what each of us chooses to do when we represent our experiences. Whose rules do we follow? Will we make our own? What is the nature of the "I," that so many of our prohibitions bury? How can we unearth some of the inner worlds that we learn so very well to hide? Are we willing to do this within social science? Do we, in fact, have the guts to say, "You may not like it, but here I am." (Krieger 1991:244)

These questions resonate with the challenges of many of the changes the 20th century saw in the cultural forms of Western same-sex experience. Such experiences shifted from being highly disparaged—stigmatized, psychiatrized, and criminalized—to being politicized, social, and "out." A new form of gayness emerged symbolically in 1969 around the Stonewall moment, the start of the Gay Liberation Front, or GLF, sparked by gay resistance to the police invasion of the Stonewall Tavern in New York City. It led on to what might be seen as a proliferation of de-essentialized "queer" forms by the start of the new century, an array of different types of experience with no clear common core. These shifts—in the changing organization of "the closet," in the structures of homophobia and heterosexism, in the blurring of boundaries and borders, in the arrival of AIDS as a major galvanizing and depressing force, in the globalization and the "glocalization" of gay experience, indeed in the postmodernization of homosexualities—have all now been much documented, discussed, and dissected in the huge literatures that constitute a lesbian/gay/bisexual/transgender/queer compendium of studies (e.g., Abelove, Barale, and Halperin 1993; Murray 1997; Nardi and Schneider 1998;

Seidman, Meeks, and Traschen 1999; Weeks 1977, 1999).

Our aim in this chapter is to address the sense that, as all of this has changed, so have the methodologies for approaching it. We are now in the midst of emerging forms of experience that are paralleled by shifting styles of interviewing and analysis. What we suggest is simply that *the sensibilities of interviewing are altered with the changing social phenomena that constitute "the interviewee."* Interviewer and interviewee are always connected by a social location or habitus. We start with a brief tour of the shifts in the interviewing of gays in North America and Europe over the past 100 years before turning to a discussion of how contemporary issues have necessitated a different procedural agenda for researching same-sex experience.

◆ Interviewing "Homosexuals"

Table 5.1 presents some of the key changes that have taken place in the interviewing of gays in the past century. The table should be seen as an unstable continuum, certainly involving much overlap, depicting trends, rather than as a designation of strict time periods.[1] Broadly, we can trace a movement from a highly positivist mode of research through one where the boundaries become weaker, and on to a situation where interviewing has been partially deconstructed.

THE EARLY DAYS: A TRADITIONAL WORLD OF RESEARCH

Traditional "homosexual" research relied on a form of positivism that drew a sharp distinction between the subjects of knowing (i.e., researchers) and the objects of study (i.e., interviewees).[2] Through standardized interviews, ostensibly disinterested researchers obtained seemingly objective accounts of the nature of homo-

sexuality. Here, "homosexuals"—a term coined by Hungarian doctor Karoly Maria Benkert in the 1860s—were interviewed as the Other. Until the latter third of the 20th century "scientists" studied homosexuals, initially as perverted, then as sick, and finally as different persons. The interviews usually aimed at explaining the properties of sexuality by referring to "an inner truth or essence—a uniform pattern ordained by nature, not connected to values and emotions" (Stein 1997:203).

This dominant pattern of research unfolded in two waves. In both, homosexuals were incited to speak through interviews about what made them that way and just how different they were. But in one wave, the interview was clearly an instrument of pathological diagnosis—strongly dehumanizing, rendering homosexuals sick and diseased, and often serving as a specific means for placing homosexuals in prison, under treatment, or worse. Medicine and psychiatry dominated. This continued until 1973, when at least the American Psychiatric Association saw fit, under pressure, to demedicalize homosexuality (Bayer 1981). Prime examples of work in this vein include Richard von Krafft-Ebing's (1899) research, the studies of George W. Henry (1941), and, in the 1950s and 1960s the research of Irving Bieber (1962) and Charles Socarides (1968).

At the same time, another more benign tendency was taking place, one that was to play a more humanizing role. In this wave, the interview became a tool of modernist democratization and ultimately of social reform. To some extent, it can be found in Freud's openness to polymorphousness and bisexuality, but it is strongly present in the important interviews of Alfred Kinsey and his associates (Kinsey, Pomeroy, and Martin 1948; Kinsey et al. 1953) and Evelyn Hooker (1957) in the United States and of Michael Schofield, alias Gordon Westwood (1961), in the United Kingdom. This more benign approach humanized the deviant, advocated tolerance, and weak-

Table 5.1 CHANGES IN INTERVIEWING REGARDING SAME-SEX EXPERIENCE

	Traditional	Modernizing	Postmodern
Kind of interviewer	Presumed heterosexual and objective interviewer	Closeted gay and heterosexual interviewers	An "out" gay or lesbian interviewer
Conception of same-sex relations	1. "Essential homosexual"; a clear type of person awaiting an interview 2. Strict closet	1. The arrival of "homosexualities"; diversities 2. Weakened closet; gradual "coming out"	1. De-essentialized homosexual; no clear type of person; multiple pathways and experiences 2. Old closets weakened; new closets grow
Types of respondents	1. Homosexual respondents hard to find; usually psychiatric patients, criminal samples 2. Exotic and stigmatized "outsider"	1. Respondents from within the gay community: often white and male 2. Homosexuals becoming "normalized"	1. Recognition of a range of experiences; queer, global, multicultural 2. Queers and gays; fracturing; a normalization of a mainstream gay with new groups on the "outside"
Questions posed	Etiology and pathology: What causes homosexuality and descriptions of pathologies and negative lives?	The "coming out" story detailing the classic life story and lifestyle	Fragmenting; de-essentialized questions; a wider range of questions, often going well beyond the issue of homo-sexualities; "queering the field"
Approach	Mainly clinical	Mainly psychological and sociological surveys	Much more active, reflexive, and reflective; the decentered, deconstructed, and self-aware interview
Wider discourses of same-sex experience	Disease discourse	Psychosocial discourses	Cultural and political discourses
Nature of interview	Subject as interview object; sometimes coercive; seen as other		Mutuality of interviewer and subject; seen as potential friend
Examples	Krafft-Ebing (1989), moving to Kinsey et al. (1948, 1953)	Bell & Weinberg (1978); Gagnon & Simon (1973)	Krieger (1983, 1991, 1996)
Politics	Traditional-conservative, often with interview as a tool of control	Modernist-liberatory, often with interview as a democratic liberalizing force	Postmodernist themes; fragmented, postmodern ethics; self-conscious, more localized, politics and change

ened the language of the exotic. It made the interview a more pedestrian affair. Findings saw continua in sexuality, a strong overlap between gay and heterosexual experience. Such studies investigated social backgrounds, early homosexual experiences, attempts to combat personal troubles, work, leisure, law, and community integration, as well as sexual adjustment.

With the exception of the work of Kinsey and his colleagues, however, little overt attention was given to the problems of interviewing themselves. Of course, there were the standard obligatory considerations of where interviews should take place (preferably in the home of the "contact") and the nature of the sample. But there was no methodological reflexivity of any kind, any sense of "active interviewing" (Holstein and Gubrium 1995). Subjects were largely taken to be passive receptacles of information, and emphasis was placed on the presentation of objective data.

This was true of the major, massive surveys that were conducted in the 1960s by the Kinsey Institute, one in Chicago as a pilot and the other in San Francisco. These studies, headed initially by John Gagnon and William Simon, and later conducted by Martin Weinberg and Alan Bell, drew from a very large subject pool established by way of advertising and recruitment in bars, gay baths, public places, and organizations, and through personal contacts. Samples of approximately 1,000 gay and 500 heterosexual men and women were obtained, and an interview schedule of some 175 pages was used, which took two to five hours for the recruited graduate student interviewers to complete. This produced some of the most widely cited findings of the late 20th century (e.g., Bell and Weinberg 1978; Bell, Weinberg, and Hammersmith 1982). But again, interview methodology followed strictly in the positivist mold, applying research practices that had by then become well established.[3]

Much, if not all, of this tradition of research has been "essentialist" in approach (Plummer 1981:57-61), an orientation that was progressively critiqued by the so-called social constructionists, who became prominent during the 1970s and 1980s.[4] The latter argued that sexuality and sexual identity are social constructions, belonging less to the biological world than to the domain of culture and meaning (Epstein 1987). Constructionists relativized the conception of gay identity and argued that the late-20th-century Western experience of same-sex intimacies was historically unique, as they simultaneously sketched the different makings of the homosexual role. They argued that the modern homosexual role emerged with the appearance of male transvestite social clubs and homosexual coteries in major cities such as London in the 17th century, with the experience of the wage labor sector and the growth of urban populations in the 18th century, and with the professionalization of medicine and the social organization of sexual "types" in the 19th century (Adam 1985; Foucault 1979).

"COMING OUT" AS A MODERNIST TALE

The rise of a lesbian and gay movement from the 1960s onward triggered a new understanding of homosexuality and a new research direction. With the redeployment of the 19th-century slang term *gay* to oppose the pathologizing term *homosexual,* the positivist approach was being slowly undone, as it was elsewhere in the social sciences. A hermeneutic or interpretive perspective emerged, and the interview increasingly became a tool for self-identification and "coming out." As researchers asked how respondents got to be gay and how they felt about it, a cultural event started to take shape through interviewing that led to the makings of the "coming out story."

These stories were typically "modernist tales," articulated in a causal language of linear progression and centered on an unproblematic identity. Interviews were presumed to be discovering the "truth" of the gay self. Starting in childhood and following through the life course in linear progression, gay interviews assumed the same sequenced and causal pattern featured in much modern biography. In gay stories, childhood was usually presented as an unhappy time, frequently the source of the individual's being gay or lesbian. There was often a strong sense of difference expressed: "I never felt as if I fit in. I don't know why for sure. I felt different. I thought it was because I was more sensitive" (Troiden 1988; cited in Savin-Williams 1990). A crucial moment appeared within this modernist narrative, usually in early adolescence, where problems led to a marked concern over being "gay." Personal difficulties abounded and were usually documented in detail: secrecy, guilt or shame, fear of discovery, and suicidal feelings. But they were then resolved in some fashion in a redemption tale, usually involving the person's meeting other lesbians or gays in the community. Finally, the individual achieved a sense of identity or self *as* gay or lesbian, along with a sense of community (see Dank [1971] in Nardi and Schneider 1998; Plummer 1995:83). This is a simplified version, but over and over again narratives of this kind were proffered in the many "coming out" interviews gathered in the 1970s and 1980s. Coming out became the central narrative of positive gay experience.

At the same time, more and more self-identified gay researchers engaged in the interview process, collapsing the old split between subject/researcher and the object/researched. Some researchers started to come out through their writings. If in some instances the interview process became a political act, it also started to imply that only gay and lesbian researchers could conduct this interviewing, because of their more authentic understanding of other gay men and lesbians. Putting it simply, the assumption was that only those who have been there can understand what it's like.

THE DRIFT TO REFLEXIVITY IN THE 1980S

Two major changes took place in the 1980s that extended these shifts in interviewing: the consolidation of feminist research practices and the arrival of AIDS research. Feminist research practices had been advocated since at least the mid-1970s. Feminists brought a heightened self-awareness and reflexivity to interview methodology, which led to a greater concern with subjects' lived and contradictory experience, along with an image of the in-

terview that was based more on friendly conversation than on "masculine" interrogation (see Reinharz and Chase, Chapter 4, this volume). This brought the researcher and the researched into greater contact and made the research process more expressly moral and political. Many feminist researchers also were lesbians, and they incorporated a mode of working that also touched specifically on lesbian issues (Krieger 1983, 1991, 1996; Stanley and Wise 1983, 1993).

AIDS and HIV research led to more community-based approaches to interviewing, although it must be said that much of this was carried out in the time-honored positivist manner, which researchers saw as the only way to gain funding. New, culturally specific practices were incorporated as gay researchers went into the field and interviewed in venues most frequented by gay men, using sexually explicit language and gay vernacular.

As a result, an interview context emerged that was based largely on gay (and lesbian) "sensibilities." Although this term may have an essentialist resonance, in practice this meant that the gay interviewer and gay interviewee could empathize around shared meanings and ways of knowing.[5] A safe environment where gay men felt at ease to talk about their sexual and relationship histories was constructed. The result was that the interview context was distinctively "gayed."

THE RISE OF QUEER THEORY AND A QUEER METHODOLOGY

It was but a few steps from this to a more developed "queer methodology." Drawing from some of the existing critical trends, but taking a lead from poststructuralism, some researchers mounted a challenge to traditional epistemologies by arguing that we have no way of accessing the reality where our theory can be grounded without some form of conceptual and linguistic ordering in which to understand experience.

Interpretation, writing, and speech acts are all practices both of and in an intertextual field. Poststructuralism radically rejected the notion of the possibility of obtaining objective reality, as it elided a reality "posited beyond the text with reference to which meaning can be stabilized among different subjects" (Smith 1996:174).

On the status of objective knowledge, the poststructuralist rejection of a one-to-one correspondence between a category and the object it denoted implied that language was no longer a transparent medium. Attention to the multiple discursivity that constituted social relations was the only alternative. On the status of subjectivity, poststructuralists rejected the notion of a unified disciplinary subject, because subjects are always "situated" or "positioned" when they enter the symbolic world. Poststructuralists thus urged us to reconcile ourselves to our having multiple and fragmented, discursively constituted subjectivities, intersected significantly by gender, race, sexuality, and class, among the many and diverse subject positions that mediate everyday life and, of course, the interview.

Queer theory works toward deconstructing discourses, and, to the extent that interviewing is discursive, this means deconstructing the interview.[6] To quote Michael Warner (1993), this leads to a stark attack on "normal business in the academy" (p. xxv). One result is the adoption of a "scavenger methodology that uses different methods to collect and produce information on subjects who have been deliberately or accidentally excluded from traditional studies of human behavior." In its most general form, this entails a refusal to abide orthodox methodology, encouraging a "certain disloyalty to conventional disciplinary methods" (Halberstam 1998: 9, 13).

In this context, the traditional "scientific" interview is devalorized and takes a much more down-to-earth role alongside any and all other methods. The very idea that various types of people named homosexuals or gays or lesbians can simply be called up for interviews becomes a key problem in itself. Instead, the researcher becomes increasingly open and sensitive to how sexuality, among a broad range of identities, is anchored in fleeting ways within the discursive contours of interviewing. The many social worlds that can, as a result, contextualize what is said during interviews are not immediately transparent, whereas others are amorphously nascent and forming. It is not always possible to see what is forming, producing subjective domains and identities that Plummer (1995) has called the worlds of "imagining-visualising-empathising" (p. 126).

The subject of inquiry ("the homosexual"), the nature of the inquiry ("the interview"), and the inquirers themselves have all become problematized and open to deconstruction. The result is that new procedural issues are being seriously considered in relation to how interviewing gets done. One of these relates to matters of *subjective representation*.[7] Here the problem arises of literally who and what is being heard through the interview. Specifically, who are these "homosexuals" being interviewed, how do they come to find their voice, and what indeed is that voice? If one is successfully coaxed into giving voice to one's experience in an interview, what are the chances that one will become the Other in the process? Homosexuals, gays, bisexuals, transgenders, lesbians, even "queer" subjects have typically been homogenized and cast into some role of Other and thus seriously misrepresented, their thoughts, language, and sentiments collapsed into categories foreign to, if not destructive of, experience. Indeed, how often are these voices mere reproductions of white, middle-class, Western gay men, as if there were indeed no other subjectivities to consider? As far as representation is concerned, doing interviews now more urgently than ever requires us to investigate simultaneously who has been excluded. And this leads to the questions of who can speak for the other, from what position, and on what basis

(Denzin 1994; Lincoln and Denzin 1994: 577).

This raises a second procedural issue centered on *legitimation*. This relates to the old problem of the validity of interviews, although now the problem becomes to sense the legitimacy of "constructing an interview" and how results get composed into a "research text." When, therefore, we come to a text about gay lives that is composed through interviews, we want some sense of how faithful it is "to the context and the individuals it is supposed to represent" (Lincoln and Denzin 1994:578).

A third and related issue is *reflexivity*, which centers on the problem of locating the connectedness between the (gay?) interviewer and (gay? bisexual? lesbian? queer?) interviewee. This alerts us to questions of whether researchers should be part of the communities they study, and to the emotional responses interviews provoke in their subjects, indeed to their erotic involvements as well. The full assembly of academic and intellectual conventions around interviewing is broached, conventions that can actually work to obscure, not discover, knowledge.

And, finally, there is the matter of interviewing's *politics, morality, and ethics*. Closely linked to all of the above is the crucial recognition that interviewing involves human dimensions. Although it may be cozy to see interviews as simply a matter of "gathering data," a deconstruction of interviewing that derives from firmly sensing what has been done to "homosexuals" through interviews in the past must be at the forefront of what it now means to "queer" the interview. We need to take account of the distinct possibility that, within the research process itself, interviews are moral and political interventions through and through, and we need to represent our findings as such.

Of course, these problems are not peculiar to the interviewing of homosexuals. The latter highlight them in different ways in relation to distinct subjectivities. In what follows, we take up the issues in greater de-

tail as they specifically relate to possibilities for queering the interview process.

◆ The Problem of Representation

Who is being re-presented in the interview? Posing the question in this way leads to the consideration of how the gay person being interviewed may become the Other within the context of being a respondent. Indeed, if we are to take Michel Foucault seriously, our interviews may show nothing but our will to power as interviewers. An interview could never really "represent" the gay or lesbian who is being interviewed as such; rather, it is one more technical display of a disciplined regimen of interviewer/author power over subjects. From this perspective, representation is a kind of authorial and cultural self-re-presentation. Interviewees' presentations are always already directly connected to the situated interviewing self of an author/researcher and his or her project (Krieger 1991).

Can the interview stories we hear from lesbians and gays and that appear in texts as diverse as Arlene Stein's *Sex and Sensibility* (1997), Gary Dowsett's *Practicing Desire* (1996), and Richard Parker's *Beneath the Equator* (1999) really represent the worlds of those studied? What does the interview come to represent? Can it reveal, legitimately, the experience of interviewees? Or does it implicate, instead, the narrower, more restricted world of the researcher, which would say more about Arlene Stein, Gary Dowsett, and Richard Parker than about their subjects themselves? Do these texts address the interests of those studied?

The key status of the interviewer/author is now put into question. Whether or not the interviewer's voice is manifest, it always deploys a unique self in the interview and claims to have some pervasive authorial functions over other subject matters that are being interpreted. Even having the

research subjects as authors does not completely solve the problem, for we are left
asking under what institutional constraints
they can come to be authors and under
what historical limitations they can speak
and write. Just when and how can stories of
such lives be told? (See Plummer 1995; see
also Briggs, Chapter 24, this volume.)

This makes interviewing and the texts
that flow from it much more problematic
than the authors of the earlier studies of gay
life could have figured. New strategies for
handling matters of representation have to
be found (see in this volume Ellis and
Berger, Chapter 23). One way may involve
a greater focus on specialized and localized
knowledges, another may focus on the creation of new modes of writing the interview.

THE INTERVIEW AS A SITE OF
LOCALIZED KNOWLEDGE

Because epistemology has traditionally
been the legacy of white, straight men, it
has had to be challenged by more specialized and marginalized knowledges. From
diverse positions—Foucauldian, standpoint theoretical, postmodern, and postcolonial—new voices have started to be
heard telling their stories (Foucault 1984;
Harding 1991; Spivak 1994). The missing
voice of "authentic" (a word with a host of
problems and that we use advisedly) gays
and lesbians under the sign of compulsory
heterosexuality in the sex/gender regime
of society can become a key to new
forms of local knowledge. The hetero-
sexual/homosexual binary is recognized as
a master rhetoric, not an essential framework, for constructing the self, sexual
knowledge, and social institutions. This
binary sex system, or power/knowledge regime, is critically assessed for how it creates
rigid psychological and social boundaries
that inevitably give rise to systems of domi-
nance and hierarchy (Sedgwick 1990; Fuss
1991; Butler 1990; Warner 1993).

AIDS interview research has, perhaps of
necessity, only partially given way to this
critical consciousness. Rather than interviewing self-identified gay men as the sole
sources to learn about the sexual practices
of same-sex experience, researchers interview "MSM" (men who have sex with
other men)—a distinction that seems to ter-
minologically suspend the issue of the interviewee's identity. This recognition of the
"collapse of identity and difference" links
up queer with AIDS activism (Edelman
1995). Although coming out of the closet is
often viewed as a gay empowerment strategy and as a supreme political act to affirm
gay visibility from heterosexism, the division between individuals who are "in" the
closet and those who are "out" has its costs,
as this not only narrowly defines the sexual
experiences of lesbians and gay men, but
also stigmatizes the former, who are "in,"
as living unhappily and privileges the latter,
who are "out," as presumably now more
satisfied with their lives and identities (see
Seidman et al. 1999).

The recent critique from "queer theorists" also receives its attention in anthropology, as Kath Weston (1998) argues.
Many lesbians and gay men do not offer the
"best" natives for study. In representation,
if not in action, they appear too modern,
too urban, too here and now, too wealthy,
and too white. Below the perceptual hori-
zon are queers with rural origins, immigrant status, empty pocketbooks, racial
identities at variance with the Anglo.
Ironically, the gay movement's problematic
tendency is to draw analogies between sexual and racial identity, as though all gays
were white and people of color could not
be gay (Weston 1998:194).

Last but not least, localization is extended as postcolonial theorists examine
the intertwining relationship between race
and sexuality.[8] Drawing heavily on the legacy of poststructuralism, queer theory, and
postcolonialism, postcolonial queer theorists contend that homosexuality is often
viewed as a white European experience,
and gay Asian British/American identity

seems to be contradictory. These theorists argue that postcolonial gay identities are not merely the additive experiences of race, gender, class, and sexuality, or simply another variation of the Western homoerotic experience; rather, they are the result of multifarious and contradictory sets of oppression within specific institutional arenas. We must understand sexual identity in terms of this "politics of difference" in order to avoid suppressing the multiple ways of experiencing homosexual desires (Takagi 1996; Hanawa 1994; Jackson and Sullivan 1999; Leong 1996; Kong 2000). Interviewing in relation to such differences can reveal and, at the same time, dissolve into multiplicities, the many ways there are to experience same-sexedness.

THE INTERVIEW AS A SHIFT IN WRITING STRATEGY

Many experiments with writing have been undertaken, pioneered by feminist researchers who have emphasized how personal experience can be used as evidence in research (see in this volume Ellis and Berger, Chapter 23). The standard mode, of course, is to use interview extracts in such a way that the representative text becomes littered with examples of first-person speech drawn out of interview findings. In this mode of representation, the interviewed gay or lesbian is engrossed by the author's own writing and scholarly authority.

What is required is a shift in style that shows textually how interviews of gay men and lesbians can be led by the researcher's vested interest. This effort would help to create a new way of looking at things by blurring representational distinctions (e.g., between philosophy and literary) and subject matters (e.g., between "hard-core" sociological writing and autobiography). Researchers can explore this shift in style by using "fictionalized" interview material to express issues of representation, subjectivity, and critique for social research (Banks

and Banks 1998). They may also explore by experimenting with the use of autovideo—that is, turning the camera back onto interviewer and interviewee (Juhasz 1995). Researchers may further explore this shift through renditions of social science that see it as drama, poetry, diary, documentaries, interactive Web sites, and more.

Ironically, at the same time, the author can often lose his or her own voice in favor of a more "subjective" one. In a series of studies and observations, Susan Krieger has pondered just how she "had a right to say something that was mine," reflecting the perspective of researchers and interviewers who figure they have no right at all to bring themselves and their feelings into their work. In several studies, such as *The Mirror Dance* (1983), *Social Science and the Self* (1991), and *The Family Silver* (1996), Krieger has tried to find ways in which she can do research and yet allow her own presence and experiences to be felt. During her research reported in *The Mirror Dance,* for example, she lived in a community of lesbians, seeing her year's participation with the group she studied as an active emotional reengagement process. Krieger describes how an understanding of her own self, worked through over time, helped her to clarify what could otherwise have been just "data."

◆ The Problem of Legitimation

Another key problem of interviewing centers on issues of legitimation and authenticity, what used to be called validity. At the simplest level, gays and lesbians may tell lies or just set out to please the interviewer to gain positive evaluations. Even if they are assumed to give authentic answers, problems still exist. As a large part of gay and lesbian interviews are usually retrospective accounts, interviewees are required to reconstruct their pasts actively in order to make sense of their present selves.

Problems of memory and accounting enter here (Plummer 2001). Even questions that do not directly ask about the past, such as "What does it mean to be gay?" and questions concerning interviewees' current opinions on love and/or sex still demand that lesbians and gays create some kind of coherent account of their responses, implicating the past. Of course, these problems are not unique to lesbian and gay interviews, but they do suggest problems that are trickier than the older ways of putting this in terms of validity and reliability.

Any attempt to overcome this authenticity problem, as it relates to narrative, risks falling back into the trap of positivism, where it is assumed that the "truth" of the past can be revealed through objective methods of investigation. How can this be overcome? Various kinds of postmodern sensibilities for "queer interviewing" suggest themselves.

One is overtly political. Foucault's (1984) subversive genealogy is a strategy that exposes how power and discourse operate together and how subordinated knowledges can be used to resist any validity-as-authority claims. Thus studying gay and lesbian identity may disturb the prevailing rigid familial, gender, and moral systems of society, but this may also reify the very categories of lesbian and gay that may fix or control conduct.

Another recent leap of the imagination may be found in Judith Halberstam's (1998) work. In examining "female masculinity," Halberstam argues that although we have started to recognize the varieties of masculinities that are linked to men, we have signally failed to develop ways of seeing that can grasp the different kinds of masculinities that women have revealed both in the past and in the present. According to Halberstam, there are aristocratic European cross-dressing women of the 1920s, butch lesbians, dykes, drag kings, tomboys, black butch-in-the-hood rappers, trans-butches, tribades, gender inverts, stone butches, female-to-male transsexuals (FTMs), and raging bull dykes. Halberstam

also detects, through examination of films as diverse as *Alien* and *The Killing of Sister George,* at least six prototypes of the female masculine: the tomboy, the predator, the fantasy butch, the transvestite, the barely butch, and the postmodern butch.

This research brings to the surface social worlds only dimly articulated hitherto, suggesting that there are more, many more, to be formulated. As far as interviewing is concerned, it signals the hugely diverse, mixed, hybridized, and newly imagined subjectivities around which questions could be prepared, responses offered, and interview material interpreted—which a single category of female, male, or even female masculinity itself would collapse into homogenized subjective meaninglessness.

The task is to subvert the unified notion of gay and lesbian identity and to paint a picture of multiple and conflicting sexual/gendered experiences. Further to the point, in these times of globalization, we can present postcolonial queer identities that offer new insights by troubling the hegemonic Western formulation of "being gay." The queer interview can be composed discursively to cause trouble.[9] Such complicated assumptions behind interviewing are made clearer, for example, by Travis Kong, one of the authors of this chapter. Kong comes from Hong Kong, has self-identified as a gay man, has been living in London for a couple of years, and works in English. Although he shares with the other two authors a sense of being a gay academic man, his postcolonial and sexual statuses inevitably affect his formulation of gayness under a Western hegemonic knowledge regime. For example, as a sexual and racial minority in a white and heterosexual society, the Chinese gay man is imagined as an exotic/erotic fantasy, as the "golden boy," as an infantilized (age), feminized (gender), and golden (race) persona who seems to suffer different forms of subordination under the hierarchies of domination in both the straight and gay worlds (Kong 2000, forthcoming).

Assumptions are usually made about what it means to be gay in the West, not the East. The Chinese construction of the individual as a "relational self" seems to be in conflict with the Western idea of coming out, in which outed gay figures are usually without blood-family ties. The possibility of leading a satisfactory life outside the family seems to be inconceivable in Asian countries, and so the problem is how to reconcile gay identity with the institution of the neo-Confucian family (see Berry 1996; Kong 2000). In the Chinese context, coming out is not a common way of asserting one's gayness, and desires do not seem to be framed in terms of political interests. Rather than the term *homosexual* (a Western medical term), *gay* (a Western construction), or even *queer* (a Western deconstruction), the term *tongzhi* (literally "comrade") has gained in popularity within gay circles in Hong Kong because of its ambiguous nature.[10] Because *tongzhi* also carries no direct sexual connotation, Hong Kong gay men feel comfortable using it. This and other kinds of non-Western "trouble" provide a culturally sensitive pretext for *normalizing* family-oriented questions in interviews with gays. Needless to say, the coming out narrative in this context might very well signal domestic reconciliation or transformation more than disengagement.

◆ Self-Reflection in the Interview Process

Another concern for gay and lesbian interviewing has to be the increased awareness of the need for self-reflexivity. Pierre Bourdieu, in *An Invitation to Reflexive Sociology* (1992), suggests that reflexivity provides a much greater awareness of the entire intellectual process. We need to look at (a) the subject of the research along with (b) the social locations in which research knowledge is produced, as well as (c) a much fuller sense of the spaces—personal, cultural, ac-

ademic, intellectual, historical—that the researcher occupies in building that knowledge. There has to be an attentiveness to what people take into research situations and take out of them, as well as to feeling, identity, and the body.

This is of particular importance in the case of in-depth interviews on gay men's private lives. Before being interviewed, many gay men want to know where both the researcher and the teller of that life are coming from, what kind of relationship they are having together, and how intimate details will be used and represented. Dan Mahoney, another of the authors of this chapter, found this self-reflexive process to be an effective strategy when he was recruiting a gay couple for an interview. In his field notes, Mahoney (2000) writes:

> Our drive back to their home outside London went particularly well. It became clear that Adam and I would get on. We both took the opportunity to ask and respond to each other's questions in a way that felt appropriate and polite. I was careful to come across as an interested and sincere person. I wanted to give the impression that I wasn't the type of researcher who was overbearing or full of myself. I felt it was important that I set the stage for the interview. I also felt that Adam was doing some preliminary assessing on his own. . . .
>
> Adam produced the fax I sent him and went about asking for clarification about the nature of the research and what I meant by storytelling. I took the opportunity to speak about the book I was writing on gay men and their families, and my interest in writing about experiences of gay men we haven't heard about before. James [Adam's partner] sat and took it all in. Adam continued to ask me questions. He wanted to know about my personal background, why I was studying in England, and why on earth I was living in Colchester. I gave him a short biogra-

phy of my life. More disclosures about my life precipitated more answers and questions about me and my research interests. I was getting the impression that they were warming up to the idea of being interviewed.

REFLEXIVITY, EMOTIONS, AND THE RESEARCHER'S SELF

The doing of interviews is personal, interactional, and emotional. It is embodied work that can have implications for the researcher as well as the researched. How does the researcher present him- or herself? How is the interaction embodied? How are feelings presented and managed (see Coffey 1999; Kleinman and Copp 1993)? In earlier work on sexual life stories, Ken Plummer (1995) describes a situation he encountered in doing life story interviewing that wasn't gay but fetishistic, and then reflects on just what the doing of such an interview meant. Plummer comments on a so-called foot fetishist:

I travel to the North of England where I meet a young man in his early twenties in a hotel lobby. We go to my hotel room, and he tells me in enormous detail of his desire to be trod upon by women in high heels. As this happens, he fantasizes a dagger being plunged into his stomach. It is a long story, which takes me through his childhood memories of this and the "driven" nature of his "single" adult life. I record the conversation, and respond very sympathetically to him; he seems a nice enough man. Back at my university, the tape is transcribed and makes fascinating reading. The secretary (of the research) names him Jack (a pseudonym, but interestingly her husband is called Jack!). This transcript is sent to Jack, who comments profusely on it. A short correspondence is set up, and I send him a copy of a key book in this field, *The Sex Life of the Foot and Shoe*. For

the past ten years, the transcript and its commentary sits in my filing cabinet. I have lost contact with him. (P. 10)

After this brief description, so much more could have been said. So Plummer continues asking questions of himself about what he was actually doing, implicating a number of his own identities in the process —as tolerant researcher, as a coparticipant in self-disclosure, and as representer of the experience under consideration.

What brought me to seek out a man who wanted to talk about his "unusual" sexual life? Why should I, in the name of Holy Social Science, want to coax anyone to tell me about their sexual lives? What brought him to the hotel room to tell me all about it? How could he produce such stories, and how did my "tolerant" responses to him actively encourage him to tell a certain sort of story? He could sense very early on that I was not going to be shocked or censorious in any way. But didn't that make him say certain things rather than others? And to leave endless undetected absences? How much of his story was a performance of a dress rehearsal he had practised many times in solitude before? What, then, was the relationship of my transcribed interview to his actual life? And how was I to write this? In his voice, or in my voice, or in his voice through my voice, or even in my voice through his voice? And then, once read by others—including me and him— what multiple interpretations would it be open to? Would there perhaps be a correct reading which would finally get us all to the truth of such foot fetishists? Or would it be used as an occasion for condemnation, curiosity, or simple titillation, or as a guide for someone else to locate their sexual nature? What would it do to Jack once published? And indeed, what has it done to him since it has *not* been published, but sits unread in a filing cabinet? And so it goes on.

> The questions proliferate. I became more and more aware of these questions at the time of doing the research, and they slowly incapacitated me. Just what *are* these sexual stories gathered for research? (P. 12)

THE BIG SILENCE: ON SEXING THE INTERVIEW

What starts to be sensed are all the typically silenced questions around an interview that more and more need to be brought to the fore. We can take all this one stage further, into slightly dangerous, certainly controversial, territory. Here we turn to the hidden dimensions of romance, passion, and sexuality that must impinge on some, maybe much, research, even if rarely spoken about. It is curious, not to say disingenuous, to find that most research is written as if such experiences quite simply never happen in people's lives. From fieldwork to interviews, as people come and go, nothing much ever appears to unfold in erotic mode. Just where is it?

Recently, a number of researchers have started to make this erotic dimension more explicit. For example, in a wonderful account of Kay, a lesbian in her 80s and one of Esther Newton's (1993) key informants at the lesbian community of Cherry Grove, Newton makes her passion and involvement very clear:

> This morning I introduced myself to a woman of eighty plus, whom I'd been wanting to meet, as she rolled toward me in her electric chair. Not only was she receptive, she clasped my arm in an intimate embrace and practically pulled me into her while we talked . . . and my heart quite turned over. Such are the perils of fieldwork. . . .
> . . . the beauty of it is I adore her even though I need her and have ulterior professional motives. (Pp. 12-14)

There surely have been other cases when, in interviews concerning sex, having actual sexual experiences could be strongly justified. Some years back, Joseph Styles (1979) wrote about how his personal sexual experiences of gay bathhouses helped him to understand others' sexualities. In the wake of an explosion of sex research around AIDS, one leading anthropologist, Ralph Bolton (1992), has indeed positively advocated sex with respondents if what the interviewer wishes to understand is their sexuality. Of course, this is a controversial area, but it is one that surely needs to be confronted and scrutinized rather than methodologically and morally silenced. Certainly, all the authors of this chapter can recall moments of feeling passion for persons we were busy interviewing, and we keep quiet about saying whether it went any further. Such stories need to be told and discussed.

◆ Toward an Ethical Strategy in Gay Interviewing

Gay interviewing often brings with it a kind of gay and lesbian sensibility that informs the questions asked, the types of relationships formed, and our ways of knowing. For some researchers, this finely tuned aesthetic facilitates the process of building a collaborative, communicative experience between interviewer and interviewee, and it suggests the need for a greater ethical awareness of this relationship. Thus many gay men, lesbians, and bisexual and transgendered people will speak about their personal experiences only when they feel safe. Getting gay men to speak openly about their subjective experiences can be very much like asking them to go through another form of coming out (Seidman et al. 1999).

Investigating the complex nature of this queer subjectivity, for some, requires the researcher to adopt a pragmatic ethical strategy. The adoption of such a perspective places emphasis on the specific cultural meanings that gay people and their communities bring to their intimate arrangement and argues against any moral imperative that values one set of experiences over another. As Seidman (1992) suggests:

> Our starting point should be an understanding of the basic assumptions of a particular society with regard to sexuality, the relationship between sex, identity, and private and public life. The existing sexual and social patterns of the society one is addressing need to be accorded a certain respect and legitimacy; these patterns should be seen as growing out of, and fitted in some useful way, to the lives of the various individuals and groups who share a history, culture and social structural position. A minimal level of respect therefore needs to be accorded existing patterns as they reflect, in part, a creative adaptation to individual or group. (P. 192)

This pragmatic of adopting an ethical strategy when investigating gay subjectivity usually comes about on a number of fronts and can be thought of as a process. Although being members, or keen supporters, of particular gay communities may provide researchers with some important insider contacts, this is no assurance that the researchers' location within these communities will mark the beginning of successful research recruitment. What appears to be more important is that researchers begin by first constructing ethical identities in the communities they wish to study, so that individuals, groups, and networks in those communities begin to see the researchers as trusted insiders (or trusted outsiders, as the case might be) who are not out to misrepresent them in their research write-ups.

Gay research can generate innovative interview practices. For example, Dan Mahoney's preferred style relies heavily on his participating as a member in gay social groups, allowing him to get to know individuals, as well as the norms, practices, and cultural nuisances of their particular community, slowly, over time. This also provides the community members the opportunity to form their own opinions and judgments of him. In such research, it is particularly important during the initial phases that the researcher be transparent about the reasons (both interpersonal and work related) he or she has become a member of the group, as well as about the point of the research and the tools and resources he or she has brought to the research context. Such interactions allow individuals and communities to make informed choices about whether they want to participate in the research. The construction of an ethical researcher in the field is an important methodological tool for building trust and cooperation.

THE ART OF AN ETHICAL STRATEGY

Forming an ethical strategy is as much art as science and figures as much in personally sensitive research of any kind as it does in the interviewing of gay people. One facet of this centers on self-presentation. The researcher's management of his or her research identity comes about through ongoing internal dialogue, as well as through the researcher's conversations with research participants. Key questions the researcher should ask him- or herself include the following: Am I describing the research correctly? Does this person understand the concepts/language I am putting forward? Am I presenting enough information about myself and my research in order for this person to make an informed choice?

A second facet relates to the interviewer's empathic stance. Adopting an ethical strategy also suggests that the interviewer constructs an empathic, emotional orientation during the interview process. When interviewers ask gay people to engage in a potentially lengthy process of disclosure, the respondents need to know that the interviewer will be open to their lived experiences and is prepared to cofacilitate the interpretations of those events. Establishing such empathic rapport in an interview is always context specific, of course. However, deep levels of disclosure will come about only if the subject senses shared understanding from the interviewer (Josselson 1995).

Herbert Rubin and Irene Rubin (1995) present a hermeneutic model of interviewing that is well suited for this style of interviewing. In their view, interviewers must understand what they have seen, heard, or experienced in the subject's terms. According to Rubin and Rubin, what interviewers hear is affected by the ongoing interpersonal relationship between themselves and their informants, a perspective we share. The research process is indeed personal, not objectively detached, as a result. This interview context makes collaboration more open to interpretation while emphasizing the active participation of the researcher in the process.

A third facet concerns borders and boundaries. It is important that interviewers be able to sense the boundaries and limitations that are associated with these relationships. Interpretive interview methods often require that gay and lesbian researchers seek out other gays and lesbians toward whom they have some affinity; otherwise, the construction of intense, ongoing interpersonal contexts is difficult. However, it is important to remember that an interview context where "friendship" is constructed can be contrived and artificial. The scheduled nature of research projects often means that interview relationships have very short life spans (Crick 1992; Coffey 1999; El-Or 1997). These fieldwork relationships are often deep and intense, but not long lasting, which places unusual boundaries on the research's interpersonal dimensions.

Interpersonal borders can shift to inhibit the research process. There are times during the interview process when subjects do not respond well to an empathic, interactive process, or are not be willing to explore feelings and emotions. There also may be clashes of personalities between the interviewer and interviewee, making the construction of an interactive context impossible. The combination of these factors can be quite disastrous. It is often at this stage that the interviewer and/or interviewee begins to disengage from the interview process, and a loss of empathy and shared understanding occurs. An ethical strategy requires the researcher to acknowledge and be more open to examining these shifts as they relate to the feelings and behaviors participants bring to the interview context (Kleinman and Copp 1993).

Interviewers need to become more aware of their own feelings and, in turn, use them to guide the research process. For example, Mahoney (2000) found that further distancing himself during the interview process resulted in a lost opportunity. He made note of the consequences of this experience in his dissertation research:

In Richard's story, I was confronted with the realisation that I didn't care for this person very much, in fact I had little empathy for him. I couldn't relate to his snobbery and I certainly couldn't relate to a person who wasn't more up front about their feelings. After much reflection and journal writing, I was able to acknowledge this discomfort openly. Acknowledging these feelings and concerns helped me to recognise the assumptions, beliefs, and life experiences I brought to this experience. It allowed me to question my own values and expectations around power relations between myself and my research collaborators. Perhaps, most importantly, it got me to acknowledge the distancing that took place between myself and Richard. This distancing prevented me from becoming more interactive in the discussion, which further prevented an expansion of our knowledge construction of his story.

Much of this bears on the ethical imperative of what might be viewed as a methodology of friendship, moving beyond the roles of traditional research procedure. The research aims at building a quite special relationship founded partly on research goals but equally on friendship. But there is a downside to this, as a number of feminists have recently noted. All is not always so well when research turns into a friendship: "As researchers and participants get acquainted, establish trust and friendship, they become vulnerable to misunderstanding, disappointment, and invaded privacy. It can lead amongst other things to false intimacies, fraudulent friendships, a deceptiveness over equal relationships, and a masking of power" (Kirsch 1999:26).

◆ Conclusion

In this chapter, we have been concerned to show, in the first instance, how interviews are not fixed in time but change with historical moments. Interviewing "gays and lesbians" at the start of the 21st century is very different indeed than interviewing "them" was at the end of the 19th century. We are now much more sensitive to issues of othering and how we construct representation. We now consciously contend with the challenges of legitimation, with what it is that is being claimed and written and how that is accomplished. Issues of reflexivity, involvement, and ethics come forth in ways that were not possible at the start of the 20th century. We have suggested that findings and research practice are bound together; what is found in an interview depends upon the historical shape of the interview. With the arrival of postmodern, poststructural, and queer sensibilities, new forms of interviewing and indeed new kinds of findings may well be in the making.

The lessons of this chapter, however, go well beyond an account of lesbian and gay interviewing. Although the changes described are striking, we would suggest that

this sense of radical historicity should now be seen as a necessary feature of all interviewing. Interviewing must be viewed as recursive: It feeds out of a historical, cultural moment from which questions and methodological strictures are mediated. In this context, interviewing is also a cultural form, providing a new cultural text of "findings," in which questions and answers become self-validating circles (Cicourel 1964; Gubrium and Holstein 1997). The short history of interviewing gays—a subjectivity that appeared only in the last decades of the 20th century with any pervasiveness—echoes this.

■ Notes

1. Terminology is always a problem. In short, *homosexual* is a term of the past, *gay* and *lesbian* are contemporary terms, and *queer* is a recent, more radical term. It is generally argued that these various terms do not depict the same phenomena, but in popular parlance they do, while highlighting key contrasting nuances.

2. There are major exceptions to this classification. The classic studies by Magnus Hirschfield in Germany in the early 20th century do not quite fit the theme of "exotic outsider." Hirschfield was a homosexual, his research was sympathetic to gays, and he was a victim of the Nazi purges. Likewise, in the 1990s, some of the major sex surveys conducted around AIDS were not conducted by gays.

3. There were other linked traditions. We are thinking especially of the urban ethnographic tradition that blossomed in the 1960s and is perhaps most keenly exemplified in the notorious work of the late Laud Humphreys (1970). He conducted interviews as well. Carol Warren (1974) was not interested in etiology, but found that her respondents in fact spent a great deal of time telling her their stories of "how they got to be this way." Warren notes, "The tales had a uniformity; they tallied well with all kinds of deterministic social science theories of dominant mothers, environment, traumas, and seduction." Warren slowly realized that "these social science rhetorics were being put to good use in the construction of members' current identities and commitments" (p. 176).

4. International conferences were organized around this theme.

5. Although the term *gay sensibility* can lead to an essentialist understanding of a common core of meaning, we wish to make it clear that it is a form of historically specific "local knowledge" and not a universal, time-free sensitivity.

6. Often distinctions are made among queer theory, queer politics, and queer culture. Here we are referring mainly to queer theory (see Stein and Plummer 1996).

7. In this and the next section, our key source of inspiration is Yvonna Lincoln and Norman Denzin's (1994) discussion of issues of representation and legitimation.

8. Examples include Edward Said's (1978) and Franz Fanon's (1970) critiques of Western representations of non-Western cultures, which show how Western abstractions (e.g., human, man, masculinity) are produced at the expense of non-Western, colonized, and localized specificities (e.g., the other, the native, femininity). In her essay "Can the Subaltern Speak?" (1994), Gayatri Chakravorty Spivak concludes that it is impossible for the subaltern to speak because she is a "female subaltern from an underprivileged third-world nation." The composition of gendered, class, and racial subordination is the ultimate silent/silenced bearer of the burdens of centuries of Western imperialist history. Contrasting with Spivak's pessimistic conclusion that "the natives have gone forever," other postcolonial theorists advance a notion of minority discourse (Deleuze and Guattari 1990) or the option of hybridity (Bhabha 1994).

9. As Jacques Derrida (1976) has noted, writing itself is a "wandering outcast" of the Western logocentric tradition, because it is always spoken rather than written language that is privileged. But writing also is a political act. Certain questions—Who is writing? Can everyone write? What does it mean to write? Write to whom? To dispatch what?—are not simply interrogative; they are questions of power.

10. The term *queer* is not commonly used in the gay community in Hong Kong. Its popularity seems to be restricted to academic circles. The term *tongzhi* was originally used by the Chinese national father Sun Yi Xian, who encouraged Chinese people to fight against the imperialist regime of the early 20th century. He said, "Evolution has not been successful; comrades should fight against it until the end." The term is believed to have been first appropriated as a synonym for gays, lesbians, and other sexual minorities after the first gay and lesbian film festival, held in 1991, which was referred to as the Tongzhi Film Festival.

■ *References*

Abelove, H., M. A. Barale, and D. M. Halperin, eds. 1993. *The Lesbian and Gay Studies Reader.* New York: Routledge.

Adam, B. 1985. "Structural Foundations of the Gay World." *Comparative Study of Society and History* 27:658-71.

Banks, A. and S. P. Banks, eds. 1998. *Fiction and Social Research: By Ice or Fire.* Walnut Creek, CA: AltaMira.

Bayer, R. 1981. *Homosexuality and American Psychiatry.* New York: Basic Books.

Bell, A. and M. S. Weinberg. 1978. *Homosexualities: A Study of Diversity among Men and Women.* London: Mitchell Beazley.

Bell, A., M. S. Weinberg, and S. K. Hammersmith. 1982. *Sexual Preference: Its Development in Men and Women.* Bloomington: Indiana University Press.

Berry, C. 1996. "Sexual DisOrientations: Homosexual Rights, East Asian Films, and Postmodern Postnationalism." Pp. 157-82 in *In Pursuit of Contemporary East Asian Culture,* edited by X. Tang and S. Snyder. Boulder, CO: Westview.

Bhabha, H. K. 1994. *The Location of Culture.* London: Routledge.

Bieber, I. 1962. *Homosexuality: A Psychoanalytic Study of Male Homosexuality.* New York: Basic Books.

Bolton, R. 1992. "Mapping Terra Incognita: Sex Research for AIDS Prevention—An Urgent Agenda for the 1990s." Pp. 124-58 in *The Time of AIDS: Social Analysis, Theory, and Method,* edited by G. H. Herdt and S. Lindebaum. Newbury Park, CA: Sage.

Bourdieu, P. 1992. *An Invitation to Reflexive Sociology.* Chicago: University of Chicago Press.

Butler, J. 1990. *Gender Trouble: Feminism and the Subversion Identity.* London: Routledge.

Cicourel, A. V. 1964. *Method and Measurement in Sociology.* New York: Free Press.

Coffey, A. 1999. *The Ethnographic Self: Fieldwork and the Representation of Identity.* London: Sage.

Crick, M. 1992. "Ali and Me: An Essay in Street-Corner Anthropology." In *Anthropology and Autobiography,* edited by J. Okely and H. Callaway. London: Routledge.

Deleuze, G. and F. Guattari. 1990. "What Is a Minor Literature?" In *Out There: Marginalization and Contemporary Cultures,* edited by R. Ferguson, M. Gever, Trinh T. M., and C. West. Cambridge: MIT Press.

Denzin, N. K. 1994. "The Art and Politics of Interpretation." Pp. 500-515 in *Handbook of Qualitative Research,* edited by N. K. Denzin and Y. S. Lincoln. Thousand Oaks, CA: Sage.

Derrida, J. 1976. *Of Grammatology.* Translated by G. C. Spivak. Baltimore: Johns Hopkins University Press.

Dowsett, G. W. 1996. *Practicing Desire: Homosexual Sex in an Era of AIDS.* Stanford, CA: Stanford University Press.

Edelman, L. 1995. "Queer Theory: Unstating Desire." *GLQ: A Journal of Lesbian and Gay Studies* 1:343-46.

El-Or, T. 1997. "Do You Really Know How They Make Love? The Limits on Intimacy with Ethnographic Informants." In *Reflexivity and Voice,* edited by R. Hertz. Thousand Oaks, CA: Sage.

Epstein, S. 1987. "Gay Politics, Ethnic Identity: The Limit of Social Constructionism." *Socialist Review* 93/94:9-54.

Fanon, F. 1970. *Black Skins, White Masks.* London: Paladin.

Foucault, M. 1979. *The History of Sexuality,* Vol. 1, *An Introduction.* Harmondsworth: Penguin.

———. 1984. "What Is Enlightenment?" In M. Foucault, *The Foucault Reader.* Edited by P. Rabinow. New York: Pantheon.

Fuss, D., ed. 1991. *Inside/Out: Lesbian Theories, Gay Theories.* New York: Routledge.

Gagnon, J. and W. Simon. 1973. *Sexual Conduct: The Social Sources of Human Sexuality.* Chicago: Aldine.

Gubrium, J. F. and J. A. Holstein. 1997. *The New Language of Qualitative Method.* New York: Oxford University Press.

Halberstam, J. 1998. *Female Masculinity.* Durham, NC: Duke University Press.

Hanawa, Y., ed. 1994. "Circuits of Desire (special issue). *Positions: East Asia Cultures Critique* 2(1).

Harding, S. 1991. *Whose Science? Whose Knowledge? Thinking from Women's Lives.* Ithaca, NY: Cornell University Press.

Henry, G. W. 1941. *Sex Variants: A Study in Homosexual Patterns,* 2 vols. New York: Hoeber & Sons.

Holstein, J. A. and J. F. Gubrium. 1995. *The Active Interview.* Thousand Oaks, CA: Sage.

Hooker, E. 1957. "The Adjustment of the Male Overt Homosexual." *Journal of Projective Techniques* 21:17-31.

Humphreys, H. L. (1970). *Tearoom trade: Impersonal sex in public places.* Chicago: Aldine.

Jackson, P. A. and G. Sullivan, eds. 1999. "Multicultural Queer: Australian Narratives" (special issue). *Journal of Homosexuality* 36(3-4).

Josselson, R. 1995. "Imagining the Real: Empathy, Narrative, and the Dialogic Self." Pp. 27-44 in *The Narrative Study of Lives,* Vol. 3, *Interpreting Experience: The Narrative Study of Lives,* edited by R. Josselson and A. Lieblich. Thousand Oaks, CA: Sage.

Juhasz, A. 1995. *AIDS TV: Identity, Community and Alternative Video.* Durham, NC: Duke University Press.

Kinsey, A. C., W. B. Pomeroy, and C. E. Martin. 1948. *Sexual Behavior in the Human Male.* Philadelphia: W. B. Saunders.

Kinsey, A. C., W. B. Pomeroy, C. E. Martin, and P. Gebhard. 1953. *Sexual Behavior in the Human Female.* Philadelphia: W. B. Saunders.

Kirsch, G. E. 1999. *Ethical Dilemmas in Feminist Research: The Politics of Location, Interpretation, and Publication.* Albany: State University of New York Press.

Kleinman, S. and M. A. Copp. 1993. *Emotions and Fieldwork.* Thousand Oaks, CA: Sage.

Kong, T. S. K. 2000. "The Voices in Between . . . : The Body Politics of Hong Kong Gay Men." Ph.D. thesis, Department of Sociology, University of Essex.

——. Forthcoming. "The Seduction of the Golden Boy: The Body Politics of Hong Kong Gay Men." *Body and Society.*

Krafft-Ebing, R. von. 1899. *Psychopathia Sexualis.* London: Rebman.

Krieger, S. 1983. *The Mirror Dance: Identity in a Women's Community.* Philadelphia: Temple University Press.

——. 1991. *Social Science and the Self: Personal Essays on an Art Form.* New Brunswick, NJ: Rutgers University Press.

——. 1996. *The Family Silver: Essays on Relationships among Women.* Berkeley: University of California Press.

Leong, R., ed. 1996. *Asian American Sexualities: Dimensions of the Gay and Lesbian Experience.* London: Routledge.

Lincoln, Y. S. and N. K. Denzin. 1994. "The Fifth Moment." Pp. 575-86 in *Handbook of Qualitative Research,* edited by N. K. Denzin and Y. S. Lincoln. Thousand Oaks, CA: Sage.

Mahoney, D. 2000. Unpublished field notes for Ph.D. thesis, Department of Sociology, University of Essex.

Murray, S. O. 1997. *American Gay.* Chicago: University of Chicago Press.

Nardi, P. M. and B. E. Schneider, eds. 1998. *Social Perspectives in Lesbian and Gay Studies: A Reader.* London: Routledge.

Newton, E. 1993. "My Best Informant's Dress: The Erotic Equation in Fieldwork." *Cultural Anthropology* 8:3-23.

Parker, R. 1999. *Beneath the Equator: Cultures of Desire, Male Homosexuality, and Emerging Gay Communities in Brazil.* London: Routledge.

Plummer, K. 1981. "Homosexual Categories: Some Research Problems in the Labelling Perspective of Homosexuality." Pp. 53-75 in *The Making of the Modern Homosexual,* edited by K. Plummer. London: Hutchinson.

——. 1995. *Telling Sexual Stories: Power, Change and Social Worlds.* London: Routledge.

——. 2000. *Documents of Life—2.* London: Sage.

Rubin, H. J. and I. S. Rubin. 1995. *Qualitative Interviewing: The Art of Hearing Data.* Thousand Oaks, CA: Sage.

Said, E. W. 1978. *Orientalism.* London: Routledge & Kegan Paul.

Sedgwick, E. K. 1990. *Epistemology of the Closet.* Berkeley: University of California Press.

Seidman, S. 1992. *Embattled Eros: Sexual Politics and Ethics in Contemporary America.* London: Routledge.

Seidman, S., C. Meeks, and F. Traschen. 1999. "Beyond the Closet? The Changing Social Meaning of Homosexuality in the United States." *Sexualities* 2:9-34.

Smith, D. E. 1996. "Telling the Truth after Postmodernism." *Symbolic Interaction* 19:171-202.

Socarides, C. 1968. *The Overt Homosexual.* New York: Grune & Stratton.

Spivak, G. C. 1994. "Can the Subaltern Speak?" In *Colonial Discourse and Post-colonial Theory: A Reader,* edited by P. Williams and L. Chrisman. Cambridge: Cambridge University Press.

Stanley, L. and S. Wise. 1983. *Breaking Out Again: Feminist Ontology and Epistemology.* London: Routledge.

——. 1993. *Breaking Out Again: Feminist Ontology and Epistemology.* 2d ed. London: Routledge.

Stein, A. 1997. *Sex and Sensibility: Stories of a Lesbian Generation.* Berkeley: University of California Press.

Stein, A. and K. Plummer. 1996. " 'I Can't Even Think Straight': 'Queer' Theory and the Missing Sexual Revolution in Sociology." Pp. 129-44 in *Queer Theory/Sociology,* edited by S. Seidman. Cambridge, MA: Blackwell.

Styles, J. (1979) "Outsider/Insider: Researching Gay Baths." *Urban Life* 8:135-52.

Takagi, D. Y. 1996. "Maiden Voyage: Excursion into Sexuality and Identity Politics in Asian America." In *Queer Theory/Sociology,* edited by S. Seidman. Cambridge, MA: Blackwell.

Warner, M. "Introduction." Pp. vii-xxxi in *Fear of a Queer Planet: Queer Politics and Social Theory,* edited by M. Warner. Minneapolis: University of Minnesota Press.

Warren, C. A. B. 1974. *Identity and Community in the Gay World.* London: John Wiley.

Weeks, J. 1977. *Coming Out: Homosexual Politics in Britain from the Nineteenth Century to the Present.* London: Quartet.

———. 1999. *Making Sexual History.* Cambridge: Polity.

Weston, K. 1998. *Long Slow Burn: Sexuality and Social Science.* New York: Routledge.

Westwood, G. 1961. *A Minority: A Report on the Life of the Male Homosexual in Great Britain.* London: Longmans.

6

INTERVIEWING OLDER PEOPLE

◆ G. Clare Wenger

It is important to start by asking two questions: Who are older people, and who are they older than? When I entered the field of gerontology more than 20 years ago, this growing area of study tended to focus on people over 65 years old. In those countries with established pension schemes, pressures existed for the field to include those "over retirement age," but differential retirement ages for men and women and, in some countries, differences in retirement policies among occupations complicated the issue. As a result, in many instances, government statistics were based on retirement ages, whereas academic researchers stuck to research on those 65+ or 60+, so that samples of men and women— then referred to as *the elderly*—would be directly comparable.

The study of gerontology, while projecting its objectivity, has been haunted by the specter of ageism. If ageist attitudes are more easily observed among health and social care professionals, they have from the outset remained only lightly disguised

among academics. Referring to older people as *the elderly* had the effect of setting apart a significant proportion of the population on the basis of age, even though that proportion could include two generations. This was recognized in the introduction of such subcategories as *the young elderly* (those aged 65-75), *the old elderly* (aged 75+), and, subsequently, *the oldest old* (aged 85+).

In a climate of growing consciousness of discrimination on the basis of ascribed characteristics and the emergence of political correctness, "the elderly" came to be perceived as a stigmatizing category. More astute readers will recognize the inherent ageism in this perception. Why should being older than others be stigmatizing, unless being old is somehow a disadvantage? We learned to refer to *elderly people*. This group was still generally considered to be those aged 65+, and so we also talked about *younger elderly people* and *older elderly people*. In the United States, the terms *elders* and *seniors* were introduced, but these never achieved general popularity outside North America, although the first is often used in the United Kingdom to refer to older members of minority ethnic groups.

At the same time, the field of gerontology (and allied service disciplines) was expanding to include concerns about preretirement, early retirement, menopause, and the impacts of aging on the social and physical aspects of people's lives. Papers presented at international gerontological conferences gradually began to focus on a much wider age range, from circum-menopausal women to centenarians. In parallel with this expansion in the definition of the field of study of gerontology, life expectancy was extending, birthrates were diminishing, and morbidity was becoming more and more concentrated into the last few years of life. Active life well into retirement became the norm for growing proportions of people, many of whom did not conform with the image of "elderly people" at all.

With a field of study or concern that includes people of roughly ages 45 to 100, the term *elderly people* began to sound embarrassingly patronizing. We were already learning to refer to children as *younger people,* and gradually *older people* and *older adults* crept into the politically correct terminology used to refer to those subject to developmental changes that occur after approximately the age of 45 or 50. These terms are not entirely satisfactory either, because everyone is older than someone. A helpful editor once changed every reference I had made to "elderly people" in a paper to "older people"—a term I had used in the same paper to refer to those aged 80 or over within the sample I was discussing—successfully destroying both the argument and the sense of the paper.

◆ *Interviewing and Heterogeneity*

I have raised this problem of definition in detail at the start of this chapter to alert the reader to the semantic as well as procedural problems that exist. It is also my intent to draw attention to the fact that getting older tends to be derogated and perceived by others as stigmatizing or embarrassing. Although we all want to live long and fulfilling lives, and wish for the same for all those whom we love, we have a tendency to see those who are achieving this goal as somehow diminished, irrespective of how these aging individuals experience the aging process.

Interviewing older people for the most part involves ascertaining what their experience of aging is like. In this chapter, I adopt the currently accepted term *older people,* but first I would like to say something about the wide heterogeneity of age and experience that this term embraces, as this affects the forms that interviewing will take. The point is that interviewing older people should not be conceived as a one-size-fits-all set of procedures; rather, it is a form of inquiry that should take into account the diverse subjects older people are now known to be. It is also important that those who interview older people try not to become preoccupied with age; they should not assume that everything under consideration is age related (Kaufman 1986; Duffy 1988).

As I noted above, those described as older people may be aged anywhere from 45 to 100 or more. This wide age range can include three generations and normally includes at least two. This fact was brought home to me vividly some years ago when I went to interview a housebound widow of 68 who was living alone in a sheltered bungalow. I was 46, and the woman's daughter, who seemed to be about my age or older, was just leaving when I arrived. Early in the lengthy interview, the 68-year-old woman commented that I had interviewed her mother the previous week. I was sure that she was mistaken and wondered whether her cognitive function was impaired. But I soon figured out that she was right; I had indeed interviewed her 92-year-old mother, and her mother had telephoned her and told her all about me. What is significant about this anecdote is not only the generational span included in our current definition of "older" people, but also my assumption that the interviewee could be impaired despite the accuracy of her observation. I will return to this aspect of interviewing older people later in the chapter.

Because the later years of life are characterized by losses of different kinds, the age range includes a broad heterogeneity. The older people become, the more likely they are to become widowed, to lose brothers and sisters, to live alone, to suffer from mobility problems, to need to use the services of health and social care providers, to lose age peers (friends and neighbors) through disability or death, to become frail, and to move into sheltered or long-term care facilities. Clearly, interviewing well people in their 60s and 70s is comparable to interviewing younger well adults, whereas interviewing frail and impaired people in their 80s and 90s calls for an approach that is sympathetic to the physical and mental energies of the respondents (see Eder and Fingerson, Chapter 2, this volume).

Other aspects of the heterogeneity of the group we call older people reflect the patterns of the individuals' earlier lives, and as people age the potential differences between them are accentuated and increase as each represents the sum of all that has gone before. Not all older people have been married, and some who married did not bear children, so not all are parents. Some older people had many brothers and sisters, whereas others were only children. Those who had no brothers, sisters, or children also have no nieces, nephews, or grandchildren. Their life experiences have been different from those of individuals who have been members of large and growing families. The life experiences of men and women are also different (see in this volume Schwalbe and Wolkomir, Chapter 3; Reinharz and Chase, Chapter 4). Men are less likely than women to become widowed and more likely to have worked full-time for a large part of their adult lives. They are

more likely than women to be receiving an occupational pension. With increasing age, more older people are women and more are middle-class as a result of differential survival. Approximately three-fourths of those aged 85+ are women, and a similar proportion of surviving men and women come from middle-class backgrounds.

All societies distinguish between those older people who are able to live independently and those who have become dependent on others for help (Amoss and Harrell 1981). In traditional societies, which have neither the concept of retirement nor pensions, old age is often defined by the ability to look after oneself. The lives of older people who must depend on others (family members, neighbors, friends, or formal services) are very different from those of individuals who remain independent. Self-image and self-esteem are affected by decline in physical capacities and by changes in personal appearance. There is no one recommended approach to interviewing older people across such differences. Although interviewers may be more likely to encounter some situations when interviewing older people than when interviewing individuals in other age groups, they should keep in mind that, as with all age groups, each older interviewee is one person, and they need to respond to each interviewee on an individual basis (Patterson and Dupree 1994).

◆ Sampling and Heterogeneity

Given the heterogeneity of the group designated as older people, it is clear that interviewing older people involves researchers in interactions with a wide range of interviewees. In addition, older people can be the subjects of a variety of types of interviewing, from clinical, therapeutic, and assessment interviews—which are more common than in other age groups (Patterson and Dupree 1994)—to research interviews. Types of interviewing are addressed elsewhere in this volume, and I will not deal with them again here, although it is worth pointing out that cognitive interviewing has been found to work better than other types in eliciting information from older people (Jobe, Keller, and Smith 1996; Mello and Fisher 1996).

Reflecting the great heterogeneity among older people, the range of reasons for interviewing is equally broad. Professionals conduct clinical or assessment interviews in order to intervene to ameliorate problems in an older person's life. Such interviews are, therefore, personal and relate to the interviewee only. They may continue over several time periods and may take a variety of forms (Edelstein and Semenchuk 1996). Interviewing skills for multidimensional assessment of older people are taught in many professional areas (Robins and Wolf 1989; Morrow-Howell 1992; Nelson 1992). In other situations, interviews are conducted as part of research projects, to gain information. The nature of the research question determines the nature of the sample and the type of interview, in addition to age heterogeneity.

The selection of samples of older people is arguably more complex than sample selection with other age groups. Population samples need to be representative of the general population of older people. However, because at any one time a small proportion of older people will be in residential care of one sort or another, population samples are often limited to "older people living in the community." Thus the oldest age groups, of which larger proportions are living in residential establishments, are often undersampled. Even if institutional residents are included in a sample, there are always some who are too mentally or physically impaired to be interviewed. The problems of interviewing older people in residential care have been identified, and the need for researchers to use observational data in addition to interviews has been stressed (West, Bondy, and Hutchinson 1991).

Even interviewing older people living in the community can be difficult, as relatives often try to avoid involvement of their oldest family members if they are at all frail. This further limits the representation of the oldest, most impaired, and family-dependent individuals. So the achievement of a truly representative population sample is difficult. Other, more purposive, samples may be easier to compile, such as samples of patients, clients, service users, sufferers of particular conditions, grandparents, those who never married, and the oldest old.

◆ Gaining Access

Having identified a sample, the interviewer must accomplish the next step: attaining access to potential interviewees. Where assessment interviews are concerned, access is part of the role relationship between the older person and a service provider, and so is usually straightforward. Where there is no formal service involvement (for instance, with doctors, community nurses, social workers, residential homes), the interviewer may approach older persons directly. An initial approach may be made by letter or by telephone, or by cold calling in person. The choice will be determined by the nature of the research, but the approach will come directly from the researcher/ interviewer. Whatever approach is used, this forms the first step in the establishment of the interview relationship.

Approach by letter can take several forms. The interviewer might invite potential interviewees to participate and ask them to notify him or her of their willingness to do so, at which time the interviewer will make contact to arrange a time and place for the interview. Or the interviewer can tell potential interviewees that they have been selected and that an interviewer will call on them unless they express their unwillingness to be involved. In the latter case, the interviewer might suggest a particular date for a meeting in the initial letter.

There are several disadvantages to an initial approach by letter. The older persons contacted may not clearly understand the reason for the requested visit. They may feel uneasy or wary about admitting a stranger into their homes or of committing themselves without knowing more about the study or the interviewer. It is therefore easier for them not to volunteer or to decline. Some older people may consult relatives or ask them to read the letter—particularly where the older person's vision is impaired—and these individuals may become concerned about the implications of the interview. They may feel that it would be irresponsible for them to encourage their older relatives (usually parents) to admit a stranger to their homes. They may be concerned about the authenticity of the approach, or, if the topic of the study has to do, for instance, with family relationships or sources of support, they may be concerned that their older relatives will put them in a bad light, whether deserved or undeserved. Approach by letter makes it relatively easy for older persons or their agents to refuse.

Telephone interviewing is becoming increasingly popular as a research technique, particularly where research topics are sufficiently well defined and interviews are likely to be short. It is less easy to reject a friendly voice on the telephone. Cultural constraints of politeness, helpfulness, and, in the case of some people, loneliness make it likely that potential interviewees will enter into conversation. The skillful interviewer will establish rapport before broaching the asking of specific questions. Older people are less likely to refuse to answer questions asked over the telephone unless they seem too intrusive or personal, or are related to money or property. Unless someone else answers the telephone, the intervention of relatives is unlikely.

However, not all older people use the telephone, and thus resulting samples are likely to be biased away from poorer respondents or consumers. Hearing loss is a problem of old age that increases with the years. Older people with a hearing loss may be reluctant to establish conversation on the telephone, may misinterpret what is said to them and give misleading answers, or do not answer incoming calls. This effect biases achieved samples toward younger respondents. Tests of telephone interviewing against face-to-face data collection produce highly correlated results. Telephone interviewing is more convenient and less expensive than in-person interviewing and is considered a practical method for collecting data from older people about function and affect (Morishita et al. 1995; see Shuy, Chapter 9, this volume).

Experience suggests that, handled sensibly, direct approaches to older people are most successful in gaining access. Direct approaches vary, from the market researcher with a clipboard filling her quota of older people on the street, through approaches made through social, sports, or religious organizations, to knocking on the door of the older person's home. Approaches made in public places and group situations are obviously different from the individual approach. However, what all these direct approaches have in common is that the potential interviewee can see the interviewer and form an impression of him or her. The interviewer has a face and an apparent personality. It is harder to reject someone face-to-face than to decline an invitation by letter or to hang up the telephone.

When calling on older persons at home, interviewers should bear in mind that older people may at times have difficulty with mobility or hearing, and may take a long time to respond to a doorbell or knock on the door. On the other hand, especially in rural areas, they may call, "Come in!" When this happens, it can put the interviewer in a quandary, because the potential interviewee may never have seen him or her before. It also raises issues of security. I usually instruct interviewers to show older respondents their identification cards, even if the respondents do not ask to see them. My hope is that this will alert the older persons to the appropriateness of seeing identification, so they might be more inclined to ask for it in the future. Moreover, anxious relatives may ask the older persons if they checked identification and remonstrate with them if they did not. This can dissuade them from agreeing to subsequent interviews.

Where the approach is made in a public place or in a group situation, the older person is more likely to feel that he or she is being included in something rather than left out. In group situations, potential respondents see others agreeing to be interviewed and again want to be included, or are at least intrigued to know what it is all about. When the approach is made on the doorstep, the presentation of the interviewer is more important. Even if the timing is inconvenient, the interviewer may be able to establish rapport and negotiate an appointment to return at a mutually convenient time.

Older people are more likely to admit women than men into their homes, although they may also be suspicious of very young women. Interviewers are also more likely to be successful if they are conventionally dressed. Based on my own experience, the interviewers with the highest success rates in acceptance by older interviewees are middle-aged or older women with outgoing personalities. The oldest interviewer I have used was 82. Other researchers have also used older interviewers and have found that, compared with interviews conducted by students, those conducted by older persons were "qualitatively and empirically more complete and useful" (Prager 1995).

Early in my career, although I already suspected that women would be more acceptable on the doorstep, particularly in isolated rural areas, I sought interviewing help from two male colleagues. At that point in the research, the interview was brief and could be conducted on the doorstep if necessary; the interviewer did not need to go into the house. Some months later in that same community, a 77-year-old woman I was interviewing said to me:

> I want to give you a piece of advice, my dear. You made a great mistake when you sent those young men round asking questions. They frightened a lot of people. Everyone was talking about them. Next time you go yourself. You're a nice young woman [actually, I was 40+] and people trust you.

The two "young men" in question were in their mid- to late 30s, established academics with very gentle personalities, and I was hard-pressed to imagine that either of them could be perceived as threatening, but to these old women living alone, men clearly could not be trusted. The only other time I used a male research assistant to do interviews, his refusal rate was higher than those of any of the women interviewers I used. On the other hand, male professional carers have commented on the fact that many older women tell them how nice it is to have a young man in the house. The professional role is clearly protective in both directions.

There can also be constraints that make older men reluctant to admit women into their homes. This may be marked in Muslim communities. On more than one occasion, men living alone explained to me that they were happy to be interviewed but they thought I ought to know they were alone in the house before they admitted me. In one case, a man I interviewed left his outside door open to protect my reputation. There is a tendency for younger people to assume that once past retirement age, older people cease to be sexual beings (Archibald and Baikie 1998). Clearly, this does not always extend to older people's own self-images.

The importance of putting respondents at ease is covered in most books on methodology (e.g., Fetterman 1998). The more common experience of interviewers who knock on the doors of older persons is that, once the interviewers have demonstrated their friendliness and eagerness to talk by showing the potential interviewees that they have information the interviewers value, the prospect of distraction and company they offer makes access easy. Although most older people are obligingly interested and pleased to help, however, interviewers do occasionally encounter reluctance or outright refusal (see Adler and Adler, Chapter 8, this volume).

When a potential respondent expresses reluctance, the skillful interviewer can often overcome that reluctance if he or she can establish the reason for it. Sometimes, a request to answer questions is anxiety provoking (perhaps particularly if the interviewer has identified him- or herself as being from a university) because questions are associated with tests, and many older persons have had only a very basic education. One woman told me that she felt she could tell me nothing. I explained that although she might feel that way, all I wanted to do was to find out about the experiences of older people, and without people like her answering questions, this was impossible to know. She then said, "But what if I give the wrong answers?" Another explanation that there were no wrong answers and a few examples of the types of questions to be asked, such as "When did you last visit the doctor?" convinced her that she could help after all. She remarked, "Oh, is that all? Why didn't you say? Come in!" Often the interviewer's offering to make an agreement with a potential interviewee that no question must be answered and that he or she can terminate the interview at any time will be enough to gain acceptance that an interview can at least be started.

In other situations, older persons' reluctance or refusal is based on the admonishment of an adult child that "I mustn't let anyone I don't know into the house." It is possible that this is also the reason for refusals when no reasons are given. Once an interviewer has established rapport with a potential interviewee, he or she may be able to overcome this reluctance by explaining that, having seen the interviewer's identity card and received a business card, the older person does know who the interviewer is; further, the interviewer can suggest that he

or she meet with the adult child to explain the study and discuss the interview. In many cases, it is clear that the older person is willing to help and would really like the company and experience but is constrained by not wanting to cause family conflict. However, it is never appropriate for the interviewer to push too hard. Discussion and negotiation are acceptable, but no must mean no in the final analysis.

Where the sample is to be drawn from service caseloads or from among the residents of a hospital or residential care home, in most developed countries access by researchers to older persons as a result of their contact with professionals must be negotiated by way of an ethics committee. Such committees are set up to protect vulnerable people from being approached by (unscrupulous) interviewers, to protect the confidentiality of the clinical or assessment interview, and to guard professionals from complaints that could be made by patients/clients or members of their families. In these sorts of situations, once ethical approval is granted, interviewers may approach older persons in their doctors' offices, in hospitals, in residential homes, or in other therapeutic contexts and seek their participation in an interview. Ethical approval is more easily achieved where research is being conducted in partnership with professionals to answer questions in which they have an interest.

In other instances, where older persons are to be interviewed independent of treatment/intervention settings, identifying individuals as, for instance, patients or sufferers of particular conditions could be seen as a breach of confidentiality. In these cases, the professionals involved may be unable to divulge the names and addresses of vulnerable people without first gaining their consent to interview. This procedure needs to be described in detail in any application for ethical approval. A professional representative then acts as an intermediary by securing the agreement of the older person before identifying him or her to the potential interviewer.

There are several difficulties associated with these types of interviews. It is sometimes impossible to get ethical approval if the committee feels that the research might undermine the profession in any way or bring to light inadequacies in a service. Much evaluation research, if it involves questions regarding current patterns of treatment or care, may be turned down because it is seen to threaten practice accepted by the profession or potentially to question the competence, sensitivity, or reliability of professionals. Generating a sample through professional approaches to patients/clients can also lead to bias in the sample. The researcher has no control over who is approached to participate, and professionals may seek to exclude especially vulnerable, sick, critical, or difficult older people because they feel they should not be bothered, would make poor interviewees, have communication difficulties, or might express negative views about the service or its providers.

◆ Confidentiality

Researchers, of course, have their own codes of ethics. Confidentiality must be maintained at all times. Most academic professional associations and institutions have their own guidelines. Once access has been granted, the researcher must protect all types of data; this includes protecting the data from access by other members of the respondents' families and service providers. There are some particular situations, however, that are more critical in the context of interviewing frail older people. Any access by unauthorized people to data that make clear that the interviewee is physically, mentally, or financially vulnerable to exploitation or abuse puts that person at risk.

Maintaining confidentiality sounds more straightforward than it is. Ethnographic approaches rely heavily on what respondents tell researchers—what others

might call gossip. Gossip is a reciprocal activity, and interviewees are likely to both volunteer information and ask questions about others they know to be part of the study. It is often difficult for interviewers to curb their spontaneity and keep the exchange of the relationship on track while also maintaining discretion about other participants. This is particularly taxing when you know that they know what they know you know and ask you about it! The other side of this coin, however, is that interviewers can, in the course of an interview, become privy to situations of risk that are not known to others.

There are many types of risk or emergency situations that interviewers can discover in the course of their contact with an older person. Some of these are straightforward. For instance, if an interviewer arrives at an older person's house to find that he or she has fallen and is in pain, the interviewer's calling an ambulance does not compromise confidentiality. For other kinds of concerns, it is advisable for researchers to develop written codes of conduct in advance. If possible, an interviewer should ask the older person's permission to seek professional help for him or her. In most cases, the older person will be relieved that somebody is taking that initiative (see below).

As rapport is established, the interviewee may divulge information that makes the interviewer become concerned about the older person's safety. In cases where the older person is at risk but is not willing for the interviewer to take any action, the interviewer needs to have a prearranged code to follow in discussion with colleagues. Such cases could involve suspected physical, psychological, or financial abuse of the older person or unmet needs for medical or instrumental assistance. Where an interviewer encounters reluctance or outright refusal of intervention, he or she may need to discuss the matter with the research director and come to a joint decision about what to do. In such instances discretion is of the utmost importance; the interviewer may have incurred an ethical or legal responsibility, but the bottom line must be the safety of the older person.

◆ Special Challenges

Older people are "just like us but they've been alive longer," as one of my interviewers once commented. Many of the general statements made about interviewing techniques in other chapters in this volume apply also to older people. In this chapter, I limit my discussion to the challenges of interviewing older people that in my experience seem different from those encountered in interviewing members of other populations, or are more likely to occur with older people. This means that I may seem to be concentrating on the "problems" of old age, but the reader should keep in mind that most older people do not suffer from infirmities that interfere with the interview process. Remember that "older people" can be any age from 45 up.

RESPONDENTS WITH SENSORY IMPAIRMENTS

Among the practical challenges that researchers may encounter in interviewing older people, impaired hearing is one of the most common. Poor hearing may make an older person less willing to be interviewed. If an individual is wearing a hearing aid or is clearly having hearing problems, the interviewer should acknowledge this and explain that he or she will speak clearly and slowly. The interviewer should tell the potential interviewee that he or she is prepared to take the time to make sure the respondent understands everything the interviewer says, and that the interview will be ended if it becomes too tiring for the interviewee.

In interviewing a person with hearing problems, the interviewer should try to ensure that the respondent can see his or her face. It is helpful in such a case for the inter-

viewer to face the light; even if they are not aware of it, most older persons with impaired hearing gain additional information from seeing facial expressions and lip reading. It may be necessary for the interviewer to sit very close to the respondent, almost knee-to-knee, particularly if the respondent also has impaired vision. My experience has been that when the interviewer is prepared to be patient and to make the effort to be understood, the older person relaxes, enjoys the interview and the interaction, and is frequently very grateful for the efforts made on his or her behalf. If a potential interviewee is profoundly deaf and uses sign language, the researcher may need to find someone who signs to conduct the interview. An alternative to this, if appropriate, is for the interviewer to read from a questionnaire or interview schedule as the interviewee follows the printed text.

Impaired vision can reduce an older person's willingness to let anyone into the house, although it does not interfere with the comprehension of questions. Interviewers should be prepared for respondents with poor sight to move close to their faces in order to try to make out their features more clearly. This can be disconcerting, particularly in most Western cultures, where people have expectations of a generous amount of personal space. The interviewer's stepping back in such a case, however, may make the older person feel threatened, as if the interviewer may have something to hide.

In the context of some illnesses—for instance, if the older person has suffered a stroke or is in the advanced stages of Parkinson's disease—speech may be affected. With goodwill and patience, it is possible to interview speech-impaired people. When a speech-impaired respondent realizes that the interviewer is prepared to be patient, the older person is likely to relax and to become more coherent. It is often useful in such situations for the interviewer to ask someone who is close to the person and understands him or her to be present during the interview, to act as an interpreter. An interviewer may be tempted to put words in a speech-impaired respondent's mouth by finishing his or her sentences. This can lead to misinformation, as it may be easier for the interviewee to agree rather than to struggle to put the interviewer right. On the other hand, sometimes such interviewer intervention can ease the experience for the interviewee by reducing the effort he or she must make to consciously form each word.

People with speech impairments are quickly tired by the effort of speaking. It is important for interviewers to remember that even if a person's speech is impaired, his or her understanding and hearing may not be. Unless the interviewer has evidence to the contrary, he or she should never ignore or shout at such a respondent. Interviewing speech-impaired persons is one of the situations in which it is probably often advantageous to interview by proxy.

USING INTERVIEW PROXIES

It is often useful to employ proxies in interviews with older people in order to ensure the representativeness of the sample. If all those who are too impaired or too ill are omitted on compassionate grounds, the sample becomes biased. In most cases, proxies for older respondents should be spouses or close relatives. Where that is not possible, the proxy should be the individual who is closest to the older person. When conducting proxy interviews, researchers should ask only questions of fact (e.g., "Can X get up and down steps without help?"), not questions requiring subjective answers involving feelings or attitudes (e.g., "Does X feel lonely often?"). On the other hand, it is valid for interviewers to record proxies' interpretations of given situations as long as they take care to analyze those interpretations as the responses of carers, friends, or spouses.

It is sometimes necessary for an interviewer to bring an interview to a close before he or she has gained all the information he or she might have wished because it is clear that the interviewee is struggling

with illness or fatigue. If the older person was enjoying the exchange, the interviewer and interviewee can plan another time to meet and continue, but if the older person's effort seems to be inappropriate or pressured, the interviewer may find it better to continue with a proxy.

Interviewers should resort to proxy interviews with people with impaired hearing only if all their efforts to make themselves understood have failed. With respondents who are blind or partially sighted, proxy interviews are usually not necessary unless the respondents' hearing is also impaired. Proxy interviews with close relatives may be indicated where respondents have speech difficulties and find the effort to speak tiring and debilitating. However, interviewers should address persons with speech difficulties directly and give them the opportunity to respond or to counter their proxies' responses. When using a proxy, the interviewer should explain to the older person that this might make the interview easier for him or her. The interviewer should also ask the older person to indicate his or her agreement or disagreement with the proxy's responses. This not only results in better data but gives the older person the chance to be involved in the interview, something many speech-impaired people enjoy.

RESPONDENTS WITH COGNITIVE IMPAIRMENT

Cognitive impairments affect approximately 7 to 10 percent of older people in the developed world, with some national variation (Saunders et al. 1989). Among those aged 80 plus, approximately 20 percent have some cognitive impairment. It is possible that greater longevity is increasing the incidence and prevalence of dementia (Melzer, Ely, and Brayne 1997). Interviewers working with older people are likely to encounter various forms of cognitive impairment, and this is one of the most difficult areas for interviewing. There are indications that different types of data collection have varied impacts on results—structured interviews have been shown to result in lower prevalence rates than physicians' clinical diagnoses based on assessment interviews (Fichter et al. 1995)—although it is not obvious why this might be. It is not possible to interview older people who are in the final stages of dementia, but it may be possible to communicate with them in other ways, and it is always possible to observe them, which may be a more appropriate way to collect data.

Most older people who are in the early stages of dementia are able to respond to interviews, although they may experience lapses in memory or word recall. A great deal depends on the subject matter. As the disease progresses, long-term memory is more resilient than short-term memory. Respondents may be able to recall accurately most of the names of the children who were in their first-grade classes at school but be unable to remember the names of all their own grandchildren.

Sometimes, interviewers may not realize that their interviewees are affected by cognitive impairments. Such individuals might present well, demonstrate good social and communication skills, and respond with answers to most questions. Their "don't knows" or "can't remembers" might seem to be perfectly plausible. However, interviewers who work with older persons must be on their guard: It is possible to conduct an entire interview and be completely unaware that most of what one has been told is inaccurate.

The following anecdote illustrates this phenomenon. At the start of a longitudinal study, a never-married woman, Miss R, had been interviewed by one of our interviewers. Subsequently, one of Miss R's friends was a subject in an intensive study of a small subsample, which I conducted. I therefore heard much about Miss R from her friend, including about the friend's disappointment when Miss R entered residential care and her friend could not see her anymore.

Eight years after the study began, I went to interview Miss R in residential care. She was sitting in her wheelchair and looking out the window of the dining room when I arrived. A care assistant took me in and said, "You have a visitor, Miss R." She had not met me before, but she looked up and said, "Oh, hello, my dear, how nice to see you. You're from the book club aren't you?" I explained who I was and why I had come. She graciously agreed that she remembered an earlier interview and was willing to talk to me. Prior to my visit, I had briefed myself by reading through her file.

I first asked her about how long she had been in the residential home and then asked about whether she had visitors. She assured me that she had regular visits from her friends and from her brother, who looked after all her affairs. I was a bit disconcerted at that, because I had read in her file that her only brother had died a few years before. It is rare, but it is always possible that there is a relative who has not been mentioned previously. She was able to tell me where her brother lived, how often he came, and when he had last been to visit.

I then asked her how she had come to be admitted to residential care. She became tearful and said that she couldn't live alone in the house after her mother died. At that point I knew that she was cognitively impaired, because her mother had died before she had moved to the village where she was originally interviewed. She became more and more distressed and told me in great detail about how she had cared for her mother for umpteen years and had promised her that she would never have to go into a nursing home. She went on to explain that when her own health failed, she had had to put her mother in a home, and that she felt she had really let her down. She was not entirely clear, but it seemed that she thought that her admission to residential care was associated with this in some way.

After Miss R recovered and we talked about other things for a while, I left. Our leave-taking was as courteous and gracious as my arrival. She thanked me for coming to see her and said how much she had enjoyed our chat. Before I left the home, I spoke with the person in charge. I felt very sad that Miss R still felt guilt about her mother. I asked about the brother. My memory was accurate—she had had only one brother and he had died long before she had entered care. "Did she tell you about her mother?" the person in charge asked. I told her that she had and commented on how sad it was that she was still feeling guilt. "But it's not true," said the staff member. "It's more tragic than that. She nursed her mother at home and her mother died in her arms. She was never in a nursing home." Somehow Miss R's admission appeared to have been transmogrified into her mother's admission. She wept about it every day.

Not only was Miss R's speech perfectly coherent throughout the interview, but her social skills were intact and she was very convincing. Had I not known anything about her previously, I would have accepted everything she told me about her brother. I was also convinced that her feelings of guilt were based on a real occurrence, even though I realized that her admission to long-term care had nothing to do with her mother's death.

The point of this anecdote is that some people with cognitive impairment can continue to present with entirely appropriate behavior and to answer questions convincingly. On the other hand, if an interviewee's answers sometimes seem incongruous, as did those mentioned in my earlier anecdote, an interviewer cannot automatically assume that the speaker is cognitively impaired. This is one of the more difficult aspects of interviewing older people. Even in the case of diagnostic interviews for dementia, some researchers have identified a need for a second witness (Walstra and van Gool 1995).

I have sometimes asked interviewers working with very old people to record how confident they are about the responses they were given. Where doubts are evident, it is often desirable, if the possibility exists, for the interviewer to check with a relative of the interviewee or with a member of resi-

dential staff; in such instances, however, the interviewer must pay attention to matters of confidentiality. Perhaps the best situation is for a relative of the older person to be present during the interview, so that he or she can indicate by a shake of the head when responses are not accurate. The interviewer can then check out those questions with the relative or others after the interview has ended. Many inaccuracies have to do with older persons' not remembering whether or not particular persons are still alive.

Still, it bears repeating that the presence of cognitive impairment or deficiency is not a reason to assume that interviewing is impossible. Although interviewing people who suffer from cognitive impairments and learning difficulties can be a challenge, researchers who treat such individuals sensitively and appropriately can be successful in completing interviews and recording useful data (McVilly 1995).

TAPE RECORDING AND COMPUTER ASSISTANCE

Sometimes it may be considered appropriate for interviewers to tape-record interviews. This is often desirable with open-ended interviews, where the discussion is free-flowing and ranges over many topics, some of which are unpredictable. Most of the older people I have interviewed have had no problem with this. As soon as the interview moves beyond the first few exchanges after the tape recorder is set up, they tend to forget it is there and are often startled when they hear the click indicating the end of a tape. Occasionally, respondents may have misgivings about being recorded. It often seems inappropriate to ask them why; they have every right to refuse. It is important in any case that the interviewer explain why he or she wants to tape the interview, to what use the tape will be put, and who else might hear it. Confidentiality must be assured.

In at least one instance when I was trying to negotiate the use of a tape recorder, the respondent told me that she did not want to be recorded because she thought her English was not very good. I reminded her that only I and perhaps a colleague would ever hear the tape, and I would have heard her speaking in any case. She was still reluctant, although she said that she wanted to be helpful. So I suggested that we record the interview, and when it was over, I would play it back to her. If at that point she did not like it, I would either erase it or leave the tape with her. She was happy with this arrangement and the interview went ahead. She had never heard her own voice before, and when I played back the tape, she kept saying, "That's right!" When I reminded her that the voice she was hearing was hers, she said, "Well, I'm not so bad in English am I? Let's hear some more." She let me keep the tape.

In survey research, interviewees' responses are often recorded on paper interview schedules, although the use of laptop computers for this purpose is becoming more common (see Couper and Hansen, Chapter 10, this volume). In such computer-assisted interviewing, the computer is programmed so that the interviewer can click on or type in responses. The program then automatically skips to the next relevant question, thus saving interviewer time. The main advantage of this method is that data can be entered into the data set as they are received. This method also reduces margins of error, because the data are not transferred again after they are recorded. Furthermore, researchers can perform partial exploratory analyses before all the data are collected.

When my colleagues and I first planned to use laptops in our research, we received a lot of criticism to the effect that the machine and its unfamiliar technology would create a barrier between the older person and the interviewer. It was also suggested that older respondents living on fixed incomes would be concerned about our using their electricity to run our computers. Our experiences were quite the opposite. The older people were fascinated by the laptops. For most of them, it was their first close contact with a computer. They seemed to be impressed that such advanced technology was being used to record their responses. In some cases, respondents came to sit next to the interviewers and soon started to respond before the interviewers could read out the questions. This was a real benefit for those with hearing impairments. Where it seemed that the cost of electricity to run the computer might be significant, we used or offered to use batteries ("I could plug this in or if you prefer we can run it on the batteries"). In other cases, we believed it would be inappropriately demeaning to indicate that we felt cost might be an issue.

USING MATERIAL CLUES

The homes of older people tend to give clues to their earlier lives. Photographs of members of several generations may be on display, for example. These clues are a useful way into discussions of topics that the interviewer wishes to explore. In the context of qualitative data collection, a comment on a picture of a grandchild can serve as a trigger for discussions about the whole family—children, grandchildren, and great-grandchildren—including all their ages, places of residence, and frequency of contact. Photographs of parents and brothers and sisters can offer similar starting places for family histories. Interviewers might also ask older people if they have pictures of themselves when they were young. Most older people enjoy reminiscing in this way and will give interviewers extensive information about their pasts.

If the interview is focused on a particular craft or skill, comments on tools of the trade in evidence can also be useful: How were they used? What did you do then? Who made the tools? What are they called?

It is often better for interviewers to look at the products of crafts and ask questions about them than to ask respondents to talk about such things in the abstract. Interviewers may also gather useful data by photographing some of their respondents' artifacts, but only after receiving the respondents' permission.

Taking photographs of older people themselves is more controversial. Some older people are happy to be photographed, whereas others are reluctant to be pictured warts and all. Women are more likely than men to be reluctant, and reluctance often increases with greater frailty. On the other hand, photographs enrich the textual data, remind the interviewer of the respondent, and often include interesting life clues for analysis. Interviewers should never photograph respondents without their permission, and they should take care to be tactful in requesting that permission.

The laws of copyright and privacy differ from country to country. In the United Kingdom, a photograph and its copyright are the property of the photographer. However, this does not mean that courtesies can be overlooked. Most of the older people my colleagues and I have photographed have been happy, even delighted, to have their likenesses used to illustrate our work. However, these have usually been posed portrait photographs. It is important that researchers employ sensitivity in using photographs of recognizable people to illustrate dependency, impairment, and other less positive aspects of old age.

INTERPERSONAL RELATIONS

One challenge of interviewing respondents of any age is to make an interview feel like a conversation. One of the normative expectations of conversation is that the interlocutors take turns and match self-disclosure with self-disclosure. Interviews tend to be one-sided, with one person doing all the asking and the other person doing all the answering. The subjects of interviews may feel that they are giving much away without getting anything in return. It is common for older people, who may be less familiar than other respondents with the concept of the research interview, to expect to exchange information with an interviewer, as they would in ordinary conversation. When interviewers ask older interviewees about how many children they have, where their children live, and what they do, this often raises the interviewees' curiosity about the interviewers' own children.

The interview's interpersonal relations are likely to vary over time. Conversation in the early stages of a relationship is structured around getting to know one another. Self-disclosure on the part of the interviewer encourages the interviewee to continue the exchange. Resistance to self-disclosure by the interviewer, on the other hand, can create a feeling of imbalance and increase the distance between interlocutors. There needs to be giving as well as receiving in these exchanges. Reciprocity is needed to maintain the relationship. For example, I have found that when I tell respondents that I have been divorced, they sometimes amend information they have previously given me about married sons or daughters, admitting that they too have been separated or divorced. The establishment of a reciprocal relationship is particularly important in the context of in-depth interviewing (Kaufman 1994). It has, however, been suggested that such relationships raise ethical dilemmas about the exploitation of respondents (Hart and Crawford-Wright 1999). It is a matter of conscience for each interviewer to decide this for him- or herself.

Where interviewing continues over an extended period of time, the relationship between interviewer and interviewee often shifts in tone. Friendship can develop, with the accretion of the norms and responsibilities associated with that relationship. Greater familiarity leads to an expectation of more disclosure and participation on the part of the interviewer. Older people may ask an interviewer for advice or help with small tasks. My own inclination is to enter freely into such relationships. There is an opposing viewpoint that suggests that growing familiarity and closeness with respondents affect the objectivity with which the researcher can view the data. This is a real concern and, again, one that each interviewer has to recognize and negotiate for him- or herself. Doctors do not treat members of their own families, but they seek to influence the behavior of their patients. Researchers, on the other hand, may need to be careful not to influence behavior, because this distorts the data.

CULTURAL SENSITIVITY

It is important that interviewers be sensitive to the different values, concerns, and expectations of respondents from different cultures, ethnic groups, and religious traditions, whatever the age of the respondents (see in this volume Dunbar, Rodriguez, and Parker, Chapter 7; Ryen, Chapter 21). In the context of the aging process, researchers should take pains to ascertain what the expectations, assumptions, and practices associated with advancing age are for the specific groups they are working with. It is possible here to cover only a few of the challenges that can arise.

In cultures where women are secluded, such as in most traditional Muslim communities, it can be difficult for interviewers to gain access to older women, who are often unlikely to venture outside the household. Women interviewers are essential for the study of women in such communities, because it is culturally inappropriate for a woman to be alone with a man who is not a relative. It is sometimes difficult even for a woman interviewer to interview a woman alone. Her husband or adult son may expect to be present and to answer most of the questions for her. Women interviewers need to be diplomatic to ensure that they are able to talk to Muslim women alone. It may be useful for the interviewer to intimate that it is women's talk—concerning specific health matters, for instance—that is to be undertaken, where it might be inappropriate for any man to be present.

Likewise, even though it is easier for both male and female interviewers to gain access to Muslim men, it is advisable that male interviewers be used. Even older respondents may not feel that they are being taken seriously if interviewed by a woman, and, in the worst-case scenario, a woman who tries to interview a man could be placed in a stigmatized category and treated accordingly.

From the Middle East to the Far East, responsibilities toward aging parents rest with sons, in contrast to the West, where daughters are more likely to be expected to provide care for frail parents. These responsibilities are deeply embedded in Eastern cultures. Unmarried women are the responsibility of their fathers and subsequently other senior male relatives, wives are the responsibility of their husbands, and widows are the responsibility of their sons. In some cultures, married women cease to belong to their families of socialization upon marriage.

In Eastern cultures, an interviewer's asking an older woman about seemingly straightforward matters of household composition can be a source of embarrassment, shame, or loss of face if the appropriate relative has not fulfilled his responsibilities to her. This was brought home forcefully to me when I visited China. While I was visiting a woman in her 70s at home, where she lived with her married son, daughter-in-law, and two adult granddaughters, she asked me (through an interpreter) about my own children. When I told her that I had three sons, she asked, "And which one do you live with?" When I told her that I did not live with any of them, she was mortified and embarrassed because she felt that she had committed a faux pas by causing a guest to lose face. My having to admit that I did not live with one of my sons was seen as the equivalent of admitting that I had not been a good mother, which was shameful and had caused the embarrassment of a guest.

Similarly, once when I was in rural India, everyone present was embarrassed when I asked an older woman how many children she had. In India, a country where arranged marriages are common, virtually everyone marries. For a woman to remain childless is both shaming and a source of sadness. The woman told me she had no children. This meant that she was dependent on the good-will of a nephew for food and shelter. All the other women present were uncomfort-able at this exchange, and my hosts apolo-gized to me for not being aware of this in advance and warning me, so that a difficult situation could have been avoided.

These two incidents illustrate how an in-terviewer's lack of knowledge of cultural implications and values can inadvertently lead to embarrassment when he or she asks questions that are perceived as insensitive or inappropriate. They underline the im-portance of the interviewer's having a good understanding of the cultural backgrounds of the individuals in the target sample. When interviewers are working with ethnic groups other than their own, it is important that they learn as much as possible about the cultures of those groups before they be-gin to interview. In most cases, it is better for interviewers to be of the same ethnic group as the interviewees. In all cases, interviews with older people should be conducted in the respondents' first lan-guages or own dialects whenever possible (Matsuoka 1993; Goldstein et al. 1996).

Other sensitive issues related to old age are death (on suicide, see Hendren 1990) and difficulties involving age-related his-torical experiences (on the Nazi Holocaust, see Kahana, Harel, and Kahana 1989). For example, it is inappropriate for interview-ers to discuss suicide with older Chinese, as they are likely to interpret this as a sugges-tion that they remove the burden of their care from their families. Likewise, inter-

viewers working with older Jews and European Gypsies need to be aware that the Holocaust is a most sensitive subject with these groups. All social groups, of course, have topics that are "not spoken about." Researchers need to identify such topics and approach them carefully. Among other subjects that are especially age sensitive are incontinence, sexuality, physical impair-ment, mental illness, cognitive deteriora-tion, inheritance, accumulated income, intergenerational conflict, divorce, and res-idential care. For example, in the United Kingdom most refusals relate to questions about income. In Japan, questions that could reveal tensions with daughters-in-law are difficult. Chinese elders do not dis-play likenesses or photographs of living rel-atives, only of the deceased. Jews do not name grandchildren after grandparents who are still alive. If you think about the way in which older people in your own so-cial group might feel about talking with a stranger about some of these topics related to themselves, you can start to see how im-portant it is for interviewers to understand about different cultures. All of these kinds of knowledge can facilitate the cultural sen-sitivity of interviewing.

◆ Ending the Interview

With older respondents, interviewers can often find it difficult to end their interviews and take their leave. In some cases, being interviewed can be tiring, upsetting, or de-bilitating; interviewers need to be aware of how the effort is affecting their interview-ees, even though they may appear to be en-joying themselves. Older people often want to help; this can be especially important to those whose mobility is impaired, because their opportunities to contribute have al-ready been reduced. Finding that they can-not do what they want to do can be upset-ting, and they often want to continue with interviews even though they are feeling a strain.

My experience is that it is usually best for the interviewer to be quite straight with a tiring interviewee. The interviewer can explain that he or she is concerned that the respondent is getting tired, and then, taking a cue from the context, suggest either that he or she come back later, preferably saying or negotiating when, or that perhaps he or she could speak with the respondent's spouse or daughter and gain agreement to this. Of course, if a respondent does not want the interviewer to talk to a proxy, the interviewer must respect this. In certain circumstances, using subterfuge may be justified. For instance, if it is clear that an interview is proving hard work for the older person but he or she is determined to go on, the interviewer can claim to have another appointment to keep, end the interview, and set a time to return and continue. Not only will this ensure that the interviewee is not overtired, but it will inevitably result in the rested interviewee's later providing more detailed and far-ranging information.

In cases where the older person is in good health, ending the interview can be difficult because the interviewee may have few opportunities to talk to someone so obviously interested as the interviewer. Just when the interviewer thinks it is time to leave, the respondent employs some delaying tactic: "Oh, before you go, I just want to show you something!" or "Now you will have a cup of tea, won't you?" Having taken up the older person's time, the interviewer may find it difficult to refuse such requests. My feeling is that interviewers have to be prepared to be generous with their time if their respondents have been generous with theirs. Many older persons may get few opportunities to chat about themselves. They may be lonely, and they may get a boost to their self-esteem by being able to make a contribution.

As noted earlier, good interviews take the form of natural conversation. There needs to be some exchange and the establishment of common ground or rapport. For lonely older persons who may not get out as much as they would like and thus have reduced opportunities for meeting people, an interview can be a highlight in their week. By the end of many interviews, the two people have developed warm feelings toward each other and mutual understandings. For the interviewer leaving may be routine, as he or she moves on to another interview, to reflect on the interview content as data, or to return to professional or family life. The older person, on the other hand, may be left alone to think over the experience and to wonder if he or she will ever see the interviewer again. The older respondent may feel a sense of loss, missing the recent interest shown by the interviewer and the company. The experience may raise feelings of regret in the older person that he or she does not have many visitors.

Clearly, the interviewer needs to establish his or her role at the beginning of the interview, but that does not prevent the respondent from having expectations or desires for further contact. In many instances, the interviewer will not be returning. In some cases, an interviewer may return frequently over a short period of time or infrequently over a longer period. In either case, a relationship inevitably develops. Ending even an embryonic relationship can be hard for vulnerable people. Where repeat interviewing has led to the development of closeness, disengagement raises ethical as well as difficult social and psychological questions. Interviewers need to give serious thought to how they handle such withdrawal.

In conducting a longitudinal study over 20 years, I formed what became socially intimate relationships with some of the respondents, on the basis of our growing knowledge of each other, although I saw most only once every 4 years. This was particularly so with older women, as women's informal interactions and friendships, compared with men's, tend to be based more on mutual exchange and disclosure. The question "When are you coming back?" was appropriate when this was the third interview. Saying "In 4 years" was often hard to do, as it seemed socially inappropriate to leave the relationship for so long. On more than one occasion, respondents told me that I should try to come back soon, as they would not live forever, or some similar sentiment. For those respondents in the intensive phase of this study with whom I became closer, disengagement after 4 years was not possible in all cases. By the end of 4 years, half the intensive sample had died, but I continued to keep in touch with some of the others who had few contacts on account of mutual affection and a sense of responsibility. If I had not done so, I felt I would not have fulfilled an obligation that I had created.

◆ Summary and Conclusion

Many of the topics covered in this chapter are also covered by other contributors to this volume. Interviewing older people is not a very different undertaking from interviewing members of any other social groups. Most interviews are exchanges between two individuals, and it is the individuality of the interviewee to which the interviewer must relate. With older people, paradoxically perhaps, it is important that the interviewer not approach the task as specifically an encounter with old age. Rather, the interviewer should see the event primarily as an encounter with another person. As I noted at the start, those described as "older people" can now include anyone aged 45 or more. If we exclude those still in full-time education, that probably means half of all adults.

Nonetheless, there are some specific considerations of which interviewers need to be aware with respect to interviewing those who, as a result of advancing age, suffer from various sensory, physical, and mental impairments. In addition to interfering with communication, these factors may also render the frail older person vulnerable, both in terms of the possible stress of the interview situation and in terms of exploitation, not only by researchers but by unscrupulous persons who could gain illicit access to the data. Researchers need to take these age-related factors into account when interviewing frail older people. Although they do not apply to the majority of people aged 45-100 plus, they are more prevalent among those over 80. Of course, researchers need to afford consideration to all those who are vulnerable as a result of physical or mental impairment, irrespective of age.

People over the age of 70 constitute the majority of those who use health and social care services. Much of the interviewing of older people, therefore, is aimed at clinical assessment or seeking information about their needs for and use of services. The problem orientation of much of the research requiring interviewing of older people has no doubt contributed to the stereotypes of older persons as vulnerable, dependent, and in ill health. However, representative population samples should include appropriate proportions of people in their 60s, 70s, and older age groups. Interviewers need to be encouraged to see interviewing older people in the same way they see interviewing younger people; that is, they should see each interviewee as a separate individual and should accommodate vulnerabilities and disadvantages as appropriate, no matter what the age of the interviewee. It is not age that makes older people different from other categories of people, it is the higher incidence of sensory and physical impairment, widowhood and other bereavements, mobility problems, reduced incomes, and negative self-image among individuals in this group that lead to their being seen as different from younger age groups. As I noted at the beginning, most older people are just like everyone else, except that they have been around longer.

■ *References*

Amoss, P. T. and S. Harrell. 1981. "Introduction: An Anthropological Perspective on Aging." Pp. 1-24 in P. T. Amoss and S. Harrell, *Other Ways of Growing Old: Anthropological Perspectives.* Stanford, CA: Stanford University Press.

Archibald, C. and E. Baikie. 1998. "The Sexual Politics of Old Age." Pp. 222-36 in *The Social Policy of Old Age: Moving into the 21st Century,* edited by M. Bernard and J. Phillips. London: Centre for Policy on Ageing.

Duffy, M. 1988. "Interviewing Older Adults." Pp. 160-78 in *Systematic Interviewing: Communication Skills for Professional Effectiveness,* edited by J. M. Dillard and R. R. Reilly. Columbus, OH: Merrill.

Edelstein, B. A. and E. M. Semenchuk. 1996. "Interviewing Older Adults." Pp. 153-73 in *The Practical Handbook of Clinical Gerontology,* edited by L. L. Carstensen and B. A. Edelstein. Thousand Oaks, CA: Sage.

Fetterman, D. M. 1998. *Ethnography: Step by Step.* 2d ed. Thousand Oaks, CA: Sage.

Fichter, M. M., I. Meller, H. Schroeppel, and R. Steinkirchner. 1995. "Dementia and Cognitive Impairment in the Oldest Old in the Community: Prevalence and Comorbidity." *British Journal of Psychiatry* 166:621-29.

Goldstein, A. E., L. Safarik, W. Reiboldt, and L. Albright. 1996. "An Ethnographic Approach to Understanding Service Use among Ethnically Diverse Low Income Families." Pp. 297-321 in *The Methods and Methodologies of Qualitative Family Research,* edited by J. F. Gilgun and M. B. Sussman. New York: Haworth.

Hart, N. and A. Crawford-Wright, A. 1999. "Research as Therapy, Therapy as Research: Ethical Dilemmas in New-Paradigm Research." *British Journal of Guidance and Counselling* 27:205-14.

Hendren, R. L. 1990. "Assessment and Interviewing Strategies for Suicidal Patients over the Life Cycle." Pp. 235-52 in *Suicide over the Life Cycle: Risk Factors, Assessment, and Treatment of Suicidal Patients,* edited by S. J. Blumenthal and D. J. Kupfer. Washington, DC: American Psychiatric Press.

Jobe, J. B., D. M. Keller, and A. F. Smith. 1996. "Cognitive Techniques in Interviewing Older People." Pp. 197-219 in *Answering Questions: Methodology for Determining Cognitive and Communicative Processes in Survey Research,* edited by N. Schwarz and S. Sudman. San Francisco: Jossey-Bass.

Kahana, B., Z. Harel, and E. Kahana. 1989. "Clinical and Gerontological Issues Facing Survivors of the Nazi Holocaust." Pp. 197-211 in *Healing Their Wounds: Psychotherapy with Holocaust Survivors and Their Families,* edited by P. Marcus and A. Rosenberg. New York: Praeger.

Kaufman, S. R. 1986. *The Ageless Self: Sources of Meaning in Late Life.* Madison: University of Wisconsin Press.

———. 1994. "In-Depth Interviewing." Pp. 123-36 in *Qualitative Methods in Aging Research,* edited by J. F. Gubrium and A. Sankar. Thousand Oaks, CA: Sage.

Matsuoka, A. K. 1993. "Collecting Qualitative Data through Interviews with Ethnic Older People." *Canadian Journal on Aging* 12:216-32.

McVilly, K. R. 1995. "Interviewing People with a Learning Disability about Their Residential Service." *British Journal of Learning Disabilities* 23:138-42.

Mello, E. W. and R. P. Fisher. 1996. "Enhancing Older Adult Eyewitness Memory with the Cognitive Interview." *Applied Cognitive Psychology* 10:403-17.

Melzer, D., M. Ely, and C. Brayne. 1997. "Cognitive Impairment in Elderly People: Population Based Estimate of the Future in England, Scotland and Wales." *British Medical Journal* 315:462.

Morishita, L., C. Boult, B. Ebbitt, and M. Rambel. 1995. "Concurrent Validity of Administering the Geriatric Depression Scale and the Physical Functioning Dimension of the SIP by Telephone." *Journal of the American Geriatrics Society* 43:680-83.

Morrow-Howell, N. 1992. "Multidimensional Assessment of the Elderly Client." *Families in Society* 73:395-407.

Nelson, G. M. 1992. "Training Adult-Service Social Workers in the Public Sector: A Core Curriculum for Effective Geriatric Social Work Practice." *Educational Gerontology* 18:163-76.

Patterson, R. L. and L. W. Dupree. 1994. "Older Adults." Pp. 373-97 in *Diagnostic Interviewing,* 2d ed., edited by M. Hersen and S. M. Turner. New York: Plenum.

Prager, E. 1995. "The Older Volunteer as Research Colleague: Toward 'Generative Participation' for older adults." *Educational Gerontology* 21:209-18.

Robins, L. S. and F. M. Wolf. 1989. "The Effect of Training on Medical Students' Responses to Geriatric Patient Concerns: Results of a Linguistic Analysis." *Gerontologist* 29:341-44.

Saunders, P. A., J. R. M. Copeland, M. E. Dewey, C. Gilmore, B. A. Larkin, H. Phateperkar, and A. Scott. 1989. "The Prevalence of Dementia, Depression and Neurosis in Later Life: Findings from the Liverpool MRC-ALPHA Study." *International Journal of Epidemiology* 22:838-47.

Walstra, G. J. M. and W. A. van Gool. "The Need for a 'Second Witness' in Diagnosing Dementia." *Journal of the American Geriatrics Society* 43:1176-77.

West, M., E. Bondy, and S. Hutchinson. 1991. "Interviewing Institutionalized Elders: Threats to Validity." *Image: Journal of Nursing Scholarship* 23:171-76.

7

RACE, SUBJECTIVITY, AND THE INTERVIEW PROCESS

◆ Christopher Dunbar, Jr.
Dalia Rodriguez
Laurence Parker

The only ethic I can find that you can hang your hat on says:
Now that I have the material, how do I treat my subjects? Do I accord
them all the humanity they deserve or do I write a crude and simplistic exposé?

David Simon, June 2000

David Simon, former reporter for the *Baltimore Sun*, goes directly to the heart of the interview process when he pointedly asks, "How do I treat my subjects?" (quoted in Scott 2000). This question focuses our attention on the subject that is taken to lie behind the interview respondent. Does the researcher/interviewer approach the respondent as if he or she were simply a vessel of answers—a mere interviewee—who can provide the information needed for a particular story or the data for a research project, or does the interviewer treat the respondent as a subject replete with a full complement of historical, biographical, and social sensibilities (see Holstein and Gubrium 1995; see also Holstein and Gubrium, Chapter 1, this volume)? Where interpretations of interview data are concerned, are we merely to report our findings and write our stories as if what we have heard is "objective" fact, or are we obligated, as C. Wright Mills (1959) passionately argues, to link the personally biographical with the social and historical?

In this chapter, we argue and present case material to show that the interview process and the interpretation of interview material must take into account how social and historical factors—especially those associated with race—mediate both the meanings of questions that are asked and how those questions are answered. Responsibility lies primarily with the interviewer and his or her sponsor, but all participants in the interview process are ultimately implicated in these concerns.

Although there is always an envisioned subject behind an interview respondent, this subjectivity—the subject or agent who produces meaningful, contextualized interview responses—becomes especially problematic when the respondent is a member of a "nonmainstream" group or population. If there are myriad assumptions made about mainstream respondents, they commonly emanate from presumed similarities between interviewer and interviewee. For nonmainstream respondents—whether they are persons of color, members of culturally distinct or enigmatic groups, or persons of nonconformist political persuasions or lifestyles, for example—the complications and uncertainties of how such subjects will be constituted virtually multiply. A common consequence, as Simon implies in the remarks quoted above, is that "crude and simplistic" portrayals of complex and nuanced experience emerge, because subjects are not accorded their due respect as distinctly situated individuals.

Here we focus on race as a distinct dimension of subjectivity. In the contemporary context of American and Western European society, being "white" is the unreflected-upon standard from which all other racial identities vary. But the meaning and consequence of that variation itself often goes unnoted. Frequently, persons of color are thought of as nonmainstream subjects in relation to a white standard—people whose social and/or personal characteristics do not reflect those that are taken for granted as "conventional" in the general population. What this might possibly mean is glossed over by attempts to standardize or normalize research perspectives and procedures.

As subjects, persons of color share the experience of other groups who have not traditionally been accorded viable subjectivities in their own right. For example, until recently, few interviewers figured that when interviewing women, they needed to take account of these respondents as special subjects distinct from the population at large (see Reinharz and Chase, Chapter 4, this volume). This was also true of interviewing men (see Schwalbe and Wolkomir, Chapter 3, this volume). Interviewers viewed both men and women simply as "respondents" for the most part, and proceeded to interview them as such, not particularly formulating questions in terms of special social or historical experiences that distinguished them as subjects. The rise of feminist consciousness and, in turn, the emergence of gender self-consciousness for men transformed female and male subjects from being generic mainstream respondents into subjects with considerable distinctions. The upshot for research, and especially interviewing, is that we are now increasingly procedurally conscious of femaleness and maleness as subject positions from which respondents may or may not speak in interview situations; we take this into account in relating to both the interview process and the interpretation of interview material. (For a discussion of "queering" as a further specification of gendered subjectivity, see Kong, Mahoney, and Plummer, Chapter 5, this volume.) We argue for a similar procedural consciousness with regard to race.

It is our view that such a sensibility as it applies to the subjectivity of racialized populations requires very special attention and needs to be heightened throughout the research process. Researchers and interviewers cannot simply apply technical skills and be straightforwardly "objective," as if respondents were people whose subjectivity could be taken for granted. Race is a category of the subject that has traditionally struck so many negative social and historical resonances that interviewers must always be vigilant for the ways it becomes insinuated into all aspects of identity and self-presentation, either by assertion or through silence. Once again following Simon, we suggest that the only *ethic* that properly applies in interviewing is one that accords the subject all the humanity he or she deserves. As we will show, it is an ethic that necessarily directs us to the racialized subject behind the respondent. Knowledge of this subject is immeasurably significant for an interviewer's understanding of what the respondent is saying, why he or she might remain silent in relation to particular interview topics, and how the interviewer might proceed to influence the context for openness and the respondent's willingness to speak honestly about his or her experiences.

This chapter proceeds in three parts. The first is a brief overview of literature on race and the interview process. It is not exhaustive; rather, we present this overview to show how a procedural consciousness in the matter of a racialized research subject has emerged. The second part of the chapter draws from Dalia Rodriguez's field research on interviewing nonwhite subjects in educational settings. As Rodriguez shows, the everyday, noninterview contexts surrounding an interview situation can help a researcher to gain deep insight into what he or she needs to take into account in approaching and interacting with respondents behind whom racialized subjects are to be found. A central proposition that emerges is that interviewing nonwhite subjects may require a researcher to conduct extensive ethnographic fieldwork, both before and during the interview process. This fieldwork should center on how the lived experiences of the members of the particular subject category under consideration can inform participants' conversation in the interview situation. Rodriguez is quite proactive in articulating an ethic of procedural consciousness as she turns methodological matters into concerted,

reflexive practice that has direct implications for the meaning of being a subject/respondent.

The third part of the chapter builds on these themes to offer insights into, and suggestions for, the interviewing of persons of color. Using as a point of departure some of the experiences Christopher Dunbar, Jr., has had in his research with African American youth, we propose some special sensibilities that might inform interview research where race is concerned. Among other things, Dunbar's experience as an African American male researcher attempting to study younger African American males suggests that the simple common ground of race provides no guarantee that the expressed subjects behind these respondents will honestly relate their experiences as black youth. The lesson, as we will show, is that respondents themselves recognize the subtleties and complexities of identity—of race and other subject positions—and this affects the kinds of subjects/respondents they will be if they choose to be interviewed.

◆ Interviewing and Race

Interviewing has always been a major methodological component of both qualitative and quantitative social research and of journalistic reporting. The art and science of hearing data has been at the center of how researchers obtain information, get the story right, and offer readers with insights into the social world of interviewees (Casey 1996; Rubin and Rubin 1995). However, the interview process, especially interviewing using "standardized" methods, has always been problematic with respect to nonmainstream subjects, especially in the area of race. Discussions of race currently center on how it plays out as a social construct, either in color-blind discourse and whiteness or from critical race perspectives and interpretations such as critical race theory, critical race feminism, Latina/o critical race theory (LatCrit), Asian/Pacific Islander positions, Tribal Nation perspectives, and race's intersections with other aspects of identity and issues of power (see, for example, Crenshaw et al. 1995; Delgado and Stefancic 1997; Ladson-Billings 1998; Lipsitz 1998; Omi and Winant 1994; Tate 1997). The debates in this area mirror conflicts in qualitative and quantitative research regarding the interview process and race. Historically, researchers have asked why interviews are done on "racialized" populations, for what purpose, and by whom (Andersen 1993; Stanfield 1993; Foster 1994).

HORIZONS OF RACIAL INTERVIEWING

The types of interviews related to race range from polls that are conducted to determine racial attitudes to in-depth focus groups and oral life histories. For example, a recent survey of racial perceptions in the United States gathered many of its data on race from organizations such as the National Opinion Research Center and the Institute for Social Research (Schuman et al. 1998). A New York Times poll measuring race relations in the United States (Sack and Elder 2000) was conducted through telephone interviews with 2,165 adults, with African Americans sampled at a higher rate than normal to permit analysis of black attitudes in greater depth. The results of these interviews indicated that both whites and blacks see some progress in the area of race relations. Many whites who were interviewed, however, expressed fatigue with race as an issue and said that they thought too much time and energy are devoted to it. This finding corresponds with the findings of other interview research conducted on the racial attitudes of white European Americans, in which whites indicated that they believed racism to be a thing of the past (Berger 1999). White respondents said they themselves were not racist, and very few respondents revealed honest, in-depth,

or self-critical feelings about race. However, in the New York Times poll and other interview studies (see, for example, Feagin 1992), African Americans in general have said that they see race as a determining factor in their lives, especially in the areas of education, housing, and employment.

These views on race have focused on the "black/white" paradigm that has been central to race-based discourse, law, and social policy. However, some have called for a broader discussion of race that includes perspectives and intersections with ethnicity. Critical race theory and its progressions into LatCrit and Asian American critical legal perspectives have been helpful with respect to providing a legal, social policy, and culturally sensitive framework from which to view race, power, and authority in the 21st century. For example, Cheryl Harris (1993) examined the role of law in shaping how white, as a race, is associated with property and power, over and against Native Americans and African Americans. The connection of "whiteness" to property rights has been used against Native Americans in the confiscation of Native lands and the relegation of indigenous populations to reservations and subordinate status. Harris notes how the connection of "whiteness" to property also has been used legally against African Americans with regard to slavery and white ownership of African chattel.

Another example of the expanding perspectives on race is the work of Robert Chang (1994) and others featured in a 1994 special issue of the Asian Law Journal of the California Law Review devoted to critical Asian American legal scholarship. Some of the articles in this issue examine the "honorary white" status of Asian Americans at various points in U.S. legal history, juxtaposing this status with discriminatory actions taken at other times, such as the forced relocation and internment of Japanese during World War II. Edward Park and John Park (1999) have called for new perspectives on race theory not just to be inclusive, but to alter fundamentally the lens through which researchers analyze Asian

American and Latino racial realities. A critical race theory position here would account for their differences related to Asian American/Pacific Islander American ethnicity, culture, and language and how this is also linked to transnational issues and racial status. It would also consider how the concepts of race and racial groups are constructed by the larger society, taking factors such as immigration and U.S. foreign policy into account in the monolithic ways Asian American populations are viewed and treated in the United States. Finally, the LatCrit movement has been important in shaping theory and documenting the racialization of Latino/a and Chicano/a groups. It has shown how the myth of assimilation has been held out to these groups, but also how they, in turn, have had to face the reality of laws and social hostility directed at them through such anti-immigration and affirmative action measures as Propositions 187 and 209 in California ("LatCrit Theory" 1997; Martinez 1999).

Interviews have emerged as one of the main ways of documenting the lived experience undergirding critical race theory. Topical oral histories, life histories, and evaluation interviews show that racism and racial discrimination play important roles in recent challenges to the prevailing notion of legal neutrality and race in the civil rights desegregation era. The thick descriptions and interviews characteristic of case study research not only serve illuminative purposes, but can be used to document institutional racism as well as stories of overt personal racism. The interviewing process yields narratives that can be used in building cases against racially biased policies and discriminatory practices, as shown in the historical and personal testimonies of African American expert witnesses in *Knight v. State of Alabama* (1991). In that case, the court found the state of Alabama guilty of perpetuating a dual, and racially discriminatory, segregated higher-education system. Interviews related to race can serve important purposes in that descriptions of discrimination can form an integral and in-

valuable part of the historical and current legal evidence in such cases.

REFLEXIVITY AND RACE

Another issue related to the interview process and race involves reflexivity in research (Pillow 2000). Too often, qualitative researchers have neglected discussions of the subjective lenses through which they view their research (Van Maanen 1988). But that has begun to change as qualitative researchers and ethnographers in particular are making efforts to write about the researcher's position and how the researcher is affected by the fieldwork and field relationships. This is especially noteworthy regarding how race and race relations shape the research and its implications (see Behar 1995; Cochran-Smith 2000). Yet this too is not without controversy, as some reflexive accounts have been criticized for being too focused on the personal tales of the researcher or for dealing too much with self-therapy as the researcher engages in ethnic or racial narcissism and confessional tales related to mistakes made in the field, rather than more directly addressing matters related to race, representation, and the reporting of data or its implications for social justice and validity (Buford and Pattillo-McCoy 2000; Deyhle and Swisher 1997).[1]

John Stanfield (1993, 1994) and Michelle Foster (1994) have criticized the use of interview data as narratives in research with respect to how they are used to describe various aspects of black life and the African American community. Both of these authors argue that narrative descriptions by white European American researchers are fraught with problems of subject exploitation. They assert that white researchers often neglect diverse discourse styles in their interview protocols and fail to deal with the plethora of power struggles that can take place between the researchers and "subjects" of color (see also Briggs, Chapter 24, this volume). Part of this criticism has led researchers to try to paint more nuanced portraits of African American life (e.g., Anderson 1990) and the experiences of other groups of color. For example, John Langston Gwaltney's (1980) interviews with African Americans reveal complexities of urban life and depths of black experience not previously told by most white researchers.

Many ethnographies have reflexively elaborated how the researchers have conducted their interviews to reflect the racial reality of aspirations and expectations concerning how to address racism in everyday life (see MacLeod 1995; Noblit 1999).[2] Nevertheless, researchers' reflections on the nuances of subject-interviewer interaction have often failed to identify important factors that revolve around race. For example, it is likely that white researchers have frequently been deliberately misled by the "trickster" discourse of African Americans and Native Americans as well (Vizenor 1988; Jeffries 1994). The trickster is an imagined amalgamative figure who uses comic discourse and language as a game to tell stories that challenge conformity and existing norms with multiple meanings. Some groups have typically used trickster discourse in relating to outsiders. For example, Native Americans have used such discourse to fool traditional anthropologists who have tried to interpret the meanings of tribal nation folklore; during slavery, the trickster was the defiant representative of African Americans against the oppression of the masters. The trickster disrupts the idea that we can know another group if we are outsiders (or, in some cases, insiders). The trickster can play a significant role in interview dialogue and data surrounding the experiences of members of groups of color and what they say about their racial experiences (Buendia 2000).

Other reflexive concerns are decidedly epistemological. Much recent research builds on the work of Maxine Baca Zinn (1979) and her insights related to insider-outsider qualitative studies with women of color. A related Chicana feminist epistemology underpins a wave of new research into the postcolonial identities that emerge as young women struggle with race, class, and gender issues growing up in Mexico and the United States (see Delgado Bernal 1998; Gonzalez 1998; Pizarro 1998; Villenas 1996).

Matters of social context and interviewing have moved in varied directions. For example, issues of race and reflexivity bear on sexual nonconformity. When analysis of race has been combined with sexual orientation, the use of narrative has been problematic for gays and lesbians of color because their stories have been used against them within homophobic institutional/political structures (Tanaka and Cruz 1998). Other issues relate to researchers of color studying and interviewing whites and examining their perspectives on race and racism (Parker 1998; Roediger 1998). Another concern for researchers is how formal interview settings may restrict more idiomatic forms of racial/cultural expression, leading to considerations of how researchers can conduct interviews in a group format/setting to facilitate talk among the participants, including the interviewer (Meacham 2000). The emerging critical race perspective and its connection, through interviews, to qualitative research has created powerful frameworks from which researchers can analyze and illustrate the larger context of the social construction of race.

◆ Understanding the Racialized Subject

Given the growing sensitivity to race in interview research, it is imperative that we examine how the racialized subject can be understood by way of interviews. The social context of racialized experience provides the backdrop against which the interview subject is constituted and understood as the interviewer attempts to elicit a full and authentic version of the interviewee's story. But what subject will be activated by interview questions? Whose voice might be heard or silenced? And how can the interviewer anticipate the narratives that will emerge and what they mean in the ongoing lives of respondents?

Dalia Rodriguez, a Latina graduate student from a working-class family in the U.S. Midwest, conducted a field study of overt and perceived racism encountered by students of color on a college campus and at the annual professional and student development conference held by the professional group Latinos in Higher Education. In the following subsections, Rodriguez presents both informal interview narratives and ethnographic descriptions of the social contexts that inform her understanding of what she hears her respondents say. In the process, she provides readers with information that gives shape to the subject behind the interview respondent. Her first-person accounts display the reflexive interplay between background knowledge derived ethnographically and experientially and the personal narratives generated by way of interview questions. This interplay fleshes out the subjects of her research; in documenting her related research experiences, Rodriguez adds rich and significant social detail as it relates to what her respondents could mean by what they say.

PROCEDURAL UNDERSTANDING

I run down the hall with my bag half open, frantically double-checking to see whether I have extra batteries for my tape recorder, extra tapes, and my interview guide. I rush into the "dungeon," the graduate student T.A. office, filled with rows of battered desks piled with old exams and papers. Okay, he's not here yet. I sit in front of my desk deciding whether or not to start grading my students' papers. Just as I pick up my pen, in walks J.R., an African American undergraduate student; he is about six feet tall, muscular, with long dreadlocks. I start by asking him about what he's study-

ing and about his future plans. He has come back to school after taking a few years off and plans to finish his bachelor's degree in December.

We then move on to the meat of the interview, and I ask him about his experience as an African American on campus. He responds:

> When I first came to this campus . . . it's just a shame that I was grouped into a group that had to prove that I belonged here. It wasn't like I was accepted with open arms by professors. Ya know, they see me . . . as a big black guy. Just having to prove myself to people, constantly . . . [I want to] start a rebellion against the status quo. Like my rhetoric professor, I used to hate going to that class. She used to dog me out about how I talk, cuz I was just fresh out of high school, and I used to speak a lot of slang then and I would turn papers in and she would say things were wrong with the paper. She told us we could pick any subject we wanted and then I wrote about my relationship with my girlfriend versus my friend. One time I was five minutes late for her class, and she marked my paper an entire grade. Since that experience I questioned myself and thought, "Man, maybe I don't belong in school." . . . You do end up second guessing yourself.

Hearing J.R. express self-doubts reminds me of my own trepidations. I think about my first year in graduate school and the constant doubting. No "hellos" in the hallway from professors, no "How ya doing?" When a professor did speak to me, it was to say, "Your work isn't good enough," or "Why is *that* [studying race] significant? *Everyone* studies race, do something different." I was constantly doubting myself, my abilities, and feeling like perhaps I'm not cut out to be an academic. I recall Jonathan, a graduate student, asking me one day, "Notice that there aren't *any* American racial/ethnic minorities in this new year's cohort?" Yes, I had heard through another graduate student of the many reasons that African Americans and Latinas/os were not being admitted that year, because the department was trying to improve its national ranking and admitting racial/ethnic minorities who were "doomed to fail" would only bring down the reputation of the program. After all, Latinos represent such a small percentage of Ph.D. recipients. Surprised to see myself and two other minorities in the program come back to finish our second year, one professor said, "Oh! You guys are back?!?! That's a surprise." I know they expected me to fail.

Hearing J.R. doubt himself angers me because I know that he deserves better, and I make every effort to encourage J.R. to continue his education. I ask him, "What are you planning on doing after you get your degree?" He responds, "I was thinking about graduate school . . . but, I don't know. . . . I don't think I have that great of a GPA, I mean I'm no A student." I can hear some confidence, along with doubt—doubt that I know he shouldn't have.

Breaking the methodological "rule" of not giving an interviewee your own personal views, I tell J.R., "I have also doubted myself . . . a lot. . . . Ya know, I study race/ethnicity issues, not simply because it's an interesting topic but also because of my personal experiences." He deserves to hear that he can make it. "You don't have to be an all-A student to apply to graduate school. That's great that you want to attend graduate school, you should still apply. . . . I'm sure that you already know this, but as an African American male, you will encounter so much more racism at every level, and don't *ever* let anyone tell you that you're not good enough. When you get ready to apply to graduate school, please call me, we'll work on your application, okay?" I scribble down my number as well as my e-mail address and tell him to contact me.

*   *   *

This instance of empathy and self-disclosure might be viewed in conventional research terms as "contamination," but one could also argue that, in this case, it further encouraged the respondent—now conceived as a capable and deserving subject—to elaborate on the racialized aspects of his student experience. Employing an approach similar to what Jack Douglas (1985) calls "creative interviewing," the interviewer forges common ground to share with the respondent, so that the subjects behind both interviewee and interviewer share a familiar, if sometimes uncomfortable, narrative space (see also in this volume Eder and Fingerson, Chapter 2; Reinharz and Chase, Chapter 4). In order to cultivate a climate of mutual disclosure, Douglas suggests to the researcher, "know thyself" (p. 51).

By reflexively constituting and engaging a racialized subject with whom she shares an appreciation for what it means to be a student of color, the interviewer provides empirical grounds for elaboration on the respondent's narrative. She thus forms a relevant procedural understanding of the respondent. J.R. continues:

> A lot of times when I walk into an administrative office, they [administrators] keep asking me if I'm in a "special program," an assisting type of program, and I have never seen them ask a white student that. There will be a white student in front of me and they ask him, "Your name, social security number, college you belong to" and that's it. Whereas every time I go up there I gotta be in some special program.

J.R. goes on to tell about constantly being questioned and having administrators and professors make assumptions about him as a black student, about how they constantly assume that he's "not good enough."

> I even had a professor tell me something about my hair, cuz ya know, I have dreadlocks. My professor told me, "I

like your hair, but a lot of professors can be intimidated by that and that maybe when you go talk to a professor, maybe you should dress up." I'm thinking, "I'm in college and everyone dresses in T-shirts and jeans and it's not like I'm at a conference, where I would dress accordingly."

Reflexively playing off her own experiences and feelings about what she is being told, the interviewer interactively crafts the subject of her interview into one to be appreciated rather than trivialized, compartmentalized, or derided. In this form of active interviewing (Holstein and Gubrium 1995), she conveys a personal appreciation for the subject's racialized experience, which in turn cultivates further narrative disclosure. Although the interviewer's building J.R.'s confidence with respect to graduate school may reap long-term benefits for J.R., the more immediate research consequence is that he continues to be forthcoming in the context of the interview; J.R. poignantly elaborates the details of how considerations of race infuse his university experience—even though race may only hover in the background of research conversations.

In this instance, the interviewer draws upon her own experience as a person of color and minority student—her autobiography and autoethnography, so to speak—to fill in some of the "humanity" that is necessary for a nuanced portrayal of the subject. Moreover, she uses her general sensitivities to racial issues—acquired experientially and ethnographically—to provide a framework for asking about, listening to, and understanding stories about the impact of race on the lives of students of color. Not only does she empathize with the respondent, she "activates" a racialized subject behind the respondent, inciting narratives that reveal the implications of race that might not otherwise become available. Following a proactive research ethic that aims to empower the racialized subject, Rodriguez is well aware of the need to sup-

port the formation of a respondent who will forthrightly speak to his racialized experiences. She attempts to introduce a kind of procedural consciousness to the interview process. Although her active engagement in the interview interaction may violate strictures of standardization, the anticipated trade-off is the likelihood of deeper and more complete, meaningful disclosure.

SPEAKING OUT AND BEING SILENCED

Being attuned to both the lived and procedural complexities of a racialized subject can help an interviewer to draw that subject out in the course of an interview. Why do some respondents nonetheless remain silent or inarticulate regarding race? Is it that they have nothing to say? Do they have no relevant experience to recount? Rodriguez's experiences with other students of color tell us that there are alternative explanations, as we hear in the following narrative and in her interactions in other educational settings.

*　　*　　*

Whenever students discussed issues in class, they, including the professor, would turn to me and ask, "What do Latinos think?" I tried to tell them, hey, yeah, sure . . . I'm Mexican, but I'm also a true cowboy! My home consists of horses and a ranch back at home—so, there's a lot more to me than being Mexican.

Although I understand the importance of speaking out, I can't help but think about one semester when I assisted in an "Introduction to Women's Studies" course. An African American student approached me about feeling exactly the same way. The prior week we had a discussion about *Skin Deep* (Hoffman 1995), a documentary film about college students of color who get together for a retreat to confront each other's attitudes about issues of race/ethnicity. I started the discussion by announcing the many events and symposia offered on campus. Because we had been discussing body image issues the previous week, I decided to offer extra credit to anyone who would attend the Latina body image issues workshop held at La Casa, the Latina/o cultural center on campus. As I continued with the announcements, I heard Linda and Jen, both sitting in the front row, right in front of me, whispering something. Linda, blonde with bright red lipstick, covered her mouth with one hand, but I distinctly heard her tell Linda, "Well, if we go you know that we'll be the only white people there," laughing underneath her breath. "Umhhh. . . . Do you have something you'd like to share with the class?" I asked, trying not to sound angry. "No," they responded. Linda and Jen looked at each other and began to laugh, while I looked at them intently and inquiringly. "No, never mind."

The task for the day was to get students to open up about issues of race, an all-too-familiar challenge I meet every single semester in every class I teach. However, I felt confident that my students would eventually talk about these sensitive issues, because we had spent weeks repeatedly discussing theoretical paradigms and sociological concepts: social conflict theory, structural functionalism, symbolic interactionism, internalized racism, and blaming the victim. I began by asking them what their initial reactions were to the film they had seen. One student commented that she really enjoyed the film and that she felt that she could relate to it because the setting was on a college campus. Others nodded in agreement.

But the students still seemed hesitant to "really talk." I kept hearing "Yes, great film," over and over again, but no one offered any specific thoughts about *why* it was a good film. Keeping in mind my pedagogical rules for getting people to "talk more," I did not ask, "Why?" but instead

asked, "What about the film did you like, specifically?" Dead silence. Hesitantly, Esther, an incoming freshman who usually sat quietly in the front row, said, "Well, I thought it was interesting to see how white students feel when they're the only ones in the room. I mean, it's more common to hear that from racial/ethnic minorities, but not from white students."

"Yes!" Tracy jumped in. "One time I was in a fashion show for an Asian American cultural event and I just remember feeling as if everyone there kept staring at me. I mean, I know they were wondering, 'How did this white girl get into this fashion show? What is *she* doing here?' "

"Yes!" other white female students chimed in. "It is alienating being the only white person in a room, you feel like everyone's staring at you." Esther again expressed how glad she was to have seen the film, because she had never "thought about how it would be to be the only white person in a room. I never realized this before but you [indicating me], Ana, and Lindsay are the only minorities in this room." All 23 white female students stared at me, waiting for me to reply.

As Beverly Daniel Tatum (1997) has noted, "Fear is a powerful emotion, one that immobilizes, traps words in our throats, and stills our tongues" (p. 194). People do not speak out about issues of race and racism for many reasons: fear of isolation from friends and family, fear of being ostracized, fear of rejection by those who are offended by what they have to say, fear of the loss of privilege that may come with speaking in support of the marginalized (Tatum 1997). Some are afraid of their own ignorance.

Karla, another student, mentioned that there was something about the film that she couldn't understand: "I couldn't understand why all of those people of color were so angry." I noticed that none of my students of color responded, nor did any of my white students. The students continued talking about being the only white students in certain situations. I finally decided that we had to address the issue of anger. I know that the reality on a predominantly white campus is that students of color are often "the only ones" in classes, at talks, and in most facets of university life. The only thing that came to mind was bell hooks's (1995) insight into how black rage has been pathologized, that there's no room even to think that African Americans (or other people of color) can feel anger because of the racism and discrimination they experience. "Rage is not necessarily pathological nor are we victims if we choose to become enraged," hooks says. "In fact, denying that rage . . . can create a cultural climate where the psychological impact of racism can be ignored and where race and racism become topics that are de-politicized" (p. 26).

"Let's go back to the issue Karla brought up, the issue of anger—what about that anger? Why do you think that the students of color were so angry?" Linda responded:

> Well, I don't know, I thought that the only thing the students of color wanted was an apology from the white students. They were so angry and I just didn't think it was fair that they yell like that. And, when they didn't get it they were pissed off. I thought that was uncalled for. Personally, I think it's ridiculous that I have to apologize for being white. I can't help it that I have what I have. I have no problem recognizing my white skin privilege, but I refuse to apologize to *anyone* for the position I'm in.

No one else seemed to want to talk about it; students began to look down at their feet or at the wall, avoiding the issue altogether. Then, one of my white liberal students spoke up:

> Well, I just don't see why people of color aren't more pissed off. I mean, really, they have every right to be. To be treated so horribly, in the past and now even, if I were them I would've done a lot more than just yell at white students.

> You guys were talking about being the only white person in a group; can you imagine what people of color feel like *every day* at this university?

After our discussion of the film, one of my students who is African American thanked me for establishing a comfortable class environment. She apologized profusely for not speaking very much in class, adding that she was simply "tired of being expected to represent all black people." It is clear that "speaking up" and "representing my racial group" are big burdens that many members of racial/ethnic minority groups carry. I can understand why students of color don't want to speak up.

*   *   *

Active, thoughtful subjects lurk behind even the most taciturn respondents. What we make of the silent (or silenced) respondent, however, involves more than recording "no opinion" on an interview code sheet. Rodriguez shows us how her own experiences with public discussions involving persons of color and topics of race shape her understanding of why respondents might be less than forthcoming in interview situations. In light of such experience, the interviewer must be especially conscious of the implications of what potential respondents might or might not say when asked interview questions. An interviewer's experiences outside the interview situation inform what he or she might hear (or not hear) within it. Equally important, they can cast experiential light on the broader social meanings of silence and speaking out on topics of race. Again, a proactive research ethic would aim to empower the subject to "speak up" concerning these matters, even when the "natural" impulse is to remain silent. The result is that the sensitive and astute researcher tries to look past and into the silences that greet interview questions in order to understand the possible categorical sources of silence.

◆ Procedural Sensibilities

Taken together, the preceding observations suggest that interviewers must be deeply familiar with the lives of potential respondents in order to cultivate and activate fully the subjects that figuratively stand behind them. Indeed, one might infer that interviewers need to be "insiders" in order to conduct productive, insightful, nuanced, and revealing interviews. Ethnographic fieldwork might provide researchers with the sorts of background knowledge they need to establish this familiarity, but actual membership in the subject groups under consideration is another avenue to the sorts of human portrayals that interview researchers often seek. This clearly implies the often-heard argument that only members of a group or a race are capable of truly understanding and representing the experiences of members of that group or race.

In this section we take issue with that view, suggesting some procedural sensibilities that even members need to take into account in seeking to know and recognize racialized subjects. Christopher Dunbar, Jr., adds to the accounts Dalia Rodriguez presents above by presenting some of his research experiences with young African American males, revealing further complexities in the study of race. Dunbar, an African American, has conducted ethnographic and interview research in a rural community in the Midwest for several years. His study focuses on school-aged African American males' encounters with schools and the criminal justice system. His insights echo Rodriguez's in many respects, and they also propel our considerations of race and the interview process in new directions, revealing the interactive subtleties of interviewing and race.

* * *

Education is like, for a black man you have to fight to stay free, you have to fight to have freedom, you got you fight to stay out of jail, you got to fight to get your education. That's for a black man. For a white man you don't got to do nothing but do it. (Bobby, quoted in Dunbar 1999:138)

Bobby, a 14-year-old African American male and a student in an alternative school, sat up from a slouched position on the floor to respond to a question about what education means to him. His analysis of his environment and perceived plight prompted him to stand up as he articulated his assessment of what it was like for him to be black and male and to live in America. He articulated his belief that success and education are inextricably linked and that a litany of obstacles stand in the way of his effort to obtain an education. His response also suggests his perception that racism is the leading cause of these blockages.

Two thoughts come to mind as I reflect on this response. First, would Bobby have responded the same way if I were someone other than an African American male? Second, could someone other than an African American male understand how profound a statement this young boy had made and its implications for him, a student who had been expelled from school?

SUBJECTS NEED TO
KNOW THE RESEARCHER

I recently told a white colleague that I had been asked to coauthor a chapter on interviewing people of color. He responded jokingly that the first thing you have to do is "be a person of color." He went on to tell me a story about another professor who had attempted to interview African American students. The professor, it seems, was unable to penetrate cultural barriers despite his best efforts. The circumstances that surround this situation are unknown to me, but it has been my experience when I interview African Americans students that, in order to have a meaningful dialogue, I have to spend time in the school so that students get to know me. That is, I need to spend time to develop and subsequently nurture a relationship with the students.

Too often, the emphasis in research efforts is disproportionately placed on the researcher's getting information from the interviewee. The greater effort is given over to uncovering or discovering some aspect of the individuals being studied. The problem with this approach is that it includes little or no exchange or disclosure about the life of the researcher. The researcher enters a situation wanting to learn everything about the interviewees without disclosing anything about him- or herself. Being approached by someone with such intentions would make many of us suspicious, yet it is the practice of many researchers. I think it is important to the success of the interview for the researcher to disclose something about him- or herself to the interviewees. This is foundation work; that is, it tells the interviewee where the researcher is coming from (see Douglas 1985).

Self-disclosure on the part of the interviewer is especially important when he or she is interviewing people of color, because, like other marginalized individuals, people of color tend to regard outsiders with suspicion. Years of misrepresentation and misinterpretation have legitimated skepticism and distrust. The question most often asked of interviewers by interviewees of color is "Who are you?" The second most frequently asked question is "Why should I talk to you?" This is clearly understandable if the researcher has not provided interviewees with any reason they should psychologically disrobe in front of strangers.

While in schools as a participant observer, I would often notice students watching me closely and listening to me. It was important for them to gauge my reactions and interactions with their peers and teachers so that they could assess whether I was someone they would talk with. For some students, it was important to determine if they could "shake me." For example, I asked one student his name, and he re-

sponded, "Eatdees." Thinking the name unusual, I asked "Eatdees what?" The student replied, "Eatdees [expletive]," referring to parts of his anatomy. I retorted, "You don't have any." The student and his peers laughed, surprised at my response. Had I responded any other way, my credibility may have gone out the window. This middle school student and his cohort determined at that moment that I was "straight" (translation: I was okay to talk with). The student immediately apologized, stopped what he was doing, and became my tour guide and informant throughout the study. From that moment on, I became an ally rather than a foe. The student took me directly to the computer room and began to pull up information on rap star Tupac Shakur, who had recently been killed. This was his effort to show me two things. First, he wanted to show off his computer skills, which he had acquired despite the fact that he was enrolled in an alternative school, where students are not typically considered to be academically inclined. Second, it was another way of saying that I was okay. This episode broke the ice, so to speak. When his peers saw him spending time with me, it provided a virtual stamp of approval.

Did my prior knowledge of the "tough-guy image" played out by these boys help me know how to respond in the situation? Did the fact that I was African American, male, and inextricably linked to "the black experience" prepare me to respond appropriately to the test imposed by these youngsters? I address these questions below.

SHARING THE SUBJECT'S EXPERIENCES

As an African American male, I shared the same race and gender as the students I interviewed. Apparently, race would not be an issue. However, it quickly became apparent that the students were deeply concerned with "who I was," well beyond my demographic characteristics. I came to the alternative school as a graduate student from a campus where many of these students had been barred. (It seems that any student placed on probation was forbidden from entering the campus unsupervised. This was a condition of probation. Most of the students in the study were on probation and therefore were barred from the campus.) So, here I was, an African American from the campus that was off-limits to them.

Many were suspicious of me; that was only reasonable. As far as many of them were concerned, I represented someone who probably did not have their interests at heart. I was simply another of the many researchers who had come and gone in their lives, intruding into their affairs until I got what I wanted. They suspected that I would eventually leave without showing a hint of gratitude for their temporary unpacking of layers of protection against further abuse (Dunbar 1999). Why would I be any different from the rest? Yes, I was indeed African American, but they were convinced that their experiences were completely different from mine. That is, our cultural and class experiences were different. In this instance, by *culture and class* I mean "the way we do things around here." Even if we were racially similar, the students had no good reason to believe that I would appreciate "the way they do things." I was a stranger to their way of life.

In fact, I grew up in a "traditional" working-class family, where I observed my parents waking up on time every day and going to work. My sisters and I went to school every day, too. That is how things were done around our house. Many of the students I interviewed were living in "nontraditional" family structures. For example, some students were being reared by grandparents or other extended family members. Others were being raised in foster homes. The ways things were done in their respective homes were often very different from my own experiences. This posed a quandary for me. It was incumbent upon me to acknowledge these "real" differences, yet I also wanted to hold on to the notion that "we" (African Americans) are all the same, that we all suffer the same indignities.

My self-perceptions have been shaped by my social and political experiences, which are not dissimilar to those that my subject, Bobby, has experienced. His words rang loud in my ear. Bobby heard what I heard as a child. Words from my grandma—"You must work twice as hard as the white man in order to succeed"—rang in concert with Bobby's predilection.

Different family structures often result in different cultural experiences. However, some social and political influences cross cultural barriers. Do you have to share the same race to understand the nuances of differences that exist among different cultures? In many instances, probably not; however, it can work to your advantage.

LISTENING, OBSERVING, AND COMMUNICATING

Most of the literature on interviewing techniques discusses the art of asking and listening but stops short of considering the use of personal reflections and experiences as these relate to the research (but see in this volume Schwalbe and Wolkomir, Chapter 3; Kong et al., Chapter 5; Adler and Adler, Chapter 8; Ellis and Berger, Chapter 23). Being "objective" is a major tenet of most interviewing techniques. My experience in interviewing people of color conflicts with this. The notion that the researcher should shelve his or her experiences, values, and beliefs to maintain objectivity does not always serve us well in the pursuit of rich interview data.

The notion of objectivity is problematic for me on two counts. First, my passion and interest for the subject matter of my research makes it difficult for me to sever my beliefs and values from my convictions. I do, however, maintain the capacity to check them. Second, especially when I have interviewed African American educators, I have found many of them looking to me to share *my* perceptions because they view me as a former teacher (this information I share early on) as well as a researcher. My providing this information opens opportunities for meaningful dialogue. Educators want to know if others in like positions face similar situations. They look to me not only as a researcher but as a resource. There is an expected exchange. Otherwise, it becomes a situation of "all give and no get." Mutual disclosure is often a more productive strategy (see Douglas 1985; see also in this volume Eder and Fingerson, Chapter 2; Reinharz and Chase, Chapter 4).

Sometimes when I interview persons of color, there seems to exist an unstated expectation that because I am a researcher—even though I am an African American—I will not understand the messages my subjects convey. I think some of this has to do with the fact that I am "the researcher" and therefore respondents think that I am "out of touch" with circumstances that exist in "their" communities. They seem to assume automatically that there are social and economic differences between us. They view me as someone "outside the loop."

To counteract this, I usually try to relate some aspect of my own experiences to potential respondents, to establish common experiential ground. Discerning what that common ground might possibly be requires close listening on the part of both interviewer and interviewee. I listen to respondents' answers to my inquiries not just for informational purposes but for procedural purposes as well. I listen to pick up the colloquial. I also listen for implicit nuances and respond accordingly, in order to indicate my understanding of what has been said. What subjects reveal conveys their perception of who they think I am and how they think I am receiving their response. They listen and watch in order to discern the way I understand their messages. When

I pull from my own experience as it relates to the subject, it conveys to them the message that I "really" understand. This two-way communication process within the interview suggests that respondents themselves recognize the subtleties of identity—of race as a subject position, not as a fixed demographic category. This, in turn, affects the kinds of subjects they will be, as well as what kind of subject they take me to be as the interviewer.

TAKING NOTE OF SUBTLE CUES

Observing facial expressions, vernacular voice intonations, nonverbal cues, and other forms of body language is an important part of interviewing African Americans. Important cues may come from a respondent's nodding his or her head or changing facial expressions that convey a look that says "I don't understand" or "I disagree," or from verbal expressions that use few words yet convey much meaning. Also, when an interviewer nods and says, "I hear ya" or, in today's vernacular, "I'm feelin' you," this can go a long way toward communicating to the respondent that the interviewer understands the point being made. It also displays a circumscribed degree of cultural familiarity without making it appear that the interviewer is "trying too hard" to fit in.

It has been my experience in interviewing African Americans that when some respondents become excited, their voices become louder. This does not signal anger; it simply means that the interview has touched on a point that is especially important to them. When Bobby began to explain what education meant to him, his voice became louder because he became excited about being asked to express himself about something of consequence to him. When he began saying, "A black man has to . . . ," I could hear the rhythm and intonation in his voice. This was an issue important to him and one that warranted further probing. His excitement indicated the importance of the question to him.

BEING AWARE OF CULTURALLY SENSITIVE QUESTIONS

When interviewees offer only short responses, it may indicate several problems. First, the question may seem too simple to the interviewee. It may appear rhetorical, or it may have been asked in a way that does not conform to the way the interviewee is accustomed to being asked such a question. The interviewer's charge is not only to ask culturally sensitive questions, but to ask questions in a culturally relevant and explicit manner.

"Wat yu trying to say, Mr. Dunbar, dat dare's somtin' wrong with my famly?" This was Bobby's response when I asked him if there was anyone at home to help him do his homework and to make sure he was in bed at a reasonable hour. Many poor African American children have been interviewed, tested, incarcerated, restrained, denied, abused, lied to, and misled so often that they have developed a keen ear for what is being asked *implicitly* (Dunbar 1999:138). Some will respond accordingly—that is, they may tell the interviewer what they think he or she wants to hear—and others will question the question. Some children have developed savvy that far exceeds their age. The art of interviewing entails framing questions in a way that allows interviewees (in this case children) to maintain their dignity while they tell the stories that are important to them. This means allowing subjects their humanity.

CAPTURING AND PRESENTING THE STORY

Had I not listened to Bobby as he lamented his educational plight, and had I not acquired prior knowledge of his cultural experiences, which were influenced by both social and political forces, and had I paid less attention to Bobby's body language as he sat up to begin his story, and were I not an African American male, perhaps I would have walked out of this interview thinking not only that Bobby was angry, but that he was particularly angry with me. However, having developed some useful sensibilities with respect to interviewing persons of color, I came away feeling excited—excited that I had struck an important chord with Bobby as a thoughtfully engaged subject. The interview ceased to be an interview. It became a conversation. It evolved into a dialogue. It became the story of a rich, nuanced, and important life.

When I set out to learn about the experiences of African American males in an alternative school, I didn't figure on writing stories. I set out to write a traditional ethnography. I planned to collect data, code themes, conduct an analysis, and write up my findings. Instead, as stories began to surface, they illuminated new dimensions of the lives of these students. I spent time with them as they were shuffled from detention center to foster care, to extended family members and back home, only to repeat the cycle. This, in turn, enriched my understanding of their interview narratives. My observations and experiences with the students reflexively informed, and were informed by, what the students themselves told me.

Stories and performance texts helped me to represent these experiences in an evocative way (see in this volume Ellis and Berger, Chapter 23). This approach allowed me to rework the data so that they highlighted the triumphs and tragedies that constituted the lives of these children. My intent was to bring their experiences to life for the reader rather than simply attempt to explain them. Turning simple tales of suffering, loss, pain, and victory into evocative performances sometimes moves audiences beyond just emotional catharsis, to reflective critical action (Denzin 1997). I wrote collective stories from the data in an effort "to give voice to silenced people to represent them as historical actors" (Richardson 1997:15).

Dramatic and nondramatic performances also emerged from the data that interrogated the meanings of the lived experiences of these students (Denzin 1997). The dramatic text evolved into poems and plays, and the nondramatic texts evolved from conversations turned into natural performances (Denzin 1997). These were simply recountings of events, tellings, and interpretations from the field. Performance texts allowed me to expose and challenge conventional understandings that are underpinned by systems of realistic interpretation and meaning. They provided me with a way "to turn the chaotic, unstructured, spontaneous moments of students into evocative performances" (Denzin 1997:94).

Using this approach to represent the experiences of these students allowed me to put faces on these children and to provide an enlightened glimpse into their lives. It further gave me an opportunity to present a critical view of alternative education that is filled with sociological implications without ostentatiously parading them as such, doing more to obfuscate than to reveal.

◆ Conclusion

The accounts of interviewing people of color presented in this chapter are just the tip of a social and historical iceberg. The biographical material expressed in interviews draws from, and is mediated by, experiences from well beyond the interview situation and any one respondent's life. These experiences vary from overt racism to subtle racism. Students of color face a constant struggle as they routinely must work to overcome obstacles—in the classroom, with other students, with professors, administrators, law enforcement officers, and judges. To do justice to their experience, interviews must reflexively engage

subjects in terms that can capture these complexities of their lives.

The perspective on interviewing that we have tried to present in this chapter focuses on the connections that can form between lived experiences and interview activities, which in traditional interviewing and conventional representation remain hidden behind shields of research practice. Emerging critical theoretical perspectives on racialized subjectivity have done much to reveal the actual, lived, racialized experiences of persons of all colors by providing both the procedural pretext for interviewing differently and an ethic to support such actions.

We have focused here on racialized youth cultures, but we believe it is important for researchers to have prior knowledge when studying racialized cultures of any kind. As we enter the field, we now find ourselves at the intersection of social class, gender, race, and other subjective sensibilities; the task is now to describe this intersection in all its complexity, not gloss it in tired and trite conventional terms. The operating principle here should be, "Do not assume that the subject behind the respondent is merely there for the asking." Rather, we must take the subject to have a biography that is socially and historically mediated, and proceed accordingly.

Equally important, as we have tried to illustrate, research practices that ostensibly only report "what's there" and ignore matters of procedural consciousness—or nonconsciousness, as the case has traditionally been—serve to suppress nonmainstream (often racialized) subjectivities. Conceiving of a "standardized" subject behind the respondent casts the subject as a mere vessel of answers that can be expressed only in conventional terms, in relation to the standards that are assumed to be in place. This cheats the experiences of those whose lives are not lived in accord with, or may even be lived against, the standard. Research practices that respect and reveal the social world of the lived subject are an important procedural step toward decomposing "standards" into the variety of historically and socially relevant experiences that characterize a diverse society.

■ Notes

1. Donna Deyhle and Karen Swisher (1997: 183) argue for research validity with regard to methods seriously grounded in social justice on tribal nation terms and long-term commitment to and involvement in challenging white supremacy over Native American affairs.

2. Jay MacLeod (1995:300) notes in his appendix how in some ways the "brothers" wanted to "look good" in terms of what they would and would not reveal about their status; he speculates that this may have been due to these interviewees' trying to put the best possible face on bad situations related to racism.

■ References

Andersen, M. L. 1993. "Studying across Difference: Race, Class, and Gender in Qualitative Research." Pp. 39-52 in *Race and Ethnicity in Research Methods,* edited by J. H. Stanfield II and R. M. Dennis. Newbury Park, CA: Sage.

Anderson, E. 1990. *Streetwise: Race, Class, and Change in an Urban Community.* Chicago: University of Chicago Press.

Behar, R. 1995. "Writing in My Father's Name: A Diary of *Translated Woman's First Year."* Pp. 65-82 in *Women Writing Culture,* edited by R. Behar and D. A. Gordon. Berkeley: University of California Press.

Berger, M. 1999. *White Lies: Race and the Myths of Whiteness.* New York: Farrar, Straus & Giroux.

Buendia, E. 2000. "Race, Method, and Narrative Structure: The Place of Trickster Discourses in Representing Whiteness." Presented at the annual meeting of the American Educational Research Association, April 24-28, New Orleans.

Buford, R. A. and M. Pattillo-McCoy. 2000. "Do You See What I See? Examining a Collaborative Ethnography." *Qualitative Inquiry* 6:65-87.

Casey, K. 1996. "The New Narrative Research in Education." Pp. 211-54 in *Review of Research in Education,* Vol. 21, edited by M. W. Apple. Washington, DC: American Educational Research Association.

Chang, R. 1994. "Toward an Asian American Legal Scholarship: Critical Race Theory, Poststructuralism, and Narrative Space." *Asian Law Journal–California Law Review* 1:3-82.

Cochran-Smith, M. 2000. "Blind Vision: Unlearning Racism in Teacher Education." *Harvard Educational Review* 70:157-90.

Crenshaw, K., N. Gotanda, G. Peller, and K. Thomas, eds. 1995. *Critical Race Theory: The Key Writings That Formed the Movement.* New York: New Press.

Delgado, R. and J. Stefancic. 1997. *Critical White Studies: Looking Behind the Mirror.* Philadelphia: Temple University Press.

Delgado Bernal, D. 1998. "Using a Chicana Feminist Epistemology in Educational Research." *Harvard Educational Review* 68:555-79.

Denzin, N. K. 1997. *Interpretive Ethnography: Ethnographic Practices for the 21st Century.* Thousand Oaks, CA: Sage.

Deyhle, D. and K. G. Swisher. 1997. "Research in American Indian and Alaska Native Education: From Assimilation to Self-Determination." Pp. 113-94 in *Review of Research in Education,* Vol. 22, edited by M. W. Apple. Washington, DC: American Educational Research Association.

Douglas, J. D. 1985. *Creative Interviewing.* Beverly Hills, CA: Sage.

Dunbar, C., Jr. 1999. "Three Short Stories." *Qualitative Inquiry* 5:130-40.

Feagin, J. 1992. "The Continuing Significance of Racism: Discrimination against Black Students in White Colleges." *Journal of Black Studies* 22:546-78.

Foster, M. 1994. "The Power to Know One Thing Is Never the Power to Know All Things: Methodological Notes on Two Studies of Black American Teachers." Pp. 129-46 in *Power and Method:*

Political Activism and Educational Research, edited by A. Gitlin. New York: Routledge.

Gonzalez, F. E. 1998. "Formations of Mexicananess: Trenzas de Identidades Multiples/Growing Up Mexicana: Braids of Multiple Identities." *International Journal of Qualitative Studies in Education* 11:81-103.

Gwaltney, J. L. 1980. *Drylongso: A Self-Portrait of Black America.* New York: Random House.

Harris, C. 1993. "Whiteness as Property." *Harvard Law Review* 106:1707-91.

Hoffman, D. 1995. *Skin Deep* (film). San Francisco: Iris Films, California Newsreel.

Holstein, J. A. and J. F. Gubrium. 1995. *The Active Interview.* Thousand Oaks, CA: Sage.

hooks, b. 1995. *Killing Rage: Ending Racism.* New York: Henry Holt.

Jeffries, R. B. 1994. "The Trickster Figure in African American Teaching Pre- and Postdesegregation." *Urban Review* 26:289-304.

Knight v. State of Alabama, 787 F. Supp. 1030 (N.D. Ala. 1991).

Ladson-Billings, G. 1998. "Just What Is Critical Race Theory and What Is It Doing in a 'Nice' Field Like Education?" *International Journal of Qualitative Studies in Education* 11:7-24.

"LatCrit Theory: Latinas/os and the Law" (symposium). 1997. *California Law Review* 85(4).

Lipsitz, G. 1998. *The Possessive Investment in Whiteness: How White People Profit from Identity Politics.* Philadelphia: Temple University Press.

MacLeod, J. 1995. *Ain't No Makin' It: Aspirations and Attainment in a Low-Income Neighborhood.* Boulder, CO: Westview.

Martinez, G. A. 1999. "Latinos, Assimilation and the Law: A Philosophical Perspective." *Chicano Latino Law Review* 20:1-34.

Meacham, S. J. 2000. "Black Self-Love, Language, and the Teacher Education Dilemma: The Cultural Denial and Cultural Limbo of African American Preservice Teachers." *Urban Education* 34:571-96.

Mills, C. W. 1959. *The Sociological Imagination.* New York: Oxford University Press.

Noblit, G. W. 1999. *Particularities: Collected Essays on Ethnography and Education.* New York: Peter Lang.

Omi, M. and H. Winant. 1994. *Racial Formation in the United States: 1960-1990.* 2d ed. New York: Routledge.

Park, E. J. W. and J. S. W. Park. 1999. "A New American Dilemma? Asian Americans and Latinos in Race Theorizing." *Journal of Asian American Studies* 2:289-309.

Parker, L. 1998. "Who Is the Master and What Are the Tools? A Critical Conversation on Race, Class, Gender, Postcolonialism and Other Standpoints in Educational Research." Presented at an interactive symposium at the annual meeting of the American Educational Research Association, April 19-24, San Diego, CA.

Pillow, W. S. 2000. "Exposed Methodology: The Body as a Deconstructive Practice." Pp. 199-220 in *Working the Ruins: Feminist Poststructural Theory and Methods in Education,* edited by E. A. St. Pierre and W. S. Pillow. New York: Routledge.

Pizarro, M. 1998. "Chicana/o Power! Epistemology and Methodology for Social Justice and Empowerment in Chicana/o Educational Communities." *International Journal of Qualitative Studies in Education* 11:57-80.

Richardson, L. 1997. *Fields of Play: Constructing an Academic Life.* New Brunswick, NJ: Rutgers University Press.

Roediger, D. R. 1998. *Black on White: Black Writers on What It Means to Be White.* New York: Schocken.

Rubin, H. J. and I. S. Rubin. 1995. *Qualitative Interviewing: The Art of Hearing Data.* Thousand Oaks, CA: Sage.

Sack, K. and J. Elder. 2000. "Poll Finds Optimistic Outlook but Enduring Racial Division." *New York Times,* July 11, pp. A1, A23.

Schuman, H., C. Steeh, L. Bobo, and M. Krysan. 1998. *Racial Attitudes in America: Trends and Interpretations.* Rev. ed. Cambridge, MA: Harvard University Press.

Scott, J. 2000. "Who Gets to Tell a Black Story?" *New York Times,* June 11, pp. 1, 16, 17, 18.

Stanfield, J. H., II. 1993. "Methodological Reflections: An Introduction." Pp. 3-15 in *Race and Ethnicity in Research Methods,* edited by J. H. Stanfield II and R. M. Dennis. Newbury Park, CA: Sage.

———. 1994. "Ethnic Modeling in Qualitative Research." Pp. 175-88 in *Handbook of Qualitative Research,* edited by N. K. Denzin and Y. S. Lincoln. Thousand Oaks, CA: Sage.

Tanaka, G. and C. Cruz. 1998. "The Locker Room: Eroticism and Exoticism in a Polyphonic Text." *International Journal of Qualitative Studies in Education* 11:137-53.

Tate, W. F., IV. 1997. "Critical Race Theory and Education: History, Theory, and Implications." Pp. 195-250 in *Review of Research in Education,* Vol. 22, edited by M. W. Apple. Washington, DC: American Educational Research Association.

Tatum, B. D. 1997. *"Why Are All the Black Kids Sitting Together in the Cafeteria?" and Other Conversations about Race.* New York: Basic Books.

Van Maanen, J. 1988. *Tales of the Field: On Writing Ethnography.* Chicago: University of Chicago Press.

Villenas, S. 1996. "The Colonizer/Colonized Chicana Ethnographer: Identity, Marginalization, and Co-optation in the Field." *Harvard Educational Review* 66:711-31.

Vizenor, G. 1988. *The Trickster of Liberty: Tribal Heirs to a Wild Baronage.* Minneapolis: University of Minnesota Press.

Zinn, M. B. 1979. "Field Research in Minority Communities: Ethical, Methodological and Political Observations by an Insider." *Social Problems* 27:209-19.

Part II

TECHNICAL CONCERNS

8

THE RELUCTANT RESPONDENT

◆ Patricia A. Adler
Peter Adler

Although it is nearly a sociological maxim that people like to talk about themselves, researchers occasionally find that potential respondents are reluctant to be interviewed. This may have nothing to do with the character of the social scientist or the intended subject, but may be rooted in social patterns that are understandable and analyzable. Researchers generally encounter two types of reluctance, involving issues of *access* and *resistance*. These are lodged in different stages of the data gathering enterprise. Individuals who are reluctant to grant access will withdraw, be reticent, or demur when the interview is initially requested. They may be hard to find and even harder to secure for permission to study. Other people may agree to be interviewed, but then resist opening up or discussing certain kinds of topics. They may not be forthcoming during part or all of the interview.

The reluctance of respondents has been noted since the earliest days of recorded reflections on social scientific interviewing. More than 30 years ago, Howard Becker and Blanche Geer (1969) addressed respondents' inability or unwillingness to discuss certain matters:

Frequently, people do not tell an interviewer all the things he might want to know. This may be because they do not want to, feeling that to speak of some particular subject would be impolitic, impolite, or insensitive, because they do not think to and because the interviewer does not have enough information to inquire into the matter, or because they are not able to. (P. 326)

Becker and Geer noted that social scientists had already begun to devise strategies to overcome such resistance, from experimenting with different approaches during the interview to probing for inconsistencies or illogicalities, to reacting to submerged data, when unearthed, in a matter-of-fact manner (see Becker 1954; Rose 1945). When resistance is not detected and overcome, they remarked, it is likely to result in significant data gaps. Further, other problems and areas of potential interest may remain undiscovered, and this can damage scholars' understanding of empirical issues and the theoretical extrapolations deriving from this base.

◆ Social Context

Now, more than ever, the reluctance of respondents may have developed into a problem of great magnitude. American society, as Jack Douglas (1971) long ago noted, is immense, highly complex, and pluralistic, composed of myriad different subgroups and subcultures, each having its cohesion and loyalty focused inward, away from the dominant, overarching society. Functioning in society's mass bureaucracy involves navigating through rules and regulations that are often more profitably skirted. Many groups operate within the context of opposition groups or movements, those who would critique, oppose, or eliminate their actions. This necessitates researchers' moving beyond the simplistic cooperation model of research to grapple with some of the characteristics of a conflictful view of social order (Douglas 1976). As a result, groups separate their terrain and knowledge into that which is publicly accessible —available to outsiders—and that which is accessible only to select companies of insiders. This may be the case for even the most seemingly innocuous groups, from informal collectives to formal organizations.

The rise of secrecy in U.S. society has been exacerbated by the expansion of litigation, as people increasingly use lawsuits as tools to force disclosures and redress grievances. To protect themselves against such damaging intrusions and costs, groups have become even more hidden. This has been made more difficult by advances in technology, which enable ever-greater surveillance over citizens (Marx 1988). Concealed audio and video devices record behavior, phone calls may be monitored and taped, Internet communication may be invaded, and secure documents and systems hacked. Records of individuals' lives, in this information age, are readily accessible to those with the necessary technological expertise, and privacy consequently has been diminished. All of these factors exacerbate individuals' reluctance to reveal too many aspects of their selves to others.

ETHICAL AND POLITICAL DEVELOPMENTS AFFECTING RELUCTANCE

In past times, research codes of ethics, both those informally taught and those formally codified by professional social science associations, privileged researchers' protection of the human subjects they studied. Scholars in training were taught through rhetoric and example that they should give careful regard to the welfare of the populations they studied. Social scientists routinely employed rules of confidentiality, safeguarding the identities of respondents in their published work. They widely practiced self-censorship (see Adler and Adler 1993), withholding information that could identify or harm respondents. They held strong loyalty tenets that allied them with the people who had opened up their lives to them and shared intimate details and experiences through their research relationships. They resisted pressures to reveal information that could threaten those relationships. For example, during John Van Maanen's (1983) study of the police, an incident occurred on a night when Van Maanen was doing a ride-along in a patrol car: A black man, in the course of being arrested, was beaten up. A dispute arose in which the man claimed he had been a victim of police brutality and the officers involved claimed he had resisted arrest. Investigators turned to Van Maanen, wanting to see if his field notes could shed some light on the competing charges. But Van Maanen withheld his notes, feeling that the loyalty bonds between his subjects and himself overrode other concerns. The research community sided with Van Maanen, and he safeguarded his subjects and data. Of course, such dilemmas can end up being quite complicated, because all sorts of legal, ethical, and moral concerns enter into the picture when researchers observe actions that are reprehensible. There may be times, therefore, when appeals to higher loyalties must supersede the protection of the people being researched.

Yet other research in the past exploited subjects for the gain of expanding scientific knowledge. Classic horror stories surfaced that generated alarm about the unchecked behavior of scientists. Among the most infamous examples are the U.S. government's medical experiments on the progression of syphilis, in which treatments that became known during the course of the research that could have reversed the fatal effects of the disease were withheld in order to preserve the original experimental design (Jones 1981), and psychological experiments on college students in which researchers tested compliance to authority by ordering subjects to administer (secretly fake) electric shocks to others strapped into electrode chairs to see how far people could be pushed to (allegedly) harm or kill others (Milgram 1965). These cases led a tide of change in public opinion, and the government sought to intervene into research behavior, turning formerly private decisions into public ones. Institutional review boards (IRBs), groups of individuals assigned to review research proposals with the intent of protecting human subjects, began to be formed in the 1970s, but this practice did not really take hold until the 1990s, when many universities mandated that all proposed research be approved by committee. IRBs privileged the moral good

of the country, the power of the law, and the protection of institutions sponsoring research (universities) from lawsuits over the informal loyalty ties between researchers and subjects. As a result, subjects could no longer be protected in the same ways as before (on the problems of protecting respondent confidentiality, see Picou 1996).

Some of the first test cases that came to national prominence in sociology shocked the research community. Mario Brajuha, a graduate student at the State University of New York at Stony Brook, was studying a restaurant when it burned down because of a fire of suspicious origin. When the police subpoenaed Brajuha's field notes, he refused to turn them over (Brajuha and Hallowell 1986). Rik Scarce, a graduate student at Washington State University, was studying animal rights activists when an animal research laboratory was invaded, equipment destroyed, and the animals "liberated." When the police subpoenaed Scarce's field notes, he refused to comply (Scarce 1994). In both of these cases, the researchers were denied the ability to shield their subjects from police inquiry, and the IRBs sided with the law. Brajuha was stripped of all rights, endured lengthy and expensive court battles, lost all his money as well as his family, and quit the field of sociology. Scarce, who was found to be in contempt of court, also experienced lengthy and expensive court battles and spent six months in jail.

A wave of concern washed over the research community as the new guidelines took effect. Researchers were mandated to place the public good over their moral obligations to respondents and deputized as agents of the state, required to report illegal and immoral behavior. As a result, when Eleanor Hubbard undertook an interview study of battered women who resisted their abuse by fighting back, she was clearly instructed that she should be vigilant in observing these "violent" women's behaviors; if they could strike their husbands, they might strike their children. She was ordered to report them to social service agencies should she see any indications of such tendencies. She was also instructed that she had to caution potential respondents, prior to obtaining their permission for interviews, that if they said anything that indicated they had taken part in illegal or immoral behavior, she was required to report them (Hubbard 1992).

Like Hubbard, all researchers now must caution respondents that the researchers' first loyalty lies with the state, and that respondents should regard researchers as deputized agents of the state. This declaration has a potentially chilling effect on research. It cannot help but exacerbate the reluctance of respondents who worry that their revelations might be used against them or their friends, colleagues, or family members. As a result, access to such respondents has been significantly diminished (Hamm and Ferrell 1998).

◆ The Spectrum of Reluctance

The variety of respondents who may feel some reluctance to be interviewed can be seen as falling along a spectrum of degrees of aversion to revealing aspects of self and/or being part of social scientific research. Depending upon their needs for secrecy or privacy, their fear of detection, and a host of other factors, individuals may want to guard themselves from talking to researchers, journalists, and a variety of other inquirers. Below, we discuss the range of respondents who might be particularly hesitant to be interviewed.

At the most anxious end of the spectrum of reluctance, more unwilling respondents, those we address specifically in this chapter, are scattered throughout society. They tend to cluster, however, around the top and bottom of the power, prestige, and socioeconomic hierarchies. In a cogent review of people who research "sensitive" topics, Claire Renzetti and Raymond Lee (1993) state:

It is probably possible for *any* topic, depending on context, to be a sensitive one. Experience suggests, however, that there are a number of areas in which research is more likely to be threatening than in others. These include (a) where research intrudes into the private sphere or delves into some personal experience, (b) where the study is concerned with deviance and social control, (c) where it impinges on the vested interests of powerful persons or the exercise of coercion or domination, and (d) where it deals with things sacred to those being studied that they do not wish profaned. (P. 6)

SECRETIVE RESPONDENTS

Some causes of reluctance can be found in individuals scattered across the wider spectrum of society. Especially fearful of being researched are people with secrets. Omnipresent in society, people with secrets live in fear that what they are hiding will be revealed to public attention. Despite the near-universal edict among social scientists that the identities of those they study must be protected, respondents who hold secrets are concerned about information leaking out. Most obvious among these are people who belong to secret societies (see Bellman 1984). This has often been an issue for anthropologists, who venture into indigenous cultures and sometimes find themselves among clandestine groups. For instance, Pamela Brink (1993) discusses the problems she encountered in studying the Annang, a covert women's cohort in a small, isolated African community. Like most secret societies, the Annang imposed sanctions against persons who revealed their secrets. This put Brink's respondents as well as Brink herself at personal risk of being "punished" several times for revealing the group's private matters.

Researchers need not venture onto foreign soil to confront such situations, however. Renée Anspach (1993) refers to the physicians in the neonatal intensive care unit she studied as members of a "closed" society. Much like a secret tribe, Anspach observes, these doctors had their own language, customs, and decisions that they sought to protect. Given the life-and-death judgments they were constantly making, these specialists feared retribution, lawsuits, or public humiliation if Anspach revealed information that was sensitive in nature. Even more radical in their secrecy were the Roman Catholic nuns who were the subjects of a study by Mary Anne Wichroski (1997). Wichroski had the challenging task of penetrating female monastic communities that practice codes of silence in truly cloistered societies. Beyond these extreme cases, many ordinary people hold secrets about themselves and others that they guard carefully, and that might be damaging to reveal.

SENSITIVE RESPONDENTS

Respondents who are being asked about delicate or sensitive topics may also display reluctance. Any personal issue that might cause embarrassment could fall into the "delicate or sensitive" category. Traditionally, people have been loath to discuss with interviewers their financial matters, health or disease issues, sexual conduct, drug use, and relational problems. Interestingly, Robert Weiss (1994:76) notes that survey researchers claim that income is, surprisingly, even more difficult to ask about than sex. Raquel Bergen (1993) endeavored to study marital rape, a highly sensitive topic about which women do not like to speak. Because obtaining access to women who had been raped in their marriages demanded that Bergen go through institutional channels, she had to obtain permission from the directors of appropriate women's organizations to do her research. Despite her gender and her background as a rape counselor, she was rejected by the vast majority of the institutions she contacted. Ironically, once she

finally gained access to women for the interviews, she had little trouble getting them to open up. Similarly, Rosalind Edwards (1993) found that asking women about their private family lives was difficult. She referred to her respondents as putting "invisible walls" around their family lives (p. 186).

In our own research on upper-level drug dealers and smugglers (Adler 1985), we would not have been able to get these people to talk about their drug use had we not admitted (and, in fact, shared with them) our own patterns of use. Because of the illicit nature of the activity under study, respondents had an obvious mistrust of anyone prying into their business. However, as K. J. Day (1985; cited in Renzetti and Lee 1993:6) avers, there is no fixed private sphere. Areas of social life commonly shielded from others include sexual and financial matters. Concerning the former, a number of researchers have attempted to uncover the sexual proclivities of Americans. In the most recent major study, Edward Laumann and his colleagues (1994) included numerous checks and balances to try to ease the way for respondents to discuss the intimacies of their bedroom behavior. Despite such assurances, surveys concerning sexual practices have repeatedly been attacked or questioned by others regarding respondents' veracity (see, especially, Ericksen 1999). Particularly disturbing to social researchers is the notion that all people, not just members of certain groups or people discussing specific subjects, have confidences that they would prefer remain unrevealed. In this regard, almost all potential respondents should be treated as reluctant.

THE ADVANTAGED

Yet another group of people who have commonly been difficult for social scientists to access are the advantaged, those in positions of wealth, status, and power. As Rosanna Hertz and Jonathan Imber (1995) note: "Few social researchers study elites because elites are by their very nature difficult to penetrate. Elites establish barriers that set their members apart from the rest of society" (p. viii).

Susan Ostrander (1984, 1995a) is one of the few sociologists who has successfully studied the upper class. Despite her success in this area, she has described in detail the arduous steps she has had to take to accomplish her various studies of elites (Ostrander 1995b). Because of their privileged position in society, upper-class individuals can parry the forays of social scientists trying to infiltrate their midst. Unlike members of downtrodden populations, who can often muster few protections to prevent people from intruding on and studying them, aristocrats in American society have many layers of shields that can keep social scientists at bay. Ostrander has proved that there are ways around these, but the relative paucity of research on the upper class serves as testimony to the difficulties researchers encounter in the field. Louis Corsino (1987) experienced some problems while he was trying to study the inner workings of political campaigns. With the knowledge and permission of the campaign managers, he researched the mayoral campaigns of Kevin White in Boston and Pete Wilson in San Diego. Despite his initial entrée, he was constantly under intense scrutiny regarding his political and research motives. Politicians, too, have been a group underresearched by sociologists, mainly because they have maintained the sanctity of access to their inner circles.

Celebrities. Another group of advantaged individuals who have traditionally been reluctant to be studied is made up of people with high visibility, such as celebrities, athletes, and opinion leaders. Used to being in the public eye and fearful of media exploitation or tabloid sensationalism, these people assiduously work to avoid being interviewed or portrayed in a negative light. This makes gaining access to them ex-

tremely trying for social scientists. Joshua Gamson (1994), one of the few relatively successful researchers into this domain, has studied entertainment industry elites (entertainers, agents, managers). Hollywood types such as these are so wary of publicity seekers that they may see the social scientist merely as another gossipmonger. Our own research on a major college basketball team offers another example (Adler and Adler 1991). Entering the scene before the team's success and celebrity had struck, we were able to gain access and full insider status. At the same time, Peter gained celebrity status during the course of the research through his membership role with the team (Adler 1984). So necessary was it for us to establish a role that approximated the lifestyle of the players and coaches that Peter became swept up in the media attention, popularity, and stardom that was bestowed on other members of this scene, and he had to work to shield himself from the prying eyes and questions of outsiders.

Malcolm Spector (1980) has also discussed a similar problem: researching public figures. In his case, he was in the midst of two public controversies involving psychiatry in which the respondents drew the attention of the media. Because of the notoriety these people had accrued, they were wary of any incursion into their lives or opinions. People in the center of a well-publicized storm are not likely to give access to social scientists or others. We noted this as residents of Boulder, Colorado, in the 1990s, when swarms of media personnel descended on the community in relation to the JonBenet Ramsey murder case and the Columbine High School killings.

Organizations and corporations. Other powerful groups in society that desire to protect themselves from social researchers are organizations and corporations. Because corporate managers must safeguard organizational goals, they serve as gatekeepers, effectively keeping out unknown or nosy intruders. Robert Thomas (1995), who has conducted several studies of corporate executives, makes the point that, even though these elites are highly visible to their shareholders and employees, this visibility is not the same as accessibility: "Gaining access can be a tough proposition, even when the point of getting in is innocuous, well-intentioned, or attractive to key people in the organization itself. One reason is that business elites are quite good at insulating themselves from unwanted disturbances" (p. 4). Thus, through a variety of methods, corporate executives strive to keep in place the kinds of shields that will keep social researchers at bay.

Michael Useem (1995) also discusses the difficult times he had in trying to interview corporate executives. Many people he wanted to interview declined to receive him, were "unavailable" when he was able to see them, or were simply not very responsive to his questions. Years ago, we attempted to study a professional football team about momentum in sport, in the wake of having done interviews with the local professional baseball team (Adler 1981). Despite the fact that we had some people on the inside who could vouch for us, the football team denied us access because another author (not a social scientist) had previously written an exposé about drug use among team members. With corporate espionage, paranoid management, and industrial takeovers so prevalent in organizational life in the global business community today, social scientists are at a disadvantage in trying to study the elite circles of large companies.

Those vulnerable to litigation. The final group of elites who are wary of social scientific researchers are people with exposure to lawsuits. For example, one of Anspach's (1993) doctors in the neonatal ward said to her: "And for your notes, this is a very difficult ethical problem, iatrogenesis. I'm not particularly anxious to be called into court, and it is not in my self-interest to have this baby survive" (p. 185). Obviously, he was well aware of her presence, afraid of the ramifications of her report, and careful to warn her that she had better protect his interests. In our ethnography of a Hawaiian resort hotel, we worked for a year and a half to get management permission to conduct research (Adler and Adler 1999). After several years in the setting, however, two lawsuits were brought by employees against the resort. After that, our research access was systematically diminished, with approval being required for management interviews and that approval increasingly denied. Many of the kinds of elites discussed above, such as public figures, "deep-pockets" corporations, people under restraining orders, and those fearful of libel suits may be equally circumspect about allowing themselves to be interviewed or to become part of a research project.

THE DISADVANTAGED

The disadvantaged make up the final group in which reluctant respondents are likely to be found. These people, who lack the power to withdraw from researchers, may simply distrust the intentions and meanings of academic research. The poor, for instance, who may be more accessible and easier to find than the rich, still have many reasons to be careful about what social scientists discover about them. One particular group of people who have frequently come under the scrutiny of sociologists are those engaged in illegal activities, such as criminals and revolutionaries, and other "hidden" populations. W. Wayne Weibel (1990) defines these individuals: "The term 'hidden populations' refers here to a subset of the general population whose membership is not readily distinguished or enumerated based on existing knowledge and/or sampling capabilities" (p. 4). Most often associated with research on deviant groups, studies of such hidden populations are characterized by the difficulty involved in locating subjects (but for discussions of the facilitative aspects of gaining access to deviant groups, see Anderson and Calhoun 1992; Tewksbury and Gagné 1997). Ralph Weisheit (1998) discusses how difficult it was for him to locate marijuana growers in rural areas. Not only were these people secretive about their activities, they were extremely scattered, living in remote locations.

Much criminological research is conducted with incarcerated populations, in part because active offenders are, as John Irwin (1972) notes, "hard to locate because they find it necessary to lead clandestine lives. Once located, they are *reluctant*, for similar reasons, to give accurate and truthful information about themselves" (p. 117; emphasis added). Bruce Jacobs (1998) describes how much difficulty he had in locating urban crack dealers. We encountered similar problems in our study of upper-level drug dealers and smugglers (Adler 1985). Although we were fortunate to have a next-door neighbor who became our key informant, we virtually had no other way to meet people than through the associates to whom we were introduced. Whenever respondents sense that the research might be threatening to them, they are likely to be cautious about allowing the inquiry to continue. Whether this is because much research deals with private aspects of people's lives, because of the possibility for information released to be incriminating, or because research impinges on political alignments in the community, social scientists can normally expect that people engaged in illegal activities will be loath to offer access (Lee 1993).

In contrast to elites who worry about lawsuits, less powerful people may be afraid of exposure to censure if they reveal too much to researchers. Subordinates in organizations who are bringing lawsuits against their employers might want to discuss their situations, but they may be under "gag orders" that prohibit them from engaging in this kind of disclosure. For example, in our study of a resort hotel, we interviewed a chef who was charging the resort with racial discrimination. While the lawsuit was pending, he could not discuss any aspects of the case or the treatment he received from the hotel's management. Less

powerful people suing large corporations or governments may be concerned about getting "SLAPPed" (Pring and Canan 1996) back—that is, being sued by the organization for defamation, libel, or any action that they bring to make the group look bad. These people also need to be careful in talking to outsiders such as researchers. Thus disgruntled employees, angry citizens, and other people dissatisfied with the status quo might make interesting respondents, but they are frequently not allowed to be interviewed about their involvement.

Finally, people who may be at risk, especially because of their subordinate status, are likely to be reluctant respondents. Ramona Asher encountered this problem in her study of women married to alcoholics. Although the wives often wanted to talk about the emotional traumas they faced, the husbands, paranoid that something unseemly about them might be revealed, attempted to block these interviews (see Asher and Fine 1991). Similarly, a lower-level pastry chef at our resort, referred to us by mutual friends, declined our request for an interview because he had heard at work that talking to us might not be good for his job. Whenever employees are in a vulnerable position because of fear about losing their jobs, they may be disinclined to grant interviews. People who have been victimized may also be afraid to talk to researchers for fear of retaliation. Julia Brannen (1988:560) provides a number of examples in which her respondents feared negative reactions from their husbands in her study of marital difficulties. Finally, as Lee (1995) points out, potential subjects who are in dangerous situations—whether physical, financial, emotional, or relational—may be well-advised to keep their mouths shut.

NONWARY RESPONDENTS

Lest readers come away with the mistaken impression that all respondents are reluctant, we should point out that John Dean, Robert Eichhorn, and Lois Dean

(1969) provide a useful guide of types of respondents at the other end of the reluctance spectrum—those who are not reticent to talk to researchers. The "nouveau-statused," for instance, are people who have just been promoted or changed positions and are likely to want to open up about their experiences. "Old-timers" are respondents who no longer have a stake in the operations of the setting or who are so secure that they do not feel they will be jeopardized by what they say. "Frustrated" people may be rebels or malcontents who want to vent about their positions or the ill treatment they are receiving. "Rookies," or naive informants, may not even realize that they are revealing intimacies of the setting. They may be so new to the place that they have inadequate knowledge of and stake in the system to protect it. "Outsiders" may be people who are somewhat connected to a scene, but have a unique vantage point external to the culture or community. "Needy" members of a scene may fasten onto researchers because they crave attention or support and will talk to any sympathetic ear. "Subordinates," although discussed above as wary respondents, may sometimes be so hostile that they are willing to speak no matter the consequences. Finally, individuals on the "outs" are people who have lost power but may still be "in the know." Members of any of these groups of people may be particularly open to being interviewed.

◆ Overcoming Reluctance

In an attempt to provide some guidelines for researchers who need to overcome reluctance on the part of respondents, we outline various strategies below. Basically, these techniques are related to the two types of reluctance noted earlier: access and resistance. Problems related to getting access to subjects have plagued social scientists since formal research procedures were established. There is a wide range of possi-

ble conditions, and different researchers have arrived at some divergent, opposing viewpoints on how to overcome reluctance.

APPROACHING RESPONDENTS

Brannen (1988) asserts that researchers' success in attaining interviews, especially about sensitive topics, may be influenced by the *relationship between researchers and respondents*. She argues that researchers may facilitate their access to respondents if they cast the interviews within a "one-off" relationship (a transitory, as opposed to in-depth association, which assures anonymity). Respondents will have less fear, and therefore will be more forthcoming, if they believe they will never cross paths with the researchers again. According to this view, there is an ironic security in detachment, which creates anonymity and more likelihood for self-disclosure on the respondents' part. Irving Seidman (1991), too, asserts that the easier the access to interviewees, the more complicated the interview. This builds on the assumption in psychiatry that people can more openly disclose to others who are uninvolved in their lives. However, this opinion goes against the philosophy of other researchers, who believe that trust is best forged between a researcher and a respondent when a more personal relationship is established. Barbara Laslett and Rhona Rapoport (1975) suggest that repeated interviews will yield the best results, because this allows for the establishment of such relationships.

By returning to the same respondents several times, researchers may be able to broach more sensitive topics, and deeper intimacy may result. Some postmodern ethnographers have advocated interactive interviewing, in which respondents and researchers share personal and social experiences in a collaborative communication process that involves multiple interview situations (see Ellis, Kiesinger, and Tillmann-

Healy 1997; see also Ellis and Berger, Chapter 23, this volume). Almost all current practitioners of ethnography have now adopted similar ideas about the importance of membership roles, contact with subjects, and in-depth involvement in subjects' lives (Adler and Adler 1987).

Feminist researchers have been at the forefront of the call to *empower respondents*. Criticizing the passive role of respondents in traditional interview situations, Ann Oakley (1981) asserts that methods such as coauthorship and collective consciousness-raising between researchers and respondents can give subjects more of a stake in the research process. Many researchers are now experimenting with various types of collaborative research ventures in which respondents are brought into the planning and analysis phases of the research (Clough 1994; Collins 1992; Smith 1989). Researchers may reduce problems of access to difficult-to-penetrate groups by entrusting group members with a say in what is written. As Bergen (1993) notes, "Research participants are empowered because they understand that their personal experiences are no longer raw material for the data mill but that they are active in sharing their stories with others and evoking change" (p. 202).

Heeding a similar cry, postmodern ethnographers believe that respondents should be given "voice" in their own stories (Denzin 1997). Merging notions of poststructuralism, feminism, and new journalism, these authors join with their respondents to produce polyvocal, subjective, poetic, and dramatic prose that incorporates equally the lives of researchers and respondents (see in this volume Ellis and Berger, Chapter 23). Central to all of these studies is the self, squarely situated in the research and openly available for inspection by those being studied (Clough 1992; Denzin 1997; Richardson 1997). Respondents are also given an opportunity to see what the researcher has written, to respond to it, and to change what gets reported (Duelli Klein 1983; Ellis et al. 1997;

Tripp 1983). Elliot Liebow (1993), for instance, went to great trouble to include what the homeless women he studied thought of his analysis, even to the extent of omitting materials to which they objected. Thus, through a variety of methods, postmodern ethnographers are bringing researchers into closer proximity to respondents, providing more mutual trust and intensifying the relationships between them. The expectation is, then, that problems of access are reduced in the process.

On a more traditional front, researchers have been debating for years the benefits of *providing goods, services, payments, or gifts* to respondents in order to gain access to them. Particularly important in research about organizations, payoffs can serve to cement the commitment that gatekeepers have to the continuation of a research project. According to Peter Yeager and Kathy Kram (1995), "The research must have an identifiable 'payoff' for the organization, and it must be presented in terms neither threatening to the organization's purpose nor foreign to its culture" (p. 46). Without some identifiable "profit," Yeager and Kram argue, organizations are not likely to welcome researchers. In studying deviant groups, often the only way researchers can get interviews is by making some monetary payoffs. Much of the research done on inner-city drug use, for instance, has relied on researchers' offering small pecuniary incentives to respondents (Hamid 1990; Johnson et al. 1985; Dunlap et al. 1990).

Survey researchers have long favored the use of incentive fees to gain the cooperation of reluctant respondents. For example, in their comprehensive study of the sexual practices of Americans, Laumann et al. (1994) found that "the judicious use of incentive is cost efficient since so much of the expense is due to interviewer travel time and costs incurred returning to residences" (p. 56).

Exchanges can be other than financial, however. For instance, Irwin (1972) frequently provided loans, transportation, accommodations, and other favors to the nonincarcerated criminals he studied. We, too, were often in the position of offering our services as baby-sitters to the drug dealers we studied to secure the research bargain (Adler 1985). By putting ourselves out and going beyond the standard relationship, we enhanced our ability to get access to dealers. In studying children, Gary Fine felt that, at times, there were benefits to be gained by offering services, such as companionship, educational expertise, praise, food, and monetary loans, to child informants (Fine and Sandstrom 1988:24). We did the same in our study of college athletes, feeding them, helping them with their studies, and providing short-term loans (Adler and Adler 1991).

However, there is not universal agreement that providing goods and services to respondents is advantageous to research projects (see Lee 1993). William Yancey and Lee Rainwater (1970) have argued that gifts or loans from affluent researchers to poor respondents can reinforce paternalistic roles and feelings of inequality. Richard Berk and Joseph Adams (1970) have warned that researchers who provide gifts to respondents may be getting "suckered." As Gary Fine and Kent Sandstrom (1988) express it: "A danger exists in providing services, even those that are not monetary. Researchers may become accepted for what they provide, not for what they are. The relationship may become commodified and instrumental" (p. 25). Thus the tying of respondents to researchers by payoffs of any kind may not necessarily produce the most trusting relationships. This issue remains highly controversial among social scientists today.

There are a number of *practical strategies* that interviewers can use to assure access to respondents. In most qualitative interviewing situations, the interviewer's goal is to be informal, nondirective, and freewheeling, because most qualitative researchers believe that a less structured atmosphere enhances rapport with subjects. They argue that it is especially important not to hurry respondents into interview sit-

uations prematurely. We made this mistake in our study of drug dealers and smugglers. Having thought that we had established a trusting relationship with one dealer's "old lady," we asked if we could interview her. Although we had not been overly specific about the scope of our research interests, we thought that she liked and trusted us and that, as a graduate student in cultural anthropology, she understood and respected academic research. However, as soon as the interview began, we realized that she felt uncomfortable discussing the drug trafficking of her friends: She ducked our questions, feigned sleepiness, and avoided direct answers. We politely left and lost all future access to her. Similarly, if researchers are too aggressive in their requests, they may scare or threaten respondents.

In order to counteract this problem, some authors have suggested that interviewers use "shallow cover" (Fine and Sandstrom 1988:19), or the "sin" of omission. Here, researchers are overt about their intentions but remain oblique or vague about their specific purpose. In Fine's (1987) case, he told the Little Leaguers he studied only that he was interested in observing the behavior of preadolescents; he did not go into any further detail about the exact nature of his study. Although this kind of approach did not work for us, it allowed Fine to remain more flexible in the research bargain and prevented him from possibly scaring off some of the children or their parents.

SPONSORSHIP

Perhaps the strategy researchers most commonly use to gain access to diffident groups is sponsorship. Made famous in sociology by such notables as Doc in *Street Corner Society* (Whyte 1943), the eponymous Tally (Liebow 1967), and Herman, the janitor whom Elijah Anderson (1976) met at Jelly's (the bar-liquor store he studied), sponsors act "in a bridging or a guiding role, serv[ing] indirectly to facilitate acceptance of the researcher" (Lee 1993: 131). One function a sponsor can serve is as a referral to others in the setting, vouching for the researcher. For instance, in our research with drug dealers, Dave, our key informant, introduced us to a wide spectrum of his associates and guaranteed our trustworthiness. Because we had housed Dave after he was imprisoned, his colleagues trusted us. These referrals were priceless, as there would have been no other way for us to gain access to members of such a concealed group. Having the backing of trusted individuals in the setting can greatly ease researchers' access. For example, Jeffrey Sluka (1990) had relatively little problem getting into a Catholic enclave in Belfast (despite the highly political and violent nature of the setting) because he initially contacted a local and trusted priest who vouched for him. Yeager and Kram (1995) found that developing a number of liaison relationships with internal groups of managers early on in their research allowed them the necessary access to sites in the banking and high-technology industries because these people referred them to others who were aware of their relationships with the sponsors.

Among some groups that are very difficult to penetrate, it may be tantamount to professional suicide for researchers not to have sponsorship networks to exploit. In explaining how he gained access to dignitaries in Hollywood, for example, Gamson (1995) states that "an outside researcher who does not tap into a relationship network, and one with a powerful individual at its center, is going to have terribly restricted access to the higher-ups in the industry elite" (p. 86). Similarly, Joan Hoffman (1980) used the sponsorship of her social ties, people she knew personally or who knew members of her family, to gain access to hospital boards of directors and their upper-class members. Without these connections, she never would have been granted permission to interview the people she did.

If all else fails, and access is either not forthcoming or summarily denied, researchers may need to "send out feelers" (Henslin 1972:63) to establish contact with the groups they want to study. Using his role as a college professor, for example, Henslin (1972) recommended that students in his classes conduct research on abortion, a highly secretive practice at the time. He encouraged anyone who had a friend or acquaintance who had had an abortion to pursue these lines. In this way, he found respondents who otherwise would have been closed off to him.

RELATIONAL GROUNDWORK

A chief difference between ethnographers and those who practice survey research or qualitative interviewing unsupported by participant observation is the kind of groundwork that ethnographers can lay in their settings. Jennifer Platt (1981) suggests that researchers interview peers with whom they already have established relationships, and Robert Burgess (1991) urges researchers to develop friendships to gain access to the groups in which they are interested. In his studies of educational settings, he became friendly with administrators and teachers in various schools. He notes that, rather than causing problems in the collection of data,

> these friendships facilitated entry to groups that would otherwise have been difficult to enter. Secondly, these friendships provided access to a different range of perspectives on the school. Thirdly, my acknowledged friendships with particular individuals gave rise to a situation where other teachers wanted to give me their views on particular matters. (P. 51)

Ethnographers have long argued that they have a greater likelihood of securing interviews if they take the time to get to know the people they are studying, to develop relationships with them, and to build trust between respondents and themselves. Ethnographers believe that laying the relational groundwork for future interviews not only enhances their access to study populations, but, based on depth, commitment, and trust, these longitudinal associations may lead to research that yields richer portraits of the subjects. Long-term, meaningful, in-depth involvement with subjects, these researchers argue, yields a greater likelihood that respondents will be available, honest, and soul-searching in discussing the research topic.

JOINT MEMBERSHIP

Finally, we and others have argued that having a membership role in a setting increases a researcher's likelihood of gaining interview access (see, e.g., Adler and Adler 1987). Ethnographers have practiced this technique for decades, but Jeffrey Riemer (1977) was the first to highlight it in his discussion of "opportunistic" research sites. Many studies have been conducted by researchers who have had access to particular groups because they were already members. For example, researchers can *take advantage of unique circumstances or timely events* to select their topics of study. Lawrence Ouellet (1994) carried out his study of truck drivers while he drove a cross-country truck route to pay his bills during graduate school. Julius Roth's (1963) research on long-term medical patients was the result of his own hospitalization. Our own work on young children's car pools began when we found ourselves ferrying kids back and forth to preschool (Adler and Adler 1984).

Researchers can also *take advantage of familiar situations* to select topics for research. In studying preadolescents, we began by observing our own children and their friends (Adler and Adler 1996). As parents in the community, we already were interested in the lives of these children. Turning this into a research setting was a natural outgrowth of our parental roles. We

were accepted and trusted by many in the setting because, as parents, we had a natural reason to be there and shared membership-related concerns and interests.

Similarly, researchers may *take advantage of their own special expertise* in selecting their research topics. Ned Polsky (1967) was an avid billiards player when he began his study of pool hustlers, and Marvin Scott (1968) was a frequent visitor at horse-racing tracks, leading him to study that world. Some autoethnographers focus primarily on their own experiences. Examples include Carolyn Ellis's (1995) study of the death of her husband, as both she and he chronicled the last months before he died of emphysema; David Karp's (1996) study of people who suffer from manic depression, a condition with which he was afflicted; and Carol Ronai's (1995) poignant study of incest survivors, of which she was one. The advantage of all such opportunistic approaches is that they facilitate entry into the setting, because the researcher already has a legitimate purpose for being there.

Not all ethnographers, of course, "exploit" their own biographies to expedite access to a research population. Often, researchers do not establish their membership in a setting until well after they have arrived there. One of the most creative examples of this is Nancy Mandell's (1988) "least-adult" role. In order to study preschool children, Mandell minimized the physical, cognitive, intellectual, and social differences between herself and the children by literally getting into the sandbox with them, putting herself eyeball to eyeball with them, ignoring their deviances and transgressions, and generally approximating, as best she could, the stance of a child. Although distrustful at first, the children came to see Mandell as much closer to them than other adults. Her observations and discussions with the youngsters were thus greatly enhanced.

At times, researchers who study social movements or proselytizing religious groups may be recruited by members

(Grills 1994; Rochford 1985). Although such recruitment may ease the researcher's entry into the group, it may also prohibit the researcher from gaining access to respondents other than through being seen as a potential convert.

◆ Overcoming Resistance

Once a researcher has gained entrée to a group, the arduous task of actually conducting the interviews ensues. There are a host of problems that may arise once interviews are granted, particularly with respondents who are reluctant to talk in the first place. Researchers hope for full and complete disclosure on the part of respondents, but there may be many reasons respondents are not forthcoming with information. Below, we outline some of the typical problems interviewers face and some strategies they might use to overcome these obstacles.

SETUP ISSUES

In arranging and negotiating interviews, interviewers' *demographic characteristics* may serve as an important link to respondents (Weiss 1994). Thus if there is an overlap between the interviewer and the interviewee in such areas as age, gender, social class, ethnicity, and general appearance, a reluctant respondent may be more prone to openness during the interview. Bergen (1993), for instance, found that her gender was a major advantage in her interviewing women about marital rape. Martin Weinberg, Colin Williams, and Douglas Pryor (1994) recruited volunteers from the Bisexual Center and the Institute for Advanced Study of Human Sexuality to conduct the interviews in their San Francisco study of bisexuals. They had hoped that this would make their respondents more comfortable with talking about their sexual orientations. However, as they note, this approach is not without its drawbacks:

> The danger of having organizational members conduct the interviews lay in the possible *reluctance* of people being interviewed to disclose something negative about being bisexual, the Bisexual Center itself, a mutual acquaintance, and the like. Similarly, there was always the chance that persons being interviewed might exaggerate their sexual history to impress a bisexual interviewer or provide acceptable responses with perceived interviewer effects. (P. 24; emphasis added)

Nevertheless, Weinberg et al. found that their respondents did prefer to discuss these intimate issues with like-minded people.

The *location* of the interview is another factor that can be important in assuring that reluctant respondents will feel comfortable. When interviews deal with highly emotional, sensitive, or private topics, it is often best if they can be conducted in places that are as secluded as possible, such as the respondents' homes. Bergen (1993) found this to be the case in her study of marital rape; she notes that "interviewing women in their homes was an important aspect of establishing a relationship and fully understanding the emotional and physical trauma that these women have suffered" (p. 207). Interviewing in a respondent's home casts a guest ambience over the researcher's presence and imbues the researcher with an aura of friendship. Other topics are best brought up in the workplace, particularly when respondents do not want to talk around other people in their homes, or when they are used to entertaining reporters at their places of business. Most critically, it is essential that researchers meet respondents at the times and places that are convenient to the respondents (Thomas 1995). For instance, in his study of Hollywood elites, Gamson (1994) conducted most interviews at respondents' workplaces, but others felt more comfortable at public meeting places, such as cafés or restaurants.

CONDUCT

The conduct of the interviewer during the course of the interview is a crucial determinant of how comfortable the respondent will be. Interviewers who are assiduous in providing reassurances can make even reluctant respondents feel at ease. John Brewer (1993) used humor, ribaldry, and self-deprecation to court and relax the police he studied in Northern Ireland. The interviewer's phrasing of the questions, too, is important; carefully worded questions can make a respondent feel less threatened, especially when the interview concerns hard-to-discuss topics such as sex. Numerous rape researchers, for example, have found that women are more likely to be willing to respond to questions about "forced or unwanted sexual intercourse" than to discuss "rape" (see Bergen 1993; Finkelhor and Yllo 1985; Russell 1990; Walker 1989). Richard Tewksbury and Patricia Gagné (1997) found that by reminding their transgendered respondents that they were not being seen as "freaks," they could greatly enhance their interviews with these respondents: "During interviews and other interactions when our research motives have been questioned or respondents have become defensive or reticent, we have been able to reestablish empathy by explaining that we believe gender is socially constructed and exists along a continuum" (p. 143).

In a similar vein, Hoffman (1980) found that "deflection" was a useful technique to use with subjects who were anxious about personal exposure. That is, although they were uncomfortable when they perceived themselves to be the objects of study, they talked more freely on generic or "external" topics. Marsha Rosenbaum (personal communication, 1999) has told us that in interviewing drug users about their behavior, she always started the conversation by asking, "Say, what sort of drugs do people use around here?" rather than asking them their drugs of choice. Anything that deflects attention away from respondents as

the main target of study can be useful for promoting conversation. Using plural and personal pronouns with respondents is yet another way to facilitate rapport and break down barriers. John Johnson (1975:108) suggests that an interviewer's using words such as *we, us, they,* and *them* can convince respondents that the interviewer is actually *of* them, not apart from them.

A common ploy that interviewers use involves "normalizing perceived deviance" (Johnson 1975). That is, interviewers are well-advised not to raise their eyebrows, change their tone of voice, or seem dismayed when respondents discuss deviant activities. For instance, in our study of preadolescents, we were frequently in a position to hear about the transgressions of young teenagers, such as cigarette smoking, cutting school, and early sexual exploits. Rather than expressing moral indignation, we either nodded affirmatively or seemingly ignored the situation. If we had reacted any differently, these youngsters would not have felt comfortable telling us about these activities.

Qualitative interviews are, by definition, flexible. Researchers are permitted to allow respondents to shape the contours of the interview. At times, this may mean that respondents ask questions about the intimate lives of interviewers; this can result in appropriate and beneficial transactions that can ease respondent reluctance (but see Weiss 1994, who questions whether self-disclosure is an effective facilitative technique). The practice of postmodern and feminist ethnographers suggests that when respondents and researchers share information, the interview context is more comfortable and the hierarchical gap between researchers and respondents is diminished (Cook and Fonow 1986; Ellis et al. 1997). Rosalind Edwards (1993), for instance, was asked to "self-disclose" about her own family life in her study of mature mother-students seeking higher education. She felt that her own revelations aided the respondents in telling her their life stories. In our study of drug dealers, we often talked about the one day that Peter had spent in jail. Although this was a rather fleeting stay, we were able to milk this piece of our history to get respondents to open up about their own prison experiences or fears about arrest. With any sensitive topic, the more researchers can indicate that they share respondents' pain or have experienced similar feelings, the more likely it is that respondents will open up (Daniels 1983).

Lee (1995), in a useful manual about dangerous fieldwork, suggests that conducting open and *simultaneous fieldwork* with other, even opposing, parties may be helpful to researchers studying controversial topics. For instance, in their study of a nude beach, Jack Douglas and Paul Rasmussen (1977) found that their talking openly to all participants in disputes concerning the beach—such as nudists, police, and property owners—made those on each side want to tell their story. So as not to be left out or misunderstood, divided factions in disagreements may become less reluctant to talk. David Gilmore (1991) refers to this as the "competition of communication," wherein each side tries to convince the researchers of the justice of its cause, increasing the amount of data made available.

Ostrander (1995b) describes several ploys that she has found to be beneficial in getting elites to let their guard down. It is easy to feel intimidated by these people, she notes, especially given that they are used to being in charge of most social situations. However, counterintuitively, she recommends that interviewers not be too deferential or overly concerned about establishing positive rapport with elite respondents; rather, interviewers should take some visible control over the situation. In one example from her studies, she was invited to breakfast at a fancy restaurant selected by a respondent. She arrived early, before he did, and although this immediately put him off guard, he eventually deferred to her. Another simple strategy she has employed

is to choose a particular spot to place her tape recorder, so that this gives her an excuse to take charge of where she and the respondent sit during the interview. Finally, Ostrander recommends that interviewers give elites the opportunity to respond directly to criticisms others have of them, thereby allowing them to express frustrations or to defend themselves.

RELATIONSHIPS

Similar to their role in affecting research access, researchers' relationships with respondents may overcome resistance during the course of interviews. "One-off" advocates continue to maintain that detachment fosters the greatest reduction of resistance, whereas those who believe that researchers should conduct multiple interviews with the same respondents and that researchers should forge relationships with respondents prior to interviewing champion greater intimacy and connection.

Researchers may also lessen respondent resistance by trying to equalize the status differentials and power inequalities between themselves and their respondents. In the difficult task of "studying up," Hoffman (1980) notes, the onus is on researchers to elevate their status and power. This earns them greater respect from respondents and a greater feeling of ease. Conversely, researchers who investigate the downtrodden and powerless should balance differences as well. In trying to get reluctant respondents to talk, interviewers should try not to appear overly above or below them. Researchers should avoid obvious displays of affluence or position and should look for areas of other personal overlap between respondents and themselves where they might forge rapport. Thus in our study of college athletes we tried to minimize the differences between our often black, inner-city, young, and inexperienced respondents and ourselves. They initially felt extremely deferential toward us, in part because of our age, race, social class, education, and position as faculty members; they called Peter "Coach" and Patti "Miss Patti." After a while, our unpretentious and unconventional behavior, and our clear desire to support them in the setting, led them to relax and treat us more as friends. They then felt more comfortable cursing in our presence, revealing their behavior and relationships, and expressing their feelings about others in the setting to us. Although many researchers agree that such status equalization diminishes interview reluctance, it cannot be overlooked that researchers can also purposely use their greater status and power in the interview setting to steamroll respondents, pushing them into answering questions without giving them the opportunity to be reticent. This occurs rarely, however.

◆ Conclusion

The litigious nature of U.S. society today and the politicization of research have influenced the core, basic character of interviewing. Compared with the past, there are now many more reasons, organizational and individual, for people to be wary of being studied. In particular, formal factors have been added to informal ones, escalating people's reluctance. As a result, some groups may be entirely lost to researchers'

views, and aspects of the lives of some others may remain hidden. Still, thoughtful and sensitive researchers can still accomplish much fruitful research. Interviews, especially when they are deep and unstructured, fundamentally remain a potentially enjoyable medium of interaction and exchange, where social scientists' interests in people and their lives can stimulate respondents to share their experiences and insights in a way that leaves all participants mutually enriched.

As society changes, it is possible that the nature of resistance might change as well. With increasing degrees of protection built into the research relationship and the increasing education of the populace, perhaps respondents in the future will be better assured that their interests will be protected. It is more likely, however, that researchers will have to continue to deal with reluctant respondents, no matter the sociohistorical times or the context of the research. Although we do not envision a time when respondent reluctance will disappear entirely, we can hope that, for the future of social science, informed respondents will be less taciturn than they are in the fairly paranoid environment in which we currently live. Thus, although the strategies described in this chapter might need to be amended in the future, researchers will always need to aware of the cautionary feelings of the people they study.

■ References

Adler, P. 1981. *Momentum: A Theory of Social Action*. Beverly Hills, CA: Sage.
———. 1984. "The Sociologist as Celebrity: The Role of the Media in Field Research." *Qualitative Sociology* 7:310-26.
Adler, P. A. 1985. *Wheeling and Dealing: An Ethnography of an Upper-Level Drug Dealing and Smuggling Community*. New York: Columbia University Press.
Adler, P. A. and P. Adler. 1984. "The Carpool: A Socializing Adjunct to the Educational Experience." *Sociology of Education* 57:200-210.
———. 1987. *Membership Roles in Field Research*. Newbury Park, CA: Sage.

————. 1991. *Backboards and Blackboards: College Athletes and Role Engulfment.* New York: Columbia University Press.

————. 1993. "Ethical Issues in Self-Censorship: Ethnographic Research on Sensitive Topics." Pp. 249-66 in *Researching Sensitive Topics,* edited by C. M. Renzetti and R. M. Lee. Newbury Park, CA: Sage.

————. 1996. "Parent-as-Researcher: The Politics of Researching in the Personal Life." *Qualitative Sociology* 19:35-58.

————. 1999. "Transience and the Postmodern Self: The Geographic Mobility of Resort Workers." *Sociological Quarterly* 40:31-58.

Anderson, E. 1976. *A Place on the Corner.* Chicago: University of Chicago Press.

Anderson, L. and T. C. Calhoun. 1992. "Facilitative Aspects of Field Research with Deviant Street Populations." *Sociological Inquiry* 62:490-98.

Anspach, R. R. 1993. *Deciding Who Lives: Fateful Choices in the Intensive-Care Nursery.* Berkeley: University of California Press.

Asher, R. and G. A. Fine. 1991. "Fragile Ties: Shaping Research Relationships with Women Married to Alcoholics." Pp. 196-205 in *Experiencing Fieldwork: An Inside View of Qualitative Research,* edited by W. B. Shaffir and R. A. Stebbins. Newbury Park, CA: Sage.

Becker, H. S. 1954. "A Note on Interviewing Tactics." *Human Organization* 12:31-32.

Becker, H. S. and B. Geer. 1969. "Participant Observation and Interviewing: A Comparison." Pp. 322-31 in *Issues in Participant Observation,* edited by G. J. McCall and J. L. Simmons. Reading, MA: Addison-Wesley.

Bellman, B. L. 1984. *The Language of Secrecy.* New Brunswick, NJ: Rutgers University Press.

Bergen, R. K. 1993. "Interviewing Survivors of Marital Rape: Doing Feminist Research on Sensitive Topics." Pp. 197-211 in *Researching Sensitive Topics,* edited by C. M. Renzetti and R. M. Lee. Newbury Park, CA: Sage.

Berk, R. A. and J. M. Adams. 1970. "Establishing Rapport with Deviant Groups." *Social Problems* 18:102-17.

Brajuha, M. and L. Hallowell. 1986. "Legal Intrusion and the Politics of Fieldwork: The Impact of the Brajuha Case." *Urban Life* 14:454-78.

Brannen, J. 1988. "The Study of Sensitive Topics." *Sociological Review* 36:552-63.

Brewer, J. D. 1993. "Sensitivity as a Problem in Field Research: A Study of Routine Policing in Northern Ireland." Pp. 125-45 in *Researching Sensitive Topics,* edited by C. M. Renzetti and R. M. Lee. Newbury Park, CA: Sage.

Brink, P. J. 1993. "Studying African Women's Secret Societies." Pp. 235-48 in *Researching Sensitive Topics,* edited by C. M. Renzetti and R. M. Lee. Newbury Park, CA: Sage.

Burgess, R. G. 1991. "Sponsors, Gatekeepers, Members, and Friends: Access in Educational Settings." Pp. 43-52 in *Experiencing Fieldwork: An Inside View of Qualitative Research,* edited by W. B. Shaffir and R. A. Stebbins. Newbury Park, CA: Sage.

Clough, P. T. 1992. *The End(s) of Ethnography: From Realism to Social Criticism.* Newbury Park, CA: Sage.

————. 1994. *Feminist Thought: Desire, Power and Academic Discourse.* Cambridge, MA: Blackwell.

Collins, P. H. 1992. "Transforming the Inner Circle: Dorothy Smith's Challenge to Sociological Theory." *Sociological Theory* 10:73-80.

Cook, J. A. and M. M. Fonow. 1986. "Knowledge and Women's Interests: Issues of Epistemology and Methodology in Feminist Sociological Research." *Sociological Inquiry* 56:2-27.

Corsino, L. 1987. "Fieldworker Blues: Emotional Stress and Research Underinvolvement in Fieldwork Settings." *Social Science Journal* 24:275-86.

Daniels, A. K. 1983. "Self-Deception and Self-Discovery in Fieldwork." *Qualitative Sociology* 6:195-214.

Day, K. J. 1985. "Perspectives on Privacy: A Sociological Analysis." Ph.D. dissertation, University of Edinburgh.

Dean, J. P., R. L. Eichhorn, and L. R. Dean. 1969. "Fruitful Informants for Intensive Interviewing." Pp. 142-44 in *Issues in Participant Observation,* edited by G. J. McCall and J. L. Simmons. Reading, MA: Addison-Wesley.

Denzin, N. K. 1997. *Interpretive Ethnography: Ethnographic Practices for the 21st Century.* Thousand Oaks, CA: Sage.

Douglas, J. D. 1971. *American Social Order.* New York: Free Press.

———. 1976. *Investigative Social Research.* Beverly Hills, CA: Sage.

Douglas, J. D. and P. K. Rasmussen, with C. A. Flanagan. 1977. *The Nude Beach.* Beverly Hills, CA: Sage.

Duelli Klein, R. 1983. "How to Do What We Want to Do: Thoughts about Feminist Methodology." Pp. 99-121 in *Theories of Women's Studies,* edited by G. Bowles and R. Duelli Klein. New York: Routledge & Kegan Paul.

Dunlap, E., B. D. Johnson, H. Sanabria, E. Holliday, V. Lipsey, M. Barnett, W. Hopkins, I. Sobel, D. Randolph, and K. Chin. 1990. "Studying Crack Users and Their Criminal Careers: The Scientific and Artistic Aspects of Locating Hard-to-Reach Subjects and Interviewing Them about Sensitive Topics." *Contemporary Drug Problems* 17:121-44.

Edwards, R. 1993. "An Education in Interviewing: Placing the Researcher and the Research." Pp. 181-96 in *Researching Sensitive Topics,* edited by C. M. Renzetti and R. M. Lee. Newbury Park, CA: Sage.

Ellis, C. 1995. *Final Negotiations: A Story of Love, Loss, and Chronic Illness.* Philadelphia: Temple University Press.

Ellis, C., C. E. Kiesinger, and L. M. Tillmann-Healy. 1997. "Interactive Interviewing: Talking about Emotional Experience." Pp. 119-49 in *Reflexivity and Voice,* edited by R. Hertz. Thousand Oaks, CA: Sage.

Ericksen, J. A., with S. A. Steffen. 1999. *Kiss and Tell: Surveying Sex in the Twentieth Century.* Cambridge, MA: Harvard University Press.

Fine, G. A. 1987. *With the Boys: Little League Baseball and Preadolescent Culture.* Chicago: University of Chicago Press.

Fine, G. A. and K. L. Sandstrom. 1988. *Knowing Children: Participant Observation with Minors.* Newbury Park, CA: Sage.

Finkelhor, D. and K. Yllo. 1985. *License to Rape: Sexual Abuse of Wives.* New York: Holt, Rinehart & Winston.

Gamson, J. 1994. *Claims to Fame: Celebrity in Contemporary America.* Berkeley: University of California Press.

———. 1995. "Stopping the Spin and Becoming a Prop: Fieldwork on Hollywood Elites." Pp. 83-93 in *Studying Elites Using Qualitative Methods,* edited by R. Hertz and J. B. Imber. Thousand Oaks, CA: Sage.

Gilmore, D. D. 1991. "Subjectivity and Subjugation: Fieldwork in the Stratified Community." *Human Organization* 50:215-24.

Grills, S. 1994. "Recruitment Practices of the Christian Heritage Party." Pp. 96-108 in *Doing Everyday Life,* edited by M. L. Dietz, R. Prus, and W. B. Shaffir. Mississauga, Ontario: Copp Clark Longman.

Hamid, A. 1990. "The Political Economy of Crack-Related Violence." *Contemporary Drug Problems* 17:31-78.

Hamm, M. S. and J. Ferrell. 1998. "Confessions of Danger and Humanity." Pp. 254-72 in *Ethnography at the Edge: Crime, Deviance, and Field Research,* edited by J. Ferrell and M. S. Hamm. Boston: Northeastern University Press.

Henslin, J. 1972. "Studying Deviance in Four Settings: Research Experiences with Cabbies, Suicidees, Drug Users, and Abortionees." Pp. 35-70 in *Research on Deviance,* edited by J. D. Douglas. New York: Random House.

Hertz, R. and J. B. Imber. 1995. "Introduction." Pp. vii-xi in *Studying Elites Using Qualitative Methods,* edited by R. Hertz and J. B. Imber. Thousand Oaks, CA: Sage.

Hoffman, J. E. 1980. "Problems of Access in the Study of Social Elites and Boards of Directors." Pp. 45-56 in *Fieldwork Experience: Qualitative Approaches to Social Research,* edited by W. B. Shaffir, R. A. Stebbins, and A. Turowetz. New York: St. Martin's.

Hubbard, E. A. 1992. "Of Course I Fight Back: An Ethnography of Women's Use of Violence in Intimate Relationships." Ph.D. dissertation, Department of Sociology, University of Colorado at Boulder.

Irwin, J. 1972. "Participant-Observation of Criminals." Pp. 117-38 in *Research on Deviance,* edited by J. D. Douglas. New York: Random House.

Jacobs, B. A. 1998. "Researching Crack Dealers: Dilemmas and Contradictions." Pp. 160-77 in *Ethnography at the Edge: Crime, Deviance, and Field Research,* edited by J. Ferrell and M. S. Hamm. Boston: Northeastern University Press.

Johnson, B., P. J. Goldstein, E. Preble, J. Schmeidler, D. S. Lipton, B. Spunt, and T. Miller. 1985. *Taking Care of Business: The Economics of Crime by Heroin Abusers.* Lexington, MA: Lexington.

Johnson, J. M. 1975. *Doing Field Research.* New York: Free Press.

Jones, J. H. 1981. *Bad Blood: The Tuskegee Syphilis Experiment.* New York: Free Press.

Karp, D. A. 1996. *Speaking of Sadness: Depression, Disconnection, and the Meanings of Illness.* New York: Oxford University Press.

Laslett, B. and R. Rapoport. 1975. "Collaborative Interviewing and Interactive Research." *Journal of Marriage and the Family* 37:968-77.

Laumann, E. O., J. H. Gagnon, R. T. Michael, and S. Michaels. 1994. *The Social Organization of Sexuality.* Chicago: University of Chicago Press.

Lee, R. M. 1993. *Doing Research on Sensitive Topics.* Newbury Park, CA: Sage.

———. 1995. *Dangerous Fieldwork.* Thousand Oaks, CA: Sage.

Liebow, E. 1967. *Tally's Corner: A Study of Negro Street Corner Men.* Boston: Little, Brown.

———. 1993. *Tell Them Who I Am: The Lives of Homeless Women.* New York: Penguin.

Mandell, N. 1988. "The Least-Adult Role in Studying Children." *Journal of Contemporary Ethnography* 16:433-68.

Marx, G. T. 1988. *Undercover.* Berkeley: University of California Press.

Milgram, S. 1965. "Some Conditions of Obedience and Disobedience to Authority." *Human Relations* 18:57-76.

Oakley, A. 1981. "Interviewing Women: A Contradiction in Terms?" Pp. 30-61 in *Doing Feminist Research,* edited by H. Roberts. London: Routledge & Kegan Paul.

Ostrander, S. A. 1984. *Women of the Upper Class.* Philadelphia: Temple University Press.

———. 1995a. *Money for Change: Social Movement Philanthropy at Haymarket People's Fund.* Philadelphia: Temple University Press.

———. 1995b. " 'Surely You're Not in This Just to Be Helpful': Access, Rapport, and Interviews in Three Studies of Elites." Pp. 133-50 in *Studying Elites Using Qualitative Methods,* edited by R. Hertz and J. B. Imber. Thousand Oaks, CA: Sage.

Ouellet, L. 1994. *Pedal to the Metal: The Work Lives of Truckers.* Philadelphia: Temple University Press.

Picou, J. S. 1996. "Sociology and Compelled Disclosure: Protecting Respondent Confidentiality." *Sociological Spectrum* 16:209-32.

Platt, J. 1981. "On Interviewing One's Peers." *British Journal of Sociology* 32:75-91.

Polsky, N. 1967. *Hustlers, Beats, and Others.* Chicago: Aldine.

Pring, G. and P. Canan. 1996. *SLAPPS: Getting Sued for Speaking Out.* Philadelphia: Temple University Press.

Renzetti, C. and R. M. Lee. 1993. "The Problem of Researching Sensitive Topics: An Overview and Introduction." Pp. 3-13 in *Researching Sensitive Topics,* edited by C. M. Renzetti and R. M. Lee. Newbury Park, CA: Sage.

Richardson, L. 1997. *Fields of Play: Constructing an Academic Life.* New Brunswick, NJ: Rutgers University Press.

Riemer, J. 1977. "Varieties of Opportunistic Research." *Urban Life* 5:467-77.

Rochford, E. B. 1985. *Hare Krishna in America.* New Brunswick, NJ: Rutgers University Press.

Ronai, C. R. 1995. "Multiple Reflections of Child Sex Abuse: An Argument for a Layered Account." *Journal of Contemporary Ethnography* 23:395-426.

Rose, A. M. 1945. "A Research Note in Interviewing." *American Journal of Sociology* 51:143-44.

Roth, J. 1963. *Timetables.* Indianapolis: Bobbs-Merrill.

Russell, D. E. H. 1990. *Rape in Marriage.* Rev. ed. Bloomington: Indiana University Press.

Seidman, I. 1991. *Interviewing as Qualitative Research: A Guide for Researchers in Education and the Social Sciences.* New York: Teachers College Press.

Scarce, R. 1994. "(No) Trial, (but) Tribulations: When Courts and Ethnography Conflict." *Journal of Contemporary Ethnography* 23:123-49.

Scott, M. B. 1968. *The Racing Game.* Chicago: Aldine.

Sluka, J. A. 1990. "Participant Observation in Violent Social Contexts." *Human Organization* 49:114-26.

Smith, D. E. 1989. "Sociological Theory: Methods of Writing Patriarchy." Pp. 34-64 in *Feminism and Sociological Theory,* edited by R. A. Wallace. Newbury Park, CA: Sage.

Spector, M. 1980. "Learning to Study Public Figures." Pp. 98-109 in *Fieldwork Experience: Qualitative Approaches to Social Research,* edited by W. B. Shaffir, R. A. Stebbins, and A. Turowetz. New York: St. Martin's.

Tewksbury, R. and P. Gagné. 1997. "Assumed and Perceived Identities: Problems of Self-Presentation in Field Research." *Sociological Spectrum* 17:127-55.

Thomas, R. J. 1995. "Interviewing Important People in Big Companies." Pp. 3-17 in *Studying Elites Using Qualitative Methods,* edited by R. Hertz and J. B. Imber. Thousand Oaks, CA: Sage.

Tripp, D. 1983. "Co-authorship and Negotiation: The Interview as Act of Creation." *Interchange* 14:32-45.

Useem, M. 1995. "Reaching Corporate Executives." Pp. 18-39 in *Studying Elites Using Qualitative Methods,* edited by R. Hertz and J. B. Imber. Thousand Oaks, CA: Sage.

Van Maanen, J. 1983. "The Moral Fix: On the Ethics of Fieldwork." Pp. 269-87 in *Contemporary Field Research: A Collection of Readings,* edited by R. M. Emerson. Boston: Little, Brown.

Walker, L. E. A. 1989. *Terrifying Love: Why Battered Women Kill and How Society Responds.* New York: HarperCollins.

Weibel, W. W. 1990. "Identifying and Gaining Access to Hidden Populations." Pp. 4-11 in *The Collection and Interpretation of Data from Hidden Populations,* edited by E. Y. Lambert. Rockville, MD: National Institute on Drug Abuse.

Weinberg, M. S., C. J. Williams, and D. W. Pryor. 1994. *Dual Attractions: Understanding Bisexuality.* New York: Oxford University Press.

Weisheit, R. A. 1998. "Marijuana Subcultures: Studying Crime in Rural America." Pp. 178-204 in *Ethnography at the Edge: Crime, Deviance, and Field Research,* edited by J. Ferrell and M. S. Hamm. Boston: Northeastern University Press.

Weiss, R. S. 1994. *Learning from Strangers: The Art and Method of Qualitative Interview Studies.* New York: Free Press.

Whyte, W. F. 1943. *Street Corner Society: The Social Structure of an Italian Slum.* Chicago: University of Chicago Press.

Wichroski, M. A. 1997. "Breaking Silence: Some Fieldwork Strategies in Cloistered and Noncloistered Communities." Pp. 265-82 in *Reflexivity and Voice,* edited by R. Hertz. Thousand Oaks, CA: Sage.

Yancey, W. L. and L. Rainwater. 1970. "Problems in the Ethnography of the Urban Underclass." Pp. 78-97 in *Pathways to Data,* edited by R. W. Habenstein. Chicago: Aldine.

Yeager, P. C. and K. E. Kram. 1995. "Fielding Hot Topics in Cool Settings: The Study of Corporate Elites." Pp. 40-64 in *Studying Elites Using Qualitative Methods,* edited by R. Hertz and J. B. Imber. Thousand Oaks, CA: Sage.

9

IN-PERSON VERSUS TELEPHONE INTERVIEWING

◆ Roger W. Shuy

In the process of gathering data, social science researchers expend considerable time and effort that can make in-person interviewing impractical. Doing fieldwork—interviewing, observing, carrying out surveys and other kinds of data gathering—is often the most difficult and time-consuming part of the research task. Because time is valuable, researchers may try to figure out ways to reduce their work, short-cutting the data gathering or finding other ways to meet deadlines and get their projects done. One method of reducing fieldwork time that researchers may consider is to conduct interviews by telephone instead of meeting with subjects in person.

In this chapter I will consider the issue of in-person versus telephone interviews as it arises in the contexts of both traditional research surveys and everyday practical interviews, such as those conducted by hearings officers, doctors, lawyers, and journalists. Certain advantages and disadvantages are associated with each type of interviewing, and researchers who decide to use the telephone may benefit from realizing what they gain and lose in the process.

Many types of research interviews, such as surveys, whether conducted by telephone or in person, entail two different tasks for the researcher. The first task is to persuade the respondent to agree to be interviewed; the second is to elicit the information desired. In everyday practical interviews, the first task is usually unnecessary, because practical considerations make respondents willing to participate.

Studies of the persuasive aspect of research interviewing have focused on issues such as cost-efficiency, interviewer bias, response rates, questionnaire uniformity, and how researchers can best obtain subject compliance. Researchers have also examined how the voice characteristics of interviewers, such as rapid speech, loudness, varied intonation, and Standard English pronunciation, impinge on respondent confidence and refusal rates. No such research, however, has looked at these same speech characteristics in respondents (Oksenberg and Cannell 1988; Holstein and Gubrium 1995). It should also be noted that the studies examining speech characteristics of interviewers have been based on psycholinguistic laboratory research using only male voices (Brown 1973), leaving the voice characteristics of female interviewers, as well as female respondents, unexamined.

My focus here will be on comparing the advantages and disadvantages of telephone and in-person interviewing as carried out both by research interviewers and by those who interview as part of their everyday practical occupations. It is my hope that researchers using both methodologies can learn from this discussion of these strengths and weaknesses.

I will also emphasize the fact that most of the research on interviewing has concentrated on the interviewer rather than on the respondent. Reports on the advantages of telephone interviewing tend to stress matters such as interviewer bias, uniformity of questions and interviewer delivery, standardization of questions, interviewers' personal safety, and how interviewers can ask questions more sensitively. Very little is said about respondents' language and comfort. Communication consists of a sender, a message, and a receiver. By analyzing only the sender (interviewer) and the message (question), most researchers examining interviewing practices have overlooked the third major component, the person who answers the questions.

As in almost every other area of life, compromises in the interviewing task can lead to unanticipated problems. Some kinds of information may be gathered from respondents just as well by means of the telephone as in person. But researchers should know in advance, or at least should anticipate, the extent to which the quality and type of information they acquire can be affected by the mode they choose for gathering it.

After I review below the advantages and disadvantages of both telephone and in-person interviewing, I will present a case study of interviewing in an everyday practical context in order to illustrate many of the consequences of the differences between these two modes of interviewing.

◆ Criteria for Deciding between Telephone and In-Person Interviewing

Following are some of the criteria that researchers and others have set forth for deciding whether interviews should be conducted by telephone or face-to-face—whether the interviewing is done in relation to the everyday practical work of life or in relation to targeted surveys or polls:

- The type of interview to be carried out (e.g., research, polling, medical, journalistic)

- The type of information sought (e.g., demographic, personal, sensitive)

- The attitudinal variability, safety, and workload of the interviewers

- The need for consistency and/or uniformity among multiple interviewers

- The social variability of individual participants (e.g., gender, race, age)

- The need for contextual naturalness of response and setting

- The need to let participants generate responses with little or no influence from the questions

- The complexity of the issues and questions

◆ The economic, time, and location constraints of the project

◆ Research on Telephone versus In-Person Interviewing

The telephone interview has swept the polling and survey industry in recent years and is now the dominant approach. There have been a few comprehensive comparisons of telephone and face-to-face interviewing, but even fewer studies comparing identical items and similar populations under the same conditions (Stokes and Yeh 1988). There have also been very few studies comparing telephone and in-person interviewing practices in practical, nonresearch settings. The reasons for the lack of comparisons are simple: (a) Such studies are very difficult to carry out, (b) they are very expensive, and (c) there has been little reason for those who interview as an integral part of their everyday work lives to veer from the traditional in-person interview. But there has been some movement to substitute telephone interviewing for in-person interviewing in bureaucratic settings of various sorts. This development has permitted a preliminary and somewhat limited comparison of telephone and face-to-face interviews, but one that allows us to compare the advantages and disadvantages of each mode.

Most of the available comparisons between telephone and in-person research interviewing concentrate on the interviewer. Some give attention to the attitudes of respondents, but even these typically focus on things that influence nonresponse (Groves 1979). Quality and quantity of responses are the focus of one report; Edith de Leeuw and Johannes van der Zouwen (1988) examined 28 studies that compared the summarized content (not the specific language) of telephone versus in-person interviews. They carried out a meta-analysis on the quantity and quality of data found in the studies, looking only at five indicators. Four of these five indicators—absence of social desirability bias (answers considered more acceptable in society), quantity of information given (responses to open questions), nonresponse to items (including "don't know"), and similarity of content of response in both modes (telephone and in person)—favored in-person interviewing, albeit with only a slight advantage. This confirms a finding from an earlier study that had concluded that the tilt of research findings is toward better-quality data in personal interviews, although the meaning of *quality* was not probed very deeply. Another comparison study found that respondents were more acquiescent, evasive, and extreme in their responses in telephone interviews than when they were interviewed face-to-face (Jordan, Marcus, and Reeder 1980).

It is difficult to assess the appropriateness of telephone interviewing versus in-person interviewing in all potential contexts. Researchers in different disciplines use interviewing for quite different purposes and seek distinct kinds of information. Some linguists, for example, interview with no particular content in mind. They simply want to obtain samples of natural, continuous speech, no matter what the respondents talk about. They place a premium on letting respondents ramble on at will, with as little participation and as few preset questions as possible from the interviewer. Ethnographers also carry out a version of this approach as relatively minor participants in the verbal exchanges they observe and analyze. In contrast, public opinion researchers focus almost totally on the content of what their respondents have to say. Their aim is often to keep respondents' verbal input to a minimum through the use of highly focused and consistent sets of questions.

The degree to which a researcher should consider either in-person or telephone interviewing more appropriate depends on many variables based on and growing out of the criteria noted above. It is possible to discern some of the advantages and disadvantages of these two interviewing modes from what is known and reported in the literature. In the following sections, I review the claimed advantages of both telephone and in-person interviewing practice.

◆ Advantages of Telephone Interviewing

Those who carry out surveys or polls for which it appears to be economically impractical to do in-person interviewing claim that there are certain advantages to telephone interviewing, as described below.

Reduced interviewer effects. Despite the lack of convincing comparisons of telephone and in-person interviewing, telephone interviewing appears to allow for fewer interviewer effects, largely because such effects can be monitored in centralized telephone research facilities (Lavrakas 1993; Frey 1989; de Leeuw and van der Zouwen 1988). The very presence of telephone interviewers together in the same facility offers them opportunities to learn from each other, in contrast to the face-to-face interviewer's conventional isolation.

Better interviewer uniformity in delivery. The vocal tone and delivery of interviewers has also been suggested as a reason telephone interviewing can be more successful than the in-person mode, because interviewer training can be more easily implemented and more successful (Oksenberg and Cannell 1988). Likewise, the shorter data collection period of telephone interviewing lends itself to closer monitoring of interviewer performance (Aquilino and LoSciuto 1990). But such findings leave unanswered the question of why in-person interviewers cannot be trained with the same efficiency.

Greater standardization of questions. Survey researchers point out that using telephone interviewing provides researchers with control over quality: "When properly organized, interviewing done by telephone most closely approaches the level of unbiased standardization that is the goal of all good surveys" (Lavrakas 1993:5). This observation is undoubtedly accurate when the goal is to have every question asked in exactly the same way.

Researcher safety. Some researchers believe that by using telephone interviewing, they can safely reach respondents in difficult-to-visit or dangerous neighborhoods, especially late at night (Groves and Kahn 1979; de Leeuw and van der Zouwen 1988).

Greater cost-efficiency and fast results. If the research goal is limited to obtaining a completed interview in a short amount of time and in a cost-effective manner, there is little reason to question that telephone interviewing should be favored over face-to-face interviews. Robert Groves (1978) notes that the speed of questioning is greater in telephone interviews than in in-person interviews, but he also observes that the faster pace is linked to shorter answers to open-ended questions. Aside from cutting down on the travel time required for in-person interviews, using the telephone results in slightly shorter actual interview events. Groves (1989) estimates that questionnaires administered over the telephone take 10 to 20 percent less time than the same questionnaires administered in person. Speed in gathering the data required in some research other than opinion surveys is also faster when the telephone is used.

In the 1990s, computer-assisted telephone interviewing and computer-assisted personal interviewing increased the efficiency of telephone interviewing (see Couper and Hansen, Chapter 10, this volume). These techniques increase efficiency because the use of computers eliminates the researcher's need to generate a sampling pool, reduces noncoverage and nonresponse errors, reduces measurement errors associated with the wording of the questionnaire and the questioner's language, and assists in the data processing of the responses.

◆ Advantages of In-Person Interviewing

In contrast with the suggested advantages of telephone interviewing, the following advantages of face-to-face interviewing over in-person interviewing have been reported.

More accurate responses owing to contextual naturalness. Naturalness comes in many shapes. What is natural in most people's use of language is the freedom to introduce topics, change the subject, interrupt, and otherwise speak in the way they do in most of their everyday conversations. Answering questions posed by an interviewer is also natural, but because most people spend very little of their talking lives being interviewed, such language behavior occupies a very minor part of their existence. This explains, in part, why many people freeze up when asked questions by teachers, physicians, or lawyers.

The problem of a lack of naturalness in telephone interviewing may not be in the telephone per se, given that much of everyday telephone conversation is not a series of questions and answers. If the in-person interview consists of only the same questions and answers that are exchanged by telephone, little is gained in terms of adapting to the more natural mode of language interaction. But face-to-face interaction compels more small talk, politeness routines, joking, nonverbal communication, and asides in which people can more fully express their humanity. And naturalness leads to open expression and comfort.

Recent research on interviewing in various professional settings, such as law (Conley and O'Barr 1998) and medicine (Roberts 1999), shows that when the goal is to elicit accurate information, natural conversation and narrative discourse are preferable to more rigid question-and-answer approaches. Judges, lawyers, and physicians often object to this notion, claiming that their time is too precious for them to wait for information to be unfolded before them in a way that is preferred by, and more natural to, witnesses and patients. Thus in the courts and in doctors' offices, natural conversation is normally subordinated to a more rigid question-and-answer format. The focus on what the lawyer or doctor wants to know, in the manner and sequence the lawyer or doctor wants it to unfold, seldom allows for witnesses or patients to tell their own stories. The above-cited researchers make a compelling case that the necessary and accurate information sought by the courts and doctors using a rigid question-and-answer format is not always revealed.

Greater likelihood of self-generated answers. It is the nature of questions to influence responses. For example, a tag question such as "You voted for Jones, didn't you?" gives the respondent very little latitude to disagree. Even yes/no questions influence answers, because they set the boundaries of answers to only two possibilities and assume that a simple yes or no represents the variability of responses that all people have. "Wh-" (what, who, what, where, when) questions are somewhat less influential, although they still focus the area of response on only the what, who, when, or where of the question, whereas the respondent may be more concerned about other things that these questions rules out. Open-ended questions influence answers the least, because they give respondents considerable leeway to take their answers wherever they want. Perhaps out of necessity, telephone interviewing tends to employ highly structured, closed-ended questions. To be sure, in-person interviews can also fall into this same pattern, asking only questions that focus the respondent on issues that are of concern to the interviewer. The virtue of the in-person interview, however, is that it has the context potential of simulating natural everyday conversation; a respondent may provide more than brief, underdeveloped answers to an interviewer's questions. The face-to-face approach encourages more self-generated responses.

Symmetrical distribution of interactive power. One of the characteristics of everyday conversation (as opposed to most interviews) is that it is mutually interactive. Both parties have the opportunity to raise topics, request clarification, change the subject, interrupt, and otherwise act conversationally normal. When one person is the designated question asker, the power of the interaction clearly falls to that person. The respondent is thus placed in a subordinate relationship to the questioner. Although question asking is central to interviewing and may have all the advantages noted above, including economy of the researcher's time, standardization of questions, and uniformity and sequencing of questions to avoid ordering effects, it also has the clear disadvantage of lack of naturalness and unequal distribution of interactive power. Just as patients and pupils who are questioned by physicians and teachers have little or no interactive power, so respondents in interviews are placed in a subordinate position. Again, not all face-to-face interviews avoid this problem, for if the in-person interaction is framed only as a version of the same questioning found in telephone interviews, little may be gained in terms of sharing power. But the face-to-face interview at least has the potential of escaping such asymmetry, largely because the in-person setting is more clearly like that of two people in everyday conversation than is the telephone interview. People expect different things from different modes of interaction.

Greater effectiveness with complex issues. When the topic of research involves issues

that require complex questions and answers, it is often more difficult to accomplish interviews over the telephone. As Paul Lavrakas (1993) notes, "It is tiresome to keep the average person on the telephone for longer than 20-30 minutes, especially for many senior citizens" (p. 6). Once again, one cause of such impatience is the absence of interactive naturalness. Whereas people do not become as fatigued or impatient in face-to-face settings, 20 minutes can seem like a long time on the telephone. When an interview requires the respondent to review documents, as in an administrative hearing interview, for example, use of the telephone can be a distinct disadvantage.

Better for older or hearing-impaired respondents. Even though some hearing-impaired individuals now have telephones equipped with amplification devices, this does not resolve all the communication issues raised by telephone interviewing. For example, linguists have found that average persons, regardless of hearing acuity, avoid requesting clarification or repetition as long as possible in conversation, choosing instead to infer meaning in the hope that they will eventually figure out what the other person has said. In the face-to-face interview, visual clues to a respondent's puzzlement or difficulty in understanding are available to the interviewer, who can then clarify without the respondent's needing to make an embarrassing request for him or her to do so.

On the other hand, A. Regula Herzog and Willard Rogers (1988), in a survey of older Americans on issues of politics, attitudes, health, well-being, and life satisfaction, found almost no difference in response distribution obtained from telephone and in-person interviews. In this study, respondents in two age groups, over 60 and under 60, were first interviewed face-to-face and then reinterviewed by telephone, so that the researchers could compare the two modes across age levels. Herzog and Rogers admit, however, that the older respondents were given more help by the interviewers in the telephone mode than they received face-to-face (see also Wenger, Chapter 6, this volume).

More thoughtful responses. Some researchers have noted that the faster pace of telephone interviews leads to less thoughtful responses (Sykes and Collins 1988). Again, the absence of visual clues is central. In face-to-face interaction there are many visual signs to encourage respondents to elaborate, clarify, or amend what they say. These visual signs are not available by telephone.

More accurate results owing to lower interviewer workload. Lavrakas (1993) asserts that the workload of telephone interviewers is higher than that of face-to-face interviewers, leading to less efficiency and less accurate results. A 20-minute telephone interview is more exhausting for both respondent and interviewer than is a 20-minute face-to-face meeting.

Better response rates. Some researchers have found that response rates for telephone interviews are typically lower than those for in-person interviews (Thornberry 1987; Lavrakas 1993; Groves and Kahn 1979; Groves, Miller, and Cannell 1987). Lavrakas (1993), in fact, notes a constant decrease in telephone response rates over the past two decades. Some effort has been made to increase telephone response rates with callbacks, but this actually can backfire by increasing the refusal rate and, in callback cases where the respondent agrees to respond, tends to result in inferior data.

Noting that there is lower cooperation on the telephone than in in-person interviews, Groves (1979) found that face-to-face respondents preferred the in-person interview, whereas fewer telephone respondents said they preferred to be interviewed over the telephone. To help assure the cooperation of respondents in telephone interviews, Groves (1979) suggests

that "perhaps the first few moments of the interaction should be designed to request no information but rather to attempt to develop trust of the interviewer by the respondent" (p. 204). This sounds very much like advice to engage in the kind of natural, everyday conversation that helps reduce asymmetrical power of the interactants discussed earlier.

Better for marginalized respondents. William Aquilino and Leonard LoSciuto (1990) found that whereas telephone and in-person interviews of white respondents concerning drug use yielded about the same responses, African Americans gave higher estimations of their marijuana and alcohol consumption in the face-to-face mode than over the telephone. There was no substantive difference between the modes, however, in questions about tobacco use, suggesting that the more sensitive the question, the more African Americans differ in their responses in the two modes of interviews. In an earlier study measuring depression among residents of Los Angeles, Carol Aneshensel and her associates (1982) found that both African Americans and Hispanics reported less depression in telephone interviews than they did in face-to-face contacts. Apparently there are different social norms among different ethnic groups about which researchers should be aware when they are planning interview research.

In his edited volume comparing National Center for Health Statistics face-to-face survey data with the Survey Research Center's telephone surveys on health issues, Owen Thornberry (1987) concludes that the lower response rates for telephone interviewing correlate with the poorly educated, younger adults, and the elderly. In a comparison of nine national surveys (five conducted in person and four by telephone), Herzog, Rodgers, and Richard Kulka (1983) found that the telephone surveys underrepresented elderly people, who were less likely to participate by telephone and were more likely to experience the telephone interview as lengthier than the in-person mode.

Better for research involving sensitive questions. Groves and Robert Kahn (1979) suggest that in the telephone mode there may be less likelihood that respondents will cast their answers to sensitive or threatening questions in the most positive light, despite the fact that the reason for this may be that telephone responses are usually briefer than in-person ones. In surveys conducted following both telephone and in-person interviews, Groves and Kahn found that a larger proportion of telephone respondents reported uneasiness about answering items on such topics as income, racial attitudes, income tax returns, health, jobs, voting behavior, and political opinions. In the case of questions about income, for example, the nonresponse rate was between two and three times greater in the telephone interviews than in the in-person interviews. It is difficult to reconcile these two rather conflicting findings about responses to sensitive questions.

In contrast, Aquilino (1994) reports that respondents in his survey of 18- to 45-year-olds in Los Angeles varied in their admissions to using illicit drugs. He found the respondents more likely to admit using marijuana, cocaine, or crack in face-to-face interviews than over the telephone. But he also found relatively similar admission rates about alcohol abuse in both modes. Perhaps the most interesting finding of Aquilino's research is that there are apparent degrees of sensitivity, with drug use being the strongest and other topics, such as alcohol abuse, less so. He concludes that confidentiality and trust factors appear to be harder for respondents to judge on the telephone. The results of this study contrast with those of an earlier survey of drinking behavior in Great Britain, in which the researchers found that telephone interviews revealed greater amounts of alcohol consumption than did face-to-face interviews (Sykes and Collins 1988).

Timothy Johnson, J. Hougland, and R. Clayton (1989) report a similar finding among college students who were asked questions about substance abuse in telephone and face-to-face modes. The students were much more open in their responses when interviewed in person. In a follow-up report, the researchers note that there were few differences in the students' reports of their use of nonillegal substances, such as tobacco and alcohol, by either males or females, but males were not as likely to report substance abuse over the telephone, suggesting that telephone interviews are not as reliable for such topics (Johnson, Hougland, and Moore 1991). On the other hand, female respondents were found to be less likely to agree to be interviewed in person about their drug use.

◆ Weighing the Advantages and Disadvantages

In the preceding sections, I have tried to indicate that a researcher's decision to carry out telephone versus face-to-face interviewing should depend on the nature of the requirements of the task, the type and depth of the responses desired, the relative need for standardization of questions, the need for cost-efficiency, the complexity of the information required, and the overall identity and makeup of the respondents.

With perhaps some justification, most comparisons of telephone interviewing and in-person interviewing have focused on the researcher's skills and on the effectiveness and standardness of the questionnaire. These are, of course, important considerations, not to be treated lightly. It is apparent, however, that most research comparing these two modes has not focused on variations in respondents' uses of language. As noted earlier, every communication is made up of a sender, a message, and a receiver. Focusing on the sender and the message covers only two-thirds of the communicative triad, whether the interviewing is conducted by telephone or in person. Traditional interview research often overlooks the receiver, with the exception of demographic information gathered before or during the interview. But such a broad demographic picture says nothing about the respondent's personal or social interactional needs, styles, patterns, or preferences. If these are discovered at all, it is during the course of the interview, often when it may be too late for the researcher to make use of the information.

Because the approaches of survey research consider the respondent and the answer to a given question to be the salient units of analysis, it would seem all the more likely that the individual and group variability of respondents should be more deeply probed, even when economic considerations make it difficult for the researcher to consider any mode of interviewing other than the telephone.

Researchers in other fields, such as anthropology, linguistics, law enforcement, medicine, and some of the other social sciences are often more concerned with variability of responses, especially those that are natural and self-generated rather than induced by a standard questionnaire. In these fields the face-to-face interview is generally considered appropriate, at least for the initial basic research. Once a researcher has found general patterns of specific answer features in smaller populations through in-person interviews, it is sometimes then useful to test these features on a larger population by telephone. For example, William Labov (1982) carried out a number of individual face-to-face interviews with a sample of the New York City population in an effort to determine the diagnostic features of New York City speech. Once he discovered salient distinctive features through these interviews, he extended his population through telephone interviews with a larger number of New Yorkers, focusing only on these few selected features.

◆ *A Case Study*

The following case study shows how all three members of the sender-message-receiver triad can be examined in the interview process. It also provides some evidence of the role of gender differences in both the interviewer and the interviewee, and the advantages of in-person interviewing for getting better responses to sensitive items, reducing the social distance between interviewer and respondent, and letting respondents self-generate what is on their minds.

In 1970, the U.S. Supreme Court held that a person's statutory entitlement to welfare benefits cannot be terminated without a predetermination interview hearing, which would satisfy the requirement of due process (*Goldberg v. Kelly* 1970). Since that time, more and more of the requirements of government agencies have come under due process protection. This means that an individual recipient of benefits can request an agency interview concerning any loss or reduction of his or her benefits. The agency conducts such an interview both to comply with the rulings and to be fair to the beneficiary—to provide the beneficiary the opportunity to challenge the agency's decision and to supplement or explain the information on which the agency has based its decision.

As early as 1987, Medicare's proposal to substitute telephone hearings for in-person interviews in terminating benefits met stiff opposition from Congress, attorneys for the elderly, and the Association of Administrative Law Judges. The concerns of Congress ultimately led to the defeat of the proposal. By the 1990s, however, things had changed and Medicare Part B hearings began to be conducted in both telephone and in-person interviews, depending on the wishes of the beneficiaries, but still without the research that Congress had found lacking in the 1980s. Concern over this lack of research, coupled with a suspicion that older Medicare recipients might not be being treated fairly or accurately, led the Senior Citizens Law Center (SCLC) to propose a comparison of whatever extant tape recordings of telephone hearing interviews were available with in-person interviews (Shuy and Staton 1994; Shuy 1998).

Interviewing in practical work contexts, of necessity perhaps, needs to stress respondent conduct and well-being as much as interviewer behavior. In the case study material, however, those who managed the interviewing in question appeared to be somewhat undecided about whether to switch from conventional in-person interviewing to telephone interviewing, primarily for economic considerations. The growing number of established in-person interview hearings required by law became an issue of cost-effectiveness. Some bureaucrats argued that the interviews could be carried out by telephone. Unfortunately, there was no research evidence that various agencies could consult to find out what they would gain or lose by switching from an in-person to a telephone mode. Nevertheless, various agencies of the federal and state governments began encouraging the use of the telephone for hearing interviews, although they left the final choices to their regional or local offices. Some interviewers chose the telephone; some chose to continue interviewing in person. Fortunately, tape recordings were made of a small sample of the telephone interviews, so that it was possible to compare these with observed in-person events. The following describes an effort made by the SCLC (in association with the Gray Panthers) to answer the question of which mode would be most appropriate for Medicare Part B interviews (Shuy 1998).

DESIGN AND PURPOSE OF THE STUDY

The research design of this study hardly qualifies as rigorous. It was possible to locate 17 previously tape-recorded telephone interviews for comparison with 8 concur-

rently tape-recorded in-person interviews. No effort could be made to be random or representative. The 25 beneficiaries were from California, Iowa, Oregon, Maryland, and Virginia. The interviews were carried out by 11 female and 7 male hearing officers.

Issues that commonly concern traditional researchers comparing the two modes of interviewing were not foremost in this study. This research was not concerned with determining a profile of the recipients' attitudes, beliefs, or knowledge. Instead, the goal was to assess such issues as fairness of treatment, the comfort of both parties, and their mutual understanding of the success or failure of the interview. To accomplish these goals, the research examined the language and communicative styles of the various participants. In short, the focus was to determine, for both the interviewers and the beneficiaries, how communicative language and style differ between telephone and in-person interviews. The type and purpose of the interviews were held constant. Also unlike past research on this topic, this study focused on the receiver of the message as well as the sender and the message itself. Of particular importance were the issues of how and if clients were permitted to present their own agendas, whether they had conversational rights, whether they were being listened to and treated fairly, and the extent to which status, age, and gender of the respondents and interviewers affected the quality of the interviews.

Such research questions are very different from issues of standardization of questionnaire and interviewer uniformity. To a lesser extent, interviewer bias was observable in this study, but not in the same way that past research has described. Underlying the study, of course, was the important question of cost-effectiveness, for this was the government's concern in the first place. It was assumed from the outset that it is less expensive to do telephone interviews than to carry out individual meetings, but at what cost to the beneficiaries and at what cost to accuracy of the transmission and exchange of information?

Applying the research discussed previously concerning the advantages of both telephone and face-to-face interviewing, I summarize the results of this study below. It should be noted, however, that among the advantages of telephone interviewing mentioned above, those related to interviewer bias, standardization of questionnaire, response rates, and safety of the interviewer are not relevant for comparison, for various reasons. Interviewer monitoring was not possible in this context, nor did a standard questionnaire exist. Response rates are irrelevant, because the beneficiaries initiated the interviews. And the safety of the interviewer was not an issue here, whether the interviews were conducted by telephone or in person.

ACHIEVING COST- AND TIME-EFFICIENCY

Contrary to the literature reporting that in-person interviews take longer than those done by telephone, no substantive elapsed time difference was found between the two modes in this study. In two of the telephone interviews, the beneficiary was represented by an attorney, and these interviews took longer than interviews with beneficiaries alone. But even including these two interviews, there was no substantive difference between telephone and in-person modes in the time taken to complete interviews.

It is likely that the cost of in-person interviews for administrative hearings is somewhat greater than that of telephone interviews, simply because of the time required for travel to the designated interview location (usually a Social Security office). But there was no distinguishable difference in elapsed time for the interviews themselves between the telephone and in-person modes.

ENSURING INTERVIEWER UNIFORMITY

Surprisingly, the greatest uniformity found among interviewers was based on gender, both of the interviewer and of the interviewee. Female telephone interviewers were consistent in reframing the interview from the formal to the informal register, in making use of language markers of the informal register (such as address forms, contractions, personal comments, feedback markers, and varying intonation patterns), in being polite through indirectness rather than directness, in making use of positive speech acts such as advising (males tended to use the more negative speech act of warning), in avoiding challenges to the beneficiary, in sharing power rather than exploiting it, in avoiding power asymmetry (by not using the first-person pronoun *I* and by avoiding *my* statements), in letting the beneficiary generate his or her own story, in avoiding displays of authority and knowledge, and in taking the beneficiary's perspective. This practice by the female interviewers contrasted sharply with that of the male interviewers, but *only* in the telephone interviews. In the face-to-face interviews, male interviewers used the language forms just noted in approximately the same manner as the female interviewers. This suggests something very interesting about the use of the telephone mode. Female interviewers seemed to be more comfortable with it than males and used it to accomplish most of the agency's stated goals for the interaction, whereas male interviewers accomplished these goals best in face-to-face interactions.

The gender of the beneficiary was also noteworthy in terms of uniformity. When females interviewed female beneficiaries, the above-noted language features were symmetrically distributed. But when males interviewed male beneficiaries by telephone, these features were even more conspicuously sparse. Power, including language power, was evident in the language of the male interviewers, and even more so when male interviewers spoke with male beneficiaries rather than with female beneficiaries. Male interviewers appeared to be concerned with winning disputed points, defending mistakes of the agency, and challenging the points made by the male beneficiaries. Interestingly, the quantity of power moves made by male interviewers was lower when male interviewers met with male or female beneficiaries face-to-face. This contrast would suggest that male interviewers are more likely to use the language advantages of the female interviewers when engaged in face-to-face interviewing, but much less so in telephone exchanges.

GETTING RESPONSES TO SENSITIVE QUESTIONS

Groves and Kahn (1979) found that in telephone surveys, direct questions about income yield the largest missing-data rates in the research. To reduce this problem, they suggest that interviewers use an unfolding procedure when respondents are reluctant to provide exact income figures, in which respondents are asked to indicate into which one of three broad income categories their incomes fall. But even with this unfolding technique, the proportion of missing data on such questions is still higher in telephone surveys than in face-to-face interviews.

Why is it that in-person interviewing yields better response rates on more sensitive items than the telephone approach? For one thing, physical presence is naturally more intimate, even for people meeting for the first time, than is nonpresent telephone communication. The personal distancing from intimacy found in telephone interviewing has advantages. For example, small talk is less necessary, saving valuable interview time. On the other hand, there can be no doubt that physical presence provides the interviewer with a larger inventory of communicative tools, including those that allow the type of inti-macy that promotes answers to sensitive questions. In addition, physical presence makes obvious the answers to some sensitive questions, such as those involving the respondent's physical and/or emotional state, and so eliminate the interviewer's need to ask; such answers are also difficult for respondents to refute with vague or inaccurate responses.

Another advantage of in-person interviewing is that physical presence makes available obvious communicative clues to the respondent's confusion, reluctance to answer, or discomfort, enabling the interviewer to rephrase a question or reframe the context in order to convert a no-answer response into a salvageable answer. This advantage was especially obvious in this study, where instances of respondents' confusion or anger were mitigated in the personal interviews much better than in the telephone mode. Once again, however, it should be noted that female telephone interviewers were much better at this than male telephone interviewers. Of course, if the point of the research is to follow the set questionnaire exactly, this is not an advantage after all.

OBTAINING CONTEXTUAL NATURALNESS

It is easy to overlook the obvious fact that the interview is only one of the many types of human communication. People engage actively in different types of communication daily, such as talk between friends and family members, talk between strangers, and talk with providers of goods and services. In most of these talking events the participants are more or less equal in power, status, and knowledge. The interview event, simply because one person asks all the questions, is fraught with the asymmetry of power. As such, it is a marked communicative episode in the respondent's day of otherwise symmetrical talk.

It would seem reasonable that interviewers would want to reduce this asymmetry as much as possible, especially because the interview is so different from the respondent's daily communication patterns. In the conventional interview event, power, status, and knowledge reside in the questioner, not in the respondent. In the administrative interviews in this study, the beneficiaries were supplicants, requesting redress for what they considered to be unfair treatment by the agency. They were the subordinates and the interviewers were the superordinates. In short, the interviews had a high probability of unequal role assignment.

Some of the administrative interviews met the agency's goal of permitting the beneficiaries to supplement or explain information in a fair way that could produce a more accurate picture of their situations. Others did not. The language of the more successful interviews can be characterized as producing an informal conversational style, sharing or giving up perceived power, letting the respondents self-generate topics, defusing the legal format, taking the beneficiary's perspective, and avoiding displays of knowledge (Shuy 1998). These qualities permitted respondents to initiate their own topics, disagree, give directives, and even ask questions. In short, the more successful interviewers reframed and reformatted the conventional question-answer interview to make the interview event more like the type of everyday conversation with which respondents were familiar, recontextualizing it and making it more natural to them. They took the respondents' perspectives and made them feel important. These interviewers let the beneficiaries be teachers while the interviewers took on the role of learners, adopting what some fieldworkers have called the "one down" position (Agar 1980).

SELF-GENERATING RESPONSES

In the hearing interviews that met the agency's goal—unveiling the respondents'

perceived new and important information as accurately and fairly as possible—the interviewers permitted, even encouraged, the respondents to bring up whatever topics they wanted, ask any questions they wanted, and otherwise talk as they might in natural, everyday conversation. It is clear that the open-ended question was highly valued as a topic introducer, with "wh-" questions used as follow-ups. For example, the female interviewers began with open-ended requests such as "Tell me anything that you would like to help me make a decision in your favor" and "I will give you the floor and you go on into what it is you wish to give me." As a side note, even when male telephone interviewers employed open-ended questions, they often posed them negatively; for example, "Why do you disagree with the denial you got from the agency?" This question, although open-ended, appears to reflect the competitive approach of the male interviewers who conducted their interviews by telephone. Curiously enough, this competitive aspect was far less evident among the male interviewers in the face-to-face mode.

One might predict that encouraging self-generated responses from interviewees would greatly extend the duration of the interviews, but as it turned out, this did not happen, except in two telephone interviews in which beneficiaries were accompanied and represented by attorneys. Those interviews took on the formulaic interview context of the courtroom, where information is unwrapped slowly and in a fashion comfortable only to lawyers. The beneficiaries in those cases played very minor roles in the interviews.

DISTRIBUTING POWER EQUALLY

Respondents' lack of power in many interview situations can be intimidating to them, and can often result in their providing imperfect, ambiguous, incomplete, or otherwise unsuccessful representations of their actual knowledge and opinions.

When interviewers permit respondents to participate in setting the agenda, to ask questions, and to change the direction of things, they surrender personal power and help to distribute power more equally between the participants.

But there is also more that interviewers can do to ensure symmetry of power, whether interviewing by telephone or in person. For example, an interviewer can make explicit statements about how important the interviewee is, tactfully demonstrating the equal status of respondent and interviewer; some of the hearing officers in this study took this approach. One positive way for an interviewer to promote equality, as noted above, is to use casual, conversational language rather than the normally more formal interview language. The use of casual address forms, contractions, added personal comments, abundant feedback markers (such as "uh-huh" uttered during responses), and conversational intonation aids this endeavor.

One significant finding of this case study is that the interviewers who managed to share power and take the perspective of the respondent were able to elicit necessary information faster and more completely than were those who did not do so. Among the remarks the interviewers made that show this perspective taking are the following:

I can appreciate your point that you've done everything you could to find out what the guidelines were and to adhere to them.

Sometimes that's the only route that you have open to you.

I can understand that since your doctor prescribed it, you feel that you know your condition.

There are also status pitfalls that interviewers can avoid, such as the use of "I" power statements ("I want you to . . ." or "I'll send you a . . . ,"); interviewers can sub-stitute passive-voice equivalents for such statements. Once again, this study revealed that male interviewers used "I" power statements far more frequently on the telephone (but not in person) than did female interviewers, suggesting a mode weakness of the telephone interview, at least for male interviewers.

ADDRESSING COMPLEX ISSUES

In the interviews conducted in this study, it was sometimes necessary for the participants to refer to previous correspondence and/or regulations found in beneficiary handbooks. When this happened during telephone interviews, interviewers and respondents spent considerable time trying to locate documents or to refer to exact pages. When a beneficiary did not have the necessary documents at hand, the interviewer had to read relevant passages aloud. This increased the time spent and introduced the additional problem of the comprehensibility of orally read materials. Interviews that did not require such searches for documentation were smooth and quick, often taking no longer than 20 or 30 minutes. When such problems arose, however, the interviews lasted up to 10 minutes longer. In contrast, during face-to-face interviews, the needed documents were immediately available for both parties to see and discuss on the spot, with little or no time added to the event.

DEALING WITH OLDER OR HANDICAPPED RESPONDENTS

In this study, the respondents were all older and/or handicapped, so a comparison between telephone and in-person interviewing is salient. In the telephone interviews, the interviewers had to ask more questions about the respondents' physical conditions than did interviewers in the in-person interviews. In addition, in-person interviewers were able to see whether hearing-impaired respondents were straining to hear what was being said and so could adjust the clarity and volume of their speech, often eliminating the respondents' need to request that they repeat questions.

◆ Related Studies of Practical Interviewing

Related research comparing telephone and in-person interviewing in the practical work context provides other information. In the 1970s, the California Unemployment Insurance Appeals Board (CUIAB) faced the problem of conducting interviews for applicants for benefits who had moved to another location, requiring split interviewing in two different sites. It was decided that experiments should be conducted to determine whether or not telephone interviews could replace this difficult task. After a lawsuit brought by an employee denied unemployment compensation had been rejected, the case was taken up the appeals ladder to the California Court of Appeals. The judge who wrote the decision supported the lower court's denial of the application, but continued to favor in-person interviews when possible (when the parties were within an hour's driving distance).

An entity called the Fair Hearing Project attempted to assist CUIAB by carrying out research on the reactions and attitudes of participants in both in-person and telephone hearing interviews. This study found that both interviewers and interviewees believed that the concerns about due process were met by the telephone interview, but, when asked to compare the two modes, the respondents were much less certain about their preference. Of the respondents surveyed, 44 percent felt that the telephone interviews provided a less extensive opportunity for the participants to question and rebut; 64 percent of the interviewers felt that telephone interviewing required more extensive preparation than the in-person mode, believed that the process of asking questions to obtain the necessary information was more difficult over the telephone, and felt that telephone hearings were more difficult to manage. A major conclusion of this research was that whenever possible, such interviews should be conducted in person (Corsi and Hurley 1979a). In a follow-up report, the researchers propose that the telephone might be substituted for in-person interviews in certain areas, especially when the claimant is represented by an attorney, but they still maintain that in-person interviews are preferable to telephone interviews (Corsi and Hurley 1979b).

Similar research by the Fair Hearing Project was carried out in the 1980s concerning a four-year study of telephone versus in-person interviewing for unemployment and welfare appeals in New Mexico (Corsi et al. 1984). It was found that appeals were more likely to be denied in telephone interviews and that the "somewhat artificial" setting caused by the telephone resulted in claimants' being less able to express themselves and more intimidated than in face-to-face interviews. Even so, 73.7 percent of the claimants reported being satisfied with the telephone interview, whereas 61.9 percent of those who were interviewed in person expressed such satisfaction. A clear conclusion of this study was that the telephone mode created savings in cost and time related to productivity improvement.

The partially conflicting findings of both the research of the Fair Hearing Project and the findings of the SCLC are due, at least in part, to the differences in what was studied and in the ages of the respondents. Whereas the SCLC (Gray Panther) study examined tape recordings of the actual language used by the parties, the Fair Housing Project concerned itself with self-reported reflections and feelings of the participants. Although both types of data can be useful, insights obtained from the actual language used during the interviewing event are seldom examined, nor were they by the Fair

Hearing Project. Likewise, the ages of the interviewees, although not reported, are another likely source of difference in findings. The younger respondents in the Fair Hearing Project were likely more familiar with using the telephone and possibly more comfortable with telephone interviewing than were the senior citizen respondents in the SCLC interviews.

◆ Summary of Relative Benefits

I began this chapter by saying that different kinds of interviews use different criteria for success and that the decision to interview by telephone or face-to-face depends on many factors. It is not my purpose to claim that one mode is better than the other for research interviewing. Factors of expedience, cost, and time may dictate the mode to be used, despite whatever else may be compromised in the process. My purpose, rather, is to point out the relative benefits of both modes and to make as clear as possible the advantages and disadvantages that are present. These can be summarized as follows:

◆ *Cost:* In most cases, research interviewing by telephone is less expensive than face-to-face interviewing.

◆ *Control:* Research has shown that situational variables are easier to control in telephone interviews than in face-to-face interviews.

◆ *Quantification of results:* For research that seeks specific responses to specific questions, telephone interviewing lends itself more readily to ease in coding and quantification of results. This is not to say that quantitative analysis is not possible with data collected in face-to-face interviews. Such analysis, however, is more difficult and time-consuming to manage, because responses are not given in a prescribed order, making eventual coding more time-consuming. Computer-assisted telephone interviewing makes such quantification even easier.

◆ *Completion time:* Although the time expended during face-to-face interviews is roughly equal to that expended during telephone interviews, in-person interviewing requires additional time for interviewers to make arrangements and travel to the interview sites.

◆ *Naturalness:* Advantages gained through telephone interviewing may be negated if it is important for the researcher to get the type of response accuracy provided by the everyday communication context found in face-to-face interaction.

◆ *Response rates:* From reports of past comparisons, it appears that better response rates are achieved in face-to-face interviewing than in telephone interviewing.

◆ *Thoughtfulness of responses:* If the goal is to probe deeply and to elicit thoughtful answers, then interviewers' letting respondents self-generate whatever is on their minds is superior to having probes controlled by a standardized set of questions, whether this is done in person or by telephone.

◆ *Complexity of issues:* Face-to-face interaction appears to be better suited than telephone interviewing for handling complex issues.

◆ *Marginalized respondents:* In-person interviewing is clearly superior to telephone interviewing with older, hearing-impaired, and minority respondents.

◆ *Sensitive questions:* Past research clearly shows that face-to-face interviews are better than telephone interviews for eliciting answers to the most sensitive questions, such as those concerning substance use, personal income, and sometimes even drinking patterns.

◆ Unresolved Issues

A number of issues remain unresolved concerning the advantages and disadvantages of telephone and in-person interviewing. As noted above, relatively little research has been done on the actual language used in interviews conducted in either mode. Researchers have looked at summaries of respondents' answers and at respondent attitudes, but few have undertaken detailed analyses of the ways interviewers and interviewees talk during interviews (see Schaeffer and Maynard, Chapter 11, this volume). Representations of attitudes, knowledge, and beliefs are always interesting self-report information, but such data are still at least a step away from much of the information discoverable in the actual language interaction. A good way for researchers to discover this information is by studying audiotapes of the spoken language and, if possible, videotapes of nonverbal aspects of in-person interviews. Because language goes by so fast and is so complex, researchers interested in studying language use in interviews will need to record interviews on video- or audiotape and then review the tapes many times for different features. Although the gap here is beginning to be filled, missing in most of the existing research comparing the two modes of interviewing is attention to the respondents' language and comfort. Perhaps it is only natural that research on interviewing would start with the sender of the message and the message itself. But with the knowledge that has been accumulated thus far, it is now important for researchers to give more attention to the receiver of the interviewer's questions.

For researchers to know exactly what they may be missing or gaining when they carry out telephone interviews rather than in-person interviews, they need reliable information based on detailed comparisons between the two modes. Also, in light of the findings of the research on the power of questioning cited above, it would be useful for future research to compare the advantages of highly structured, standardized question sequences with the responses obtained through freer and more natural forms of discourse. If the experience of linguistics and anthropology is in any way helpful, it may show that respondents who give single answers to directed interview questions may respond quite differently if given the chance to generate their own information. Realizing that the collaborative nature of communication is compromised when the major role of one party is to answer the questions of another (Cicourel 1964; Holstein and Staples 1992), we need to know more about how telephone and face-to-face interviewing each suit this human condition.

Finally, we need to know considerably more about the role of gender in interviewing. Some past research has pointed out gender differences in respondents, particularly with respect to sensitive topics, such as substance abuse (Cahalan 1968; Johnson et al. 1991; Murphy and Binson 1988). In a consumer attitude survey, Groves and Nancy Fultz (1985) analyzed the effects of interviewer gender on response rates and found that female interviewers were more successful at getting responses than were male interviewers. However, the results were confounded, as Groves and Fultz admit, by the fact that the male interviewers were less experienced than the females. In any case, the sole focus was on response rate rather than on quality or type of response. Judson Landis, Daryl Sullivan, and Joseph Sheley (1973), in analyzing questions about women's rights, found that male interviewers got more feminist responses from female respondents than did female interviewers. It is clear that some question topics elicit responses that vary depending on the gender of the interviewer. It would be useful to know more about how gender-based responses are the same or different in telephone versus in-person interview contexts.

■ *References*

Agar, M. 1980. *The Professional Stranger: An Informal Introduction to Ethnography.* New York: Academic Press.

Aneshensel, C. S., R. R. Fredrichs, V. A. Clark, and P. A. Yokopenic. 1982. "Measuring Depression in the Community: A Comparison of Telephone and Personal Interviews." *Public Opinion Quarterly* 46:110-21.

Aquilino, W. S. 1994. "Interview Mode Effects in Surveys of Drug and Alcohol Use: A Field Experiment." *Public Opinion Quarterly* 58:210-40.

Aquilino, W. S. and L. A. LoSciuto. 1990. "Effects of Interview Mode on Self-Reported Drug Use." *Public Opinion Quarterly* 54:362-95.

Brown, R. 1973. *A First Language: The Early Stages.* Cambridge, MA: Harvard University Press.

Cahalan, D. 1968. "Correlates of Respondent Accuracy in the Denver Validity Survey." *Public Opinion Quarterly* 32:606-21.

Cicourel, A. V. 1964. *Method and Measurement in Sociology.* New York: Free Press.

Conley, J. M. and W. M. O'Barr. 1998. *Just Words: Law, Language, and Power.* Chicago: University of Chicago Press.

Corsi, J. R. and T. L. Hurley. 1979a. "Attitudes toward the Use of the Telephone in Administrative Fair Hearings: The California Experience." *Administrative Law Review* 31:247-83.

———. 1979b. "Pilot Study Report on the Use of the Telephone in Administrative Fair Hearings." *Administrative Law Review* 31:485-524.

Corsi, J. R., L. B. Rosenfeld, G. D. Fowler, K. E. Newcomer, D. C. Niekerk, and J. D. Bell. 1984. "Major Findings of the New Mexico Experiment of Teleconferenced Administrative Fair Hearings." *University of Miami Law Review* 38:647-55.

de Leeuw, E. D. and J. van der Zouwen. 1988. "Data Quality in Telephone and Face-to-Face Surveys: A Comparative Meta-analysis." Pp. 283-300 in *Telephone Survey Methodology,* edited by R. M. Groves, P. P. Biemer, L. E. Lyberg, J. T. Massey, W. L. Nicholls II, and J. Waksberg. New York: John Wiley.

Frey, J. H. 1989. *Survey Research by Telephone.* 2d ed. Newbury Park, CA: Sage.

Goldberg v. Kelly, 397 U.S. 254 (1970).

Groves, R. M. 1978. "On the Mode of Administering a Questionnaire and Responses to Open-Ended Items." *Social Science Research* 7:257-71.

———. 1979. "Actors and Questions in Telephone and Personal Interview Surveys." *Public Opinion Quarterly* 43:190-205.

———. 1989. *Survey Errors and Survey Costs.* New York: John Wiley.

Groves, R. M. and N. H. Fultz. 1985. "Gender Effects among Telephone Interviewers in a Survey of Economic Attitudes." *Sociological Methods & Research* 14:31-52.

Groves, R. M. and R. L. Kahn. 1979. *Surveys by Telephone: A National Comparison with Personal Interviews.* New York: Academic Press.

Groves, R. M., P. V. Miller, and C. F. Cannell. 1987. "Differences between the Telephone and Personal Interview Data." Pp. 11-19 in *An Experimental Comparison of Telephone and Personal Health Interview Surveys* (Vital and Health Statistics Series 2, Data Evaluation and Methods Research, No. 106), edited by O. T. Thornberry. Hyattsville, MD: U.S. Department of Health and Human Services.

Herzog, A. R. and W. L. Rodgers. 1988. "Interviewing Older Adults: Mode Comparison Using Data from a Face-to-Face Survey and a Telephone Resurvey." *Public Opinion Quarterly* 52:84-99.

Herzog, A. R., W. L. Rodgers, and R. A. Kulka. 1983. "Interviewing Older Adults: A Comparison of Telephone and Face-to-Face Modalities." *Public Opinion Quarterly* 47:405-18.

Holstein, J. A. and J. F. Gubrium. 1995. *The Active Interview.* Thousand Oaks, CA: Sage.

Holstein, J. A. and W. G. Staples. 1992. "Producing Evaluative Knowledge: The Interactional Bases of Social Science Findings." *Sociological Inquiry* 62:11-35.

Johnson, T. P., J. G. Hougland, and R. R. Clayton. 1989. "Obtaining Reports of Sensitive Behavior: A Comparison of Substance Use Reports from Telephone and Face-to-Face Interviews." *Social Science Quarterly* 70:174-83.

Johnson, T. P., J. G. Hougland, and R. W. Moore. 1991. "Sex Differences in Reporting Sensitive Behavior: A Comparison of Interview Methods." *Sex Roles* 24:669-80.

Jordan, L. A., A. C. Marcus, and L. G. Reeder. 1980. "Response Styles in Telephone and Household Interviewing: A Field Experiment." *Public Opinion Quarterly* 44:210-22.

Labov, W. A. 1982. *The Social Stratification of English in New York City.* Washington, DC: Center for Applied Linguistics.

Landis, J. R. 1973. "Feminist Attitudes as Related to Sex of Interviewer." *Pacific Sociological Review* 16:305-14.

Lavrakas, P. J. 1993. *Telephone Survey Methods: Sampling, Selection, and Supervision.* 2d ed. Newbury Park, CA: Sage.

Murphy, P. A. and D. Binson. 1988. "Who Says 'No' to Whom: Respondent Interaction in Refusal to Sensitive Questions." Presented at the annual meeting of the American Association of Public Opinion Research, Toronto.

Oksenberg, L. and C. F. Cannell. 1988. "Effects of Interviewer Vocal Characteristics on Nonresponse." Pp. 257-69 in *Telephone Survey Methodology,* edited by R. M. Groves, P. P. Biemer, L. E. Lyberg, J. T. Massey, W. L. Nicholls II, and J. Waksberg. New York: John Wiley.

Roberts, F. D. 1999. *Talking about Treatment: Recommendations for Breast Cancer Adjuvant Therapy.* New York: Oxford University Press.

Shuy, R. W. 1998. *Bureaucratic Language in Government and Business.* Washington, DC: Georgetown University Press.

Shuy, R. W. and J. J. Staton. 1994. "A Linguistic Comparison of Telephone and In-Person Hearings." Pp. 1-87 in *Telecommunications and Public Benefit Hearings,* edited by B. Brewer, A. J. Chiplin, Jr., and B. D. Fretz. Washington, DC: National Senior Citizens Law Center.

Stokes, L. and M.-Y. Yeh. 1988. "Searching for Causes of Interviewer Effects in Telephone Surveys." Pp. 357-62 in *Telephone Survey Methodology,* edited by R. M. Groves, P. P. Biemer, L. E. Lyberg, J. T. Massey, W. L. Nicholls II, and J. Waksberg. New York: John Wiley.

Sykes, W. and M. Collins. 1988. "Effects of Mode of Interview: Experiments in the UK." Pp. 301-20 in *Telephone Survey Methodology,* edited by R. M. Groves, P. P. Biemer, L. E. Lyberg, J. T. Massey, W. L. Nicholls II, and J. Waksberg. New York: John Wiley.

Thornberry, O. T., ed. 1987. *An Experimental Comparison of Telephone and Personal Health Interview Surveys* (Vital and Health Statistics Series 2, Data Evaluation and Methods Research, No. 106). Hyattsville, MD: U.S. Department of Health and Human Services.

10

COMPUTER-ASSISTED INTERVIEWING

◆ **Mick P. Couper**
Sue Ellen Hansen

Computer-assisted data collection methods are having a profound effect on survey interviewing. In this chapter we explore several themes related to this impact. Although computer-assisted telephone interviewing (CATI) has been around for several decades (see Shuy, Chapter 9, this volume), the revolution in survey methods began to be felt with the introduction of computer-assisted personal interviewing (CAPI) in the early 1990s (see Couper and Nicholls 1999). More recently, with the development of methods that reduce the role of the interviewer (e.g., audio computer-assisted self-interviewing) or eliminate the interviewer entirely (e.g., Web surveys), renewed attention has been focused on the role of the survey interviewer in an automated data collection environment. Despite major changes in the survey process over the past several years, only recently has research attention been

focused on the effects of the introduction of computers on the interviewing situation and on the role and task of the survey interviewer.

In this chapter we review the effects of the data collection revolution on survey interviewers and respondents. We explore how the work of interviewers has changed under computer-assisted interviewing (CAI). Our central thesis is that CAI and paper-and-pencil (P&P) surveys differ in many ways for both interviewers and respondents, and for the interaction between the two. This does not mean that one technology (paper or computer) is necessarily better than the other; rather, the two are qualitatively different. Furthermore, we believe that many of the effects of technology may be mediated by the particular design or implementation of a survey, rather than by fundamental features of the technology. These design differences may in turn reflect organizational philosophies (e.g., related to control of interviewers), constraints of particular software used (in the case of CAI), or design choices on the part of those implementing the survey (whether on paper on computer). To understand the effects of CAI on interviewers and respondents, it is important to understand the contexts in which particular survey instruments are created.

We begin with a brief review of the recent history of computer-assisted methods and their impacts on the survey endeavor. We then turn to an examination of the effects of the new technology on interviewers and on interactions between interviewers and respondents. We end with a discussion of some of the newer methods of data collection that includes some speculation on their possible impacts on the role of the survey interviewer.

We preface this discussion with a note that computer-assisted interviewing is widely viewed as a tool of standardized survey interviewing. In other words, CAI is seen as a means to ensure greater control over the interview process or to increase standardization. However, this is not an inherent feature of computer assistance, and instruments can be designed to provide interviewers with more (rather than less) flexibility (see, e.g., Conrad and Schober 1999; Belli, Shay, and Stafford 1999). It is not our goal to join this debate; we merely want to note that standardized interviewing is the dominant viewpoint from which CAI has been developed and evaluated.

◆ Computer-Assisted Interviewing Methods

Computer-assisted telephone interviewing, first used in 1971, was the earliest form of computer-based survey data collection to gain widespread use. Improved data quality was among the potential benefits that early proponents claimed for the new technol-

ogy. Such data quality was to come through (a) systematic control over the scheduling of calls and callbacks, (b) automatically tailored wording of complex questions based on prior responses, (c) computer-controlled branching between questions or sections of the instrument, (d) automatic range and consistency checks, and (e) careful monitoring of interviewer performance (Nicholls 1988). CATI also permitted study (and thereby control or improvement) of interviewer behavior and performance through its audio and video monitoring capabilities and automated call records (Couper and Nicholls 1999). Although these are now all standard features of most CAI surveys, the evidence of their effects on data quality is relatively modest.

Even before the advent of laptop computers, survey research realized the potential of extending computer assistance to face-to-face or personal-visit interviewing. In the late 1980s, computer-assisted personal interviewing was used for the first time in the Netherlands, and soon thereafter it was rapidly adopted in the United States and Europe. Today, most large-scale government and academic surveys in the United States are conducted using CAPI. During the progression from the early mainframe-based CATI days to PC-based CAPI systems, the software and interviewing systems became increasingly complex, to a point where many CAI surveys can no longer be replicated on paper. These complexities include features such as randomization of question order, tailored text (fills), on-line range and consistency checks, complex branching or skip instructions, links to external databases, on-line coding, and presentation of multimedia content. As a result, much of the development and testing effort has focused on program correctness or functionality rather than on optimal design from the interviewer's viewpoint, or usability.

Despite the rapid technological advances in survey data collection over the past few decades, most of the research has examined the quality of the resultant data rather than the process of data collection itself. For all the supposed benefits CAI was to bring in terms of data quality, a thorough review of the literature on data quality comparisons between CAI and paper-and-pencil interviewing led William Nicholls, Reginald Baker, and Jean Martin (1997) to conclude that data quality has been largely unaffected or only marginally improved by the introduction of CAI.

There are several indicators of data quality that researchers can examine to compare P&P and CAI methods. The first is the effect on skip errors. We should expect that, if the instrument is programmed correctly, skip errors would be eliminated in computer-assisted interviewing. In an early comparison of CATI and P&P, Robert Groves and Nancy Mathiowetz (1984) found that in one complex sequence of items (containing 28 questions and 42 possible paths), 1.8 percent of CATI entries were inappropriate, compared to 8.8 percent of non-CATI entries. Randy Olsen (1992), reporting results from the CAPI versus P&P experiment in round 12 of the National Longitudinal Survey—Youth Cohort, found that the percentage of invalid skips went from an already low 0.97 percent in P&P to 0.02 percent in CAPI. Gary Catlin and Susan Ingram (1988) compared discrepancy (or edit failure) rates between CATI and P&P in the Canadian Labor Force Survey. For the relatively straightforward household docket portion of the interview, the discrepancy rates were similar (0.7 percent in CATI and 0.6 percent in P&P), whereas for the more complex labor force questionnaire, the rates were significantly lower in CATI (1.8 percent in CATI, 4.6 percent in P&P). These findings suggest that the benefits of skip error or edit failure reductions in CAI are realized only when the instrument is very complex. Even so, these interviewer mistakes are not a large source of overall error in P&P surveys.

Given the evidence of general respondent indifference toward the technology used (which we will discuss later in this chapter), we would not expect large differences in the proportions of "don't know" and "refused" responses, and the research evidence bears this out. Groves and Mathiowetz (1984), for example, found comparable levels of item nonresponse for demographic and income questions in CATI and P&P. Jean Martin, Colm O'Muircheartaigh, and John Curtice (1993) similarly found proportions of "don't knows" and refusals to be identical in P&P and CAPI.

Another early concern in the transition to CAI was related to the length and quality of responses to open-ended questions. It was believed that interviewers could not type as fast as they could write. The evidence from comparisons on labor force surveys in France and Canada suggest these fears were unfounded. Bernard (1989) compared industry and occupation questions in CAPI and P&P and found no differences in the average length or number of words in the recorded responses. She also found identical coding rates for the two approaches. Catlin and Ingram (1988) obtained similar results in their comparison of CATI and P&P. Again, the conclusion of these studies is that CAI does no worse than paper-and-pencil interviewing.

A further source of initial concern was the possibility of keying errors associated with an interviewer's typing in a number to correspond with the selected answer in CAI, as opposed to checking a box in P&P. John Kennedy, Jennie Lengacher, and Loren Demerath (1990) found an average of only 0.62 percent keying errors over four CATI surveys, but did not collect comparable data from P&P surveys. Lynn Dielman and Mick Couper (1995) examined keying errors in a CAPI survey and found only 16 such errors out of more than 16,000 questions examined, for an error rate of 0.095 percent. James Lepkowski and his colleagues (1995) used behavior and error coding to examine responses to an even larger number of comparable CATI and P&P questions in the Panel Survey of Income Dynamics. They found recording error rates to be identical at 0.1 percent. As we shall see later, some studies have found keying errors to be not a fundamental feature of CAI surveys, but rather a consequence of particular instrument design decisions. However, in general, entry errors appear to be no more (or less) of a concern in computer-assisted interviewing than in paper-and-pencil surveys.

Finally, a number of studies have compared the substantive distributions obtained from CAI and P&P surveys. Generally the distributions are similar, and where significant differences are found, these do not lend themselves to easy interpretation (e.g., Olsen 1992). Thus, despite the early claims of improved data quality resulting from the switch to computer-assisted methods, it is probably fair to say that, in general, data quality is no worse in CAI than it is in P&P interviewing. (There are two notable exceptions in which dramatic improvements in data quality have come from extensions of computer-assisted methods—audio computer-assisted self-interviewing, or audio-CASI, and dependent interviewing in panel surveys, in which data collected in a previous wave are fed back to respondents for review and confirmation.)

Where substantive differences have been found in comparisons of CAI with equivalent P&P surveys, the post hoc explanation in many cases has been that the designs or layouts of the two versions differed (e.g., Baker, Bradburn, and Johnson 1995; Bergman et al. 1994; see also Nicholls et al. 1997). Although many of these are seemingly innocuous changes of layout (e.g., separation of items across screens in CAI) rather than wording, they nonetheless convey different expectations of what kinds of information are required and thereby influence the responses obtained.

When the technology (i.e., paper or computer) alone is considered, rather than the technology with any concomitant change in instrument design, there has been found to be remarkably little change in the quality of the data collected. This should not be taken to imply that the advent of CAI has had minimal impact on interviewers and their work. Rather, it may suggest that although the *process* of interviewing has changed, the *outcome* is largely unaffected by the switch, at least as a result of computer assistance per se. This should not come as a big surprise, as many CAI surveys have been designed to be as comparable as possible to their P&P predecessors, in many cases to preserve the integrity of lengthy time series of trend data. One explanation may thus be the explicit efforts researchers have made to keep designs equivalent or comparable. Another may be that well-trained interviewers are compensating for instrument design flaws (in both paper-and-pencil and computer-assisted methods) in ways that mask the effects of the technologies. We should thus look more closely at the effects of computer assistance on the process of data collection, and particularly on the role of interviewers and their interactions with survey respondents.

◆ Effects of CAI on Interviewers and Respondents

Concerns about interviewers' use of computer software have been raised since the early days of CATI. Key among these is the problem of "segmentation," first identified by Robert Groves, Marianne Berry, and Nancy Mathiowetz (1980; see also House and Nicholls 1988). Segmentation arises from the fact that, because of the limited screen real estate in CAI, the interviewer sees only a small segment of the instrument at a time. Although this may have the benefit of focusing the interviewer on the immediate task at hand, the interviewer may lose a sense of the "big picture" of the interview, making his or her navigation (movement) through the instrument (other than the regular forward movement dictated by the program) more difficult and providing the interviewer little feedback on his or her progress through the instrument. As Groves et al. (1980) note: "With a paper questionnaire, no one has to explain to the interviewer how to flip backwards a page or two. But the designer of the on-line questionnaire must anticipate such needs and make explicit provision for them" (p. 519). Although some progress has been made in reducing the segmentation effect through judicious software design (see Sperry et al. 1999), this issue remains a common complaint of CAI interviewers.

With the advent of CAPI, additional concerns were raised about the effects of the new technology on interviewers. This was especially true of hardware and ergonomic issues, such as the heavy weight of the computer, low battery life, small screen size and low visibility, and slowness of the computer. The early machines did indeed suffer from a number of these limitations, but improvements in hardware and software over time appear to have eased these burdens for interviewers. With some exceptions (e.g., doorstep interviews and exit polls), concern about the feasibility of the current generation of laptop computers for CAPI surveys has waned. As a consequence, it seems, more attention is now being paid to software issues, some of which have been with us since the early days of CATI. Furthermore, as graphical user interfaces (e.g., Windows) become more common, increasing the range of options available to survey designers, the issue of software design is again becoming prominent in CAPI as well as in CATI.

Despite these concerns, both empirical and anecdotal evidence suggests that interviewers have adopted CAPI with enthusiasm (e.g., Baker and Wojcik 1992; Couper and Burt 1994; Edwards et al. 1993). Most of the initial concerns about in-person interviewers' ability to conduct computer-assisted interviews were unfounded. The reasons most often given for the positive reactions to the new technology relate to a sense of increased professionalism, of being on the cutting edge (see Nicholls and Groves 1986; Weeks 1992).

Interviewers using computers also report being relieved that they no longer have to worry about following complex skips, and being happy with the fact that their work is done when the interview is completed. In the days of P&P interviewing, an interviewer had a great deal of clerical work to perform before and after each interview. In some surveys (such as the Current Population Survey, or CPS), this involved transcribing details from previous waves of data collection onto the interviewing form, using optical mark recognition "bubbles." Similarly, after completing an interview, the interviewer had to clean up the questionnaire to prepare it for coding and keying, including at times rewriting or expanding upon hastily scribbled marginal notes. Many interviewers viewed these tasks as tedious and uninteresting, and certainly less important than their real task of interacting with sample respondents. Mick Couper and Geraldine Burt (1993) asked CPS interviewers in an open-ended question what they liked most about using a computer for interviewing: 47 percent mentioned the elimination of editing and transcription activities, 19 percent mentioned the ease or efficiency of interviewing, 18 percent mentioned the reduction of paperwork, and 16 percent mentioned the automation of skips and branching. On the other hand, 36 percent of the interviewers mentioned slow speed as the feature they enjoyed least about CAPI; this was followed by battery problems (19 percent), backing up to change answers in the instrument (11 percent), and weight of the computer (10 percent). In response to a later set of closed-ended questions, 81 percent agreed that using a computer enhanced the professional image of interviewers, and 39 percent agreed that using a computer slowed the interview down relative to paper and pencil (Couper and Burt 1994). Brad Edwards and his colleagues (1993) found that almost 40 percent of interviewers surveyed preferred P&P over CAPI for correcting errors.

Although interviewers generally express enthusiasm for CAPI, the number of interviewer complaints about features of the hardware and software suggest that optimal CAI design has not yet been achieved, and there is room for improvement of the interviewing systems being used. Increasingly, research attention has moved way from issues of feasibility (Is CAPI possible?) to issues of usability (How can the systems be optimized for the task?).

Respondent reactions to CAI appear equally as positive as those of interviewers. Several researchers have asked respondents how they feel about CAPI in sets of debriefing questions at the ends of interviews (e.g., Baker and Wojcik 1992; van Bastelaer, Kerssemakers, and Sikkel 1987).[1] We caution against overinterpretation of the results of such research, as the demand characteristics of the interview situation may make it hard for respondents to express negative attitudes to interviewers about an experience they just went through. Nonetheless, there is no evidence that suggests overt negative reactions to CAPI on the part of respondents. Furthermore, the introduction of CAI has appeared to have no effect on survey refusal rates (e.g., Bergman et al. 1994; de Leeuw and Nicholls 1996), suggesting that respondents are, at the very least, indifferent about the use of computers for interviewing. But, as we have already implied, the effects of the introduction of computers on respondents may be felt indirectly through changes in the behavior of the interviewer or the process of the interview. After all, the interviewer serves as intermediary between the computer and the respondent, and so any effects on the respondent (other than direct reactions to the presence of the computer) are likely to be mediated through the interviewer. For this reason, most of our work has focused on the interviewer's interactions with the CAI system.

◆ CAI Design and Interviewer-Computer Interaction

It is clear from our own work that the design of the computerized instrument has an impact on the way the interview is conducted. This is not a particularly new idea, but it is one that has received little research attention until recently. It has long been accepted that the design or layout of paper questionnaires can affect the data collection process. Several nonexperimental studies have demonstrated this for both interviewer-administered and self-administered surveys (e.g., Sanchez 1992; Smith 1995). Despite this, theory development on design issues other than question wording has been slow.[2] Furthermore, it appears to be presumed that in interviewer-administered surveys, well-trained interviewers can compensate for poor design, and in any case format, layout, and other design issues are not worthy of research attention. With the advent of CAPI, and particularly the range of design features made possible by the introduction of graphical user interfaces, this issue is becoming more salient in computer-assisted surveys. But this has already been recognized by Carol House and William Nicholls (1988), who note that a change to CAI "modifies the role of both survey interviewer and questionnaire designer. The interviewer becomes more dependent on the work of the designer" (p. 421).

That design is an important element of computer-assisted surveys (and indeed surveys of all types) is supported by evidence of several different types. The evidence provided by Maria Sanchez (1992) and Tom Smith (1995) comes from natural experiments of unintended layout changes in paper questionnaires. Sanchez (1992) examined the results when the layout of the same series of questions was changed in two similar surveys. She found that for one question, the number of "not ascertained" responses declined from 9 percent to 2 percent; for another, the number of interviewer failures to probe declined from 8.8 percent to 0.8 percent as a result of the changed designs. Similarly, Smith (1995) found wide variation (1.7 percent to 11.8 percent) in the number of missing answers to a follow-up question on religion across years of the General Social Survey. He concludes that placement of the identically worded questions contributed to this variation. In the surveys with high rates of missing data, the follow-up question appeared at the top of the reverse side of a page, making it more likely to be skipped.

Early indicators of possible design difficulties in CAI came from interviewer reports from debriefing surveys. For example, in response to Couper and Burt's (1993) questionnaire, 60 percent of CPS interviewers reported difficulties backing up and changing answers in the CAPI instrument. In fact, 52 percent reported having difficulty with a particular feature of the CAPI instrument that prevented them from backing up to the household roster once the roster had been completed.

Another source of information about interviewer difficulties in interacting with CAI instruments lies in keystroke or trace files. These automatic by-products of many CAI software systems provide records (with varying levels of detail across different software systems) of the functions used or keys pressed by interviewers during the interview. Studies have generally found that interviewers use certain CAI functions (e.g., on-line help and backup) less frequently than might be expected. For example, Mick Couper and Jay Schlegel (1998) found that CAPI interviewers in the National Health Interview Survey (NHIS) rarely used on-line help, with only 9 percent of all interviews showing any help access and an average use of 14 times per 100 interviews. The relatively infrequent use of on-line help parallels the findings of other researchers (Baker 1992; Couper, Sadosky, and Hansen 1994; Sperry et al. 1999). What this does not reveal is why interviewers do not use on-line help. Do they not need the information? Do they not find the available information useful? Or do they not know how to access help during an interview?

Similar results have been found for interviewers' backing up during interviews. Although backing up one item at a time is a common procedure familiar to most interviewers, "jumpback" functions (which allow an interviewer to return to an earlier point in the interview) are extremely rare. Couper and Schlegel (1998) found that whereas 78 percent of the interviews they examined contained at least one single-item backup, less than 3 percent contained jumps back. Perhaps more illuminating from their keystroke file analysis is an examination of the targets of these backups and the reasons the interviewers backed up. We return to a few illustrative examples later.

Couper, Sue Ellen Hansen, and Sally Sadosky (1997) found that function key errors were not uncommon. In some cases, interviewers pressed a function key instead of the adjacent key, or instead of the equivalent numeric key on the laptop keyboard, indicating possible problems remembering the functions or dealing with the compact laptop keyboard in a live interviewing environment.

In general, the studies reveal that although, overall, interviewers appear quite comfortable with CAPI, there are instances where instrument design may lead to problems that can be revealed only through more detailed examination of the process. For example, the item illustrated in Figure 10.1 was found to be the target of a disproportionately large number of backups in the NHIS (about 13 backups for every 100 times the screen was accessed; see Couper and Schlegel 1998). At first blush this item appears unremarkable, until we note that it was the fifth in a series in which the previous four items all had two response options: (1) Yes and (2) No. The fifth item changed response format as shown. It was

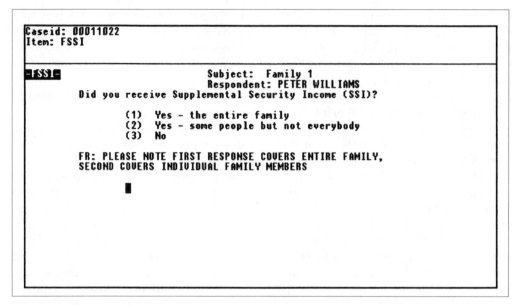

```
Caseid: 00011022
Item: FSSI

-FSSI-                    Subject:  Family 1
                          Respondent: PETER WILLIAMS
         Did you receive Supplemental Security Income (SSI)?

                  (1)  Yes - the entire family
                  (2)  Yes - some people but not everybody
                  (3)  No

         FR: PLEASE NOTE FIRST RESPONSE COVERS ENTIRE FAMILY,
         SECOND COVERS INDIVIDUAL FAMILY MEMBERS

             █
```

Figure 10.1. Example of Question Producing Large Number of Backups

found that 87 percent of the backups to this item were from a follow-up question asked only of those who answered 2. Of these, 97 percent returned to this item and changed the answer from 2 to 3. This suggests that changing the pattern of response options (i.e., inconsistent design) in this series of questions produced errors that were detected only because the follow-up question did not make sense for a "no" answer.

Harley Frazis and Jay Stewart (1998) report on a similar effect for the following question in the Current Population Survey:

> Did you ever get a High School diploma by completing High School OR through a GED or other equivalent?
>
> 1. Yes, completed High School
> 2. Yes, GED or other equivalent
> 3. No

Again, there is nothing remarkable about this question, unless one again considers that the rest of the instrument uses 1 for yes and 2 for no. This question is asked only of those with less than high school education, and of these, 12 percent selected option 2.

Using external data, Frazis and Stewart estimate that almost all of these responses are spurious, and the true population estimate for these additional GEDs is closer to 400,000 than the 4.8 million estimated using the question above.

These examples show how the shift from paper to CAI has changed the interviewer data entry task from checking boxes closely associated with response options to entering numbers not necessarily visually associated with response options. A change in response option codes should have little or no effect on data quality in a paper interview, but can have a dramatic effect in CAI.

Another example comes again from the NHIS (see Hansen, Couper, and Fuchs 1998). In usability laboratory observations of NHIS interviews, we found one screen to be particularly problematic (see Figure 10.2). The interviewer's task is to read the first three names displayed, press [Shift-F6] to activate the bottom screen, then [PgDn] to see the remaining names to be read. The interviewer is then to return to the top of the initial screen to finish reading the question and enter the responses. In only 5 of the 18 usability interviews we observed in

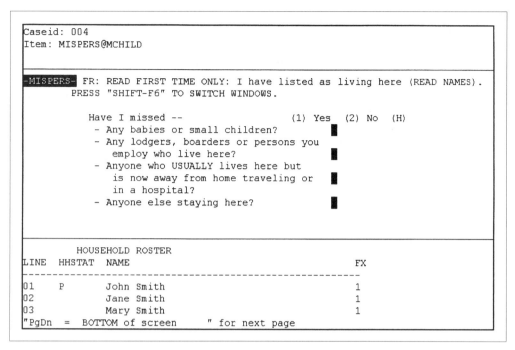

```
Caseid: 004
Item: MISPERS@MCHILD


-MISPERS- FR: READ FIRST TIME ONLY: I have listed as living here (READ NAMES).
         PRESS "SHIFT-F6" TO SWITCH WINDOWS.

         Have I missed --            (1) Yes  (2) No  (H)
           - Any babies or small children?        ▮
           - Any lodgers, boarders or persons you
             employ who live here?                ▮
           - Anyone who USUALLY lives here but
             is now away from home traveling or   ▮
             in a hospital?
           - Anyone else staying here?            ▮



              HOUSEHOLD ROSTER
LINE  HHSTAT  NAME                              FX
------------------------------------------------------------
01    P       John Smith                        1
02            Jane Smith                         1
03            Mary Smith                         1
"PgDn  =  BOTTOM of screen      " for next page
```

Figure 10.2. Example of Complex Interviewer Function

which there were more than three family members was there an attempt to use the [Shift-F6] function to see the remaining names, and in all 5 cases the attempt was unsuccessful. Later trace file analysis of more than 16,000 interviews from the field revealed that in households with four or more persons, the [Shift-F6] function was used less than 6 percent of the time it was required. This clearly indicates a function that is not working as intended, a fact that could only have been revealed by an examination of the process of the interview rather than the resulting data.

We found many other examples like these in the NHIS (an instrument we have studied in some detail). In all of these examples, the interviewers had been using the CAPI survey instruments for several months before these observations were made, and so the blame for the difficulties cannot be placed on interviewer inexperience. Some of the problems were identified through usability evaluations of the instruments, whereas others were revealed through trace file analysis of field inter-

views. Together with a growing body of evidence from other surveys, this suggests that the design of CAI surveys does affect the interviewer's interaction with the instrument (see Couper 1999b). Some elements of an interviewer's work have been eliminated or improved under CAI, whereas other interviewing tasks may have become more difficult. It is important for researchers to understand what these are and to find ways to overcome these obstacles to smooth and effective administration of a survey instrument.

In summary, the design of survey instruments (both paper and computer) affects the conduct of the interview in ways that the field is only now beginning to explore systematically. In paper surveys, interviewers have to handle the complex tasks of following skip patterns and judging the appropriateness of answers. On the computer, branching and edit checks are now invisible to the interviewer. This means the interviewer must place trust in the designer to make the correct decisions and to anticipate all possible contingencies that may occur in the field. Although some interviewing tasks have been automated, freeing the interviewer of these concerns, the computer typically exercises greater control over the flow of the interview, and interviewer flexibility in dealing with unusual situations may have been reduced. This also means that there are circumstances in which the interviewer may be completely unaware of problems, as in the example above from Frazis and Stewart (1998). In other words, there may be both advantages and disadvantages to computerization of the survey interview. Design and research activities should focus on maximizing the potential benefits of CAI while minimizing the drawbacks.

Thus far we have examined only the interviewer-computer interaction. In the next section, we bring the third player in the interaction—the respondent—into consideration and examine the impact of CAI on the interviewer-respondent interaction and the triadic relationship among interviewer, computer, and respondent (see also Schaeffer and Maynard, Chapter 11, this volume).

◆ Effect of CAI on Interviewer-Respondent Interaction

Previous research has tended to focus on the interviewer-respondent interaction and on the respondent's cognitive processes in answering survey questions (see Schwarz and Sudman 1996; Sirken et al. 1999; Sudman, Bradburn, and Schwarz 1996). In contrast, the interaction between the interviewer and the survey instrument (whether paper or computer based) and the effects of instrument design on the interaction between interviewer and respondent have been largely unexplored. The survey instrument itself places cognitive demands on the interviewer, and these may interfere with the communication demands of interacting with the respondent. However, in CAI additional cognitive demands may be placed on the interviewer. The interviewer's focus of attention is divided between the computer and the respondent and so tends to shift between the two throughout the survey interview. Depending on the cognitive demands of one, the interviewer may be more or less able to attend to the cognitive demands of the other. Computer assistance may further divide the interviewer's attention between the task at hand (e.g., recording the respondent's answer) and how to perform that task (e.g., typing the number associated with the response and pressing the [Enter] key). Thus an interviewer's attention in a computer-assisted interview may be divided in multiple ways. Interaction with the computer involves the interviewer's reading questions from the computer screen and entering data at the computer keyboard, and also attending to how the computer supports those tasks. The interviewer is also simultaneously attending to the respondent's answers and, if necessary, engaging in extended conversational turns with the respondent in order to elicit codable responses to enter on the computer. The computer may also serve to divide the respondent's attention, which may be focused either on the interviewer's questions and other contributions to conversation or on the interviewer's actions in relation to the computer. The interviewer's success in managing these multiple tasks as well as the survey instrument's design, which may or may not facilitate or support the interviewer, may well affect the interviewer's ability to collect the information desired in the manner prescribed.

We present a model of this three-way interaction in Figure 10.3 (see also Couper 1999a; Hansen 2000). The separate bidirectional interactions between interviewer and computer and between interviewer and respondent may affect one another, as represented by the curved and dashed bidirectional line. The interviewer, respondent, and computer all have potential impacts on the interviewing tasks of each

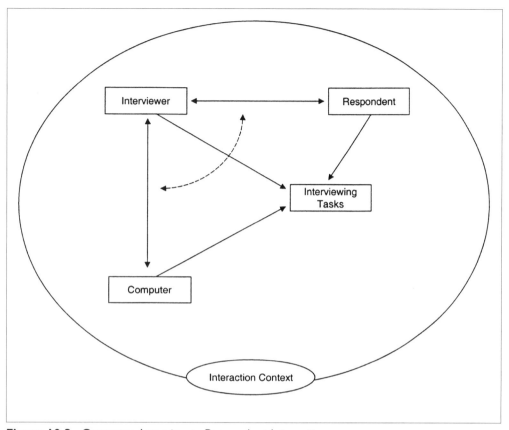

Figure 10.3. Computer-Interviewer-Respondent Interaction

(for example, ask question, understand question, respond, record response, deliver next question) and the question-response outcome, and each is affected by the environment or survey setting, including mode and method of survey administration. For example, the interaction contexts or environments of personal and telephone interviews differ and thus may differ in how they affect interaction. The personal interview is conducted face-to-face by an interviewer using a laptop computer, and takes place in a setting that may make the presence, and hence effect, of the computer more salient. On the other hand, a telephone interview is typically conducted by an interviewer using a desktop computer, with larger keyboard and screen display than are available in a laptop, making it easier for the interviewer

to interact with the computer, and the respondent sees neither the computer nor the interviewer.

This model of interaction in the computer-assisted survey interview could be generalized to represent other types of interactions involving the focused exchange of information between two people, one of whom is using a computer in the performance of a job (for example, a bank teller or emergency dispatch operator). Within this class, interactions vary in terms of who initiates the interaction, the participants' understanding of their respective roles, and external constraints placed on interaction. In the survey interview, the interviewer initiates interaction and may have a clearer understanding of the respondent's role than does the respondent, and standardization places considerable constraints on the behavior of the participants that are typically not present in other interactions of this type.

These types of interactions have generally received little attention in the literature on human-computer interaction or in the literature on computer-supported cooperative work (see Couper 1999a). Two exceptions are David Greatbatch and his colleagues' work on doctor-patient interactions before and after the introduction of desktop computers for record keeping (Greatbatch et al. 1993, 1995a, 1995b) and Jack Whalen's (1995a, 1995b) analysis of calls to an emergency dispatch center that used a computer-aided dispatch (CAD) system.

Greatbatch et al. (1993) found that both computer-assisted and paper-based records create a "tool-saturated" environment, dividing the doctor's attention between the interaction with the patient and the tools used to review and update patient records and to prescribe treatments. However, computers lack the "ecological mobility" of paper and pen, and thus change the nature of doctor-patient consultations in ways similar to what we have observed in interviewer-respondent interactions (see Hansen 2000).

Whalen (1995b) demonstrates how the features and structural properties of the CAD system can both facilitate and constrain interaction. The data entry form used by the emergency call takers he studied was designed to "standardize and routinize the recording of information and the processing of emergencies." However, Whalen notes that, rather than being a neutral, standardized instrument, the CAD system could be "characterized as a kind of ubiquitous and obligatory work instrument that call-takers must . . . manage and come to terms with over the course of each and every phone call," and that "call-takers must do this while they are simultaneously engaged in interaction with citizen callers" (p. 192).

Our research is finding parallels with these studies in the computer-assisted survey interview setting. For example, we have observed in a series of laboratory-based interviews that the complex situation described above and illustrated in Figure 10.2 led interviewers to adopt a variety of strategies in order to complete the task required by the computer, at times soliciting respondents' help in repeating the names of household members.

Another set of examples focused on the effect of CAI on standardization. As we have discussed, CAI is believed to help enforce standardization in two ways: by standardizing question wording through the programmed tailoring of questions to fit a respondent's characteristics and by eliminating skip errors through the enforced display of all appropriate questions. The goal of these programming efforts is to ensure that the interviewer both reads the appropriate question and does so in the prescribed manner, exactly as worded (e.g., Fowler and Mangione 1990). Despite the large amount of programming effort that goes into tailoring "fills" in CAI to facilitate the reading of the question text, there is little empirical evidence on its efficacy— that is, on the extent to which tailoring text facilitates the interviewer's reading of questions.

In a series of analyses based on coding of videotaped survey interactions, Hansen (2000) has explored the effect of these instrument design features on two indicators of standardization: not asking a question and not reading a question as worded. She found that, contrary to expectation, computer assistance did not decrease the likelihood of an interviewer's having problems reading a question, relative to paper and pencil. Regardless of technology, features of the question, such as name fills, emphasis, parenthetical text, alternative wording, and other customization features, had significant effects on interviewers' problems with reading questions as worded.

Computer assistance also did not appear to increase the likelihood of an interviewer's asking questions. However, Hansen's analysis of items not asked showed that a large number of questions not asked were in the household roster section of the interview and could be linked to design decisions that introduced problems in interviewer-respondent interaction. When household roster items were removed from analysis, computer assistance significantly decreased questions not asked, as expected. These results, and others from the qualitative analysis of these interactions (Hansen et al. 1998; Hansen, Fuchs, and Couper 1997), reveal that when computer-assisted instruments are not designed to accommodate the interviewer's tasks, rather than increasing standardization (relative to paper and pencil) as expected, they may actually impede the interviewer's execution of the tasks as intended, leading to changes in the interviewer-respondent interaction.

Thus, contrary to the expectation that CAI will help achieve the explicit goals of standardization, we have seen numerous instances of interviewers departing from standardization or scripted interaction and customizing the interaction with the respondent to deal with some of the constraints placed on them by the survey instrument (such as not asking awkward questions that the computer delivers, or not reading questions as automatically tailored by CAI). As currently implemented in most surveys, CAI is less flexible than paper instruments, requiring (we believe) greater ingenuity on the part of the interviewer to balance the demands of interacting with the respondent and meeting the data needs of the researcher (as embodied in the CAI program).

We have seen the presence of the computer in CAI affect the interaction in survey interviews in several ways. First, on the outbound computer-interviewer communication, the instrument may affect the way the interviewer asks the question (as noted above from Hansen's analysis). Second, on the inbound interviewer-computer interaction, the instrument may affect the way the

interviewer enters the response provided by the respondent (see our earlier examples regarding inconsistent response options). Third, the computer (especially in CAPI) may indirectly affect the interviewer-respondent interaction, with increased attention of the interviewer to the computer (particularly when interviewer-computer interaction breaks down) leading to loss of eye contact or other changes in rapport between interviewer and respondent. Similar effects have also been noted in paper-and-pencil surveys. Further research is needed to determine when and how such effects may lead to differences in the quality of the data collected through computer-assisted surveys.

◆ Changes in Survey Interviewing

We end this chapter with a brief look at other trends in computer-assisted survey data collection that may affect survey interviewing, particularly the role of the survey interviewer. As early as 1984, the European Society for Market Research (ESOMAR) held a conference with the title "Are Interviewers Obsolete?" With recent developments in automated self-administered methods, such as audio-CASI, interactive voice response, and Web surveys, this question continues to be raised (see, e.g., Baker 1999).

The proponents of the new methods claim that interviewers are not only expensive but prone to make errors and influence respondents in the responses given, especially to socially sensitive questions. Some see computers as a replacement technology (e.g., Black 1998) that indeed has the potential to make interviewers obsolete. This view focuses primarily on the limitations of survey interviewers rather than on their strengths for survey data collection. It also gets at the heart of the standardization debate (see Beatty 1995). If standardization simply means reading the question exactly as worded with the same tone and inflection every time, this could be done better by a computer than by a human. Similarly, computers may eliminate skip errors (to the extent they are programmed correctly) and may not exert the same social influences on a respondent as a live interviewer. This implies that standardization of the stimulus is important, rather than standardization of the meaning of the questions.

But this ignores the important role that interviewers play in gaining cooperation from sample persons, in motivating them throughout what are often long and complex interviews, in explaining and clarifying complex concepts and ambiguous questions, in probing inadequate answers, and so on. Although it may be true that many questions, and indeed many surveys, may be administered by computers without a major loss of data quality (ignoring the nonresponse problem), there remains a large class of surveys for which interviewer administration seems essential and is likely to remain so for some time to come.

The newer methods of data collection have evolved to meet a variety of specialized needs or to seize opportunities offered by new technological developments. An example of the former is audio-CASI. The development of this method stemmed from the recognition that answers to sensitive questions are subject to social desirability biases when the questions are administered by an interviewer (Sudman and Bradburn 1982). For many years, paper-and-pencil surveys on sensitive topics such as sexual behavior and illicit drug use have included self-administered components for the most sensitive items. The effectiveness of this approach for increasing reports of socially undesirable behavior is well established. But this method still presents a threat in that others (e.g., family members) could possibly see the respondent's answers being recorded. An early precursor of audio-CASI involved the respondent's using a personal stereo cassette player (e.g., a Walkman) to listen to a tape on which the questions were recorded and enter responses onto an answer sheet that was devoid of the question wording (Camburn, Cynamon, and Harel 1991).[3] This approach had the advantage of increased privacy and reduced literacy requirements (respondents could listen to the questions, rather than having to read them). However, the prerecorded nature of the tape made it extremely difficult to implement skips or conditional questions, or to tailor wording based on previous answers. Hence audio-CASI, in which the respondent listens to the questions on a headset plugged into the computer and answers by entering responses on the computer screen, was developed at approximately the same time. Initially, audio-CASI made use of the multimedia capabilities of the Apple Macintosh laptop (Johnston and Walton 1995); the technology was then adapted for use with DOS-based laptop computers (O'Reilly et al. 1994). This method is now widely used in surveys on sensitive topics, with demonstrated gains in data quality (see Tourangeau and Smith 1996, 1999; Turner et al. 1999).

As currently implemented, audio-CASI remains part of an interviewer-administered survey. The interviewer gains cooperation from the selected household, selects a random sample person, and typically administers a large part of the interview. In preparation for the audio-CASI portion of the interview, the interviewer sets up the equipment, explains the operation to the respondent, and remains available in case the respondent needs assistance while completing the self-administered portion. In a large number of cases, the interviewer may actually administer the questions him- or herself or assist the respondent more directly than is intended (see Couper and Rowe 1996; Couper and Stinson 1999). The interviewer thus remains an integral part of the data collection operation. Nonetheless, there are questions about how long the self-administered part of the interview can or should be—some suggest the entire interview should be self-administered, with the interviewer's only role being to obtain cooperation and then to drop off and pick up the equipment.

Other newer methods of automated data collection obviate the need for an interviewer altogether. These methods are the functional equivalent of mail surveys, but computer assistance can offer the power and complexity of an interviewer-administered survey without the cost and unreliability, some claim. The most powerful of these at present are surveys on the World Wide Web (for a review, see Couper 2000; see also Mann and Stewart, Chapter 12, this volume). Web surveys are proliferating at a rate unprecedented in the survey industry, but at a pace quite in line with the general move toward Internet use. Often these new technologies are being adopted more for reasons of competitiveness than quality. Proponents of Web surveys are claiming, as have the proponents of many new technologies, that the new methods will replace traditional survey methodologies such as random-digit dialing telephone surveys and make interviewers obsolete (Black 1998). We believe that such pronouncements of the imminent demise of interviewers are premature. Instead, we expect to see an increasing fragmentation of the survey industry, with some sectors (dominated by market research) embracing Internet-based methods and others (mainly government and academic surveys) staying largely with interviewer-administered surveys for household populations. It is unclear where the smaller academic research centers and political polling organizations (both dominated by low-margin, rapid-turnaround telephone surveys with high turnover of interviewing staff) may fall.

These are either the best of times or the worst of times for survey interviewers. We predict that although the interviewing profession may appear to be under threat, it will certainly not disappear. Rather, interviewers will become more specialized—as well as better trained and better paid—as more and more is being asked of them. The straightforward surveys that could just as easily be administered by computers can be,

and are being, moved to automated methods, leaving the difficult, complex, intrusive surveys requiring a high degree of accuracy to be administered by a smaller cadre of well-trained interviewers. Thus the ranks of survey interviewers may well shrink over the next few years, but those who remain will be better trained, better paid, and better motivated—in other words, more professional.

If this is the case, then the issue of control versus flexibility, and the role of the computerized instrument therein, becomes even more salient. The model under which the computer controls the interaction is one in which there is little trust in the interviewer's ability to administer a standardized survey instrument appropriately while trying to adapt the interview to the needs, interests, and abilities of the respondent. Under this model, the interviewer simply carries out the instructions of the designer as embodied in the computer program. The program typically leaves the interviewer (and thereby also the respondent) with little flexibility to accommodate answers or situations that are outside the "normal range" anticipated by the designer. However, there are efforts under way to design CAI instruments that facilitate the task of the interviewer and provide greater flexibility (e.g., Conrad and Schober 1999; Belli et al. 1999).

Along with an increasing awareness of the professionalism of survey interviewers, we may see a growing recognition that CAI systems need to be designed to facilitate, rather than control, the task of interviewing. Rather than controlling the interview flow and interaction, well-designed CAI software could give the interviewer more freedom to execute the goals of the survey rather than blindly follow the successive commands presented by the computer. If standardization of meaning or understanding is the goal, then any effort that could accommodate the varying needs of respondents and assist in the variety of interviewing situations that develop is desirable. The CAI system should assist the interviewer in a manner that motivates the respondent to provide the most honest and accurate information possible, with minimal burden.

In summary, then, the introduction of computer-assisted interviewing has had profound effects on survey data collection and continues to do so. Although many researchers made the transition to CAI some time ago, there is still much we do not know about the role of the computer in the survey interview. Our work, consistent with that of Greatbatch et al. (1993) and Whalen (1995b), has shown that the computer is not a passive, neutral tool; rather, it is an active part of the survey interaction. We look forward to further research on this topic.

■ Notes

1. There is not likely to be much effect in CATI, as respondents are generally unaware of the technology being used by the interviewer at the other end of the telephone. Where comparisons have been made, few respondent differences have been found (e.g., Groves and Mathiowetz 1984).

2. Cleo Jenkins and Don Dillman (1997) have articulated a set of theoretical propositions regarding self-administered paper surveys, but this has not yet led to much empirical work on the issue.

3. This approach is still in use at the U.S. Bureau of the Census (see Bass and Downs 1999).

■ References

Baker, R. P. 1992. "New Technology in Survey Research: Computer-Assisted Personal Interviewing (CAPI)." *Social Science Computer Review* 10:145-57.

———. 1999. "The CASIC Future." In *Computer Assisted Survey Information Collection*, edited by M. P. Couper, R. P. Baker, J. Bethlehem, C. Z. F. Clark, J. Martin, W. L. Nicholls II, and J. M. O'Reilly. New York: John Wiley.

Baker, R. P., N. M. Bradburn, and R. A. Johnson. 1995. "Computer-Assisted Personal Interviewing: An Experimental Evaluation of Data Quality and Costs." *Journal of Official Statistics* 11:415-31.

Baker, R. P. and M. S. Wojcik. 1992. "Interviewer and Respondent Acceptance of CAPI." Pp. 613-21 in *Proceedings of the Bureau of the Census 1992 Annual Research Conference*. Washington, DC: U.S. Bureau of the Census.

Bass, L. E. and B. A. Downs. 1999. "What Can the SPD Adolescent SAQ Tell Us about the Well-Being of Adolescents in the Aftermath of the 1996 Welfare Reform Act?" Presented at the annual meeting of the Population Association of America, New York.

Beatty, P. 1995. "Understanding the Standardized/Non-standardized Interviewing Controversy." *Journal of Official Statistics* 11:147-60.

Belli, R. F., W. Shay, and F. Stafford. 1999. "Computerized Event History Calendar Methods: A Demonstration of Features, Functions and Flexibility." Presented at the annual meeting of the American Association for Public Opinion Research, May, St. Petersburg Beach, FL.

Bergman, L. R., K.-E. Kristiansson, A. Olofsson, and M. Säfström. 1994. "Decentralized CATI versus Paper and Pencil Interviewing: Effects on the Results in the Swedish Labor Force Surveys." *Journal of Official Statistics* 10:181-95.

Bernard, C. 1989. *Survey Data Collection Using Laptop Computers* (Report No. 01/C520). Paris: INSEE.

Black, G. S. 1998. "The Advent of Internet Research: A Replacement Technology." Presented at the annual meeting of the American Association for Public Opinion Research, May, St. Louis, MO.

Camburn, D., D. Cynamon, and Y. Harel. 1991. "The Use of Audio Tapes and Written Questionnaires to Ask Sensitive Questions during Household Interviews." Presented at the National Field Technologies Conference, San Diego, CA.

Catlin, G. and Ingram, S. 1988. "The Effects of CATI on Costs and Data Quality: A Comparison of CATI and Paper Methods in Centralized Interviewing." Pp. 437-52 in *Telephone Survey Method-*

ology, edited by R. M. Groves, P. P. Biemer, L. E. Lyberg, J. T. Massey, W. L. Nicholls II, and J. Waksberg. New York: John Wiley.

Conrad, F. G. and M. F. Schober. 1999. "A Conversational Approach to Text-Based Computer-Administered Questionnaires." In *Proceedings of the Third ASC International Conference, Edinburgh, September 22-24,* edited by R. Banks et al. Chesham, England: Association for Statistical Computing.

Couper, M. P. 1999a. "The Application of Cognitive Science to Computer Assisted Interviewing." In *Cognition and Survey Research,* edited by M. G. Sirken, D. J. Herrmann, S. Schechter, N. Schwarz, J. M. Tanur, and R. Tourangeau. New York: John Wiley.

———. 1999b. "Usability Evaluation of Computer Assisted Survey Instruments." In *Proceedings of the Third ASC International Conference, Edinburgh, September 22-24,* edited by R. Banks et al. Chesham, England: Association for Statistical Computing.

———. 2000. "Web Surveys: A Review of Issues and Approaches." *Public Opinion Quarterly* 64(4): 464-494.

Couper, M. P. and G. Burt. 1993. "The Impact of Computer-Assisted Personal Interviewing (CAPI) on Interviewer Performance: The CPS Experience." Pp. 189-93 in *Proceedings of the Joint Statistical Meeting of the American Statistical Association, Section on Survey Research Methods, 1992.* Alexandria, VA: American Statistical Association.

———. 1994. "Interviewer Attitudes toward Computer-Assisted Personal Interviewing (CAPI)." *Social Science Computer Review* 12:38-54.

Couper, M. P., S. E. Hansen, and S. A. Sadosky. 1997. "Evaluating Interviewer Performance in a CAPI Survey." In *Survey Measurement and Process Quality,* edited by L. E. Lyberg, P. P. Biemer, M. Collins, E. D. de Leeuw, C. Dippo, N. Schwarz, and D. Trewin. New York: John Wiley.

Couper, M. P. and W. L. Nicholls II. 1999. "The History and Development of Computer Assisted Survey Information Collection." In *Computer Assisted Survey Information Collection,* edited by M. P. Couper, R. P. Baker, J. Bethlehem, C. Z. F. Clark, J. Martin, W. L. Nicholls II, and J. M. O'Reilly. New York: John Wiley.

Couper, M. P. and B. Rowe. 1996. "Evaluation of a Computer-Assisted Self-Interview (CASI) Component in a CAPI Survey." *Public Opinion Quarterly,* 60:89-105.

Couper, M. P., S. A. Sadosky, and S. E. Hansen. 1994. "Measuring Interviewer Behavior Using CAPI." Pp. 845-50 in *Proceedings of the Joint Statistical Meeting of the American Statistical Association, Section on Survey Research Methods, 1993.* Alexandria, VA: American Statistical Association.

Couper, M. P. and J. Schlegel. 1998. "Evaluating the NHIS CAPI Instrument Using Trace Files." Presented at the annual meeting of the American Association for Public Opinion Research, May, St. Louis, MO.

Couper, M. P. and L. L. Stinson. 1999. "Completion of Self-Administered Questionnaires in a Sex Survey." *Journal of Sex Research* 36:321-30.

de Leeuw, E. D. and W. L. Nicholls II. 1996. "Technological Innovations in Data Collection: Acceptance, Data Quality and Costs." *Sociological Research Online* 1(4):1-19. Available Internet: http://www.socresonline.org.uk/socresonline/1/4/leeuw.html

Dielman, L. and M. P. Couper. 1995. "Data Quality in a CAPI Survey: Keying Errors." *Journal of Official Statistics* 11:141-46.

Edwards, B., D. Bittner, W. S. Edwards, and S. Sperry. 1993. "CAPI Effects on Interviewers: A Report from Two Major Surveys." Pp. 411-28 in *Proceedings of the Bureau of the Census 1993 Annual Research Conference.* Washington, DC: U.S. Bureau of the Census.

Fowler, F. J., Jr. and T. W. Mangione. 1990. *Standardized Survey Interviewing: Minimizing Interviewer-Related Error.* Newbury Park, CA: Sage.

Frazis, H. and J. Stewart. 1998. "Keying Errors Caused by Unusual Keypunch Codes: Evidence from a Current Population Survey Test." Pp. 131-33 in *Proceedings of the Joint Statistical Meeting of the American Statistical Association, Section on Survey Research Methods, 1997.* Alexandria, VA: American Statistical Association.

Greatbatch, D., C. Heath, P. Campion, and P. Luff. 1995a. "How Do Desk-Top Computers Affect the Doctor-Patient Interaction?" *Family Practice* 12(1):32-36.

Greatbatch, D., C. Heath, P. Luff, and P. Campion. 1995b. "Conversation Analysis: Human-Computer Interaction and the General Practice Consultation." In *Perspectives on HCI: Diverse Approaches,* edited by A. F. Monk and G. N. Gilbert. London: Academic Press.

Greatbatch, D., P. Luff, C. Heath, and P. Campion. 1993. "Interpersonal Communication and Human-Computer Interaction: An Examination of the Use of Computers in Medical Consultations." *Interacting with Computers* 5:193-216.

Groves, R. M., M. Berry, and N. A. Mathiowetz. 1980. "Some Impacts of Computer Assisted Telephone Interviewing on Survey Methods." Pp. 519-24 in *Proceedings of the Joint Statistical Meeting of the American Statistical Association, Section on Survey Research Methods, 1979.* Alexandria, VA: American Statistical Association.

Groves, R. M. and N. A. Mathiowetz. 1984. "Computer Assisted Telephone Interviewing: Effect on Interviewers and Respondents." *Public Opinion Quarterly* 48:356-69.

Hansen, S. E. 2000. "Asking Questions with Computers: Interaction in the Computer Assisted Standardized Survey Interview." Ph.D. dissertation, University of Michigan.

Hansen, S. E., M. P. Couper, and M. Fuchs. 1998. "Usability Evaluation of the NHIS Instrument." Presented at the annual meeting of the American Association for Public Opinion Research, May, St. Louis, MO.

Hansen, S. E., M. Fuchs, and M. P. Couper. 1997. "CAI Instrument Usability Testing." Presented at the annual meeting of the American Association for Public Opinion Research, May, Norfolk, VA.

House, C. C. and W. L. Nicholls II. 1988. "Questionnaire Design for CATI: Design Objectives and Methods." Pp. 421-26 in *Telephone Survey Methodology,* edited by R. M. Groves, P. P. Biemer, L. E. Lyberg, J. T. Massey, W. L. Nicholls II, and J. Waksberg. New York: John Wiley.

Jenkins, C. R. and D. A. Dillman. 1997. "Towards a Theory of Self-Administered Questionnaire Design." In *Survey Measurement and Process Quality,* edited by L. E. Lyberg, P. P. Biemer, M. Collins, E. D. de Leeuw, C. Dippo, N. Schwarz, and D. Trewin. New York: John Wiley.

Johnston, J. and C. Walton. 1995. "Reducing Response Effects for Sensitive Questions: A Computer-Assisted Self Interview with Audio." *Social Science Computer Review* 13:304-9.

Kennedy, J. M., J. E. Lengacher, and L. Demerath. 1990. "Interviewer Entry Error in CATI Interviews." Presented at the International Conference on Measurement Errors in Surveys, November, Tucson, AZ.

Lepkowski, J. M., S. A. Sadosky, M. P. Couper, L. Carn, S. Chardoul, and L. J. Scott. 1995. "Exploring Mode Differences in Interviewer Entry Errors." Pp. 521-26 in *Proceedings of the Joint Statistical Meeting of the American Statistical Association, Section on Survey Research Methods, 1979.* Alexandria, VA: American Statistical Association.

Martin, J., C. O'Muircheartaigh, and J. Curtice. 1993. "The Use of CAPI for Attitude Surveys: An Experimental Comparison with Traditional Methods." *Journal of Official Statistics* 9:641-62.

Nicholls, W. L., II. 1988. "Computer-Assisted Telephone Interviewing: A General Introduction." Pp. 377-86 in *Telephone Survey Methodology,* edited by R. M. Groves, P. P. Biemer, L. E. Lyberg, J. T. Massey, W. L. Nicholls II, and J. Waksberg. New York: John Wiley.

Nicholls, W. L., II, R. P. Baker, and J. Martin. 1997. "The Effect of New Data Collection Technologies on Survey Data Quality." Pp. 221-48 in *Survey Measurement and Process Quality,* edited by L. E. Lyberg, P. P. Biemer, M. Collins, E. D. de Leeuw, C. Dippo, N. Schwarz, and D. Trewin. New York: John Wiley.

Nicholls, W. L., II and R. M. Groves. 1986. "The Status of Computer-Assisted Telephone Interviewing: Part I. Introduction and Impact on Cost and Timeliness of Survey Data." *Journal of Official Statistics* 2:93-115.

Olsen, R. J. 1992. "The Effects of Computer-Assisted Interviewing on Data Quality." Working Paper No. 36, European Scientific Network on Household Panel Studies, University of Essex.

O'Reilly, J. M., M. Hubbard, J. Lessler, P. P. Biemer, and C. F. Turner. 1994. "Audio and Video Computer Assisted Self-Interviewing: Preliminary Tests of New Technologies for Data Collection." *Journal of Official Statistics* 10:197-214.

Sanchez, M. E. 1992. "Effect of Questionnaire Design on the Quality of Survey Data." *Public Opinion Quarterly,* 56:206-17.

Schwarz, N. and S. Sudman, eds. 1996. *Answering Questions: Methodology for Determining Cognitive and Communicative Processes in Survey Research.* San Francisco: Jossey-Bass.

Sirken, M. G., D. J. Herrmann, S. Schechter, N. Schwarz, J. M. Tanur, and R. Tourangeau, eds. 1999. *Cognition and Survey Research.* New York: John Wiley.

Smith, T. W. 1995. "Little Things Matter: A Sampler of How Differences in Questionnaire Format Can Affect Survey Responses." Pp. 1046-51 in *Proceedings of the Joint Statistical Meeting of the American Statistical Association, Section on Survey Research Methods, 1994.* Alexandria, VA: American Statistical Association.

Sperry, S., B. Edwards, R. Dulaney, and D. E. B. Potter. 1999. "Evaluating Interviewer Use of CAPI Navigation Features." In *Computer Assisted Survey Information Collection,* edited by M. P. Couper, R. P. Baker, J. Bethlehem, C. Z. F. Clark, J. Martin, W. L. Nicholls II, and J. M. O'Reilly. New York: John Wiley.

Sudman, S. and N. M. Bradburn. 1982. *Asking Questions: A Practical Guide to Questionnaire Design.* San Francisco: Jossey-Bass.

Sudman, S., N. M. Bradburn, and N. Schwarz. 1996. *Thinking about Answers: The Application of Cognitive Processes to Survey Methodology.* San Francisco: Jossey-Bass.

Tourangeau, R. and T. W. Smith. 1996. "Asking Sensitive Questions: The Impact of Data Collection Mode, Question Format, and Questions Context." *Public Opinion Quarterly* 60:275-304.

———. 1999. "Collecting Sensitive Information with Different Modes of Data Collection." In *Computer Assisted Survey Information Collection,* edited by M. P. Couper, R. P. Baker, J. Bethlehem, C. Z. F. Clark, J. Martin, W. L. Nicholls II, and J. M. O'Reilly. New York: John Wiley.

Turner, C. F., B. H. Forsyth, J. M. O'Reilly, P. C. Cooley, T. K. Smith, S. M. Rogers, and H. G. Miller. 1999. "Automated Self-Interviewing and the Survey Measurement of Sensitive Behaviors." In *Computer Assisted Survey Information Collection,* edited by M. P. Couper, R. P. Baker, J. Bethlehem, C. Z. F. Clark, J. Martin, W. L. Nicholls II, and J. M. O'Reilly. New York: John Wiley.

van Bastelaer, R. A., F. Kerssemakers, and D. Sikkel. 1987. "A Test of the Netherlands' Continuous Labor Force Survey with Hand-Held Computers: Interviewer Behavior and Data Quality." Pp. 37-54 in *Automation in Survey Processing,* edited by R. J. Mokken et al. Voorburg/Heerlen: Netherlands Central Bureau of Statistics (CBS Select 4).

Weeks, M. F. 1992. "Computer-Assisted Survey Information Collection: A Review of CASIC Methods and Their Implications for Survey Operations." *Journal of Official Statistics* 8:445-65.

Whalen, J. 1995a. "Expert Systems versus Systems for Experts: Computer-Aided Dispatch as a Support System in Real-World Environments." Pp. 161-83 in *The Social and Interactional Dimensions of Human-Computer Interaction,* edited by P. J. Thomas. Cambridge: Cambridge University Press.

———. 1995b. "A Technology of Order Production: Computer-Aided Dispatch in Public Safety Communications." Pp. 187-203 in *Situated Order: Studies in the Social Organization of Talk and Embedded Activities,* edited by P. ten Have and G. Psathas. Washington, DC: University Press of America.

11

STANDARDIZATION AND INTERACTION IN THE SURVEY INTERVIEW

◆ Nora Cate Schaeffer
Douglas W. Maynard

Survey interviews conduct measurement by question. That is, surveys use questions to collect measurements from a sample in order to estimate characteristics of a population. The "objective" data obtained by survey interviews are achieved in the interaction between respondents and interviewers who have been trained to behave in a standardized manner. Over the years, both critics (e.g., Briggs 1986; Cicourel 1974; Mishler 1986; Suchman and Jordan 1990) and practitioners (e.g., Cannell and Kahn 1968) of standardized survey interviewing have considered how the fundamentally social nature of the interview affects the data produced there.

Both groups view the interaction between the interviewer and the respondent as critical to judgments about the quality of the data (e.g., Cicourel 1982; Schuman 1982). Thus critics have presented examples of the awkward, and even bizarre, interactions that sometimes occur in survey interviews as evidence that the resulting data cannot be valid. Practitioners view such individual incidents as resulting from unusual circumstances or "bad" survey questions, and they consider adherence to rules of standardization to improve the quality of the data in the aggregate (e.g., Cannell, Lawson, and Hausser 1975). Practitioners and critics of surveys both view respondents' answers as

AUTHORS' NOTE: We would like to thank Colm O'Muircheartaigh, Jennifer Dykema, Frederick Conrad, and Michael Schober for their comments on an earlier version of this chapter.

constructed during the interaction, but they evaluate the effects on the resulting data differently (see Holstein and Gubrium 1995; Tourangeau, Rasinski, and Rips 2000).

In the past decade, survey researchers and other social scientists have revisited the debate about standardization (e.g, Beatty 1995), a debate that has a long history (see O'Muircheartaigh 1997). The latest round of the debate has been accompanied by a new set of studies of interaction in the survey interview. Some of these studies extend traditional methods used by survey researchers for studying the interview by experimenting with styles of interviewing and analyzing detailed coding of the interaction between the interviewer and respondent. Other studies, deriving from a tradition of studies of work and the production of scientific knowledge, have used concepts and methods from ethnomethodology and conversation analysis.

In this chapter, we first review the justification for standardization in the survey interview; we summarize recent debates, discuss different varieties of standardization, and consider standardization's limits and limitations. As we consider the limits of standardization, we focus on the role of *tacit and commonsense knowledge* in the conduct of the survey interview. In the second main section of the chapter, we argue for studying interaction in the survey interview using an approach we call *analytic alternation*. Because of the tension between the procedures for social measurement and the practices of talk and interaction, interviewers *alternate* between following the rules of standardization and using the tacit knowledge available to competent social actors who must solve problems that arise as their work tasks unfold. *Analytic* alternation means following the situated oscillations between formal rule following and tacit practices that interviewers enact in concert with survey respondents. Following this procedure, we outline the role of tacit knowledge in survey interviewing and consider, as an illustration, the *interviewing*

sequence by which the survey instrument is administered.

In the third major section of the chapter we review recent studies of survey interaction. Some of these studies involve coding behavior so that the effects of different techniques for questioning or probing can be examined; other studies are experiments that test how the style of interviewing affects the respondent's motivation, understanding, and other phenomena; and a third group of studies use ethnomethodological and conversation-analytic approaches to examine the detail of situated work methods and the practices of talk and social interaction. Finally, we consider the challenges this research poses for improving measurement in the social sciences.

◆ Standardization: Why and What

The justification for standardization lies in the logic of scientific measurement applied to social phenomena. Investigators who analyze survey data would like the variation they observe in data to result from variation in the concept being measured. For example, if different respondents report different levels of self-esteem, the different levels of self-esteem recorded in the data should reflect true differences between respondents in their levels of self-esteem. If interviewers behave differently with different respondents, however, the distribution of answers may reflect variation in the behavior of interviewers rather than variation in levels of self-esteem among respondents.

In addition, interviewers can introduce errors—by their expectations that respondents will have consistent attitudes or that respondents with specific social characteristics will have certain beliefs—that can affect the accuracy of responses. This is sometimes referred to as *biasing* answers. The model that divides total error into variance and bias has dominated the way statisticians think about error: "Interviewer variance represents the error about the 'expected value' for all the interviewers, while net interviewer bias represents the deviation of this expected value from the true population mean" (Hyman et al. [1954] 1975:322).

The varied practices that researchers refer to as *standardization* evolved in response to early studies, such as those described by Herbert Hyman and his colleagues ([1954] 1975), that demonstrated how the behavior of interviewers affects "error" in survey estimates. Hyman et al. found that ratings made by interviewers and the numbers of responses recorded to open questions were substantially affected by interviewer variance (p. 257; see also the summary in Groves 1989:380-81). Individual studies also found substantial gross errors (for example, those introduced through the expectations or reactions of the interviewer) that could affect many interviewers but not increase inter-interviewer variation (Hyman et al. [1954] 1975:252-74). Hyman et al. summarize the effects of the interviewer on the distribution of answers as follows: "The only reasonable answer seems to be that absolutely anything can happen" (p. 271).

Standardization addresses both components of interviewer error. The rules of standardization attempt to hold the behavior of the interviewer constant, thereby to reduce variable error. Recent studies in centralized telephone facilities where standardization is practiced, for example, have found that the component of variance due to differences in the behavior of the interviewer across respondents (interviewer variability) is usually quite small for most types of survey items (e.g., Mangione, Fowler, and Louis 1992; Groves and Magilavy 1986). This is so even though there are many lapses in achieving the ideal of standardization (see, e.g., Oksenberg, Cannell, and Kalton 1991). When standardization is successful, it makes the net effect of the interviewer in the aggregate very small, in the specific sense that it reduces the interviewer's contribution to

variance. Standardization also reduces bias by reducing the number of opportunities for the interviewer's expectations or opinions (for instance) to intrude on the process by which the respondent's answer is generated, interpreted, or recorded.

Standardization does not eliminate the effect of the interviewer on the individual respondent. An interviewer who follows the rules of standardization might react to a respondent's ambiguous answer by repeating all the response categories, for example, instead of using his or her own beliefs about the respondent's likely answer to choose which response categories to repeat. The standardized practice of repeating the response categories not only affects how respondents express their answers, but over the course of the interview probably has the desirable effect of training respondents to choose a category from among those offered as part of subsequent questions. Nevertheless, if standardization were comprehensive and perfectly implemented, we could say that the interviewer did not affect the respondent—in the very specific sense that the effect of any interviewer would be the same as the effect of any other interviewer.

THE RECENT DEBATE ABOUT STANDARDIZATION

In advocating standardization, Hyman et al. ([1954] 1975:21) still worried that researchers might focus on improving reliability and neglect the more difficult problem of increasing validity. Decades later, Lucy Suchman and Brigitte Jordan (1990) argued that standardization is itself a substantial threat to the validity of the resulting data (see also Briggs 1986; Mishler 1986). They presented illustrations in which the rigidities of standardization led to awkward interactions and answers that might be inaccurate. They proposed letting both the respondent and the interviewer see the instrument and allowing "the interviewer to talk about the questions, to offer clarifications and elaborations, and to engage in a limited form of recipient design and common-sense inference" (p. 240; we discuss recipient design later in the chapter).

Subsequent discussions of standardization among survey practitioners have been influenced by studies that examine social-information-processing models of the process of answering a survey question (see, e.g., Sudman, Bradburn, and Schwarz 1996; Tourangeau et al. 2000). Much of the research developed within this framework has focused on improving the respondent's comprehension of survey questions and increasing the accuracy of the information a respondent retrieves from memory. Some of this research has experimented with relaxing the constraints of standardization to improve retrieval (e.g., Means et al. 1991). More recent studies have modified standardization with the aim of helping respondents understand survey concepts (we discuss this research later in the chapter).

Nevertheless, suggestions for loosening the constraints of standardization raise the anxieties of many survey researchers. The concerns of survey practitioners include, for example, that questions about events and behaviors require different measurement practices than questions about subjective things such as attitudes; that a system of standardization must be suitable for the requirements of recruiting, training, and supervising interviewers for very large surveys; and that innovations not increase interviewer variance. Discussions about standardization in the past decade have focused researchers' attention on several topics that have been examined in the studies we review later: how standardized interviewers actually behave, how their behavior affects the answers given by respondents, how conversational practices from other sorts of talk might be used in standardized interviewing, and how standardization might be changed to improve both the quality of the interaction and the quality of the resulting data.

STANDARDIZATION: VARIETIES AND PRACTICES

In debates about interviewing, "standardization" is sometimes assigned the role of "straw object"—as though there were one method of standardization that all survey researchers agree is best, that provides guidelines for all situations that an interviewer might encounter, and that interviewers could implement perfectly even when questions are poorly written. The reality has always been more complex than this caricature. There are no received tablets on which the rules of standardization are inscribed, and the practices of standardization have developed at various sites, each of which has its own traditions.

The rules that Floyd Fowler and Thomas Mangione codify in *Standardized Survey Interviewing* (1990) are comprehensive, grounded in the rationale for standardization, and refined through many years of practice and observation. Fowler and Mangione describe four principles of standardized interviewing:

1. Read questions as written.

2. Probe inadequate answers nondirectively.

3. Record answers without discretion.

4. Be interpersonally nonjudgmental regarding the substance of answers. (P. 35)

These principles would probably be almost universally accepted among survey researchers, but the specific practices derived from these principles can vary. At various sites, researchers and staff charged with supervising field operations have developed their own specifications for training interviewers derived from general principles (see Viterna and Maynard forthcoming).

The rules of standardization assembled by Michael Brenner (1981:19-22) illustrate this variation. Brenner allows the interviewer to "show an interest in the answers given by the respondent," to "volunteer" clarification "when necessary," and to "obtain an adequate answer by means of nondirective probing, repetition of the question or instruction, or nondirective clarification" when the respondent gives an inadequate answer. If a respondent asks for clarification, the interviewer must provide clarification, but nondirectively, by using "predetermined clarifications." These clarifications appear to be similar to the information that is sometimes provided to interviewers in "question-by-question specifications" or to the interviewers in the experiments on "flexible" or "conversational" interviewing described below (Schober and Conrad 1997; Conrad and Schober 2000). Both practices offer a contrast to Fowler and Mangione's recommendations for restraining the discretion of interviewers.

The variability in the practice of standardization can also be seen in the differing ways in which Fowler and Mangione's first principle is implemented. Although the general principle that the question must initially be read exactly as worded is probably the basic technique of standardization, and is even part of a variant method variously labeled *flexible* or *conversational* interviewing (Schober and Conrad 1997; Conrad and Schober 2000), some survey centers also accept a process that has been called *verification* as a legitimate technique of standardization. Verification acknowledges that respondents sometimes provide information before the interviewer asks for it, and that if an interviewer ignores the fact that he or she has already heard the answer to a question, the interaction may be awkward for both the interviewer and the respondent. For example, when the interviewer has already been told the respondent's age in one context, instead of asking a later, scripted question about the respondent's age, the interviewer might say, "I think you said earlier that you were 68 years old. Is that correct?"

The second principle, to probe nondirectively, can also be implemented in different ways. So, for example, Fowler and Mangione (1990:39-40) require interviewers to repeat all the response categories when they probe closed questions. There is substantial research showing that the meaning of any individual category depends on the entire set of categories (see, e.g., Schaeffer and Charng 1991; Smit, Dijkstra, and van der Zouwen 1997) to support this stipulation. But Johannes van der Zouwen (forthcoming) describes a practice he calls "tuning" in which the interviewer needs to repeat only the categories that appear to be in the vicinity of the respondent's answer. Tuning is itself similar to a technique called "zeroing in" that Fowler and Mangione (1990:41) describe for numerical answers.

Furthermore, practitioners recognize that there are situations in which the behavior of the interviewer cannot be completely standardized, such as the probing of "don't know" answers. Such answers, which require that the interviewer diagnose the "reason" for the "don't know," are a source of interviewer variation (Fowler and Mangione 1990:44; Mangione et al. 1992). When investigators train interviewers using "question-by-question specifications" of objectives, they recognize that the interviewer may need this information, the application of which cannot be prespecified, to diagnose and correct respondents' confusions and misunderstandings. That interviewers become less standardized when they actually use the information provided to them during training is part of the tension latent in traditional styles of standardization.

THE LIMITS OF STANDARDIZATION: ALTERNATION TO THE TACIT REALM

Listening to a survey interview, it is easy to conclude both that standardization is essential and that it will never be implemented perfectly and comprehensively, because no set of rules can cover every contingency. For example, when survey practitioners first documented how interviewers followed respondents' answers with feedback, the researchers' impulse was to standardize that feedback. Controlled feedback (e.g., "thank you," "that information is helpful") is intended to provide positive reinforcement for thoughtful behavior by the respondent without evaluating the content of the answer. Some experiments with controlled feedback suggest that it may improve the accuracy of reports (Cannell, Miller, and Oksenberg 1981; but see also Miller and Cannell 1982), possibly because it teaches respondents what kinds of effort and answers the interviewer wants. This tactic extends the reach of standardization, and the use of feedback could be enhanced by an understanding of the features of various acknowledgment tokens (Maynard and Marlaire 1992). But, despite researchers' best efforts, interviewers may vary in how they use feedback, respondents may perceive that feedback evaluates the content of their answers, and respondents may react to feedback in unpredictable ways.

Survey practitioners often must accept data produced in "messy" interactions as good enough for the purposes and budget at hand. Survey practitioners explicitly or implicitly recognize that interviewers inevitably must alternate between the rules of standardization and supplementing those rules. By using the term *alternate,* we mean that interviewers deploy resources of an "interactional substrate"—basic skills for engaging meaningfully with respondents—in pursuit of answers. These skills are presumed by, and yet are largely ignored in, the rules of standardized interviewing (Marlaire and Maynard 1990; Maynard and Marlaire 1992). The reliance of survey researchers on the interactional competence of interviewers acknowledges that *tacit knowledge* is required to implement and supplement formal, standardizing rules.

◆ Tacit Knowledge and Interaction in the Survey Interview

Before we discuss the problem of tacit knowledge, we need to define an approach to the survey interview called *critical remediation* (Maynard and Schaeffer 2000). The approach derives from work done by researchers who have studied the survey interview from a critical, "qualitative" methodological orientation (e.g., Cicourel 1974; Suchman and Jordan 1990; Briggs 1986; Mishler 1986).

CRITICAL REMEDIATION

Some qualitative researchers have suggested that survey researchers do not understand respondents' commonsense knowledge. From the critics' perspective, utterances or questions in the survey interview are never self-evident in terms of meaning; they are always occasioned and gain their sense only against a background of unspoken meanings and aspects of settings (Cicourel 1974: 196). In Elliot Mishler's (1986:22) terms, the problem is that survey research is a "context-stripping procedure" in which investigators "pretend" that the context does not affect the meaning of questions and answers. Context and meaning comprise actors' commonsense ways of thinking, conversing, acting, and deciding, or, in a phrase, their "essential sociocultural grounds of meaning" as these reside in the "life setting" of the respondent (Mishler 1986:23). These matters are particularly important when there are variations in respondents' cultural backgrounds (see also Briggs 1986). This is the "critical" part of critical remediation.

Qualitative researchers have also argued that, because the interview involves the use of language, "structural and transformational linguistics, cognitive psychology, developmental psycholinguistics, and linguistically oriented anthropological works on componential analysis and the ethnography of speaking" need to be taken into account in the design of survey interviews (Cicourel 1964:108, 198). In addition, "retrospective talk" as it occurs in a survey interview is very different from speech events in day-to-day experience (Cicourel 1974:179). Linguistic, psycholinguistic, and sociolinguistic investigations, it is argued, could redress survey researchers' neglect of language use and interaction. This is the "remedial" part of critical remediation. These perspectives would enable investigators to appreciate more fully the character of talk in the interview.

Although such discussions of the survey interview raise important points, many of these issues have been recognized and studied within the survey methodological tradition itself. For example, more than 45 years ago, Robert Kahn and Charles Cannell (1957:16) argued that interviews are a "specialized pattern of verbal interaction," and, more recently, Louise Kidder (1981: 146) has suggested that surveys rely on "verbal reports" whose properties require investigation. In proposing that survey researchers should better appreciate *respondents'* life worlds, some qualitative investigators have bypassed the concerns of survey methodologists and have been preoccupied with what survey researchers miss, how they distort, and what they should do better. Such preoccupations mean that some critics have done with respect to interviewers precisely what they accuse survey researchers of doing with respect to respondents: They have ignored and misrepresented the *interviewers'* life worlds—or everyday work worlds—and failed to comprehend that the survey interview enterprise is a complex set of actions and activities. In other words, such critics have avoided immersion in the world of the researcher and interviewer in the way they recommend that the researcher and interviewer should enter the world of the respondent.

ANALYTIC ALTERNATION

To enter the world of the interviewer, we draw on the "Ethnomethodological Studies of Work" program in the arena of science studies and other professional endeavors (Heritage 1984b; Lynch 1992; see Maynard and Schaeffer 2000). The thrust of this research is to comprehend analytically the concreteness, specificity, and detail involved in actual work, including how practitioners use technologies. If we become concerned with the *survey interviewer's* work, we take a new approach to studying the survey interview. We consider the survey enterprise as a kind of "formal analytic" inquiry, providing a vast set of instructions for how investigations can proceed. These instructions—including procedures for standardization, as used in specific instances—necessarily and repeatedly raise an ethnomethodological question. To paraphrase Harold Garfinkel (1996:19): What more is there to instructions and instructed actions than a survey center—with its manuals, procedures, instruments, and other kinds of instructions—can provide? The "what more" question points to the tacit knowledge that interviewers use to handle the problems that emerge during the interview.

Analytic alternation, in the context of the survey interview, is a means of investigating practitioners' work. Practitioners' work involves both adherence to formal inquiry—the use of rules, procedures, and instruments for conducting the interview—and the exercise of taken-for-granted, tacit skills. Practitioners *alternate* from one orientation and set of competencies to the other. These skills are exhibited in the produced, orderly detail of everyday talk and embodied action that reflexively supports and helps achieve the accountability of the formal inquiry. *Accountability* means that the interview gets done in ways that are acceptably—for all practical purposes—standardized and scientific.

A straightforward example of interviewer alternation is to be found in a glance at any survey research center: We can observe interviewers engaged in computer-aided telephone interviewing to be gazing at and reading verbatim to their respondents from scripted interviews on the screens in front of them, with hands and fingers tethered to keyboards on the desks, and entering codes for heard responses that correspond to the proper categories as displayed on the screens. The interviewers, for some duration, appear to be formal analytic or standardized homunculi, enacting what the survey instruments on their computer screens tell them to do as they talk, listen, and type.

At singular and unpredictable moments, however, interviewers will glance away from the screens, move their hands from the keyboards, and gesture more or less expansively, producing talk that is neither scripted nor otherwise predesigned, in order to handle some departure from the routine, with the aim of being able to return to that routine. For example, an interviewer may find it necessary to gesture while explaining something learned during training about the survey to a respondent. Although the gesturing is not something that the respondent sees, it might help the interviewer in articulating a point, or in emphasizing a significant piece of talk, or some other aspect of the verbal presentation. When the point has been made, the interviewer returns gaze and hands back to the computer and keyboard. At these moments of departure, interviewers alternate from the formal to the tacit realm and engage practices designed to provide for alternation again back to the formal.

This is only a more visible manifestation of what we mean by alternation, for even when they read scripts more or less verbatim, interviewers, in interaction with respondents, are engaged in performances that improvise on those scripts. For example, the script does not tell the interviewer how to manage turn taking with the respondent; instead, interviewer and respondent use a familiar "interviewing sequence"

(which we discuss below). *Analytic* alternation refers to studying departures from, and improvisations on, scripts as orderly practices. That is, interactions, as manifestations of tacit and commonsense knowledge, are sites of pattern and organization and therefore need to be appreciated analytically in their own terms. Recent studies of interaction in the interview are beginning to provide such an appreciation. Tacit knowledge is not only necessary and inescapable; beyond this, it inescapably shapes social measurement.

THE "INTERVIEWING SEQUENCE" IN THE SURVEY AND OTHER ENVIRONMENTS

One form of tacit knowledge exhibited in the survey is the question-answer-acknowledgment series of turns—the "interviewing sequence"—that participants produce. In analyzing this sequence as a generic form, we are reminded that the survey is only one type of "interview." Dictionary definitions, for example, suggest that the interview is a "formal consultation" used to evaluate qualifications or "a meeting at which information is obtained (as by a reporter, television commentator, or pollster) from a person" (*Merriam-Webster's Collegiate Dictionary*, 10th edition). Accordingly, the survey has a relationship to other interviews, all of which embody the interviewing sequence but, as we discuss below, with "third-turn acknowledgments" of various configurations. For example, physicians and nurses often interview their patients to obtain medical histories, teachers and psychologists interview students as part of teaching and testing, employers interview prospective employees in making hiring decisions, and newscasters interview government officials and others as part of their programming. The survey can be compared to these other kinds of interviews to specify some of its distinctive characteristics.

A comparison of survey interviews and other interviews is instructive. For example, a prominent feature of the medical interview is how questioning builds in certain biases. Physicians and other health professionals do not exhibit the disinterest and objectivity required of survey interviewers; instead, during history taking they "build their questions so as to convey a form of relatedness and concern for the welfare of the patient" (Boyd and Heritage forthcoming). Questions in medical interviews are built with presuppositions and preferences that suggest optimistic, "no problem" answers. Medical personnel do not ask questions such as "Is your father dead?" but rather "Is your father alive?" They would not ask, "Are your bowel movements problematic?" but rather "Are your bowel movements normal?" Similarly, British health visitors in interaction with mothers who have recently given birth construct their questions about the process of childbirth in ways that favor "no problem" responses, stringing together proposals to the mother about having a "normal pregnancy" and a "normal delivery," saying "she's bottle-feeding?" and the like in a way that suggests they expect positive answers. Heritage (forthcoming) calls this the principle of optimization.

Interview questions in medical contexts also embody what Harvey Sacks, Emanuel Schegloff, and Gail Jefferson (1974) call "recipient design," which refers to a "multitude of respects in which the talk by one party in a conversation is constructed or designed in ways which display an orientation and sensitivity to the particular other(s) who are the coparticipants" (p. 727). Such recipient design is exhibited in the following questions from a physician to a 50-year-old divorced woman whom the doctor knows to have had a tubal ligation procedure: "Are you using any contraception? Is that necessary for you?" These questions exhibit the physician's understanding of the women's circumstances (Boyd and Heritage forthcoming). Heritage (forth-

coming) demonstrates that health visitors' questions to new parents also exhibit such recipient design. By contrast with social surveys and medical interviews, the standardized survey interview is designed to obviate any practices of optimization or recipient design that would increase the likelihood of obtaining biased answers from respondents. Standardized survey interviews are, in Heritage's (forthcoming) phrase, built to be "essentially anonymous" (on the anonymous way in which survey participation is solicited, see also Maynard and Schaeffer 1997).

ACKNOWLEDGMENT TURNS

One contribution of a comparison of surveys with other forms of interviewing is that it makes our understanding of what standardization overcomes—such as optimization and recipient design—more specific. A second contribution is that it describes issues surrounding the third, "acknowledgment," turn of the interviewing sequence. Acknowledgments are what survey researchers refer to as *feedback*. Acknowledgments include subtle forms of interviewer behavior, which may be influential, as well as the more formal tokens that interviewers use after a respondent has produced an answer to a survey question. Research on educational testing and occupational and news interviews shows how this third turn contributes to making the "outputs" from such diverse interviews *collaborative productions*.

Viewing interview outputs as collaborative productions goes against stimulus-response and other bipartite models of the interviewer-interviewee relationship that presume that interviewers are neutral conduits of questions that interviewees answer according to their own abilities, willingness to disclose, and so on. Research that examines interaction shows how the interviewer enters into the answering behavior and

A

S:	1→	.hh When do you get out. Christmas week or the week before Christmas.
		(0.3)
G:	2→	Uh::m two or three days before Ch[ristmas.]
S:	3→	[Oh:,]

B

T:	1→	((Holding up card)) This is the long word. Who knows what it says?
S:	2→	Cafeteria.
T:	3→	Cafeteria, Audrey, good for you!

products of interviewees. Just one example from an educational testing situation illustrates how this happens. Children often learn from the examination experience itself, and from such patterns as the pacing of questions, the parsing of stimulus items, and the reactions of test administrators, whether their answers are on the right track. On the way to producing answers, using these cues, they can modify what they end up saying and fashion answers that more or less reflect the social environment as much as their own solitary efforts (Marlaire and Maynard 1990; Maynard and Marlaire 1992; Mehan 1973; Mehan, Hertweck, and Meihls 1986). Collaborative production of "answers" also occurs in teaching (as opposed to testing) environments, and it is a feature that Michael Schober and Frederick Conrad (forthcoming) argue is present in the survey interview.

The more formal forms of feedback described in interactional research are third-turn acknowledgments. In conversation, such third turns follow information-seeking question-answer sequences (turns 1 and 2) and register that the information is informative to the questioner (Heritage 1984b: 285-86). Turns in Excerpt A are labeled with numbers.

The "Oh" in turn 3 indicates a "change of state" in the answer recipient's knowledge (Heritage 1984a). In educational settings, question-answer or "instructional" sequences involve teachers asking "known-information" questions, as in Excerpt B,

from Hugh Mehan (1979:52-53). In such instructional sequences, the third-turn response evaluates a student's answer.

In contrast with conversational and educational settings, there are other institutional settings in which questioners *withhold* third-turn responses of either variety (indicating a change of knowledge state or evaluation of an answer). Prominent among these are courtrooms (Atkinson and Drew 1979), job interviews (Button 1987), and news interviews (Heritage and Greatbatch 1991). These venues have in common that interviewers (lawyers or employers or newscasters, as the case may be) are soliciting answers for an *overhearing audience* of some kind who may do their evaluations of interviewees and their answers at some distance from the interview itself. By refraining from any kind of post-answer commentary, interviewers exhibit themselves as conduits for those answers to flow to those audiences—who are then in the position of supplying that commentary in another social context aside from the interview itself.

A rule that forbids third-turn responses may be clearer than protocols under which interviewers are not enjoined from such productions but are still not supposed to comment on the content of the answers. This dilemma of being permitted to respond but in restricted ways characterizes the survey interview, and it is also present in educational testing interviews. Indeed, the protocols for tests such as the Woodcock-

Johnson Psychoeducational Battery may warn administrators, "Be careful that your pattern of comments does not indicate whether answers are correct or incorrect" (Mehan et al. 1986:96-97). Administrators may produce "neutral" acknowledgments ("okay," "thank you," and the like) after a child has answered a test item. However, research demonstrates that administrators sometimes alter their third-turn responses *systematically,* using "good" when an answer is correct and "okay" when it is incorrect, for example; they may also give encouraging nonvocal signals by smiling or nodding when a child's answer is right and appearing more taciturn when it is wrong (Maynard and Marlaire 1992).

The concern that most survey centers have in regard to third-turn "feedback" is no doubt well placed. Survey researchers have long recognized that fine gradations in such responses potentially influence the answers of respondents (Marquis, Cannell, and Laurent 1972). Although most survey centers have protocols that attempt to standardize the use of feedback, such standards are by no means uniform *across* survey centers (Viterna and Maynard forthcoming). Practitioners agree on the principle that feedback should not evaluate the content of the answer, but specific rules about the frequency, content, and purpose of feedback vary (whether it should be used to sustain motivation, to take notice of the respondent's level of effort, to take notice that the respondent's answer meets task requirements, to provide reassurance, and so on).

CONVERSATION WITH A PURPOSE

The survey interview has long been described as a "conversation with a purpose" (Bingham and Moore 1924, cited by Cannell and Kahn 1968; see also Schaeffer, 1991). In this regard, it is like interviewing behavior in other settings, including both conversation (where participants may go on fact-finding excursions) and institu-

tional settings such as schools, courtrooms, and news organizations. Both parties to an interview use tacit knowledge and taken-for-granted procedures to produce and answer interview questions; the interviewer uses these skills to respond or withhold responses in particular ways. The survey interview shares generic practices for asking, answering, and acknowledging answers with other interview forms. The survey interview is relatively distinctive in its practices for maintaining the anonymity of questions and acknowledging answers without evaluating their content. Studies of interaction in the survey interview, such as those we review next, implicitly or explicitly recognize the interviewing sequence as the base form for the interview.

◆ Recent Studies of Interaction in the Survey Interview

In the past decade, the methods used to study what happens during the survey interview and the goals of this research have become increasingly more diverse (on earlier studies, see Schaeffer 1991). Explicitly or implicitly, these various research efforts recognize how tacit knowledge is embedded in the conduct of a survey interview. The research we review here includes studies that have described and coded the behavior of standardized interviewers and respondents, experiments that have compared the effects of different styles of interviewing, and investigations that we will characterize roughly as ethnomethodological and conversation analytic. Studies in the last group have examined details of the interaction between the interviewer and respondent in order to map the interactional resources participants use to create survey data. But the other studies can also contribute to our understanding of how interviewers and respondents alternate between following the rules of standardization and using daily interactional competence. The studies we summarize vary in whether they are primarily descriptive or attempt to show how the participants' behavior affects the quality of survey data.

CONCEPTUAL MODELS

Social-information-processing models have motivated research that has increased and complicated our understanding of how respondents answer survey questions. However, we still lack a general conceptual framework that focuses on the interaction in the interview and that could guide research about how the interviewer's behavior affects the respondent and subsequently the respondent's answers. Early research about interviewing invoked concepts such as "rapport," acquiescence, and social desirability to speculate about the mechanisms that might intervene between the interviewer's behavior and the respondent's answer (see, e.g., Goudy and Potter 1975; Weiss 1968, 1970). But that research did not explicate what these mechanisms might actually look like in the interaction.

An attempt to incorporate the interaction in the interview appears in Johannes van der Zouwen, Wil Dijkstra, and Johannes Smit's (1991:420) model of interviewing "style" and the experiments they based on this model. The model specifies that interviewing style, which consists of specific behaviors, can affect the "respondent's willingness to provide adequate answers" and the adequacy of the cues the interviewer provides the respondent. The effect of the interviewer's behavior is modified by the respondent's certainty about his or her answer (a respondent who is more uncertain will pay more attention to cues provided by the interviewer's behavior) and the difficulty of the task (the style of interviewing will have little impact if questions are easy and do not present many possibilities for suggesting answers). Questions that are difficult, but for which the inter-

viewer cannot suggest answers, are likely to benefit from a personal style of interviewing because it increases the respondent's motivation to be accurate and complete. For questions that are easy (and so do not require as much motivation) but susceptible to suggestions by the interviewer, a formal style of interviewing may obtain higher-quality data.

We have taken a less formal approach to describing how the interaction in the interview affects the data (Schaeffer and Maynard 1996). Drawing on discussions of "social cognition" and studies of interaction in other contexts, we have argued that social-information-processing models of the response process are limited. We have illustrated how part of what these models label as "cognitive processing" is actually accomplished in the interaction between the interviewer and the respondent, and not inside the respondent's head. That "processing" also relies on aspects of the way language is used in interaction (e.g., Clark and Schober 1992).

More complete models of how the interaction in the interview affects responses could help researchers consider alternatives to strict standardization more systematically, just as the van der Zouwen et al. model directs our attention to assessing the motivation of the respondent and the adequacy of the cues provided by the interviewer. Both these projects—developing better models and designing variants of traditional standardization—could benefit from a better understanding of what interviewers and respondents actually do in survey interviews.

An initial list of the activities we observe interviewers performing that researchers should take into account in devising styles of standardization might include the following: reading questions, repeating information the respondent has given earlier as a "verification" of an answer to a current question, responding to comments respondents make about the survey question, responding to other comments made by respondents, proposing solutions to a possible comprehension problem, proposing a change in the structure of the task, proposing further choices or actions to the respondent, and providing acknowledgment or acceptance. Each of these activities can be analyzed as part of tasks that might be the subject of interviewing rules and training.

For example, the observation that interviewers sometimes propose a solution to a possible comprehension problem or propose a change in the task can lead to an examination of what situations lead to interviewer intervention, what behavior of respondents' interviewers treat as indicating problems in comprehension, what behavior of respondents' interviewers treat as indicating problems with the structure of the question-and-answer task, what techniques interviewers use to clarify questions or modify the task, and so on. Thus we can observe survey interviewers treating respondents' delays in answering and their "reportings" of material related to the topic of the question as though these behaviors indicate some problem in comprehension (we provide an example of this later). Interviewers may then "remedy" these problems by providing preemptive probes, repeating the question, and so on (Schaeffer and Maynard forthcoming; see also Schaeffer, Maynard, and Cradock 1993). The effectiveness of the techniques interviewers use can be tested in experiments, and those found to be successful can be used to expand the repertoire of survey interviewing.

DESCRIBING THE BEHAVIOR OF STANDARDIZED INTERVIEWERS

The justification for rules of standardization continues to receive support from recent studies that examine interviewer effects (e.g., Mangione et al. 1992). Research also shows how departures from standardization can affect the validity of answers. For example, Smit, Dijkstra, and van der

Zouwen (1997) used a question that evoked a response before the response categories were presented to compare experimentally the effects of three different ways of having interviewers present the response categories. After the respondent "interrupted" with an answer, the interviewer presented (a) the three categories adjacent to the category the respondent's answer suggested, (b) a single category in the direction suggested by the respondent, or (c) the category that seemed closest to the answer given by the respondent. The results suggest that respondents are more likely to choose the category mentioned by the interviewer; in addition, the relationship of the item with the respondent's age varied depending on which technique the interviewer used. In an additional experimental manipulation that compared neutral and suggestive probes, Smit et al. found that the probes influenced the subsequent answer in one of two cases they examined. This finding complements that of an earlier experiment that showed that when interviewers briefly expressed an opinion on a topic related to the survey questions, the distribution of answers was affected (Dijkstra 1987).

Research that examines the behavior of standardized interviewers suggests, however, that departures from standardization sometimes increase the accuracy of answers. Jennifer Dykema, James Lepkowski, and Steven Blixt (1997) analyzed a study of health-related events and experiences that included a record check of respondents' answers for several questions. For only 1 of 10 items was there a relationship between reading the question exactly as worded and the accuracy of the answer—and for that case the relationship was not in the predicted direction. Dykema and her colleagues note that there may be something about the specific items involved that accounts for this finding. Furthermore, the deviations from standardization that account for this relationship when it occurs are unlikely to be random or haphazard alterations of question wording. The effect is likely to be due either to wording changes that are tailored to the situation in some way or to other interviewer behaviors that happen to be correlated with question wording changes. (For example, experienced interviewers may be both most likely to alter the wording of questions and most adept at identifying when respondents misunderstand questions.) In later analyses of these data, Robert Belli and colleagues find evidence that when interviewers modify the wording of the question, accuracy is improved for younger, but not for older respondents (Belli, Weiss, and Lepkowski 1999). Some of the mechanisms that produce these results may be those examined in recent experiments that let interviewers depart from standardization to try to improve respondents' comprehension of questions (see our later discussion).

EXPERIMENTING WITH THE STYLE OF INTERVIEWING TO IMPROVE SURVEY DATA

Experiments that compare styles of interviewing presume an analysis that identifies the components of interviewing "style." Such an analysis identifies behaviors of the interviewer—such as those discussed earlier—that could distinguish styles of interviewing and that are expected to affect the validity or reliability of resulting data. Experimental variations of interviewing styles can focus on any of the goals of standardized measurement, including reducing error variation and increasing the accuracy of individual answers. Borrowing from social-information-processing models of the question-answering process, one might propose modifying practices of standardization to improve the respondent's comprehension of survey concepts, improve the respondent's recall, clarify the format in which the response is to be provided, motivate the respondent to be accurate, and so on.

The goal of improving recall has long been a focus of experiments with interviewing techniques, such as controlled feedback, anchoring dates to fix reference periods, beginning the interview with a "free-flowing discussion" of the topic, and using various techniques to stimulate recall of events. Some of the techniques in these experiments could be used in standardized interviews (e.g., controlled feedback), but others involve substantially loosening the practices of standardization (e.g., varying the order of topics, free recall) (for examples, see discussions in Cannell, Marquis, and Laurent 1977; Means et al. 1989; Oksenberg et al. 1992). Many—perhaps most—of these techniques have not found their way into large-scale production interviewing. This is probably at least partly because they pose challenges (and additional expense) for the training and supervising of interviewers and for the recording and processing of data.

The motivation of the respondent has also been addressed in experiments with interviewing techniques. When respondents are asked to sign a form on which they commit themselves to working hard, reporting appears to improve (see, e.g., Cannell et al. 1981). In Dijkstra's (1987) comparison of formal and personal (elsewhere labeled "socioemotional"; see Dijkstra and van der Zouwen 1988) interviewing, both styles are essentially standardized, but the personal style attempts to increase the respondent's motivation by telling the interviewer during training that a good relationship with the respondent is important for getting accurate information and by allowing the interviewer to express sympathy toward the respondent (e.g., "How nice for you!"). Respondents interviewed in the personal style performed better on a map-drawing task, provided more irrelevant information, and had lower social desirability scores than did respondents interviewed in the formal style. Respondents in the two styles were similar in the amount of relevant information they provided and in their

```
43   IV:    .hhh Naow (0.3) Last week
44          (0.5)
45   IV:    did you (.) do any work at all including work for pay or
46          other types of compensation
47   FR:    N:ow are you asking this of me? [personally?  ]
48   IV:                                    [You yeah ub] you
49          personally .hh be[cause] I'm speaking with=
50   FR:                     [(   )]
51   IV:    =you pers- and then the next question will be (.)
52          concerning (.) your husband=
53   FR:    =Oh um
54          (0.7)
55   IV:    [So do y-]
56   FR:    [I'm on ma]ternity lea- maternity leave right now=
57   IV:    =Okay so nother words you are .hhh w- last week you
58          actually did not work [right?  ]
59   FR:                          [No did] not work=
60   IV:    =O:kay (.) for any pay
61   FR:    Right
```

tendency to be influenced by an opinion the interviewer provided (as part of an experimental treatment) during the course of the interview.

Subsequent analyses of this experiment examined how participants behaved in the two styles of interviewing. Interviewers in the formal and personal styles appeared similar in how often they deviated from the wording of the question in the questionnaire and in how often they "chose" an answer based on information provided by the respondent, but interviewers in the personal style were more likely to emit "irrelevant behaviors" and more likely to "hint" at an answer (asking leading questions or suggesting an answer) (Dijkstra and van der Zouwen 1988). Analyses of the interaction sequences indicate that interviewers trained in the personal style are more likely than interviewers trained in the formal style to use leading probes, and that these probes are usually "in line" with information already provided by the re-

spondent. Respondents are likely to accept suggestions made by the interviewer, particularly when the interviewer uses the personal style (van der Zouwen et al. 1991).

Another important goal of interviewing, suggested by models of the response process, is to improve the respondent's understanding of the task. Survey questions can never apply perfectly to every respondent's situation. Thus interviewers regularly encounter respondents who have trouble classifying themselves using the available response categories. These problems occur when respondents present situations that the researcher expected to be infrequent in the sample or did not anticipate in the design of the instrument. The interactional trajectory of these occasions shows that correctly classifying the respondent using survey concepts is the interviewer's, not the respondent's, business, as the interaction between an interviewer (IV) and female respondent (FR) shown illustrates (see Schaeffer and Maynard forthcoming).

At line 56, the respondent produces a "report" of information relevant to the question, but does not provide a formatted answer. Paul Drew (1984) has shown that in other contexts, it is up to the recipient of a report to gather the upshot, as this interviewer does beginning at line 57.

The sort of directive probe used by this interviewer is probably unacceptable in most versions of standardization. We speculate, however, that at least some investigators would be comfortable with an intervention that presented a portion of the concept definition tailored for this respondent, such as, "And did you get paid for that maternity leave?" or "Did you have a job to which you expected to return after your maternity leave?" or whatever the relevant distinction might be. The clarification the interviewer presents at lines 48-52 is tailored in this way: She uses a contrast with "your husband" (he is presumably in the "common ground" of the interview) to clarify that "you" means only the respondent.

Under the strongest version of the flexible style of standardization examined by Schober and Conrad (1997; Conrad and Schober 2000) in their innovative series of experiments, the initiative shown by this interviewer in diagnosing the source of the difficulty would be within the range of acceptable behavior, as would the directive probe (M. F. Schober, personal communication, March 1, 2000). Schober and Conrad tested the impact of allowing interviewers to determine when they should help respondents by clarifying survey concepts and authorizing interviewers to define survey concepts in their own words, sometimes in combination with instructions to respondents that explained that survey concepts could differ from everyday concepts and encouraged respondents to ask for help. Respondents are much more likely to ask for clarification in the flexible style of interviewing (of the questions that mapped onto respondents' situations in complicated ways, 2 percent elicited questions in standardized interviews and 34 percent did so in conversational interviews; see Bloom and Schober 1999), which began with extensive instruction about the importance of asking for clarification (see also Schober, Conrad, and Fricker 1999). Either the respondents' requests or the initiative taken by the interviewer, or the combination, appears to be effective: Respondents with complicated situations were significantly more likely to give accurate answers when they were interviewed with the flexible style. The increased accuracy comes at an increased cost (which is sometimes substantial) in interview time for both straightforward and complex situations (Schober et al. 1999).

The technique of authorizing interviewers to diagnose and intervene to correct possible problems in understanding and applying survey concepts faces a number of challenges. It is true that instruments cannot always anticipate or handle all situations respondents might present. However, instruments should be designed to handle complex situations that affect significant proportions of the sample. Because situations that instruments cannot handle will always arise, training interviewers in how to intervene properly could increase validity, even if it took more interviewing time for the affected cases.

The operational problems these techniques face in gaining acceptance include the cost of having the interviewer take the initiative when it might not be needed and the cost of training interviewers to use these techniques in surveys in which there are many concepts. There are also other unknowns: whether respondents will continue to ask questions and indicate when they need help during long interviews, whether interviewers can retain concepts over long field periods in which any given definition may be required only rarely, how the techniques might be applied to questions about subjective things (or how interviewers might manage alternating between strict standardization for subjective questions and flexible interviewing for other questions), how interviewers might be monitored and supervised in their use of these techniques, and what the impact on interviewer variance in a full-scale study might be (see also Schaeffer and Royston 1999).

ETHNOMETHODOLOGICAL AND CONVERSATION-ANALYTIC STUDIES OF INTERACTION

Many recent studies of interaction in the survey interview draw on ethnomethodology and conversation analysis, two interrelated subfields in sociology that regard concrete activities of participants in everyday life as a site of intelligible organization that is available for close scientific analysis (Maynard and Clayman 1991; see also Garfinkel 1967, 1996; Heritage 1984b). Ethnomethodology started with a concern for members' "accounting practices," or the devices by which intelligibility is sustained in and through concrete concerted actions. It has made large contributions to the study of practices in the workplace and in scientific laboratories (Lynch 1992). Consequently, it has implications for the study of survey interviewing as a work practice (Maynard and Schaeffer 2000; Lynch forthcoming).

Conversation analysis describes and analyzes the orderly properties of conversational interaction as the achievements of participants. Rather than being a product of external influence, processes of conversational interaction have their own internal constraints, or are under *local control* (Zimmerman 1988:408). For instance, Sacks et al. (1974) note that in taking turns at talk, participants have three ordered options: (a) a current speaker may select the next speaker, (b) a next speaker may self-select, or (c) a current speaker may continue. With this system of turn taking in conversation, participants have an *intrinsic* motivation for listening to one another, independent of other motivations including interest, deference, or politeness.

Potential next speakers must listen to a current speaker to find out whether they have been selected to take the next turn, to discover when the current turn ends and it is appropriate to start speaking, and to know what they may be constrained to say next, given what has been said in the turn of talk under way. This intrinsic motivation for listening means that conversation is largely self-governing with respect to the orderly achievement of mutual understanding. If the displayed understanding in that next turn does not align with the speaker's own, then the *next* turn of speaker can be devoted to correcting the matter. *Repair* of all kinds of conversational trouble usually exhibits sequentially systematic properties (Schegloff, Jefferson, and Sacks 1977). Robert Moore and Douglas Maynard (forthcoming) discuss how conversation repair intertwines with the *probing* of uncodable answers to survey questions. Turn-taking and repair mechanisms are part of the *local* control mechanisms for maintaining orderliness in conversational interaction.

Conversational and Interactional Sequencing

As we discussed earlier, Suchman and Jordan (1990) have observed that the survey interview is under external control. Survey design governs both what participants in the interview talk about and how they talk (through question-answer sequences). This means that ordinary resources for establishing shared understanding in conversation are prohibited in the interview. For instance, whereas participants in conversation are free to elaborate on what their presumptive worldviews are, what their utterances mean, and what the sources of any misunderstandings are, interviewers and respondents are severely constrained from such elaboration.

The critique of Suchman and Jordan (1990) and others (see our earlier discussion) focuses on how the survey interview differs from, and is inferior to, conversation in the establishment of mutual understanding and meaning, rather than on what characterizes the performance of the survey interview *as a standardized interview* for purposes of social measurement. Schegloff (1990), in a response to Suchman and Jordan, suggests that inquiry is possible "into the features of the survey interview as an organized occasion of talk in interaction" (p. 249; see also Schegloff forthcoming). Such inquiry would recognize that "all talk-in-interaction faces certain generic organizational problems, and will perforce adopt some organized solution to them." Such generic organizational problems include procedures for allocating turns of talk; interactional constraints on coherence; repair of troubles in speaking, hearing, understanding, and so on; an overall structural organization; and a variety of other matters depending on the nature of the survey and its substantive topic.

"Preference structures" provide an example of interactional constraints. The concepts of "preference" and "preference structure" in conversation refer to ways in which agreement (preferred) and disagreement (dispreferred) and other paired conversational actions (acceptance/rejection, offering/requesting, and so on) are asymmetrical in terms of their conversational enactment. Even when participants may "want" to disagree with someone, they often display their disagreements in a *dispreferred* fashion. Thus the term *preference* refers to structural properties of and systematic practices in conversation (see Pomerantz 1984; Sacks 1987). Nora Cate Schaeffer (1991) has argued that preference structure may intrude on the survey interview in a way that affects respondents' answers.

Because the fundamental framework for doing conversation analysis is sequential organization, the organization of question-answer sequences, which dominate the survey interview, is of natural interest. We have referred to the sequence in which an interviewer asks a question as written and a respondent answers in the format requested as *paradigmatic* (Schaeffer and Maynard 1996). This ideal sequence presumes that the cognitive processing required to produce an answer occurs "inside the respondent's head." But, as discussed earlier, we have shown how the *concerted* participation in the interview radically enters into the cognitive processes researchers often assign to the respondent (Schaeffer and Maynard 1996). Respondents do not simply react to the wording of the survey questions, and interviewers are not only a conduit of the questions. Attention to question-answer sequences and ways in which respondents solicit interviewer help, or in which interviewers offer help, reveals a more complicated and interactive picture.

Monograph Studies of Interaction in the Survey Interview

Hanneke Houtkoop-Steenstra's book *Interaction and the Standardized Survey Interview* (2000) is the most extensive conversation-analytic study to date of question-and-answer sequences during the survey interview. Houtkoop-Steenstra's empirical investigation starts with a consideration of "participant roles" in the interview, suggesting that the interview implicates more than just an "interviewer" and a "respondent." Using Erving Goffman's (1979) concept of "footing," which refers to the stances that participants take in relation to their talk, Houtkoop-Steenstra describes how interviewers exhibit themselves as "animators" (Goffman 1979) or "relayers" (Levinson 1988) of text that is designed by others, the "author" (Goffman 1979) or "formulator" (Clark 1996). Accordingly, when respondents ask for clarification or have other difficulties, interviewers comment in ways that indicate such a participation status, such as "I just ask questions here." Or, in other circumstances, interviewers may refer to distant participants who design the instrument items, with phrases such as "They're asking . . . ." From time to time, interviewers may step out of their animating stance altogether, saying (for example) "I'm sorry" when a respondent reports a sad incident.

Elsewhere in her book, Houtkoop-Steenstra addresses the topics of redundant questions, the structure of question turns, and the field coding of questions. Redundant questions are those for which a respondent has already provided relevant information in response to a previous question. Although some centers use the "verification" procedure we described earlier, there are circumstances in which redundant questions still pose problems. In such circumstances, it appears that the Dutch survey interviewers Houtkoop-Steenstra studied become more "conversational," whereas U.S. interviewers may be stricter in following rules of standardization. Houtkoop-Steenstra also addresses the organization of question turns in interviews (see also Houtkoop-Steenstra forthcoming). Survey researchers have observed that when a "question" is followed by a definition, respondents may interrupt before the definition is read (e.g., Cannell et al. 1989); Schaeffer (1991) has shown how work by conversation analysts could be used to understand why such a question might frequently be interrupted.

Using specifications provided by Sacks et al.'s (1974) foundational work on turn taking, Houtkoop-Steenstra (2000) describes how many survey questions are vulnerable to interruption because they can be heard to implicate a response from the respondent before the scripted question is complete. Realizing this, interviewers often modify such questions in the course of producing them, although this reduces standardization. In the final chapter of *Interaction and the Standardized Survey Interview,* Houtkoop-Steenstra deals with "field coding" of answers to open questions, arguing that, in a variety of ways, interviewers are prompted to modify such questions, sometimes, for example, producing candidate answers on behalf of their respondents, who can confirm such candidates. Although this may compromise standard-

ization, features of interaction may naturally occasion such interviewer behavior.

Another major conversation-analytic work on the survey is Robert Moore's (1999) doctoral dissertation on "repair" and its relation to "probing" in the survey interview. Moore discusses respondents' requests for repeats and clarifications of survey questions and interviewers' queries about inadequately formulated answers. A phenomenon related to repair, and to Houtkoop-Steenstra's consideration of question structure, is how interviewers handle "premature" answers or those that occur before a question has been completely read because respondents figure they have enough information. It is important to note that repair in conversation is related to the achievement of understanding (Schegloff et al. 1977), but in the survey interview, standardization may impede practices of repair and therefore interfere with such understanding (see also Moore and Maynard forthcoming).

Finally, Maynard et al. (forthcoming) have edited a collection of studies on interaction in the survey interview. Topics covered include theoretical orientations toward studying such interaction, the organization of questions and interviewing sequences, and data quality.

Recruiting Survey Participants

Robert Groves, Robert Cialdini, and Mick Couper (1992) propose that interaction is also one of the critical elements in a theory of survey *participation.* Conversation-analytic investigations add to other studies of survey interview openings that attempt to identify the tacit means by which scripted introductions are made to work on behalf of recruiting respondents to the interview. In one article, we have examined the practices by which interviewers open their encounters with potential respondents and make requests for participation, as well as the complementary means by which call recipients accept or decline such requests (exercising their "gatekeeping" capacity) and the methods by which both participants close and terminate the encounter when a respondent refuses the request (Maynard and Schaeffer 1997; see also Maynard and Schaeffer forthcoming-a).

Groves et al. (1992) introduce the concept of "tailoring" for understanding the work of soliciting participation. Successful interviewers, they argue, tailor the scripted instructions for recruiting participants to specific concerns and objections that potential survey respondents may raise. They search for cues about a householder who answers the door or telephone and should be able to size up a situation quickly and apply the appropriate persuasive messages. Couper and Groves (forthcoming) show some suggestive evidence that the more interviewers tailor their introductions, the more likely they are to get cooperation. And we have examined in detail the real-time devices of talk and embodied behavior by which an interviewer "tailors" the callback to a selected respondent who had previously refused participation in a survey and successfully obtains participation of the household, if not that particular respondent (Maynard and Schaeffer forthcoming-b). Through a variety of tacit and persuasive methods, the interviewer obtains permission to call back later, and, upon making that callback, the interviewer obtains a completed interview.

◆ Conclusion

The questions used in survey measurement are similar to everyday questions—which are a resource in many familiar types of talk. As a result, however, survey interviews are prey to a tension between the everyday task of "getting information" and the scientific task of "measurement." In resolving this tension, interviewers alternate between following the rules of standardization and, for circumstances such rules cannot foresee or prescribe how to handle,

deploying their tacit knowledge and interactional competence in pursuit of survey answers.

Recent studies of interaction in the survey interview have documented the limits of standardization but also the resourcefulness of interviewers in pushing those limits in pursuit of answers. For example, detailed studies of interaction from a conversation-analytic standpoint describe ways that interviewers diagnose problems in comprehension (Schaeffer and Maynard forthcoming). Subsequent studies suggest that the validity of survey data might be enhanced if interviewers are authorized to intervene with clarifications when they determine that respondents do not understand survey concepts. Such innovations could improve the quality of survey data if they are shown to reduce total error—considering effects on both reliability and validity.

The fate of the innovative methods of interviewing examined by past research, however, suggests that improving survey measurement will require that researchers grapple with the operational issues involved in putting a "prototype" style of interviewing into "production." The challenges include devising methods that large field staffs can be trained to use reliably at an acceptable cost. New interviewing methods also will require guidelines for monitoring the quality of interviewers' behavior as well as appropriate instruments and data processing procedures.

In addition to their contribution to our understanding of the survey interview, the findings of the studies examined here may have implications for our understanding of how the interviewer affects what is observed in other sorts of interviews. The controls provided by standardization make the survey interview a useful site in which to observe features of social life operating (e.g., Schuman and Ludwig 1983). For example, race-of-interviewer effects in studies of racial attitudes are not methodological artifacts, but a reflection of the way respondents consider the race of the person with whom they are speaking when they talk about race. Respondents' sensitivity to the race of the person with whom they are speaking is a feature not only of survey interviews, but of social life, and one that researchers can describe systematically— if somewhat "thinly"—by examining its operation in survey interviews (see also Dunbar, Rodriguez, and Parker, Chapter 7, this volume). Similarly, the tacit knowledge that people require to interact at all forms the necessary grounding of social measurement and interviews of any sort. Tacit knowledge is necessary and inescapable, and it inescapably shapes social measurement.

■ *References*

Atkinson, J. M. and P. Drew. 1979. *Order in Court: The Organization of Verbal Interaction in Judicial Settings.* London: Macmillan.

Beatty, P. 1995. "Understanding the Standardized/Non-standardized Interviewing Controversy." *Journal of Official Statistics* 11:147-60.

Belli, R. F., P. S. Weiss, and J. M. Lepkowski. 1999. "Dynamics of Survey Interviewing and the Quality of Survey Reports: Age Comparisons." Pp. 303-26 in *Cognition, Aging, and Self-Reports*, edited by N. Schwarz, D. Park, B. Knauper, and S. Sudman. Philadelphia, PA: Psychology Press.

Bingham, W. and B. Moore. 1924. *How to Interview.* New York: Harper & Row.

Bloom, J. E. and M. F. Schober. 1999. "Respondent Cues That Survey Questions Are in Danger of Being Misunderstood." In *Proceedings of the Joint Statistical Meeting of the American Statistical Association, Section on Survey Research Methods, 1998.* Alexandria, VA: American Statistical Association.

Boyd, E. A. and J. Heritage. Forthcoming. "Taking the Patient's Personal History: Questioning during Verbal Examination." In *Practicing Medicine: Talk and Action in Primary Care Encounters*, edited by J. Heritage and D. W. Maynard. Cambridge: Cambridge University Press.

Brenner, M. 1981. "Aspects of Conversational Structure in the Research Interview." Pp. 19-40 in *Conversation and Discourse*, edited by P. Werth. London: Croom Helm.

Briggs, C. L. 1986. *Learning How to Ask: A Sociolinguistic Appraisal of the Role of the Interview in Social Science Research.* Cambridge: Cambridge University Press.

Button, G. 1987. "Answers as Interactional Products: Two Sequential Practices Used in Interviews." *Social Psychology Quarterly* 50:160-71.

Cannell, C. F. and R. L. Kahn. 1968. "Interviewing." Pp. 526-95 in *Handbook of Social Psychology,* Vol. 2, edited by G. Lindzey and E. Aronson. Reading, MA: Addison-Wesley.

Cannell, C. F., G. Kalton, L. Oksenberg, and K. Bischoping. 1989. *New Techniques for Pretesting Survey Questions* (Final Report, Grant No. HS 05616). Washington, DC: National Center for Health Services Research and Health Care Technology Assessment.

Cannell, C. F., S. A. Lawson, and D. L. Hausser. 1975. *A Technique for Evaluating Interviewer Performance.* Ann Arbor: University of Michigan, Survey Research Center of the Institute for Social Research.

Cannell, C. F., K. H. Marquis, and A. Laurent. 1977. *A Summary of Studies of Interviewing Methodology* (Vital and Health Statistics Series 2, Data Evaluation and Methods Research, No. 69). Rockville, MD: National Center for Health Statistics.

Cannell, C. F., P. V. Miller, and L. Oksenberg. 1981. "Research on Interviewing Techniques." Pp. 389-437 in *Sociological Methodology 1981*, edited by S. Leinhardt. San Francisco: Jossey-Bass.

Cicourel, A. V. 1964. *Method and Measurement in Sociology.* New York: Free Press.

———. 1974. *Theory and Method in a Study of Argentine Fertility.* New York: John Wiley.

———. 1982. "Interviews, Surveys, and the Problem of Ecological Validity." *American Sociologist* 17:11-20.

Clark, H. H. 1996. *Using Language.* Cambridge: Cambridge University Press.

Clark, H. H. and M. F. Schober. 1992. "Asking Questions and Influencing Answers." Pp. 15-48 in *Questions about Questions: Inquiries into the Cognitive Bases of Surveys,* edited by J. M. Tanur. New York: Russell Sage Foundation.

Conrad, F. G. and M. F. Schober. 2000. "Clarifying Question Meaning in a Household Telephone Survey." *Public Opinion Quarterly* 64:1-28.

Couper, M. P. and R. M. Groves. Forthcoming. "Introductory Interactions in Telephone Surveys and Nonresponse." In *Standardization and Tacit Knowledge: Interaction and Practice in the Survey Interview,* edited by D. W. Maynard, H. Houtkoop-Steenstra, J. van der Zouwen, and N. C. Schaeffer. New York: John Wiley.

Dijkstra, W. 1987. "Interviewing Style and Respondent Behavior: An Experimental Study of the Survey Interview." *Sociological Methods & Research* 16:309-34.

Dijkstra, W. and J. van der Zouwen. 1988. "Types of Inadequate Interviewer Behavior in Survey-Interviews." Pp. 29-35 in *Data Collection and Scaling,* edited by W. E. Saris and I. N. Gallhofer. New York: St. Martin's.

Drew, P. 1984. "Speakers' Reportings in Invitation Sequences." Pp. 129-51 in *Structures of Social Action: Studies in Conversation Analysis,* edited by J. M. Atkinson and J. Heritage. Cambridge: Cambridge University Press.

Dykema, J., J. M. Lepkowski, and S. Blixt. 1997. "The Effect of Interviewer and Respondent Behavior on Data Quality: Analysis of Interaction Coding in a Validation Study." Pp. 287-310 in *Survey Measurement and Process Quality,* edited by L. E. Lyberg, P. P. Biemer, M. Collins, E. D. de Leeuw, C. Dippo, N. Schwarz, and D. Trewin. New York: John Wiley.

Fowler, F. J., Jr. and T. W. Mangione. 1990. *Standardized Survey Interviewing: Minimizing Interviewer-Related Error.* Newbury Park, CA: Sage.

Garfinkel, H. 1967. *Studies in Ethnomethodology.* Englewood Cliffs, NJ: Prentice Hall.

———. 1996. "Ethnomethodology's Program." *Social Psychology Quarterly* 59:5-21.

Goffman, E. 1979. "Footing." *Semiotica* 25:1-29.

Goudy, W. J. and H. R. Potter. 1975. "Interview Rapport: Demise of a Concept." *Public Opinion Quarterly* 39:529-43.

Groves, R. M. 1989. *Survey Errors and Survey Costs.* New York: John Wiley.

Groves, R. M., R. B. Cialdini, and M. P. Couper. 1992. "Understanding the Decision to Participate in a Survey." *Public Opinion Quarterly* 56:475-95.

Groves, R. M. and L. J. Magilavy. 1986. "Measuring and Explaining Interviewer Effects in Centralized Telephone Surveys." *Public Opinion Quarterly* 50:251-66.

Heritage, J. 1984a. "A Change-of-State Token and Aspects of Its Sequential Placement." Pp. 299-345 in *Structures of Social Action: Studies in Conversation Analysis,* edited by J. M. Atkinson and J. Heritage. Cambridge: Cambridge University Press.

———. 1984b. *Garfinkel and Ethnomethodology.* Cambridge: Polity.

———. Forthcoming. "Ad Hoc Inquiries: 'Routine' Question Design in an Open Context." In *Standardization and Tacit Knowledge: Interaction and Practice in the Survey Interview,* edited by D. W. Maynard, H. Houtkoop-Steenstra, J. van der Zouwen, and N. C. Schaeffer. New York: John Wiley.

Heritage, J. and D. Greatbatch. 1991. "On the Institutional Character of Institutional Talk: The Case of News Interviews." Pp. 93-137 in *Talk and Social Structure: Studies in Ethnomethodology and Conversation Analysis,* edited by D. Boden and D. H. Zimmerman. Berkeley: University of California Press.

Holstein, J. A. and J. F. Gubrium. 1995. *The Active Interview.* Thousand Oaks, CA: Sage.

Houtkoop-Steenstra, H. 2000. *Interaction and the Standardized Survey Interview: The Living Questionnaire.* Cambridge: Cambridge University Press.

———. Forthcoming-b. "Questioning Turn Format and Turn-Taking Problems in Standardized Survey Interviews." In *Standardization and Tacit Knowledge: Interaction and Practice in the Survey Interview,* edited by D. W. Maynard, H. Houtkoop-Steenstra, J. van der Zouwen, and N. C. Schaeffer. New York: John Wiley.

Hyman, H. H., W. J. Cobb, J. J. Feldman, C. W. Hart, and C. H. Stember. [1954] 1975. *Interviewing in Social Research.* Chicago: University of Chicago Press.

Kahn, R. L. and C. F. Cannell. 1957. *The Dynamics of Interviewing: Theory, Technique, and Cases.* New York: John Wiley.

Kidder, L. H. 1981. *Research Methods in Social Relations.* New York: Holt, Rinehart & Winston.

Levinson, S. 1988. "Putting Linguistics on a Proper Footing: Explorations in Goffman's Concepts of Participation." Pp. 161-227 in *Erving Goffman: Exploring the Interaction Order,* edited by P. Drew and A. Wootton. Boston: Northeastern University Press.

Lynch, M. 1992. "Extending Wittgenstein: The Pivotal Move from Epistemology to the Sociology of Science." In *Science as Practice and Culture,* edited by A. Pickering. Chicago: University of Chicago Press.

———. Forthcoming. "The Living Text: Written Instructions and Situated Action in Telephone Surveys." In *Standardization and Tacit Knowledge: Interaction and Practice in the Survey Interview,* edited by D. W. Maynard, H. Houtkoop-Steenstra, J. van der Zouwen, and N. C. Schaeffer. New York: John Wiley.

Mangione, T. W., F. J. Fowler, Jr., and T. A. Louis. 1992. "Question Characteristics and Interviewer Effects." *Journal of Official Statistics* 8:293-307.

Marlaire, C. L. and D. W. Maynard. 1990. "Standardized Testing as an Interactional Phenomenon." *Sociology of Education* 63(2):83-101.

Marquis, K. H., C. F. Cannell, and A. Laurent. 1972. *Reporting Health Events in Household Interviews: Effects of Reinforcement, Question Length, and Reinterviews* (Vital and Health Statistics Series 2, Data Evaluation and Methods Research, No. 45). Rockville, MD: U.S. Department of Health and Human Services.

Maynard, D. W. and S. E. Clayman. 1991. "The Diversity of Ethnomethodology." *Annual Review of Sociology* 17:385-418.

Maynard, D. W., H. Houtkoop-Steenstra, J. van der Zouwen, and N. C. Schaeffer, eds. Forthcoming. *Standardization and Tacit Knowledge: Interaction and Practice in the Survey Interview.* New York: John Wiley.

Maynard, D. W. and C. L. Marlaire. 1992. "Good Reasons for Bad Testing Performance: The Interactional Substrate of Educational Exams." *Qualitative Sociology* 15:177-202.

Maynard, D. W. and N. C. Schaeffer. 1997. "Keeping the Gate: Declinations of the Request to Participate in a Telephone Survey Interview." *Sociological Methods & Research* 26:34-79.

———. Forthcoming-a. "Opening and Closing the Gate: The Work of 'Optimism' in Recruiting Survey Respondents." In *Standardization and Tacit Knowledge: Interaction and Practice in the Survey Interview,* edited by D. W. Maynard, H. Houtkoop-Steenstra, J. van der Zouwen, and N. C. Schaeffer. New York: John Wiley.

———. Forthcoming-b. "Standardization and Its Discontents: Standardization, Interaction, and the Survey Interview." In *Standardization and Tacit Knowledge: Interaction and Practice in the Survey Interview,* edited by D. W. Maynard, H. Houtkoop-Steenstra, J. van der Zouwen, and N. C. Schaeffer. New York: John Wiley.

———. 2000. "Toward a Sociology of Social Scientific Knowledge: Survey Research and Ethnomethodology's Asymmetric Alternates." *Social Studies of Science* 30:323-70.

Means, B., A. Nigam, M. Zarrow, E. F. Loftus, and M. S. Donaldson. 1989. *Autobiographical Memory for Health-Related Events.* Rockville, MD: National Center for Health Statistics.

Means, B., G. E. Swan, J. B. Jobe, and J. L. Esposito. 1991. "An Alternative Approach to Obtaining Personal History Data." Pp. 167-84 in *Measurement Errors in Surveys,* edited by P. P. Biemer, R. M. Groves, L. E. Lyberg, N. A. Mathiowetz, and S. Sudman. New York: John Wiley.

Mehan, H. 1973. "Assessing Children's Language Using Abilities: Methodological and Cross Cultural Implications." Pp. 309-43 in *Comparative Social Research: Methodological Problems and Strategies,* edited by M. Armer and A. D. Grimshaw. New York: John Wiley.

———. 1979. *Learning Lessons.* Cambridge, MA: Harvard University Press.

Mehan, H., A. Hertweck, and J. L. Meihls. 1986. *Handicapping the Handicapped: Decision-Making in Students' Educational Careers.* Stanford, CA: Stanford University Press.

Miller, P. V. and C. F. Cannell. 1982. "A Study of Experimental Techniques for Telephone Interviewing." *Public Opinion Quarterly* 46:250-69.

Mishler, E. G. 1986. *Research Interviewing: Context and Narrative.* Cambridge, MA: Harvard University Press.

Moore, R. J. 1999. "Achieving Understanding in the Standardized Interview: A Conversation Analytic Study of Talk in Telephone Surveys." Ph.D. dissertation, Department of Sociology, Indiana University.

Moore, R. J. and D. W. Maynard. Forthcoming. "Achieving Understanding in the Standardized Survey Interview: The Organization of Repair." In *Standardization and Tacit Knowledge: Interaction and Practice in the Survey Interview,* edited by D. W. Maynard, H. Houtkoop-Steenstra, J. van der Zouwen, and N. C. Schaeffer. New York: John Wiley.

Oksenberg, L., T. Beebe, S. Blixt, and C. F. Cannell. 1992. *Research on the Design and Conduct of the National Medical Expenditure Survey Interviews.* Ann Arbor, MI: Institute for Social Research.

Oksenberg, L., C. F. Cannell, and G. Kalton. 1991. "New Strategies for Pretesting Survey Questions." *Journal of Official Statistics* 7:349-65.

O'Muircheartaigh, C. A. 1997. "Measurement Error in Surveys: A Historical Perspective." Pp. 1-25 in *Survey Measurement and Process Quality,* edited by L. E. Lyberg, P. P. Biemer, M. Collins, E. D. de Leeuw, C. Dippo, N. Schwarz, and D. Trewin. New York: John Wiley.

Pomerantz, A. 1984. "Agreeing and Disagreeing with Assessments: Some Features of Preferred/Dispreferred Turn Shapes." Pp. 57-101 in *Structures of Social Action: Studies in Conversation Analysis,* edited by J. M. Atkinson and J. Heritage. Cambridge: Cambridge University Press.

Sacks, H. 1987. "On the Preferences for Agreement and Contiguity in Sequences in Conversation." Pp. 54-69 in *Talk and Social Organization,* edited by G. Button and J. R. E. Lee. Clevedon, England: Multilingual Matters.

Sacks, H., E. A. Schegloff, and G. Jefferson. 1974. "A Simplest Systematics for the Organization of Turn-Taking for Conversation." *Language* 50:696-735.

Schaeffer, N. C. 1991. "Conversation with a Purpose—or Conversation? Interaction in the Standardized Interview." Pp. 367-91 in *Measurement Errors in Surveys,* edited by P. P. Biemer, R. M. Groves, L. E. Lyberg, N. A. Mathiowetz, and S. Sudman. New York: John Wiley.

Schaeffer, N. C. and H.-W. Charng. 1991. "Two Experiments in Simplifying Response Categories: Intensity Ratings and Behavioral Frequencies." *Sociological Perspectives* 34:165-82.

Schaeffer, N. C. and D. W. Maynard. 1996. "From Paradigm to Prototype and Back Again: Interactive Aspects of Cognitive Processing in Standardized Survey Interviews." Pp. 65-88 in *Answering Questions: Methodology for Determining Cognitive and Communicative Processes in Survey Research,* edited by N. Schwarz and S. Sudman. San Francisco: Jossey-Bass.

———. Forthcoming. "Occasions for Intervention: Interactional Resources for Comprehension in Standardized Survey Interviews." In *Standardization and Tacit Knowledge: Interaction and Practice in the Survey Interview,* edited by D. W. Maynard, H. Houtkoop-Steenstra, J. van der Zouwen, and N. C. Schaeffer. New York: John Wiley.

Schaeffer, N. C., D. W. Maynard, and R. Cradock. 1993. "Negotiating Certainty: Uncertainty Proposals and Their Disposal in Standardized Survey Interviews." Working Paper No. 93-25, Center for Demography and Ecology, University of Wisconsin–Madison.

Schaeffer, N. C. and P. Royston. 1999. "Exploring the Interview Process." In *A New Agenda for Interdisciplinary Survey Research Methods: Proceedings of the CASM II Conference,* edited by M. Sirkin, T. Jabine, G. Willis, M. Elizabeth, and C. Tucker. Hyattsville, MD: Centers for Disease Control and Prevention, National Center for Health Statistics.

Schegloff, E. A. 1990. "Discussion of Suchman and Jordan: 'Interactional Troubles in Face-to-Face Survey Interviews.' " *Journal of the American Statistical Association* 85:248-50.

———. Forthcoming. "The Survey Interview as a Form of Talk in Interaction." In *Standardization and Tacit Knowledge: Interaction and Practice in the Survey Interview,* edited by D. W. Maynard, H. Houtkoop-Steenstra, J. van der Zouwen, and N. C. Schaeffer. New York: John Wiley.

Schegloff, E. A., G. Jefferson, and H. Sacks. 1977. "The Preference for Self-Correction in the Organization of Repair in Conversation." *Language* 53:361-82.

Schober, M. F. and F. G. Conrad. 1997. "Does Conversational Interviewing Reduce Survey Measurement Error?" *Public Opinion Quarterly* 61:576-602.

————. Forthcoming. "A Collaborative View of Standardized Survey Interviews." In *Standardization and Tacit Knowledge: Interaction and Practice in the Survey Interview,* edited by D. W. Maynard, H. Houtkoop-Steenstra, J. van der Zouwen, and N. C. Schaeffer. New York: John Wiley.

Schober, M. F., F. G. Conrad, and S. S. Fricker. 1999. "When and How Should Survey Interviewers Clarify Question Meaning?" In *Proceedings of the Joint Statistical Meeting of the American Statistical Association, Section on Survey Research Methods, 1998.* Alexandria, VA: American Statistical Association.

Schuman, H. 1982. "Artifacts Are in the Mind of the Beholder." *American Sociologist* 17:21-28.

Schuman, H. and J. Ludwig. 1983. "The Norm of Even Handedness in Surveys as in Life." *American Sociological Review* 48:112-20.

Smit, J. H., W. Dijkstra, and J. van der Zouwen. 1997. "Suggestive Interviewer Behavior in Surveys: An Experimental Study." *Journal of Official Statistics* 13:19-28.

Suchman, L. and B. Jordan. 1990. "Interactional Troubles in Face-to-Face Survey Interviews." *Journal of the American Statistical Association* 85:232-41.

Sudman, S., N. M. Bradburn, and N. Schwarz. 1996. *Thinking about Answers: The Application of Cognitive Processes to Survey Methodology.* San Francisco: Jossey-Bass.

Tourangeau, R., K. Rasinski, and L. Rips. 2000. *The Psychology of Survey Response.* Cambridge: Cambridge University Press.

van der Zouwen, J. Forthcoming. "Why Study Interaction in Survey Interviews?" In *Standardization and Tacit Knowledge: Interaction and Practice in the Survey Interview,* edited by D. W. Maynard, H. Houtkoop-Steenstra, J. van der Zouwen, and N. C. Schaeffer. New York: John Wiley.

van der Zouwen, J., W. Dijkstra, and J. H. Smit. 1991. "Studying Respondent-Interviewer Interaction: The Relationship between Interviewing Style, Interviewer Behavior, and Response Behavior." Pp. 419-37 in *Measurement Errors in Surveys,* edited by P. P. Biemer, R. M. Groves, L. E. Lyberg, N. A. Mathiowetz, and S. Sudman. New York: John Wiley.

Viterna, J. S. and D. W. Maynard. Forthcoming. "Varieties of Standardization: Practice in Academic Survey Centers." In *Standardization and Tacit Knowledge: Interaction and Practice in the Survey Interview,* edited by D. W. Maynard, H. Houtkoop-Steenstra, J. van der Zouwen, and N. C. Schaeffer. New York: John Wiley.

Weiss, C. H. 1968. "Validity of Welfare Mothers' Interview Responses." *Public Opinion Quarterly* 32:622-33.

————. 1970. "Interaction in the Research Interview: The Effects of Rapport on Response." In *Proceedings of the Meeting of the American Statistical Association, Section on Social Statistics, 1969.* Alexandria, VA: American Statistical Association.

Zimmerman, D. H. 1988. "On Conversation: The Conversation Analytic Perspective." Pp. 406-32 in *Communication Yearbook 11,* edited by J. A. Anderson. Newbury Park, CA: Sage.

12

INTERNET INTERVIEWING

◆ **Chris Mann**
Fiona Stewart

Interviews provide ready access to human experience in our everyday world. Now researchers in the 21st century are challenged by the simultaneously familiar yet mysterious worlds that lie "behind the screen" of the computer. They are the three-dimensional worlds of friends, colleagues, and strangers manifested in on-screen text. They are also the virtual worlds of on-line communities with their own images, rules, and interpersonal dynamics created in text. Sitting at a computer, using the Internet, researchers can interview disembodied people from across the earth and also the personae who frequent the imagined environments of cyberspace.

In this chapter we discuss interviewing using widely available Internet technology. First, we describe the key characteristics of computer-mediated communication and identify pioneering studies that have used this medium for interviewing (also see

Couper and Hansen, Chapter 10, this volume). We then consider some of the more important costs and benefits of conducting interviews on-line. Next, we discuss in detail the different kinds of expertise that researchers might need in order to conduct quantitative and qualitative interviews on-line. Finally, we consider options that might become available to researchers using the Internet as an interviewing medium in the future.

◆ *Computer-Mediated Communication*

Computer-mediated communication (CMC) allows computer users to interact directly with each other, using text, via keyboards. Text-based CMC is available in two main modes. Asynchronous CMC, the feature of most e-mail messaging systems, allows users to type extended messages that are then electronically transmitted to recipients who can read, reply, print, forward, and file them at any time they choose. Synchronous CMC, or "real-time chat," involves the interchange of messages between two or more users simultaneously logged on at different computers or computer terminals.

CMC systems also divide into semi-private and public arenas. The former include e-mail, one-to-one discussions using "chat" software, and conferences/forums (asynchronous discussion groups). These systems allow the interviewer (and participants) some level of control with regard to the nature and content of interaction. Public areas of CMC, in contrast, are beyond the direct control of the interviewer, and interaction may be extremely volatile (McLaughlin, Osborne, and Smith 1995). The main public arenas using CMC are bulletin board systems (BBSs) and news groups, such as those found in Usenet, the WELL, and ECHO, and undirected real-time chat systems such as those found in most Internet relay chat (IRC) and MU* environments.[1] Whichever modes they adopt for interviewing, researchers are becoming aware that CMC has characteristics that do not fit within more traditional modes of data collection (Mann and Stewart 2000); these characteristics are challenging some standard assumptions about language (Herring 1996), interpersonal relationships (Walther 1996), and group dynamics (Lea 1992; Garton, Haythornthwaite, and Wellman 1999).[2]

Although Internet use is still evolving, the potential of CMC as an interviewing medium has already been recognized, and pioneering studies have begun to identify the possibilities and pitfalls of Internet interviewing. Some researchers adopt CMC as an interviewing medium because it seems the "logical" (O'Connor and Madge 2000), indeed "the only authentic and congruent" (Smith-Stoner and Weber 2000) method of investigating Internet usage. Research has

focused on the demographics of Internet use (Kehoe and Pitkow 1996) and also many aspects of on-line experience. Some investigations are associated with discussions of Internet culture (Baym 1995; Turkle 1995) and the impact of this culture, or variations of this culture (Shields 1996), on debates around identity (Bruckman 1992; Reid 1991), gender (Matheson 1992; Bannert and Arbinger 1996; Spender 1995), race (Burkhalter 1999), and cross-cultural relations (Hantrais and Sen 1996).

Other interviewers have investigated the experiences of people engaged in such on-line activity areas as distance learning (Salmon 2000; Smith-Stoner and Weber 2000), gay men's chat (Shaw 1997), virtual worlds (Correll 1995), use of Web sites (O'Connor and Madge 2000) and e-mail-mediated help services (Hahn 1998), virtual focus groups (Sweet 1999), on-line versions of a subculture (Hodkinson 2000), rural women's use of interactive communication technology (Daws 1999), and the empowering use of technology for people with disabilities (Seymour, Lupton, and Fahy 1999).

In addition, as Joseph Walther (1999) has pointed out, interviewers may use "computer-based tools and computer-accessible populations to study human behavior in general" (p. 1). Some examples of researchers who have used CMC to interview people about off-line experiences are Fiona Stewart, Elizabeth Eckerman, and Kai Zhou (1998), who collected data on a range of health issues and practices using on-line or "virtual" focus groups involving participants from the Fiji Islands, China, Australia, and Malaysia; Elizabeth Anders (2000), who conducted an international study of issues faced by women with disabilities in higher education; Anne Ryen and David Silverman (2000), who undertook a case study of an Asian entrepreneur in Africa; and Chris Mann, who looked in depth at factors that might relate to differences in academic performance among undergraduates (this research is discussed in Mann and Stewart 2000).

In these studies, the researchers chose CMC because it eliminated constraints that would have made face-to-face (FTF) research impractical. It allowed researchers to interview participants on different continents, to maintain day-by-day contact with many students throughout the course of work on their degrees, and to reach people who would have been unable to participate face-to-face because of disability, financial difficulties, and/or language and communication differences. Yet other interviewers have capitalized on the anonymity of the technology to access the voices of members of socially marginalized communities, such as gay fathers (Dunne 1999) and men who might have avoided discussing emotions if interviewed face-to-face (Bennett 1998). Psychologists are also beginning to explore CMC as a research medium (Senior and Smith 1999). For instance, on-line discussion groups have enabled researchers to access and then interview individuals with specific disorders, such as panic attacks (Stones and Perry 1998).

Clearly, CMC interviewing has a great deal to offer, but is it an interviewing medium suitable for all inquiries and all potential interviewees? This question can be answered only with reference to the methodological choices made in any research study. Research questions may focus on the form/nature or the extent/prevalence of phenomena. Generally, nonstandardized qualitative interviews, conducted with individuals or groups, investigate the former; standardized quantitative interviews map the latter. As other chapters in this book describe, qualitative and quantitative methods have costs and benefits at both practical and methodological levels. A particularly significant factor in this context is that the majority of conventional qualitative interviews are conducted face-to-face, whereas larger-scale quantitative interviews are frequently self-administered (see in this volume Shuy, Chapter 9; Couper and Hansen, Chapter 10). These

issues will come into play in the next section, where we discuss whether CMC increases the benefits and/or reduces the costs associated with off-line research.

◆ Some Costs and Benefits of Internet Interviewing

The costs and benefits of Internet interviewing can be assessed along a number of dimensions, some of which parallel traditional interviewing concerns and some of which are unique to the Internet medium. Let us begin by considering the first challenge that faces all interviewers: gaining access to participants.

SAMPLING AND RECRUITMENT

There is no doubt that the unrepresentativeness of current Internet access remains the greatest problem for data collection on-line. Given that only approximately 0.01 percent of the world's population was on-line at the start of 2000, it is not surprising that some writers focus on the "cyberspace divide" (Loader 1998) and the ascendancy of the literate and the computer literate in this mode of communication. Microsoft's Bill Gates (1997) has admitted that, in terms of the Internet, the problem of "the haves versus the have-nots has many dimensions: rich versus poor, urban versus rural, young versus old, and perhaps most dramatically, developing countries versus developed countries" (p. 34). Interviewers need to be aware that access to and use of the Internet is a matter not only of economics, but also of one's place in the world in terms of gender, culture, ethnicity, and language (Mann and Stewart 2000).

The patchiness of Internet access has clear implications for interviewing approaches that seek representative sampling. In statistical terms, large samples (which are certainly possible with e-mail-based and, in particular, Web-page-based surveys) do not mean anything unless they are representative of a target population, a goal that currently would clearly be difficult to attain except for specialized populations. With regard to the latter, Georgia Tech University's Graphics, Visualization, and Usability (GVU) Center's series of World Wide Web surveys attempted to identify the demographics of the Internet population itself (Kehoe and Pitkow 1996).[3] E-mail surveys have also been used to study small-scale homogeneous groups of on-line users (Parker 1992; Smith 1997; Tse et al. 1995; Winter and Huff 1996). Resourceful use of the Internet can expand the boundaries of how such interviewees may be identified. A variety of on-line formats, such as chat rooms, mailing lists, BBSs, and conferences, focus on specific topics, drawing together geographically dispersed participants who may share interests, experiences, or expertise. With a growing total of more than 25,000 news groups accessible to more than 40 million users (Kennedy 1998), the Internet is an extremely convenient way of identifying people with similar interests.

These same arenas are also available to qualitative researchers who seek purposive rather than representative samples of participants. The virtuality of the medium offers unprecedented possibilities for extending the range of participants beyond those who are available for FTF interviewing, such as mothers at home with small children, shift workers, and people with disabilities. The Internet also offers researchers a possible means of communicating with people in sites to which access is restricted (such as hospitals, religious communities, prisons, government offices, the military, schools, and cults).

The technology can offer interviewers practical access to sites previously "closed" to researchers with visible attributes that would make them stand out within the population of interest, such as age, gender, ethnicity, or even physical "style" (bikers, surfers, Goths, punks, jet-setters and so on)—although there are ethical considerations surrounding researchers' disguising their identities to become acceptable to insiders. CMC also extends the possibilities of conducting research in politically sensitive or dangerous areas (see Lee 1993). Physical distance and the possibility of anonymity offer protection to both researchers and participants (see, for instance, Coomber's 1997 study of illicit drug dealers). Political and religious dissidents or human rights advocates might feel able to participate in on-line interviews without excessive risk. Researchers can access censored and/or politically or militarily sensitive data without needing to be physically in the field. They can interview people living or working in war zones, or sites of corruption or criminal activity, or places where diseases are rife, without needing to grapple with the danger—and the bureaucracy—involved in actually visiting the area. The disembodiment of CMC also allows researchers to distance themselves physically from ideological camps, reducing the likelihood of suspicion and innuendo that might alienate some participants. Researchers could communicate, for instance, with both police and criminals without being seen visiting either; or researchers could interview both Israelis and Palestinians, say, without leaving themselves open to charges of spying.

Many interviewers recruit on-line participants using the Internet itself; another option for recruitment is to include a contact e-mail or Web address when advertising the research more conventionally in publicity leaflets and journals. Recruiting individual participants involves acquiring their e-mail addresses, either through earlier interaction (on- or off-line) or by soliciting responses from Internet users. Placing a request for contacts or information when logging onto appropriate Internet sites is one possibility (Kehoe and Pitkow 1996). Some researchers also target individuals by writing to their e-mail addresses, which are generally attached to postings in many public CMC environments. However, this can create problems if the researcher moves directly to sending research materials without first gaining a user's consent. Cooperative participants can also assist with recruitment by "snowballing" messages using the "forwarding" option provided by e-mail software (Hodkinson 2000).

Other options for interviewers are to invite participation passively by posting recruitment messages that set out to attract anyone who happens to "surf" or "lurk" around chat rooms and conference areas linked to particular Web sites, or to set up their own Web sites with "hotlinks" that draw in potential participants (O'Connor and Madge 2000). However, a certain degree of proactivity is needed to attract participants. Interviewers who advertise their research need a "hook" that will gain attention. For instance, Ross Coomber (1997) targeted drug dealers in news groups by using the subject headline "Have You Ever Sold Powdered Drugs? If So, I Would Like Your Help." Coomber also suggests that recruitment messages should be posted on a weekly basis, as news group posts are gradually replaced and sites attract new visitors all the time.

Why should individuals participate in on-line interview research at all? As with conventional research, they may be attracted by material reward or may have altruistic reasons. However, once interviewees are recruited, CMC offers them many bonuses. They can participate at their convenience from their own homes or places of work. Women, older people, and members of socially marginalized groups can communicate from familiar and physically safe environments. CMC is also experienced as relatively trouble-free, eliminating the "hassle" of finding pen and paper, buying stamps, and keeping FTF appointments. It is possible that low technical skills, particularly keyboarding skills, may marginalize some participants. On the other hand, CMC is generally informal and conversational in style and thus accessible to the everyday writer.

Sustaining CMC interaction over time, in view of both Internet "churn" (loss of access to the technology) and the ease with which participants can disappear without a trace into cyberspace, presents researchers with a new challenge. Early evidence suggests that, as in conventional research, the participants' commitment to the research purposes is a paramount factor in ensuring continuity of communication (Mann and Stewart 2000).

EXPENSE AND TIME

The lower cost of Internet research in relation to other modes is one of its most powerful advantages (and one that may increasingly encourage research sponsors to inquire whether conventional fieldwork could not be conducted through CMC). Once the necessary computer equipment has been acquired, the principal expenses for users of standard CMC are Internet service provider fees and telephone costs. In some parts of the world, phone calls for Internet use are already free, and, in a highly competitive and rapidly changing market, free Internet access is becoming increasingly available. For users with institutional access to the Internet, the cost to researchers or projects may be zero.

However, low-cost access to the online community has different implications for virtual versions of FTF and self-administered interviews. With conventional FTF interviewing, time and travel expenses can lead to compromises regarding where interviews are held and with whom. These problems are compounded as the research extends further afield. Interstate or interregional comparisons increase time and expense as the researcher and/or participants have to travel to different locations and conduct multiple sessions. In addition, venues for FTF interviews need to be easily accessible to participants in terms of location, timing (before work, in the evening, after children are dropped at day care), lifestyle (some participants may require child-care facilities, others may need on-site venues in businesses, schools, or hospitals), and physical access. Interviewers will also have their own requirements for FTF venues, depending upon the nature of the research (such as on-site if the research concerns a nursing home, or in a neutral location if it concerns abused wives). The requirements of researcher and participants can lead to costs in terms of the time to organize (and frequently reorganize) interview venues as well as the usage costs themselves.

In contrast, CMC is a practical and cost-efficient way of conducting in-depth interviews with individuals or groups who are geographically distant, and it also facilitates collaboration between colleagues who may be at different sites, even on different continents (Cohen 1996). With on-line participation, the venue becomes the sites at which CMC is available. There may still be site-related hire costs (such as usage rates in cybercafés), and there will still be considerations about the impacts of the venue (e.g., is computer access in a public, professional, or home context?). In practical terms, however, many of the difficulties and financial considerations associated with organizing FTF venues disappear. A further consideration is that, with on-line research, interaction results in the immediate production of a text file. Unlike in research using FTF interviews, the researcher has no need to budget for recording equipment, transcribing equipment, or transcription costs, and delays caused by transcription are eliminated.

The Internet also offers researchers the potential for substantial financial savings when their studies involve self-administered interviews (Bachmann, Elfrink, and Vazzana 1996; Mehta and Sivadas 1995). E-mail and Web-page-based surveys eliminate paper, are cheap to send, and, once initial start-up costs have been met, involve minimal costs for implementation and analysis (Sheehan and Hoy 1999). Apart from the benefit to researchers of direct ac-

cess to large numbers of people, the speed of response in such surveys offers substantial time-cost savings. Comparative studies confirm that e-mail questionnaires are returned faster than their paper equivalents (Schaefer and Dillman 1998; Comley 1996). Web-page-based surveys can speed up responses even further (Comley 1996; Smith, 1997); studies have shown that hundreds of responses may be generated over a single weekend (Sheehan and Hoy 1999), and there are anecdotal accounts of "thousands of responses" being received within a few hours (Gjestland 1996). However, savings are not automatic. E-mail surveys can consume time if the researcher has to search around for addresses, if many addresses turn out to be invalid, and if the form of the survey has to be explained to participants. There are also hidden costs associated with the level of technology involved. As we shall discuss below, researchers may need to set aside a considerable period for coping with the technical challenges and problems that might be involved in implementing on-line surveys (Couper, Blair, and Triplett 1999).

WORKING WITH DIGITAL DATA

Working with digital data offers researchers substantial benefits but also presents them with great challenges. There is no doubt that the technological base of the interviewing medium complements the computerized practices that are becoming so familiar to researchers. Individual interviews and even large databases from CMC surveys can be moved effortlessly into other computer functions. Electronic messages can be recalled on a computer monitor, saved and accessed in word-processing packages, and stored either as hard-copy printouts or on computer diskettes or compact discs.

The analysis of interview data can also benefit from the development and convergence of technologies. For instance, interview data can be moved directly into qualitative or quantitative analysis software packages (Creswell 1997; Fielding and Lee 1998; Tesch 1990) that might themselves interconnect (some qualitative software packages already have SPSS export facilities). There is likely to be a huge increase in such interconnection of digital processes in the future.

On the other hand, working with digital data in a virtual environment, researchers cannot avoid engaging with legal and ethical issues that are still in a state of flux. Research projects may involve interviewers in the processes of

> authentication (checking that someone is who he claims to be, or a website what it seems to be); authorisation (controlling access in a sophisticated . . . way); confidentiality (keeping private information private); integrity (ensuring that information has not been tampered with); and non-repudiation (being sure the terms of a transaction are binding and legitimate). ("Future of the Internet," 1999:35)

Many of these areas require further legal definition and link in with other issues of intellectual property, security (including personal security from virtual assault, harassment, and stalking), encryption, digital signatures, and certification (see Kramarae and Kramer 1995; Thomas, Forcht, and Counts 1998). Researchers cannot overlook these issues, as some countries are establishing laws concerning, for instance, data protection and/or encryption that would apply to data generated in academic as well as commercial research.

The confusion about the legal implications of on-line research is matched by a lack of clarity about "good practice" on-line. There is little agreement about how to proceed ethically in a virtual arena, and few research practice conventions are available. Researchers are just beginning to grapple with the implications of the legal and ethi-

cal minefield and to discuss issues of confidentiality, participant risk, and informed consent in on-line research (Mann and Stewart 2000). As funding bodies and institutional review boards are adopting mandatory good-practice norms for on-line research, it would be politic for interviewers who intend to work on-line to give time to these issues and to find out at early stages of their research about current discussions that may have impacts on their research designs.[4]

◆ Technical Skills and Standardized Interviews

Dorothy Myers (1987) suggests that there are two kinds of experts on-line: the technically astute and the "relationally" astute (that is, the social experts who nurture and direct on-line relationships and create interpersonal bonds). On-line interviewers certainly need competence in both these areas, but do they need expertise? A great deal depends on the type of interview. As we shall discuss, conducting standardized interviews on-line is technically taxing. In a review of on-line surveys, Christine Smith (1997) concludes that "the lack of standardization among operating systems, servers, and browsers creates a challenging milieu in which a researcher must be technologically savvy as well as methodologically sound." For nonstandardized qualitative interviews, the technology may be more accessible but the acquisition of relational expertise is emphasized. Face-to-face, the human interviewer "can be a marvelously smart, adaptable, flexible instrument who can respond to situations with skill, tact, and understanding" (Seidman 1991:16); the challenge is to transfer these qualities on-line.

The technical challenges faced by researchers who have attempted structured interviews on-line have been documented more extensively than the work of researchers using qualitative approaches. Studies of self-completion surveys conducted on-line began to be published around the end of 1995 (for reviews, see Comley 1996; Couper et al. 1999; Witmer, Colman, and Katzman 1999) and offer considerable practical insights for any researcher who intends to use CMC in this way. We next consider the demands for technical expertise placed on researchers conducting standardized interviews using e-mail and the World Wide Web.

E-MAIL SURVEYS

In an e-mail survey, the questions are usually sent to respondents as the text of a conventional e-mail message. To complete the survey, respondents use the "reply" facility of their e-mail system and add their answers to the text of the returned message. The answers received can then be typed into an analysis program in the same way as for a conventional survey. Alternatively, a program can be written that will interpret the e-mailed responses and read the answers directly into a database; this approach offers significant savings in terms of data entry. Commercial survey-creation programs are available that, as well as assisting in producing the text of a survey, can carry out this interpretation of replies, provided the survey has been completed correctly (see also Smith 1997).[5]

Text-based e-mail surveys are convenient for respondents because they require no facilities or expertise beyond those the respondents use in their day-to-day e-mail communication. However, technical problems still arise. The size of the survey may also be a difficulty. Peter Comley (1996), for instance, had to split his survey into two e-mails. Some organizations use e-mail systems that convert messages over a certain size (such as questionnaires) into attachments. In one study a number of employees reported that they had received attach-

ments but didn't know what to do with them (Couper et al. 1999).

A further drawback is that a text survey can appear dry and uninteresting. E-mail in its simplest form does not allow formatting of text (e.g., use of boldface, italics, different fonts). In addition, the researcher has no control over the format of the responses. There is nothing to prevent a respondent from answering outside the boxes, selecting three choices where only one is required, or deleting or altering questions. In a study conducted by Mick Couper and his associates (1999), 21 percent of all e-mail respondents did not make use of the reply feature as intended, but used a word processor or text editor instead. In such cases, researchers may still be able to interpret what respondents mean, as with badly completed paper questionnaires, but the need to edit responses removes the advantages of automated data entry and can greatly increase per case costs.

If all potential respondents are using relatively modern e-mail systems that can understand HTML, the researcher can alleviate some design problems by using an HTML-based e-mail survey.[6] Because HTML uses only standard text characters, the survey is still sent as the text of an e-mail. But because the e-mail system interprets HTML commands, the message can be laid out in an attractive way. In addition, the researcher has control over participants' responses: Answers can be typed only in text-entry boxes, and if only one choice is required, only one will be accepted. HTML-based e-mail combines these advantages (usually associated with Web-based surveys) with the direct response advantage of e-mail. However, until HTML-enabled e-mail systems become more common, these benefits are possible only if the survey participants are within a defined population where the researcher knows what systems they are using.

A further possibility is for the researcher to present the survey not in the body of the e-mail message itself but as a file (for example, a word processor document or a spreadsheet) attached to the e-mail. The respondent opens the attached file, completes the survey using the relevant program, saves the file, and then attaches the saved file to a return e-mail. This gives the researcher control over the appearance of the survey, but completion and return require that respondents have more technical ability. In addition, respondents must all have access to the program (such as Microsoft Word or Microsoft Excel) in which the attached document was created. As with HTML-based mail, the approach is suitable only for a defined population where the researcher knows the abilities of the respondents or can provide them with training and support. In addition, some organizations may prohibit users from receiving e-mail attachments because of fears about viruses.

Researchers can overcome some of these problems by using survey-creation software to produce self-contained interactive survey programs.[7] The software allows researchers to create elegant, responsive, and efficient surveys, and the survey programs can produce formatted answer files that can be mailed back to interviewers for automated input to a database. However, such programs have a number of limitations. For example, a program created for the Windows operating system will not run on a Macintosh, and vice versa. Even with a single operating system, researchers may run into unexpected technical difficulties when trying to run their programs on the wide range of computers likely to be used by respondents; Couper et al. (1999) found problems with all seven of their pretest subjects. For instance, the program files produced may be large (in the case of Couper et al.'s study, approaching one megabyte), which may result in unacceptable volumes of Internet traffic and may be beyond the size permitted for incoming e-mail attachments. Because of such problems, most of the e-mail surveys reported to date have used the straightforward text-based route. However, Couper et al. (1999) "remain optimistic about the potential for e-mail as an alternative to the traditional mail survey" (p. 54).

WEB-PAGE-BASED SURVEYS

David Schaefer and Don Dillman (1998) note that their experiment with e-mail surveys "revealed the possibility that [these] represent only an interim surveying technology" (p. 392). Many researchers are turning their attention to the World Wide Web as a more suitable medium for administering questionnaires (for further information, see Comley 1996; Kehoe and Pitkow 1996; Coomber 1997; O'Connor and Madge 2000; for a comparison with e-mail surveys, see Patrick, Black, and Whalen 1995). However, the main drawback of the Web approach is the high level of technical expertise that researchers must acquire or have available to them. This includes the knowledge of HTML required to create the Web pages. Survey-creation programs, as discussed previously, can provide "what you see is what you get" editing of pages, removing much of the mystery of HTML, but identifying and learning a suitable program presents another hurdle to be overcome. Once the pages have been created, they must be uploaded to a host Internet server, another technically complex procedure (Mann and Stewart 2000).[8]

Why might researchers grapple with the challenges attendant on using the Web to interview? A Web-page-based survey has the advantage that it appears identical (subject to the browser used) to all respondents. Through the use of text formatting, colors, and graphics, the survey can be given an attractive appearance. Web-page-based surveys are also easy for respondents to complete, typically by selecting responses from predefined lists or entering text in boxes and then simply clicking a "submit" button when finished. The data received by the researcher are in a completely predictable and consistent format, making automated analysis possible without the editing that may be necessary with text-based e-mail surveys.

Despite the technical challenges involved, Christine Smith (1997) has predicted that Web-based survey software will soon become an indispensable research tool, "along with or even instead of analytical tools like SPSS." The significant advantages that Web-page-based surveys offer suggest they will become more and more common, especially for commercial market research. It may not be long before the creation of Web survey pages is routinely taught in social science research methods courses.

◆ Relational Skills and Nonstandardized Interviews

In nonstandardized interviews, the focus moves from the preformulated ideas of the researcher to "the meanings and interpretations that individuals attribute to events and relationships" (May 1993:94). It is this emphasis that leads many practitioners to refer to such interviews as qualitative, and it is to the relational skills required in such interviews that we now turn.

SOFTWARE OPTIONS IN NONSTANDARDIZED INTERVIEWS

Researchers are familiar with the methodological reasons that might inform a decision to interview one-to-one or in groups (Mann and Stewart 2000). However, when interviewing is conducted on-line, the decision to use in-depth interviews or "virtual" focus groups involves further issues relating to temporality—that is, whether interviews should take place synchronously (with delayed response) or in "real" or syn-

chronous time. There are various forms of software available:

Individual Interview
Options Software

◆ *E-mail:* E-mail allows asynchronous interviews one-to-one.

◆ *Real-time one-to-one chat:* Software such as AOL's Instant Messenger and ICQ (I Seek You; see www.icq.com) allows users to chat in real time one-to-one (or with groups of people).

Group Interview
Options Software

◆ *Real-time many-to-many chat:* This is communication in which messages are written and read at the same time, although in different places. What one person types is visible to everyone else on the same "channel." Chat software can range from "shareware" (software programs that are freely downloadable, such as mIRC; see www.mirc.com) to licensed software packages such as Hotline Client and FirstClass Conferencing, which are ideal for moderated real-time focus groups.[9] Typically, a chat program will have a conversation flow area, where a participant can read all contributions, as well as a separate composition area, where participants can write their own messages.

◆ *Asynchronous many-to-many conferencing:* In this form of communication, as in e-mail, participants can respond to messages from other participants at some time in the future. Unlike e-mail, however, conferencing is conducted at a "conference site" (as opposed to individual e-mail addresses), which can have restricted or public access. A typical conference site may be a type of folder, like the one that appears on both Macintosh and Windows computer screens. Conferencing provides an effective means of conducting non-real-time on-line focus groups. Conferencing systems include FirstClass (from SoftArc, Inc.) and CoSy (from Softwords Research International). In addition, both Microsoft and Netscape have their own systems and distribute them widely in combination with software and system packages. Conferencing systems are also known as groupware systems, of which Lotus-Notes (from Lotus) is perhaps the best known.

CMC AND THE DEVELOPMENT OF RAPPORT IN NONSTANDARDIZED INTERVIEWS

Generating textual data using e-mail or chat software is rarely a technical challenge (although group software involves extra complications). However, nonstandardized interviews also require researchers to acquire "relational" expertise. Successful qualitative interviewing depends upon interviewers' developing rapport with participants (Fontana and Frey 1994). Traditionally, this has been associated with a mutual reading of presentation of self. In any social situation, each party makes a swift appraisal of the other's age, gender, and ethnicity; of accent, dress, and personal grooming; of conventionality, eccentricity, and subcultural markers; of confidence levels, physical attractiveness, and friendliness or restraint. In addition, oral dimensions of language (pitch, tone, and so on) might identify whether what is said is spoken from a position of confidence, doubt, irony, and so forth. The sense of the other attained by such means allows each person to assess (a) how others are interpreting what he or she says and (b) the genuineness of intent in queries and responses.

If, as a result of this delicate interaction, participants come to trust in the sincerity and the motivation of the interviewer, they may be prepared to share in-depth insights into their private and social worlds. At the same time, the interviewer will increasingly be able to sense the appropriateness of questions and the meaningfulness of answers. Reading signs of the other is a human characteristic that many FTF qualitative researchers develop to the level of a skill. But is it possible to "connect" at these emotional and mental levels when communicating on-line?[10] Is it possible for an interviewer to develop rapport with participants whom he or she may never have seen or heard? We posed these questions to two researchers who had conducted qualitative e-mail interviews. They responded differently:

> Generating an atmosphere of rapport online can be a problem, and given the lack of tone or gesture and the length of time between exchanges it can lead to something of a formal, structured interview. This is in contrast to the spontaneous speeding up, slowing down, getting louder, getting quieter, getting excited, laughing together, spontaneous thoughts, irrelevant asides etc. etc. which I have experienced in off-line interviews. The best words I can think of to separate off-line from E-mail interviews then, are FLOW, and DYNAMICS, both of which, in my view are liable to contribute to greater depth and quality of information in an off-line interview than over e-mail. (P. Hodkinson, e-mail communication, March 1999)

> Is rapport online possible? Absolutely!!!! Rapport comes from being very up front with what you are doing and responding as you would with anyone. Laughing, listening and connecting are the key. (M. J. Smith-Stoner, e-mail communication, March 1999)

These perspectives reflect current debates about in-depth communication online. In one view, CMC cannot achieve the highly interactive, rich, and spontaneous communication that can be achieved in FTF interviewing. Communication differences between media are often conceptualized in terms of bandwidth, or the "volume of information per unit time that a computer, person, or transmission medium can handle" (Raymond 1993, cited in Kollock and Smith 1996:15). CMC is said by some to have a narrow or lean bandwidth, in contrast to the "rich" bandwidth of FTF interaction (see Sala 1998). As it allows insufficient transmission of social cues to establish the human "presence" of the other, CMC is seen as impersonal and distancing (Hewson, Laurent, and Vogel 1996; Kiesler, Siegel, and McGuire 1984; Short, Williams, and Christie 1976). Particularly in groups, the psychological distances separating participants and the depersonalization of "the other" that can result may lead to various kinds of unsociable behavior, such as flaming (Dubrovsky, Kiesler, and Sethna 1991). When CMC is seen as an "impoverished" communication environment (Giese 1998), it is not surprising that it is mainly considered appropriate for tasks requiring little social interaction or intimacy (Rice and Case 1983). Walther's (1992) review of this literature sums up the implications for research if CMC is viewed in this way: If investigations seek "information that is ambiguous, emphatic, or emotional . . . a richer medium should be used" (p. 57).

If CMC is indeed a "lean" communication medium that is neither conducive to establishing good interpersonal relationships nor capable of addressing delicate information, then it is clear that the work of the on-line qualitative interviewer will be challenging, if not doomed to failure from the beginning. However, relational development theorists have challenged these findings, pointing out that most assumptions about interpersonal relationships (such as the need for physical proximity) predate CMC and may not be fully applicable to on-line settings (Lea and Spears 1995; Parks and Floyd 1996). In his review of nonexperimental studies of CMC, Walther (1992) found evidence that warm relationships can and do develop on-line.

He points out that the same motives that drive people in other contexts drive them in CMC. People want to interact, they seek social reward, they want to be liked. Thus research interactants, like communicators in any context, will "desire to transact personal, rewarding, complex relationships and . . . they will communicate to do so" (p. 68). We shall now consider factors that might contribute to the successful development of rapport on-line.

USING TECHNOLOGY TO CREATE RAPPORT

Some on-line interviewers use linguistic conventions available in CMC to help convey the mood of the communication and to make social and emotional connections. Electronic paralanguage consists of repetitions, abbreviations, and verbal descriptions of feelings and sounds, such as "hehehe" for laughter, "lol" for "lots of laughs," and "LJATD" for "let's just agree to disagree" (discussion going nowhere).

"Emoticons"—such as :-) for smiling/happy and :-o for surprise/shock—offer interviewers another textual means to show feelings and to soften the potentially distancing abruptness of some CMC messages by adding humor or whimsicality (Murphy and Collins 1997). However, the use of emoticons is not transparent in communicative terms. First, emoticons may reflect the social and communicative practices of a subculture (see Baym 1995). Second, emoticons may not always work cross-nationally. In Japan, where signs of respect are finely graduated and where relationships develop in indirect ways, a highly complex system of emoticons attempts to parallel some of the delicacy of FTF interaction. However, these emoticons are not familiar to most Western interviewers. Such emoticons are read in a traditional horizontal format rather than sideways: -o-) for "I'm sorry"; (^o^;) for "excuse me!"; (^o^) for happy; (^-^;; for awkward (see Aoki 1994).

Emoticons may also be "read" in different ways by participants in a research project. To some, they may indicate a friendly but rather impersonal approach (Aycock and Buchignani 1995). To others, as with varying responses to such friendship gestures as handshakes and open body language in FTF research, they may seem an inappropriate way of "doing research." They can also be seen as lazy and unimaginative, possibly alienating some members of sophisticated on-line communities. As Stacy Horn (1998) has warned, it is possible that "people will assume that you are without language, or conversation and suggest that you go back to America Online (a place known for its liberal use of emoticons)" (p. 63). It would seem that interviewers should use electronic paralanguage judiciously. Even if they do, in the opinion of one participant in Mann's study of academic performance at the University of Cambridge, CMC will never be subtle enough to compare to FTF interaction:

> You'll see people annotate their mails using smilies, HTML-style tags, capital letters, etc., but even so there is no reliable way of conveying tone. How you say something is often more important than what you say—and e-mail doesn't have this dimension. (Quoted in Mann and Stewart 2000:14)

Clearly, qualitative interviewers who seek to establish rapport on-line need to look beyond electronic paralanguage. In the following sections we discuss factors that have seemed of most importance in interview studies.

IMPORTANCE OF SHARED RESEARCH AGENDA FOR RAPPORT

Participants with a superficial interest in the research topic may be initially intrigued and attracted by the option of interacting on-line, but this might not be enough to sustain their ongoing interest without the impetus of enthusiasm and focus that can be injected in the FTF setting by a skilled interviewer who is "firing on all cylinders." On-line, interviewers may not be able to offer enough verbal "dazzle" to compensate for the charm or charisma that can be so effective face-to-face. If participants have no particular vested interest in a study or a low boredom threshold, there may be a tendency for less involved participants to drop away:

> The longest of my e-mail interviews has been a few weeks . . . usually I found that people lost interest before I am able to get to the same degree of detail as a face to face interview. (P. Hodkinson, e-mail communication, March 1999)

However, a shared research agenda and/or being given an opportunity to be "heard" in a meaningful way can "lead virtual relationships to become very personal very quickly" (Smith-Stoner and Weber 2000). In these circumstances, interest in the interaction is sustained.

> Respondents often spoke of the value of our dialogues for helping them to make sense of their lives. They remarked on the time they had taken in thinking through their responses (some taking several hours) and messages were usually very long. (Dunne 1999:3)

Marilyn Smith-Stoner and Todd Weber (2000), who report having had excellent rapport with their participants, point out that the women they interviewed were very enthusiastic about the research topic: It did not "require any selling at all." Not only did these women want to tell their stories, they "expressed deep satisfaction with the process and were grateful to be able to do in online." A similar overlap of appreciating methodological and personal factors ensured the effectiveness of O'Connor's real-time focus group discussions with new parents:

The interviews all provided high levels of self-consciousness, reflexivity and interactivity. Whether it was owing to the nature of the interviewees (self-selected, motivated, frequent on-line users), or owing to the nature of the subject matter, clearly very close to the hearts of the women involved, it is difficult to judge. (O'Connor and Madge 2000:4)

ESTABLISHING TRUST AS A BASIS FOR RAPPORT

It is generally recognized that mutual trust is the basis for the development of rapport in interviews. One way for researchers to dispel respondents' feelings of caution and to increase trust is to be as open as possible about the purposes and processes of the research. For semistructured interviews, the researcher can do this by making an interview schedule available well before the interview and inviting clarifying questions. Another way for the researcher to display "openness" would be to inform participants fully about the time frame of the interaction. Some researchers may conclude that in-depth research, particularly regarding sensitive topics, would benefit if people met face-to-face before attempting to conduct an on-line relationship.

There are, however, precedents for researchers' conducting deeply personal interviews without ever meeting the respondents in person. One means of establishing trust, and bridging the geographic and perhaps personal distance that may characterize on-line interviews (Moore 1993), is for interviewers and participants to share information about themselves (Murphy and Collins 1997). Richard Cutler (1995) has suggested that the more an individual discloses personal information on-line, the more others are likely to reciprocate, and the more individuals know about each other, the more likely it is that trust, satisfaction, and a sense of being in a safe communication environment will ensue.

Caroline Bennett (1998), in her in-depth e-mail interviews, sought to establish relationships that would "nurse" equal degrees of self-disclosure between herself and her coinvestigators. She made initial disclosures about herself to encourage this pattern of discourse, and her participants responded in kind.

Technical ease of contact in CMC gives researchers the option of repeating interview interactions over time. There is evidence that trust and warmth in CMC relationships increases over extended interactions (Walther 1992). As Nancy Baym (1995) notes, "In CMC, as in real life, relationships take time to build" (p. 158). This has been the experience of qualitative researchers who have used sequential one-to-one e-mail interviews (Bennett 1998; Dunne 1999; Mann and Stewart 2000). However, findings from sequential interviews using e-mail suggest that the outcomes in terms of intimacy are not predictable. In part, this reflects differences in research design. In Gill Dunne's (1999) study of gay fathers, it was the participants' strong desire to be "heard" that led spontaneously to interviewer-participant closeness. This continued after the formal closure of the research and, in some cases, led to FTF meetings. In other studies, the development of long-term relationships was a part of the research design (see Mann and Stewart 2000; Ryen and Silverman 2000; Bennett 1998). Both Bennett and Anne Ryen and David Silverman (2000) sought to strengthen relational bonds through on-line disclosure, phone calls, exchange of photographs, and, in Ryen's case, some FTF meetings. In Chris Mann's research into experiences of higher education, extended relationships were the inevitable result of Mann's contacting students regularly over the course of their work on their degrees. There, the aim was to establish mutual trust rather than intimacy, thus Mann did not initiate talk about herself, nor did she see students face-to-face. This was not a misguided attempt to claim research "neutrality"; rather, Mann accepted that she was a very minor part of the students' lives and preferred to keep the focus of the interaction on the issues and students' perspectives on the issues.

In all these studies, the interviewers may be presumed to have different agendas. It is perhaps unsurprising that this should lead interviewers to different conclusions about whether electronic communication can sustain personal relationships over time. For Bennett and Ryen, the intensity of the relationship with participants seemed to peak and then falter somewhat, leading Bennett to admit that "maintaining long-term relationships is much more difficult than it appears" (e-mail communication, March 1999). In Bennett's study the frequency of on-line interaction over a seven-month period might explain a participant's disengagement due to pressures of time and a (sometimes reluctant) need to prioritize other commitments. Another possibility might have been a sense (from the participant's point of view) that all that could be said had been said. Ryen suggests that, as the novelty of the research project wears off, a participant might use the interaction for more instrumental purposes. In her case study, Ryen's e-mail correspondent seemed to move from commitment to the research process to a general desire to keep in touch because the interviewer might prove a possible useful contact in his business world. In Mann's study, a "slow and steady" approach to developing relationships within a time-limited, albeit extensive (three- to four-year) period was required. The interviewer-student relationships lacked the intensity of the relationships in Bennett's and Ryen's studies, but, perhaps for that very reason, most of the relationships were sustained for the duration of the research.

Considering these differing research patterns, it seems likely that human relationships have the same kind of variability on-line as they do in "real life." Some remain at a constant level of good neighborliness, whereas others reach deeper levels of intimacy that must increase (which would alter the research relationship), change in

nature, or diminish. Although the ease and availability of CMC allows for extended communication, it does not follow that the technology can circumvent those life patterns.

INTERACTIVE SKILLS

There are several key areas where on-line interviewers may have to adapt expertise gained in FTF interviews in order to increase rapport in a virtual venue. We discuss these areas briefly below.

Reassurance

Cooperating in research in general, and on-line research in particular, may be a new and challenging experience for many people. Working one-to-one, participants may need regular confirmation that they are communicating in appropriate ways, that their contributions are valued, and that the faceless researcher is trustworthy. In on-line groups, participants may become anxious about how the group is operating or about what is expected of them, and facilitators have to be alert to signs of confusion or withdrawal into silence (Sweet 1999). It seems that in most on-line interviews participants benefit from frequent and explicit verbal assurances from the researcher.

Listening

An attentive pause to listen is a key feature in FTF interviewing skills. However, this may be a luxury in some CMC contexts. For instance, the characteristic rapid fire of chat can preclude pausing, whether it be for thought or for effect. In addition, participants may experience an interviewer's pause to listen not as attentiveness but as indifference, as absence. Cues that an interviewer is listening reassure participants of continuing interest. An interviewer who listens too much (read as being absent from the screen) may cause participants in focus groups to feel "leaderless and uncomfortable" (Gaiser 1997). Similarly, interviewers in turn may be unsure whether "silences" in real-time chat are "owing to the fact that the participant is thinking, is typing in a response and has not yet hit the return button, or has, in fact, declined to answer the questions" (O'Connor and Madge 2000:2).

Nonresponse in a virtual venue can undermine a developing sense of rapport. It is clear that on-line listening needs to be expressed as words, not silence. An interviewer may express listening with interest by "responding promptly to questions, overtly expressing interest in particular points made, asking follow up questions, or perhaps enthusiastically sharing similar experiences to that described by the interviewee" (P. Hodkinson, e-mail communication, March 1999). Meanwhile, the interviewer is also "listening" to the written script created by participants. The researcher needs to be alert to changes in the tone of the conversation, to any fracture in the flow of a response that might point to a reluctance to speak or a failure to understand language or concepts, and to verbal "cues" that might suggest that participants would be happy to talk more about something if asked. Marilyn Smith-Stoner notes ways in which participants flag that they are prepared to talk in more detail:

> Often they put a tag line at the end of the phrase—"let me know if you want to know more"—or they bring the subject up more than once. I think many people need to be invited to expound on a topic, they are courteous about people's time and don't want to abuse it. (E-mail communication, March 1999)

Verbal Expertise

Sustaining rapport depends upon an interviewer's skill in dealing with sensitive issues and/or potentially embarrassing or conflictual interaction. How can researchers negotiate delicate interaction on-line? As with reassurance, language has to be ex-plicit. Nuances in tone of voice, facial expression, and subtlety of gesture are unavailable. However, the use of mild imperatives (for example, "You may want to check out") and mitigation ("if you'd like") show how the skillful choice of words can avoid making presumptions about the reader (Galegher, Sproull, and Kiesler 1998:517). In real-time interaction, interviewers have to make rapid choices about how to handle sensitive issues. For Henrietta O'Connor and Clare Madge (2000), who interviewed together, the interaction felt abstracted from real life, and on-line language use often seemed inadequate: "There were occasions when we were 'lost for words,' taking some time to decide on what to send as a message, because we felt like our written comments sounded banal or our questions too direct and leading" (p. 3).

E-mail allows more time for interviewers to choose their words in one-to-one or asynchronous group interactions. For instance, in Wendy Seymour et al.'s (1999) asynchronous long-term conferencing study, in which the participants had disabilities, an exacerbation of a disability could interrupt the process of some interviews:

> These events required gentle and sensitive communication to ensure that participants did not feel pressured to continue, so that they felt valued, and so that they would feel welcome to continue with the project once the episode had passed. (P. 3)

Anne Ryen was afraid that sensitive issues might arise when she was conducting interviews over a long period with someone on another continent (Tanzania/Kenya versus Norway) and from another culture (Asian versus Norwegian). Her approach was to try to clear the ground at an early stage in the interaction, as she did in the following e-mail communication with a research subject:

> Well, I am very happy indeed that you will go on with the interview. If there

are questions you find odd, or that you do not "appreciate," please do not hesitate to tell me. That is the only way to make me learn or to avoid repeating the mistake . . . (e-mail 10.12.98). (Quoted in Ryen, e-mail communication, March 1999)

This direct approach, where the interviewer makes no attempt to disguise the possibility that questions might come across as crass or impertinent, may also be a way to negotiate the questions themselves. This is an approach Mann has used in her own research: "I should like to ask you more about something you said, but if you feel my question is too intrusive please do not bother to reply to this—I shall not bring it up again" (see Mann and Stewart 2000).

Explaining Absences

Finally, absence, in terms of long gaps in communication in asynchronous studies, can be deeply unsettling for both interviewers and participants. Committed participants may take time to explain irregular messages. In Ryen's study, her correspondent's laptop broke down while he was traveling. However, he phoned to inform her of this. In Mann's study, students frequently e-mailed to explain that work had taken over their time. Similarly, Mann alerted students when she would be away at conferences. Interviewers have greater responsibility than participants to explain absences, even though, as Bennett (1998) discovered, this can be a taxing process:

For example, when I was ill in bed I still had to check in with my co-investigators; write replies, explain that I was ill and that my conversations would only be short, but thus maintaining the link between us. Whilst this may seem to make online interaction appear both tenuous and transient, I would argue that it is simply the nature of the environment that makes it so, and not the people who are involved. (P. 39)

However, as Bennett points out, neglecting to explain absences can seriously jeopardize the rapport that has been built up in earlier interactions.

RELATIONAL EXPERTISE IN GROUP DISCUSSIONS

In one-to-one investigations, qualitative researchers who ask questions are usually referred to as interviewers. However, asking questions in groups requires additional skills, as suggested by such titles as *moderator* and *facilitator*. David Morgan (1988) has argued that the key role of the focus group moderator is "to control the assembly and the running of the session" (p. 15). This is a task with multiple strands, and it is clearly a challenge to transfer these skills on-line. In another view, a moderator is a "person who reminds, tracks, clarifies, prompts, reviews, distills, negotiates, mitigates, mediates, arbitrates" (Davis and Brewer 1997:70). In the fast-paced and hectic environment of real-time chat, flexibility and patience (with everyone involved) are definite virtues (Sweet 1999). From a human relations perspective, the task of moderating/facilitating groups has two principal aspects: (a) developing rapport between all interactants and (b) providing a noncontentious atmosphere for all—even at the cost of exerting control over the few. We discuss these issues next.

DEVELOPING RAPPORT AMONG MULTIPLE PARTICIPANTS

Many of the participants who are prepared to join on-line group discussions already have experience in chat rooms, so they are adept at creating on-line relationships quickly. However, as Casey Sweet (1999) reports, the guided group discussion "draws participants out and personalities begin to emerge, thereby creating a dynamic that develops during the group and varies just like in-person groups. . . . The amount of interaction between online participants can vary and may be influenced by the topic and moderator" (p. 3).

The initial moments of an on-line focus group are perhaps the most crucial, as this is when introductions are made and group rapport is first attempted. In the Young People and Health Risk study (Stewart et al. 1998), rapport was encouraged in two ways. First, the facilitator posted a welcome message in a non-real-time conference center ahead of time. This message sought to set the tone and atmosphere for the on-line groups to follow. Second, as the group facilitator, Stewart entered the young women's real-time focus group with the following lines:

Fiona Stewart: Welcome Yellow Beijing—I am fiona the controller, please introduce yourselves and tell the other girls about your hobbies, your subjects at school and then we can proceed. Have you read the welcoming message?

It was anticipated that messages such as this would create a sense of personal connection among the young people participating, who resided in four different countries. Another approach that facilitators can use to encourage group rapport is to ask all participants about their immediate physical environments (Sweet 1999).

CONTROL IN GROUPS

In a face-to-face focus group, a facilitator may choose to be passive, exercising "mild, unobtrusive control over the group" (Krueger 1988:73), but in an on-line focus group this is rarely possible. Certain procedures have been shown to ensure the smooth running of group interviews (Sweet 1999; Mann and Stewart 2000). First, by establishing their expectations, facilitators can minimize participant confusion and enhance adherence to both subject matter and protocol. Second, facilitators need to state some ground rules. In cyberspace, arguments and disagreements "can erupt with

little warning" (Horn 1998:56), and facilitators do not have the option of ignoring outrageous, patently false, or volatile comments. Rules are one means by which facilitators can manage the potential for conflict, although it can rarely be eliminated. Some listowners, such as Horn (1998), in ECHO, develop "mission statements" as the baseline rule of conduct. This can prove an effective mechanism for facilitating discussion and containing conflict, although its ongoing implementation is not without problems.

Rule setting is important for managing the volatility of real-time groups. It also acts as a means of encouraging effective group self-management, which is particularly important in asynchronous groups. Rules make explicit the ways in which participants may engage in the on-line discussion and can set a positive tone for the interaction. However, there is also a risk that the facilitator may inadvertently create a hostile and unwelcoming environment by seeking to establish behavioral guidelines. The facilitator's challenge is to introduce rules in a way that is positive and acceptable to participants.

Facilitators also rely on text to maintain order in on-line groups. Because a facilitator cannot use body language, such as shuffling papers or turning away (Krueger 1988:84), the style of the textual communication must be clear and precise. Such facilitation can range from subtle to more assertive and formal approaches. Sweet has found that subtle approaches can sometimes be more successful on-line than face-to-face:

> I find in FTF groups that some dominators can push a position over and over and over again even after I, as moderator, have repeated it to them and asked them to indicate if I have heard correctly. Online, I find they can fizzle out, or if I put it in print that, "I understand your point of view to be . . . ," or "you dislike the idea because . . . ," they seem

to back off. They don't seem to have the same impact on the group as FTF. (E-mail communication, March 1999)

Facilitator intervention on-line may seem overbearing when compared with FTF conventions, but it is sometimes the only response to a fast-moving situation. Real-time groups are characterized by high interactivity, and a facilitator may not be able to intervene quickly enough to prevent an outburst of flaming. Even if the facilitator steps in promptly, there is no guarantee that intervention will be successful. The example below is taken from the Young People and Health Risk study (Mann and Stewart 2000:147). In this extract, although flaming did not occur, the young male participants did need to be reprimanded. As facilitator, however, Stewart was not sure that her request for an apology would be honored. She was thankful when it was.

Facilitator: Does anyone know what the health pyramid is?

Red Beijing: We know many good jokes

Facilitator: Red oz why don't you explain what the health pyramid is?

Red Australia: i don't like fiona

Facilitator: I beg your parden red oz

Facilitator: you should apologise for saying that

Red Australia: can you tell me a joke?

Red Australia: sorry

Red Beijing: the health pyramid is the meaning of different food. for example, bread meat milk

As we see, the need to reprimand participants can detract from the quality of the discussion. In the on-line environment there is no such thing as a quiet word in the ear of an individual participant. What is more, in the middle of attempting to obtain a public apology, the facilitator may need to repeat a particular question, even if this means spending more time than anticipated on a particular subject. In the example above, it was only after the facilitator pursued a line of questioning about the health pyramid that the participants contributed meaningfully to the dialogue. This was despite the fact that discussion and the flow of the dialogue had been disrupted for only a moment.

◆ *Conclusion*

In this chapter we have focused on the costs and benefits of using the Internet to interview and the skills that researchers may require to interview effectively on-line. As we have seen, researchers who consider conducting interviews on-line have many factors to weigh in the balance. The excitement of working with an interviewing medium that is not constrained by boundaries of time and space, and that offers digital data literally at one's fingertips, is matched by the growing realization that the virtual venue makes practical, legal, ethical, and interpersonal demands that move beyond the knowledge and expertise that researchers may have acquired in conducting off-line interview studies.

In addition, as long as CMC remains a text-based interchange, there are factors—such as the nature of language use on-line and the implications of disembodiment for issues of identity and/or power relations in cyberspace—that many researchers would wish to consider in designing their studies (Mann and Stewart 2000). It could be argued that using CMC to conduct interviews calls for such intensification of technical and interpersonal skills that only interviewers with considerable expertise in conventional research could feel confident about moving to a virtual venue. However, although pioneering researchers have alerted prospective on-line interviewers to some of the challenges of the medium, the majority of these pioneers have retained their initial excitement with regard to Internet interviewing. Most seem determined to develop the skills needed to conduct on-line interviewing in current circumstances and also to keep abreast of rapid technological developments that promise to extend interviewing possibilities in terms of both scope and style.

As we have discussed, the main barrier to more widespread participation in on-line interviews lies in the hardware and (in some countries) infrastructure costs associated with the desktop computer/modem/landline technology that currently dominates Internet access. Truly global access will require the development of other technologies, and the shape of these is becoming clear. Already, some mobile phones can be used to send and receive e-mail (Alanko et al. 1999). E-mail will also soon be offered as an offshoot of digital television (in conjunction with a telephone connection). Phones and other mobile devices, such as personal organizers or Palm Pilots, will use wireless application protocol to "gain access to the Internet using a 'microbrowser,' which displays web pages specially formatted for tiny screens" ("Future of the Internet" 1999:30). If such devices follow the pattern of mobile voice telephony, we can expect that hardware costs will drop dramatically after the first couple of years (although usage costs may remain high) and that these devices will prove especially popular in countries (not only developing countries) where conventional telephone services are inadequate or unreliable.

For researchers, these developments offer the exciting prospect of Internet-based communication (and hence research) with a far wider spectrum of socioeconomic groups and nationalities than is currently available. They also hold the promise of new forms of interviewing. Text-based CMC may eventually be seen as one of many ways to interview using the Internet, and as new technologies develop, new interviewing skills will develop to meet them.

■ Notes

1. ECHO and WELL (Whole Earth 'Lectronic Link) are on-line towns emanating from New York and California. MU* environments, which include MUDS and MOOs, are multiuser, text-based, role-playing areas of CMC.

2. See Mann and Stewart (2000) for discussion of these issues.

3. The GVU Center uses repeat participation in Web surveys to map current and changing Internet user characteristics and attitudes (see Kehoe and Pitkow, 1996; see also www.gvu.gatech.edu/user_surveys/). More than 55,000 respondents were involved in the first five surveys, and new versions of the survey are sent out biannually.

4. The Economic and Social Research Council, which is a core funding body for social science research in the United Kingdom, has already responded to European Union data protection legislation with a guidance document relating to copyright and confidentiality. The Scientific Freedom, Responsibility and Law Program within the American Association for the Advancement of Science convened a workshop in 1999 to examine the challenges facing scientists conducting Internet research involving human subjects. The outcomes of the workshop deliberations were used to draft a chapter for the *Guidebook for Institutional Review Boards on Internet Research,* produced by the NIH Office for Protection from Research Risks in 2000. The latest information is available at the AAAS Web site (see www.aaas.org/spp/dspp/sfrl/projects/intres/main.htm).

5. As of March 2000, available survey-creation programs included

> MaCATI (www.senecio.com),
> Survey Internet (www.aufrance.com),
> Survey Said (www.surveysaid.com),
> Survey Select (www.surveyselect.com),
> SurveySolutions (www.perseus.com),and
> SurveyTracker (www.surveytracker.com).

MaCATI's editing program is for the Macintosh only, and it has versions of its data collection program for the Mac, Windows, and Java. All of the other programs listed run under Windows only. Smith (1997) has pointed out that although Web survey development software is increasingly available, packages have huge variations in terms of price, functions, and server compatibility. It remains to be seen which, if any, of these packages will become the standard.

6. HTML stands for HyperText Markup Language, which is the coding system used to create pages that can be displayed by Web browsers. It consists of a series of "tags" that give instructions to the browser about how to display the text. For example, the text "<b>bold words<bsb> and <i>italic words<bsi>" would be displayed by a Web browser (or HTML-enabled e-mail system) as **bold words** and *italic words*. However, if the same text were read using a standard e-mail system, all the characters would be displayed exactly as typed: <b>bold words<bsb> and <i>italic words<bsi>. Originally, authors created HTML documents by typing the tags using a text editor. However, it is increasingly common to create HTML using "what you see is what you get" editing programs, where the author applies the formatting required (such as bold or italic) and the program automatically adds the relevant tags.

7. An example of such software is Perseus SurveySolutions Interviewer (www.perseus.com).

8. In this context, a server is a large computer that forms part of the worldwide network of permanently connected computers that is the Internet. Your pages are held on your host server. When someone requests a page, the request is routed to your host server and the page information is passed back to the requester's computer via the network.

9. FirstClass Conferencing has real chat and asynchronous conferencing options.

10. Patricia Wallace (1999) provides an excellent psychological framework for asking these questions.

■ *References*

Alanko, T., M. Kojo, M. Liljeberg, and K. Raatikainen. 1999. "Mobile Access to the Internet: A Mediator-Based Solution." *Internet Research: Electronic Networking, Applications and Policy* 9:58-65.

Anders, E. 2000. "Women with Disabilities: Higher Education, Feminism and Social Constructions of Difference." Ph.D. thesis, Deakin University, Melbourne.

Aoki, K. 1994. "Virtual Communities in Japan." Presented at the Pacific Telecommunications Council Conference.

Aycock, A. and N. Buchignani. 1995. "The E-Mail Murders: Reflections on 'Dead' Letters." Pp. 184-231 in *CyberSociety: Computer-Mediated Communication and Community,* edited by S. G. Jones. Thousand Oaks, CA: Sage.

Bachmann, D., J. Elfrink, J., and G. Vazzana. 1996. "Tracking the Progress of E-Mail vs. Snail-Mail." *Marketing Research* 8:30-35.

Bannert, M. and P. Arbinger. 1996. "Gender-Related Differences in Exposure to and Use of Computers: Results of a Survey of Secondary School Students." *European Journal of Psychology of Education* 11:269-82.

Baym, N. 1995. "The Emergence of Community in Computer-Mediated Communication." Pp. 139-63 in *CyberSociety: Computer-Mediated Communication and Community,* edited by S. G. Jones. Thousand Oaks, CA: Sage.

Bennett, C. 1998. "Men Online: Discussing Lived Experiences on the Internet." Honors dissertation, James Cook University, Townsville, Queensland, Australia.

Bruckman, A. 1992. "Identity Workshops: Emergent Social and Psychological Phenomena in Text-Based Virtual Reality." MIT Media Laboratory. Unpublished manuscript. Available from author (e-mail): Bruckman@media.mit.edu

Burkhalter, B. 1999. "Reading Race Online: Discovering Racial Identity in Usenet Discussions." Pp. 60-75 in *Communities in Cyberspace,* edited by M. A. Smith and P. Kollock. London: Routledge.

Cohen, J. 1996. "Computer Mediated Communication and Publication Productivity among Faculty." *Internet Research: Electronic Networking, Applications and Policy* 6(2-3):41-63.

Comley, P. 1996. "The Use of the Internet as a Data Collection Method." Presented at the ESOMAR/EMAC Symposium, Edinburgh.

Coomber, R. 1997. "Using the Internet for Survey Research." *Sociological Research Online* 2(2). Available Internet: http://www.socresonline.org.uk/socresonline/2/2/2.html

Correll, S. 1995. "The Ethnography of an Electronic Bar: The Lesbian Cafe." *Journal of Contemporary Ethnography* 24:270-98.

Couper, M. P., J. Blair, and T. Triplett. (1999). "A Comparison of Mail and E-Mail for a Survey of Employees in US Statistical Agencies." *Journal of Official Statistics* 15:39-56.

Creswell, J. W. 1997. *Qualitative Inquiry and Research Design: Choosing among Five Traditions.* Thousand Oaks, CA: Sage.

Cutler, R. H. 1995. "Distributed Presence and Community in Cyberspace." *Interpersonal Communication and Technology: An Electronic Journal for the 21st Century* 3(2):12-32. Available Internet: http://jan.ucc.nau.edu/~ipct-j/1995/n2/cutler.txt

Davis, B. H. and J. P. Brewer. 1997. *Electronic Discourse: Linguistic Individuals in Virtual Space.* Albany: State University of New York Press.

Daws, L. 1999. "Cattle, Special Education, Old Hats and Rain: Investigating Rural Women's Use of Interactive Communication Technologies." Center for Policy and Leadership Studies, Queensland University of Technology, Kelvin Grove. Unpublished manuscript. Available from author (e-mail): l.daws@qut.edu.au

Dubrovsky, V. J., S. Kiesler, and B. N. Sethna. 1991. "The Equalization Phenomenon: Status Effects in Computer-Mediated and Face-to-Face Decision-Making Groups." *Human-Computer Interaction* 6:119-46.

Dunne, G. 1999. "The Different Dimensions of Gay Fatherhood: Exploding the Myths." Report to the Economic and Social Research Council, London School of Economics.

Fielding, N. G. and R. M. Lee. 1998. *Computer Analysis and Qualitative Research.* Thousand Oaks, CA: Sage.

Fontana, A. and J. H. Frey. 1994. "Interviewing: The Art of Science." Pp. 361-76 in *Handbook of Qualitative Research,* edited by N. K. Denzin and Y. S. Lincoln. Thousand Oaks, CA: Sage.

"The Future of the Internet." *Economist,* November 13, 1999.

Gaiser, T. 1997. "Conducting On-Line Focus Groups." *Social Science Computer Review* 15:135-44.

Galegher, J., L. Sproull, and S. Kiesler. 1998. "Legitimacy, Authority, and Community in Electronic Support Groups." *Written Communication* 15:493-530.

Garton, L., C. Haythornthwaite, and B. Wellman. 1999. "Studying On-Line Networks." In *Doing Internet Research: Critical Issues and Methods for Examining the Net,* edited by S. G. Jones. Thousand Oaks, CA: Sage.

Gates, W. 1997. "Keynote Address." In *The Harvard Conference on the Internet and Society.* Cambridge, MA: O'Reilly.

Giese, M. 1998. "Self without Body: Textual Self-Representation in an Electronic Community." *First Monday* 3(4) [On-line]. Available Internet: http://www.firstmonday.dk/issues/issue3_4/giese/

Gjestland, L. 1996. "Net? Not Yet." *Marketing Research* 8:26-29.

Hahn, K. L. 1998. "Qualitative Investigation of an E-Mail Mediated Help Service." *Internet Research: Electronic Networking, Applications and Policy* 8:123-35.

Hantrais, L. and M. Sen. 1996. *Cross-National Research Methods in the Social Sciences.* Guildford, England: Biddles.

Herring, S. C., ed. 1996. *Computer-Mediated Communication: Linguistic, Social and Cross-Cultural Perspectives.* Amsterdam: John Benjamins.

Hewson, C., D. Laurent, and C. Vogel. 1996. "Proper Methodologies for Psychological and Sociological Studies Conducted via the Internet." *Behavior Research Methods, Instruments and Computers* 28:186-91.

Hodkinson, P. 2000. "The Goth Scene as Trans-Local Subculture." Ph.D. dissertation, Center for Urban and Regional Studies, University of Birmingham.

Horn, S. 1998. *Cyberville: Clicks, Culture, and the Creation of an Online Town.* New York: Warner.

Kehoe, C. M. and J. E. Pitkow. 1996. "Surveying the Territory: GVU's Five WWW User Surveys." *World Wide Web Journal* 1(3):77-84.

Kennedy, A. 1998. *The Internet and the World Wide Web: The Rough Guide.* London: Penguin.

Kiesler, S., J. Siegel, and T. McGuire. 1984. "Social Psychological Aspects of Computer-Mediated Communication." *American Psychologist* 39:1123-34.

Kollock, P. and M. Smith. 1996. "Managing the Virtual Commons: Cooperation and Conflict in Computer Communities." Pp. 109-28 in *Computer-Mediated Communication: Linguistic, Social and Cross-Cultural Perspectives,* edited by S. Herring. Amsterdam: John Benjamins.

Kramarae, C. and J. Kramer. (1995). "Legal Snarls for Women in Cyberspace." *Internet Research: Electronic Networking, Applications and Policy* 5(2):14-24.

Krueger, R. A. 1988. *Focus Groups: A Practical Guide for Applied Research.* Newbury Park, CA: Sage.

Lea, M., ed. 1992. *Contexts of Computer-Mediated Communication.* Brighton, England: Harvester-Wheatsheaf.

Lea, M. and R. Spears. 1995. "Love at First Byte? Building Personal Relationships over Computer Networks." In *Under-studied Relationships: Off the Beaten Track,* edited by J. T. Wood and S. Duck. Thousand Oaks, CA: Sage.

Lee, R. M. 1993. *Doing Research on Sensitive Topics.* Newbury Park, CA: Sage.

Loader, B. D., ed. *Cyberspace Divide: Equality, Agency and Policy in the Information Society.* London: Routledge.

Mann, C. and F. Stewart. 2000. *Internet Communication and Qualitative Research: A Handbook for Researching Online.* London: Sage.

Matheson, K. 1992. "Women and Computer Technology: Communicating for Herself." Pp. 66-88 in *Contexts of Computer-Mediated Communication,* edited by M. Lea. Brighton, England: Harvester-Wheatsheaf.

May, T. 1993. *Social Research: Issues, Methods and Processes.* Buckingham: Open University Press.

McLaughlin, M. L., K. Osborne, and C. Smith. 1995. "Standards of Conduct in Usenet." Pp. 90-112 in *CyberSociety: Computer-Mediated Communication and Community,* edited by S. G. Jones. Thousand Oaks, CA: Sage.

Mehta, R. and E. Sivadas. 1995. "Comparing Response Rates and Response Content in Mail versus Electronic Mail Surveys." *Journal of the Market Research Society* 37:429-39.

Moore, M. 1993. "Theory of Transactional Distance." In *Theoretical Principles of Distance Education,* edited by D. Keegan. London: Routledge.

Morgan, D. L. 1988. *Focus Groups as Qualitative Research.* Newbury Park, CA: Sage.

Murphy, K. L. and M. P. Collins. 1997. "Communication Conventions in Instructional Electronic Chats." *First Monday* 2(11) [On-line]. Available Internet: http://www.firstmonday.dk/issues/issue2_11/murphy/

Myers, D. 1987. "Anonymity Is Part of the Magic: Individual Manipulation of Computer-Mediated Communication Context." *Qualitative Sociology* 10:251-66.

O'Connor, H. and C. Madge. 2000. "Cyber-Parents and Cyber-Research: Exploring the Internet as a Medium for Research." Center for Labour Market Studies, University of Leicester. Unpublished manuscript.

Parker, L. 1992. "Collecting Data the E-Mail Way." *Training and Development,* July, pp. 52-54.

Parks, M. and K. Floyd. 1996. "Making Friends in Cyberspace." *Journal of Communication* 46(1):80-97.

Patrick, A. S., A. Black, and T. E. Whalen. 1995. "Rich, Young, Male, Dissatisfied Computer Geeks? Demographics and Satisfaction from the National Capital FreeNet." Pp. 83-107 in *Proceedings of Telecommunities 95: The International Community Networking Conference,* edited by D. Godfrey and M. Levy. Victoria, BC: Telecommunities Canada. Available Internet: http://debra.dgbt.doc.ca/services-research/survey/demographics/vic.html

Raymond, E., ed. *The New Hacker's Dictionary.* 2d ed. Cambridge: MIT Press.

Reid, R. 1991. "Electropolis: Communication and Community on Internet Relay Chat." Honors thesis (electronically distributed version), Department of History, University of Melbourne.

Rice, R. E. and D. Case. 1983. "Electronic Message Systems in the University: A Description of Use and Utility." *Journal of Communication* 33(1):131-52.

Ryen, A. and D. Silverman. 2000. "Marking Boundaries: Culture as Category Work." *Qualitative Inquiry* 6:107-27.

Sala, L. 1998. "The Paradox: Megabandwidth and Micromedia." Presented at the International Sociology Conference. Montreal.

Salmon, G. 2000. *E-Moderating: The Key to Teaching and Learning Online.* London: Kogan Page.

Schaefer, D. and D. A. Dillman. 1998. "Development of a Standard E-Mail Methodology: Results of an Experiment." *Public Opinion Quarterly* 62:378-97.

Seidman, I. 1991. *Interviewing as Qualitative Research: A Guide for Researchers in Education and the Social Sciences.* New York: Teachers College Press.

Senior, C. and M. Smith. 1999. "The Internet . . . A Possible Research Tool?" *Psychologist* 12:442-44.

Seymour, W., D. Lupton, and N. Fahy. 1999. "Negotiating Disability, Technology and Risk: Towards a New Perspective." Report, School of Social Work and Social Policy, University of South Australia, Magill.

Shaw, D. 1997. "Gay Men and Computer Communication: A Discourse of Sex and Identity in Cyberspace." Pp. 133-46 in *Virtual Culture: Identity and Communication in Cybersociety,* edited by S. G. Jones. Thousand Oaks, CA: Sage.

Sheehan, K. B. and M. G. Hoy. 1999. "Using E-Mail to Survey Internet Users in the United States: Methodology and Assessment." *Journal of Computer-Mediated Communication* 4(3) [On-line]. Available Internet: http://www.ascusc.org/jcmc/vol4/issue3/sheehan.html

Shields, R., ed. 1996. *Cultures of Internet: Virtual Spaces, Real Histories, Living Bodies.* London: Sage.

Short, J., E. Williams, and B. Christie. 1976. *The Social Psychology of Telecommunication.* London: John Wiley.

Smith, C. B. 1997. "Casting the Net: Surveying an Internet Population." *Journal of Computer-Mediated Communication* 3(1) [On-line]. Available Internet: http://www.ascusc.org/jcmc/vol3/issue1/smith.html

Smith-Stoner, M. J. and T. A. Weber. 2000. "Developing Theory Using Emergent Inquiry: A Study of Meaningful Online Learning for Women." Ph.D. dissertation, California Institute of Integral Studies. Available from authors (e-mail): mssrn@aol.com

Spender, D. 1995. *Nattering on the Net: Women, Power and Cyberspace.* Melbourne: Spinifrex.

Stewart, F., E. Eckerman, and K. Zhou. 1998. "Using the Internet in Qualitative Public Health Research: A Comparison of Chinese and Australian Young Women's Perceptions of Tobacco Use." *Internet Journal of Health Promotion,* December 29 [On-line]. Available Internet: http://www.monash.edu.au/health/IJHP/1998/12

Stones, A. and D. Perry. 1998. "Preliminary Evaluation of the World Wide Web as a Tool for Data Collection in the Area of Panic Research." Presented at the Computers in Psychology Conference, April, University of York.

Sweet, C. (1999) "Anatomy of an On-Line Focus Group." *Quirk's Marketing Research Review,* December. Available Internet: http://www.quirks.com/articles

Tesch, R. 1990. *Qualitative Research: Analysis Types and Software Tools.* New York: Falmer.

Thomas, D. S., K. Forcht, and P. Counts. (1998). "Legal Considerations of Internet Use: Issues to Be Addressed." *Internet Research: Electronic Networking, Applications and Policy* 8:70-74.

Tse, A. C. B., K. C. Tse, C. H. Yin, C. B. Ting, K. W. Yi, K. P. Yee, and W. C. Hong. 1995. "Comparing Two Methods of Sending Out Questionnaires: E-Mail versus Mail." *Journal of the Market Research Society* 37:441-46.

Turkle, S. 1995. *Life on the Screen: Identity in the Age of the Internet.* London: Weidenfeld & Nicolson.

Wallace, P. 1999. *The Psychology of the Internet.* New York: Cambridge University Press.

Walther, J. B. 1992. "Interpersonal Effects in Computer-Mediated Interaction: A Relational Perspective." *Communication Research* 19:52-90.

———. 1996. "Computer-Mediated Communication: Impersonal, Interpersonal, and Hyper-personal Interaction." *Communication Research* 23:3-43.

———. 1999. "Researching Internet Behavior: Methods, Issues and Concerns." Presented at the National Communication Association Summer Conference on Communication and Technology, July, Washington, DC.

Winter, D. and C. Huff. 1996. "Adapting the Internet: Comments from a Women-Only Electronic Forum." *American Sociologist* 27:30-54.

Witmer, D., R. Colman, and S. Katzman. 1999. "From Paper-and-Pencil to Screen-and-Keyboard: Toward a Methodology for Survey Research on the Internet." Pp. 145-63 in *Doing Internet Research: Critical Issues and Methods for Examining the Net,* edited by S. G. Jones. Thousand Oaks, CA: Sage.

13

TRANSCRIPTION QUALITY

◆ Blake D. Poland

The transcription of audiotaped interviews as a method for making data available in textual form for subsequent coding and analysis is widespread in qualitative research. Yet, until relatively recently, little attention had been paid to methodological aspects of transcription, despite the theoretical and interpretive consequences of various approaches to defining and attending to transcription quality.

In this chapter, I explore the issue of transcription quality from a number of vantage points. I take the emerging literature on this topic as my point of departure, noting that the researcher is frequently exhorted to be ever more vigilant in the application of a growing number of possible conventions and measures to ensure that transcripts are verbatim facsimiles of what was said in interviews (Edwards and Lampert 1993; Du Bois et al. 1993; Psathas and Anderson 1990). In the opening sections, I review several potential challenges to transcription quality, together with a number of suggested notational conventions that have been devised to assist transcribers in catching features of interest in the translation from spoken to written word.

A second vantage point from which to examine these issues takes inspiration from the postmodern turn in the social sciences. A growing number of voices in the emerging methodological literature on transcription call for a more explicitly reflexive stance vis-à-vis the inherently representational and interpretive nature of transcription (Mishler 1991; Lapadat and Lindsay 1999; Kvale 1996). These authors question

AUTHOR'S NOTE: The views expressed here do not necessarily represent those of the University of Toronto and remain the sole responsibility of the author. I am grateful to Norman Denzin, Joan Eakin, and two anonymous reviewers for comments on earlier drafts of this chapter.

not only the possibility of the verbatim transcript, but the implicit ontological and epistemological baggage that this kind of method talk conceals. Thus in subsequent sections of the chapter, I will problematize and deconstruct the notion of "verbatim" to reveal the nature of the transformations it frequently imposes on the data. In other words, data are (re)constructed in the process of transcription as a result of multiple decisions that reflect both theoretical and ostensibly pragmatic considerations. These vital insights, however, are typically accompanied by few suggestions for rigor in this aspect of qualitative research other than the general call to reflexivity. Thus I conclude the chapter by considering what the reflexive qualitative researcher might do to enhance the quality of transcription as a vital aspect of rigor in qualitative research.

My focus in this chapter is on the issues involved in the production of transcripts that are meant to be analyzed primarily for *what* is said, rather than *how* it is said. At several points I will make reference to the unique notational conventions and transcription requirements of conversation analysis, the preoccupation of which is the sequential development of talk. However, the latter is not my primary focus.

◆ Getting It Right

Many qualitative researchers, it would appear, do not give transcription quality a second thought. If they do, their concern is most often with ensuring the accuracy of verbatim accounts by minimizing sources of error in the transcription process. Insofar as these preoccupations are embedded in what Jaber Gubrium and James Holstein (1997) refer to as the "idiom" of "naturalistic method talk," it reflects a bias toward a realist ontology that is particularly evident, for example, in qualitative research in the health sciences. That is to say, from a naturalistic idiom, it is typically (if tacitly) assumed not only that the research interview

adequately captures social reality as it is experienced and expressed by respondents, but that the translation to audiotape and then text is not inherently problematic, so long as careful attention is given to ensuring accuracy of transcription.

Although the importance of ensuring that interview or focus group transcripts are verbatim accounts of what transpired is widely acknowledged (e.g., McCracken 1988; Patton 1990), it does not yet appear to be standard practice for qualitative researchers to consider transcription quality prior to their undertaking the analysis of textual data. A literature review conducted in 1995 of more than a decade of *Qualitative Sociology*, back issues of *Qualitative Health Research*, and more than a dozen frequently cited qualitative research textbooks and sourcebooks revealed very little substantive discussion of strategies for monitoring and improving transcription quality.[1]

Several resources have become available since 1995 (see Kvale 1996; Lapadat and Lindsay 1999; Seale 1999), but this literature is still relatively new. I would argue that, with the possible exception of the literature on transcription notation in conversation analysis, systematic and comprehensive attention to issues of transcription quality has yet to become routine practice in qualitative research. Of particular note is the absence of discussion of these issues in much of the literature on the rigor of qualitative research.[2]

CHALLENGES TO TRANSCRIPTION QUALITY

In this subsection I consider several challenges to transcription quality and their possible origins. This is not intended as an exhaustive treatment of the subject; rather, I offer this discussion to stimulate reflection on and examination of these issues as they affect the quality of qualitative research.

Table 13.1   EXAMPLES OF TRANSCRIPTION "ERRORS"

As Recorded on Transcript	As Recorded on Audiotape
. . . it's kind of been a tough function but we, you would go with whatever the problems with health policies are . . .	it's been kind of a tacit assumption that we would go with whatever the province's health policies are . . .
. . . the government is almost saying to non-smokers well, you know, you were taught, like you either—	the government is almost saying to non-smokers "Well, you know, here its law. Its OK to stand up and give smokers hell"
. . . a broken cigarette is an (awful?) game. Now that's a proactive message	"A broken cigarette is a little freedom gained": now that's a proactive message.
You got to inhale all the diesel fumes. And that's worse, the way I see it anyway.	You've got to inhale all the diesel fumes. And that's worse than any cigarette ever will be.
I have no doubt that communities are the way to God!	I have no doubt that communities are the way to go.
. . . I think we we're a blast with a really good investigative team . . .	. . . I think we were blessed with a really good investigative team . . .
. . . a more direct interactive community confrontation model . . . and intimate health promotion projects don't recognize that need, that we've got to build in a consultation more process more	. . . a more direct interactive community consultation model . . . and community health promotion projects have recognized that need and have tried to build in a consultation process
I think unless we want to become like other countries, where people have, you know, democratic freedoms . . .	I think unless we want to become like other countries, where people have no democratic freedom . . .

SOURCE: Poland (1993).

My observations regarding challenges to transcription quality and strategies for addressing them arose initially from my dissertation research (Poland 1993; Poland et al. 1994).[3] As part of that research, the Brantford study, I reviewed interview transcripts on a computer screen while the interview or focus group tapes were running so as to identify and correct what I perceived as discrepancies between what was recorded in writing and what I felt fairly certain had actually been said during the interviews, as well as to refamiliarize myself with the material prior to coding. (I had been the interviewer/facilitator for all of the interviews and focus group discus-sions.) At first, I kept a running tally of the number of discrepancies and maintained a cut-and-paste file of them that contained both versions of each—the excerpt as it appeared in the transcript and as I felt it should have appeared. Table 13.1 displays some examples from the entries in this file. I reviewed every transcript in my collection, and although the process of maintaining such a file became overly time-consuming and I eventually discontinued it, the information that I compiled helped me to generate the typology of challenges to transcription quality discussed below.

Even when a transcriber attempts to produce a verbatim account by remaining faithful to the original language and flow of the discussion, and even when the transcriber has a suggested syntax to follow in transcription (more on this later), there are a number of logistical and interpretive challenges to the translation of audiotape conversation into textual form. Drawing on my review of transcription quality in the aforementioned Brantford study, I have identified transcribers' problems with sentence structure, the use of quotation marks, omissions, and mistaking words or phrases for others. Each of these challenges is briefly discussed below.

Because people often talk in run-on sentences (actually, the concept of "sentence" does not translate well into oral tradition, or vice versa), transcribers must make judgment calls during the course of their work about where to begin and end sentences. The insertion of a period or a comma can sometimes alter the interpretation of the text. For example, "I hate it, you know. I do" carries a different meaning from "I hate it. You know I do." Although the original meaning and intent may be clear from the intonation and pacing of speech in the audiotape, it may be much less so in the transcript, unless these features are meticulously cataloged as well (see the discussion of notation systems to follow).

A second challenge identified in the Brantford study involved the failure of transcripts to indicate when people are paraphrasing or mimicking others, or when respondents quote things they told themselves or others told them. In these cases, the intonation and context of the testimony help, but transcribers who do not have a stake in the content of the material and are struggling word for word to get the material committed to paper may not catch what is going on, or may not judge the distinctions to be significant. The danger in a transcriber's failing to include quotation marks and/or annotations such as "(mimicking voice)" is that what a respondent was trying to convey as being someone else's thinking or reaction appears in the written text as if it were the respondent's own.

A third challenge revealed by the Brantford study involved omissions that occur when transcribers go forward and backward in the tape when they need to listen to a passage more than once, with the danger that they do not pick up exactly where they left off and pieces are lost. For example, in one case "I lost a very close friend to cancer" should have read "I lost a very close friend to lung cancer." The omission of the word "lung" was significant given the focus of the study on smoking cessation.

A fourth challenge for transcribers is the mistaking of words for other similar words that may or may not make sense in the context of what is being said. This is particularly apt to happen in passages that are difficult to discern due to problems of poor tape quality (more on this later). But it was not limited to those occasions alone in the Brantford study. On a number of occasions, transcribers' misinterpretations reversed the meaning of what was said. For example, in one case "consultation" was substituted for "confrontation," and "an evaluation model" became "and violation of the model" (see Table 13.1).

In some cases the mistaken wording made some sense (was plausible, although perhaps unlikely) in the immediate context of the sentence in which it was located, but not in the wider context of the interview. In other cases what was written in the transcript seemed bizarre and nonsensical even within the particular sentence or paragraph in which it appeared. In the most ambiguous places, researchers interpolate what makes sense to them as being what was likely uttered during the course of an interview.[4]

To discern the more plausible of several possible readings of an audio passage, then, the transcriber and/or researcher draws on powerful, if implicit, social conventions about the organization of speech and communicative competence to interpolate or adjudicate such apparent anomalies, under the assumption (when passages are unclear) that alternate bizarre phrasings would not have been intended and were therefore not uttered. In essence, confirmation is sought in terms of the coherence (see Hodder 1994) of the utterance with the phrases immediately preceding and following it, as well as with the rest of the respondent's testimony and whatever other knowledge the researcher has about the respondent and his or her social location and biography. The trustworthiness of such corroborating evidence, in turn, is ascertained in terms of prolonged engagement and other aspects of credibility, as described by Egon Guba and Yvonna Lincoln (1989) and others. A transcriber struggling to decipher what is being said from one utterance to the next cannot generally be expected to keep track of the larger context of what is being said as a basis for assessing the plausibility of alternate assessments of what is being said. Furthermore, when the substantive focus is quite outside the experience and/or expertise of the transcriber, such interpolation becomes less likely.

Many challenges associated with transcription quality can be attributed to the poor quality of some tape recordings (more on this later). Transcriber fatigue and lack of familiarity with the topic area can also contribute to the number of errors that creep into the transcription. Less controllable, but sometimes also a factor, is the clarity, speed, and accent of speech used by interviewees. With increasing ethnic and racial diversity in our populations and mounting pressure on researchers to include (and researchers' interest in including) diverse cultural perspectives in research studies, a number of challenges associated with cross-cultural research will also need to be addressed. For example, in cases where minority community members or translators are hired to interview (or assist in the interviewing of) respondents in languages other than those spoken by the principal investigator or the majority of the research team, the translation of audiotaped information or of interview transcripts must be considered. This introduces yet another layer of interpretation in the interview-tape-transcript interface.

ETHICAL CONSIDERATIONS

One of the most disconcerting moments in my dissertation research came when I reviewed several of the transcripts that had been completed by someone the project's primary transcriber had enlisted to assist her. This person (a legal secretary) took it upon herself to tidy up the discussion so that it would *read* better, just as she would have been expected to do with dictated correspondence at work. Michael Patton (1990) tells a similar story about an experience of one of his graduate students. And a colleague of mine recently discovered that her transcribers found the interview material they were working on so depressing and traumatic that they were altering the testimonies of respondents to make them sound more upbeat.[5] Such deliberate attempts to manipulate the data generally reflect transcribers' honest desires to be helpful, based on their own notions of what the transcripts should look like.

Verbal interactions follow a logic that is different from that for written prose, and therefore tend to look remarkably disjointed, inarticulate, and even incoherent when committed to the printed page. Inherent differences between the spoken tongue and the written word mean that transcripts of verbal conversations do not measure up well to the standards we hold for well-crafted prose (or even formal speeches), with the result that participants often come across as incoherent and inarticulate (Kvale 1988).

Ironically, this impression may be reinforced by an insistence on verbatim transcription in which all pauses, broken sentences, interruptions, and other aspects of the messiness of casual conversation are faithfully reproduced, despite what this messiness might lead one to presume about the participants. Some transcribers (particularly those accustomed to preparing correspondence based on dictated notes) find it difficult to resist the impulse to tidy up their transcriptions so that the participants do not appear so thoroughly inarticulate. The disjuncture between what coheres in natural talk and what demonstrates communicative competence in written prose comes as a shock to many respondents when they are asked or are offered the opportunity to review the transcripts of their interviews. Speaking from experience, I should add that interviewers themselves can find their own contributions, committed to paper, a rude awakening.

The potential for respondents (or classes of respondents) to be made to appear inarticulate as a result of the liberal use of verbatim quotes in the published results of a study has important ethical implications. In addition, verbatim quotes often make for difficult reading. The impact of quotes from respondents can often be greater if the researcher subjects them to a little skillful editing, without substantially altering the gist of what was said. Frequently, colleagues and I have been asked by editorial reviewers to tidy up quotes used in our publications. Usually, we consent in the interest of providing a more readable text. However, it is my opinion that although the tidying of quotations may be appropriate when an author is writing up qualitative research for publication, this should occur after the analysis has taken place and should be done by the researcher (not the transcriber), who should take care that what is removed does not appreciably alter the meaning of what was said (see Morse 1994:232). The author may wish to note in the text that "some transcription details have been omitted in the interest of readability" as a way of indicating to colleagues that the original transcripts paid closer attention to detail.

On the other hand, in cases where transcripts will be examined by a number of investigators and students who are part of a research team (which is increasingly the case in multidisciplinary research), ethical considerations might call for identifying information to be removed from transcripts prior to analysis. This is particularly the case when transcripts are made available for secondary analysis at a later date—for example, as part of a student dissertation after project funding has expired. The removal of identifying information becomes potentially problematic when this includes not simply the elimination of names but also the removal of other information that might allow analysts to identify individual respondents by virtue of their locations, social networks, job titles, organizations of employment, or other distinguishing features. The risk here is that removing too much identifying information could compromise future researchers' ability to contextualize the testimony of the respondents adequately as a basis for analysis, even though this practice may be defensible on ethical grounds.

Ethical issues also attend the unintentional misrepresentation of respondents, as when, for example, testimony is misunderstood or errors in transcription substantially alter the gist of what was intended, as is the case in several of the examples in Table 13.1. Giving study participants the opportunity to verify the transcripts or initial analyses may be one way for researchers to address this possibility. However, it is preferable that researchers forewarn respondents in these cases about how they are likely to appear on paper, for reasons that are elaborated above. (I discuss some other complications that may arise during member checking in a subsequent section of this chapter.)

I have noticed that a number of researchers today are including in the research proposals they submit for ethical review the stipulation that interview audiotapes will be erased as soon as transcripts are completed. This reflects a laudable concern for respondent confidentiality, but I am concerned that the erasure of audiotapes at an early stage in a research project will ensure that many decision points—regarding how difficult passages were transcribed and the application of the anointed syntax in practice, for example—will become irretrievable.

◆ *Problematizing "Verbatim"*

As previously noted, the transcript, as text, is frequently seen as unproblematic and given a privileged status in which its authority goes unquestioned (see Denzin 1994). This position may even be enhanced by an emphasis on accuracy of transcription. The conventional understanding of transcription error is in terms of the discrepancy between the written record (transcript) and the audiotape recording of the research interview upon which it is based. The notion of a verbatim transcript, therefore, is limited to a faithful reproduction of the oral record, the latter being taken as the indisputable record of the interview (problems with tape quality excepted).

However, many aspects of interpersonal interaction and nonverbal communication are not captured in audiotape records, so that the audiotape itself is not strictly a verbatim record of the interview. In other words, concern with ensuring that transcripts are accurate may unreflexively conflate lived experience of the one-on-one conversation with recorded speech (tapes), and this speech with the written word (transcript). In the words of Ann Oakley (1981), "Interviewing is rather like a marriage: everybody knows what it is, an awful lot of people do it, and yet behind each closed door there is a world of secrets" (p. 41). Those "secrets" include many nonverbal aspects of the interview context that are often not recorded on tape: body language, facial expressions, eye gazes (Bloom and Lahey 1978, cited in Lapadat and Lindsay 1999), nods, smiles or frowns (Kvale 1996), the physical setting, the ways

participants are dressed, and other factors affecting the tone of the interview (Fontana and Frey 1994). Raymond Gorden (1980) identifies four types of nonverbal communication that are salient in this context:

> *Proxemic* communication is the use of interpersonal space to communicate attitudes; *chronemic* communication is the use of pacing of speech and length of silence in conversation; *kinesic* communication includes any body movements or postures; and *paralinguistic* communication includes all the variations in volume, pitch and quality of voice. (P. 335)

Even when aspects of emotional context are expressed with an oral component, such as intonation of voice, pauses, sighs, and laughter, these are not easily or straightforwardly translated into the written record. There may also be considerable variability in the extent to which verbal cues such as abandoned utterances, garbles, and verbal disruptions (Hughes, McGillivray, and Schmidek 1997, cited in Lapadat and Lindsay 1999) are adequately captured in transcription. These may require a standardized syntax for reliable encoding in the transcript, as well as a fuller accounting of the interview context that draws on field notes.[6]

Further, the dialogue that is captured on tape is framed not only by the immediate microcontext of the research interview (a stilted environment itself), but by a broader macrocontext of historically and socially located events. Because context is both "infinitely delicate and infinitely expandable" (Cook 1990, cited in Lapadat and Lindsay 1999:72), its apprehension is inherently incomplete and selective (on the importance of context, see also Kvale 1996).

We might do well then to ask, echoing Steinar Kvale (1995), "What is a valid translation from oral to written language?"

(p. 27). The socially constructed nature of the research interview as a coauthored conversation-in-context must be acknowledged, instead of a quasi-positivist reification of the transcript as data about the interviewee, frozen in time (and space) (Kvale 1988; Richardson 1993). As text, the transcript is also open to multiple alternative readings, as well as reinterpretation, with every fresh reading (Denzin 1995; Kvale 1995).

The central issue, then, is what kind of text we envisage a transcript to be. How do we construct the transcript as an object of research? As recorded conversation? Phenomenological experience? Literary text? Linguistic data set? Dialogue? Narrative? (See Kvale 1988.) The reification of the transcript as synonymous with the interview, but also as a privileged text revealing the truth about the researched, glosses over these important distinctions (Kvale 1995). A modernist obsession with transcription accuracy, which problematizes transgressions in the privileged written text while simultaneously concealing the author in the writing up of interviews in conventional scientific prose, constructs issues of validity and reliability in terms of findings rather than tellings (Richardson 1993; see also Denzin 1994; Kvale 1995).

A number of authors have articulated and advanced alternative criteria for evaluating the quality of qualitative research (Lincoln and Guba 1985; Guba and Lincoln 1989; Corbin and Strauss 1990; Altheide and Johnson 1994; Hall and Stevens 1991), although none has addressed specifically the issue of transcription quality. Taken together, however, these authors raise issues of voice, representation, authenticity, audience, positionality, and reflexivity. This raises the possibility that our fixation on the depth interview and its textual representation in the form of transcripts is blinding us to the possibility and value of other ways of capturing voice, such as through self-stories and personal experience stories (Denzin 1995; see also Ellis and Berger, Chapter 23, this volume). In this context, theatrical and poetic representations of research data and/or findings are particularly well suited to convey the emotional content of the material.

I would therefore suggest that we can usefully focus our attention on the trustworthiness of transcripts as research data by examining how faithfully they reproduce the oral (tape) record, while also being mindful of the limitations of these media to portray the full flavor of the interview. We must also take into account the potential for contested meanings and divergent interpretations of the gist and significance of what is being said, particularly when speech is garbled or poorly captured on tape. This may encourage us to examine reflexively our assumptions about transcription (and transcription quality) and its role in the research process, as well as to take the steps necessary to ascertain and document the trustworthiness of transcription as an aspect of rigor in qualitative research.

No doubt there are readers who will see these perspectives (error as real and yet also individually and socially constructed and contestable) as fundamentally contradictory. I think it is possible, indeed reasonable and defensible, to attend to many straightforward determinants of transcription quality (e.g., quality of audiotape recording, use of notational syntax to capture aspects of interaction more consistently, training of transcribers) while simultaneously maintaining a reflexive skepticism regarding the multiple interpretive acts that constitute the transcription process and their impact on the process of translating (re-presenting) the interview as audio recording and then as textual data. Putting it differently, I might say that such a position approximates that described by Martin Hammersley (1992) as subtle realism, or by David Altheide and John Johnson (1994) as analytic realism, in which it is assumed that knowable phenomena can be known only in cultural, social, politically situated ways (as situated human construction). Thus, by implication, researchers must consider the relationships among substance, observer, interpretation, audience, and style. This is broadly consistent with a critical realist stance. Indeed, this observation underscores the indivisibility of methodological issues (namely, transcription) from theoretical and epistemological ones.

◆ Strategies for Maximizing Transcription Quality

As with other aspects of qualitative research, there may be no singular approved approach to transcription divorced from the context and aims of the research project. However, several strategies are available for qualitative researchers to consider employing or adapting to their situations for the purpose of enhancing transcription quality. These include strategies for maximizing the audio quality of tape recordings, for using notation systems, for working with transcribers, for reviewing the quality of transcription, for using member checks, for flagging ambiguity in the interview, for using field notes or other sources as corroborating evidence in the interpolation of difficult passages, and for reporting on transcription quality in published research findings. Each of these is discussed below.

TAPE QUALITY

Much aggravation (for both researcher and transcriber) can be prevented by the interviewer's ensuring the quality of the original tape recording. Excessive background noise, weak batteries, a dirty recording head, placement of the recording device or microphone too far away from the respondent, the use of low-quality cassettes, and people speaking too softly to be heard well are all factors in the quality of the audio recording. Several suggestions for ensuring

the audio quality of tape recordings are outlined in Table 13.2.

NOTATION SYSTEMS AND CONVENTIONS FOR TRANSCRIPTION

By failing to establish a priori a clear and consistent syntax for transcribers to use in recording pauses, laughter, interruptions, intonations, and so forth in the written text, the researcher does little to encourage consistency in the way these are handled within and between transcripts. Several notation systems have been developed and proposed over the years (Edwards and Lampert 1993; Psathas and Anderson 1990; Silverman 1993). Which one a researcher selects (or whether and how a researcher adapts an existing system or develops one for his or her own use) depends on which features the researcher considers important to capture, given the inevitable trade-off between level of detail and the resources required to achieve it. Thus it is neither appropriate nor possible to specify a priori what constitutes the most appropriate (or rigorous, or highest-quality) universal notation system. The researcher's decisions about what to include and how to do so must be informed by the theoretical stance and empirical focus of the study, as well as by such pragmatic considerations as the availability of sufficient resources.

Those researchers who are interested in detailed, turn-by-turn conversation analysis (CA) are especially concerned with pauses, overlaps, stretched sounds, intonations, partial words, and expressions of agreement, acknowledgment, surprise, and so on (see Atkinson and Heritage 1984). Such details of talk assume great significance because they reveal *how* things are said (and not only *what* is said). In these cases, even more careful precision in transcription is required, including the insertion of special codes to convey details that normally do not get committed to paper during the transcription process.

Table 13.2   STRATEGIES FOR ENSURING HIGH-QUALITY TAPE RECORDING

I. Equipment
   a. Use electrical outlet and outside mike whenever possible.
   b. If you use batteries, check them.
   c. Clean tape recorder heads regularly.
   d. Take along extra tape cassettes (and batteries).

II. Before interview
   a. Choose a place that's quiet and free from interruptions.
   b. Place microphone close to respondent, then speak loud enough so we hear what you're saying; most important, we want to hear the answer.
   c. Set recorder on stable surface.
   d. Test the recording system.

III. During interview
   a. Speak clearly and not too fast—respondent is likely to do the same.
   b. Ask respondent to speak clearly.
   c. Make test with respondent, then rewind and listen so respondent can hear whether she/he is speaking distinctly; if not, say, "The recorder does not seem to be picking up well. Could you speak up a little?" Whether the problem is mechanical or personal, correct it before continuing.
   d. Avoid using voice activation feature (if available), as it may fail to record the first few words spoken after each pause (also, lengths of pauses cannot be judged).
   e. Don't rustle papers, cups, bottles, and so on near the microphone.
   f. Watch for tape breakage and tangling.
   g. Repeat test if tape change is necessary.
   h. At end of interview, say, "This is the end of interview with . . . ."

IV. After interview
   a. Listen to tape—make notes, list proper names (or pseudonyms) and unfamiliar terminology.
   b. Label tapes and return them to appropriate containers.
   c. Keep tapes and recorder in good condition—do not touch tape or expose it to extreme temperatures.
   d. Consider making backup copies of tapes before turning them over to the transcriber.

SOURCE: Adapted from Patton (1990).

CA is concerned with the methods by which people produce orderly social interaction. This includes the ways in which conversation is structured, not only by implicit cultural norms (regarding appropriate turn taking and the like), but by the institutional and/or situational context of interaction, which may invoke competing discourses and opportunities for the display of social competence (see Silverman 1993). David Silverman and his colleagues provide a convincing demonstration of the potential benefits of going beyond verbatim transcription to the use of the syntax of conversation analysis in terms of the sometimes profound effects this had on the way the transcripts were coded by the research project team (see Clavarino, Najman, and Silverman 1995; Silverman 1993). Similarly, Elliot Mishler (1991) compares the yield and impact of the use of several different approaches to notation and representation (poetic, narrative, discursive). And, taking the discussion in a different direc-

Table 13.3   SAMPLE TRANSCRIPTION NOTATION SYSTEM ORIENTED TO CONVERSATION ANALYSIS REQUIREMENTS

[Mo:	C2: quite a [while [yea	Left brackets indicate the point at which a current speaker's talk is overlapped by another's talk.
=	W: that I'm aware of= C: =Yes. Would you confirm that?	Equal signs, one at the end of a line and one at the beginning of the next, indicate no gap between the two lines.
(.4)	Yes (.2) yeah	Numbers in parentheses indicate elapsed time in silence in tenths of a second.
(.)	to get (.) treatment	A dot in parentheses indicates a tiny gap, probably no more than one-tenth of a second.
::	O:kay?	Colons indicate prolongation of the immediately prior sound. The length of the row of colons indicates the length of the prolongation.
WORD	I've got ENOUGH TO WORRY ABOUT	Capitals, except at the beginnings of lines, indicate especially loud sounds relative to the surrounding talk.
.hhhhh	I feel that (.2) .hh	A row of h's prefixed by a dot indicates an inbreath; without a dot, an outbreath. The length of the row of h's indicates the length of the in- or outbreath.
( )	future risks and ( ) and life ( )	Empty parentheses indicate the transcriber's inability to hear what was said.
(word)	Would you see (there) anything positive	Parenthesized words are possible hearings.
(( ))	confirms that ((continues))	Double parentheses contain author's descriptions rather than transcriptions.
.,?	What do you think?	Punctuation indicates speaker's intonation.

SOURCE: Adapted from Silverman (1993).

tion, Candace West (1996) points out the need to fit both transcription conventions and analytic questions to the level of detail that can possibly be recorded.

Detailed CA notation systems can help resolve some ambiguities in interpretation. To illustrate, the careful inclusion of pregnant pauses and interjections such as "yes-mm" and "uh-huh" could indicate receipt or assent (or resistance, in the case of refusals to provide the usual affirming responses to the speech of another). These subtleties (which can be significant) tend to be missed in less stringent transcription practices, particularly when they are overlaid with the speech of another. Without clear direction from the research team on how to handle these situations, transcribers are faced with determining on a case-by-case basis which interjections are consequential enough to be included—a situation that can be fraught with uncertainty (yielding inconsistent results).

Gail Jefferson is generally credited with developing the core features of CA transcription conventions (see Jefferson 1984;

see also Sacks, Schegloff, and Jefferson 1974; Atkinson and Heritage 1984; Psathas 1995). Drawing on these and other sources, Silverman (1993) has produced a more concise rendition that remains true to the original objectives; Silverman's recommendations are displayed in Table 13.3.

On the other hand, this level of attention to detail can prove exhausting for transcribers and researchers alike. There is a limit to the degree of painstaking attention to detail that can be demanded of a transcriber in applying an elaborated system of codes. Whether or not this is warranted depends entirely on what the researchers wish to get out of the transcription. In studies with large sample sizes (60-100+ interviews), when analysis may be more superficial and limited to the cataloging of opinions or experiences, close attention to conversational dynamics may be unnecessary. On the other hand, in studies where sample sizes are smaller and where the features of interaction will be scrutinized (especially in naturally occurring talk such as the analysis of doctor-patient communication), it may be vitally important to employ notational systems of the type described in Table 13.3.

In Table 13.4, I offer an abbreviated set of instructions for transcribers that might be an alternative to Silverman's syntax of conversation analysis. Again, which of these, or which of several other conventions, a researcher uses will depend on the hypotheses, theoretical orientation, and nature of the data at hand. The schema in Table 13.4 calls for less detail in some areas than is stipulated in CA transcription. For example, short pauses are indicated by a series of dots (. . .) and longer ones by the word *pause* in parentheses; in CA, pauses are timed to tenths of a second. In addition to a formalized notation system for capturing these elements, Lori d'Agincourt-Canning and Susan Cox (2000) recommend that researchers give transcribers lists of jargon or special terms, with correct and phonetic spellings, to help them handle any terminology with which they may be unfamiliar.

SELECTING TRANSCRIBERS

The discussion in this chapter assumes that transcription is being done by individuals hired specifically for that purpose, rather than by the interviewers or researchers themselves. This practice is increasingly common in naturalistic qualitative inquiry, particularly in the health sciences, in contrast to conversation analysis, where the painstaking work of transcription is invariably undertaken by the researcher. The contracting out of transcription to paid employees presents a number of unique challenges with respect to transcription quality, although many of the issues raised in this chapter also pertain to transcription undertaken by interviewers and researchers.

Given the interpretive work involved in transcription, researchers need to consider carefully who might be the most appropriate persons to undertake this task. This is particularly so when the roles of interviewer, transcriber, analyst, and primary author of publications arising from a research study are embodied by different people. One might well ask whether persons with secretarial training and experience but little prior involvement in, or understanding of, qualitative research are appropriate candidates for making the myriad interpretive decisions involved in the transcription process, despite these persons' considerable technical skills.

It has been my observation that such divisions of labor (paid interviewer, transcriber, student/staff analyst, and principal investigator or coinvestigator) are increasingly common in large, externally funded research projects in the health sciences. The disruption of the continuity that might previously have been expected as a result of the same individual's embodying these roles has the potential for ruptures in understanding to occur in the process of translating data across media. I would suggest that

Table 13.4   ALTERNATIVE ABBREVIATED INSTRUCTIONS FOR TRANSCRIBERS

It is important for qualitative research that transcripts be verbatim accounts of what transpired in the interview; that is, they should not be edited or otherwise "tidied up" to make them "sound better."

Pauses	Denote short pauses during talking by a series of dots (. . .), the length of which depends on the amount of time elapsed (e.g., two dots for less than half a second, three dots for one second, four dots for one and a half seconds). Denote longer pauses with the word pause in parentheses. Use "(pause)" for two- to three-second breaks and "(long pause)" to indicate pauses of four or more seconds.
Laughing, coughing, etc.	Indicate in parentheses; for example, "(coughs)," "(sigh)," "(sneeze)." Use "(laughing)" to denote one person, "(laughter)" to denote several laughing.
Interruptions	Indicate when someone's speech is broken off midsentence by including a hyphen (-) at the point where the interruption occurs (e.g., "What do you-").
Overlapping speech	Use a hyphen to indicate when one speaker interjects into the speech of another, include the speech of the other with "(overlapping)," then return to where the original speaker was interrupted (if he or she continues). For example: R: He said that was impos- I: (overlapping) Who, Bob? R: No, Larry.
Garbled speech	Flag words that are not clear with square brackets and question mark, if guessing what was said (e.g., "At that, Harry just [doubled? glossed?] over"). Use x's to denote passages that cannot be deciphered at all (number of x's should denote approximate number of words that cannot be deciphered). For example, "Gina went xxxxx xxxxx xxxxx, and then [came? went?] home."
Emphasis	Use caps to denote strong emphasis; for example, "He did WHAT?" (Do not use boldface or underlining because such formatting is often lost when text files are imported into qualitative analysis software programs.)

such ruptures also attend the loss of intimacy with the fullness of the context of the data that occurs when investigators (or students or others undertaking secondary analysis) work directly from the transcripts without prior involvement in the interview or transcription phases, and often without having listened to any of the interview audiotapes.

WORKING WITH TRANSCRIBERS

Transcriber training should probably include at least one session in which the researcher introduces the syntax to be used and goes over a section of tape with the transcriber(s), answering questions that may arise in the course of applying the guidelines to an actual study interview.[7] The researcher should also make an attempt to review several of the initial transcripts, so that misunderstandings can be cleared up early in the process. I would recommend that researchers meet at regular intervals with all transcribers, in addition to reviewing their work early on in the process to ensure comparability (if there is more than one transcriber) and dependability.

In my experience, I have found that it helps if transcribers are informed about the nature and purpose of the research. It is even better if those doing the transcription have themselves undertaken social science research (perhaps as students), so that they are generally knowledgeable about the process. The tenets of hermeneutic science are often difficult to identify and convey adequately to transcribers without postsecondary education in the relatively short orientation periods available. Transcribers with primarily secretarial backgrounds have the technical skills required but find it harder to understand the research enterprise and topics under investigation than do transcribers with more education. In my experience this is reflected in the nature of the interpretive decisions such transcribers make in the course of transcription. On the

other hand, they may have insights into the life worlds of the researched that are unavailable to the study investigators by virtue of their class location, race, and/or gender.

Indeed, researchers should not overlook the opportunity to involve transcribers in the study beyond their function as recorders. After all, other than the interviewers and one or two study investigators, transcribers are the only people to be exposed to the interviews in their entirety. In the Brantford study, the transcriber was encouraged to provide feedback (typically in writing at the end of the interview file) about her reactions to the interview—not only its content, but also her perceptions of the nature and quality of interaction between interviewer and interviewee (the time she took to provide her reactions was included as paid time). The quality of the transcriber's contributions in this vein was variable, but I frequently found her input to be worthwhile.[8] It may also be useful for researchers to contact transcribers for regular debriefings, by phone or in person, particlarly when the material being transcribed is emotionally charged (d'Agincourt-Canning and Cox 2000). If the project employs more than one transcriber, and resources allow for it, the researcher may have the opportunity to engineer some overlap in the transcribers' workloads so as to identify and explore some of the differences that may arise in transcription of the same interview tape(s). There may be yet other ways in which researchers may engage the transcriber-as-hired-hand in making suggestions and modifications to the transcription syntax, the coding of data, the data entry of codes (when using computer analysis software), and so forth. In other words, researchers should not overlook opportunities to engage transcribers more fully in their research projects. Of course, in these cases it is important for researchers to remember to acknowledge the contributions of the transcribers in conference presentations and publications (d'Agincourt-Canning and Cox 2000).

REVIEWING
TRANSCRIPTION QUALITY

It is unlikely that all discrepancies in interpretation between transcriber and interviewer/investigator regarding the translation of data from audiotape to written text can be prevented, even with well-trained transcribers working from high-quality recordings and supported by clear guidelines for transcription. On the other hand, reviewing all transcripts is time-consuming and expensive, and may not be justified. Transcription costs alone average $100 (for four to six hours) per interview (more for focus group discussions), depending on length and complexity, to which one would have to add at least another $50 of paid research staff time for reviewing transcription quality (unless this is done by the study investigators, for whom time is also at a premium).

For many studies, the addition of an extra step of this nature would represent a significant increase in costs and a setback in time. Given these limitations, two alternatives seem appropriate in this context, and these are not mutually exclusive. One option is for the researchers to consider not having all of the interviews transcribed in their entirety. Investigators (or research staff) could listen to the interview tapes and identify sections (using tape counter numbers) for subsequent transcription, for example. This would have the added benefit of ensuring that research staff/investigators involved in analysis (but who did not complete some or all of the interviews themselves) will have listened to the audiotapes of all the interviews. Alternatively, the researchers could review a subset of transcripts (selected purposefully or randomly) to highlight themes and phenomena around which subsequent (selective) transcription efforts (and analysis) would be focused. This would also help the researchers avoid the possibility (in larger studies) of their being overwhelmed by the volume of material to be analyzed.[9]

A second option (which may be exercised in concert with the first) is for the researchers to be selective in their review of transcript quality. They could review a small proportion of the transcripts, randomly or purposively selected, to gauge the quality of transcription overall. They should bear in mind, however, that transcription quality can be highly variable, as I found it to be in the Brantford study. Some transcripts (notably where the quality of the tape recording was poor) had errors affecting up to 60 percent of passages, whereas I judged many others to be virtually error-free. Such variability calls into question the viability of the practice of selecting a small (e.g., 10 percent) random sample of transcripts for closer scrutiny on the assumption that what holds for those will generally hold for the others. On the other hand, the effort required to assess transcription quality and effect remedial action will usually preclude an exhaustive review of all transcripts. One strategy a researcher might use would be to gravitate toward examining those texts that transcribers themselves identify as having been particularly difficult to produce. The researcher could select these plus a small sample of other transcripts for review onscreen while the interview tape is rolling. Keeping a tally of the number of minor (semantic) and major (meaning-reversing) errors will help the researcher to determine the extent of the problem and to decide whether a full review of the remainder of the transcripts is called for. In many cases, a researcher's documenting the quality of transcription in a sample of transcripts will itself be a marked improvement over conventional practice.

MEMBER CHECKING

The nature of transcription as an interpretive activity surfaces the possibility that multiple interpretations will not be easily resolved and that different people checking transcription quality may generate different versions of the interview transcript. Although the documentation of these differences may be instructive, the argument might be made that the interviewer (using his or her field notes and other recollections of the interview experience) should be the one to review the transcript, rather than a relative newcomer to the study hired for this purpose. In some cases, respondents themselves may also be of assistance in sorting out particularly ambiguous passages, as Guba and Lincoln (1989) advocate under the rubric of member checks for establishing the credibility of research (see also Bloor 1983).

This strategy presents other challenges, however. Despite the many merits of checking back with respondents, either on a routine or an ad hoc basis, the use of this strategy for the validation of the trustworthiness of transcription is potentially problematic. When a researcher presents a transcript to a respondent for review, what he or she typically gets back are not only corrections to (perceived) errors in transcribing, depending on the person's recollections of what was said, but also attempts to clarify, justify, or perhaps even revoke or alter aspects of what was said (Hoffart 1991). Such member checking may be an important and valued addition or component of the research process. It allows for the gathering of additional information, permits respondents to validate or clarify the intended meaning behind certain statements, or comment on the overall adequacy of the interview (Lincoln and Guba 1985). This highlights the ways in which respondents may reinterpret or try to alter their testimonies upon further reflection or later in time.

Some researchers also value an ethical stance in which respondents retain ultimate control over how their stories are reported and interpreted, regardless of the number of changes they request or the nature of those requests. Although giving respondents the power to revoke or alter their testimony is laudable, researchers need to be aware of the anxiety they may help to create in respondents when they give those

who have been interviewed the opportunity to see their words in print. In my experience, no matter how many times promises of confidentiality and anonymity are repeated, when respondents see their own words in print, the possibility of sensitive material being made available to others seems to be highlighted. This appears to be particularly so for professionals who may have made comments about their colleagues or employers that could be damaging if revealed. I suspect that this is partly because we typically associate print material with dissemination and communication (i.e., text is printed for the purpose of sharing with others), and because most professionals in North America are acutely aware of the dangers of particular materials falling into the wrong hands. Stories of leaked confidential memos pepper the popular press, and this does little to reassure respondents when they see their own testimony in print.

Nevertheless, the distinction between what was originally intended and what was actually said (let alone what the respondent wishes to change or retract) is not addressed by a focus on transcription quality per se (i.e., ensuring that what was said—and how it was said—is accurately committed to paper). But the clarification of intended meaning may be as important as (or more important than) the establishment of the accuracy of transcripts as privileged texts. These observations reinforce a point made earlier—that transcripts are, at best, partial accounts of the encounters between researcher and researched, rather than simply windows into the lives of the researched (Kirk and Miller 1986; Kvale 1988).

FLAGGING AMBIGUOUS MATERIAL IN THE INTERVIEW

Ideally, some of the ambiguities that are most salient to the research study will be flagged during the interview. The interviewer can create opportunities within the interview for the respondent to clarify earlier statements or to validate the initial interpretations of the interviewer, rather than wait until after the interview is complete and the transcript in hand.

USE OF FIELD NOTES AND OBSERVATIONAL DATA

As noted above (in the context of the interpolation of meaning in difficult passages), field notes may also help researchers to clarify some aspects of the interview context (see Atkinson and Coffey, Chapter 20, this volume). Details pertinent to the setting or other aspects of the respondent's life, the researcher's relationship with the researched, and so forth may have a bearing on how statements in the interviews are heard or interpreted. Of course, this assumes that field notes are not a gold standard against which to assess transcription, but are themselves necessarily partial interpretive accounts. Indeed, researchers must pay attention to what conventions will guide what is transcribed "in the field," including how to represent conversation (see West 1996).

REPORTING ON TRANSCRIPTION QUALITY

The suggestions contained in this chapter have a number of implications for how research might be carried out as well as how it might be reported and written up. One could envisage a "methods" section of a research paper or report containing a description of the steps taken to ensure audiotape quality, the directions provided to transcribers, and an assessment of the trustworthiness of the transcription based on a review of selected transcripts, in the context of an explicit acknowledgment of the interpretive nature of the transcription process. As with other aspects of the qualitative research process, researchers should ideally provide sufficient information to allow others to assess the trustworthiness of the data and subsequent interpretations, although there will typically be limited space in peer-review journal articles in which to do so.

◆ The Future of Transcription

New technologies may eclipse or transform the transcription process as we know it. It is possible, for example, that voice-recognition software will improve sufficiently in accuracy to permit the automation of transcription. This could represent a considerable savings in both time and money, and would remove some of the drudgery (albeit drudgery that earns many people a living) associated with preparing interview data for analysis. However, because this software is not designed to represent many aspects of the verbal record that might be of interest to researchers (e.g., pauses, sighs, intonations, laughter), programs would have to be adapted for use in qualitative research (perhaps to suit particular notational conventions, such as a particular program for conversation analysis). In any case, it is noteworthy that automation cannot do away with the many interpretive issues that normally arise in the course of transcription; however, it may make them more arbitrary and less visible or available for scrutiny.

It is possible that new information technologies will allow researchers to skip transcription altogether. As storage media increasingly permit the collection of larger sound files (spurred by developments of MP3 and other resources on the World Wide Web), it may be possible to develop qualitative analysis software that will work directly with audio material. Audio passages (and perhaps even video passages) could be coded and retrieved for analysis in presumably much the same manner that sections of transcript text currently are, with much more of the interaction preserved for analysis. A combination of voice-recognition software and audiovisual storage capabilities might even allow for streaming video images alongside the automatically generated transcript text (simultaneous code and retrieve). Indeed, such capabilities are already to be found in the KIT program (see Tesch 1990; Kvale 1996). To quote Kvale (1996), in the KIT program,

> the tape recording is transferred to a compact disk, converted into digital form, and stored in the computer. During replay the speech can be coded on the monitor, comments on the passages can be written down, and central passages for later reporting can be transcribed. The coded passages can be retrieved for relistening, or recoding and other functions of the analysis program can be conducted—in this case, by working directly with the recorded interview instead of with the transcripts. (Pp. 174-75)

Although Kvale is optimistic that "many methodological and theoretical problems of transforming oral speech into written texts are simply bypassed when the analyst works directly on recordings of the live conversations" (p. 175), Judith Lapadat and Anne Lindsay (1999) remain skeptical of this claim. As long as scientific results are disseminated in written form (which continues to be the primary, although no longer the only, medium), transcription of at least some material is virtually inevitable, although at least with systems like KIT, more of the data in their raw form are available in the analysis phase. Nevertheless, audio passages (and even streaming video) do not capture all elements of the interview experience. Rather than being embedded in transcription notation conventions, many of the decisions regarding what to capture and how to do so would conceivably simply be deferred to the coding phase, with potentially unsatisfactory results (less predictable or uniform, for example). In other words, it is unlikely that technology will enable researchers to bypass the thorny issues of interpretation involved in the preparation of data for analysis. Would we really want it any other way?

■ Notes

1. The qualitative research sourcebooks examined in this review included *Analyzing Everyday Explanation* (Antaki 1988), *In the Field* (Burgess 1984), *Doing Qualitative Research* (Crabtree and Miller 1992), *Interpretive Interactionism* (Denzin 1989), *Handbook of Qualitative Research* (Denzin and Lincoln 1994), *Ethnography: Step by Step* (Fetterman 1989), *The Interpretation of Cultures* (Geertz 1973), *Using Computers in Qualitative Research* (Fielding and Lee 1991), *The Long Interview* (McCracken 1988), *Qualitative Data Analysis* (Miles and Huberman 1984), *Successful Focus Groups* (Morgan 1993), *Qualitative Evaluation and Research Methods* (Patton 1990), *Everyday Understanding* (Semin and Gergen 1990), *Qualitative Methodology and Sociology* (Silverman 1985), *Interpreting Qualitative Data* (Silverman 1993), *Qualitative Analysis for Social Scientists* (Strauss 1987), and *An Introduction to Qualitative Research Methods* (Taylor and Bogdan 1984). Of these, only David Morgan's (1993) edited collection and Michael Patton's (1990) volume make more than passing reference to the issue of transcription quality, and both are cursory and selective in their treatment of the topic.

2. I have consulted the following sources on rigor in qualitative research: Cobb and Hagemaster (1987), Strauss and Corbin (1990), Daly and McDonald (1992), Engel and Kuzel (1992), Guba and Lincoln (1989:chap. 8), Hall and Stevens (1991), Hammersley (1992: chap. 4), Italy and McDonald (1992), Kuzel and Like (1991), LeCompte and Goetz (1982), Lincoln and Guba (1985:chap. 11), Morse (1991a, 1991b), Silverman (1993:chap. 7), and West (1990).

3. An earlier paper on the issue of transcription quality was published in *Qualitative Inquiry* (Poland 1995) and was subsequently revised and updated for inclusion in this volume.

4. Such interpolations should probably be identified as such in transcripts through the use of square brackets ([. . .]) and/or question marks, or some other consistent syntax (see Table 13.3).

5. Exposing transcribers to potentially traumatic testimonies also raises ethical considerations, insofar as the provision of emotional supports should be considered.

6. Others argue that researchers must entertain entirely different approaches to data representation if they are to convey adequately the emotional content of the lived experience of study participants (regarding poetic representations, for example, see Richardson, Chapter 42, this volume).

7. Ideally, there might be more than one such session and more than one tape used (pulling, for example, from a recording judged to be difficult to understand or from different types of interviews or topic areas), particularly where a fairly detailed syntax is to be used.

8. This was so even, or perhaps especially, when her assessment of an interview was at odds with mine, forcing me to reexamine my assumptions or conclusions about the interview.

9. Kvale (1988) discusses the ways in which the combination of large (excessive?) data sets and computer analysis software may compromise the research by seducing the researcher into substituting the search and retrieval of character strings for a more carefully thought-out analysis plan (when plans for the analysis of interview material are formulated after a large number of transcripts have been amassed).

■ *References*

Altheide, D. L. and J. M. Johnson. 1994. "Criteria for Assessing Interpretive Validity in Qualitative Research." Pp. 485-99 in *Handbook of Qualitative Research*, edited by N. K. Denzin and Y. S. Lincoln. Thousand Oaks, CA: Sage.

Antaki, C., ed. 1988. *Analyzing Everyday Explanation: A Casebook of Methods*. Newbury Park, CA: Sage.

Atkinson, J. M. and J. Heritage, eds. 1984. *Structures of Social Action: Studies in Conversation Analysis*. Cambridge: Cambridge University Press.

Bloom, L. and M. Lahey. 1978. *Language Development and Disorders*. New York: John Wiley.

Bloor, M. J. 1983. "Notes on Member Validation." Pp. 156-72 in *Contemporary Field Research: A Collection of Readings,* edited by R. M. Emerson. Boston: Little, Brown.

Burgess, R. G. 1984. *In the Field: An Introduction to Field Research*. London: George Allen & Unwin.

Clavarino, A. M., J. M. Najman, and D. Silverman. 1995. "The Quality of Qualitative Data: Two Strategies for Analyzing Medical Interviews." *Qualitative Inquiry* 1:223-42.

Cobb, A. K. and J. N. Hagemaster. 1987. "Ten Criteria for Evaluating Qualitative Research Proposals." *Journal of Nursing Education* 26(4):138-43.

Cook, G. 1990. "Transcribing Infinity: Problems of Context Representation." *Journal of Pragmatics* 14:1-24.

Corbin, J. and A. L. Strauss. 1990. "Grounded Theory Research: Procedures, Canons, and Evaluative Criteria." *Qualitative Sociology* 13:3-21.

Crabtree, B. F. and W. L. Miller. 1992. *Doing Qualitative Research*. Newbury Park, CA: Sage.

d'Agincourt-Canning, L. and S. M. Cox. 2000. *Mere Words on a Page? Transcription as Embodied Labor*. Presented at the Sixth Annual Qualitative Health Research Conference, Banff, Alberta.

Daly, J. and I. McDonald. 1992. "Covering Your Back: Strategies for Qualitative Research in Clinical Settings." *Qualitative Health Research* 2:416-38.

Denzin, N. K. 1989. *Interpretive Interactionism*. Newbury Park, CA: Sage.

———. 1994. "The Art and Politics of Interpretation." Pp. 500-515 in *Handbook of Qualitative Research,* edited by N. K. Denzin and Y. S. Lincoln. Newbury Park, CA: Sage.

———. 1995. "On Hearing the Voices of Educational Research." *Curriculum Inquiry* 25:313-30.

Denzin, N. K. and Y. S. Lincoln, eds. 1994. *Handbook of Qualitative Research*. Newbury Park, CA: Sage.

Du Bois, J. W., S. Schuetze-Coburn, S. Cumming, and D. Paolino. 1993. "Outline of Discourse Transcription." Pp. 45-87 in *Talking Data: Transcription and Coding in Discourse Research*, edited by J. A. Edwards and M. D. Lampert. Hillsdale, NJ: Lawrence Erlbaum.

Edwards, J. A. and M. D. Lampert, eds. 1993. *Talking Data: Transcription and Coding in Discourse Research*. Hillsdale, NJ: Lawrence Erlbaum.

Engel, J. and A. Kuzel. 1992. "On the Idea of What Constitutes Good Qualitative Inquiry." *Qualitative Health Research* 2:504-10.

Fetterman, D. M. 1989. *Ethnography: Step by Step*. Newbury Park, CA: Sage.

Fielding, N. G. and R. M. Lee, eds. 1991. *Using Computers in Qualitative Research*. Newbury Park, CA: Sage.

Fontana, A. and J. H. Frey. 1994. "Interviewing: The Art of Science." Pp. 361-76 in *Handbook of Qualitative Research*, edited by N. K. Denzin and Y. S. Lincoln. Newbury Park, CA: Sage.

Geertz, C. 1973. *The Interpretation of Cultures: Selected Essays*. New York: Basic Books.

Gorden, R. L. 1980. *Interviewing: Strategy, Techniques, and Tactics*. 3d ed. Homewood, IL: Dorsey.

Guba, E. G. and Y. S. Lincoln. 1989. *Fourth Generation Evaluation*. Newbury Park, CA: Sage.

Gubrium, J. F. and J. A. Holstein. 1997. *The New Language of Qualitative Method*. New York: Oxford University Press.

Hall, J. M. and P. E. Stevens. 1991. "Rigor in Feminist Research." *Advances in Nursing Science* 13(3):16-29.

Hammersley, M. 1992. *What's Wrong with Ethnography? Methodological Explorations*. London: Routledge.

Hodder, I. 1994. "The Interpretation of Documents and Material Culture." Pp. 393-402 in *Handbook of Qualitative Research*, edited by N. K. Denzin and Y. S. Lincoln. Newbury Park, CA: Sage.

Hoffart, N. 1991. "A Member Check Procedure to Enhance Rigor in Naturalistic Research." *Western Journal of Nursing Research* 13:522-34.

Hughes, D., L. McGillivray, and M. Schmidek. 1997. *Guide to Narrative Language: Procedures for Assessment*. Eau Claire, WI: Thinking Publications.

Italy, J. and I. McDonald. 1992. "Covering Your Back: Strategies for Qualitative Research in Clinical Settings." *Qualitative Health Research* 2:416-38.

Jefferson, G. 1984. "Caricature versus Detail: On Capturing the Particulars of Pronunciation in Transcripts of Conversational Data." *Tilberg Papers on Language and Literature No. 31*, University of Tilberg, Netherlands.

Kirk, J. and M. L. Miller. 1986. *Reliability and Validity in Qualitative Research*. Newbury Park, CA: Sage.

Kuzel, A. and R. Like. 1991. "Standards of Trustworthiness for Qualitative Studies in Primary Care." In *Primary Care Research: Traditional and Innovative Approaches*, edited by P. Norton. Newbury Park, CA: Sage.

Kvale, S. 1988. "The 1000-Page Question." *Phenomenology + Pedagogy* 6(2):90-106.

———. 1995. "The Social Construction of Validity." *Qualitative Inquiry* 1:19-40.

———. 1996. *InterViews: An Introduction to Qualitative Research Interviewing*. Thousand Oaks, CA, Sage.

Lapadat, J. C. and A. C. Lindsay. 1999. "Transcription in Research and Practice: From Standardization of Technique to Interpretive Positionings." *Qualitative Inquiry* 5:64-86.

LeCompte, M. D. and J. P. Goetz. 1982. "Problems of Reliability and Validity in Ethnographic Research." *Review of Educational Research* 52(1):31-60.

Lincoln, Y. S. and E. G. Guba. 1985. *Naturalistic Inquiry*. Beverly Hills, CA: Sage.

McCracken, G. 1988. *The Long Interview*. Newbury Park, CA: Sage.

Miles, M. B. and A. M. Huberman. 1984. *Qualitative Data Analysis: A Sourcebook of New Methods*. Beverly Hills, CA: Sage.

Mishler, E. G. 1991. "Representing Discourse: The Rhetoric of Transcription." *Journal of Narrative and Life History* 1:255-80.

Morgan, D. L., ed. 1993. *Successful Focus Groups: Advancing the State of the Art*. Newbury Park, CA: Sage.

Morse, J. M. 1991a. "Evaluating Qualitative Research." *Qualitative Health Research* 1:283-86.

———. 1991b. "On the Evaluation of Qualitative Proposals." *Qualitative Health Research* 1:147-51.

———. 1994. "Designing Funded Qualitative Research." Pp. 220-35 in *Handbook of Qualitative Research*, edited by N. K. Denzin and Y. S. Lincoln. Newbury Park, CA: Sage.

Oakley, A. 1981. "Interviewing Women: A Contradiction in Terms?" Pp. 30-61 in *Doing Feminist Research,* edited by H. Roberts. London: Routledge & Kegan Paul.

Patton, M. Q. 1990. *Qualitative Evaluation and Research Methods.* 2d ed. Newbury Park, CA: Sage.

Poland, B. D. 1993. "From Concept to Practice in Community Mobilization for Health: A Qualitative Evaluation of the Brantford COMMIT Intervention For Smoking Cessation." Ph.D. dissertation, McMaster University.

———. 1995. "Transcript Quality as an Aspect of Rigor in Qualitative Research." *Qualitative Inquiry* 1:290-310.

Poland, B. D., S. M. Taylor, J. Eyles, and N. F. White. 1994. "Qualitative Evaluation of the Brantford COMMIT Intervention Trial: The Smokers' Perspective." *Health and Canadian Society* 2:269-316.

Psathas, G. 1995. *Conversation Analysis: The Study of Talk-in-Interaction.* Thousand Oaks, CA: Sage.

Psathas, G. and T. Anderson. 1990. "The 'Practices' of Transcription in Conversation Analysis." *Semiotica* 78:75-99.

Richardson, L. 1993. "Poetics, Dramatics, and Transgressive Validity: The Case of the Skipped Line." *Sociological Quarterly* 34:695-710.

Sacks, H., E. A. Schegloff, and G. Jefferson. 1974. "A Simplest Systematics for the Organization of Turn-Taking in Conversation." *Language* 50:696-735.

Seale, C. 1999. *The Quality of Qualitative Research.* Thousand Oaks, CA, Sage.

Semin, G. R. and K. J. Gergen, eds. 1990. *Everyday Understanding: Social and Scientific Implications.* Newbury Park, CA: Sage.

Silverman, D. 1985. *Qualitative Methodology and Sociology.* Aldershot, England: Gower.

———. 1993. *Interpreting Qualitative Data: Methods for Analysing Talk, Text and Interaction.* London: Sage.

Strauss, A. L. 1987. *Qualitative Analysis for Social Scientists.* New York: Cambridge University Press.

Strauss, A. L. and J. Corbin. 1990. *Basics of Qualitative Research: Grounded Theory Procedures and Techniques.* Newbury Park, CA: Sage.

Taylor, S. J. and R. Bogdan. 1984. *An Introduction to Qualitative Research Methods.* 2d ed. New York: John Wiley.

Tesch, R. 1990. *Qualitative Research: Analysis Types and Software Tools.* New York: Falmer.

West, C. 1996. "Ethnography and Orthography: A Modest Proposal." *Journal of Contemporary Ethnography* 25:327-52.

West, P. 1990. "The Status and Validity of Accounts Obtained at Interview: A Contrast between Two Studies of Families with a Disabled Child." *Social Science and Medicine* 30:1229-39.

14

COMPUTER-ASSISTED ANALYSIS
OF QUALITATIVE INTERVIEW DATA

◆ **Clive F. Seale**

Social researchers have long appreciated the usefulness of computers for data analysis. Statistical software run on increasingly powerful personal computers has automated mathematical calculations on large data sets to the extent that quantitative analysis can be increasingly interactive. Analysts can run procedures and get instant feedback on the results, freeing up time for the creative interplay of ideas and research data. In the humanities, the development of software based on various elaborations of string searches for content analysis has led to new conceptions of what is possible in linguistic analysis (Miall 1990). Computer-assisted qualitative data analysis software (CAQDAS) for social research data is a more recent development that, unlike statistical or string-search software, has depended largely on the proliferation of personal computers since the early 1980s. In this chapter, I assess the contribution that CAQDAS can make to a variety of analytic approaches to interview data. As far as possible, I use examples from completed research studies to illustrate what is feasible. Additionally, I argue that CAQDAS should not be viewed in isola-

AUTHOR'S NOTE: Many people helped me with this chapter by sending published and unpublished materials for review. I am particularly grateful to Jenny Brightman, Russell Bernard, Katie Buston, James Carey, Alan Cartwright, Susanne Friese, Harshad Keval, Odd Lindberg, Kati Rantala, Anna Triandafyllidou, Birrell Walsh, and Mitchell Weiss. A special thanks to Ann Lewins and her associates, whose contribution through the University of Surrey CAQDAS Networking Project has been important both in the writing of this piece and in supporting an international community of CAQDAS users over several years.

tion; other forms of computer-assisted data analysis (including the ones mentioned above) have a great deal to offer if used in combination with CAQDAS.

Initially, I outline the history of CAQDAS in social research and summarize the key procedures enabled by this family of software. I do not attempt to provide the finer details of individual programs, as these change from one release to the next. Suffice it to say that programs vary, and if particular features are unavailable on one, they are available on another. (For those readers who wish to explore particular packages, I provide a list of some useful resources following the endnotes to this chapter.) I then consider actual usage of these features in published, and some unpublished, social research involving interview data. It will become clear that, as in statistical software, users of CAQDAS generally exploit only the basic features of packages, with advanced usage being less common. As well as demonstrating the advantages that CAQDAS offers, I discuss some of its limitations. Finally, I consider examples of more advanced usage, linking this with a discussion of changing conceptions of the links between social theory and contemporary research practice.

Computer programs are both technical tools and rhetorical devices. The rhetorical presence of CAQDAS is exploited both by software designers in their marketing and by users in their strategic presentations to grant-making bodies, readers of research reports, and the like. Many features of the software serve as symbols to address the subcultural preoccupations of different groupings within the research community. In particular, CAQDAS programs address the quantitative/qualitative divide by presenting features appealing to scientific conceptions of rigor on the one hand and promising theoretical sophistication on the other. The fact that many of these features are not much used in actual research studies should give us pause for reflection on software design as a system for symbolic representation.

◆ The Development of CAQDAS

The chief contribution of CAQDAS is automation of the retrieval of text segments (for instance, sections of an interview) that have been categorized as examples of some analytic concept. Such categorization of data is often called *coding,* although some—for example, the creators of the CAQDAS program NUD*IST—prefer the term *indexing* on the grounds that *coding* carries with it unwelcome empiricist connotations (Kelle 1997). To appreciate the difference computers make to code-and-retrieve operations, it is instructive to consider what preceded the development of CAQDAS.

As Nigel Fielding and Ray Lee (1998) point out, the coding of responses to open questions in survey data was a well-described procedure in market research for some time before methodologists dealing with unstructured qualitative data gave accounts of coding. Additionally, in the 1940s, market researchers began to explore the possibilities of coding less structured interview material. Fielding and Lee observe that the first sustained sociological discussion of coding unstructured data is found in publications associated with Howard Becker et al.'s *Boys in White* (1961). However, it is clear that basic indexing operations were used before this. For example, William Foote Whyte (1981), in his appendix to the third edition of *Street Corner Society* (first published in 1943), describes his initial difficulty in deciding whether to organize his field notes "topically, with folders for rackets, the church, the family, and so on" (p. 308), or according to the different social groups he was observing. Eventually, as the volume of material "grew beyond the point where my memory would allow me to locate any given item rapidly" (p. 308), Whyte devised what he calls "a rudimentary indexing system" (p. 308), which served both to reduce his data and to remind him what was in the folders. Other researchers have used card indexes, different colored pens, scissors and tape, and a host of other manual devices to organize masses of otherwise unwieldy materials.

Becker (1970), however, is rightly identified as expounding a more systematic approach to coding and retrieval, which coincided with his concern to address with methodological rigor the problems of inference and proof from fieldwork data. Becker wanted researchers to be able to avoid anecdotalism, identify negative instances, produce quasi-statistics, and thereby represent without analytic bias the full range of phenomena in a data set. To this end, he recommended that coding should be done inclusively, so that all instances of a relevant phenomenon would be made available for inspection and perhaps further analysis.

At around the same time, Barney Glaser and Anselm Strauss (1967) were developing their approach to grounded theorizing (see Charmaz, Chapter 15, this volume). Like Becker, they built on earlier attempts at imposing analytic rigor on qualitative data (for example, analytic induction) and on an appreciation of developments in quantitative data analysis that involved a creative interaction between theoretical ideas and data (e.g., Lazarsfeld and Rosenberg 1955). The rigor and system made available by procedures such as the constant comparison of properties and their categories to generate theory, all of which were based on a fundamental code-and-retrieve logic, had a wide appeal that continues to this day. Aside from the real analytic gains, a generation of qualitative researchers learned the strategic advantages of citing grounded theory on grant application forms. Early CAQDAS programs (such as the Ethnograph and NUD*IST) were designed in large part to relate to the analytic logic of grounded theorizing, so that the basic procedures they make available reflect this tradition in sociological ethnography.

The advantages of automated code and retrieval, compared with manual versions of the same thing, can be illustrated with an example from my own use of the Ethnograph on data derived from interviews with people recalling the last year of life of deceased relatives or friends. This was an unusually large data set for the Ethnograph— in the version I was using then, only 80 interviews could be processed at any one time (I had a total of 639), so I had to repeat many operations several times. Nevertheless, computerized retrieval saved me a lot of clerical work that would have been necessary with manual methods. Using the "filter" operation, which enables the user to select interviews according to the values of "face sheet" variables (for example, the age or gender of the interviewee), I was able to carry out selective retrievals of coded segments. Thus I compared people who had died in hospitals with people who had died in private homes, selecting the segments where interviewees described learning of the deaths. Respondents whose deceased relatives or friends had lived alone at home and had died there often described finding the person dead; in hospitals, on the other hand, people were never "found dead" in this way, as hospital personnel ensured that relatives and friends "learned" of deaths before they witnessed the bodies (Seale 1995a). In this and other publications, I was also able to present counts of the numbers of times particular respondents said particular kinds of things, regardless of where the sentiments were expressed in the interviews (e.g., Seale 1995b, 1996). I made further comparisons of groups of interviewees (for instance, reports for people who had cancer were different in various respects from reports for people who had other kinds of illnesses) and identified negative instances, where particular examples ran counter to the majority picture. In this respect, the software's requirement that I code systematically and the tireless capacity of the computer to confront the analyst with all coded instances enforced a rigor that might otherwise have been daunting to achieve.

Aside from improving on manual methods, the basic procedures made feasible by the Ethnograph also demonstrate the advantages of dedicated CAQDAS programs compared with other software, such as databases and word processors. Anna Triandafyllidou (1999; Triandafyllidou and Fotiou 1998) has used FoxPro 2.0, a database management system, for the analysis of interviews and press reports on the topic of immigration policy. To include original text in the retrievals, however, Triandafyllidou had to type these into the database, because other links between the database and the raw transcripts were not feasible. Retrievals were therefore largely confined to the number of times a phenomenon occurred, with the user then having to locate relevant examples manually. Significantly, Triandafyllidou's research reports are thin on illustrative quotations, although theoretically the analysis is sophisticated. The macros in word processors can also be adapted to "spike" text segments that contain code words and store these in separate files (Bernard and Ryan 1998), but for researchers to undertake such do-it-yourself computer programming to mimic the most basic (code-and-retrieve) feature of a dedicated CAQDAS program seems unnecessarily time-consuming.

Beyond coding for retrieval, CAQDAS programs are capable of performing a variety of more advanced procedures; I will list these briefly here and, for the most part, illustrate them in use later in this chapter. Data entry varies from the restrictive to the inclusive. A restrictive program allows for text files only, shaped in a particular way and subject to a line limit, with additional restrictions as to the number of data files processed. An inclusive program allows users to import text files in any format (for example, downloaded from the Internet, with graphics and colors in place) as well as to attach, code, and search audio, video, and scanned images. Inclusivity also allows for the coding of "off-line" documents (such as handwritten notes stored in a filing cabinet but not scanned into a computer file) so that the phenomena occurring in these are reported in search operations. For specialist transcription, it is helpful if transcripts can be linked to audio files, so that the user can play these back while reading the transcripts; it is also helpful if the program allows the user to designate special characters and sections of transcript separately from the rest (so that they are not reported in string searches, for example). Brian Torode (1998) notes that his use of Code-A-Text for conversation analysis was greatly facilitated by such features. A program's ability to recognize special characters is also helpful if the researcher is working with a non-Western alphabet.[1] Allowing the user to edit original text without disturbing attached codes is also a feature of some more recent CAQDAS programs. Most programs allow users to attach analytic memos, in which they may explore emerging ideas, or definitions of code words.

I have noted above CAQDAS programs' capacity to search for segments according to "filter" variables, as demonstrated in the example from my own research; this is a basic feature of a code-and-retrieve program. Beyond this, programs can feature a variety of Boolean search combinations. For example, I might have asked the Ethnograph to show me segments in which respondents discussed the quality of health care and the topic of pain so that I could investigate the adequacy of care for this problem. This would have involved a simple overlap between two codes. Other kinds of Boolean searches involve manipulation of "and," "or," and "not in" commands to specify the conditions under which segments should be retrieved. Alternatively, users can specify proximity searches—that is, searches for differently coded segments that occur within specified distances of each other. Such searches can help an analyst to test hypotheses; for example, a researcher may ask whether event A always precedes event B, or whether this sequence occurs only under certain conditions of C.

The results of searches can be displayed as segments of original data, and some programs allow for both expanded and restricted views of these. At times, the researcher may need to see the text that occurs on either side of a coded segment, in order to see its context (an expanded view). Statistical output is another way to view the results of searches, and the ability to create data matrices amenable to statistical analysis by other software is now a common feature of CAQDAS programs. For example, such a feature would have allowed me to compare the number of statements made by men and women indicating satisfaction or dissatisfaction with the quality of care for various symptoms. Alternatively, I might have searched for word strings and compared the incidence of adjectives to describe, say, the experience of pain between different groups of interviewees.

The analytic operations developed in the humanities computing tradition for linguistic analysis are increasingly supported by CAQDAS programs for social research data. The capacity to do automatic searches for strings of letters (and therefore words) is fundamental to these operations. Some CAQDAS program developers remain suspicious of such "autocoding," as it raises the specter of automatic thinking. The Ethnograph, for example, stops at each "hit" of a string and requires the user to indicate whether a code should be applied in each case. This means that "I had a pain here" can be coded differently from "the doctor was a pain in the ass." Other developers feel that this approach is unnecessarily restrictive. NUD*IST, for example, will index every segment containing the word *pain* and retrieve these for inspection in one sweep; winMAX generates "key word in context" (KWIC) lists from such searches; and Code-A-Text allows for user-defined dictionaries, so that the user can identify counts of the percentages of words in each segment that belong to specific word groups. Other features of string searches that are useful include the use of "wild-card" letters (so that "coug*" returns "cough," "coughing," "coughed," and so on) and pattern searching, whereby a particular pattern of characters is identified

(for example, all words ending with "ing" and no more than 10 characters long). These latter features, however, are more likely to be found in specialist software for linguistic content analysis, such as concordance programs, which are relatively underused in qualitative social research, in spite of a "turn to language" in the contemporary social theories that increasingly influence social researchers.

A further advanced feature of some CAQDAS programs is the capacity to draw conceptual maps that assist the development of theoretical models. Concepts can be linked with various kinds of connecting lines to indicate different kinds of relationships (for example, A causes B, A is a strategy for doing B, A loves B). Freestanding graphical modelers exist, but some CAQDAS programs (e.g., ATLAS.ti, NVivo) incorporate this feature, with the added advantage that elements of the model are linked to data files. Researchers can also use graphical modeling to represent and compare the "cognitive maps" of individual interviewees, and some specialist software exists for this purpose.

◆ CAQDAS in Use

For this section, I draw on a collection of studies that have used CAQDAS on interview data. I generated the list of studies by visiting the Web sites of CAQDAS developers, by conducting on-line searches of bibliographic databases in which CAQDAS programs are mentioned as well as a fairly random perusal of journals reporting social research, and by making announcements that I was searching for such material in e-mail discussion groups. Fielding and Lee (1998) report the first study of the CAQDAS-using community, based on focus groups involving researchers. I felt that the next step would be to analyze (mostly) published studies reporting on interview data and using CAQDAS, to see the extent to which CAQDAS has influenced analytic style as well as to assess whether the features made available by the software are used in practice.

Fielding and Lee (1995) conducted an analysis of the Ethnograph network licenses and found that the largest group of users was in educational research, followed by nursing research, sociology, anthropology, other health disciplines, and psychology. Additionally, in their 1998 study of users in the United Kingdom, Fielding and Lee found that data derived from interviews were the most common form of data on which CAQDAS was used. The use of CAQDAS to analyze purely observational or documentary data was rare; such data sources were more often used in combination with interviews. Fielding and Lee also found little use being made of the more advanced features of CAQDAS described in the preceding section. In particular, any "theory building" occurred "off-line," if at all. I had no trouble finding articles involving qualitative interviews done by educational and nursing researchers that involved basic code-and-retrieve procedures. In what follows, I first discuss the enhanced rigor that CAQDAS can help deliver and then give an account of typical code-and-retrieve usage before going on to less common studies.

ANALYTIC RIGOR

One of the major potential advantages of CAQDAS is that the approach encourages (but does not enforce) rigor. As an early enthusiast, Michael Agar (1983) exemplifies this in his report of interviews with drug users. Exploring the opinions his respondents expressed about other people in their lives, he compared an earlier "intuitive," or manual, analysis with an approach supported by CAQDAS. The computer search confronted him with more negative instances than he had uncovered in his manual analysis, because "the computer coding forced a more careful reading and recall of the interview, though perhaps

I would have picked up the additional material with another direct reading of the transcript" (p. 23). He concludes that CAQDAS "doesn't get tired and miss sections of data" (p. 26). Agar also mentions that CAQDAS displays data in a publicly falsifiable way, a theme taken up by Fielding and Lee (1998), who argue that by forcing researchers to become explicit about the underlying operations of data analysis, CAQDAS creates an auditable trail that ought to enhance the credibility of findings.

Reports of interrater reliability exercises supported by CAQDAS serve to emphasize the contribution it can make to rigor and public accountability (Carey, Morgan, and Oxtoby 1996; Northey 1997). Significantly, however, William Northey (1997) takes a step back from a traditional conception of such reliability exercises by abstaining from the view that disagreements between coders should always be reconciled. Instead, using examples generated from interviews with family members about their conflicts, he recommends that researchers use NUD*IST simply to display instances of segments included under a code, so that auditors or readers have a chance to see the kinds of instances that contribute to a category. He thus performs the familiar balancing act of retaining constructivist credentials while addressing scientific concerns, precisely the discursive terrain that CAQDAS programs as a whole must negotiate.

Agar (1983) mentions colleagues who made disparaging references to the "science points" he was earning by using a computer for qualitative analysis. More serious extensions of this sentiment are expressed in the generalized fear that the search for CAQDAS-inspired rigor might impose a rigid, quasi-positivist analytic style (Hesse-Biber 1995; Buston 1997). In part, these fears reflect the traditional paranoia of qualitative researchers that quantification will take over, fueled by the capacity of CAQDAS to generate counts of code words. Some CAQDAS studies are indeed little more than extensions of quantitative work, and certain kinds of CAQDAS may build in such assumptions. For example, the U.S. Centers for Disease Control developed CDC EZ-Text for use in analyzing responses to open questions in structured interviewing studies. The program depends on all respondents' having been asked the same questions, and users must record missing data if this has not been done (Carey et al. 1998).

At the opposite extreme, however, some studies using CAQDAS programs seem to show no sign of any influence toward systematic analysis. Examples include Sue Middleton's (1996) report on interviews with teachers in New Zealand and Blake Poland's (1995) account of the experience of restrictions on smoking in Canadian public places. Both of these studies used NUD*IST, according to information gleaned from the developer's Web site, yet they share a common characteristic, hard to convey without presenting the full report, of impressionistic and anecdotal reporting of data. Both Middleton and Poland focus on presenting general arguments or surveys of their topics—in Middleton's case a historical account of discipline in schools, and in Poland's an account of the growth and scope of antismoking policy. Both authors drop extracts from interviews into their text where the interviewees' personal experiences appear to support the authors' general narratives. Neither reports any coding, searching, or accounting for negative instances. It is, in theory, possible that these authors' general narratives are the products of more rigorous analytic procedures supported by CAQDAS and then hidden from view. Alternatively, these examples suggest that although CAQDAS can enhance analytic rigor, this is not an inevitability.

CODE-AND-RETRIEVE STUDIES

More commonly, however, researchers who have used CAQDAS report unstructured or loosely structured qualitative interviewing with coding and retrieval of coded segments that vary in complexity. Retrieval, for example, can be based on a simple search of all instances of a code in a data set or can involve filtering and other operations. Coding varies from somewhat descriptive, "in vivo" concepts that rely on the categories that interviewees themselves appear to be using to codes derived from theoretical literature, codes based on prior hypotheses, and codes created with the help of some form of abductive reasoning that approximates grounded theorizing.[2] Some researchers exploit CAQDAS autocoding features; others do not. There is nothing in the design of CAQDAS programs that enforces in vivo coding, but in practice it is quite common because it is an obvious thing for a researcher to do when working from a commonsense conception of research practice.

A good example of in vivo coding is found in research conducted by Jillian MacGuire and Deborah Botting (1990), who interviewed 17 nurses about the introduction of a new way of organizing work in a hospital setting. The researchers' analysis, using the Ethnograph, focused on the impact of the change on nurses' knowledge of patients, on communication among staff, and on staff members' relationships with patients and relatives. MacGuire and Botting developed 58 codes to summarize the data. For example, they subcoded segments marked as being about "communication" according to five categories of persons with whom nurses said they communicated. They could then retrieve segments about communication with relatives separately from segments about communication with patients or other staff and summarize the main points made.

Katie Buston's (1997) use of NUD*IST in her interview study with 112 young people experiencing chronic illness represents a step up from this. The abductive nature of Buston's coding is clear in that she drew on concepts such as "loss of self" and "stigma" from the sociological literature and "denial" from psychiatric ideas, as well as such in vivo concepts as "money worries" and "thoughts about the future." Additionally, Buston reports the use of face sheet variables as filters; she compared people with different kinds of health problem, people of different genders, people in different age groups, and people with different scores on a standardized psychiatric measure. She found autocoding to be helpful for dealing with a common problem of emergent coding schemes: After 15 interviews had been coded, it became clear that many of the young people with asthma were concerned about a shortage of affordable nebulizers. A string search for "nebulizer" identified instances where this was discussed in the already-coded interviews, so that Buston could inspect and code these accordingly without having to read the entire transcript again.

Buston's study shows that as we move up in levels of sophistication in code-and-retrieve studies, CAQDAS use increasingly involves creative and flexible adaptation of software features. Lyn Richards (1995), reporting on interviews with women experiencing menopause, describes the insertion of code words at the data entry stage and how she used the automatic string-search feature of NUD*IST to find and index these at a later stage. Maree Johnson and her colleagues (1999), in a study of bilingual staff in health care settings, categorized interviewees according to their degree of fluency in their second language and the extent to which their jobs involved complex communication across languages. These became filter variables in later searches the researchers conducted using NUD*IST; this allowed them to examine how combinations of these qualities resulted in different kinds of experiences for the staff involved. Sharon Hoerr, David Kallen, and Marcia Kwantes (1995) clearly wanted to go beyond the limitations of their software (the Ethnograph) in comparing counts of particular words used by interviewees to describe obese friends and strangers. Although they could feasibly have used the Ethnograph, Hoerr and her

colleagues probably conducted such an analysis manually, as this program is limited in its string-searching capacities, although not in the filter operations that Hoerr et al. exploited at other stages of their analysis.

PATTERN ANALYSIS OR GROUNDED THEORIZING?

It is common for researchers doing this kind of work to claim that they are using grounded theory. Fielding and Lee (1998) report that in a bibliographic search, 31 percent of 163 articles cited John Seidel, the author of the Ethnograph, and also contained references to the writings of Glaser and Strauss (1967) on grounded theory methodology. The claim to having done grounded theory, however, is less than convincing in some cases, and clearly a rhetorical purpose is served by such announcements. It is helpful to distinguish between what might be termed the "pattern analysis" (L. Richards, personal communication) of studies like the code-and-retrieve ones described above and studies that really seem to have used the operations described in grounded theory methodology.[3]

Patricia Sharpe and Jane Mezoff (1995) present the results of an interview study in which Ethnograph was used; participants were 20 older women who were interviewed regarding their beliefs about diet and health. Sharpe and Mezoff claim that their "data coding and analysis were based on the constant comparison method" (p. 9) and discuss the generation of "higher order categories based on properties and dimensions the concepts share; and delineating relationships or themes among the categories" (p. 9). They also describe "a movement between inductive and deductive thinking" (p. 9) and cite Anselm Strauss and Juliet Corbin (1990). Their results, however, suggest a far less complex procedure, being a straightforward listing, with illustrative examples, of the main beliefs that were presented by interviewees. We learn, for example, that many of the women believed that eating fruits and vegetables and avoiding alcohol and sweets is a good way to stay healthy. Many of the women liked to cook and bake for their families and took pride in the compliments they received for this. Some of the diabetic women, however, had some ideas that were not in line with current dietary recommendations for this condition. It is hard to see how this worthy but descriptive pattern analysis required the conceptual operations of grounded theorizing.

John Lange and Sue Burroughs-Lange (1994), on the other hand, are more convincing in their claims to have used grounded theory. Their study involved the use of NUD*IST to analyze interviews with 12 teachers about how they gained their professional knowledge. Like Sharpe and Mezoff, Lange and Burroughs-Lange describe the use of constant comparison and refer to Strauss and Corbin (1990), specifically referring to "our grounded theory." NUD*IST "ensured that the mechanics of the field research did not draw attention away from the analytic process" (p. 620) and that it "greatly enhances the generating and testing of theorizing possibilities" (p. 621). Their analysis led them to a "transformational model of continuous professional learning" (p. 621) in which teachers moved from an initial state of professional certainty to one of "feeling comfortable" (p. 621). Realizing this transformation involved an initial perception of professional challenges triggered by a variety of encounters. Gradually gaining an understanding of the nature of these challenges, the teachers then drew on a variety of sources (their own experience, elements in the school context, or national educational initiatives) to meet these challenges and to develop strategies for resolving uncertainty and for moving on professionally. Lange and Burroughs-Lange lay out this simple sequential model of challenges, encounters, understanding, sources, resolutions, and professional growth as a series of concepts, each of which summarizes a number of subconcepts. They illustrate these with examples that demonstrate the plausibility of links they make between categories and properties in the model, so that their claim to have created a grounded theory appears fully justified.

The dividing line between computer-assisted grounded theorizing and pattern analysis is sometimes not easy to draw—I have chosen the examples above to make the distinction easy to perceive. The fuzziness of this boundary appears to encourage some authors to exploit the rhetorical advantages inherent in making grounded theory announcements, which are apparently all the more plausible if a "theory-building" CAQDAS program is also seen to be involved.

CONCEPTUAL MAPPING

It is difficult to find studies that show clear uses made of conceptual mapping software, a feature promoted by developers who wish to stress the theory-building aspects of their products. Lange and Burroughs-Lange (1994), Johnson et al. (1999), and Linda Kittell, Phyllis Mansfield, and Ann Voda (1998) present graphical models of the concepts emerging from their research, but it is clear that these were created on paper rather than with the use of mapping software. Kittell et al., for example, present a flowchart to summarize typical career patterns of the responses to menopausal change evident in their interviews with women. This is a device commonly used to summarize qualitative data (e.g., see Taraborrelli 1993; Seale 1998), and a computer is not needed to make such a drawing. Inclusion of this feature in CAQDAS programs clearly serves the rhetorical purposes of software developers.

In fact, I was able to collect only one example of the use of this feature: Susanne Friese's (1999) account of her interviews with shoppers exhibiting different degrees of addiction to compulsive buying. Using ATLAS.ti, Friese interviewed 55 shoppers about their behavior and analyzed the data so as to exploit a variety of CAQDAS features. She made links with quantitative measures and based filtering operations on scores on these variables. Counts of coded segments appear frequently in Friese's text, as well as numerous verbatim extracts to illustrate these. Figure 14.1 reproduces Friese's ATLAS-generated conceptual map summarizing the links made by addicted buyers that they perceived led to, or were associated with, episodes of impulse buying. Because Friese displays similar maps for less addicted buyers, the reader is presented with a quick comparative summary of how these people experienced and explained their behavior. The result of Friese's use of these CAQDAS-inspired analytic devices is a striking and evocative report.

REASONING WITH NUMBERS

Quantitative and qualitative data can be combined in a variety of ways (see Seale 1999:chaps. 8-9). This is increasingly done in research projects, because most practicing social researchers recognize the relative autonomy of their craft from the absolutist epistemological and theoretical debates that once appeared to divide them. CAQDAS programs generally provide support for quantification, and this has been used in interview studies in a variety of ways.

At the most straightforward level, CAQDAS can be useful in providing counts of events, whether these are code words attached to data files or words embedded in text data. The problem of anecdotalism, whereby analysts select illustrative examples that support a general point without saying how common equivalent examples are or mentioning any systematic skews in their distribution, can thereby be addressed. My own studies have exploited this element of CAQDAS, as shown in the following two extracts:

It was very common for the people living on their own to be described either as not seeking help for problems that they had (65 instances covering 48 people), or refusing help when offered (144 instances in 83 people). Accounts of this often stressed that this reflected on the character of the person involved, although other associations were also made. In particular, 33 speakers gave 44 instances where they stressed the independence this indicated: "(She) never really talked about her problems, was very independent. . . "; "(She) was just one of those independent people who would struggle on. She wouldn't ask on her own"; "She used to shout at me because I was doing things for her. She didn't like to be helped. She was very independent." Being "self sufficient," "would not be beaten," and being said to "hate to give in" were associated with resisting help. (Seale 1996:84)

More commonly, however, the event of telling [a diagnosis of terminal illness] was described in a positive light. A content analysis of adjectives and adverbs used in these descriptions shows how speakers used them to reflect on the character of the teller: nice, nicely or very nice (12 instances), kind or kindly (12), good, really, very or ever so good (8), sympathetic (6), understanding (5), compassionate (2), great (2), wonderful (2), caring or very caring (2) and well (2). There was one instance each for the following: friendly, tactful, professionally, concerned, marvellous, willing, excellent, lovely, forthcoming, gently, helpful and considerate. A typical comment was made by the wife of a man who had died of cancer:

They were very *kind*, they couldn't have done more. They made me a cup of tea and a young ladydoctor —she was *lovely*—she stayed with me a while and told me . . . they

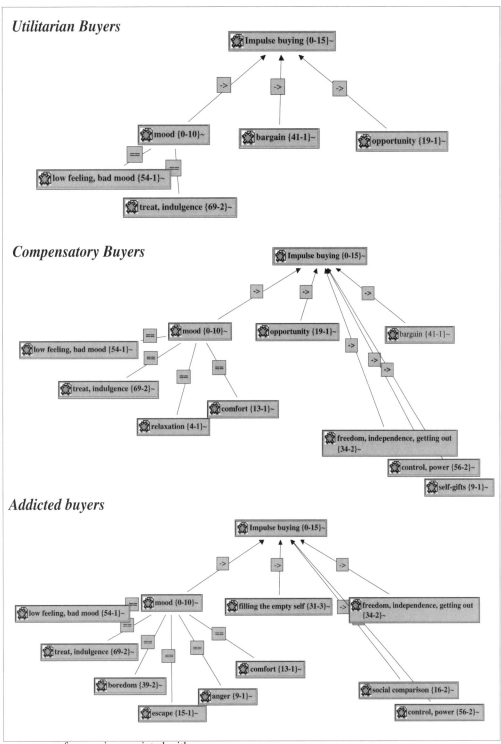

-> reason for; == is associated with

Figure 14.1. Reasons for Impulse Buying

SOURCE: Friese (1999).

couldn't do anything. I knew that really and I didn't blame them. (Seale 1995b:603)

The first of these relies on a count of code words, the second on a count of words generated by a string search of selected segments that shared a common code. In both cases the counts are designed to generate greater credibility, as readers would otherwise have to trust the author to have selected adjectives that were illustrative or common.

A step further toward quantitative methodology is represented by studies involving the use of measurement devices. For example, a sample survey might include qualitative data, derived either from unstructured interview data or from responses to open questions in structured survey instruments. R. Raguram et al. (1996) present a study of this sort, in which Textbase Alpha was used to analyze interviews with psychiatric patients in South India. Standardized quantitative measures showed that patients reporting depressive symptoms (for example, sadness, anxiety, fear) scored higher on a measure of stigma than did patients reporting somatoform symptoms (for example, limb and joint pain, headache). Qualitative analysis showed why and helped demonstrate the human impacts of the things that were being measured. Thus a patient who said, "I feel lonely . . . sad . . . like crying most of the time," also said, "I don't want anybody to know about my problem. I think others may say bad things about our family as a whole because of me. It would also affect my marriage." A patient who said, "If I walk I get pain in the back or thigh. I have pain all over," also said, "My friends know my problems. My in-laws, daughters all know about my aches and pains. The family understands my suffering" (p. 1047). The researchers, supported by systematic coding and retrieval, could generate lists of similar statements, filtered according to scores on the quantitative measures.

Causal reasoning in qualitative work is anathema to some, but others are less wary of it, and some specialist CAQDAS programs have been developed for this purpose. Conventional causal analysis through automated hypothesis testing is supported by HyperRESEARCH, which requires "factual" coding rather than "heuristic" indexing. For example, a heuristic coder might mark a text passage as being about the topic of religion; a "factual" coder might record whether or not the respondent indicates he or she believes in a god. Sharlene Hesse-Biber and Paul Dupuis (1995) give an example of hypothesis testing from a study of the causes of anorexia, testing the proposition that weight loss relates to certain antecedent conditions. A logical relationship between factual coding categories was written along the following lines: "*If* mother was critical of daughter's body image *and* mother-daughter relationship was strained *and* daughter experiences weight loss, *then* count as an example of mother's negative influence on daughter's self-image." Once particular interviews were identified as containing the codes involved, the researchers could retrieve the text for further examination in order to see whether support for this causal interpretation could be justified for each case.

"Qualitative comparison analysis" (Ragin 1987, 1995) is a method for causal reasoning that involves Boolean algebra. The relevant calculations are assisted by two CAQDAS programs: QCA and AQUAD. A detailed specification of this method is inappropriate here (for simplified explanations, see Seale 1999:chap. 9; Becker 1998:chap. 5); suffice it to say that from case study material the minimum conditions necessary to produce an outcome are specified through the analysis of "truth tables" that record the presence or absence of candidate causal factors. Thomas Schweizer (1991, 1996) used this in his secondary analysis of data from a Chinese village to establish what caused certain individuals to prosper and others to suffer during the momentous political and social changes that occurred in China between 1950 and 1980. Kati Rantala (1998) used QCA in an interview study of 14 teenagers attending art classes in Finland to establish a typology of their motivations for this activity.

Clearly, CAQDAS presents researchers with the possibility of incorporating numbers and statistical reasoning of various sorts. As in the examples discussed in the earlier section on rigor, it is clear that CAQDAS does not compel researchers to do this kind of work. But the encouragement to code systematically, as well as the capacity to search automatically for strings, places researchers in a position where quantification of qualitative events is made easy.

TURNING TO LANGUAGE

A variety of analytic approaches to research data driven by developments in social theory have emerged in recent years. Initially represented by conversation analysis and membership categorization work derived from the ethnomethodological tradition (for a review, see Silverman 1993; see also Baker, Chapter 19, this volume), more recently these have come to include several varieties of discourse analysis (Potter and Wetherell 1987; see also Schaeffer and Maynard, Chapter 11, this volume) and narrative analysis (Riessman 1993; see also Riessman, Chapter 16, this volume). These share an interest in the investigation of the effects of language, occurring either in talk or written texts, these commonly being either recordings or transcripts of interview material. CAQDAS remains relatively underused for these analytic purposes, so it is appropriate that I approach the topic of possible future developments by reviewing the possible role CAQDAS can play in this kind of work.

In one sense, of course, an interest in computerized analysis of language predates the development of CAQDAS programs for social research data. Linguists and litera-

ture specialists have long used computers to generate concordances and other string-search software to analyze literary style or language-in-use through quantitative content analysis. As noted earlier, some CAQDAS programs have features enabling elements of this approach. It is my belief that the intelligent use of CAQDAS could, in the future, assist in merging these linguistic analytic strategies with sociological concerns.

H. Russell Bernard and Gery Ryan (1998) express a similar conception in their useful review of approaches to text analysis. For them, the link is made in part through cognitive anthropology, which, among other things, has involved linguistic analysis in order to generate cognitive maps shared by people in a culture (see, e.g., Agar 1979, 1980). They report that this can involve the construction of what one author has called "personal semantic networks" (Strauss 1992), mapping the ideas that, say, interviewees express. Steve Cropper, Colin Eden, and Fran Ackermann (1990) describe software designed to assist the cognitive mapping of interview accounts; they use this technique in management consultancy exercises, citing personal construct theory as an antecedent. The software enables users to compare and combine the different maps generated in individual interviews, so that they can observe changes over time in a single person or group of people or make comparisons between people. Kathleen Carley and Michael Palmquist (1992), using STARTUP and CodeMap software, show how this can be applied in educational research, demonstrating how students' ideas (expressed in before-after interviews) about how they approach writing tasks change as a result of a course of instruction. The software is at one level a more elaborate version of the graphical mapping add-ons to conventional CAQDAS programs described earlier, but rather than being an end stage of analysis, it is used to generate more complex and revealing reports.

For Bernard and Ryan (1998), "schema analysis" represents a productive merging of the linguistic and sociological traditions. They illustrate this with anthropological studies of storytelling in Indian and Inuit cultures, but they could equally well have applied it to contemporary research interviews. Benjamin Colby (1966; Colby, Kennedy, and Milanesi 1991), for example, has developed a computer program (called SAGE) to analyze both the overall structural features and the linguistic content of stories. Initially, in work derived from interviews, he compared the words used by Zuni informants (a crop-growing group) with those used by Navajo (a sheepherding group). Crop growers are concerned with weather conditions above all; sheepherders are concerned with finding good grazing land and protection from stormy weather. Words concerning different forms of moisture (snow, rain, clouds) were accordingly found more often in Zuni stories than in Navajo stories, where storms, wind, and cold featured more frequently. Because traveling was more a feature of Navajo lifestyle, in Navajo stories home was depicted as a place of rest after a journey, and arrival home was often the end of the story; for Zuni, home was where things happened and events there occurred at the start of stories. Colby then became interested in identifying common structures in folktales and in using a computer to analyze the linguistic content of particular points in tales in order to reveal underlying cultural themes. In this respect his work develops that of Vladimir Propp (1968) on the structures of Russian folktales and of Catherine Riessman (1993) on the narrative structures of interview material.

Discussions of the uses of string searches appear from time to time in the CAQDAS literature. For example, Karl Moore, Robert Burbach, and Roger Heeler (1995), in a market research context, describe the use of CATPAC for the automated analysis of the language of interviews. They analyze answers to a question about breakdowns in contemporary family life, revealing systematic differences between respondents who blamed "internal" factors (divorce, money problems, and so on) and those who blamed "external" factors (the government, economy, crime).

The numerous messages posted by participants in e-mail discussion groups that support users of such CAQDAS programs provide more varied insights into the uses of string searching for linguistically oriented analysis. A recent exchange, involving John Seidel (the maker of the Ethnograph) and Lyn Richards (one of the developers of NUD*IST) focused on the merits and demerits of what the discussants called "autocoding." The use of this term to describe string searching is revealing, and predictably discussion focused initially on fears that this equated to automated thinking. Reference was made to the "shotgun correlations" that one sometimes sees in quantitative work, where a researcher generates a massive bivariate correlation matrix and selects the significant combinations on which to build an argument. The dangers of this were rapidly illustrated by subsequent discussants:

> [I attended] a seminar recently where . . . they counted the occurrences of key words in presidential addresses from the American Sociological Association and from the American Political Science Association. . . . They found that political scientists talk about politics and sociologists talk about society. Mmm. Then there was a set of words that both used. I wanted an analysis of the meanings, the use of argument, the structure of reasoning . . . but no, this was all too complex, let's just count the words! (Ezzard, personal communication 1999)

But this was then followed by users reporting instances of the usefulness of automated string searching. One user (Walsh) sensed that "opening doors" was an important metaphor for one interviewee in a study, and so used a string search to bring up rapidly all segments of her talk that contained this string, discarding false "hits." Another user (Downing) was interested in the way in which informants discussed "responsibility," as she was interested in how interviewees defined themselves as acting responsibly in the face of genetic risk, and so ran "check searches" on this word, its derivations, and related terms. Alan Cartwright, the developer of Code-A-Text, observed that a word concordance, if done at the outset of data analysis, could be useful in identifying themes that might not occur to the analyst by identifying key words, or those that were used very frequently. Walsh added that with string searches, one could find things where one least expected them, and this could have a suddenly great significance, like the Roman coins that someone once found in India.

Michael Fisher then reminded the discussants of his published example of the usefulness of string searches, in which he describes searching for word strings associated with "discipline" and "children" in a corpus of interviews in order to identify text segments in which parents discussed this aspect of their approach to child rearing (Fisher 1997). This is rather similar to the study reported by Anni George and Surinder Jaswal (1993), who describe how they searched for words associated with "honor" and "shame" in interviews with women in Bombay talking about their personal lives. Because these concepts rarely co-occurred in a text segment (unlike children and discipline), the researchers became aware of an important difference between public reputation and private morality. Fisher (1997) refers to this kind of analysis as "aerial reconnaissance" of data: It is useful for identifying broad patterns that deserve further detailed investigation "on the ground" but that might not be seen if the aerial view were not first taken.

The discussion ended with contributions pointing to the advantages offered to ana-

lysts of social research data of the more sophisticated aspects of the linguistic analysis tradition. Walsh described the need for semantic proximity software that could generate and sort a list of words in a document that are close in meaning to a chosen word. Peladeau announced that a beta version of WordStat that he was developing would do this, drawing on an electronically stored thesaurus. Klein referred to (unnamed) software that could detect negation automatically (thus distinguishing between "I like tea" and "I don't like tea"). For some, such contributions may once again raise the specter of automated thinking taking over analysis. A standard response to this kind of fear is that the technical tools of CAQDAS can take over only if the analyst allows them to do so.

HYPERTEXT

On a related issue, a development in CAQDAS that is explicitly derived from the preoccupations of contemporary social theory with linguistic representation is the exploitation of hypertext links. Although this builds on Ian Dey's (1993) earlier work, it is largely promoted by Paul Atkinson and his colleagues (Weaver and Atkinson 1995; Coffey, Holbrook, and Atkinson 1996), who draw on a poststructuralist critique of modes of representation in ethnographic writing (see, e.g., Atkinson 1990). This development addresses the complaint of some users of code-and-retrieve packages (e.g., Armstrong 1995; Sprokkereef et al. 1995) that these fragment data, encouraging the analyst to look across interviews rather than retain the whole context. Miriam Catterall and Pauline Maclaren (1997) develop this argument to say that coding and retrieval of segments out of their original context "freezes" the analysis of focus group data, making the analyst blind to the fact that participants often change their views during the course of a discussion—this change being the point of interest for many who run such groups.

Atkinson and his colleagues construct their work as a response to these concerns while drawing on a fashionable deconstruction of the conventional relationship between author and audience. Hypertext links allow the "analyst" of data, or the "reader" of an electronic report, to click on a highlighted word or icon and go instantly to some link that has been previously made. Thus a click on a code word might lead to an associated segment of text or to a picture or sound file illustrating the concept. This feature will be familiar to users of the Internet. It avoids decontextualization because the link does not retrieve a segment, but shows it in its original location, surrounded, for example, by the rest of the interview in which the segment of speech occurs. Additionally, the analyst can attach explanations, interpretations, and memos to particular links. Amanda Coffey and Paul Atkinson (1996) argue that, as an example, "we might also attach additional details, such as career details of particular respondents, their family trees, or details about their domestic lives" (p. 183). The reader is then able to explore original data in as much depth as he or she desires, and is thereby free of the need to attend to an overarching and exclusive presentation by a single author.

Although this is an interesting development in a new mode of presentation, it seems unlikely that readers will wish to do away with all modes of traditional representation in favor of such a deconstructable authorial presence. Many readers look to researchers for authoritative and concise statements delivered from a position of defensible expertise, based on a rigorous methodological approach that does not involve sharing methodological anxieties with the reader or pass over to them the hard work of drawing general conclusions about a disparate mass of loosely structured material.

◆ Conclusion

Many of the features of CAQDAS programs can be understood as rhetorical devices designed to appeal to both social scientists and social theorists. The more advanced features often seem to serve as symbols, helping software developers gain a foothold in the various cultures of qualitative work rather than being widely used in analysis. In this respect, however, CAQDAS is no different from other kinds of computer software. Like the word processor I am using to produce this text, CAQDAS programs have a basic core of frequently used procedures alongside a large variety of more advanced and more rarely used features. These core features—code-and-retrieve capabilities, automated string-search capabilities, and so on—have proven helpful to many qualitative researchers who have made the move to computer-assisted analysis.

Daniel Dohan and Martin Sanchez-Jankowski (1998) take the view that no single "killer app" has yet emerged from the CAQDAS scene. They define this as "a computer application that makes use of the computer irresistibly compelling by doing tasks unmanageable without computer assistance, in the fashion that spreadsheet programs *Visicalc* and *Lotus 1-2-3* motivated United States businesses to place personal computers on employees' desks" (p. 492). In part, they argue, this is due to the variety of conceptions of qualitative work that exist; those interested in exploring the "crisis of representation" brought about by postmodern critiques (Lincoln and Denzin 1994) pursue analytic directions that are rather different from those pursued by social researchers working in more pragmatic or scientifically oriented settings. Spreadsheets can solve common bureaucratic and organizational problems, but the problems faced by social researchers (such as issues of validity and reliability) cannot be resolved by computer programs because there are differing underlying conceptions about their nature and importance, as reflected in creative epistemological and political debates that characterize the research scene (Seale 1999). Social research can be conceived as a craft skill that draws on underlying philosophical and theoretical debates, using a variety of tools and procedures to explore particular research problems. CAQDAS is clearly something that can assist the craft of social research, as I hope has been demonstrated in this review, but it is unlikely and indeed undesirable that any single "killer app" should substitute for creative thinking about data analysis.

■ Notes

1. Developments in voice-recognition software seem set to transform the time-consuming business of interview transcription over the next few years. It is unlikely that CAQDAS programs will ever be able to transcribe automatically direct from tape, but transcribers who listen to tapes and speak the words into computers will work faster than typists once word recognition improves to an acceptable level.

2. I assume that it is by now a fairly well accepted point that pure induction cannot be plausibly proposed as a basis for grounded theory.

3. These involve theoretical sampling; constant comparison of categories and their properties, and how these interact; and open, axial, and selective coding (Glaser and Strauss 1967; Strauss and Corbin 1990).

■ Useful Web Resources

Details of how to join user discussion groups are available at the sites listed below. Demonstration versions of the packages can be downloaded from these sites or the links they provide. Scolari distributes CAQDAS programs in the United Kingdom.

ATLAS.ti: The Knowledge Workbench
(for ATLAS.ti):
   http://www.atlasti.de
CAQDAS Networking Project,
Surrey University:
   http://www.soc.surrey.ac.uk/caqdas
QSR International (for NUD*IST/NVivo):
   http://www.qsr.com.au
Qualis Research Associates
(for The Ethnograph):
   http://www.qualisresearch.com
Scolari: Sage Publications Software
(for CAQDAS programs):
   http://www.scolari.co.uk

■ References

Agar, M. 1979. "Themes Revisited: Some Problems in Cognitive Anthropology." *Discourse Processes* 2:11-31.
———. 1980. "Getting Better Quality Stuff: Methodological Competition in an Interdisciplinary Niche." *Urban Life* 9:34-50.
———. 1983. "Microcomputers as Field Tools." *Computers in the Humanities* 17:19-26.
Armstrong, D. 1995. "Finding a 'Role' for the ETHNOGRAPH in the Analysis of Qualitative Data." Pp. 63-80 in *Studies in Qualitative Methodology*, Vol. 5, *Computing and Qualitative Research*, edited by R. G. Burgess. Greenwich, CT: JAI.
Atkinson, P. A. 1990. *The Ethnographic Imagination: Textual Constructions of Reality*. London: Routledge.
Becker, H. S. 1970. "Problems of Inference and Proof in Participant Observation." Pp. 25-38 in H. S. Becker, *Sociological Work: Method and Substance*. Chicago: Aldine.

———. 1998. *Tricks of the Trade: How to Think about Your Research While You're Doing It.* Chicago: University of Chicago Press.

Becker, H. S., B. Geer, E. C. Hughes, and A. L. Strauss. 1961. *Boys in White: Student Culture in Medical School.* Chicago: University of Chicago Press.

Bernard, H. R. and G. W. Ryan. 1998. "Text Analysis: Qualitative and Quantitative Methods." Pp. 595-646 in *Handbook of Methods in Cultural Anthropology,* edited by H. R. Bernard. Walnut Creek, CA: AltaMira.

Buston, K. 1997. "NUD*IST in Action: Its Use and Its Usefulness in a Study of Chronic Illness in Young People." *Sociological Research Online* 2(3). Available Internet: http://www.socresonline. org.uk/socresonline/2/3/6.html

Carey, J. W., M. Morgan, and M. J. Oxtoby. 1996. "Intercoder Agreement in Analysis of Responses to Open-Ended Interview Questions: Examples from Tuberculosis Research." *Cultural Anthropology Methods* 8(3):1-5.

Carey, J. W., P. H. Wenzel, C. Reilly, J. Sheridan, and J. M. Steinberg. 1998. "CDC EZ-Text: Software for Management and Analysis of Semistructured Qualitative Data Sets." *Cultural Anthropology Methods* 10(1):14-20.

Carley, K. and M. Palmquist. 1992. "Extracting, Representing and Analyzing Mental Models." *Social Forces* 70:601-36.

Catterall, M. and P. Maclaren. 1997 "Focus Group Data and Qualitative Analysis Programs: Coding the Moving Picture as Well as the Snapshots." *Sociological Research Online* 2(1). Available Internet: http://www.socresonline.org.uk/socresonline/2/1/6.html

Coffey, A. and P. A. Atkinson. 1996. *Making Sense of Qualitative Data Analysis: Complementary Strategies.* London: Sage.

Coffey, A., B. Holbrook, and P. A. Atkinson. 1996. "Qualitative Data Analysis: Technologies and Representations." *Sociological Research On-line* 1(1). Available Internet: http://www.socresonline. org.uk/socresonline/1/1/4.html

Colby, B. N. 1966. "The Analysis of Culture Content and the Patterning of Narrative Concern in Texts." *American Anthropologist* 68:374-88.

Colby, B. N., S. Kennedy, and L. Milanesi. 1991. "Content Analysis, Cultural Grammars and Computers." *Qualitative Sociology* 14:373-84.

Cropper, S., C. Eden, and F. Ackermann. 1990. "Keeping Sense of Accounts Using Computer-Based Cognition Maps." *Social Science Computer Review* 8:345-66.

Dey, I. 1993. *Qualitative Data Analysis: A User-Friendly Guide for Social Scientists.* London: Routledge.

Dohan, D. and M. Sanchez-Jankowski. 1998. "Using Computers to Analyze Ethnographic Field Data: Theoretical and Practical Considerations." *Annual Review of Sociology* 24:477-98.

Fielding, N. G. and R. M. Lee. 1995. "Confronting CAQDAS: Choice and Contingency." Pp. 1-24 in *Studies in Qualitative Methodology,* Vol. 5, *Computing and Qualitative Research,* edited by R. G. Burgess. Greenwich, CT: JAI.

———. 1998. *Computer Analysis and Qualitative Research.* Thousand Oaks, CA: Sage.

Fisher, M. 1997. *Qualitative Computing: Using Software for Qualitative Data Analysis.* Aldershot, England: Ashgate.

Friese, S. 1999. *Self Concept and Identity in a Consumer Society: Aspects of Symbolic Product Meaning.* Marburg, Germany: Tectum.

George, A. and S. Jaswal. 1993. "An Example of Searching for Words Using GOfer." *Cultural Anthropology Methods* 5(3):12.

Glaser, B. G. and A. L. Strauss. 1967. *The Discovery of Grounded Theory: Strategies for Qualitative Research.* Chicago: Aldine.

Hesse-Biber, S. 1995. "Unleashing Frankenstein's Monster? The Use of Computers in Qualitative Research." Pp. 25-42 in *Studies in Qualitative Methodology,* Vol. 5, *Computing and Qualitative Research,* edited by R. G. Burgess. Greenwich, CT: JAI.

Hesse-Biber, S. and P. Dupuis. 1995. "Hypothesis Testing in Computer-Aided Qualitative Data Analysis." Pp. 129-35 in *Computer-Aided Qualitative Data Analysis: Theory, Methods and Practice,* edited by U. Kelle. London: Sage.

Hoerr, S. L., D. Kallen, and M. Kwantes. 1995. "Peer Acceptance of Obese Youth: A Way to Improve Weight Control Efforts?" *Ecology of Food and Nutrition* 33:203-13.

Johnson, M., C. Noble, C. Matthews, and N. Aguilar. 1999. "Bilingual Communicators within the Health Care Setting." *Qualitative Health Research* 9:329-43.

Kelle, U. 1997. "Theory Building in Qualitative Research and Computer Programs for the Management of Textual Data." *Sociological Research Online* 2(2). Available Internet: http://www.socresonline.org.uk/socresonline/2/2/1.html

Kittell, L. A., P. K. Mansfield, and A. M. Voda. 1998. "Keeping Up Appearances: The Basic Social Process of the Menopausal Transition." *Qualitative Health Research* 8:618-33.

Lange, J. D. and S. G. Burroughs-Lange. 1994. "Professional Uncertainty and Professional Growth: A Case Study of Experienced Teachers." *Teaching and Teacher Education* 10:617-31.

Lazarsfeld, P. F. and M. Rosenberg. 1955. *The Language of Social Research: A Reader in the Methodology of Social Research.* Glencoe, IL: Free Press.

Lincoln, Y. S. and N. K. Denzin. 1994. "The Fifth Moment." Pp. 575-86 in *Handbook of Qualitative Research,* edited by N. K. Denzin and Y. S. Lincoln. Thousand Oaks, CA: Sage.

MacGuire, J. M. and D. A. Botting. 1990. "The Use of the ETHNOGRAPH Program to Identify the Perceptions of Nursing Staff Following the Introduction of Primary Nursing in an Acute Medical Ward for Elderly People." *Journal of Advanced Nursing* 15:1120-27.

Miall, D. S., ed. 1990. *Humanities and the Computer: New Directions.* Oxford: Clarendon.

Middleton, S. 1996. "Uniform Bodies? Disciplining Sexuality in School 1968-1995." *Women's Studies Journal* 12(2):9-35.

Moore, K., R. Burbach, and R. Heeler. 1995. "Using Neural Nets to Analyze Qualitative Data." *Marketing Research* 7(1):35-39.

Northey, W. F. 1997. "Using QSR NUD*IST to Demonstrate Confirmability in Qualitative Research." *Family Science Review* 10:170-79.

Poland, B. D. 1995. "Smoking, Stigma and the Purification of Public Space." Pp. 208-25 in *Putting Health into Place: Landscape, Identity and Well-Being,* edited by R. A. Kearns and W. M. Gesler. Syracuse, NY: Syracuse University Press.

Potter, J. and M. Wetherell. 1987. *Discourse and Social Psychology: Beyond Attitudes and Behaviour.* London: Sage.

Propp, V. I. 1968. *The Morphology of the Folktale.* 2d rev. ed. Edited by L. A. Wagner. Austin: University of Texas Press.

Ragin, C. C. 1987. *The Comparative Method: Moving beyond Quantitative and Qualitative Strategies.* Berkeley: University of California Press.

———. 1995. "Using Qualitative Comparative Analysis to Study Configurations." Pp. 177-89 in *Computer-Aided Qualitative Data Analysis: Theory, Methods and Practice,* edited by U. Kelle. London: Sage.

Raguram R., M. G. Weiss, S. M. Channabasavanna, and G. M. Devins. 1996. "Stigma, Depression, and Somatization in South India." *American Journal of Psychiatry* 153:1043-49.

Rantala, K. 1998. "Art as Communicative Practice for Teenagers." *Young: Nordic Journal of Youth Research* 6(4):39-58.

Richards, L. 1995. "Transition Work! Reflections on a Three-Year NUD*IST Project." Pp. 105-40 in *Studies in Qualitative Methodology,* Vol. 5, *Computing and Qualitative Research,* edited by R. G. Burgess. Greenwich, CT: JAI.

Riessman, C. K. 1993. *Narrative Analysis.* Newbury Park, CA: Sage.

Schweizer, T. 1991. "The Power Struggle in a Chinese Community, 1950-1980: A Social Network Analysis of the Duality of Actors and Events." *Journal of Quantitative Anthropology* 3:19-44.

———. 1996. "Actor and Event Orderings across Time: Lattice Representation and Boolean Analysis of the Political Disputes in Chen Village, China." *Social Networks* 18:247-66.

Seale, C. F. 1995a. "Dying Alone." *Sociology of Health and Illness* 17:376-92.

———. 1995b. "Heroic Death." *Sociology* 29:597-613.

———. 1996. "Living Alone towards the End of Life." *Ageing and Society* 16:75-91.

———, ed. 1998. *Researching Society and Culture.* London: Sage.

———. 1999. *The Quality of Qualitative Research.* London: Sage.

Sharpe, P. A. and J. S. Mezoff. 1995. "Beliefs about Diet and Health: Qualitative Interviews with Low Income Older Women in the Rural South." *Journal of Women and Aging* 7(1-2):5-18.

Silverman, D. 1993. *Interpreting Qualitative Data: Methods for Analysing Talk, Text and Interaction.* London: Sage.

Sprokkereef, A., E. Lakin, C. J. Pole, and R. G. Burgess. 1995. "The Data, the Team and the ETHNOGRAPH." Pp. 81-104 in *Studies in Qualitative Methodology,* Vol. 5, *Computing and Qualitative Research,* edited by R. G. Burgess. Greenwich, CT: JAI.

Strauss, A. L. and J. Corbin. 1990. *Basics of Qualitative Research: Grounded Theory Procedures and Techniques.* Newbury Park, CA: Sage.

Strauss, C. 1992. "What Makes Tony Run? Schemas as Motive Reconsidered." Pp. 191-224 in *Human Motives and Cultural Models,* edited by R. G. D'Andrade and C. Strauss. Cambridge: Cambridge University Press.

Taraborrelli, P. 1993. "Becoming a Carer." Pp. 172-86 in *Researching Social Life,* edited by N. Gilbert. London: Sage.

Torode, B. 1998. "Narrative Analysis Using Code-A-Text." *Qualitative Health Research* 8:414-32.

Triandafyllidou, A. 1999. " 'Racists? Us? Are You Joking?': The Discourse of Social Exclusion of Immigrants in Greece and Italy." Pp. 186-205 in *Eldorado or Fortress? Migration in Southern Europe,* edited by R. King, G. Lazaridis, and C. Tsardanidis. London: Macmillan.

Triandafyllidou, A. and A. Fotiou. 1998. "Sustainability and Modernity in the European Union: A Frame Theory Approach to Policy-Making." *Sociological Research Online* 3(1). Available Internet: http://www.socresonline.org.uk/socresonline/3/1/2.html

Weaver, A. and P. A. Atkinson. 1995. *Microcomputing and Qualitative Data Analysis.* Aldershot, England: Avebury.

Whyte, W. F. 1981. *Street Corner Society: The Social Structure of an Italian Slum.* 3d ed. Chicago: University of Chicago Press.

Part III

ANALYTIC OPTIONS

15

QUALITATIVE INTERVIEWING AND GROUNDED THEORY ANALYSIS

◆ Kathy Charmaz

Novices raise two fundamental questions about qualitative interviewing: (a) How do you do it? and (b) How do you analyze your interview data? In this chapter, I address how grounded theory methods shape qualitative interviewing in relation to personal narratives and guide analysis of interview data. Essentially, grounded theory methods consist of flexible strategies for focusing and expediting qualitative data collection and analysis. These methods provide a set of inductive steps that successively lead the researcher from studying concrete realities to rendering a conceptual understanding of them. The founders of grounded theory, Barney G. Glaser and Anselm L. Strauss (1967), aimed to develop middle-range

theories from qualitative data. Hence they not only intended to conceptualize qualitative data, but planned to demonstrate relations between conceptual categories and to specify the conditions under which theoretical relationships emerge, change, or are maintained.

Grounded theory methods consist of guidelines that aid the researcher (a) to study social and social psychological processes, (b) to direct data collection, (c) to manage data analysis, and (d) to develop an abstract theoretical framework that explains the studied process. Grounded theory researchers collect data and analyze it simultaneously from the initial phases of research. Researchers cannot know exactly what the most significant social and social

AUTHOR'S NOTE: Thanks are due to Jaber F. Gubrium, James A. Holstein, and Sally Hutchinson for their extensive critiques of an earlier draft of this chapter. I also thank Wanda Boda, Maureen Buckley, Noel Byrne, Scott Miller, Leilani Nishime, Tom Rosin, and Elisa Valesquez, participants in a Sonoma State University faculty writing seminar, for their comments on a preliminary statement of these ideas.

psychological processes are in particular settings, so they start with areas of interest to them and form preliminary interviewing questions to open up those areas. They explore and examine research participants' concerns and then further develop questions around those concerns, subsequently seeking participants whose experiences speak to these questions. This sequence is repeated several times during a research project. Hence grounded theory methods keep researchers close to their gathered data rather than to what they may have previously assumed or wished was the case. These methods give researchers tools for analyzing data as well as for obtaining additional focused data that inform, extend, and refine emerging analytic themes. Thus the interviews that grounded theory researchers conduct are focused; grounded theory methods create a tight fit between the collected data and analysis of those data.

In-depth qualitative interviewing fits grounded theory methods particularly well. At first glance, the advantages of qualitative interviewing for conducting a grounded theory analysis seem unassailable. An interviewer assumes more direct control over the construction of data than does a researcher using most other methods, such as ethnography or textual analysis. As John Lofland and Lyn Lofland (1984, 1995) have noted, the interview is a directed conversation. Grounded theory methods require that researchers take control of their data collection and analysis, and in turn these methods give researchers more analytic control over their material. Qualitative interviewing provides an open-ended, in-depth exploration of an aspect of life about which the interviewee has substantial experience, often combined with considerable insight. The interview can elicit views of this person's subjective world. The interviewer sketches the outline of these views by delineating the topics and drafting the questions. Interviewing is a flexible, emergent technique; ideas and issues emerge during the interview, and the

interviewer can then immediately pursue these leads.

Grounded theory methods depend upon a similar kind of flexibility. In addition to picking up and pursuing themes in interviews, grounded theorists look for ideas by studying data and then returning to the field to gather focused data to answer analytic questions and to fill conceptual gaps. Thus the combination of flexibility and control inherent in in-depth interviewing techniques fits grounded theory strategies for increasing the analytic incisiveness of the resultant analysis. Grounded theory interviewing differs from in-depth interviewing as the research process proceeds in that grounded theorists narrow the range of interview topics to gather specific data for their theoretical frameworks.

Throughout this chapter, I draw upon my earlier grounded theory studies of how adults with serious chronic illnesses experienced their conditions. After completing a doctoral dissertation in this area based on notes from 55 interviews (Charmaz 1973), I conducted 115 more intensive interviews, almost all of which were tape-recorded. These interviews focused on the effects of illness upon the self and relationships among self, time, and illness (Charmaz 1987, 1991a). The English language does not include a full, explicit, and shared vocabulary for talking about time. Thus the open-ended nature of grounded theory methods and the emphasis on emergent ideas in this approach proved especially helpful for the study of implicit meanings of time. My next project looked directly at what it means to have a chronically ill body; that work built upon earlier data and 25 new focused interviews for which there was a detailed interview guide, 12 of which were conducted with earlier participants (Charmaz 1995a, 1999).

In the past, most discussions of grounded theory have taken data collection practices for granted, giving them scant attention. Glaser and Strauss (1967; Glaser 1978) stressed the analysis and its resultant strengths. They redirected qualitative research to turn toward theoretical statements and reduced the distance between empirical research and theorizing. Yet data and theorizing are intertwined. Obtaining rich data provides a solid foundation for developing robust theories. Grounded theorists must attend to the quality of their data. Thus in the following pages I not only outline the logic of grounded theory but also attempt to show how researchers can obtain and use rich data with which to construct viable grounded theories.

◆ Variations on Grounded Theory

All variants of grounded theory include the following strategies: (a) simultaneous data collection and analysis, (b) pursuit of emergent themes through early data analysis, (c) discovery of basic social processes within the data, (d) inductive construction of abstract categories that explain and synthesize these processes, (e) sampling to refine the categories through comparative processes, and (f) integration of categories into a theoretical framework that specifies causes, conditions, and consequences of the studied processes (see Charmaz 1990, 1995b, 2000; Glaser 1978, 1992; Glaser and Strauss 1967; Strauss 1987, 1995).

Grounded theory methods have taken two somewhat different forms since their creation: constructivist and objectivist (Charmaz 2000). The constructivist approach places priority on the phenomena of study and sees both data and analysis as created from the shared experiences of researcher and participants and the researcher's relationships with participants (see Charmaz 1990, 1995b, 2000; Charmaz and Mitchell 1996, 2001). In this view, any method is always a means, rather than an end in itself. Methods do not ensure knowing; they may only provide more or less useful tools for learning. Constructivists study how participants construct

meanings and actions, and they do so from as close to the inside of the experience as they can get. Constructivists also view data analysis as a construction that not only locates the data in time, place, culture, and context, but also reflects the researcher's thinking. Thus the sense that the researcher makes of the data does not inhere entirely within those data.

Objectivist grounded theory, in contrast, emphases the viewing of data as real in and of themselves. This position assumes that data represent objective facts about a knowable world. The data already exist in the world, and the researcher finds them. In this view, the conceptual sense the grounded theorist makes of the data derives from the data: Meaning inheres in the data and the grounded theorist discovers it (see, e.g., Strauss and Corbin 1990; Glaser and Strauss 1967; Glaser 1978). This perspective assumes an external reality awaiting discovery and an unbiased observer who records facts about it. Objectivist grounded theorists believe that careful application of their methods produces theoretical understanding. Hence their role becomes more that of a conduit for the research process than that of a creator of it. Given these assumptions, proponents of objectivist grounded theory would argue for a stricter adherence to grounded theory steps than would constructivists.[1]

Objectivist grounded theorists also assume (a) that research participants can and will relate the significant facts about their situations, (b) that the researcher remains separate and distant from research participants and their realities, (c) that the researcher represents the participants and their realities as an external authority, and (d) that the research report offers participants a useful analysis of their situations. Interviewers who subscribe to these assumptions look for explicit themes, gather findings (i.e., facts), and treat their analytic renderings as objective.

The dual roots of grounded theory in Chicago school sociology and in positivism have produced both advantages and ambiguities. The Chicago school pragmatist, symbolic interactionist, and field research traditions that Anselm Strauss brought to grounded theory give this method its open-ended emphasis on process, meaning, action, and usefulness.[2] Barney Glaser's positivism imbued grounded theory with empiricism, rigorous codified methods, and its somewhat ambiguous specialized language.[3] Glaser and Strauss (1967) developed grounded theory methods to codify explicit procedures for qualitative data analysis and to construct useful middle-range theories from the data.

My approach to grounded theory builds upon a symbolic interactionist theoretical perspective with constructivist methods (Charmaz 1990, 1995b, 2000). I make the following assumptions: (a) Multiple realities exist, (b) data reflect the researcher's and the research participants'[4] mutual constructions, and (c) the researcher, however incompletely, enters and is affected by participants' worlds. This approach explicitly provides an *interpretive* portrayal of the studied world, not an exact picture of it (Charmaz 1995b, 2000; Guba and Lincoln 1994; Schwandt 1994).[5] The researcher aims to learn participants' implicit meanings of their experiences to build a conceptual analysis of them. A constructivist approach takes implicit meanings, experiential views, and grounded theory analyses as constructions of reality. A constructivist approach to grounded theory complements symbolic interactionism because both emphasize the study of how action and meaning are constructed.

◆ Grounded Theory Interviewing as Unfolding Stories

Interview data are useful for grounded theory studies that address individual experience. For example, many people experience disrupted lives because of grief, illness, marital dissolution, or financial crises, but they may not have sustained contact with other people who face similar troubles (Charmaz 1991a; Stephenson 1985). A researcher can create an interpretive analysis of their experiences through qualitative interviewing.[6] Grounded theorists aim to explain social and social psychological processes. In my work, such processes have included situating the self in time, disclosing illness, and adapting to impairment. In researching these processes, I had to identify the conditions and sequences surrounding what chronically ill people did and what happened to them as a result. A hazard in such an undertaking is the possibility that the researcher will aim to define the analytic story at the expense of the participant's story. Thus the researcher needs to achieve a balance between hearing the participant's story and probing for processes.

A grounded theory interviewer's questions need to define and to explore processes. The interviewer starts with the participant's story and fills it out by attempting to locate it within a basic social process. The basic grounded theory question driving a study is, "What is happening here?" (Glaser 1978). In this case, the "happening" is the experience or central problem addressed in the research. Most grounded theory interview studies do not look at what is happening in the construction of the story during the interview. Objectivist grounded theorists view interview questions as the means for gathering "facts." In this view, interview questions are more or less useful tools to obtain these facts. In contrast, constructivist grounded theorists see an interview as starting with the central problem (which defines suitable participants for the study) but proceeding from how interviewer and subject co-construct the interview. Their constructions are taken as the grist of the study, but constructivists frame much of this material as "views," rather than hard facts. Constructivists emphasize locating their data in context. Thus they may attend to the context of the specific interview, the context of the individual's life, and the contextual aspects of the study and research problem within the setting, society, and historical moment.[7] Objectivists, in contrast, concentrate on the specific data they have and treat. Thus their analyses may glow with accuracy but fade in context. Both constructivist and objectivist grounded theorists try to get at key events, their contexts, and the processes that contribute to shaping those events.

The first question may suffice for the first interview if stories tumble out. Receptive "uh huhs" or a few clarifying questions or comments may keep a story coming when the participant can and wants to tell it. I choose questions carefully and ask them slowly to foster participants' reflections. Grounded theory researchers use in-depth interviewing to explore, not to interrogate (Charmaz 1991b). Framing questions takes skill and practice. Questions must both explore the interviewer's topic and fit the participant's experience. As is evident below, questions must be sufficiently general to cover a wide range of experiences as well as narrow enough to elicit and explore the participant's specific experience.

I list some sample questions below to illustrate how grounded theory interviewers frame questions to study process. These questions also reflect a symbolic interactionist emphasis on learning participants' subjective meanings and on stressing participants' actions. The questions are intended to tap individual experience. For a project concerning organizational or social processes, I direct questions to the collective practices first and then later attend to the individual's participation in and views of those practices (see also in this volume DeVault and McCoy, Chapter 18). The questions below are offered merely as examples. I have never asked all of them in a single interview, and often I do not get beyond the initial set of questions in one session. I seldom take an interview guide with me into an interview, as I prefer to keep the interaction informal and conversational.

Researchers who are working on grounded theory studies of life disruptions or of deviant behaviors of some kind risk being intrusive. Participants may tell stories during interviews that they never dreamed they would tell. Their comfort should be of higher priority for the interviewer than obtaining juicy data. Thus concluding questions should be slanted toward positive responses, to bring the interview to closure on a positive note. No interview should end abruptly after the interviewer has asked the most searching questions or when the participant is distressed. The rhythm and pace of the interview should bring the participant back to a normal conversational level before the interview ends. The following examples of interview questions illustrate the above points.

EXAMPLES OF GROUNDED THEORY INTERVIEW QUESTIONS

Initial Open-Ended Questions

1. Tell me about what happened [or how you came to _____].

2. When, if at all, did you first experience _____ [or notice _____]?

3. [If so,] What was it like? What did you think then? How did you happen to _____? Who, if anyone, influenced your actions? Tell me about how he/she or they influenced you.

4. Could you describe the events that led up to _____ [or preceded _____]?

5. What contributed to _____?

6. What was going on in your life then? How would you describe how you viewed _____ before _____ happened? How, if at all, has your view of _____ changed?

7. How would you describe the person you were then?

Intermediate Questions

1. What, if anything, did you know about _____?

2. Tell me about your thoughts and feelings when you learned about _____.

3. What happened next?

4. Who, if anyone, was involved? When was that? How were they involved?

5. Tell me about how you learned to handle _____.

6. How, if at all, have your thoughts and feelings about _____ changed since _____?

7. What positive changes have occurred in your life [or _____] since _____?

8. What negative changes, if any, have occurred in your life [or _____] since _____?

9. Tell me how you go about _____. What do you do?

10. Could you describe a typical day for you when you are _____? [Probe for different times.] Now tell me about a typical day when you are _____.

11. Tell me how you would describe the person you are now. What most contributed to this change [or continuity]?

12. As you look back on _____, are there any other events that stand out in your mind? Could you describe it [each one]? How did this event affect what happened? How did you respond to _____ [the event; the resulting situations]?

13. Could you describe the most important lessons you learned about _____ through experiencing _____?

14. Where do you see yourself in two years [five years, ten years, as appropriate]? Describe the person you hope to be then. How would you compare the person you hope to be and the person you see yourself as now?

15. What helps you to manage _____? What problems might you encounter? Tell me the sources of these problems.

16. Who has been the most helpful to you during this time? How has he/she been helpful?

Ending Questions

1. What do you think are the most important ways to _____? How did you discover [or create] them? How has your experience before _____ affected how you handled _____?

2. Tell me about how your views [and/or actions depending on topic and preceding responses] may have changed since you have _____?

3. How have you grown as a person since _____? Tell me about your strengths that you discovered or developed through _____. [If appropriate] What do you most value about yourself now? What do others most value in you?

4. After having these experiences, what advice would you give to someone who has just discovered that he or she _____?

5. Is there anything that you might not have thought about before that occurred to you during this interview?

6. Is there anything you would like to ask me?

There is overlap in the questions above, and this is intentional. Such overlap allows the interviewer to go back to an earlier thread to gain more information or to winnow unnecessary or potentially uncomfortable questions. Taking notes on key points during the interview helps as long as it does not distract either interviewer or participant. Notes remind the interviewer to return to earlier points and suggest how he or she might frame follow-up questions.

Grounded theory researchers must guard against forcing data into preconceived categories (Glaser 1978). Interviewing, more than other forms of qualitative data collection, challenges researchers to create a balance between asking significant questions and forcing responses. An interviewer's questions and interviewing style shape the context, frame, and content of the study. Subsequently, a naive researcher may inadvertently force interview data into preconceived categories. Asking the wrong questions can result in the researcher's forcing the data, as can the way questions are asked, with which emphasis, and with what kind of pacing.

By asking the wrong questions, the interviewer will fail to elicit the participant's experience in his or her own language. Such questions superimpose the researcher's concepts, concerns, and discourse upon the subject's reality—from the start. Grounded theory analysis attempts to move inductively upward from data to theoretical rendering. When either forced or superficial questions shape the data collection, the subsequent analysis suffers. Thus researchers need to be constantly reflexive about the nature of their questions and whether they work for the specific participants.

The focus of the interview and the specific questions will likely differ depending on whether the interviewer adopts a constructivist or an objectivist approach. A constructivist would emphasize the participant's definitions of terms, situations, and events and try to tap the participant's assumptions, implicit meanings, and tacit rules. An objectivist would be concerned with obtaining accurate information about chronology, events, settings, and behaviors. Then, too, Glaser's (1978) influence would produce questions different from those likely to be used by proponents of Strauss and Corbin's (1990, 1998) version of grounded theory.

On a more general level, all interviewers need to be aware of the assumptions and perspectives they might import into interview questions. Consider the following:

◆ Tell me about the stressors in your situation.

◆ What coping techniques do you use to handle these stressors?

These questions might work well with a sample of research participants, such as nurses, who are familiar with the terms *stressors* and *coping techniques,* as long as the interviewer asks participants to define these terms at some point. However, the thought of identifying sources of stress and having explicit techniques for dealing with them may not have occurred to many other participants, such as elderly nursing home patients. The interviewer must pay attention to language, meaning, and participants' lives.

Like other skilled interviewers, grounded theory interviewers must remain active in the interview and alert for interesting leads (for suggestions, see Gorden 1987; Holstein and Gubrium 1995; Rubin and Rubin 1995; Seidman 1998). Sound interviewing strategies help the interviewer to go beyond commonsense tales and subsequent obvious, low-level categories that add nothing new. Any competent interviewer shapes questions to obtain rich material and simultaneously avoids imposing preconceived concepts on it. Keeping the questions open-ended helps enormously. When participants use expressions from the lexicon of their experience, such as "good days" and "bad days," the interviewer can ask for more detail. Consider the difference between these interview questions:

◆ Tell me what a "good" day is like for you.

◆ Do you feel better about yourself on a "good" day?

The first leaves the response open to the experiences and categories of the participant, inviting the participant to frame and explore his or her own views of a good day. The second closes down the discussion and relegates the answer to a yes or no. This question also assumes both the definitional frame and that participant and interviewer share it.

A basic rule for grounded theorists is, *Study your data.* Nonetheless, grounded theory interviewers must invoke another rule first: *Study your interview questions!* Being reflexive about how they elicit data, as well as what kinds of data they obtain, can help grounded theory interviewers to amass a rich array of materials.

◆ Multiple Sequential Interviews

Unfortunately, grounded theory studies have come to be identified with a "one-shot" interviewing approach (Creswell 1997). However, multiple sequential interviews form a stronger basis for creating a nuanced understanding of social process. Ethnography, case studies, historical research, and content analysis are also suitable methods for grounded theory analysis (see Charmaz and Mitchell 2001; see also Atkinson and Coffey, Chapter 20, this volume).

One-shot interviewing undermines grounded theory research in several ways. The logic of the grounded theory method calls for the emerging analysis to direct data gathering, in a self-correcting, analytic, expanding process. Early leads shape later data collection. Again, paying attention to language helps to advance a constructivist approach. Rather than glossing over a participant's meaning, a constructivist asks for definitions of it. For example, the interviewer's request above, "Tell me what a 'good' day is like for you," elicits the properties of a "good" day and how the participant constructs his or her definition. New questions arise as the researcher talks to more people and gains greater understanding of their situations. One useful way for the researcher to check leads and to refine an analysis is to go back and ask earlier participants about new areas as these are uncovered. When interviewers rely on one-shot interviewing, they miss opportunities to correct earlier errors and omissions and

to construct a denser, more complex analysis. Consequently, the contribution of the research to a theoretical rendering of the empirical phenomenon also has less power.

Interviewers who must use single interviews can attempt to mitigate these problems by ensuring that later interviews cover probing questions that address theoretical issues explicitly. An interview may capture a participant's views and preferred self-presentation at one point in time. Both can change. The present frames any view of the past (Mead 1932). As the present changes, so also may the participant's view of past events and of self. For example, one participant told me she had glossed over earlier events in a preceding interview because she could not face what they implied about her marriage. She had not acknowledged what an earlier set of medical tests indicated. At the time, her husband refused to drive her to the hospital for the tests and took little interest in their outcome. By downplaying the seriousness of the tests, she also diminished the significance of his actions.[8] Multiple interviews chart a person's path through a process. Conducting multiple interviews also fosters trust between interviewer and interviewee, which allows the interviewer to get closer to the studied phenomenon.

Multiple sequential interviews also permit independent checks over time. Through multiple interviews, the participant's story gains depth, detail, and resonance. Yet the significance of conducting multiple interviews transcends the simple aim of prompting a fuller story. Multiple interviews allow the researcher to hear about events when participants are in the middle of them, not only long afterward. For example, in my own research I was able to listen to a young woman's accounts of shifts in her definitions of trusted relationships as her experience changed over the course of years.

The logic of grounded theory demands that the interviewer successively ask more questions about participants' experiences that probe for theoretical insights. Through the early data analysis, the researcher's questions aim to explore leads about the studied process much more than about individual proclivities. The grounded theory interview develops through a shaped, but not determined, process.

Interviewers then have the opportunity to follow up on earlier leads, to strengthen the emerging processual analysis, and to move closer to the process itself. One-shot interviews often leave the researcher outside of the phenomenon and contribute to the objectivist cast of many grounded theory works. The interviewer may visit the phenomenon and at least peek at it, if not engage it, but he or she does not enter it and live in it. The one-shot interviewer need not sustain his or her gaze or become immersed in either the participant's realities or the participant's feelings (although listening to tapes and reading transcripts over and over may seem like immersion in the field). Grounded theory researchers often lay out general parameters of a topic as external observers but remain apart from it (Charmaz and Mitchell 2001).[9] The externality and objectivism in much grounded theory data collection and analysis has granted grounded theory credibility at the cost of the full realization of its phenomenological potential.[10]

◆ Grounded Theory Guidelines for Analyzing Data

Grounded theory provides researchers with guidelines for analyzing data at several points in the research process, not simply at the "analysis" stage.

CODING DATA

Coding is the pivotal first analytic step that moves the researcher from description toward conceptualization of that description. Coding requires the researcher to attend closely to the data. Nonetheless, the

codes reflect the researcher's interests and perspectives as well as the information in the data. Researchers who use grounded theory methods do so through the prism of their disciplinary assumptions and theoretical perspectives.[11] Thus they already possess a set of "sensitizing concepts" (Blumer 1969; van den Hoonaard 1997) that inform empirical inquiry and spark the development of more refined and precise concepts. Symbolic interactionism provides a rich array of sensitizing concepts, such as "identity," "self-concept," "negotiation," and "definition of the situation." The idea of identity has served as a sensitizing concept for me, alerting me to look for its implicit meanings in the lives of participants (Charmaz 1987). In my research on the lives of the chronically ill, I saw identity and threats of the loss of identity as connected with a variety of participants' actions and concerns, such as identity goals, that formed an identity hierarchy. Participants moved up and down this identity hierarchy as their physical conditions and social circumstances changed.

Grounded theorists draw upon sensitizing concepts to begin coding their data, although usually they do so implicitly. Constructivist grounded theory encourages researchers to be reflexive about the constructions—including preconceptions and assumptions—that inform their inquiry. Objectivist researchers minimize this reflexivity to the extent that they treat the researcher as a tabula rasa who conducts inquiry without prior views or values. If researchers make their sensitizing concepts more explicit, they can then examine whether and to what extent these concepts cloud or crystallize their interpretations of data. Researchers can use sensitizing concepts if they spark ideas for coding and take the nascent analysis further and drop them if they do not. Questions that researchers might ask about sensitizing concepts include the following: (a) What, if anything, does the concept illuminate about these data? (b) How, if at all, does the concept specifically apply here? (c) Where does the concept take the analysis? As researchers answer such questions, they make decisions about the boundaries and usefulness of the sensitizing concept. Extant concepts are expected to earn their way into a grounded theory analysis (Glaser 1978).

From a grounded theory perspective, the first question to ask and to pursue is, "What is happening in the data?" (Glaser 1978). Constructivist grounded theorists acknowledge that they *define* what is happening in the data. Objectivist grounded theorists assume they *discover* what is happening in the data.

Grounded theory coding is at least a two-step process: (a) Initial or open coding forces the researcher to begin making analytic decisions about the data, and (b) selective or focused coding follows, in which the researcher uses the most frequently appearing initial codes to sort, synthesize, and conceptualize large amounts of data.[12] Thus coding entails the researcher's capturing what he or she sees in the data in categories that simultaneously describe and dissect the data. In essence, coding is a form of shorthand that distills events and meanings without losing their essential properties. During the coding process, the researcher (a) studies the data before consulting the scholarly literature, (b) engages in line-by-line coding, (c) uses active terms to define what is happening in the data, and (d) follows leads in the initial coding through further data gathering. Studying successive interviews helps the researcher to stay close to the studied empirical world and thus lessens the probability that he or she will force borrowed concepts on it (Glaser 1978, 1992; Melia 1996). Similarly, coding each line with active terms prompts the researcher to link specific interview statements to key processes that affect individuals or specific groups. After the grounded theorist defines these processes, he or she gathers more data about them. Grounded theory coding can lead the researcher in unanticipated directions; for example, the researcher may find that he or she needs to obtain new kinds of data from the partici-

pants or to increase the interview sample to include another type of participant.

Initial coding helps the grounded theory researcher to discover participants' views rather than assume that researcher and participants share views and worlds. Should ambiguities arise, the grounded theorist returns for another interview. Through additional interviews, the researcher can check whether and how his or her interpretations of "what is happening" fit with participants' views. In the sample of initial coding displayed in Table 15.1, the excerpt is from an interview with a woman I had interviewed over a seven-year period. She had become increasingly disabled during that time from the effects of lupus erythematosus and Sjögren's syndrome, combined with back injuries. I tried to understand how this woman's statements about her physical suffering affected her situation at work. Although I had conducted previous interviews with her, this one focused on her experiencing bodily limitations. Hence the interview questions frame the content, which, in turn, shapes the codes constructed in analysis of the data. Certainly my theoretical interests in the social psychology of time and of the self informed my coding of her experience. Note the specificity of the codes in relation to the interview statements.

The line-by-line coding in Table 15.1 generated several categories: "suffering as a moral status," "making a moral claim," and "having a devalued moral status because of physical suffering" (Charmaz 1999). Line-by-line coding prompts the grounded theorist not only to study the interviews, but to examine how well the codes capture participants' implied and explicit meanings. By keeping these codes active, I preserve process and can later discern sequences after examining multiple interviews. By defining processes early in the research, the grounded theorist avoids limiting the analyses of interviews to typing people into simplistic categories. By conducting multiple sequential interviews, the researcher

---

Table 15.1   INITIAL CODING

Christine Danforth, a 43-year-old receptionist, had returned to work after eight recent hospitalizations and a lengthy convalescence from a flare-up of lupus erythematosus and Sjögren's syndrome (see Charmaz 1999). A statement from her interview and the initial coding of the statement appear below.

Initial Coding	*Interview Statement*
Recounting the events Going against medical advice Being informed of changed rules Suffering as a moral status Accounting for legitimate rest time Distinguishing between "free" and work time Receiving an arbitrary order Making a moral claim Finding resistance; tacit view of worth Having a devalued moral status because of physical suffering Taking action Learning the facts Making a case for legitimate rights Trying to establish entitlement Meeting resistance Comparing prerogatives of self and other Seeing injustice Making claims for moral rights of person-hood	And so I went back to work on March 1st, even though I wasn't supposed to. And then when I got there, they had a long meeting and they said I could no longer rest during the day. The only time I rested was at lunchtime, which was my time, we were closed. And she said, my supervisor, said I couldn't do that anymore, and I said, "It's my time, you can't tell me I can't lay down." And they said, "Well you're not laying down on the couch that's in there, it bothers the rest of the staff." So I went around and I talked to the rest of the staff, and they all said, "No, we didn't say that, it was never even brought up." So I went back and I said, "You know, I just was talking to the rest of the staff, and it seems that nobody has a problem with it but you," and I said, "You aren't even here at lunchtime." And they still put it down that I couldn't do that any longer. And then a couple of months later one of the other staff started laying down at lunchtime, and I said, you know, "This isn't fair. She doesn't even have a disability and she's laying down," so I just started doing it.

can establish the conditions under which individuals move between categories.

Grounded theory requires the researcher to make comparisons at each level of analysis. Action codes show what is happening, what people are doing. These codes move the researcher away from topics, and if they address structure, they reveal how it is constructed through action. I try to make action in the data visible by looking at the data as action. Hence I use terms such as *going, making, having,* and *seeing.* Using action codes helps the researcher to remain specific and not take leaps of fancy. In addi-

tion, action codes help the grounded theorist to compare data from different people about similar processes, data from the same individuals at different times during the course or trajectory of the studied experience, new data with a provisional category, and a category with other categories (Charmaz 1983, 1995b; Glaser 1978, 1992; Strauss 1987).

In selective or focused coding, the researcher adopts frequently reappearing initial codes to use in sorting and synthesizing large amounts of data. Focused codes are more abstract, general, and, simultane-

Table 15.2 SELECTIVE OR FOCUSED CODING

Selective Coding	Interview Statement
Going against medical advice	And so I went back to work on March 1st, even though I wasn't supposed to. And then when I got there, they had
Suffering as a moral status	a long meeting and they said I could no longer rest during the day. The only time I rested was at lunchtime, which
Making a moral claim	was my time, we were closed. And she said, my supervisor, said I couldn't do that anymore, and I said, "It's
Having a devalued moral status because of physical suffering	my time, you can't tell me I can't lay down." And they said, "Well you're not laying down on the couch that's in there, it bothers the rest of the staff." So I went around
Making a case for legitimate rights	and I talked to the rest of the staff, and they all said, "No, we didn't say that, it was never even brought up." So I
Seeing injustice	went back and I said, "You know, I just was talking to the rest of the staff, and it seems that nobody
Making claims for moral rights of personhood	has a problem with it but you," and I said, "You aren't even here at lunchtime." And they still put it down that I couldn't do that any longer. And then a couple of months later one of the other staff started laying down at lunchtime, and I said, you know, "This isn't fair. She doesn't even have a disability and she's laying down," so I just started doing it.

ously, analytically incisive than many of the initial codes that they subsume (Charmaz 1983, 1995b; Glaser 1978). They also cover the most data, categorize those data most precisely, and thus outline the next phase of analytic work, as indicated in Table 15.2. Selective coding must take into account a careful study of the initial codes. Note that I include the same data as displayed in Table 15.1 to show which codes I chose to treat in greater analytic detail.

These codes cut across multiple interviews and thus represent recurrent themes. In making explicit decisions about which focused codes to adopt, the researcher checks the fit between emerging theoretical frameworks and their respective empirical realities. Of the initial codes listed in Table 15.1, "suffering as a moral status" received analytic treatment. Within the same study, comparisons of different interviews netted similar statements about learning about

having an impaired and unpredictable body and how to monitor it.

The reciprocal relation between the coding of data and the creation of analytic categories now becomes apparent: Grounded theorists develop categories from their focused codes. Subsequently, they construct entire analytic frameworks by developing and integrating the categories.

MEMO WRITING

Memo writing links coding to the writing of the first draft of the analysis; it is the crucial intermediate step that moves the analysis forward. Grounded theorists use memos to elaborate processes defined in their focused codes. Hence memo writing prompts them to raise their codes to conceptual categories. Through memo writing, researchers take these codes apart analytically and, by doing so, "fracture" the data.

That is, they define the properties of each category; specify conditions under which each category develops, is maintained, and changes; and note the consequences of each category and its relationships with other categories. As researchers analyze categories, they ground them in illustrative interview excerpts included in their memos. Thus memos join data with researchers' original interpretations of those data and help researchers to avoid forcing data into extant theories. Memos can range from loosely constructed "freewrites" about the codes to tightly reasoned analytic statements.

Memo writing helps grounded theorists to do the following:[13]

◆ Stop and think about the data

◆ Spark ideas to check out in further interviews

◆ Discover gaps in earlier interviews

◆ Treat qualitative codes as categories to analyze

◆ Clarify categories—define them, state their properties, delineate their conditions, consequences, and connections with other categories

◆ Make explicit comparisons—data with data, category with category, concept with concept

The researcher's gains from memo writing go beyond the specific analytic procedures. Memo writing helps the researcher to spark fresh ideas, create concepts, and find novel relationships. This step spurs the development of a writer's voice and a writing rhythm. Memo writing is much like focused freewriting for personal use (see Elbow 1981). Memos should be written quickly—as fully as possible, but not perfectly. Aiming for perfection is a worthy goal for revising drafts. At the memo-writing stage, however, researchers need to explore their ideas and aim for spontaneity,

writing down questions and musings for later checking. Memos may read like letters to a close friend rather than like stodgy scientific reports. Through memo writing, the researcher begins analyzing and writing early in the research process and thus avoids becoming overwhelmed by stacks of undigested data. This step keeps the researcher involved in research and writing. Furthermore, memos explicitly link data gathering, data analysis, and report writing. They provide the foundation upon which whole sections of papers and chapters can later be built. One latent benefit of memo writing is the increased sense of confidence and competence it can instill in the researcher (Charmaz 1999).

The excerpt below is the first section of an early memo from one of my studies; it is followed by a brief discussion of the published work that covers the same material (Charmaz 1991a). I wrote this memo quickly after comparing data from a series of recent interviews.

Example of a Grounded Theory
Memo: "Suffering as a Moral Status"

Suffering is a profoundly moral status as well as a physical experience. Stories of suffering reflect and redefine that moral status. With suffering comes moral rights and entitlements as well as moral definitions—when suffering is deemed legitimate. Thus the person can make certain moral claims **and** have certain moral judgments conferred upon him or her.

> Deserving
> Dependent
> In need

Suffering can bring a person an elevated moral status. Here, suffering takes on a sacred status. This is a person who has been in sacred places, who has seen known what ordinary people have not. Their stories are greeted with awe and wonder. The self also has elevated status. . . .

Although suffering may first confer an elevated moral status, views change. The moral claims from suffering typically narrow in scope and in power. The circles of significance shrink. Stories of self within these moral claims may entrance and entertain for a while, but grow thin over time—unless someone has considerable influence or power. The circles narrow to most significant others.

The moral claims of suffering may only supersede those of the healthy and whole in crisis and its immediate aftermath. Otherwise, the person is less. WORTH LESS. Two words—now separate may change as illness and aging take their toll. They may end up as "worthless." Christine's statement reflects her struggles at work to maintain her value and voice.

And so I went back to work on March 1st, even though I wasn't supposed to. And then when I got there, they had a long meeting and they said I could no longer rest during the day. The only time I rested was at lunchtime, which was my time, we were closed. And she said, my supervisor, said I couldn't do that anymore, and I said, "It's my time, you can't tell me I can't lay down." And they said, "Well you're not laying down on the couch that's in there, it bothers the rest of the staff." So I went around and I talked to the rest of the staff, and they all said, "No, we didn't say that, it was never even brought up." So I went back and I said, "You know, I just was talking to the rest of the staff, and it seems that nobody has a problem with it but you," and I said, "You aren't even here at lunchtime." And they still

put it down that I couldn't do that any longer. And then a couple of months later one of the other staff started laying down at lunchtime, and I said, you know, "This isn't fair. She doesn't even have a disability and she's laying down," so I just started doing it.

Christine makes moral claims, not only befitting those of suffering, but of PERSONHOOD. She is a person who has a right to be heard, a right to just and fair treatment in both the medical arena and the workplace.

In the sections of the memo excerpted above, I addressed the following concerns: (a) establishing suffering as moral status, (b) explicating the tacit moral discourse that occurs in suffering, and (c) sketching a moral hierarchy. I realized that the term *stigma* did not capture all that I saw in key interviews. Subsequently, I recoded earlier interviews and talked further with select participants about these areas, then formed questions to ask other participants. In this way, I thought I might tap participants' unstated assumptions that would shape my developing categories. Objectivist grounded theory guidelines suggest that the direct relationship between data and categories generates definitive and obvious categories (Charmaz 1983; Glaser 1978, 1992; Glaser and Strauss 1967). That may not be true. If researchers bring similar perspectives to the same data, they may define similar categories; otherwise, they may not. Categories denote researchers' ways of asking and seeing as well as participants' ways of experiencing and telling.

Slight differences from the memo above are evident in the more developed published version (Charmaz 1999). In the published work, I discuss a range of social conditions that affect the hierarchy of moral status in suffering and describe more empirical examples. In conducting my research, I find it helpful to include the exact wording of interview excerpts in my memos from the start. After exhausting the analytic potential of categories in a memo, I can take the memo further by relating it to relevant literatures.

THEORETICAL SAMPLING

Theoretical sampling—that is, sampling to develop the researcher's theory, not to represent a population—endows grounded theory studies with analytic power. Grounded theorists return to the field or seek new cases to develop their theoretical categories. Thus theoretical sampling builds a pivotal self-correcting step into the analytic process. Predictable gaps become apparent when researchers raise their codes to analytic categories and find that some categories are incomplete or lack sufficient evidence. Obtaining further data to fill these gaps makes the categories more precise, explanatory, and predictive. For example, I sought further data on the elevated moral status of suffering to flesh out that category. When categories are incomplete, grounded theorists interview select participants about specific key ideas to extend, refine, and check those categories. Thus I returned to earlier participants to learn more about bodily suffering and, later, sought new interviewees and read personal accounts to illuminate the categories.

Theoretical sampling helps grounded theorists to do the following:

◆ Gain rich data

◆ Fill out theoretical categories

◆ Discover variation within theoretical categories

◆ Define gaps within and between categories

Through theoretical sampling, a researcher can define the properties of a category, the conditions under which it is operative, and

how and when it is connected with other categories. For example, I needed to explore "making moral claims" with a number of participants to discern to what extent the category was evident and when and how it fit into my emerging analytic framework and the participants' experience. That meant comparing interview excerpts from the same person to discover when he or she did or did not make moral claims, how this person may have learned to make such claims, what the properties of this experience were, and when, if at all, making moral claims reflected definitions of self. Then I compared different participants' interview excerpts. For example, when Christine says, "and I said, you know, 'This isn't fair. She doesn't even have a disability and she's laying down,' so I just started doing it," she is doing more than just recounting a past event; she is making moral claims.

Theoretical sampling relies on comparative methods. Through comparative methods, grounded theorists define the properties of categories and specify the conditions under which categories are linked to other categories. In this way, categories are raised to concepts in the emerging theory. By the time a researcher conducts theoretical sampling, he or she will have developed a set of relevant categories for explaining the data. Presumably, a grounded theorist will keep seeking data to check a category until it is "saturated" (i.e., no new information is found). In practice, saturation tends to be an elastic category that contracts and expands to suit the researcher's definitions rather than any consensual standard (see also Morse 1995).

After deciding which categories best explain what is happening in the study, the grounded theorist treats these categories as concepts. In this sense, these concepts are useful for understanding many incidents or issues in the data (Strauss and Corbin 1990). Strauss (1987) suggests that researchers conduct theoretical sampling early in the research, but I recommend conducting it later in order to allow relevant data and analytic directions to emerge without being forced. Theoretical sampling undertaken too early may bring premature closure to the analysis.

INTEGRATING THE ANALYSIS

Memo writing provides researchers with the material from which they can draft papers or chapters. Grounded theorists decide which memos to use on the basis of their analytic power for understanding the studied phenomenon; they may set aside other memos for later projects (Charmaz 1990). Theoretical sampling sharpens concepts and deepens the analysis. Then the work may gain clarity and generality that transcends the immediate topic. But how do the memos fit together?

Writing memos during each phase of the analysis prompts the researcher to make the analysis progressively stronger, clearer, and more theoretical. Each memo might be used as a section or subsection of a draft of a research paper. Some sets of memos fit together so well that ordering them seems obvious. The researcher's integration of the memos may simply reflect the theoretical direction of the analysis or stages of a process. But for many topics, researchers must create the order and make connections for their readers. How do the ideas fit together? What order makes most sense? The first draft of a paper may represent a researcher's first attempt to integrate a set of memos into some kind of coherent order.

Researchers go about integrating their memos in many ways, but the steps generally include sorting the memos by the titles of categories, mapping several ways to order the memos, choosing an order that works for the analysis and the prospective audience, and creating clear links between categories. When ordering memos, a grounded theorist may think about how a particular order reflects the logic of partici-

pants' experience and whether it will fit readers' experience. The grounded theorist will attempt to create a balance between these goals, which may mean collapsing categories for clarity and readability.

Grounded theory methods provide the researcher with powerful tools for honing an analysis. One inherent danger in using these tools is that the researcher may create a scientistic report overloaded with jargon. Like other social scientists, grounded theorists may become enamored of their concepts, especially because they provide a fresh handle on the data.

◆ Conclusion

A grounded theory interview can be viewed as an unfolding story. It is emergent although studied and shaped. It is open-ended but framed and focused. It is intense in content yet informal in execution—conversational in style but not casual in meaning. The relationship of the research participant to the studied phenomenon as well to the interviewer and the interview process also shapes the type, extent, and relative depth of the subsequent story. This unfolding story arises as interviewer and participant together explore the topic and imprint a human face upon it. The story may develop in bits and pieces from liminal, inchoate experience. It may tumble out when participants hold views on their experience but are not granted voices to express those views or audiences to hear them.

Interviews may yield more than data for a study. Research participants may find the experience of being interviewed to be cathartic, and thus the interviews may become significant events for them. Furthermore, participants may gain new views of themselves or their situations. Many participants gain insights into their actions, their situations, and the events that shape them.

Simply telling their stories can change the perspectives participants take on the events that constitute those stories and, perhaps, the frames of the stories themselves. These shifts in perspective may range from epiphanies to growing realizations.

The kinds of research stories told are likely to differ between constructivist and objectivist renderings of data. The constructivist approach leans toward a story because it rests on an interpretive frame. Like a story, a constructivist grounded theory may contain characters and plots, although they reflect reality rather than dramatize it. Unlike a story such as an ethgraphic tale, with rich description of people and events, a constructivist grounded theory stresses the analytic and theoretical features of the study processes. An objectivist grounded theory study takes the form of a research report prepared by an unbiased observer. Thus it looks more like a traditional quantitative study than a story, emphasizing parsimony, clarity, comprehensiveness, and analytic power. Objectivist grounded theorists attempt to specify the applicability and limits of their analyses through explicit conditional statements and propositions, whereas constructivists weave these into the narrative.

Grounded theory interviews are used to tell a collective story, not an individual tale told in a single interview. The power of grounded theory methods lies in the researcher's piecing together a theoretical narrative that has explanatory and predictive power. Thus inherent tensions are apparent between the emphasis on the subjective story in the interview and the collective analytic story in grounded theory studies. Grounded theorists place a greater priority on developing a conceptual analysis of the material than on presenting participants' stories in their entirety.

Are these inherent tensions irresolvable? No, not if the researcher intends to follow grounded theory strategies and stays on the analytic path. Not if the researcher outlines the place of interview stories in the final report and the research participant agrees. Not if the researcher believes that reciprocities are possible between interviewer and participant during the interview process itself. Priorities may legitimately differ during data collection and analysis. So, too, may the roles of researcher and participant. Although roles are always emergent and may take novel turns, clarity about reciprocities and ethics can mitigate later dilemmas. The interviewer can minimize the hierarchical nature of the relationship between interviewer and participant through active involvement in that relationship (see also Fontana and Frey 1994). The interviewer can give full attention to what the participant wants to tell—even when it seems extraneous or requires additional visits. And the interviewer can pace the interview to fit the participant's needs first. During data collection, then, participants take precedence. During analysis and presentation of the data, the emerging grounded theory takes precedence.

Tensions between participants' stories and grounded theory analyses may be more academic than actual. Postmodernists who take a literary turn may argue for telling research participants' whole stories, yet participants may not. Whether participants wish to have themselves and their stories captured in prose and revealed in public remains an empirical question as much as an ethical issue. Not every participant finds the prospect appealing—especially if the story reveals private, unmanageable, or discreditable concerns.

Taking a different stance, there is no inherent reason grounded theorists cannot include fuller stories or, for that matter, move closer to a narrative style. Grounded theorists are not prevented from exploring and adopting other genres to some extent simply because earlier grounded theorists adopted the style of scientific reportage. The potential exists for discovery and innovation. In the meantime, grounded theorists need to remain reflexive during all phases of their research and writing. In this way, they may learn how their grounded theory discoveries are constructed.

■ Notes

1. For a more complete statement of contrasts distinguishing constructivist and objectivist grounded theory, see Charmaz (2000).

2. Robert Prus (1987, 1996) discusses a complementary approach for using symbolic interactionism as a guiding perspective for the development of conceptual analyses of data.

3. Since the foundational statements of grounded theory were made, Anselm Strauss and Juliet Corbin (1990, 1998) have added dimensionalizing, verification, axial coding, and the conditional matrix to the grounded theory lexicon. Glaser (1992) contends that these procedures subvert grounded theory analyses. Phyllis Noerager Stern (1994a) asserts that they erode grounded theory, and Linda Robrecht (1995) states that axial coding adds undue complexity. Ian Dey (1999) has examined the logic of grounded theory, and he notes that Glaser and Strauss use the term *categories* inconsistently in their works.

4. I use the term *participants* to indicate their contribution to the research.

5. Earlier major grounded theory statements took a more objectivist position (see Charmaz 1983; Glaser and Strauss 1967; Glaser 1978; Strauss and Corbin 1990, 1998).

6. If these individuals were to become involved with informal support groups or formal organizations that focus on their problem, then a combination of interviews and ethnographic research would be the best choice (see Gubrium and Holstein 1997).

7. Gale Miller (1997) provides a nice statement addressing the need for placing texts into contexts.

8. This example comes from data collected for the study reported in my book *Good Days, Bad Days* (Charmaz 1991a).

9. This difference suggests Henri Bergson's ([1903] 1961) distinction between two ways of studying phenomena: going around them as contrasted with entering them.

10. Holly Skodol Wilson and Sally Hutchinson (1991) provide a statement about the use of grounded theory and hermeneutic approaches. I argue for less fidelity to method and more fidelity to the studied phenomenon.

11. For other statements of the steps of the method in addition to those already cited, see the work of W. Carole Chenitz and Janice Swanson (1986), Stern (1994b), and Strauss and Corbin (1994).

12. Strauss and Corbin (1990, 1998) introduce a third step in coding, axial coding, which aims to code the dimensions of a property. For example, expanded time and spatial horizons are properties of a good day. Using axial coding would lead me to analyze further what expanded time and space include. Glaser (1992) views axial coding as unnecessary; I find that it adds complexity to the method but may not improve the analysis.

13. This list is adopted in part from Charmaz (1999:376-77).

■ References

Bergson, H. [1903] 1961. *An Introduction to Metaphysics.* Translated by M. L. Andison. New York: Philosophical Library.
Blumer, H. 1969. *Symbolic Interactionism: Perspective and Method.* Englewood Cliffs, NJ: Prentice Hall.
Charmaz, K. 1973. "Time and Identity: The Shaping of Selves of the Chronically Ill." Ph.D. dissertation, School of Nursing, University of California, San Francisco.
———. 1983. "The Grounded Theory Method: An Explication and Interpretation." Pp. 109-26 in *Contemporary Field Research,* edited by R. M. Emerson. Boston: Little, Brown.
———. 1987. "Struggling for a Self: Identity Levels of the Chronically Ill." Pp. 283-321 in *Research in the Sociology of Health Care,* Vol. 6, *The Experience and Management of Chronic Illness,* edited

by J. A. Roth and P. Conrad. Greenwich, CT: JAI.

———. 1990. " 'Discovering' Chronic Illness: Using Grounded Theory." *Social Science and Medicine* 30:1161-72.

———. 1991a. *Good Days, Bad Days: The Self in Chronic Illness and Time.* New Brunswick, NJ: Rutgers University Press.

———. 1991b. "Translating Graduate Qualitative Methods into Undergraduate Teaching: Intensive Interviewing as a Case Example." *Teaching Sociology* 19:384-95.

———. 1995a. "Body, Identity, and Self: Adapting to Impairment." *Sociological Quarterly* 36:657-80.

———. 1995b. "Grounded Theory." Pp. 27-49 in *Rethinking Methods in Psychology,* edited by J. A. Smith, R. Harré, and L. van Langenhove. London: Sage.

———. 1999. "Stories of Suffering: Subjects' Stories and Research Narratives." *Qualitative Health Research* 9:362-82.

———. 2000. "Grounded Theory: Objectivist and Constructivist Methods." Pp. 509-35 in *Handbook of Qualitative Research,* 2d ed., edited by N. K. Denzin and Y. S. Lincoln. Thousand Oaks, CA: Sage.

Charmaz, K. and R. G. Mitchell. 1996. "The Myth of Silent Authorship: Self, Substance, and Style in Ethnographic Writing." *Symbolic Interaction* 19: 285-302.

———. 2001. "An Invitation to Grounded Theory in Ethnography." Pp. 160-174 in *Handbook of Ethnography,* edited by P. A. Atkinson, A. Coffey, S. Delamonte, J. Lofland, and L. H. Lofland. London: Sage.

Chenitz, W. C. and J. M. Swanson, eds. 1986. *From Practice to Grounded Theory: Qualitative Research in Nursing.* Reading, MA: Addison-Wesley.

Creswell, J. W. 1997. *Qualitative Inquiry and Research Design: Choosing among Five Traditions.* Thousand Oaks, CA: Sage.

Dey, I. 1999. *Grounding Grounded Theory: Guidelines for Qualitative Inquiry.* San Diego: Academic Press.

Elbow, P. 1981. *Writing with Power: Techniques for Mastering the Writing Process.* New York: Oxford University Press.

Fontana, A. and J. H. Frey. 1994. "Interviewing: The Art of Science." Pp. 361-76 in *Handbook of Qualitative Research,* edited by N. K. Denzin and Y. S. Lincoln. Thousand Oaks, CA: Sage.

Glaser, B. G. 1978. *Theoretical Sensitivity.* Mill Valley, CA: Sociology Press.

———. 1992. *Basics of Grounded Theory Analysis: Emergence vs. Forcing.* Mill Valley, CA: Sociology Press.

Glaser, B. G. and A. L. Strauss. 1967. *The Discovery of Grounded Theory: Strategies for Qualitative Research.* Chicago: Aldine.

Gorden, R. L. 1987. *Interviewing: Strategies, Techniques, and Tactics.* 4th ed. Homewood, IL: Dorsey.

Guba, E. G. and Y. S. Lincoln. 1994. "Competing Paradigms in Qualitative Research." Pp. 105-17 in *Handbook of Qualitative Research,* edited by N. K. Denzin and Y. S. Lincoln. Thousand Oaks, CA: Sage.

Gubrium, J. F. and J. A. Holstein. 1997. *The New Language of Qualitative Method.* New York: Oxford University Press.

Holstein, J. A. and J. F. Gubrium. 1995. *The Active Interview.* Thousand Oaks, CA: Sage.

Lofland, J. and L. H. Lofland. 1984. *Analyzing Social Settings.* 2d ed. Belmont, CA: Wadsworth.

———. 1995. *Analyzing Social Settings.* 3d ed. Belmont, CA: Wadsworth.

Mead, G. H. 1932. *Philosophy of the Present.* LaSalle, IL: Open Court.

Melia, K. M. 1996. "Rediscovering Glaser." *Qualitative Health Research* 6:368-78.

Miller, G. 1997. "Contextualizing Texts: Studying Organizational Texts." Pp. 77-91 in *Context and Method in Qualitative Research,* edited by G. Miller and R. Dingwall. Thousand Oaks, CA: Sage.

Morse, J. M. 1995. "The Significance of Saturation." *Qualitative Health Research* 5:147-49.

Prus, R. C. 1987. "Generic Social Processes: Maximizing Conceptual Development in Ethnographic Research." *Journal of Contemporary Ethnography* 16:250-93.

———. 1996. *Symbolic Interaction and Ethnographic Research: Intersubjectivity and the Study of Human Lived Experience.* Albany: State University of New York Press.

Robrecht, L. C. 1995. "Grounded Theory: Evolving Methods." *Qualitative Health Research* 5:169-77.

Rubin, H. J. and I. S. Rubin. 1995. *Qualitative Interviewing: The Art of Hearing Data.* Thousand Oaks, CA: Sage.

Schwandt, T. A. 1994. "Constructivist, Interpretivist Approaches to Human Inquiry." Pp. 118-37 in *Handbook of Qualitative Research,* edited by N. K. Denzin and Y. S. Lincoln. Thousand Oaks, CA: Sage.

Seidman, I. 1998. *Interviewing as Qualitative Research: A Guide for Researchers in Education and the Social Sciences.* 2d ed. New York: Teachers College Press.

Stephenson, J. S. 1985. *Death, Grief, and Mourning: Individual and Social Realities.* New York: Free Press.

Stern, P. N. 1994a. "Eroding Grounded Theory." Pp. 212-23 in *Critical Issues in Qualitative Research Methods,* edited by J. M. Morse. Thousand Oaks, CA: Sage.

———. 1994b. "The Grounded Theory Method: Its Uses and Processes." Pp. 116-26 in *More Grounded Theory: A Reader,* edited by B. G. Glaser. Mill Valley, CA: Sociology Press.

Strauss, A. L. 1987. *Qualitative Analysis for Social Scientists.* New York: Cambridge University Press.

———. 1995. "Notes on the Nature and Development of General Theories." *Qualitative Inquiry* 1:7-18.

Strauss, A. L. and J. Corbin. 1990. *Basics of Qualitative Research: Grounded Theory Procedures and Techniques.* Newbury Park, CA: Sage.

———. 1994. "Grounded Theory Methodology: An Overview." Pp. 273-85 in *Handbook of Qualitative Research,* edited by N. K. Denzin and Y. S. Lincoln. Thousand Oaks, CA: Sage.

———. 1998. *Basics of Qualitative Research: Techniques and Procedures for Developing Grounded Theory.* 2d ed. Thousand Oaks, CA: Sage.

van den Hoonaard, W. C. 1997. *Working with Sensitizing Concepts: Analytical Field Research.* Thousand Oaks, CA: Sage.

Wilson, H. S. and S. A. Hutchinson. 1991. "Triangulation of Qualitative Methods: Heideggerian Hermeneutics and Grounded Theory." *Qualitative Health Research* 1:263-76.

16

ANALYSIS OF PERSONAL NARRATIVES

♦ Catherine Kohler Riessman

It is a common experience for investigators to craft interview questions carefully only to have participants respond with lengthy accounts, long stories that appear on the surface to have little to do with the questions. I became aware of this in the early 1980s while researching the topic of divorce. After completing a household interview with a divorcing spouse, I would note upon listening to the tape that a respondent had gone "on and on." Asking a seemingly straightforward question (e.g., "What were the main causes of your separation?"), I expected a list in response but instead got a "long story." Those of us on the research team interpreted these stories as digressions.

Subsequently, I realized that participants were resisting our efforts to fragment their experiences into thematic (codable) categories—our attempts, in effect, to control meaning. There was a typical sequence to the moments of resistance: The long story began with the decision to marry, moved through the years of the marriage, paused to reenact especially troubling incidents, and ended often with the moment of separation (Riessman 1990a). If participants resisted our efforts to contain their lengthy narratives, they were nonetheless quite aware of the rules of conversational storytelling. After coming to the end of the long and complex story of a marriage, a participant would sometimes say, "Uh, I'm afraid I got a little lost. What was the question you asked?" With such "exit talk," the interviewer could move on to the next question.

Looking back, I am both embarrassed and instructed. These incidents underscore the gap between the standard practice of research interviewing on the one side and the life world of naturally occurring conversa-

---

AUTHOR'S NOTE: I thank Elliot Mishler, Paul Rosenblatt, Jay Gubrium, and Jim Holstein for comments on earlier versions of this chapter. The Narrative Study Group provided valuable input for my analysis of Gita's narrative.

tion and social interaction on the other (Mishler 1986). Although dehumanizing research practices persist, feminists and others in the social sciences have cleared a space for less dominating and more relational modes of interviewing that reflect and respect participants' ways of organizing meaning in their lives (DeVault 1999; see also Reinharz and Chase, Chapter 4, this volume). We have made efforts to give up communicative power and follow participants down their diverse trails. The current wellspring of interest in personal narrative reflects these trends.

◆ The Narrative Turn

The burgeoning literature on narrative has touched almost every discipline and profession. No longer the province of literary study alone, the "narrative turn" has entered history (Carr 1986; Cronon 1992; White 1987), anthropology and folklore (Behar 1993; Mattingly and Garro 2000; Rosaldo 1989; Young 1987), psychology (Bruner 1986, 1990; Mishler 1986, 2000b; Polkinghorne 1988; Rosenwald and Ochberg 1992; Sarbin 1986), sociolinguistics (Capps and Ochs 1995; Gee 1986, 1991; Labov 1982; Linde 1993), and sociology (Bell 1988, 1999, 2000; Chase 1995; Boje 1991; DeVault 1991; Frank, 1995; Holstein and Gubrium 2000; Williams 1984). The professions, too, have embraced the narrative metaphor, along with investigators who study particular professions. These include law ("Legal Storytelling" 1989), medicine (Charon 1986; Greenhalgh and Hurwitz 1998; Hunter 1991; Hydén 1997; Kleinman 1988), nursing (Sandelowski 1991), occupational therapy (Mattingly 1998), and social work (Dean 1995; Laird 1988). Storytelling, to put the argument simply, is what we do when we describe research and clinical materials, and what informants do with us when they convey the details and courses of

their experiences. The approach does not assume objectivity; rather, it privileges positionality and subjectivity.

Narrative analysis takes as its object of investigation the story itself. I limit discussion here to first-person accounts in interviews of informants' own experience, putting aside other kinds of narratives (e.g., about the self of the investigator, what happened in the field, media descriptions of events, or the "master narratives" of theory).[1] My research has focused on disruptive life events, accounts of experiences that fundamentally alter expected biographies. I have studied divorce, chronic illness, and infertility, and I draw on examples from my work throughout the chapter.

Narrative analysis, however, is not only relevant for the study of life disruptions; the methods are equally appropriate for research concerning social movements, political change, and macro-level phenomena (see in this volume Cándida Smith, Chapter 17). Because storytelling "promotes empathy across different social locations," regarding the U.S. abortion debate William Gamson (1999:5) argues, for example, that storytelling has counteracted excessive abstraction, bridging policy discourse and the language of women's life worlds; storytelling has fostered the development of constituencies—communities of action. Ken Plummer (1995:174) puts it vividly: "Stories gather people around them," dialectically connecting the people and social movements. The identity stories of members of historically "defiled" groups, such as rape victims, gays, and lesbians, reveal shifts in language over time that shape, and were shaped by, the mobilization of these actors in collective movements. Examples here are "Take Back the Night" and gay rights groups (see Kong, Mahoney, and Plummer, Chapter 5, this volume). "For narratives to flourish, there must be a community to hear; . . . for communities to hear, there must be stories which weave together their history, their identity, their politics" (Plummer 1995:87).

Storytelling is a relational activity that encourages others to listen, to share, and to empathize. It is a collaborative practice and assumes that tellers and listeners/ questioners interact in particular cultural milieus and historical contexts, which are essential to interpretation. Analysis in narrative studies opens up forms of telling about experience, not simply the content to which language refers. We ask, "Why was the story told that way?" (Riessman 1993).

The study of personal narrative is a type of case-centered research (Mishler 2000b). Building on the kind of analysis articulated most vividly by C. Wright Mills (1959), the approach illuminates the intersection of biography, history, and society. The "personal troubles" that participants represent in their narratives of divorce, for example, tell us a great deal about social and historical processes—contemporary beliefs about gender relations and pressures on marriage at a junction of American history (Riessman 1990a). Similarly, coming out stories, in which narrators proclaim their gayness to themselves and to others, reveal a shift in genre over time; the linear, "causal" modernist tales of the 1960s and 1970s have given way in contemporary stories to identities that blur and change (Plummer 1995). Historical shifts in understanding and growing politicization occur in the stories of women with cancer whose mothers were exposed to diethylstilbestrol (DES) during their pregnancies (Bell 1999). Illness narratives reveal "deeply historicized and social view[s] of health and illness," as Vieda Skultans (1999:322) shows with post-Soviet women patients' accounts of hardship, whose explanations are erased in their physicians' biomedical definitions of problems. As Mills said long ago, what we call "personal troubles" are located in particular times and places, and individuals' narratives about their troubles are works of history as much as they are about individuals, the social spaces they inhabit, and the societies they live in. The analysis of personal narratives can illuminate "individual and collective action and meanings, as well as

the processes by which social life and human relationships are made and changed" (Laslett 1999:392).

◆ Defining Narratives for Analysis

There is considerable variation in how investigators employ the concept of personal narrative and, relatedly, in the methodological assumptions investigators make and the strategies they choose for analysis. These are often tied to disciplinary background. In one tradition of work, typical of social history and anthropology, the narrative is considered to be the entire life story, an amalgam of autobiographical materials. Barbara Myerhoff's (1978) work offers an early example of the life story approach and illustrates its potentials and problems. Myerhoff constructs compelling portraits of elderly Eastern European Jews who are living out the remainder of their lives in Venice, California. She builds these portraits from the many incidents informants shared with her during extended fieldwork. She artfully "infiltrates" her informants, "depositing her authorial word inside others' speech" to speak her truth without "erasing the others' viewpoint and social language" (Kaminsky 1992:17-18). In this genre, the stories that informants recount merge with the analyst's interpretation of them, sometimes to the point that stories and interpretation are indistinguishable.

In a very different tradition of work, the concept of personal narrative is quite restrictive, used to refer to brief, topically specific stories organized around characters, setting, and plot. These are discrete stories told in response to single questions; they recapitulate specific events the narrator witnessed or experienced. William Labov's (1982) work illustrates this approach. For example, Labov analyzes the common structures underlying a series of bounded (transcribed) stories of inner-city violence told in response to a specific question. Narrators recapitulate sequences of actions that erupt and bring the danger of death. The approach has been extended by others who include more than brief episodes to analyze a variety of experiences (Attanucci 1991; Bamberg 1997a; Bell 1988; Riessman 1990b).

In a third approach, personal narrative is considered to encompass large sections of talk and interview exchanges—extended accounts of lives that develop over the course of interviews. The discrete story as the unit of analysis of Labov's and others' approach gives way to an evolving series of stories that are framed in and through interaction. Elliot Mishler (2000b), for example, studied the trajectories of identity development among a group of artists/craftspersons that emerged from his extended interviews with them. The approach is distinguished by the following features: presentation of and reliance on detailed transcripts of interview excerpts, attention to the structural features of discourse, analysis of the coproduction of narratives through the dialogic exchange between interviewer and participant, and a comparative orientation to interpreting similarities and contrasts among participants' life stories (see also Bell 1999).

Despite differences in these approaches, most investigators share certain basic understandings. Narration is distinguished by ordering and sequence; one action is viewed as consequential for the next. Narrators create plots from disordered experience, giving reality "a unity that neither nature nor the past possesses so clearly" (Cronon 1992:1349).[2] Relatedly, narrators structure their tales temporally and spatially; "they look back on and recount lives that are located in particular times and places" (Laslett 1999:392). The temporal ordering of a plot is most familiar and responds to the characteristic Western listener's preoccupation with time marching forward, as in the question, "And then what happened?" But narratives can also be or-

ganized thematically and episodically (Gee 1991; Michaels 1981; Riessman 1987). Narrators use particular linguistic devices to hold their accounts together and communicate meaning to listeners (for a review, see Riessman 1993:18-19). Human agency and imagination are vividly expressed:

> With narrative, people strive to configure space and time, deploy cohesive devices, reveal identity of actors and relatedness of actions across scenes. They create themes, plots, and drama. In so doing, narrators make sense of themselves, social situations, and history. (Bamberg and McCabe 1998:iii)

If all talk in interviews is not narrative (there are questions and answers about demographic facts, listings, chronicles, and other nonnarrative forms of discourse), how does an investigator discern narrative segments for analysis? Sometimes the decision is clear: An informant signals that a story is coming and indicates when it is over with entrance and exit talk (Jefferson 1979). In my divorce interviews, for example, responding to a question about the "main causes" of separation, one man provided a listing and then said, "I'll clarify this with an example," an utterance that introduced a lengthy story about his judging a dog show, an avocation his wife did not share. He exited from the story many minutes later by saying, "That is a classic example of the whole relationship . . . she chose *not* to be with *me*." As the story was especially vivid, I used it along with others to theorize about gender differences in expectations of companionate marriage in the contemporary United States (Riessman 1990a:102-8).

Stories in research interviews are rarely so clearly bounded, however, and often there is negotiation between teller and listener about placement and relevance, a process that can be analyzed with transcriptions that include paralinguistic utterances ("uhms"), false starts, interruptions, and other subtle features of interaction. Deciding which segments to analyze and putting boundaries around them are interpretive acts that are shaped in major ways by the investigator's theoretical interests.

Deciding where the beginnings and endings of narratives fall is often a complex interpretive task. I confronted the problem in a study of stigma and infertility as I began to analyze a woman's narrative account of her multiple miscarriages. The research was conducted in Kerala, South India, and elsewhere I describe the fieldwork (Riessman 2000a, 2000b). At a certain point in the project, I began to focus on identity development for women beyond childbearing age, how older women construct identities that defy stigma and the master narrative of motherhood.

Below, I present a portion of an interview with a woman I call "Gita," who is 55 years old, married, childless, Hindu, and from a lower caste. Because of progressive social policies and related opportunities in Kerala, Gita is educated, has risen in status, and works as a lawyer in a small municipality. The interaction represented in this extract took place after she and I had talked (in English) for nearly an hour in her home about a variety of topics, most of which she introduced. These included her schooling, how her marriage was arranged, and her political work in the "liberation struggle of Kerala." We enter the interview as I reintroduce the topic of infertility. My transcription conventions are adapted from those recommended by James Gee (1986).[3]

Although Gita could answer my question "Were you ever pregnant?" directly with a yes, she chooses instead to negotiate a space in the interview to develop a complex narrative. She describes terminated pregnancies, going to a political demonstration, and coming home to her husband's anger, whereupon the scene shifts to the actions of her in-laws and her husband's refusal to be examined for infertility. This was unlike other women's accounts about failed pregnancies in my interviews. Although temporally organized, Gita's plot spans many years and social settings, and

emotions related to the events are absent. She makes no reference to sadness, disappointment, or other feelings common to narratives of miscarriage and infertility.

In an effort to interpret this segment of the interview, I struggled to define its boundaries. Initially, I decided to conclude my representation of the narrative with what seems like a coda at the end of Scene 4: "But afterwards I never became— [pregnant]." The utterance concludes the sequence about pregnancies—the topic of my initial question. Ultimately, however, I decided to include the next scene, which communicates various family members' responses and the reported speech of Gita's husband ("No, no, I will not go to a lady doctor"). The change in decision coincided with a theoretical shift in my thinking about identity construction. I became interested in how women in South India resist stigma when infertility occurs (Riessman 2000b). It was crucial, then, to include the episode about the in-laws, the interaction with the gynecologist, and the husband's response to the request that he be tested.

Although not my focus here, the narrative excerpt could have been analyzed as an interactional accomplishment, that is, as a joint production of the interviewer and the respondent. Such a focus would require retranscription so as to include all of my utterances (deleted and marked with == in the interview excerpt), the ways I elicited and shaped the narrative (for examples of this approach, see Bell 1999; Capps and Ochs 1995; Mishler 1997; Riessman 1987; see also Poland, Chapter 13, this volume). The narrative also could have been analyzed with a primary focus on cultural context, centering on the prominent role of the wife's in-laws, for example, in defining and managing infertility in India (for an example, see Riessman 2000a). And the narrative could have been analyzed in terms of problems it solves for the narrator—an angle into the text I will develop shortly— and other problems that narrative creates. Investigators interested in psychological processes, narrative therapy, and change

Cathy:	Now I am going to go back and ask some specific questions. Were you ever pregnant?	
Gita:	Pregnant means—You see it was 3 years [after the marriage] then I approached [name of doctor] then she said it is not a viable—[pregnancy]. == So she asked me to undergo this operation, this D&C and she wanted to examine him [husband] also.	Scene 1
	Then the second time in 1974-in 75, next time—four months. Then she wanted [me] to take bed rest advised me to take bed rest.	Scene 2
	Because I already told you it was during that period that [name] the socialist leader led the gigantic procession against Mrs. Indira Gandhi, the Prime Minister of India, in Delhi.	Scene 3
	And I was a political leader [names place and party] I had to participate in that.	
	So I went by train to Delhi but returned by plane. After the return I was in [name] Nursing Home for 16 days bleeding.	
	And so he [husband] was very angry he said "do not go for any social work do not be active" this and that. But afterwards I never became—[pregnant] ==	Scene 4
	Then my in-laws, they are in [city] they thought I had some defect, really speaking. So they brought me to a gynecologist, one [name], one specialist.	Scene 5
	She took three hours to examine me and she said "you are perfectly-[normal], no defect at all" even though I was 40 or 41 then. "So I have to examine your husband."	
	Then I told her [doctor] "You just ask his sister." She was—his sister was with me in [city]. So I asked her to ask her to bring him in. He will not come. Then we went to the house so then I said "Dr. [name] wants to see you." Then he [husband] said "No, no, I will not go to a lady doctor." Then she [sister-in-law] said she would not examine him they had to examine the—what is it?—the sperm in the laboratory. But he did not allow that.	

(White and Epston 1990; Josselson and Lieblich 1993; McLeod 1997) might explore Gita's account of infertility for its closed, sealed-off features; Gita displays a set of understandings that seem to defy redefinition and change. Or silence about emotions might be a focus. These are just a few of the analytic strategies available.

Across the board, the discernment of a narrative segment for analysis—the representations and boundaries chosen—is strongly influenced by the investigator's evolving understandings, disciplinary preferences, and research questions. In all of these ways, the investigator variously "infiltrates" the text. Unlike some of the life story approaches mentioned earlier, especially Myerhoff's, my approach here includes detailed transcripts of speech so that readers can, to a much greater degree, see the stories apart from their analysis.[4] The selves of storyteller and analyst then remain separate (Laslett 1999).

◆ *Analyzing Narrative as Performance*

Personal narratives serve many purposes— to remember, argue, convince, engage, or entertain their audiences (Bamberg and McCabe 1998). Consequently, investigators have many points of entry. Personal narratives can be analyzed textually (Gee 1986; Labov 1982), conversationally (Polanyi 1985), culturally (Rosaldo 1989; Mattingly and Garro 2000), politically/historically (Mumby 1993; White 1987), and performatively (Langellier 1989).[5] It is the last of these analytic positions that I emphasize primarily here. A story involves storytelling, which is a reciprocal event between a teller and an audience. When we tell stories about our lives we perform our (preferred) identities (Langellier 2001).

As Erving Goffman (1959, 1981) suggests with his repeated use of the dramaturgical metaphor, social actors stage performances of desirable selves to preserve "face" in situations of difficulty, thus managing potentially "spoiled" identities. Relatedly, gender identity is performed, produced for and by audiences in social situations. To emphasize the performative element is not to suggest that identities are inauthentic, but only that they are situated and accomplished in social interaction.

Applying these insights to interviews, informants negotiate how they want to be known by the stories they develop collaboratively with their audiences. Informants do not reveal an essential self as much as they perform a preferred one, selected from the multiplicity of selves or personas that individuals switch among as they go about their lives. Approaching identity as a "performative struggle over the meanings of experience" (Langellier 2001:3) opens up analytic possibilities that are missed with static conceptions of identity and by essentializing theories that assume the unity of an inner self.

Personal narratives contain many performative features that enable the "local achievement of identity" (Cussins 1998). Tellers intensify words and phrases; they enhance segments with narrative detail, reported speech, appeals to the audience, paralinguistic features and gestures, and body movement (Bauman 1986). Analysts can ask many questions of a narrative segment in terms of performance. In what kind of a story does a narrator place herself? How does she locate herself in relation to the audience, and vice versa? How does she locate characters in relation to one another and in relation to herself? How does she relate to herself, that is, make identity claims about who or what she is (Bamberg 1997b)?

Social positioning in stories—how narrators choose to position audiences, characters, and themselves—is a useful point of entry because "fluid positionings, not fixed roles, are used by people to cope with the situations they find themselves in" (Harré and van Langenhove 1999:17). Narrators can position themselves, for example, as victims of one circumstance or another in their stories, giving over to other characters rather than themselves the power to initiate action. Alternatively, narrators can position themselves as agentic beings who assume control over events and actions, individuals who purposefully initiate and cause action. They can shift among positions, giving themselves active roles in certain scenes and passive roles in others. To create these fluid semantic spaces for themselves, narrators use particular grammatical resources to construct who they are. Verbs, for example, can frame actions as voluntary rather than compulsory. Other grammatical forms intensify vulnerability (Capps and Ochs 1995). These positionings of the self in personal narratives signify the performance of identity. They are enacted in an immediate discursive context, the evolving interview with a listener/questioner, and can be analyzed from detailed transcriptions.

I illustrate this approach by returning to Gita's narrative account in the transcript excerpt above. In the larger research project from which the transcript is taken, I show how the cultural discourse of gender defines women by their marital and childbearing status. In South India, married women face severe stigma when they cannot, or choose not to, reproduce (Riessman 2000b). Self-stigma was a recurring theme in my interviews, even as historical developments in contemporary India are enabling some women to resist the "master narrative" of motherhood. Gita deviated from the general pattern. She was beyond childbearing age, and the absence of motherhood did not seem to be a particularly salient topic for her (I was always the one to introduce it); she did not express sadness or negative self-evaluation about not having had children, as younger women did. It turned out that Gita had built a life around principles other than motherhood; she is a lawyer and political activist. Close examination of the narrative reveals precisely how she constructs this preferred, positive identity, solving the problem of stigma and subordination as a childless woman in South India. She resists the dominant cultural narrative about gender identity with an autobiographical account that transforms a personal issue into a public one (Richardson 1990).

Gita carefully positions the audience (me) and various characters in constructing her story, which is, as I noted earlier, a complex performance that I have represented in five scenes. Each scene offers a snapshot of action located in a particular time and setting. Unlike narratives in the discrete story approach (Labov 1982), Gita's narrative is complex in its organization. Attention to how scenes are organized within the performance is my analytic point of entry.

The first two scenes are prompted by an audience request ("Were you ever pregnant?"), my attempt to position Gita in a world of fertility. She reluctantly moves into the role of pregnant woman in these brief scenes, quickly chronicling two pregnancies several years apart (the outcomes of which I attempt to clarify, in lines deleted from the transcript). She does not provide narrative detail, elaborate meanings, or describe emotions associated with the miscarriages; the audience must infer a great deal. Gita constructs the first two scenes with only one character aside from herself, her doctor. She "approached" the doctor, who "asked" her to have a D&C. In a quick aside, she states that the doctor wanted to examine the husband, but we infer that this did not happen. With this utterance, Gita prefigures her husband's responsibility, anticipating the final scene and the moral of the narrative. Gita again casts the doctor as the active agent in Scene 2; she "wanted" and "advised" Gita to take bed rest. Through her choices of verbs and the positioning of characters, Gita constructs scenes in which she has a relatively minor role. From the lack of narrative detail, the audience assumes that the events in the plot up to this point are not particularly salient for Gita.

The narrator's position and the salience of the events change dramatically in the third scene. Gita shifts topics, from pregnancy "to what I already told you," which is the primacy of her political world. She now constructs a scene in which *she* is the central character, the agent of action, a "political leader" in her Kerala community who "had to" participate in a demonstration in Delhi against Mrs. Indira Gandhi, who was seeking reelection. Verbs frame the narrator's intentional actions, situated as political exigencies, and there is considerable narrative elaboration, which is a sharp contrast to the spare, "passive" grammar of the previous scenes, in which Gita was the object of the doctor's actions.[6] As Gita locates her private fertility story in the larger public story of India's socialist movement, the audience is not left wondering which is more important. Ignoring her doctor's advice "to take bed rest" during her second pregnancy, she traveled to Delhi to participate in a mass demonstration, which probably involved a three-day train trip in 1975. Despite her return by plane and a 16-day nursing home stay for "bleeding," the audience infers that Gita lost the pregnancy (a fact I confirm a few moments later in lines not included here). She constructs a narrative around oppositional worlds—family life on one side and the socialist movement of India on the other. The personal and the political occupy separate spheres of action and, as such, do not morally infringe upon each other.

Moving along, in the next two scenes Gita shifts the plot to the family world. In Scene 4, she again introduces her husband as a character and reports that he was "very angry" at her "social work," meaning her political activism. She communicates a one-way conversation; Gita does not give herself a speaking role. She positions herself only as the object of her husband's angry speech. We do not know what she said to him, if anything. Her passive positioning in this scene contrasts with her activity in the previous one. Is she displaying here the typical practice in South Indian families, which is that wives are expected to defer to their husbands' authority (Riessman 2000b)? If so, her choice of language is

instructive; he said "this and that." Could she be belittling her husband's anger and directives? She concludes Scene 4 with a factual utterance: "But afterwards I never became—[pregnant]".

In the fifth and final lengthy scene, Gita introduces new characters—her parents-in-law, an infertility specialist, a sister-in-law—and an intricate plot before the narrative moves toward its moral point, which is that Gita's infertility is not her responsibility. The final scene is most elaborate, suggesting importance. Gita's performance of identity is quite vivid here. She begins by constructing a passive, stigmatized position for herself: Her in-laws "brought" her for treatment to a gynecologist in the major South Indian city where the parents live because "they thought I had some defect." As in earlier scenes involving pregnancy, others suggest or initiate action.[7] She intensifies meaning and thematic importance with repetition ("defect") in the next stanza; the gynecologist determined after a lengthy examination that Gita has "no defect at all." She is "perfectly" normal. Blame for her infertility, Gita intimates, resides elsewhere. Using the linguistic device of reported speech, she performs several conversations on the topic of getting her husband tested. Everyone is enlisted in the effort—gynecologist, sister-in-law—but he refuses: "No, no, I will not go to a lady doctor." Nor is he willing to have his sperm tested in a laboratory. (Gita returned several other times in our interview to his refusal to be tested.) The narrator has crafted a narrative performance in which she has no responsibility whatsoever.[8]

Readers might question Gita's attributions. She ignored her physician's advice to "take bed rest" during her second pregnancy, choosing to travel instead to Delhi. She gave primacy to political commitments, valuing work in the socialist movement over her gendered position in the home. She was also "40 or 41" years old when she was finally examined by a specialist. Age may have been a factor. Gita had conceived twice, but could not sustain

pregnancies, implying a possible "defect."
Gita's performance, however, suggests how
she wants to be known as a "perfectly" normal woman "with no defect at all." The
way she organizes scenes within the narrative performance, the choices she makes
about positioning, and the grammatical resources she employs put forth the preferred
identity of committed political activist, not
disappointed would-be mother.

Later in the interview (in a portion not
extracted here), she supported this interpretation. Resisting once again my positioning of her in the world of biological fertility, she said explicitly, "Because I do not
have [children], I have no disappointments,
because mine is a big family." She continued
with a listing of many brothers, their children, and particular nieces who "come here
every evening . . . to take their meals." With
these words, she challenged my bipolar notions of parenthood—either you have children or you don't. Gita performs a gender
identity that resists the master cultural narrative in place in her world: that biological
motherhood is the central axis of identity
for women. Elsewhere, I historicize Gita's
life chances and locate her in an evolving
cultural discourse about women's "proper"
place in modern India, a "developing" nation that is formulating new spaces other
than home and field in which women may
labor (Riessman 2000b).

The analytic strategy I have illustrated is
generalizable. Narrators can emplot events
in their lives in a variety of ways. They "select and assemble experiences and events so
they contribute collectively to the intended
point of the story . . . why it is being told, in
just this way, in just this setting" (Mishler
2000a:8). How narrators accomplish their
situated stories conveys a great deal about
the presentation of self (Goffman 1959). To
make the process visible, we can analyze
scenes in relation to one another, how narrators position characters and themselves,
and we can "unpack" the grammatical resources they select to make their moral
points clear to the listener. Interpretation
requires close analysis of how narrators po-

sition audiences, too, and, reciprocally,
how the audience positions the narrator.
Identities are constituted through such
performative actions, within the context of
the interview itself as a performance. Audiences, of course, may "read" events differently than narrators do, resulting in contested meanings.

◆ The "Truths" of Personal Narrative

I stated at the outset that my approach to
narrative analysis assumes not objectivity
but, instead, positionality and subjectivity. The perspectives of both narrator and
analyst can come into view. As the Personal Narratives Group (1989) articulates,
"truths" rather than "the" truth of personal
narrative is the watchword.

Not all scholars who work with personal
narratives would agree (see in this volume
Cándida Smith, Chapter 17). Daniel Bertaux (1995) believes that "every life story
contains a large proportion of factual data
which can be verified" (p. 2), for example,
with respect to the dates and places of biographical events. Locating himself in the
"realist" research tradition, Bertaux argues
that informants' stories collected from the
same milieu can serve as documentary
sources for investigating the world "out
there." Although acknowledging that informants do not "tell us the whole truth
and nothing but the truth," Bertaux claims
that by collecting many stories from the
same milieu, a researcher can uncover "recurrent patterns concerning collective phenomena or share collective experience in a
particular milieu" (p. 2).

Those working from social constructionist or performative perspectives approach the issue of truth differently. Verification of the "facts" of lives is less salient
than understanding the changing meanings
of events for the individuals involved, and
how these, in turn, are located in history

and culture. Personal narratives are, at core, meaning-making units of discourse. They are of interest precisely because narrators interpret the past in stories rather than reproduce the past as it was.

Returning to Gita's narrative account of infertility, it is irrelevant whether the events "really" occurred just as she reports them. Gita was one informant in a larger project about identity for childless women, and she clearly performs one strategic solution to the problem infertility poses for her; she is "perfectly" normal, with "no defect at all." As noted earlier, it is possible to question her causal attributions. It also goes without saying that the passage of time since the miscarriages has softened their emotional impact, and consequently she can be silent about her feelings. As all narrators do, Gita presents past events from the vantage point of present realities and values. Not unlike other women I interviewed who were beyond childbearing age, she minimizes the significance of biological motherhood and emphasizes, instead, occupational and political identities. The truths of narrative accounts lie not in their faithful representation of a past world, but in the shifting connections they forge among past, present, and future.

The complex relationships among narrative, time, and memory are currently a vital topic of research and theorizing (Freeman 1998, forthcoming; for a review, see Hinchman and Hinchman 1997). Storytelling among those with chronic illnesses offers a case in point. Serious illness interrupts lives (Charmaz 1991) and occasions the "call for stories" (Frank 1995:53). Friends want to know "what happened," and stories provide maps for the ill themselves "to repair the damage that illness has done to the ill person's sense of where she is in life, and where she may be going" (Frank 1995:53). Yet the storylines or plots into which the seriously ill pour their experience may be at variance with biomedical plots. Patients with incurable cancers, for example, construct "restitution" narratives that suggest positive end points, whereas others represent themselves in "chaos" narratives, where continuity between past and future is unclear (Frank 1995). Oncologists are often asked about time, and they construct narratives of hope for families that blur endings and leave the future ambiguous (Good et al. 1994). For both practitioner and patient, a storyline locates the threatening illness in an imagined life trajectory (Mattingly 1994; Riessman 1990b).

The meanings of life events are not fixed or constant; rather, they evolve, influenced by subsequent life events. According to Mishler (1999), "As we access and make sense of events and experiences in our pasts and how they are related to our current selves, we change their meanings" (p. 5). Ends beget beginnings, in other words (Mishler 2000a). Personal narratives—the stories we tell to ourselves, to each other, and to researchers—offer a unique window into these formations and reformations: "We continually restory our pasts, shifting the relative significance of different events for whom we have become, discovering connections we had previously been unaware of, repositioning ourselves and others in our networks of relationships" (Mishler 1999:5).

A useful way to see how identities can shift over time is to look at "turning points" in stories—moments when the narrator signifies a radical shift in the expected course of a life. For example, in my research on divorce, it was common for informants to report moments when they realized retrospectively, "This is it"—the marital relationship had crossed a line beyond repair. Such turning points often coincided with incidents of physical violence, directed toward either the spouse or a child. One woman said: "That was the last straw. You just don't hit me. . . . I wasn't going to stay around to be hit again." Another woman, who had been physically abused for years, spoke of "the final blow": Her husband "punched our oldest daughter across the living room . . . if he was going to start doing that to the kids, that was it." A divorcing man told a long narrative about his wife's open infidelity, culminating in a moment when he hit her. He said to himself, "This is it . . . there wasn't any reason to be there other than to hurt" (Riessman 1990a). Such turning points fundamentally change the meaning of past experiences and consequently individuals' identities. "They open up directions of movement that were not anticipated by and could not be predicted by their pasts"—an insight Mishler (1999: 7-8) applies to the narratives of sexual abuse survivors. Past abuse is given new significance as women move out of destructive relationships and construct new identities.

The "trustworthiness" of narrative accounts cannot be evaluated using traditional correspondence criteria. There is no canonical approach to validation in interpretive work, no recipes or formulas. (For a review of several approaches that may be useful in certain instances, see Riessman 1993:64-69.)

◆ Conclusion

I began this chapter with an account of my difficulty in doing research interviews with individuals whose lives had been disrupted and being initially annoyed at interviewees' lengthy and convoluted responses. Since then, many investigators have given a name to my problem—these were "narratives"— and offered analytic solutions for working with interview responses that do not require fragmenting them. The field now named *narrative analysis* has grown rapidly, and no review can be complete and summarize the many types of work that are evident today. I have purposively bounded the field, focusing on the personal narrative and emphasizing the performative dimension, but I have also pointed the reader toward other perspectives. (For reviews and typologies of research strategies, see Cortazzi 1993; Langellier 1989; Mishler 1995; Riessman 1993.)

Narrative analysis has its critics, of course (Atkinson 1997; Atkinson and Silverman 1997). Its methods are not appropriate for studies of large numbers of nameless, faceless subjects. The approach is slow and painstaking, requiring attention to subtlety: nuances of speech, the organization of a response, relations between researcher and subject, social and historical contexts. It is not suitable for investigators who seek a clear and unobstructed view of subjects' lives, and the analytic detail required may seem excessive to those who orient to language as a transparent medium.

Narrative methods can be combined with other forms of qualitative analysis (for an example, see Riessman 1990a), even with quantitative analysis.[9] Some fancy epistemological footwork is required, because the interpretive perspective that typically underlies narrative work is very different from the realist assumptions of some forms of qualitative analysis and certainly of quantification. Combining methods forces investigators to confront troublesome philosophical issues and to educate readers about them. Science cannot be spoken in a singular, universal voice. Any methodological standpoint is, by definition, partial, incomplete, and historically contingent. Diversity of representations is needed. Narrative analysis is one approach, not a panacea; it is suitable for some situations and not others. It is a useful addition to the stockpot of social research methods, bringing critical flavors to the surface that otherwise get lost in the brew. Narrative analysis allows for the systematic study of personal experience and meaning. The approach enables investigators to study the "active, self-shaping quality of human thought, the power of stories to create and refashion personal identity" (Hinchman and Hinchman 1997:xiv).

Narratives are a particularly significant genre for representing and analyzing identity in its multiple guises in different contexts. The methods allow for the systematic study of experience and, for feminist researchers such as myself, the changing meanings of conditions that affect women disproportionately, including domestic violence, reproductive illness, and poverty. Personal narratives provide windows into lives that confront the constraints of circumstances. Attention to personal narratives in interviews opens discursive spaces for research subjects, representing them as agents acting in life worlds of moral complexity.

■ Notes

1. There are, of course, narrative sites other than interviews (see Ochs, Smith, and Taylor 1989; Polanyi 1985; Gubrium and Holstein 2000).

2. There is lively philosophical debate in this area about whether primary experience is "disordered"—that is, whether narrators create order out of chaos (see Hinchman and Hinchman 1997:xix-xx).

3. I have grouped lines about a single topic into stanzas, which I have then grouped into scenes. Because of the narrative's direct performative reference, I have organized it into "scenes" rather than "strophes," as Gee (1986) does. I have deleted brief exchanges between Gita and me, questions I ask to clarify what she has said, which are marked ==.

4. Transcriptions, of course, are themselves theory-laden; how we choose to represent spoken dialogue is not independent of theoretical goals (see Ochs 1979; Mishler 1991; Kvale 1996:chap. 9; Poland 1995).

5. Lisa Capps and Elinor Ochs (1995) provide a compelling analysis of conversations with a single narrator over several years. They combine textual and conversational approaches in their study of the discourse of a woman suffering from agoraphobia (severe panic attacks).

6. The verb construction *had to* is, in fact, ambiguous. It might refer to others' expectations that Gita participate in the political demonstration, a consequence of her leadership role in the community, or it might refer to an "inner" compulsion to participate, arising out of her own political convictions and priorities. The narrative context supports the latter interpretation.

7. Infertility is a family event in the Indian context, and husbands' relatives often suggest and initiate treatment for daughters-in-law, including medical and religious cures (Riessman 2000a, 2000b).

8. The physiological responsibility for infertility in this and the other cases is unclear. India's infertility clinics require both spouses to be tested, and about a third of the time the problem lies in the sperm. Elsewhere, I have described Indian women's management of male responsibility; they do not disclose it to deflect stigma but, in an effort to keep families together, absorb the "fault" themselves (Riessman 2000b).

9. The material in this paragraph is adapted from Riessman (1993:70).

■ References

Atkinson, P. 1997. "Narrative Turn or Blind Alley?" *Qualitative Health Research* 7:325-44.
Atkinson, P. and D. Silverman. 1997. "Kundera's *Immortality:* The Interview Society and the Invention of Self." *Qualitative Inquiry* 3:304-25.
Attanucci, J. 1991. "Changing Subjects: Growing Up and Growing Older." *Journal of Moral Education* 20:317-28.
Bamberg, M. G. W., ed. 1997a. "Oral Versions of Personal Experience: Three Decades of Narrative Analysis" (special issue). *Journal of Narrative and Life History* 7(1-4).
———. 1997b. "Positioning between Structure and Performance." In "Oral Versions of Personal Experience: Three Decades of Narrative Analysis" (special issue), edited by M. G. W. Bamberg. *Journal of Narrative and Life History* 7:335-42.
Bamberg, M. G. W. and A. McCabe. 1998. "Editorial." *Narrative Inquiry* 8(1):iii-v.
Bauman, R. 1986. *Story, Performance, and Event: Contextual Studies of Oral Narrative.* Cambridge: Cambridge University Press.
Behar, R. 1993. *Translated Woman: Crossing the Border with Esperanza's Story.* Boston: Beacon.

Bell, S. E. 1988. "Becoming a Political Woman: The Reconstruction and Interpretation of Experience through Stories." In *Gender and Discourse: The Power of Talk,* edited by A. D. Todd and S. Fisher. Norwood, NJ: Ablex.

———. 1999. "Narratives and Lives: Women's Health Politics and the Diagnosis of Cancer for DES Daughters." *Narrative Inquiry* 9(2):1-43.

———. 2000. "Experiencing Illness in/and Narrative." In *Handbook of Medical Sociology,* 5th ed., edited by C. E. Bird, P. Conrad, and A. M. Fremont. Upper Saddle River, NJ: Prentice Hall.

Bertaux, D. 1995. "A Response to Thierry Kochuyt's 'Biographic and Empiricist Illusions: A Reply to Recent Criticism.'" *Biography & Society* (annual newsletter of Research Committee 38, International Sociological Association), pp. 2-6.

Boje, D. M. 1991. "The Storytelling Organization: A Study of Story Performance in an Office-Supply Firm." *Administrative Science Quarterly* 36:106-26.

Bruner, J. 1986. *Actual Minds, Possible Worlds.* Cambridge, MA: Harvard University Press.

———. 1990. *Acts of Meaning.* Cambridge, MA: Harvard University Press.

Capps, L. and E. Ochs. 1995. *Constructing Panic: The Discourse of Agoraphobia.* Cambridge, MA: Harvard University Press.

Carr, D. 1986. *Time, Narrative, and History.* Bloomington: Indiana University Press.

Charmaz, K. 1991. *Good Days, Bad Days: The Self in Chronic Illness and Time.* New Brunswick, NJ: Rutgers University Press.

Charon, R. 1986. "To Render the Lives of Patients." *Literature and Medicine* 5:58-74.

Chase, S. E. 1995. *Ambiguous Empowerment: The Work Narratives of Women School Superintendents.* Amherst: University of Massachusetts Press.

Cortazzi, M. 1993. *Narrative Analysis.* London: Falmer.

Cronon, W. 1992. "A Place for Stories: Nature, History, and Narrative." *Journal of American History* 78:1347-76.

Cussins, C. M. 1998. "Ontological Choreography: Agency for Women Patients in an Infertility Clinic." In *Differences in Medicine: Unraveling Practices, Techniques, and Bodies,* edited by M. Berg and S. Mol. Durham, NC: Duke University Press.

Dean, R. G. 1995. "Stories of AIDS: The Use of Narrative as an Approach to Understanding in an AIDS Support Group." *Clinical Social Work Journal* 23:287-304.

DeVault, M. L. 1991. "Talking and Listening from Women's Standpoint: Feminist Strategies for Interviewing and Analysis." *Social Problems* 37:96-116.

———. 1999. *Liberating Method: Feminism and Social Research.* Philadelphia: Temple University Press.

Freeman, M. 1998. "Mythical Time, Historical Time, and the Narrative Fabric of the Self." *Narrative Inquiry* 8(1):1-24.

———. Forthcoming. "The Presence of What Is Missing: Memory, Poetry, and the Ride Home." In *Between Fathers and Sons: Critical Incident Narratives on the Development of Men's Lives,* edited by R. J. Pellegrini and T. R. Sarbin. Thousand Oaks, CA: Sage.

Frank, A. W. 1995. *The Wounded Storyteller: Body, Illness, and Ethics.* Chicago: University of Chicago Press.

Gamson, W. A. 1999. "How Story Telling Can Be Empowering." Presented at the conference "Toward a Sociology of Culture and Cognition," November 12-13, Rutgers University, New Brunswick, NJ.

Gee, J. P. 1986. "Units in the Production of Narrative Discourse." *Discourse Processes* 9:391-422.

———. 1991. "A Linguistic Approach to Narrative." *Journal of Narrative and Life History* 1:15-39.

Goffman, E. 1959. *The Presentation of Self in Everyday Life.* Garden City, NY: Doubleday.

———. 1981. *Forms of Talk.* Philadelphia: University of Pennsylvania Press.

Good, M.-J. D., T. Munakata, Y. Kobayashi, C. Mattingly, and B. J. Good. 1994. "Oncology and Narrative Time." *Social Science and Medicine* 38:855-62.

Greenhalgh, T. and B. Hurwitz, eds. 1998. *Narrative Based Medicine: Dialogue and Discourse in Clinical Practice.* London: BMJ.

Gubrium, J. F. and J. A. Holstein, eds. 2000. *Institutional Selves: Troubled Identities in a Postmodern World.* New York: Oxford University Press.

Harré, R. and L. van Langenhove. 1999. "Introducing Positioning Theory." Pp. 14-31 in *Positioning Theory*, edited by R. Harré and L. van Langenhove. Malden, MA: Blackwell.

Hinchman, L. P. and S. K. Hinchman. 1997. "Introduction." In *Memory, Identity, Community: The Idea of Narrative in the Human Sciences*, edited by L. P. Hinchman and S. K. Hinchman. Albany: State University of New York Press.

Holstein, J. A. and J. F. Gubrium. 2000. *The Self We Live By: Narrative Identity in a Postmodern World*. New York: Oxford University Press.

Hunter, K. M. 1991. *Doctors' Stories: The Narrative Structure of Medical Knowledge*. Princeton, NJ: Princeton University Press.

Hydén, L. C. 1997. "Illness and Narrative." *Sociology of Health and Illness* 19:48-69.

Jefferson, G. 1979. "Sequential Aspects of Storytelling in Conversation." In *Studies in the Organization of Conversational Interaction*, edited by J. Schenkein. New York: Academic Press.

Josselson, R. and A. Lieblich, eds. 1993. *The Narrative Study of Lives*, Vol. 1, *The Narrative Study of Lives*. Newbury Park, CA: Sage.

Kaminsky, M. 1992. "Introduction." In B. Myerhoff, *Remembered Lives: The Work of Ritual, Storytelling, and Growing Older*. Ann Arbor: University of Michigan Press.

Kleinman, A. 1988. *The Illness Narratives: Suffering, Healing, and the Human Condition*. New York: Basic Books.

Kvale, S. 1996. *InterViews: An Introduction to Qualitative Research Interviewing*. Thousand Oaks, CA: Sage.

Labov, W. 1982. "Speech Actions and Reactions in Personal Narrative." In *Analyzing Discourse: Text and Talk*, edited by D. Tannen. Washington, DC: Georgetown University Press.

Laird, J. 1988. "Women and Stories: Restorying Women's Self-Constructions." In *Women in Families: A Framework for Family Therapy*, edited by M. McGoldrick, C. Anderson, and F. Walsh. New York: Norton.

Langellier, K. 1989. "Personal Narratives: Perspectives on Theory and Research." *Text and Performance Quarterly* 9:243-76.

———. 2001. " 'You're Marked': Breast Cancer, Tattoo, and the Narrative Performance of Identity." In *Narrative and Identity: Studies in Autobiography, Self, and Culture*, edited by J. Brockmeier and D. Carbaugh. Amsterdam: John Benjamins.

Laslett, B. 1999. "Personal Narratives as Sociology." *Contemporary Sociology* 28:391-401.

"Legal Storytelling" (special issue). 1989. *Michigan Law Review* 87(8).

Linde, C. 1993. *Life Stories: The Creation of Coherence*. New York: Oxford University Press.

Mattingly, C. 1994. "The Concept of Therapeutic 'Emplotment.' " *Social Science and Medicine* 38:811-22.

———. 1998. *Healing Dramas and Clinical Plots: The Narrative Structure of Experience*. New York: Cambridge University Press.

Mattingly, C. and L. C. Garro, eds. 2000. *Narrative and Cultural Construction of Illness and Healing*. Berkeley: University of California Press.

McLeod, J. 1997. *Narrative and Psychotherapy*. Thousand Oaks, CA: Sage.

Michaels, S. 1981. " 'Sharing Time': Children's Narrative Styles and Differential Access to Literacy." *Language and Society* 10:423-42.

Mills, C. W. 1959. *The Sociological Imagination*. New York: Oxford University Press.

Mishler, E. G. 1986. *Research Interviewing: Context and Narrative*. Cambridge, MA: Harvard University Press.

———. 1991. "Representing Discourse: The Rhetoric of Transcription." *Journal of Narrative and Life History* 1:255-80.

———. 1995. "Models of Narrative Analysis: A Typology." *Journal of Narrative and Life History* 5:87-123.

———. 1997. "Narrative Accounts in Clinical and Research Interviews." In *The Construction of Professional Discourse*, edited by B.-L. Gunnarsson, P. Linell, and B. Norberg. London: Longman.

———. 1999. "Time's Double Arrow: Re-presenting the Past in Life History Studies." Presented at Radcliffe Murray Center conference "Lives in Context: The Study of Human Development," November 12-13, Cambridge, MA.

———. 2000a. "Narrative and the Paradox of Temporal Ordering: How Ends Beget Beginnings." Presented at the Conference on Discourse and Identity, Clark University.

———. 2000b. *Storylines: Craftartists' Narratives of Identity.* Cambridge, MA: Harvard University Press.

Mumby, D. K. 1993. *Narrative and Social Control: Critical Perspectives.* Newbury Park, CA: Sage.

Myerhoff, B. 1978. *Number Our Days.* New York: Simon & Schuster.

Ochs, E. 1979. "Transcription as Theory." In *Developmental Pragmatics,* edited by E. Ochs and B. B. Schieffelin. New York: Academic Press.

Ochs, E., R. Smith, and C. Taylor. 1989. "Dinner Narratives as Detective Stories." *Cultural Dynamics* 2:238-57.

Personal Narratives Group. 1989. "Truths." In Personal Narratives Group, *Interpreting Women's Lives: Feminist Theory and Personal Narratives.* Bloomington: Indiana University Press.

Plummer, K. 1995. *Telling Sexual Stories: Power, Change and Social Worlds.* New York: Routledge.

Poland, B. 1995. "Transcription Quality as an Aspect of Rigor in Qualitative Research." *Qualitative Inquiry* 1:290-310.

Polanyi, L. 1985. "Conversational Storytelling." Pp. 183-201 in *Handbook of Discourse Analysis,* Vol. 3, edited by T. A. van Dijk. London: Academic Press.

Polkinghorne, D. E. 1988. *Narrative Knowing and the Human Sciences.* Albany: State University of New York Press.

Richardson, L. 1990. *Writing Strategies: Reaching Diverse Audiences.* Newbury Park, CA: Sage.

Riessman, C. K. 1987. "When Gender Is Not Enough: Women Interviewing Women." *Gender & Society* 1:172-207.

———. 1990a. *Divorce Talk: Women and Men Make Sense of Personal Relationships.* New Brunswick, NJ: Rutgers University Press.

———. 1990b. "Strategic Uses of Narrative in the Presentation of Self and Illness." *Social Science and Medicine* 30:1195-1200.

———. 1993. *Narrative Analysis.* Newbury Park, CA: Sage.

———. 2000a. " 'Even If We Don't Have Children [We] Can Live': Stigma and Infertility in South India." In *Narrative and Cultural Construction of Illness and Healing,* edited by C. Mattingly and L. C. Garro. Berkeley: University of California Press.

———. 2000b. "Stigma and Everyday Resistance Practices: Childless Women in South India." *Gender & Society* 14:111-35.

Rosaldo, R. 1989. *Culture and Truth: The Remaking of Social Analysis.* Boston: Beacon.

Rosenwald, G. C. and R. L. Ochberg, eds. 1992. *Storied Lives: The Cultural Politics of Self-Understanding.* New Haven, CT: Yale University Press.

Sandelowski, M. 1991. "Telling Stories: Narrative Approaches in Qualitative Research." *Image: Journal of Nursing Scholarship* 23(3):161-66.

Sarbin, T. R., ed. 1986. *Narrative Psychology: The Storied Nature of Human Conduct.* New York: Praeger.

Skultans, V. 1999. "Narratives of the Body and History: Illness in Judgement on the Soviet Past." *Sociology of Health and Illness* 21:310-28.

White, H. 1987. *The Content of the Form: Narrative Discourse and Historical Representation.* Baltimore: Johns Hopkins University Press.

White, M. and D. Epston. 1990. *Narrative Means to Therapeutic Ends.* New York: Norton.

Williams, G. 1984. "The Genesis of Chronic illness: Narrative Reconstruction." *Sociology of Health and Illness* 6:175-200.

Young, K. G. 1987. *Taleworlds and Storyrealms: The Phenomenology of Narrative.* Boston: Martinus Nijhoff.

17

ANALYTIC STRATEGIES FOR ORAL HISTORY INTERVIEWS

◆ Richard Cándida Smith

Two understandings of the past confront each other across the tape recorder. In the encounter between scholar and informant, oral history interviews juxtapose the oldest and newest forms of historical method. For millennia, communities created and preserved their understanding of the past through spoken accounts passed entirely by word of mouth. No less today than in the past, people create and sustain a shared imaginative life wherever they gather and converse, be it at the kitchen table, the tavern counter, the street corner, the wedding reception, or the office lunchroom. Oral history interviews tap into a continuous outpouring of words that provide matrices defining both community and individual identity.[1] Informal collective modes of knowledge permeate the background of contemporary oral history

interviews, even though academic researchers conduct interviews primarily to collect firsthand testimony that may assist them in describing historical events or the experience of social processes. In the unusual exchange that occurs specifically for an oral history interview, collectively generated popular understandings of the past enter scholarly discourse in a verbatim record accessible for scholarly analysis.[2]

In this chapter, I explore how scholars have used narrative analysis to understand more fully the historical foundations of the personal experience documented in oral history interviews. I begin with Luisa Passerini's (1987b) now classic model of interviews as drawing upon preexisting oral cultural forms that translate historical processes into symbolically mediated experiences. In the second section, I discuss how scholars have explored tensions and con-tradictions within narrative structures as the starting points for their analyses. In conclusion, I look at efforts to rethink the ways in which memory encodes historical processes into experience and the conse-quent possibilities for oral history inter-views to augment historical understanding.

In common with other types of evi-dence, interviews contain a mix of true and false, reliable and unreliable, verifiable and unverifiable information. Details of ac-counts can often be incorrect. Interviews may contradict each other, and, occasion-ally, interviewees provide inconsistent ac-counts in different interview situations. Re-searchers need to approach oral sources with cautious skepticism. A good starting point for evaluating the veracity of oral tes-timony can be found in Paul Thompson's (1988:240-41) extrapolation to interviews of three basic principles fundamental to all historical research: (a) Assess each inter-view for internal consistency; (b) cross-check information found in interviews with as many other published, oral, and archival sources as possible; and (c) read the inter-view with as wide a historical and theoreti-cal understanding of relevant subjects as possible.[3]

Narrative analysis allows for a historical interpretation of interview-based source material that is not dependent upon the ul-timate veracity of the accounts provided. Even if only tacitly expressed, explanatory assumptions affect every aspect of an inter-view, from the organization of the story line or the plot to the presentation of personali-ties and events, to patterns of factual errors, omissions, and contradictions. The stories that interviewees share provide insight into the narrative and symbolic frameworks they use to explain why things turned out as they did. The first step in using interviews to reconstruct links among personal experi-ence, collective memory, and broad histori-cal processes is to address the role of story-telling in popular consciousness.

◆ Popular Memory and Oral Narratives: The Translation of History into Experience

In approaching interviews, whether un-earthed in the course of archival research or taped specifically for one's own project, making them speak intelligibly can initially prove a frustrating challenge. Confronting the transcripts of the 67 interviews that constituted the core set of sources for the study reported in her book *Fascism in Pop-ular Memory*, Luisa Passerini (1987b: 10-16) at first felt that there was an impassable gulf separating popular expression from scientific historical understanding. The in-terviews were full of anecdotes, irrelevan-cies, inaccuracies, contradictions, silences, and self-censorship, as well as out-and-out lies. The interviews contained plenty of col-orful material, but the scattered recollec-tions offered few immediately clear insights into the period or the effects of the fascist dictatorship on the lives of working-class Italians.

Passerini addressed her problem of mak-ing her interviews speak historically by do-ing some reading in anthropology and folk-lore. The perspectives she acquired helped her to think about how people use language to synthesize their experience into memo-rable images that make for interesting, of-ten dramatic conversation. She looked for recurrent motifs in her interviews, many of which had documentable roots in Italian peasant folktales and folk songs. Everyday storytelling conventions might in them-selves be historical evidence of past social relations.

Although the interviews were ostensibly firsthand testimony, personal experience dissolved into deeply rooted oral cultural forms that provided a ready set of stereo-types for structuring memories and filling them with meaning (see Narayan and George, Chapter 22, this volume). The interviews, Passerini concluded, provided evidence of how communities had talked about the past and arrived at collective conclusions as to what had happened to them all. With these insights, Passerini advanced a sophisticated reconstruction of recurrent patterns within her subjects' representations. Different interviewees used the same narrative structures to recount the stories of their lives, an understanding that syntagmatic analysis could decode. The same metaphors occurred across interviews, used to emphasize conclusions about the meanings of past events. The personalities narrators ascribed to themselves and to others involved stereotyped character traits. Through analysis of these and other paradigmatic elements, Passerini (1987b:1-4, 8-11, 51-52) focused on narrative forms present in all interviews and used to express judgments and relationships (see also Passerini 1988; Portelli 1991:1-26).

Passerini no longer viewed interviews as products of narrators' immediate, personal memories. They provided no privileged access to actual historical experiences. Without external supporting evidence, one could never be certain that even deeply emotional accounts were factual firsthand reports of events the interviewee had undergone. Narrators often borrowed available mythic forms to articulate emotional truths they had formed about their pasts. For all intents and purposes, the past disappeared into a narrative structure of plot turns and symbolic motifs that embedded speakers in a particular discursive community.

THE RECORD OF
A CULTURAL FORM

The cornerstone of Passerini's (1987b) textual analysis is her definition of the oral history interview as the record of a cultural form. "When someone is asked for his life-story," she writes, "his memory draws on pre-existing storylines and ways of telling stories" (p. 8). Thus *memory,* as the term is used in the title of her book, is not a psychological category but the "transmission and elaboration of stories handed down and kept alive through small-scale social networks—stories which can be adapted every so often in a variety of social interactions, including the interview" (p. 19). Three critical elements follow from this definition:

1. Interviews are windows into collective thought processes; incidents and characters, even if presented in an individualized performative style, are conventionalized and shaped by a long history of responses to previous tellings.

2. Interviews draw upon a repertoire of oral-narrative sources that affect interviewees' selection of form and imagery; these sources include conversational storytelling, jokes, church sermons, political speeches, and testimonies given at Bible study groups and political party training schools.

3. Silences and other ruptures point to aspects of experience not fully mediated by group interpretation of past events.

The ideas, images, and linguistic strategies found in oral narratives constitute what Passerini (1987b) calls the "symbolic order of everyday life" (p. 67). What she means by this concept might be illustrated by an anecdote a woman factory worker recounted to Passerini about defending, in the years after World War II, her right to wear red overalls:

[The management] asked me, "And is it because you like red or is it because you are a Communist?" I replied: "Because I like red, because I'm a Communist, because I wear what colour I like, and because G. doesn't give me overalls and I don't want to spend money on his account. Why haven't I the right to wear what colour I like?"

To which Passerini (1987b) comments, "The girl's reply summarises rather better than we could the multiplicity of meanings that a red outfit could assume in the daily struggle and balance of forces in the factory" (p. 106).

READING FOR SYMBOLIC ORDER

Passerini argues that reading for the symbolic order of her interviews illuminates an otherwise invisible subjective experience of the fascist period. Her aim is a broader interpretation of subjectivity as a historical rather than a natural phenomenon. She demonstrates the conventionalized nature of narratives by comparing written and oral self-representations of workers. When picking up pen to write about their lives, working-class authors typically adopt the literary conventions of the classic novel. They focus their narratives on a process of education and growth, a movement that dramatizes the hero's increasing competence in handling life's challenges. Passerini's narrators, on the other hand, showed no growth but tended toward stereotypical, timeless, "fixed" identities that closely corresponded to age, gender, and skill levels. Women, for example, particularly those born before 1900, often presented themselves as "born rebels." Men, however, described themselves as capable workers with "instinctive" or "natural" know-how, a convention that preserved traditional patriarchal and artisanal virtues when such roles no longer had any direct relationship to actual working conditions.

Such stereotypes are neither self-deceptions nor reductive but ultimately valid representations of reality. Passerini (1987b) observes that many (although not all) women who characterized themselves as "born rebels" exhibited socially and politically conservative attitudes in their testimonies. The "rebel" self-appellation, she concludes, was part of a complex reaction to the radical changes industrialization brought to women's social roles:

> The stereotypical notion of "having the devil in her" justifies and explains certain innovative choices made in moments of crisis—the decision to marry without her father's permission, the wish to work in the factory even after the birth of her son, the call for a different division of labor in the house. (P. 28)

The "rebel woman" image, deriving from Italian folklore traditions about women's supposed propensity for sweeping away conventions, is what Passerini calls a "survival." Urban working-class women reworked the tradition and changed its content to fit the emotionally ambiguous and unsettling circumstances of their lives. The power of the image derived precisely from its not being "true." The symbol helped women narrate to each other their confusions over female identity in a changing society. Modern Italy remained oppressive of women but nonetheless demanded that they abandon stable relationships promising, even if not always delivering, reciprocal responsibilities within family relationships. A self-proclaimed character trait mitigated compulsory social transformations through an assumption of responsibility that, because it was inborn rather than acquired, evaded questions of choice and decision. The symbol allowed for the transmission of an awareness of oppression and a sense of otherness from the social order within which working-class women lived. It helped them develop an openness to change, which they nonetheless often resented, as they forged new lifeways for themselves. Self-representation necessarily involves an individual's acquiescence to the role his or her character plays in supporting group interpretations of historical events and processes (Passerini 1987b:27-28).

Stereotypical self-representations typically lend themselves more readily to humorous accounts than to tragic accounts of the past. Retelling anecdotes about individuals' lives is a form of entertainment in which the community can identify and interpret factors shaping life patterns. There is room for both tears and laughter, but humor is more likely to succeed in providing a satisfactory resolution to the tensions crystallized in an anecdote. In a collective storytelling situation, response shapes the way an individual comes to tell an oft-repeated story, causing him or her to drop those elements that elicit indifference or antagonism and sharpen those that promote good company.

Passerini recorded several brutal accounts of fascist terror, but her subjects spoke of life under fascism much more frequently with humor, laughter, and even joviality. The absurd posturing and venality of the regime loomed larger in their collective memory than its viciousness. Were the interviews evidence of a more benign image of fascism than that presented by other sources? Hardly. Behind the laughter, Passerini uncovered a complex of social and psychological forces that etched a darker picture.

Passerini notes that the humor in her interviews conducted in the 1970s, as well as that found in police documents from the 1930s, most frequently took the form of self-ridicule. One could interpret this recurrent feature as a marker of shame and guilt, as even an uneasy admission of complicity when daily life required some form of cooperation with the rulers of the nation. Passerini (1987b:125) observes, however, that although any form of antifascist statement was dangerous, police authorities were more likely to be lenient if a violator of public order appeared to be a drunk, playing the fool and making statements in jest. Police records show that verbal antifascism evaded judicial proceedings if it

took the form of regression to childhood language and humor.

In analyzing working-class humor, Passerini did not look for hidden political meanings. She understood humor as at once a symptom of the regimentation of life under fascism and a sign of resistance to it. In the fascist period, popular culture was a substitute for politics. A sense of self distinct from that of the oppressor could be expressed through jokes and laughter instead of through political action. When the world situation changed and the Allied invasion precipitated the collapse of Mussolini's government, laughter could suddenly turn into actual resistance, fueling an armed political warfare that previously would have been futile. The hidden side of humor suddenly became visible. Laughter and self-ridicule had all along been weapons of struggle, preserving identity against a hated regime intent on eradicating the rights of individuals to have personal opinions, to reflect on their lives, or to make judgments of any kind about the state of the nation. Humor helped express working-class self-identity, as well as a sense of pride in having endured and survived to have the last laugh.

Passerini's observations on Italian women's resistance of fascist demographic policy illustrate her use of oral sources to reveal the intersection of historical processes and personal experience in the generation of new possibilities for self-understanding. The natalist policies of the fascist regime subjected women to constant propaganda praising large families as a sign of femininity. Mothers were offered significant material inducements to bear additional children. Passerini's (1987b:155) interviews reveal that this propaganda had some continuing subjective effect: Even antifascist women praised themselves as being "fertile" and dismissed their enemies as "barren."[4] Nonetheless, birthrates continued to decline, and the number of illegal abortions, the most widespread form of birth control, continued to rise among the working classes. One-third of the women interviewed acknowledged having had abortions in those years, and Passerini assumed that other women interviewed for the project must also have had abortions but did not want to discuss this aspect of their past.

How had these women learned about birth control, given that they lived in a culture in which the practice was universally condemned? Passerini could not find evidence of underground traditions passed from mother to daughter, nor did she find evidence of working-class women's having access to or knowledge of middle-class birth control methods. Knowledge about abortion apparently spread clandestinely through social networks contained within the community and the age group most concerned about pregnancy. The choice to have an abortion was difficult and involved a radical break with community traditions. All dominant ideological institutions—the Fascist and Communist Parties and the Catholic Church—equally condemned abortion. A woman arrested for ending a pregnancy faced heavy legal penalties, with little likelihood of sympathy or support from anyone. Even 40 years later, the subject remained painful for the women who elected to share this part of their experience, although they defended their choice as an effort to make their lives better than those of their mothers or grandmothers. Passerini (1987b) concludes that, to some degree, their understanding of past behavior was influenced by feminist ideas of the 1970s retrospectively projected onto their actions in the 1930s. Still, she argues, "the fact that the meaning of actions is perceived with the wisdom of hindsight, when they had not been so clear and conscious for our subjects in the past, does not diminish the importance of their intuition in the present" (p. 181).

This aspect of Passerini's analysis suggests a model for understanding the subjective ground of ideological change. The women had recognized a need so strong that they ignored both universal ideological condemnation and heavy legal penalties.

This new behavior, conflicting with preexisting community values, made the women particularly receptive to new ideas, new values, and new ideologies that might justify what self-interest had said was necessity. A tentative process of ideological shift had begun documented by a retrospective effort to justify past transgressions that subsequently could be more broadly recognized as heroic.

LINKING PERSONAL AND HISTORICAL TIME

The conceptual tools Passerini chose are particularly suitable for reading contradictions in interview texts. Silences, self-censorship, lies and exaggerations, an overabundance of insignificant episodes told in minutest detail, the reworking of the past in terms that serve present-day interests—these offer rich sources for historical insight because such narrative blemishes indicate areas of conflict: The individual and the group could not arrive at a satisfying way of narrating painful or contentious events. Symbolic turns within a text link personal and historical time. All oral history interviews, Passerini (1987a) has written, involve

> decision-making about the relationship between the self and history, be it individual history or general.... The problem is [to determine] what forms the idea of historical time takes at different levels of abstraction and in various philosophical or daily conceptions; and in what ways the idea of historical time is connected with historical narration and self-representation. (P. 412)

Two different but subjectively undifferentiated conceptions of time alternate in interviews. These modes of temporal experience are markedly more complex than the common observation that interviews involve a retrospective reworking of past experience into terms meaningful for the

present. Interviews include a linear conception of change, and interviewees feel obligated to explain differences between the
present and the past. Spiraling around efforts to understand change by narrating its
causes and effects, however, is a condition
of atemporality, in which a "fixed" identity
locates the speaker in an eternal present.
Passerini (1987a:420) argues that this combination reflects a desire to see change in
the surrounding world but not in oneself,
because recognition of personal temporality involves acceptance of death. The idea
of personal time is inseparable from an idea
of a tragic fate. A fixed identity is a narrative strategy, an imaginative leap that allows a speaker to talk about historical
change and still repress confrontation with
mortality.

Symbols fuse judgment of historical
events with retreats into the imaginary.
Analysis of the "symbolic order of everyday
life" found in interviews allows historians
to separate these two aspects of consciousness. Symbolization is the process that mediates the ongoing, continuous dislocation
of the self between the real and the imaginary. Symbols through such mediation constitute subjective experience as both encounter and evasion of history. Reflection
on individual historical experience takes on
the forms of literary expression: Through
metaphor and other verbal juxtapositions,
interviews create their experience as symbolic expressions. In a particularly elo-
quent account, a woman told Passerini how
the fascists administered castor oil to political opponents to humiliate them in front of
their neighbors. She linked a number of distinct anecdotes about fascist terror by leap-
ing from feces to menstrual blood to the
blood of victims of politically motivated
beatings. The connections between the episodes emerged in the narrator's metonymic
stringing together of images linked by the
transformation of bodily discharges. Feces,
menstrual blood, and blood from beatings
became symbols for each other, and the
ensemble illuminated for Passerini a past
emotion that continued to live through a

linguistic, aesthetic device. Tracing the
shifts among these three symbols, she argues that shame, vulnerability, and rage still
defined her interviewee's subjective experience of the fascist years. Metaphorical
leaps are seldom arbitrary, even when
clumsy, misguided, or fabulous. Narrative
figures refer the listener (and subsequently
the analyst) to an aspect of the speaker's
mental representations that most clearly
express her understanding of historical reality. Displaced meaning allows speakers to
redescribe—in other words, reinterpret—
experiences in ways that are more emotionally satisfying to them than usages that are
more literal would allow.[5]

By focusing on oral narratives as cultural
objects, Passerini shows that what one
might dismiss as malapropism can be a key
to reading oral texts. However, if meta-
phoric figures used by interviewees are
never arbitrary, critical readings can easily
be. Passerini locates the solution to this
problem in the simple but fundamental observation that the structures of oral narratives arise to communicate ideas and
feelings within a group. The narrative traditions of that group necessarily limit interpretations of figurative representations to
what members of that group would likely
find intelligible. Individuals push the boundary of sense at the risk of becoming incom-
prehensible. The guarantee that narrative
structure must contribute to sense combines with the performative opportunities
in every speech situation to generate a field
of regularities and innovations vital to
understanding the play of ideas within
popular memory. Every interview contains
within it a guide to the plotlines and symbolic structures of the interviewee's most
important communities, as well as evidence
of the social tensions narratives express and
often displace. Passerini applied ethnographic and folkloric study of Italian working-class and peasant cultures along with
psychological theory to decode the historically specific meaning of symbol systems used to narrate the experience of
fascism. Underlying her method was a

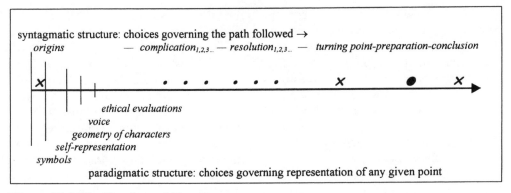

Figure 17.1. The Two Axes of Narratives

semiotic approach to language acts such as storytelling. Many scholars working with life history and oral history sources have found that before they can interpret the symbolic orders converting historical events into personal experience, they first need to analyze the narrative structures interviewees use to convey that experience.

◆ Syntagmatic and Paradigmatic Analysis: The Organization of Plot and Symbol

Contemporary thought on narrative is structured by two contradictory ideas: Language is a set of rules that impose categories of knowledge upon speakers, but all performative acts are unique expressions that push against boundaries established by genre, content, or form of expression. Researchers undertaking analysis of the linguistic aspects of interviews begin by identifying regular verbal and narrative patterns, knowing that performance will never be precisely regular. This distinction parallels the relation of speech to language in the semiotic theories of Ferdinand de Saussure, who held that languages are best understood not as they are actually spoken but as ideal forms comprising regular value distinctions combined in predictable sets.

These recurrent codings render historical forces into narrative symbols and meaningful explanatory narratives (Culler 1986; Gadet 1989; Harris 1988; Holland 1992).

Narratives have two axes. In Figure 17.1, syntagmatic structure appears as a horizontal arrow that represents the emplotted, temporal dimension of narration: how a story begins and what problem is posed, what complications mark change in the development of the problem, what the turning point is that makes the conclusion inevitable, how the story concludes, with what kind of resolution. Paradigmatic analysis focuses on recurrent images that can appear at any point in the story. It describes and explains symbolic vocabulary and the ways in which associational registers express both judgments and affective responses.

Both syntagmatic analysis and paradigmatic analysis look for coded regularities. Because these understandings expressed through regularities in the interview arise in communicative acts, repetition of storytelling motifs across interviews with different informants provides evidence of a shared construction of the past. Whether marked by individual variations or presented in a stereotyped form, narrative and symbolic structures tend to reappear in different interviews conducted in the same community. Recurrent images found in more than one interview reveal a storytelling language that provides a finite set of preferred expressive forms for the recollection of experience. Analysis of regularities across interviews can help define the boundaries of discursively defined communities—that is, of groups of people who may or may not know each other personally, but who are connected through shared languages (Joutard 1981; Joyner 1979; McMahan 1989:89-90; Tonkin 1992:97-112).

SYNTAGMATIC ANALYSIS

Syntagmatic analysis focuses on strategies of emplotment. Any story, whether a firsthand account of a specific event, a humorous anecdote, or a life history recounted across several sessions, must have a starting point, markers of transition, a turning point, and a conclusion. Emplotment involves the selection and highlighting of some events as most important. Other aspects may simply be dropped from the account altogether for the sake of narrative efficiency. Narrative form may also require the hypothetical construction of past events that may or may not have occurred but that the logic of the plotline demands. The conclusion determines that logic. Narratives are teleological, meaning that every story element flows from an effort to make the ending appear necessary and intelligible. Choices of significant details reveal "causes" that explain the inevitability of the conclusion. One may like the outcome or not, but narration enacts a process of coming to terms with the state of affairs that the narrator assumes characterize the conclusion.

One can find a clear example of syntagmatic analysis in Elliot G. Mishler's (1992) use of interviews to study career paths. Mishler categorizes an anecdote as articulating an "on-line" choice when the episode led to the narrator's taking another step toward his ultimate career goal. Even events that occur before the "turning point," the account in the story in which the narrator becomes aware of his goal,

take their meaning from the conclusion. Complications and resolutions account for an accretion of factors that ultimately made the final status of the narrator inevitable. Mishler categorizes anecdotes about events that took the narrator away from his goal as "off-line" choices. The alternation of on-line and off-line choices develops dramatic tension. Adjusting the tempo of alternation heightens or diminishes the tension by increasing or decreasing the feeling that a detour could have affected the ultimate outcome. Dramatic tension is a narrative effect, as the outcome, even if unknown to the audience, is pregiven. The sequence presents the factors that had to be addressed and the obstacles that had to be overcome for the outcome to occur. Interviews can be broken down into discrete sections, each of which is defined by its relation to the plot. Off-line choices present complications, whereas on-line choices present resolutions that allow the story to continue. The presentation of each episode underscores the "logic" of the outcome. Mishler's approach allows for analytic abstraction to replace a sequence of anecdotes with a structure of episodes, each articulating an important step in the movement to achieved identity (pp. 2-25, 28-33).

In Mishler's case study of a furniture craftsman, the outcome is satisfactory, and the story affirms the ability of the narrator to overcome his own confusions by taking a dramatic leap into a new line of work (see Table 17.1). Mishler identifies "intuition" as the causal factor the narrator uses to explain his ultimate ability to overcome a previous personal history determined more by chance events than by active decision making (see episode 7 in Table 17.1, the turning point). "Intuition" does not appear as a direct explanation in every episode, but each episode is presented in a way that supports the explanatory framework the interviewee has developed to explain his personal history. To understand a narrative is to have command of the rules governing the selection and ordering of events into a plot. The events that serve as plotting points are

Table 17.1   ACHIEVING A CRAFT IDENTITY: THE NARRATIVE OF AN ARTIST-FURNITURE MAKER

Narrative Episode	Identity Narrative: Interview Excerpts
1. Origins	"My beginnings were in—uh I did a little bit of woodworking when I was a kid, mostly with wooden boats."
2. Complication1	"I'm one of those people really vague about what I wanted to do. I—I entered— I got accepted to college as a chemical engineer, because I was interested in plastics at the time."
3. Resolution1	"I decided I wanted to do something else. . . . I started in an undergraduate program as an architect."
4. Complication2	"And ah after school I had a job for a while with a firm. ah The firm . . . collapsed. Folded. And uh I met an architect, and he and I decided to design some geodesic domes, and do that kind of thing."
5. Resolution2	"And I met a third-generation craftsman in Indiana, who uh allowed me to share his shop space with—And ah that's when I really started to do woodworking. . . . But he just knew so much technically, and I learned an awful lot."
6. Complication3	"I felt like I was wasting all my—my ah schooling as a landscape architect. So [we] moved [and] I started working as a landscape architect. And I did that for five and a half years."
7. Turning point	"And ah it just wasn't what I wanted to do for the rest of my life. . . . So I did a search, and uh decided to go to graduate school in furniture. . . . I made the—ah the decision to ah, go into furniture. Just in that I had an intuitive sense about woodworking, which I didn't about landscape architecture."

symbols in that they merge description with ethical evaluation. The evaluation appears to be the result of examining consequences, but it flows from the principles that narrators assume can and do provide explanation of the concluding point.

This distinctly conservative aspect of narration reconciles narrators (and their communities) to the patterns of change they have experienced. At times, however, the conclusion can be unbearable. Utopian aspiration refuses reconciliation and prompts a reconstruction of memory

so that possibilities for change are accentuated. In his essays "The Death of Luigi Trastulli: Memory and the Event" and "Uchronic Dreams: Working-Class Memory and Possible Worlds," Alessandro Portelli (1991:1-26, 99-116) analyzes patterns of narrative reconfiguration he found in interviews with working-class residents of Terni, Italy. Their reconstructions of the past were factually wrong. Their accounts merged or scrambled events and at times referred to events that never occurred. In effect, their collective stories had created an alternative chronology that allowed them to maintain their own historical experience.

Portelli argues that chronological inaccuracy in the narrative helped the community maintain a sense of continuing to have a future and retaining the possibility of political resurgence during a time of retreat. Notwithstanding modernization of economic structures, the growth of educational opportunities, and a growing differentiation occurring as a result of individuals' differing personal responses to a changing society, the community maintained its political cohesion. Portelli's analysis suggests that the community's ability to maintain identity rested on a utopian, historically inaccurate, but culturally effective myth of the past. The narratives kept alive an alternative future that preserved for several decades the possibility of independent, worker-based action, even if, for the most part, members of the community were actively participating in the reconstruction of Italian society around international markets.

Disjunction between discursive and pragmatic behavior may be quite widespread and could provide insight into discrepancies in the political, economic, social, and cultural actions of social groups. The disjunction between subjective and objective factors in social relationships is an area for which oral history documents provide ideal sources of evidence. Paul Ricoeur's (1983:52-87) model of threefold mimesis may help researchers to see how individual textual configurations (mimesis$_2$) found in oral history interviews intersect with collective processes of prefiguration (mimesis$_1$) and refiguration (mimesis$_3$). *Prefiguration* refers to the metaphorical transpositions that are normally available and allowed in a community, which for these purposes we can define as a group built around regularly shared communicative acts. *Refiguration* refers to the process of reconstruction of texts into experiences of meaning. In simplified terms, prefigured time (ideology) becomes

refigured time (experience) through the mediation of configured time (narrative accounts).

Prefiguration sets limits as to what will be a refigurable text—that is, one that potential audiences will accept as meaningful. Nonetheless, prefigurative conventions do not predetermine the shape of any configured text. Texts are propositions that members of a community put forward to each other. Texts must convince others that the narration accounts for what a group accepts as fact. Texts prove their aptness as explanations by providing satisfying understandings of the present and by identifying key events that others will accept as suitable evidence for the conclusion proffered (Ricoeur 1973).

As individual performances of collective prefigurations circulate with varying degrees of success, ideology becomes a fluid part of individual lives and social relations. Accepted narratives create a temporal world within which people have "experiences" that they can continue to share; that is, they have a sense of actions that remain meaningful and related logically to conclusions understood as "necessary" or, less strongly, "probable." Action may not necessarily be dependent upon narrative explanations available to a group, but stories that people exchange and accept as satisfying help establish a sense of proper, effective action, which can then be configured into new narratives. The truth of narratives rests on their ability to instigate and sustain new action. One of the values of examining how oral history interviews emplot explanatory frameworks is the degree to which they can point researchers to preferred actions as well as to likely blockages, clues that will assist with the identification and reading of other sources.

PARADIGMATIC ANALYSIS

Paradigmatic analysis complements the study of emplotment by examining recurrent symbols and other expressive motifs that are the basic constructive units of narrative flow. Oral accounts in particular tend to synthesize complex series of events into readily comprehensible and expressible images. Symbols take their place within stories as instantiations of narrative logic (Allen 1982; Ashplant 1998; McMahan 1989:100-105; Tonkin 1992:126-30). For example, in my work on interviews recorded with painters in California (Cándida Smith 1989, 1995), I found that the special quality of light and climate in the state was a recurrent symbolic motif. Interviewees used the image to articulate a special condition that shaped their work and set them apart from painters in other parts of the world. The motif appeared to the interviewees as an indubitable natural fact that explained the particularities of painting in the region. In fact, the symbol as deployed in narratives had little to do with nature but appeared typically when interviewees wanted to encapsulate their sometimes pleasant, sometimes difficult relationship to society into a ready metaphor. In one interview recorded over several sessions, the narrator described California light as clarifying and liberatory to underscore the freedom he felt when he began painting and exhibiting. Several sessions later, he described California light as blinding and stultifying as he discussed a point when his career had reached a dead end. In either case, light was not a physical phenomenon but a symbolic displacement of professional self-representation. The value that the symbol expressed depended in both cases upon its location within a narrative plotline and the conclusion it had to reinforce (Cándida Smith 1989:3-4).

Symbols often appear in patterned relationships. Women painters in post-World War II California, for example, often found as they struggled to establish their careers that critics couched favorable reviews in highly sexualized terms. Joan Brown was "everybody's darling," according to one writer, who proceeded to describe her as a talented, energetic "receptacle of attitudes" for the "germinating" ideas of her (male) teachers. In the several oral history interviews conducted with Brown over a 30-year period, she alternated two distinctive voices as she recounted her life story. One voice used humorous hyperbole to accentuate the surreality of commerce and business and those who live within that world. This inflection drew a veil across painful elements of her life by rendering them into sharp, quick, brittle images designed to shock and get a laugh. The other voice used more expansive, philosophical language to express the wonder and excitement that a once young woman felt embarking on her career. Painting was explicitly a symbol for a journey of initiation that would ultimately result in wisdom and inner peace.

Brown never recursively marked the transition between these two voices. Her vocabulary and sentence structures changed unself-consciously as she went back and forth between the two modes of her career. She was, however, quite aware of a double self-representation that enacted her response to the sexualization of herself and her art. She used archly stereotypical sexual imagery to portray herself in interaction with the absurd world of career building. She presented herself as a compulsive liar who used dress and appearance to make fools of people she encountered. This mendacious, opportunistic character appeared in her accounts as a person who drank too much, participated in parties to excess, and let herself be carried to unspecified extremes by others. Opposed to a gendered, sexualized conception of self, another voice called within the interviews, invoking the deeper reality of an initiate who survived spiritually through recurrent journeys into the alternative worlds that painting realized for her. This self-consciously degendered self-representation gave her strength to stand her ground and make difficult practical career decisions that alienated critics, curators, and gallery owners (Cándida Smith 1995:172-89).

The recurrence of paradigmatic motifs across interviews and their structural logic suggests that they are not simply individual performative expressions. They help articulate the logic of a communication by stressing the justice of a conclusion. Self-representation is a privileged symbolic feature of oral narrations because it articulates the moral position that the speaker has taken on the turning point and its consequences. Eva M. McMahan (1989), building on the theoretical work of Livia Polanyi (1985), argues that the framing of a speaker's evaluative conclusions is particularly strong in oral narratives as they establish the relationship between speaker and listeners. McMahan (1989) states that

> the teller must constantly address the implicit evaluative response of the listener: "So what?" The teller must show that the story is both topical and meaningful—that it makes a point. Generally, the interviewee as storyteller is expected to "(a) tell a topically coherent story; (b) tell a narratable story—one worth building a prolonged telling around; (c) introduce the story so that the connection with previous talk is clear; (d) tell a story that begins at the beginning, that is, one in which time moves ahead reasonably smoothly except for flashbacks that seem to serve a justifiable purpose in the telling; and, (e) evaluate states and events so that it is possible to recover the core of the story and thereby infer the point being made through telling." (Pp. 80-82; McMahan quotes Polanyi 1985:200)

In oral accounts, bracketing sections are frequently introduced so that the narrator can comment explicitly on the ethical meaning of the story, just in case listeners do not quite intuit how to feel the symbols. The narrator may elicit responses from listeners, often by asking questions. By the end of the story, as the conclusion becomes inevitable, McMahan argues, ethical evaluation begins to merge with self-representation. How listeners respond to the story determines how they respond to the storyteller, and through the account an ethical relationship has been proposed, if not established (pp. 89-92, 93-96).

Just as emplotment can lead to a reimagination and reordering of events to strengthen the inevitability of the conclusion, paradigmatic elements may be reworked to strengthen the moral evaluation and consequently the subject position that the storyteller takes in relation to his or her listeners. Mariano Vallejo, in his testimonial collected in 1874 for Hubert Bancroft's multivolume history of California, discussed at length a meeting he claimed took place in 1846, on the eve of the American invasion of Mexico. Subsequent historians have largely dismissed Vallejo's account as legendary and in the process missed the vital political content his possible fabulation conveys. As war loomed, Californio leaders convened to discuss their options. Nominally, they were citizens of Mexico, but since a local revolution in 1836, California had been for all practical purposes autonomous of the central government. Vallejo's story condensed a series of debates that occurred within Californio society over many years into the arguments of one evening. As Rosaura Sánchez (1995) has analyzed the anecdote, the participants in the debate represented four positions. Spokesmen for a liberal, federalist, republican future opposed those who were promonarchist. Liberals were evenly divided between those who favored immediate independence and those, like Vallejo, who sought annexation to the United States. The monarchists were divided between those who wanted British annexation and those who sought French intervention. The characters presented in the anecdote articulate a geometry of political positions. Whether or not the meeting actually occurred, the characters were paradigmatic inventions that allowed the speaker to articulate his evaluation of the meeting and its ultimate consequences.

Throughout his account, Vallejo editorialized on the strengths and weaknesses of each position. He linked the arguments to several practical issues for Californio society, such as trade and property regimes, while he ignored other issues entirely, such as slavery and implications for relations with the indigenous peoples. Vallejo's anecdote, however symbolic, articulated in crystalline form the competing ideological positions of his people in 1846 while explaining the political strategies that he and others followed. He defended his support for annexation to the United States by articulating his understanding of the American Revolution of 1776 and its, to his mind, still-universal promises of freedom, equality, and due process of law. He structured his account largely to convince his listeners, primarily the Anglo-American readers who would encounter him either directly in the transcript of his interview or indirectly through Bancroft's history, of their hypocrisy. His overall testimonial builds around his protest of the theft of the Californios' property and their political marginalization. American expansion had in fact betrayed the hopes that Vallejo and others had felt 30 years earlier. He wanted to convince his listeners that the outcome might have been very different had the Californios adopted policies opposed to annexation by the United States. Vallejo's account, motivated by moral fervor and foregrounding political and ideological choices of his people, still provides an important corrective to accounts that present westward expansion as a story with only American actors (Sánchez 1995:245-48).

◆ Recuperating Experience Back into History

In the context of narrative analysis, the "data" of interviews are first and foremost the ways in which a person has reconstructed the past to negotiate an ever-fluid process of identity construction. The subjective position in narration differs from psychological consciousness in its exterior manifestation and the element of self-

reflective purpose. Vallejo's interview unfolds as a conscious effort to speak through his interviewers to a broad public. Although this is not uncommon, particularly in interviews with elite figures, many interviews remain within the local, intimate historical contexts that stories shared between friends help establish. In a world of close acquaintances, anecdotes convey possibly useful impressions about what individuals might expect in future encounters. The cues are couched in explanations that, however trivial in form, remove arbitrariness from the relationship. Fred will flame you at the least provocation because "he's always like that." Characterization in this case is more of a predication than an explanation, but it serves to warn those who must or might be exposed to Fred of what to expect (Cándida Smith 1995:xxi-xxvi; Clark, Hyde, and McMahan 1980; Frank 1979; Halbwachs 1993:38; Thompson 1988:150-65).

In reading emplotment and paradigm codes, scholars often must assign meanings and values to these images that they may not have had in their original context in order to make them speak to a broader historical context. Isabelle Bertaux-Wiame (1982:192-93), for example, analyzed interviews with migrants from the countryside into Paris and found recurrent patterns in the choices of pronouns used by the interviewees. Men typically used first-person singular forms to speak of themselves as actors making decisions and changing their lives and those of their families. Women, on the other hand, tended to avoid first-person singular forms and to speak more usually either with first-person plural forms or with the impersonal third-person pronoun *on* (one). This observation allowed Bertaux-Wiame to develop a rich psychological argument about gendered conceptions of power and historical action prevalent among the French working class at a particular historical conjuncture. She readily acknowledges that her categories would seem irrelevant and foreign to the narrators whose accounts stimulated her insight. Many historians might likewise question the validity of her interpretation. Gendered selection of pronouns became meaningful because Bertaux-Wiame turned to feminist theory for assistance in reading "data" that would otherwise be ignored. Interpersonal relations symbolized through the selection of pronouns would likely not register as relevant to the study of larger transpersonal social forces without a theoretical perspective that reread intimate interactions as dialectically constituted with political and economic structures.

The distinction between psychological consciousness and narrative self is foundational to the examination of regularities, whether syntagmatic or paradigmatic, within interviews. The narrative self takes shape in the unfolding stories within which it is deployed as one of several codes. Changes in self-representation do not provide evidence in and of themselves about how people "felt." Such studies trace instead how understandings of the self have grown from and altered in relation to other social and cultural phenomena *also* represented within a narrative.

Symbolic contradictions within narrative texts indicate areas of conflict about how to represent and understand the past. The storyteller and his or her group could not arrive at a satisfying way of narrating painful or contentious events, so they deflected issues into a variety of evasive symbolic strategies. Isolation of contradictory, confused, and evasive elements within a narrative has served historical analysis by highlighting areas of concern that communities have not been able to resolve narratively. Analysis presents a field of symbolic measures that in and of themselves are subject to multiple interpretations, but these areas of contention themselves reveal places for further historical contextualization and exploration. Careful analysis of the subject positions contained within these symbols in particular can elucidate a pattern of self-imagining that includes perceptions of the dangers that "others" pose (Passerini 1987a).

Conflicts between identity and subjectivity may be a recurrent paradigmatic feature in interviews. The challenge of reconciling differences between the subject position assigned a person due to his or her social classification with a more complex, varied sense of relationships may reveal itself at the paradigmatic level through such measures as Joan Brown's double self-representation. The challenge may also appear in performative tensions that undercut a narrator's ability to articulate either a clear ethical evaluation or a clear self-representation.

Feminist scholars in particular have worked with contradictions in self-representation to identify the translation of gendered power structures into historically situated experience of gender relations. Women's accounts of their lives negotiate, as Joan Brown's does with great elegance, the discrepancy between the self-image they have developed in the course of their everyday activities and the images of themselves that they receive from men. Kathryn Anderson and Dana C. Jack (1991) argue that women's oral history interviews usually have two channels working simultaneously across the episodes narrated. On the one hand, many women may tell their stories using dominant, masculinist emplotment and paradigmatic codes. They enunciate through the selection of complications, resolutions, turning point, and conclusion, as well as through the symbols used, concepts and values that affirm male supremacy, and the appropriateness of women's reduced social position. Within the performance, however, there may be a muted story that expresses painful disappointments and resentments as a set of ironies that suggest the purely fictional character of dominant values. Anderson and Jack advise that interviewers and analysts should focus on difficult choices that women have had to make in their lives, much as Passerini did when probing for information on birth control and abortion. They also advise paying careful attention to expressions of pain and subjects that address the margins of acceptable behavior, particularly feelings and behaviors that the interviewees themselves identify as "unwomanly." Stereotypes about women invoked in the interview provide the analyst with an opportunity to see efforts to reconcile derogatory images with an interviewee's positive self-images. In these areas, narrative structures will be less likely to effect a comfortable ethical evaluation that reconciles the interviewee and her listeners to the inevitability of the conclusion. Anecdotes and images that women use to address their weakness in a situation often lead to a layering of codes conveying the storyteller's intellectual and emotional conflict. In these situations, logic collapses and the storyteller abruptly tacks on a conclusion to a story that was headed in another direction. A pat ending realigns her account with dominant values in her community but does so in a way that signals an experience of tensions (see also Borland 1991; Passerini 1987b:138-49).

Catherine Kohler Riessman (1992), in her work on women's accounts of abusive marriages, has observed critical differences in how women relate stories of victimization and stories of resistance. At the beginning of the 1980s, stories about marital rape were difficult to narrate, in part because the term itself did not yet have currency. Neither laws nor social custom recognized a wife's right to refuse sexual relations with her husband. As a political movement developed to demand legal change, new narrative structures emerged that helped women transform brutal facts in their lives into communicable experience. In seeking security and the right to divorce, abused women learned to speak to each other, to counselors, and to lawmakers. A shared language allowed for crisp, articulate stories in which the pain endured was coded typically in inflections of speech patterns, such as the introduction of unusually long pauses. Stories of resistance typically became less articulate when self-defense was angry or violent. Not even the women involved were sure that their

efforts to protect themselves from further abuse were ethical. Riessman (1992) observes that the language structures surrounding abusive marriages provide "for women's depressed emotions but not for their rage" (p. 246). Consequently, narration of anger is more episodic and confused, as if the storyteller herself had to struggle to understand her emotions and actions, which are ostensibly out of character for a "good" woman. A political movement had succeeded by establishing one emplotment code, which then blocked positive reception of alternative narratives arriving at conclusions less consonant with the nobility of victimhood.

Emplotment structures as well as symbolic motifs established in one discourse are then available for use in other situations. Work on narrative plotlines, and the subject positions they entail, allows for analysis of individual narrating style. William R. Earnest (1992) has examined the relation of workplace narratives to typical patterns for the interviewee's life story. In an interview with an employee in an automobile factory, Earnest noticed a syntagmatic pattern that recurred across several sessions. A grievance about work conditions in the factory welled up with considerable bitterness, but then the issues in dispute found resolution through a pattern of "self-effacement, criticism of other workers, sympathy for management rationales, and then final absolution of management" of any responsibility for the problem (pp. 257-58). When the questioning turned to family background and personal life, Earnest heard the same syntagmatic pattern applied to the interviewee's relationship with his father. Whenever anger at paternal neglect flared up, the interviewee's story line displaced his rage into criticism of others in the family. Family stories paralleled workplace stories by concluding with the interviewee's acceptance of his father's rationales and affirmation of father-son identity. The interviewee was unconscious of this storytelling pattern. When told of it, he was surprised and doubtful, but he accepted the validity of the conclusion when shown the evidence. Confronting his experience as a narrative effect jolted him into reexamining his memories and his organization of his recollections into discrete episodes directing him to preordained conclusions. The interviewee was thrown out of experience into a historical reconsideration of how he had come to form his social relationships.

His self-reexamination began with his examination of the points in his narratives where he felt the most tension. The movement toward reevaluating the codes he used to create meaning arose, according to George Rosenwald's (1992) analysis of this case, from a conflict between identity and subjectivity that the interview process brought to the surface. Rosenwald contends that the culture-specific narrative rules ensuring intelligibility also govern identity. In opposition to the relatively stable and stabilizing patterns of self that arise as one talks in ways that are comprehensible to others, Rosenwald poses the force of subjectivity, which he defines as the "restlessness of desire" (p. 265). Recursive recognition of the rules of narration can allow normally repressed imagination of other ways of being to enter into the storytelling process.

The introduction of such self-reflection into oral history interviews is not common—at least not as a conscious aim of the interviewer and the narrator. Portelli (1997), however, in his recent work on genre in oral history, suggests that the encounter of historian and interviewee, each with such different strategies for understanding the past, must inevitably generate cognitive tension. One way interviewers have coped with this has been by effacing themselves and allowing narrators to tell their stories with a minimum of response or guidance. That strategy imposes highly artificial requirements upon dialogic exchanges. No matter how silent interviewers strive to be, they are not invisible, and the interview situation, although drawing upon narrative repertoires that interviewees have developed, has little in common with everyday conversation.

"What is spoken in a typical oral history interview has usually never been told *in that form* before," Portelli (1997:4) argues. Even if interviewees rely upon twice-told tales to answer questions posed to them, they have usually never previously strung their stories together in a single, extended account. Narrators are also aware, like Mariano Vallejo, that they speak through their interviewers to a larger audience. Portelli notes that this leap into an imagined public realm often involves a marked change in diction. Interviewees begin to speak in a formally correct style. Even more important, Portelli adds, "the novelty of the situation and the effort at diction accentuate a feature of all oral discourse—that of being a 'text' in the making, which includes its own drafts, preparatory materials, and discarded materials" (p. 5). The task that the narrator faces is new and not reducible to the rules of everyday conversation, even if words and anecdotes spring largely or exclusively from that source.

What distinguishes oral history from folklore, Portelli (1997) claims, is the move away from "storytelling," from the sharing of familiar accounts with workmates, friends, and family that help bind them together into communities. Narrators discover a genre of discourse that Portelli calls "history-telling" (p. 6). Flowing out of researchers' theoretical and analytic assumptions, interview questions challenge narrators to transform their personal anecdotes. The process provokes narrators to reflect consciously upon the larger historical and social meanings of what has happened to them as individuals.

The relationship at the heart of oral history, as Portelli describes it, is a groping toward mutual understanding that is equally taxing for both parties to the interview. Interviewers must work to understand the connections that narrators are providing as they consider additional lines of questioning that will build upon rather than cut short the dialogue. Historians' questions ask narrators to apply their experiences to frameworks that they may never have thought with before, but that they need to intuit if they are to respond with helpful and relevant information. An attempt to reconstruct memory so that it can speak to history proceeds within this dialectic, which if it breaks down leads to an interview lacking in either texture or information. Successful oral history interviews take on a special verbal quality that Portelli calls "thick dialogue," and the recorded conversation ceases to be a rehearsal of comfortable and conventional formulas and becomes a deeper probing of what happened and why.

Oral history has been part of a broader deontological trend in the social sciences. Collaboration between historian and narrator has helped generate greater understanding that personal experience has historical impact and is not simply an aftereffect of social process. The possibility of communication, and not simply translation, across quite different modes of representing the past rests in an understanding of the symbolic structures that narrators use to posit themselves as subjects who know the objects of their worlds—past, present, and future—in specific, practical, and community-based ways. A focus on the practical underpinnings of meaning systems reintegrates ethics, politics, and knowledge.

Memory and history confront each other across the tape recorder. Separately, both struggle with syntagmatic and paradigmatic codes that structure comprehension of what the present situation means. From their collaboration occasionally emerges a richer, more nuanced understanding of the past, the power of which lies in its having transcended the particular languages that engulf both participants in the interview. (On the alienation of both academic and community understandings of the past through the oral history process, see Friedlander 1975:xxiii-xxvii.) The first step in analyzing oral history interviews is to recognize that they are not raw sources of information. Oral sources are themselves already analytic documents structured with complex codes and achieved meanings. An analyst can make visible neither the limitations nor the critical capacities of those meanings without delving into the text of the interview and beginning a process of dialogue with its narrator.

■ Notes

1. Jan Vansina's *Oral Tradition: A Study in Historical Methodology* (1965) is the classic text on oral tradition. On the relationship between oral tradition and oral history, see Elizabeth Tonkin (1992) and Isabel Hofmeyr (1992). On the selectivity of sources and the relation of oral traditions to documentary archives, see Michel-Rolph Trouillot (1995).

2. A large literature has developed on the social construction of memory. The classic sociological texts were written by Maurice Halbwachs prior to World War II. Lewis Coser has edited a selection of Halbwachs's work in a volume titled *On Collective Memory* (1993). See also the work of Alan Confino (1997), Susan Crane (1997), Noa Gedi and Yigal Elam (1996), Patrick H. Hutton (1993, 1997), Andreas Huyssens (1995), Iwona Irwin-Zarecki (1994), Jacques Le Goff (1992), Allan Megill (1989), Pierre Nora (1989), Jeffrey K. Olick and Joyce Robbins (1998), Michael Roth (1995), Michael Schudson (1995), David Thelen (1989), Frances Yates (1966), and James Young (1993).

3. For recent discussions of rules of evidence and verifiability in historical investigation after the narrative turn, see Joyce Appleby, Lynn Hunt, and Margaret Jacob (1994), Susan Stafford Friedman (1995), Lynn Hunt (1996), David Lowenthal (1989), Allan Megill (1998), and Peter Novick (1988). For classic discussions of the historical method, see Raymond Aron (1961), Lee Benson and Cushing Strout (1965), Marc Bloch (1953), Fernand Braudel (1980), R. G. Collingwood (1946), William Dray (1957), Louis Mink (1965, 1970), and Paul Veyne (1984).

4. Fascist demographic propaganda drew upon preexisting ideas and cultural expressions, which may explain to a degree the hold such

ideas had on women, even those who did not act in conformity with older ideals of femininity.

5. For the classic account of displacement through narrative figures, see Aristotle's *Poetics*

(1982:secs. 1451b5-6, 1458a18-23, 1457b6). See also Roland Barthes (1982), Seymour Chatman (1975), Leon Golden (1962), and Paul Ricoeur (1977).

■ *References*

Allen, B. 1982. "Recreating the Past: The Narrator's Perspective in Oral History." *Oral History Review* 10:33-45.

Anderson, K. and D. C. Jack. 1991. "Learning to Listen: Interview Techniques and Analyses." Pp. 11-26 in *Women's Words: The Feminist Practice of Oral History,* edited by S. B. Gluck and D. Patai. New York: Routledge.

Appleby, J., L. Hunt, and M. Jacob. 1994. *Telling the Truth about History.* New York: Norton.

Aristotle. 1982. *Poetics.* New York: Norton.

Aron, R. 1961. *Introduction to the Philosophy of History: An Essay on the Limits of Historical Objectivity.* Boston: Beacon.

Ashplant, T. 1998. "Anecdote as Narrative Resource in Working-Class Life Stories." Pp. 99-113 in *Narrative and Genre,* edited by M. Chamberlain and P. Thompson. London: Routledge.

Barthes, R. 1982. "Introduction to the Structural Analysis of Narrative." Pp. 251-95 in R. Barthes, *A Roland Barthes Reader.* New York: Hill & Wang.

Benson, L. and C. Strout. 1965. "Causation and the American Civil War: Two Appraisals." Pp. 74-96 in *Studies in the Philosophy of History: Selected Essays from History and Theory,* edited by G. H. Nadel. New York: Harper Torchbooks.

Bertaux-Wiame, I. 1982. "The Life History Approach to the Study of Internal Migration." Pp. 186-200 in *Our Common History: The Transformation of Europe,* edited by P. Thompson. London: Pluto.

Bloch, M. 1953. *The Historian's Craft.* New York: Alfred A. Knopf.

Borland, K. 1991. " 'That's Not What I Said': Interpretive Conflict in Oral Narrative Research." Pp. 63-76 in *Women's Words: The Feminist Practice of Oral History,* edited by S. B. Gluck and D. Patai. New York: Routledge.

Braudel, F. 1980. *On History.* Chicago: University of Chicago Press.

Cándida Smith, R. 1989. "Exquisite Corpse: The Sense of the Past in Oral Histories with California Artists." *Oral History Review* 17:1-34.

———. 1995. *Utopia and Dissent: Art, Poetry, and Politics in California.* Berkeley: University of California Press.

Chatman, S. 1975. "The Structure of Narrative Transmission." Pp. 213-57 in *Style and Structure in Literature: Essays in the New Stylistics,* edited by R. Fowler. Ithaca, NY: Cornell University Press.

Clark, E. C., M. J. Hyde, and E. M. McMahan. 1980. "Communicating in the Oral History Interview: Investigating Problems of Interpreting Oral Data." *International Journal of Oral History* 1:28-40.

Collingwood, R. G. 1946. *The Idea of History.* Oxford: Oxford University Press.

Confino, A. 1997. "Collective Memory and Cultural History: Problems of Method." *American Historical Review* 102:1386-1403.

Crane, S. 1997. "Writing the Individual Back into Collective Memory." *American Historical Review* 102:1372-85.

Culler, J. D. 1986. *Ferdinand de Saussure.* Ithaca, NY: Cornell University Press.

Dray, W. 1957. *Laws and Explanations in History.* London: Oxford University Press.

Earnest, W. R. 1992. "Ideology Criticism and Life-History Research." Pp. 250-64 in *Storied Lives: The Cultural Politics of Self-Understanding,* edited by G. C. Rosenwald and R. L. Ochberg. New Haven, CT: Yale University Press.

Frank, G. 1979. "Finding a Common Denominator: A Phenomenological Critique of Life History Method." *Ethnos* 7:68-94.

Friedlander, P. 1975. *The Emergence of a UAW Local, 1936-1939: A Study in Class and Culture.* Pittsburgh, PA: University of Pittsburgh Press.

Friedman, S. S. 1995. "Making History: Reflections on Feminism, Narrative, and Desire." Pp. 11-54 in *Feminism beside Itself,* edited by D. Elam and R. Wiegman. New York: Routledge.

Gadet, F. 1989. *Saussure and Contemporary Culture.* London: Hutchison Radius.

Gedi, N. and Y. Elam. 1996. "Collective Memory: What Is It?" *History and Memory* 8:30-50.

Golden, L. 1962. "Catharsis." *Proceedings of the American Philological Association* 43:51-60.

Halbwachs, M. 1993. *On Collective Memory,* edited by L. Coser. Albany: State University of New York Press.

Harris, R. 1988. *Language, Saussure, and Wittgenstein: How to Play Games with Words.* London: Routledge.

Hofmeyr, I. 1992. " 'Nterata'/'The Wire': Fences, Boundaries, Orality, Literacy." Pp. 69-92 in *International Annual of Oral History, 1990: Subjectivity and Multiculturalism in Oral History,* edited by R. J. Grele. New York: Greenwood.

Holland, N. N. 1992. *The Critical I.* New York: Columbia University Press.

Hunt, L. 1999. "Psychoanalysis, the Self, and Historical Interpretation," presented at the symposium "History and the Limits of Interpretation," March 15-17, Rice University, Houston. Available Internet: http://www.ruf.rice.edu/~culture/papers/hunt.html

Hutton, P. H. 1993. *History as an Art of Memory.* Hanover, NH: University Press of New England.

———. 1997. "Mnemonic Schemes in the New History of Memory." *History and Theory* 36:378-91.

Huyssens, A. 1995. *Twilight Memories: Marking Time in a Culture of Amnesia.* New York:

Irwin-Zarecki, I. 1994. *Frames of Remembrance: The Dynamics of Collective Memory.* New Brunswick, NJ: Rutgers University Press.

Joutard, P. 1981. "A Regional Project: Ethnotexts." *Oral History* 9:47-51.

Joyner, C. W. 1979. "Oral History as Communicative Event: A Folkloristic Perspective." *Oral History Review* 7:47-52.

Le Goff, J. 1992. *History and Memory.* New York: Columbia University Press.

Lowenthal, D. 1989. "The Timeless Past: Some Anglo-American Historical Preconceptions." *Journal of American History* 75:1263-80.

McMahan, E. M. 1989. *Elite Oral History Discourse: A Study of Cooperation and Coherence.* Tuscaloosa: University of Alabama Press.

Megill, A. 1989. "Recounting the Past: 'Description,' Explanation, and Narrative in Historiography." *American Historical Review* 94:627-53.

———. 1998. "History, Memory, and Identity." *History and the Human Sciences* 11:37-62.

Mink, L. 1965. "The Autonomy of Historical Understanding." *History and Theory* 5:24-47.

———. 1970. "History and Fiction as Modes of Comprehension." *New Literary History* 1:556-69.

Mishler, E. G. 1992. "Work, Identity, and Narrative: An Artist-Craftsman's Story." Pp. 21-40 in *Storied Lives: The Cultural Politics of Self-Understanding,* edited by G. C. Rosenwald and R. L. Ochberg. New Haven, CT: Yale University Press.

Nora, P. 1989. "Between Memory and History: *Les Lieux de mémoire.*" *Representations* 26:7-25.

Novick, P. 1988. *That Noble Dream: The "Objectivity Question" and the American Historical Profession.* Cambridge: Cambridge University Press.

Olick, J. K. and J. Robbins. 1998. "Social Memory Studies: From 'Collective Memory' to the Historical Sociology of Mnemonic Practices." *Annual Review of Sociology* 22:105-40.

Passerini, L. 1987a. "Documento autobiografico e tempo storico." *Rivista di Storia Contemporanea* 16:412-20.

———. 1987b. *Fascism in Popular Memory: The Cultural Experience of the Turin Working Class.* Cambridge: Cambridge University Press.

———. 1988. "Conoscenza storica e fonti orali." Pp. 31-66 in L. Passerini, *Storia e soggetività: Le fonti orali, la memoria.* Florence: La Nuova Italia.

Polanyi, L. 1985. "Conversational Storytelling." Pp. 183-201 in *Handbook of Discourse Analysis,* Vol. 3, edited by T. A. van Dijk. London: Academic Press.

Portelli, A. 1991. *The Death of Luigi Trastulli and Other Stories: Form and Meaning in Oral History.* Albany: State University of New York Press.

———. 1997. *The Battle of Valle Giulia: Oral History and the Art of Dialogue.* Madison: University of Wisconsin Press.

Ricoeur, P. 1973. "The Model of the Text: Meaningful Action Considered as a Text." *New Literary History* 5:91-117.

———. 1977. *The Rule of Metaphor: Multidisciplinary Studies of the Creation of Meaning in Language.* Toronto: University of Toronto Press.

———. 1983. *Time and Narrative,* Vol. 1. Chicago: University of Chicago Press.

Riessman, C. K. 1992. "Making Sense of Marital Violence: One Woman's Narrative." Pp. 231-49 in *Storied Lives: The Cultural Politics of Self-Understanding,* edited by G. C. Rosenwald and R. L. Ochberg. New Haven, CT: Yale University Press.

Rosenwald, G. C. 1992. "Conclusion: Reflections on Narrative Self-Understanding." Pp. 265-89 in *Storied Lives: The Cultural Politics of Self-Understanding,* edited by G. C. Rosenwald and R. L. Ochberg. New Haven, CT: Yale University Press.

Roth, M. S. 1995. *The Ironist's Cage: Memory, Trauma, and the Construction of History.* New York: Columbia University Press.

Sánchez, R. 1995. *Telling Identities: The Californio Testimonios.* Minneapolis: University of Minnesota Press.

Schudson, M. 1995. *Memory Distortion: How Minds, Brains, and Societies Reconstruct the Past.* Cambridge, MA: Harvard University Press.

Thelen, D. 1989. "Memory and American History." *Journal of American History* 75:117-29.

Thompson, P. 1988. *The Voice of the Past.* Oxford: Oxford University Press.

Tonkin, E. 1992. *Narrating Our Pasts: The Social Construction of Oral History.* Cambridge: Cambridge University Press.

Trouillot, M.-R. 1995. *Silencing the Past: Power and the Production of History.* Boston: Beacon.

Vansina, J. 1965. *Oral Tradition: A Study in Historical Methodology.* London: Routledge & Kegan Paul.

Veyne, P. 1984. *Writing History: Essay on Epistemology.* Middletown, CT: Wesleyan University Press.

Yates, F. 1966. *The Art of Memory.* Chicago: University of Chicago Press.

Young, J. E. 1993. *The Texture of Memory: Holocaust Memorials and Meaning.* New Haven, CT: Yale University Press.

18

INSTITUTIONAL ETHNOGRAPHY

Using Interviews to Investigate Ruling Relations

◆ **Marjorie L. DeVault**
Liza McCoy

Social researchers use interviews in various ways, but they usually think of interviews as sources for learning about individual experience. In this chapter, we discuss interviewing as part of an approach designed for the investigation of organizational and institutional processes. In this alternative to conventional forms of interview research, investigators use informants' accounts not as windows on the informants' inner experience but in order to reveal the "relations of ruling" that shape local experiences (Smith 1996).

We use the term *institutional ethnography* (IE), following Canadian sociologist Dorothy E. Smith, to refer to the empirical investigation of linkages among local settings of everyday life, organizations, and translocal processes of administration and governance. These linkages constitute a complex field of coordination and control that Smith (1999) identifies as "the ruling relations"; these increasingly textual forms of coordination are "the forms in which power is generated and held in contemporary societies" (p. 79).

Smith (1987) introduced the term *institutional ethnography* in writing about a "sociology for women," illustrating with her studies of mothers' work at home in relation to their children's schooling, but she understands the approach as having wide application. Those who have followed Smith in developing IE have investigated many different social processes, including the regulation of sexuality (Smith 1998;

Khayatt 1995; Kinsman 1996); the organization of health care (Campbell 1988, 1995, 1999; Diamond 1992; Mykhalovskiy 2000; Mykhalovskiy and Smith 1994; Smith 1995), education (Griffith 1984, 1992; Andre Bechely 1999; Stock 2000), and social work practice (de Montigny 1995; Parada 1998); police and judicial processing of violence against women (Pence 1997); employment and job training (K. M. Grahame 1998); economic restructuring (McCoy 1999); international development regimes (Mueller 1995); planning and environmental policy (Turner 1995; Eastwood 2000); the organization of home and community life (DeVault 1991; Luken and Vaughan 1991, 1996; Naples 1997); and various kinds of activism (Walker 1990; Ng 1996).

Over the past two decades, a loosely organized network of IE researchers has emerged in North America, the members of which meet regularly to share developing projects and refinements of these methods.[1] This chapter surveys the work of that network. In preparing the discussion that follows, we have examined published examples of IE research, interviewed practitioners (individually and in small groups), and collected accounts of research practices and reflections via e-mail. We understand IE as an emergent mode of inquiry, always subject to revision and the improvisation required by new applications. Thus we wish to emphasize that we do not intend any prescriptive orthodoxy. Rather, we hope to introduce this approach, provide practical information about it that is often unarticulated in published work, and reflect on unresolved issues of research practice. Because many of the specifics of IE interviews are the same as the "good practices" used by researchers conducting other kinds of interviews (methods of gaining access, building rapport, probing for specific accounts, listening carefully, and so on), we highlight distinctive practices associated with IE studies.

In the following section, we provide an introduction to this research approach and consider various uses of interviewing in IE projects. Next, we discuss the conduct of interviews. The subsequent section foregrounds the key role of texts and institutional discourses in IE research, showing how interviews can be oriented toward these aspects of social organization. We then turn to analysis and writing in relation to IE interviews.

◆ Institutional Ethnography as a Mode of Inquiry

Dorothy Smith proposes IE as part of an "alternative sociology," an approach she describes as combining Marx's materialist method and Garfinkel's ethnomethodology with insights from the feminist practice of consciousness-raising. "In different ways, all of these ground inquiry in the ongoing activities of actual individuals" (Smith 1999:232, n. 5). Analytically fundamental to this approach is an ontology that views the social as the concerting of people's activities. This is an ontology shared by phenomenologists, symbolic interactionists, and ethnomethodologists. Smith expands this through the concept of social relations, which, as in Marx, refers to the coordinating of people's activities on a large scale, as this occurs in and across multiple sites, involving the activities of people who are not known to each other and who do not meet face-to-face.

In contemporary global capitalist society, the "everyday world" (the material context of each embodied subject) is organized in powerful ways by translocal social relations that pass through local settings and shape them according to a dynamic of transformation that begins and gathers speed somewhere else (e.g., if the local hospital closes, the explanation will not be wholly local). Smith (1990) refers to these translocal social relations that carry and accomplish organization and control as "relations of ruling":

They are those forms that we know as bureaucracy, administration, management, professional organization, and the media. They include also the complex of discourses, scientific, technical, and cultural, that intersect, interpenetrate, and coordinate the multiple sites of ruling. (P. 6)

A central feature of ruling practice in contemporary society is its reliance on text-based discourses and forms of knowledge, and these are central in IE inquiries (a topic we return to later).[2]

Building on this conception of ruling, Smith's notion of institution points to clusters of text-mediated relations organized around specific ruling functions, such as education or health care. *Institution,* in this usage, does not refer to a particular type of organization; rather, it is meant to inform a project of empirical inquiry, directing the researcher's attention to coordinated and intersecting work processes taking place in multiple sites. For example, when health care is considered as an institution, what comes into view is a vast nexus of coordinated work processes and courses of action—in sites as diverse as hospitals, homes, doctors' offices, community clinics, elementary schools, workplaces, pharmacies, pharmaceutical companies, advertising agencies, insurance companies, government ministries and departments, mass media, and medical and nursing schools. Obviously, institutions cannot be studied and mapped out in their totality, and such is not the objective of institutional ethnography. Rather, the aim of the IE researcher is to explore particular corners or strands within a specific institutional complex, in ways that make visible their points of connection with other sites and courses of action. Thus Tim Diamond is studying the organization of health benefits in the United States, which he examines in its character as a text-mediated relation connecting the activities of individuals, their employers, insurance companies, hospitals, pharmacies, and so on (focus group, August 1999).

Institutional ethnography takes for its entry point the experiences of specific individuals whose everyday activities are in some way hooked into, shaped by, and constituent of the institutional relations under exploration. The term *ethnography* highlights the importance of research methods that can discover and explore these everyday activities and their positioning within extended sequences of action. When interviews are used in this approach, they are used not to reveal subjective states, but to locate and trace the points of connection among individuals working in different parts of institutional complexes of activity. The interviewer's goal is to elicit talk that will not only illuminate a particular circumtance but also point toward next steps in an ongoing, cumulative inquiry into translocal processes. As Peter Grahame (1999) explains, "The field continuously opens up as the researcher explores the institutional nexus that shapes the local" (p. 7; see also P. R. Grahame 1998).

The researcher's purpose in an IE investigation is not to generalize about the group of people interviewed, but to find and describe social processes that have generalizing effects. Thus interviewees located somewhat differently are understood to be subject, in various ways, to discursive and organizational processes that shape their activities. These institutional processes may produce similarities of experience, or they may organize various settings to sustain broader inequalities (as explored in DeVault 1999:chap. 5); in either case, these generalizing consequences show the lineaments of ruling relations. For example, George W. Smith (1998) treated the gay young men he interviewed not as a population of subjects, but as informants knowledgeable about school life for gay youth. He explains:

The interviews opened various windows on different aspects of the organization of this regime. Each informant provides a partial view; the work of institutional ethnography is to put together an integrated view based on these otherwise truncated accounts of schools. (P. 310)

The general relevance of the inquiry comes, then, not from a claim that local settings are similar, but from the capacity of the research to disclose features of ruling that operate across many local settings.

IE studies can "fit together"—much like the squares of a quilt (Smith 1987)—because they share the same organizing ontology and the same focus on generalizing processes of ruling. Thus Janet Rankin's (1998) study of nurses' work and administrative categories in a British Columbia hospital extends the analysis in Eric Mykhalovskiy's (2000) study of health services research and hospital restructuring in Ontario, and both extend the analysis in Liza McCoy's (1999) study of accounting texts and restructuring in another area of the public sector in Canada. This does not mean that the three studies consciously locate their analyses in relation to one another, but that through the analytic frame they share they can be seen to be describing different moments and aspects of the same generalizing set of relations.

Dorothy Smith's work on the social organization of knowledge predates the emergence of feminist sociology, but her formulations gained increasing power as she situated them within a community of activist feminist scholars seeking a transformative method of inquiry (DeVault 1999). IE researchers generally have critical or liberatory goals; they undertake research in order to reveal the ideological and social processes that produce experiences of subordination. For example, in Smith's classic feminist text *The Everyday World as Problematic* (1987), the idea is to "begin from women's experiences" and to take as the problematic for the research the question of how such experiences are produced. This notion shares with much feminist writing an interest in women's previously excluded views, but it uses women's accounts only as a point of entry to a broader investigation (see also Reinharz and Chase, Chapter 4, this volume). The idea is to shift from a focus on women themselves (as in a sociology "of women") to a kind of investigation that could be useful in efforts to change the social relations that subordinate women (and others).

IE researchers aim at specific analyses of social coordination; the liberatory potential of the approach comes from its specification of possible "levers" or targets for activist intervention. Some IE research has emerged directly from the researcher's position as activist (G. W. Smith 1990; Pence 1997); these projects may be driven and targeted directly toward questions arising from activist work. Some academic researchers work collaboratively with activists: Roxana Ng with garment workers' unions, Marie Campbell with people who have disabilities, and Mykhalovskiy and McCoy with AIDS activists, for example. And some academics (and other professionals) research processes that shape their own work settings, often exploring the peculiar ways in which they themselves are implicated in ruling relations despite their intentions (de Montigny 1995; Parada 1998). Whatever the position of the researcher, the transformative potential of IE research comes from the character of the analysis it produces; it is like a "map" that can serve as a guide through a complex ruling apparatus.

POSSIBLE SHAPES OF IE PROJECTS

Institutional ethnography is driven by the search to discover "how it happens," with the underlying assumptions that (a) social "happening" consists in the concerted activities of people and (b) in contemporary society, local practices and experiences are tied into extended social relations or chains of action, many of which are mediated by documentary forms of knowledge. IE researchers set out to provide analytic descriptions of such processes in actual settings.

There is no "one way" to conduct an IE investigation; rather, there is an analytic project that can be realized in diverse ways. IE investigations are rarely planned out fully in advance. Instead, the process of inquiry is rather like grabbing a ball of string, finding a thread, and then pulling it out; that is why it is difficult to specify in advance exactly what the research will consist of. IE researchers know what they want to explain, but only step by step can they discover whom they need to interview or what texts and discourses they need to examine. In the discussion that follows, we describe some common "shapes" or trajectories of IE research.

BEGINNING WITH EXPERIENCE

A common—even a "classic"—IE approach (recommended by Dorothy Smith 1987) begins with the identification of an experience or area of everyday practice that is taken as the experience whose determinants are to be explored. The researcher seeks to "take the standpoint" of the people whose experience provides the starting point of investigation. For example, George Smith (1988) begins from the experience of gay men who were arrested by police in a series of sweeping raids on gay bathhouses; Didi Khayatt (1995) begins from the experience of young lesbian women in high school; Campbell and her associates begin from the experience of people attempting to live independently with physical disabilities (see Campbell 1998, 1999); Diamond (1992) begins from the experience of people, mostly women, who work as nursing assistants in nursing homes for the elderly; and Susan Turner (1995) begins from the experience of community residents seeking to stop a developer from destroying a wooded ravine. In all of these studies, the researchers go on to investigate the institutional processes that are shaping that experience (e.g., the work of policing, the work of teaching and school administration, the organization of

home-care services, the administration of Medicare and nursing homes, the organization of municipal land-use planning). The research follows a sequence: (a) identify an experience, (b) identify some of the institutional processes that are shaping that experience, and (c) investigate those processes in order to describe analytically how they operate as the grounds of the experience.

The researcher can employ a range of data collection techniques to explore the experience that provides the starting place and identifies the problematic. Most common among these techniques are interviews and focus groups, participant observation, and the researcher's reflection on her or his own experience, all of which serve to generate descriptions of what people do in their everyday lives. The analytic enterprise is paramount, however, and ways of realizing it are diverse. Many IE researchers use individual and group interviews. For example, Khayatt (1995) conducted interviews with young lesbians. Campbell and her associates conducted interviews with people living with disabilities (see Campbell 1998). Paul Luken and Suzanne Vaughan (1998; Vaughan and Luken 1997), along with older women informants, generated oral histories regarding the women's housing activities. Dorothy Smith, Liza McCoy, and Paula Bourne (1995) conducted focus group interviews with girls in secondary school. And Darien Taylor and associates (forthcoming) conducted focus groups with men and women living with HIV/AIDS about their experience of looking after their health. Through informants' stories and descriptions, the researcher begins to identify some of the translocal relations, discourses, and institutional work processes that are shaping the informants' everyday work.

Some IE researchers spend considerable time at this point of entry (for it can take time to understand the complexity of an experience, and data from this exploration can provide material with much analytic potential). In other cases, a researcher may begin from an experience that he or she knows something about, or where the problematic is already clear (e.g., G. W. Smith 1990; Walker 1990). Eventually, however, the researcher will usually need to shift the investigation to begin examining those institutional processes that he or she has discovered to be shaping the experience but that are not wholly known to the original informants. Thus a second stage of research commonly follows that usually involves a shift in research site, although not in standpoint. Often, this shift carries the investigation into organizational and professional work sites. At this stage, other forms of research and analysis may come to be used. The researcher may employ observation and the analysis of naturally occurring language data to examine institutional work processes, for example. Or the researcher may use text and discourse analysis to examine the textual forms and practices of knowledge that organize those work processes. But interviews continue to play an important role here as well, whether as the primary form of investigation or as a way of filling in the gaps of what the researcher can learn through observation and document analysis.

A common aspect of IE research at this second stage involves the researcher's investigating institutional work processes by following a chain of action, typically organized around and through a set of documents, because it is texts that coordinate people's activity across time and place within institutional relations. For example, Turner (1995) traced the trajectory of a developer's planning proposal as it passed through a review process involving the city planning office, the local conservation authority, the railroad company, and a meeting of the city council.

RESEARCH FOCUSED ON "RULING" PROCESSES

In some IE research, the point of entry is in organizational work processes and the activities of the people who perform them.

Rather than arriving at these processes through an exploration of the experience of people who are the objects of that work or who are in some way affected by it, the researcher in this type of IE jumps right into the examination of organizational work sites. The researcher knows about a set of administrative or professional practices and sets about studying how they are carried out, how they are discursively shaped, how they organize other settings. For example, Mykhalovskiy (2000) investigated health services research and its use in health care restructuring. Dorothy Smith and George Smith (1990) researched the organization of skills training in the plastics industry. Elizabeth Townsend (1998) studied the work of professionals in the mental health system and the contradictions between their professional goal of empowering people and system processes organized to control deviance. And Alison Griffith (1998) investigated the legislative and policy bases for educational restructuring in Ontario. This type of IE emphasizes the detailed examination of administrative and professional work processes.

CONCEPTUALIZATION AND PLACE OF INTERVIEWING

Interviewing is present in some form in just about all IE studies. But "interviewing" in IE is perhaps better described as "talking with people," and IE uses of interviewing should be understood in this wide sense, as stretching across a range of approaches to talk with informants. At one end of the continuum are planned interviews, where the researcher makes an appointment with someone for the purpose of doing a research interview. Then there is the kind of "talking with people" that occurs during field observation, when the researcher is watching someone do his work and asks him to explain what he is doing, why he did what he just did, what he has to think about to do the work, where this particular document goes, and so on. "Informal," on-the-spot interviews can be combined with later "formal" or planned interviews, in which the researcher brings to the longer interview a set of questions or topics based on the earlier observation-and-talk. Yet in IE, investigation through "talking with people" is not necessarily confined to settings and occasions that occur during formal field research. Because IE researchers are investigating widespread institutional and discursive processes in which the researcher is located as well as the informants, opportunities to talk with people about institutional processes can arise for the researcher serendipitously, as it were, in her or his daily life of going shopping, talking with friends, seeking medical care, and so on, depending on the topic of the research (see also Atkinson and Coffey, Chapter 20, this volume).

Further, "talking with people" is not necessarily done one-to-one. At the planned end of the continuum, a number of recent IE studies have used focus groups to generate group conversations about shared experiences (Smith et al. 1995; Campbell 1999; Stock 2000). And Tim Diamond reports that his research into health insurance draws on collective interviews he holds with his students during class, in which participants collaborate in developing an account of how health care is covered in the news and on television (focus group, August 1999). Such an approach works in IE because institutional processes are standardized across local settings, so any group of informants encounters those processes in some way.

"Talking with people" is also a wide term in the sense that it includes more than the usual research format (whether formal or informal) of asking questions and listening to answers. Eric Mykhalovskiy comments: "Describing interviews as a set of questions doesn't get at the actual work involved. For me, analytic thinking begins in the interview. It's like an analytic rehearsal. I'm checking my understanding as it develops; I offer it up to the informant for confirmation or correction" (interview, September 1999; see also Charmaz, Chapter 15, this volume).

◆ Conducting IE Interviews

IE interviewing is open-ended inquiry, and IE interviewers are always oriented to sequences of interconnected activities. They talk with people located throughout these institutional complexes in order to learn "how things work." In many investigations, informants are chosen as the research progresses, as the researcher learns more about the social relations involved and begins to see avenues that need exploration. Given that the purpose of interviewing is to build up an understanding of the coordination of activity in multiple sites, the interviews need not be standardized. Rather, each interview provides an opportunity for the researcher to learn about a particular piece of the extended relational chain, to check the developing picture of the coordinative process, and to become aware of additional questions that need attention.

Dorothy Smith reports that when she conducted interviews jointly with George Smith, in their study of the organization of job training (Smith and Smith 1990), they thought of their talk with informants as a way to build "piece by piece" a view of an extended organizational process. Rather than using a standard set of questions, they based each interview in part on what they had learned from previous ones. She explains: "You have a sense of what you're after, although you sometimes don't know what you're after until you hear people telling you things. . . . Discovering what you don't know—and don't know you don't know—is an important aspect of the process" (interview, September 1999). As in any qualitative interviewing, there is a balance to be achieved between directing the interview toward the researcher's goals and encouraging informants to talk in ways that reflect the contours of their activity. The distinctiveness of IE interviews is produced by the researcher's developing knowledge of institutional processes, which allows a kind of listening and probing oriented toward institutional connections. Again, Smith explains, "The important thing is to think organizationally, recognizing you won't know at the beginning which threads to follow, knowing you won't follow all possible threads, but noting them along the way."

IE researchers often think of interviewing as "coinvestigation." Such an approach is evident in Gary Kinsman and Patrizia Gentile's (1998) discussion of the oral history narratives they collected from gay men and lesbians affected by Canadian national security campaigns of the late 1950s and early 1960s. They see the first-person narratives as both a "form of resistance to the official security documents" (p. 8) and a basis from which to build a critical analysis of those documents. Because people were affected differently, the narratives took different shapes, and the researchers found that their providing some historical context often helped informants remember and reconstruct their experiences. They describe their interviewing as "a fully reflexive process in which both the participant and the interviewer construct knowledge together" (p. 58).

Most IE interviewers tape conversations with informants, both as an aid in making notes and to preserve details whose relevance may not be immediately obvious. Transcripts of interviews are important texts in themselves, facilitating analysis and providing a way for research participants to "speak" in published accounts of the research. Diamond, however, is concerned about privileging the textual representation over the embodied actuality of the research conversation. We are always in our bodies, he reminds us; in fact, Smith's concept of the "everyday" begins from that fundamental fact. People's descriptions of their work activities and lived experiences are often produced gesturally as well as verbally, and our understanding of that work and that experience arises for us, in part,

through our bodily response to their gestures. "IE, in insisting on bodies being there, sensitizes us to bodies as part of the data. . . . It's not about just words but how the words live in embodied experience" (T. Diamond, personal communication, December 1999).

INTERVIEW STRATEGIES

IE interviewing is typically organized around the idea of work, defined broadly, or "generously" (Smith 1987). Whether it is the paid work of an organizational position, the activist work of challenging a regime, or some "everyday life work" such as parenting or managing an illness, the point of interest is the informant's activity, as it reveals and points toward the interconnected activities of others. The idea of work provides a conceptual frame and guides interview talk; the point is not to insist on the categorical status of any activity, but to hold in place a conception of the social as residing in the concerting of people's actual activities.

The generous understanding of work deployed by IE researchers is related to early feminist insights about women's unpaid and often invisible work—the recognition that although various kinds of work sustain social life, some are uncompensated, unacknowledged, or mystified as aspects of personality (e.g., women's "caring" work, as explored in DeVault 1991). An IE study aims at a picture that displays all the activity sustaining a particular institutional nexus or arena, and this analytic goal gives rise to several distinctive strategies for the conduct of interviews. In the following subsections, we identify several kinds of work and discuss strategies associated with each.

Work Practices of Everyday Life

Some researchers conduct IE interviews with a view to understanding the everyday/

everynight experiences of people living particular lives—single mothers, people with AIDS or disabilities, older women, or immigrant women, for example. In these interviews researchers seek detailed accounts of activities: What do mothers do when their children have trouble at school? How do individuals work at managing their health? What work do older women do to maintain their housing? How do immigrant women seek employment, education, or training? Ellen Pence began her research by "talking to women who used the police and courts. I would ask what went right or wrong"; these conversations gave her a view of the efforts battered women made to seek help (focus group, August 1999). Similarly, Nancy Naples (1998) studied the implementation of the 1988 Family Support Act in an Iowa jobs program that allowed recipients to work toward a college degree. She collected interview, observational, and documentary data on the policy, but the grounding for her study came from interviews with women in the program. Her interviews produced accounts of the women's everyday routines, which she used to uncover the tensions between their lives as mothers and college students and the demands of the program—thus bringing an "everyday life" dimension to policy analysis.

Given the conceptual frame discussed above, the interviewer approaches these conversations as explorations of work practices in everyday life; the point is to learn about what the informant actually does. Informants may or may not think of what they do as a form of "work"; the interviewer may use the rubric of work in questioning, but there is no need to insist on explicit talk of work or agreement about the status of the activity. When Smith and Griffith interviewed mothers, for example, "It worked well to take them through the school day, to ask them what they did at each point, such as what is involved in getting the kids ready for school, getting them there on time." Smith finds that guiding the interview in this way often has the result of

"training the informant": "I tell people what I'm interested in, things I'd like to hear about, rather than asking questions. . . . Some people happily go on at a level of expanding practice, and some don't. So that's maybe a good reason to do multiple interviews" (interview, September 1999). Similarly, Diamond elicits "stories" as the basis for his research into the organization of health care: "Sometimes I just say, I want to talk about health insurance in the U.S. People jump in with long stories. . . . Invariably people will talk about employment, because that's the intervening institution—people need to be employed or connected to someone employed to have health insurance" (focus group, August 1999). In a study of a public school choice program, Lois Andre Bechely interviewed parents using the program. She notes:

> Getting people to continue to talk about the details of their "work" can be a challenge. . . . And in the case of parents (and this is almost always the mothers), not all of them saw their involvement as work—it was just what they did—while others did actually use words like, "it's my job," etc. (E-mail communication, September 1999)

Taylor and associates (forthcoming) found that although the notion of work was useful to them, conceptually, in establishing the framework of their group interviews, it was counterproductive when used with informants, for whom it evoked a prevalent normative standard of the "good patient" who conscientiously works at "managing" his or her health, against which many informants perceived themselves as delinquent. The researchers had the delicate job of figuring out how to ask people what they did around their health without suggesting that they should have been doing more or otherwise.

Interviews about everyday life work may also be used to point toward the work practices of others. For example, George Smith (1998) emphasizes that the gay students he interviewed were not meant to be "objects of study"; although their narratives could be interpreted as accounts of "work" they do as students (e.g., to "fit in," or pass), he uses their stories as windows on the work processes that affect them—both the "everyday work" of students upholding a heterosexist regime through surveillance and gossip and the paid work of teachers and administrators, which was not organized to interrupt that regime and sometimes reinforced it.

Some IE researchers attempt to conduct such interviews with a view to more than data collection, seeking to share insights with informants in the course of interviewing. Diamond says of his interviews on health insurance, "Together we construct a critique of benefits" (focus group, August 1999). And Gerald de Montigny, commenting on his studies of youth in state care, reports:

> My big challenge is that when I do an interview, I do so not only as an ethnographer, but from the standpoint of wanting to be a skilled social work interviewer. . . . I do not feel that I am able to explicate in my interviews the complex social forces at play in these youth's lives, though as a social worker, I do try to help them to understand the play of forces across the landscape of the everyday experiences. (E-mail communication, September 1999)

Whether such dual goals are achievable— and if so, how—appears to be among the unresolved questions of IE interviewers.

Frontline Organizational Work

Frontline professionals, such as teachers, nurses, trainers, social workers, community agency personnel, and other bureaucrats, often become informants in IE research. Individuals in such positions are especially important because they make the linkages between clients and ruling discourses, "working up" the messiness of an everyday circumstance so that it fits the categories and protocols of a professional regime. In some studies, such individuals are interviewed as intermediary actors in an institutional complex: Kamini Maraj Grahame (1998, 1999), for example, interviewed intake workers who screened Asian immigrant women into job training, showing that funding formulas organized their work such that they tracked the women into employment streams compatible with local employers' needs. Similarly, Smith and Griffith's interviews with teachers showed how they are located between parents, concerned with particular children, and school district practices, designed for standardized processing of groups (Smith 1987). And Yoko Ueda (1995) interviewed human resource professionals to learn about corporate personnel policies that shaped the family work of Japanese expatriate wives in Toronto. In other studies, researchers may be more directly focused on the work situations of these frontline workers and concerned with the organization and control of such work. For example, Campbell's (1988, 1992; Campbell and Jackson 1992) studies of nursing work are designed to illuminate the mechanisms of managerial control that have increasingly limited nurses' autonomy in care work. Similarly, Ann Manicom's (1995) examination of "health work" undertaken by teachers in low-income schools explores how these teachers are drawn into work that goes beyond official accounts of their jobs.

Here again, IE researchers seek detailed accounts of work processes, but interviewing frontline workers presents its own distinctive challenges. These workers have been trained to use the very concepts and categories that IE researchers wish to unpack, and they are accustomed to speaking from within a ruling discourse. Thus the interviewer must find ways of moving the talk beyond institutional language to "what actually happens" in the setting. Campbell teaches such interviewing strategies in part by offering the following advice:

Listen to the person tell her story. Pay attention to the sequencing. Then ask yourself, can you tell exactly how she gets from one point to another? If not, ask questions; clarify, so that you can. (Interview, January 2000)

Such strategies require practice, because "we're all very good at filling in the blanks." But the organizational orientation of IE researchers leads them, with practice, to see both gaps in these accounts and the kinds of filling in necessary for a fuller organizational analysis. The challenge of moving beyond institutional language is so central to IE interviewing that we return to it in the following section.

In some studies that are focused more explicitly on change, interviews might include discussion of possible modifications of frontline work. For example, Pence's (1997) study of safety for battered women involved interviews with the various workers who serve the women as advocates, hospital, and criminal justice workers. As she gained an understanding of the interlocking activities of these workers, she could see that women's safety was only one of the concerns that shaped their work and, in fact, was often subordinated to organizational imperatives. She and her team began to ask workers not only how the system operated, but also how it might be organized differently. She explains:

We ask, "Is there something you don't have in your job, that if you did have, would help prevent that woman getting beat up?" "If you were going to build victim safety into this process, how would you do it?" . . .

It's an eye-opener. People in an institution rarely get asked, do you want to change something as basic as a form you fill out every day. How would you change it? Usually people totally get into it. And when you ask them, "Why is this on the form?" or "Why does the form ask that?" they can be quite in-

sightful [about how the form works in the system], even though they might never have thought about it that way before. (focus group, August 1999)

As with everyday experience interviews, then, some researchers orient toward the dual goals of analysis and change; but these intriguing possibilities require partnerships with activists and practitioners that are not easily established and may not always be feasible.

"Ruling" Work

IE researchers are always interested in moving beyond the interchanges of frontline settings in order to track the macroinstitutional policies and practices that organize those local settings. Thus interviews are often conducted with managers and administrators who work at the level of translocal policy making and implementation, and these interviews also require a distinctive orientation and strategy. Kamini Maraj Grahame (1998, 1999), who studied federally funded job training for immigrant women in the United States, emphasizes the complexity of this kind of institutional process and the amount of "legwork and conversation" required even to have a sense of where in the structure one might need to conduct interviews. She learned about various parts of the institutional complex of job training while working in and with community organizations, and eventually conducted interviews not only with clients of and workers in those organizations, but also with managers working in the local, state, and federal agencies that funded and oversaw the programs. With each interviewee, she focused on that worker's role in the overall job training system. She would ask, "What do *you* do?" Recognizing that she was interviewing each at a particular point in time, and therefore at a particular point in what she came to call "the training cycle," she would ask what the interviewee was doing that day or week, and then, "Why are you doing this now?" Whenever someone mentioned a document, she would ask to see a copy of it and then ask what the worker did with that document. In these ways, she built an accumulating understanding of how work processes were textually linked across sites and levels of administration. (We address this kind of textual coordination again below.)

Grahame found that she often had to proceed without a clear sense of where interviewing would take her: "Someone in the federal government says something I have no way of making sense of—seeing the relevance of—until I go back to an interview I did at a community organization. Then I can put it all together." Because the information gained in interviews requires this kind of synthesis, she feels it is very important to tape and transcribe whenever possible. "Taping allows me to go back and forth and have things make sense in a way they did not initially," she explains. "It's a very complex enterprise, and there's no time to go back and redo interviews" (focus group, August 1999).

Often, interviews with managers and administrators are conducted in the later phases of IE studies, so that researchers can use information gained from clients and frontline workers to direct the interviewing. For example, Lois Andre Bechely reports:

As I got farther up the chain of command, I had already done preliminary analysis of parent interviews and policy documents and my questions were focused on trying to uncover the social and textual organization of school choice practices that parents encounter and participate in. (E-mail communication, September 1999)

Andre Bechely used her knowledge as a former teacher to organize questions for administrators, but the talk still proceeded in the searching and open manner characteristic of IE interviewing.

The openness of such interviewing allows informants to speak in the forms appropriate to their work. For example, McCoy's (1998, 1999) study of restructuring in Canadian community colleges and the forms of accounting coordinating that process is based on interviews conducted almost entirely with managers. Her informants often talked about new cost accounting documents by enacting speech situations, that is, reporting what was said in the past or what might be argued in future negotiations. McCoy (1998) points out:

It is not to be supposed that these enactments exactly match what was said or what will be said; their usefulness as data in this kind of study lies in what they suggest about what can possibly or appropriately be [said], and especially, how what can be said depends on and is oriented to the textual forms through which events and activities are known in authoritative ways. (Pp. 416-17)

Such reports give a strong sense of the discursive character of the work of ruling in this kind of setting.

Processing Interchanges

IE researchers are especially alert to the points where work processes intersect, points that Pence (1997) has labeled "processing interchanges":

Processing interchanges are organizational occasions of action in which one practitioner receives from another a document pertaining to a case (e.g., a 911 incident report, a warrant request, or a motion for a continuance), and then makes something of the document, does something to it, and forwards it on to the next organizational occasion for action. It is the construction of these processing interchanges coupled with a highly specialized division of labor that accomplishes much of the ideological work of the institution. Workers' tasks are shaped by certain prevailing features of the system, features so common to workers that they begin to see them as natural, as the way things are done and—in some odd way—as the only way they could be done, rather than as planned procedures and rules developed by individuals ensuring certain ideological ways of interpreting and acting on a case. (P. 60)

In her study of the processing of domestic violence cases, Pence attends to the spaces and tools that organize the tasks of workers—how dispatchers use computers, police use Dictaphones, and so on—and to the forms required at each point of connection. As she points out, it is not "the woman who was beaten who moves from one point to the next in the stages of case processing"; rather, the "file stands in for the woman who was assaulted" (p. 67). In studying how this extremely important file is produced, Pence watched workers in these processing interchanges and also asked them about their work, querying police officers, for instance, on "how they decide when to write a report, how they decide what to record in their narratives, and how much leeway they have in making these decisions" (p. 71). At each processing interchange, she explains, "an institutional investigation helps to determine how such an objective (i.e. accounting for victim safety) could be incorporated into the design at each of these occasions" (p. 89). Working with practitioners in the system, Pence has developed an "audit" procedure—basically, an IE investigation—to be used collaboratively to provide "a place for advocates and practitioners to work together" (p. 187).

Campbell (1998, 1999) has used a similar approach in her participatory research project on home support for people with disabilities. Her team used interview material to identify processing interchanges they

wished to examine in detail, and Campbell and her assistants arranged for team members to conduct observations of these moments in the management of home support. Watching a scheduler work at a computer screen, for example, they asked questions to help her make explicit the kinds of choices she was making. "People think the computer does it," Campbell notes, "but that glosses the judgment involved in her work" (interview, January 2000). The researchers found that "continuity" in scheduling home support workers was important for people with disabilities and a goal shared by workers in the system. As they observed the scheduler, however, they found that "her talk open[ed] up the organizational priorities that interfere with the Client-focus of her work" (p. 6).

Both Pence and Campbell have found that working with a team to investigate interchanges provides opportunities for participants to come to a fuller shared understanding of organizational action. Campbell reports that team members would sometimes "clash" over differing perspectives: "The professionals would say, 'You're not seeing this right; this is what's happening.' And people with disabilities would say, 'But it doesn't feel that way; here's how it feels' " (interview, January 2000).

As facilitator, Campbell would let such discussion proceed, and then ask, "Now whose standpoint are we taking?" Team members could then respond, "Oh yes, the standpoint of people with disabilities" (interview, January 2000). In this kind of exchange, Campbell is reminding her research team of the way that a notion of "standpoint" anchors the research in the relevancies of a particular group. The point is not that "people with disabilities" share a determinate standpoint, or that the perspectives of the professionals should be ignored or discounted. Rather, the idea is to consider how the perspectives from different locations illuminate the relevant social relations while keeping in mind the questions focused by the concerns of people living with disabilities.

SELECTING INFORMANTS

The preceding discussion provides some context for understanding IE approaches to the selection of interviewees. Because IE researchers are not oriented toward descriptive reporting on a population, they do not think of informants as a "sample." Still, when exploring the ground of everyday experience, some IE investigators seek informants who can report on varied circumstances and situations. For example, Smith and Griffith (1990) interviewed both middle-class and working-class mothers; Manicom (1995) spoke with teachers in schools serving middle-class and poor students; Smith et al. (1995) sought high school girl informants in different kinds of school situations. Some researchers make special efforts to include perspectives they believe are missing: Didi Khayatt, for example, found it relatively easy to interview middle-class lesbians in Egypt, but had to make special efforts to find working-class informants (focus group, October 1999).

Such efforts are common to many kinds of interview studies. However, IE researchers aim not for categorical descriptions, but for analyses that trace how the people living in these different circumstances are drawn into a common set of organizational processes. Some report that attention to differences among informants can easily pull them toward the kinds of categorical analyses embedded in ruling process, as when Smith and Griffith (1990) found themselves thinking much like school administrators about the class composition of student groups. One solution is for researchers to conceive of this kind of selection in terms of diversity of experience rather than categorically. For example, when interviewing people living with HIV/AIDS about their health work, Taylor and associates (forthcoming) thought about diversity among their informants' circum-

stances, reasoning that they needed to include women caring for children, people living in prison, people on welfare, and so forth.

As discussed above, IE studies are rarely based solely on such a group of interviews; rather, they almost always use such interviews as pointers toward informants working in other settings. Those interviewees might be chosen in more varied ways. Some researchers follow "chains of action" (e.g., McCoy 1998; K. M. Grahame 1999). Some choose informants located in and around sites of confrontation; George Smith (1990), for example, located the "field" of the AIDS bureaucracy through work with other activists attempting to gain access to treatments. And in some studies, it seems useful for researchers to select "good thinkers" as interviewees. When Pence interviewed police, for example, she sought those who wrote especially complete or useful reports:

> If you read 50 police reports, you can say, "I want to talk to the cop who wrote these four." But I also try to interview one dud, so I can see how much is the institutional process and how much is the person. (focus group, August 1999)

Often, as George Smith (1990) explains, researchers simply rely on informants they encounter as their investigations proceed, using each conversation to expand understanding of the terrain.

Clearly, the selection of informants is more open-ended in IE investigations than it is in more conventional positivist studies, but the process is not haphazard. Rather, fieldwork and interviewing are driven by a faithfulness to the actual work processes that connect individuals and activities in the various parts of an institutional complex. Rigor comes not from technique—such as sampling or thematic analysis—but from the corrigibility of the developing map of social relations. When George Smith (1990) was learning about placebo-controlled trials of experimental AIDS treatments, for example, he did not need to identify recurring "themes" in the accounts of multiple physician informants. Rather, he sought their help in filling in his knowledge of how such trials work, continuing to "check" the account he was building as he proceeded with the investigation, and returning to physician (and other) informants as needed when questions or inconsistencies arose.

◆ *Interviewing about Textual Practices*

A prominent aspect of institutional ethnography is the recognition that text-based forms of knowledge and discursive practices are central to large-scale organization and relations of ruling in contemporary society. To use an organic metaphor, textual processes in institutional relations are like a central nervous system running through and coordinating different sites. To find out how things work and how they happen the way they do, a researcher needs to find the texts and text-based knowledge forms in operation. Thus IE investigation often involves close attention to textual practices, and interviewing is an important strategy in this regard.

When IE researchers talk about texts, they usually mean some kind of document or representation that has a relatively fixed and replicable character, for it is that aspect of texts—that they can be stored, transferred, copied, produced in bulk, and distributed widely, allowing them to be activated by users at different times and in different places—that allows them to play a standardizing and mediating role. In this view, a text can be any kind of document, on paper, on computer screens, or in computer files; it can also be a drawing, a photograph, a printed instrument reading, a video or sound recording, and so on.

Much IE research has focused on standardized texts used in professional and bureaucratic settings, such as care pathway forms in hospitals (Mykhalovskiy 2000), intake forms and applications at an employment agency (Ng 1996), patients' charts (Diamond 1992), nursing worksheets (Rankin 1998), forms for calculating teachers' workloads (McCoy 1999), course information sheets used in competency-based education reform (Jackson 1995), and safety assessment forms used by child protection workers (Parada 1998). Other bureaucratic texts studied have included job descriptions (Reimer 1995) and developers' maps used in land-use planning (Turner 1995). Griffith (1998) and Ng (1995) have examined legislative texts. Sometimes IE researchers look at the creation or generation of texts, such as the work of producing a newsletter for doctors (Mykhalovskiy 2000), creating materials for job skills training (Smith and Smith 1990), or taking wedding photographs (McCoy 1987, 1995).

IE researchers are also interested in the text-mediated discourses that frame issues, establish terms and concepts, and in various ways serve as resources that people draw into their everyday work processes, for example, health services research (Mykhalovskiy 2000), the literature on child development (Griffith 1984, 1995), the literature on "deviant" sexuality as an aspect of the policing of gay men (Kinsman 1989), the terms of an international development regime (Mueller 1995), and popular cultural discourses of femininity (D. E. Smith 1990:chap. 6). Whatever the text or textual process, in IE research it is examined for the ways it mediates relations of ruling and organizes what can be said and done.

LISTENING FOR TEXTS

At the early stages of research, when researchers are just beginning to learn about the institutional processes that shape the relations they are studying, they are alert to catch informants' references to texts or text-mediated processes. Sometimes these are fairly easy to catch, as when an informant mentions a specific document and how it functions. In the following extract, for example, a college administrator talks about a bureaucratic "D form":

> Well, that's the problem. We mounted programs and the last thing that's looked at is the return. Because the ministry—when we mount a program —has a little clause at the bottom of the D form, that simply says, you've got to make this work, we're not going to give you any more money than the funding units for it. So, if you want to put it on, fine. It's a disclaimer by the ministry of any acceptance of any debts that this program mounting creates.

At this point, or perhaps later in the interview, the researcher might ask to see a copy of the D form and, if possible, get one to take away with her. She will also want to learn more about how the D form is used: When is it filled out? By whom? What resources and future activities depend on the D form? In this way, the researcher begins to see how local settings are tied into extended institutional relations and at the same time lays the groundwork for future interviews ("Who could I talk to about that?").

Sometimes the researcher suspects that a textual process lies behind the description an informant is giving. It is not uncommon for informants who work in bureaucratic settings to use glosses and metaphors, as in the following example, where a college administrator is describing the work of a committee that recommends "per diem prices":

> And they report to the College Committee presidents who agree or disagree with their recommendation. And then that's sent on to the Ministry of Skills Development who again have to nod their approval. And finally to the federal government who have to pay the per diem. And they nod their approval or whatever.

Experience suggests that this "nodding" occurs textually, and an IE researcher interested in this process might go on to ask explicitly what form the reporting and the approval take. She might also want to discover which office or person does the approving on behalf of the ministry.

Not all the texts mentioned will become focal in the analysis, but in the early stages of studies some researchers like to map out the main textual processes at work in an institutional setting. In some cases, "mapping" might precede the initial interviews. Pence explains:

> We get together a prep work of documents and legislation. We used to start by going out and blindly interviewing. Now we prepare. But we do find out things [about texts] when we interview that we didn't know were there. (focus group, August 1999)

ASKING ABOUT TEXTS

However texts come to be identified as central to the relations under study—whether through exploratory interviews, through prep work, or through the researcher's prior knowledge—the research at some stage may involve interviews with people who can talk in detail about a text or those aspects of a textual process they know. One effective way for an interviewer to structure such an interview is to sit down with the informant and the text in question and talk very concretely about what is in the text and how the informant works with it. Diamond reports: "I ask people to bring a pay stub to the interview, so we can look at that text. We explore together: Where is health care in this pay stub?" (focus group, August 1999).

If the document in question is a standardized form, some researchers like to do the interview around a form that has been completed, rather than a blank one, as that will result in more concrete description. For example, when Dorothy Smith was interviewing a probation officer about a presentencing investigation form, she worked from an actual, completed form to ask about the sources of information (predominantly textual) and the practices of judgment that went into filling it out (interview, September 1999). When McCoy (1987) was interviewing a wedding photographer, she and the photographer worked from a set of photographs he had recently taken; as they looked through the stack of proofs, he talked about how he had worked with actual people and actual equipment on that specific day to make those pictures.

In other cases, the text in question is not one the informant creates or completes, but one he or she activates in some way, such as a report or a memo. Here the interviewer might focus on practices of reading to learn how the text is taken up in an actual setting, within an accountable work process. A transcript excerpt provided by Eric Mykhalovskiy illustrates this:

Eric Mykhalovskiy: So when you get those reports, what are you looking for? . . . How do they inform your thinking?

Informant (hospital administrator): Hmm. Well, certainly we look at the average length of stay, the time line. So if all of a sudden, I mean, we're averaging around five days, so if all of a sudden we're up to six, then that would concern me.

What the researcher wants to learn about the text and the practices of making or using it will vary, depending on the nature of the text and the focus of the investigation, but in general IE researchers are after the following:

1. How the text comes to this informant and where it goes after the informant is done with it

2. What the informant needs to know in order to use the text (create it, respond to it, fill it out, and so on)

3. What the informant does with, for, and on account of the text

4. How this text intersects with and depends on other texts and textual processes as sources of information, generators of conceptual frames, authorizing texts, and so on

5. The conceptual schema that organizes the text and its competent reading.

THE PROBLEM AND RESOURCE OF INSTITUTIONAL LANGUAGE

Institutional work processes are organized by conceptual schemes and distinctive categories. These are the terms in which the accountability of the work is produced, and procedures of accountability provide one of the main ways that various local settings are pulled into translocal relations. IE therefore pays strong attention to institutional categories and the interpretive schemata that connect them.

In interviews, it is common—and understandable—that people in an institutional setting describe their work using the language of the institution. This is especially the case with people who have been taught a professional discourse as part of their training or people whose work requires them to provide regular accounts of institutional processes. "Some people do jobs where public relations is part of their job, so they are doing that work while talking to me" (K. M. Grahame, focus group, August 1999). The challenge for the institutional ethnographer is to recognize when the informant is using institutional language. Not to do so is to risk conducting interviews that contain little usable data beyond the expression of institutional ideology in action, because institutional language conceals the very practices IE aims to discover and describe. Dorothy Smith elaborates:

> These terms are extraordinarily empty. They rely on your being able to fill out what they could be talking about. During the interview, you do that filling in while you listen, but when you look at the transcript afterward, the description isn't there. (Interview, September 1999)

As an example, Ann Manicom reports:

> One challenge I've faced in interviewing professionals is . . . to get them beyond saying something like, "Well, I have a lot of ADHD kids" to getting them to actually describe day-to-day work processes. The discourses are of course also interesting and an important piece of the analysis, but shifting them out of the discourse is important for actual descriptions of the work process. (E-mail communication, September 1999)

An informant's comment that she has "a lot of ADHD kids" would not be treated by an IE researcher as a straightforward description of her work, although it does show the teacher using institutional concepts to make sense of and to talk about her day-to-day actuality. Within the institution of schooling, it is certainly a competent description—other teachers would nod in sympathy and feel that they knew exactly what the teacher was talking about. A school administrator would understand something about that classroom relevant to her work of allocating resources. This is because the term references a discourse and practice of knowledge operative within the institution. An interviewer who knows something about teaching and professional discourses might also find, as Smith suggests above, that she too knows what the teacher is talking about. An alert IE researcher, however, would try to get the teacher to describe, for example, what

these "ADHD kids" are like: what they do or need, and in what ways their needs complicate or add to her teaching work. The researcher would try to learn how the teacher uses the ADHD concept to organize her work with the children and her conferences with their parents. Furthermore, the researcher might try to learn how ADHD as a category operates in the administration of schooling: for example, in some school districts, classroom assistants and other resources are allocated through a procedure that takes into account the number of students in a class who are entered in school records as having "special needs," such as ADHD. An IE researcher encountering institutional language has thus a twofold objective: to obtain a description of the actuality that is assumed by, but not revealed in, the institutional terms, and, at the same time, to learn how such terms and the discourses they carry operate in the institutional setting.

◆ Analysis and Presentation

As IE is fundamentally an analytic project, we cannot terminate this discussion of interviewing at the moment when the tape recorder is turned off and the researcher packs up her or his notes to go home. In this section we briefly address the work that comes after the interview has been taped and transcribed. The studies we have referred to and cited throughout the chapter provide further advice and models for analysis.

IE researchers tend not to use formal analytic strategies such as interpretive coding. Some use qualitative data analysis software to group chunks of transcript, sometimes pages in length, by theme or topic; others contend that the logic of these programs runs against that of the IE approach. The software seems to work best for IE analysis when the grouping is done rather simply, something like the indexing for a book (D. Smith, personal communication), sticking closely to topics of talk and references to institutional sites and processes. For example, a researcher might collect in one file everything informants said about using AIDS service organizations, in another the informants' stories about the work and challenges of finding suitable doctors, and so on. A researcher examining chains of action or process interchanges could use the software to group informants' comments around particular sites, texts, or moments in the process. This kind of computer-aided sorting works at a fairly primary level and offers researchers a manageable way to work with large numbers of interviews; it still leaves the analytic work to be done, as always, through writing, thinking, and discussion with collaborators and colleagues.

Just as projects have different shapes, IE researchers aim toward different kinds of analyses. Some use their data to map out complex institutional chains of action; others describe the mechanics of text-based forms of knowledge, elaborate the conceptual schemata of ruling discourses, or explicate how people's lived experience takes shape within institutional relations. John McKendy (1999), who interviewed men incarcerated for violent crimes, focuses his analysis on the informants' stories and the interview itself as a conversation, but in a way that makes visible the juxtaposition of primary narratives and ideological, institutionally oriented accounts:

> In doing the analysis now . . . I am on the lookout for segments of the interviews where "fault lines" can be detected, as the two modes of telling—the narrative and the ideological—rub up against each other. I want to examine how such junctures are occasioned within the flow of the interview, what kinds of narrative problems they pose for the speakers, and what methods speakers improvise to handle (overcome, resist, circumvent) these problems. (P. 9)

Townsend (1996, 1998) took her data—participant observation notes, interview transcripts, and documents—and addressed them through three analytic processes. First she "undertook the rather arduous task of describing the everyday world of occupational therapy" (1998:19). Then she "trac[ed] the social processes that connect the work being studied with the work of others. . . . Through a back-and-forth method of exploration, [she] traced connections between what occupational therapists do and the documentation and other processes that govern that work" (p. 21). Finally, she examined the "ideological character" of the institutional process: the ways that "occupational therapists and the people with whom occupational therapists work are conceptualized and categorized in mental health services, then coordinated and controlled through textual facts about these categories rather than through face-to-face supervision" (p. 24).

In general, IE analysts look at interview data as raising questions; according to Khayatt, the key is to ask, "How is it that these people are saying what they're saying?" She adds, "This methodology allows you to go back to a political-economic context for the answer" (focus group, October 1999). Ng and Griffith agree that analysis is always a matter of moving back and forth between collected speech and the context that produced it. For Ng (1996, 1999), whose research explores the work experiences of immigrant women, the analytic focus is how these women are drawn into institutional processes. She believes that conventional analyses of immigrants' lives often "produce ethnicity" through particular kinds of analytic work on interview data, linking informants' comments back to their "home cultures." Her goal, instead, is to find clues to "how things happen" for the people identified as immigrants in Canadian institutions. Griffith says of analysis: "It's never instances, it's always processes and coordination. It's all these little hooks. To make sense of it, you have to understand not just the speech of the moment, but what it's hooked into" (focus group, October 1999).

Many IE researchers find that they collect considerably more information than they use in a single analysis, because the analysis eventually follows some more specific thread of social organization. Dorothy Smith explains: "You don't have to use the whole interview. You can be quite selective, because you're not interested in all aspects of the institutional process" (interview, September 1999).

WRITING STRATEGIES

Two general strategies for presenting interview-based analyses can be discerned in published IE studies. In one, the writer uses interview data to produce a description, in the writer's voice, of the institutional processes under examination. Usually this account is a composite built up from multiple sources: people's explanations, documents, and so on. Knowledge gleaned through interviews with informants in different institutional locations is rolled together into a description of how a complex institution "works." The individual informants, however, do not "speak" in the text.

Researchers employing an alternative strategy use quoted excerpts from interviews to carry forward the description and analysis in the final text. George Smith (1998) uses the notion of the "exhibit" to specify a distinctive use of interview excerpts:

> As exhibits, the excerpts create windows within the text, bringing into view the social organization of my informants' lives for myself and for my readers to examine. Though what is brought into view emerges out of the dialogic relations of the interview, excerpts must not be read as extensions of my description. As exhibits, they make available the social organization of the everyday school lives of the individuals I interviewed. Dialogically they enter

> the actual social organization of schools into the text of the analysis. (p. 312)

Some writers combine these strategies, using composite accounts where analytically appropriate as well as bringing forward exhibits, descriptions, and life stories from the transcripts:

> In general, I use informants' descriptions when the matter is their actual work and the experience of doing it; I use my own description (based on multiple sources) when I am describing generalized relations or chains of action that transcend the local experience of any one informant. (McCoy 1999:47)

Institutional ethnographers try to maintain a focus on institutional relations not just during interviews, but in analysis and writing as well. This can be a challenge, because apparently minor features of presentation format, such as the identification of speakers, can support or interrupt that focus. For example, writing procedures that tag all quotes, regardless of topic, with the gender, race, and class status of the speaker risk inviting an individualizing line of analysis, in which class and ethnicity are treated as inherent in individuals rather than produced through coordinative social processes. Consequently, some IE writers suppress personal information about informants in order to keep the focus on the institutional processes they are describing; they identify quoted speakers only by their location in the institutional work process of which they speak (e.g., nurse, client, teacher, administrator). On the other hand, IE writers using life stories to examine an experience and elaborate a problematic usually find it analytically important to include biographical details and to distinguish speakers from each other through the use of pseudonyms.

It is sometimes useful for writers to instruct their readers in how to read interview excerpts. Campbell (1999) introduces her team's report with some comments about how excerpts should be understood:

> Viewed from the standpoint of what might be called "the official work processes" of community health, people with disabilities are clients. . . . In Project Inter-Seed's research we found that the person on the receiving end is not passive but must claim his or her place as an active participant in health care. . . . We ask you to think differently about clients and to read the word client in this report as a *job title (i.e., Client)*. It signifies that Clients work, including conducting relationships with people in the health care system, orienting Home Support Workers, managing different workers in their home in order to work towards having their individual health needs met. The understanding of people with disabilities as actively engaged in Home Support work helps set the frame for our discussions. (Pp. 1-2)

As in most aspects of IE, there is no fixed writing format to which all practitioners adhere; instead, writers have the goal of keeping the institution in view and different ways of realizing that goal.

◆ *Conclusion*

In one view, our brief discussion here risks misrepresenting institutional ethnography, because of the artificiality of separating out the "interview" parts of the approach. For practitioners, IE always combines theory and method, and these are understood not as dichotomized "ingredients" for an analysis, but as constituting a coherent approach to "writing the social" (Smith 1999). We have also been concerned with the danger of reifying the approach as technique. (Indeed, the IE focus on "ruling" prompts de Montigny to ask, skeptically, "What social forces of funding, or recognition, or careers

compel us to label and name that which we do as 'IE'?"; e-mail communication, September 1999.) These risks seem worth taking, however, because we believe that IE approaches offer distinctive advantages for researchers seeking to unmask the relations of ruling that shape everyday life.

Dorothy Smith's writing has been taken up in sociology as critique and revision of core theoretical concerns of the discipline, but the IE approach to empirical investigation has fit less comfortably within academic sociology, because its focus is not on theory building but on "what actually happens."[3] Much of the work we have discussed here, and much development of IE approaches, has occurred among professionals concerned with their relations to clients and the forces shaping their work or among activists working to understand the institutions they confront and seek to change. In addition, many IE researchers have found that the approach is a powerful teaching tool, because it can provide anyone with a strategy for investigating the lineaments of ruling (Naples forthcoming).

Institutional ethnography is one of the new modes of inquiry that have grown from the cracks in monolithic notions of "objective" social science, as women of all backgrounds, people of color, and others previously excluded from knowledge production have found space and "voice" to explore their experiences and pose questions relevant to their lives. In this context, the distinctiveness of IE lies in its commitment to going beyond the goal of simply "giving voice."

Ann Manicom reports that her feminist students—sensitized to the occlusion and misrepresentation of women's experience in so much traditional social science—sometimes worry about "imposing" extended analyses:

> So the work to be done is to help them think more deeply, first about the notion of "women's voices," and secondly about the notion of going "beyond" voice. The first process makes problem-

atic any simplistic notion of "experience" arising in any one of us as individuals; the second brings into view how the traces of social relations are already in women's accounts of their experience. Thus, what is called for in IE is not so much "going beyond" as it is tracing more intently what is already there to be heard. (E-mail communication, September 1999)

Such analyses are directed toward ruling processes that are pervasive, consequential, and not easily understood from the perspective of any local experience. But the IE approach suggests that an understanding grounded in such a vantage point is possible, and necessary, if we are to build upon excluded perspectives the kind of "map" of institutional processes that might be used in making changes to benefit those subject to ruling regimes.

■ Notes

1. The group includes several generations of Smith's students from the University of British Columbia and the Ontario Institute for Studies in Education (University of Toronto) and has attracted increasing numbers of other scholars. During the past decade, informal meetings have evolved into more regular conferences at York University and OISE, including a 1996 workshop sponsored by the American Sociological Association's Sex and Gender Section. Members of the group have collected exemplars of the approach in publications such as Campbell and Manicom's (1995) edited collection; a special symposium in *Human Studies* titled "Institutions, Ethnography, and Social Organization" (1998); and a forthcoming special issue of *Studies in Cultures, Organizations and Societies* on institutional ethnography (Smith forthcoming).

2. Although this approach shares with Foucault an interest in texts, power, and governance, there are some central differences that are particularly significant for empirical research. In Foucault's work and in work taking up his approach, for example, the notion of discourse designates a kind of large-scale conversation in and through texts; Smith works with a wider notion of discourse that is consistent with her social ontology and her commitment to grounding inquiry in the activities of actual individuals. For Smith, *discourse* refers to a field of relations that includes not only texts and their intertextual conversation, but the activities of people in actual sites who produce them and use them and take up the conceptual frames they circulate. This notion of discourse never loses the presence of the subject who activates the text in any local moment of its use.

3. Smith's critique involves seeing the enterprise of theory building as implicated in ruling relations. The revision it calls for is one of orientation: Rather than building theory, the researcher seeks to explicate how the categories of social theory work, in concert with related institutional processes, to regulate activities in local sites.

■ References

Andre Bechely, L. N. 1999. "To Know Otherwise: A Study of the Social Organization of Parents' Work for Public School Choice." Ph.D. dissertation, University of California, Los Angeles.

Campbell, M. 1988. "Management as 'Ruling': A Class Phenomenon in Nursing." *Studies in Political Economy* 27:29-51.

———. 1992. "Nurses' Professionalism: A Labour Process Analysis." *International Journal of Health Services* 22:751-65.

———. 1995. "Teaching Accountability: What Counts as Nursing Education?" Pp. 221-33 in *Knowledge, Experience, and Ruling Relations,* edited by M. Campbell and A. Manicom. Toronto: University of Toronto Press.

————. 1998. "Research on Health Care Experiences of People with Disabilities: Exploring the Everyday Problematic of Service Delivery." Presented at the conference "Exploring the Restructuring and Transformation of Institutional Processes: Applications of Institutional Ethnography," October, York University, Toronto.

————. 1999. "Home Support: What We've Learned about Continuity and Client Choice." Discussion paper, Project Inter-Seed: Learning from the Health Care Experiences of People with Disabilities, University of Victoria and South Vancouver Island Resource Centre for Independent Living, Victoria, BC.

Campbell, M. and N. Jackson. 1992. "Learning to Nurse: Plans, Accounts and Action." *Qualitative Health Research* 2:475-96.

Campbell, M. and A. Manicom, eds. 1995. *Knowledge, Experience, and Ruling Relations.* Toronto: University of Toronto Press.

de Montigny, G. 1995. *Social Working: An Ethnography of Front-Line Practice.* Toronto: University of Toronto Press.

DeVault, M. L. 1991. *Feeding the Family: The Social Organization of Caring as Gendered Work.* Chicago: University of Chicago Press.

————. 1999. *Liberating Method: Feminism and Social Research.* Philadelphia: Temple University Press.

Diamond, T. 1992. *Making Gray Gold: Narratives of Nursing Home Care.* Chicago: University of Chicago Press.

Eastwood, L. 2000. "Textual Mediation in the International Forest Policy Negotiation Process." Presented at the conference "Making Links: New Research in Institutional Ethnography," May, Ontario Institute for Studies in Education, Toronto.

Grahame, K. M. 1998. "Asian Women, Job Training, and the Social Organization of Immigrant Labor Markets." *Qualitative Sociology* 21:75-90.

————. 1999. "State, Community and Asian Immigrant Women's Work: A Study in Labor Market Organization." Ph.D. dissertation, University of Toronto.

Grahame, P. R. 1998. "Ethnography, Institutions, and the Social Organization of Knowledge." *Human Studies* 21:347-60.

————. 1999. "Doing Qualitative Research: Three Problematics." *Discourse of Sociological Practice* 2(1):4-10.

Griffith, A. I. 1984. "Ideology, Education, and Single Parent Families: The Normative Ordering of Families through Schooling." Ph.D. dissertation, University of Toronto.

————. 1992. "Educational Policy as Text and Action." *Educational Policy* 6:415-28.

————. 1995. "Mothering, Schooling, and Children's Development." Pp. 108-21 in *Knowledge, Experience, and Ruling Relations,* edited by M. Campbell and A. Manicom. Toronto: University of Toronto Press.

————. 1998. "Educational Restructuring in Ontario." Presented at the conference "Exploring the Restructuring and Transformation of Institutional Processes: Applications of Institutional Ethnography," October, York University, Toronto.

"Institutions, Ethnography, and Social Organization" (symposium). 1998. *Human Studies* 21:347-436.

Jackson, N. 1995. " 'These Things Just Happen': Talk, Text, and Curriculum Reform." Pp. 164-80 in *Knowledge, Experience, and Ruling Relations,* edited by M. Campbell and A. Manicom. Toronto: University of Toronto Press.

Khayatt, D. 1995. "Compulsory Heterosexuality: Schools and Lesbian Students." Pp. 149-63 in *Knowledge, Experience, and Ruling Relations,* edited by M. Campbell and A. Manicom. Toronto: University of Toronto Press.

Kinsman, G. 1989. "Official Discourse as Sexual Regulation: The Social Organization of the Sexual Policing of Gay Men." Ph.D. dissertation, University of Toronto.

————. 1996. *The Regulation of Desire: Homo and Hetero Sexualities.* Montreal: Black Rose.

Kinsman, G. and P. Gentile. 1998. " 'In the Interests of the State': The Anti-gay, Anti-lesbian National Security Campaign in Canada." Preliminary research report, Laurentian University, Sudbury, Ontario.

Luken, P. C. and S. Vaughan. 1991. "Elderly Women Living Alone: Theoretical and Methodological Considerations from a Feminist Perspective." *Housing and Society* 18:37-48.

———. 1996. "Narratives of Living Alone: Elderly Women's Experiences and the Textual Discourse on Housing." Presented at the annual meeting of the Society for the Study of Social Problems, New York.

———. 1998. "Talk about Race and Housing." Presented at the annual meeting of the Society for the Study of Social Problems, San Francisco.

Manicom, A. 1995. "What's Health Got to Do with It? Class, Gender, and Teachers' Work." Pp. 135-48 in *Knowledge, Experience, and Ruling Relations,* edited by M. Campbell and A. Manicom. Toronto: University of Toronto Press.

McCoy, L. 1987. "Looking at Wedding Pictures: A Study in the Social Organization of Knowledge." M.A. thesis, University of Toronto.

———. 1995. "Activating the Photographic Text." Pp. 181-92 in *Knowledge, Experience, and Ruling Relations,* edited by M. Campbell and A. Manicom. Toronto: University of Toronto Press.

———. 1998. "Producing 'What the Deans Know': Cost Accounting and the Restructuring of Post-secondary Education." *Human Studies* 21:395-418.

———. 1999. "Accounting Discourse and Textual Practices of Ruling: A Study of Institutional Transformation and Restructuring in Higher Education." Ph.D. dissertation, University of Toronto.

McKendy, J. 1999. "Bringing Stories Back In: Agency and Responsibility of Men Incarcerated for Violent Offences." Unpublished manuscript.

Mueller, A. 1995. "Beginning in the Standpoint of Women: An Investigation of the Gap between *Cholas* and 'Women of Peru.' " Pp. 96-107 in *Knowledge, Experience, and Ruling Relations,* edited by M. Campbell and A. Manicom. Toronto: University of Toronto Press.

Mykhalovskiy, E. 2000. "Knowing Health Care/Governing Health Care: Exploring Health Services Research as Social Practice." Ph.D. dissertation, York University.

Mykhalovskiy, E. and G. W. Smith. 1994. *Getting Hooked Up: A Report on the Barriers People Living with HIV/AIDS Face Accessing Social Services.* Toronto: Ontario Institute for Studies in Education.

Naples, N. 1997. "Contested Needs: Shifting the Standpoint on Rural Economic Development." *Feminist Economics* 3:63-98.

———. 1998. "Bringing Everyday Life to Policy Analysis: The Case of White Rural Women Negotiating College and Welfare." *Journal of Poverty* 2:23-53.

———. Forthcoming. "Negotiating the Politics of Experiential Learning in Women's Studies: Lessons from the Community Action Project." In *Locating Feminism,* edited by R. Wiegman. Durham, NC: Duke University Press.

Ng, R. 1995. "Multiculturalism as Ideology: A Textual Analysis." Pp. 35-48 in *Knowledge, Experience, and Ruling Relations,* edited by M. Campbell and A. Manicom. Toronto: University of Toronto Press.

———. 1996. *The Politics of Community Services: Immigrant Women, Class and State.* Halifax, Nova Scotia: Fernwood.

———. 1999. "Homeworking: Dream Realized or Freedom Constrained? The Globalized Reality of Immigrant Garment Workers." *Canadian Woman Studies* 19(3):110-14.

Parada, H. 1998. "Restructuring Families and Children in the Child Welfare Bureaucracy." Presented at the conference "Exploring the Restructuring and Transformation of Institutional Processes: Applications of Institutional Ethnography," October, York University, Toronto.

Pence, E. 1997. "Safety for Battered Women in a Textually Mediated Legal System." Ph.D. dissertation, University of Toronto.

Rankin, J. 1998. "Health Care Reform and the Restructuring of Nursing in British Columbia." Presented at the conference "Exploring the Restructuring and Transformation of Institutional Processes: Applications of Institutional Ethnography," October, York University, Toronto.

Reimer, M. 1995. "Downgrading Clerical Work in a Textually Mediated Labour Process." Pp. 193-208 in *Knowledge, Experience, and Ruling Relations,* edited by M. Campbell and A. Manicom. Toronto: University of Toronto Press.

Smith, D. E. 1987. *The Everyday World as Problematic: A Feminist Sociology.* Boston: Northeastern University Press.

———. 1990. *Texts, Facts and Femininity: Exploring the Relations of Ruling.* New York: Routledge.

———. 1996. "The Relations of Ruling: A Feminist Inquiry." *Studies in Cultures, Organizations and Societies* 2:171-90.

———. 1999. *Writing the Social: Theory, Critique, Investigations.* Toronto: University of Toronto Press.

———, ed. Forthcoming. "Institutional Ethnography" (special issue). *Studies in Cultures, Organizations and Societies.*

Smith, D. E. and A. I. Griffith. 1990. "Coordinating the Uncoordinated: Mothering, Schooling, and Social Class." Pp. 25-44 in *Perspectives on Social Problems: A Research Annual,* edited by G. Miller and J. A. Holstein. Greenwich, CT: JAI.

Smith, D. E. and G. Smith. 1990. "Re-organizing the Jobs Skills Training Relation: From 'Human Capital' to 'Human Resources.' " Pp. 171-96 in *Education for Work, Education as Work: Canada's Changing Community Colleges,* edited by J. Muller. Toronto: Garamond.

Smith, D. E., L. McCoy, and P. Bourne. 1995. "Girls and Schooling: Their Own Critique." Gender and Schooling Paper No. 2, Centre for Women's Studies in Education, Ontario Institute for Studies in Education.

Smith, G. W. 1988. "Policing the Gay Community: An Inquiry into Textually-Mediated Social Relations. *International Journal of the Sociology of Law* 16:163-83.

———. 1990. "Political Activist as Ethnographer." *Social Problems* 37:629-48.

———. 1995. "Accessing Treatments: Managing the AIDS Epidemic in Ontario." Pp. 18-34 in *Knowledge, Experience, and Ruling Relations,* edited by M. Campbell and A. Manicom. Toronto: University of Toronto Press.

———. 1998. "The Ideology of 'Fag': The School Experience of Gay Students." *Sociological Quarterly* 39:309-55.

Stock, A. 2000. "An Ethnography of Assessment in Elementary Schools." Ph.D. dissertation, University of Toronto.

Taylor, D., M. Bresalier, L. Gillis, C. McClure, L. McCoy, E. Mykhalovskiy, and M. Webber. Forthcoming. "Making Care Visible: Exploring the Everyday Work of People Living with HIV/AIDS." Report for the AIDS Program Committee, Toronto.

Townsend, E. A. 1996. "Institutional Ethnography: A Method for Analyzing Practice." *Occupational Therapy Journal of Research* 16:179-99.

———. 1998. *Good Intentions Overruled: A Critique of Empowerment in the Routine Organization of Mental Health Services.* Toronto: University of Toronto Press.

Turner, S. M. 1995. "Rendering the Site Developable: Texts and Local Government Decision Making in Land Use Planning." Pp. 234-48 in *Knowledge, Experience, and Ruling Relations,* edited by M. Campbell and A. Manicom. Toronto: University of Toronto Press.

Ueda, Y. 1995. "Corporate Wives: Gendered Education of Their Children." Pp. 122-34 in *Knowledge, Experience, and Ruling Relations,* edited by M. Campbell and A. Manicom. Toronto: University of Toronto Press.

Vaughan, S. and P. C. Luken. 1997. "Here and There/Now and Then: The Social Organization of Women's Moving Experiences." Presented at the annual meeting of the Pacific Sociological Association, San Diego, CA.

Walker, G. A. 1990. *Family Violence and the Women's Movement: The Conceptual Politics of Struggle.* Toronto: University of Toronto Press.

■ *Interviews*

Campbell, Marie. Telephone interview with M. L. DeVault, January 2000.
Diamond, Timothy. IE focus group conducted by L. McCoy, Duluth, MN, August 1999.
Grahame, Kamini Maraj. IE focus group conducted by L. McCoy, Duluth, MN, August 1999.
Griffith, Alison I. IE focus group conducted by L. McCoy, Toronto, October 1999.
Khayatt, Didi. IE focus group conducted by L. McCoy, Toronto, October 1999.
Mykhalovskiy, Eric. Interview conducted by L. McCoy, Toronto, September 1999.
Ng, Roxana. IE focus group conducted by L. McCoy, Toronto, October 1999.
Parada, Henry. IE focus group conducted by L. McCoy, Duluth, MN, August 1999.
Pence, Ellen. IE focus group conducted by L. McCoy, Duluth, MN, August 1999.
Smith, Dorothy E. IE focus group conducted by L. McCoy, Duluth, MN, August 1999.
———. Interview conducted by M. L. DeVault and L. McCoy, Toronto, September 1999.

19

ETHNOMETHODOLOGICAL ANALYSES OF INTERVIEWS

◆ Carolyn D. Baker

Although ethnomethodology is not typically associated with interview research, in this chapter I demonstrate a number of ways in which ethnomethodological ideas can be applied in the analysis of interview data. Such analysis provides for readings of the data that go well beyond the conventional "content" or "thematic" explications, where interviewee talk is seen as information about interior or exterior realities. Instead, ethnomethodological analyses draw attention to the interactive work that occurs during the questioning and answering process, understood as a place in the social world equally as "real" as any other, and where the participants undertake conversational interaction using resources recruited from their memberships in other settings. Such analyses attend to *how* participants do the work of conversational interaction, including how they make sense of each other, how they build a "corpus of interview knowledge," how they negotiate identities, and how they characterize and connect the worlds they talk about.

Ethnomethodology is a distinctive enterprise within the social sciences. Founded in the work of Harold Garfinkel (1967) and of Harvey Sacks, whose writings are collected in *Lectures on Conversation* (1992), ethnomethodology has been described as a "radical respecification" of the human sciences (Button 1991) because of the unique approach it takes to the study of social organization and social order. Most centrally, and most simply, ethnomethodologists are concerned with studying the resources and methods with which ordinary members go about making sense of the

AUTHOR'S NOTE: I wish to thank Mike Brown, Mike Emmison, and Eleni Petraki for comments on an earlier draft of this chapter. I am grateful to Jay Gubrium, James Holstein, and David Silverman for their helpful reviews.

settings, the people, and the events they encounter. John Heritage (1984) puts it this way:

> The term "ethnomethodology" . . . refers to the study of a particular subject matter: the body of common-sense knowledge and the range of procedures and considerations by means of which the ordinary members of society make sense of, find their way about in, and act on the circumstances in which they find themselves. (P. 4)

The reference to "ordinary" members is meant to draw attention to the sense-making accomplishments of any people anywhere and is a response and an alternative to sociologies that start with the assumptions of grand theories and/or assume that the (social) scientist's knowledge is of an inherently different order than the ordinary person's. Importantly, ethnomethodology does not compete with other sociologies for the mantle of explaining the social world. Ethnomethodology is concerned with *explicating how* things are *accomplished* by members to have the character that they do in any given site in the social world. Therefore, the topics that ethnomethodologists can study are limitless. Ethnomethodological inquiry is inspired by a sense of fascination with how people accomplish their identities, their activities, their settings, and their sense of social order.

An important recognition about ethnomethodology's interests in interview data is that ethnomethodologists do not use interviews to collect data in the manner that other social scientists do. Instead, ethnomethodologists study interviews as instances of settings—like other interactional events that are not interviews—in which members use interactional and interpretive resources to build versions of social reality and create and sustain a sense of social order. Interviews, then, are seen as a particular subset of interactional settings and as events that members make happen

thoroughly inside and as part of the social worlds being talked about, rather than as "outside" or "time out" from those social worlds. Understood this way, interviews are treated not so much as techniques for getting at information (although, commonsensically, people orient to them in this way), but more as in-their-own-right-analyzable instances of talk-in-interaction (see Baker 1997). Looked at and analyzed this way, interviews can yield new orders of insight about a range of matters, such as the production of situated identities and the moral work of accounting. This range of matters turns out to be (un)surprisingly large and, further, can connect in unanticipated ways with the topics of interviews (see Schaeffer and Maynard, Chapter 11, this volume).

In this chapter, I identify several keys to understanding the ethnomethodological approach to the analysis of interview data. These keys are as follows: (a) studying the interview as conversational interaction, (b) treating interview materials as accounts rather than reports, (c) looking for membership categorization work within the interaction and within accounts, (d) finding the production of identities, and, relatedly, (e) finding versions of worlds talked about in the interaction, in the accounts, and in the membership categorization work. These keys are connected, such that turning any one of them to open an analysis gives access to the next key, and the next. I use a number of extracts from different interview studies to demonstrate how to turn these keys. Although I have organized the chapter to focus on each of the five keys separately, each extract and discussion section contains reflections of the others.

◆ The Interview as Conversational Interaction

I discuss the first key in relation to an interview with a call taker for a technical support line for software users that took place in Sydney, Australia. Pam is a technician who answers calls from clients about their problems with computer software. The interviewer is Carolyn, a member of the research team present at the work site that is audiorecording calls to the help line and videotaping the call takers at work.[1] Interviews with call takers were organized spontaneously, and there was no set of guiding questions; call takers were simply asked to talk about their experiences as call takers and to share their insights into the work that they do. In the extract presented below, the interviewer's first turn captures precisely the ethnographic fact that the researchers have been witnesses to the work about which they will now interview the call takers.[2]

The first turns of this extract show the conversational work that is done by the participants in making the interview happen *as an interview*. Words are parts of utterances that are treated as activities (Turner 1974). The analysis of conversational interaction involves tracing the work that is done turn-by-turn by each speaker in relation to prior turns and in orientation to next turns. The sequential analysis of conversational interaction is most highly developed in the field known as conversation analysis (CA), which originated in the work of Harvey Sacks, Emanuel Schegloff, and Gail Jefferson (1974) and is closely related to ethnomethodology. Rather than drawing on the specialized terminology of CA here, I will provide a reading of each extract in less technical ethnomethodological terms.

We can focus first on the interviewer's work in talking with Pam, the technical support call taker. The first turn is an offer of a description characterizing the call taker's work, a selection of first topic, and an invitation for Pam to respond. It is also a selective characterization of what the researcher noticed as remarkable in Pam's work, and therefore a kind of self-description of the researcher's identity as a stranger to this form of work. Pam agrees

with this description, but not with the same sense of awe offered by the interviewer; Pam turns the remarkable into the mundane (turn 2). The interviewer then produces a comment that reinstates her initial assessment of the work as remarkable or extraordinary (turn 3). Pam responds by again downplaying the interviewer's characterization, and her response includes an account of how the long time is not so exceptional as to be marveled at (turn 4). The interviewer offers agreements over the course of Pam's ensuing talk (turns 5, 7, 9). After Pam concludes her account of why she does not mind long calls, the interviewer provokes some further talk about the nature of the calls by supplying yet more descriptions of Pam's work (turns 11, 13, 15), with which Pam agrees.

These comments—these "noticings"—are expressed as if from Pam's perspective. The interviewer is offering Pam some further descriptions of what her work might be like. Pam then begins a lengthy turn describing how she thinks during these long calls, describing her motivations and the callers' motivations and needs—a veritable jackpot of talk for the interviewer.

The first few lines of this extract show how deeply the interviewer has shaped the beginning of the interview. This shaping has involved characterizations of Pam and of the interviewer herself as a witness and a stranger to the work. It has involved finding things to marvel at, things that Pam makes unremarkable in her early accounts and disclaimers. Although there are no questions and no answers in this extract, as there are in many interviews, there is a clear initiation-reply format, and the exchange is oriented to by both speakers *as* an interview, as can be seen in the asymmetry of the talk, with the subject being Pam and her work. The study of *how* Carolyn and Pam converse to arrive at descriptions of Pam's work that might later be taken to be "interview data" shows that the social organization of the talk is fundamental to the production of such data. Any interview is by definition an instance of conversational

EXTRACT 1

Turn	Speaker	
1	Carolyn:	you spent a lot of time with some of those (0.2) people yesterday (.) a long time
2	Pam:	you learn patience haha
3	Carolyn:	boy
4	Pam:	ha well it's part of the job really (.) because if I wasn't on the phone to them (.) I'd be on the phone to another customer
5	Carolyn:	mm
6	Pam:	anyway like I'd be sitting there on the phone anyway
7	Carolyn:	yeah
8	Pam:	so (0.4) it doesn't really make it a lot different I'm happy to sit there as long as we fix the problem (0.4) it's like nice to 'cause if you're on a long call like that it's usually like troubleshooting rather than knowing the exact answer
9	Carolyn:	yep yep
10	Pam:	so (.) it's really good to (0.2) sit there and actually find out what does cause that problem (.) part of a learning process (1.0) so (0.4) that's (0.2) that's the reason I don't mind sitting on long calls
11	Carolyn:	and it's it's (0.2) there are all these gaps where (0.2) you know the person at the other end is trying something
12	Pam:	yeah
13	Carolyn:	and (.) and you sort of have to wait
14	Pam:	yeah
15	Carolyn:	and you don't know how long it's going to take

interaction, and this is deeply consequential for what interviewers and interviewees might say and hear. Relatedly, Mark Rapley and Charles Antaki (1998), who have studied interviewers' conversational work in "view-soliciting" open-ended interviews, conclude that "some of the things in interviewers' talk . . . do not so much solicit views as act positively to generate and shape them" (p. 605). An ethnomethodological analysis of interview talk calls into serious question the conventional social scientific characterization of interviewing as a form of data *collection*—which presumes that the data preexist the interview.

This first extract also illustrates what James Holstein and Jaber Gubrium (1997) call "active interviewing," during which "the active interviewer's role is to incite respondents' answers, virtually *activating narrative production* . . . by indicating—even suggesting—narrative positions, resources, orientations and precedents" (p. 123). The conduct of an active interview as proposed by Holstein and Gubrium (1997) is built on an appreciation that "any attempt to strip interviews of their interactional ingredients will be futile" (p. 114; see also Holstein and Gubrium 1995). These interactional ingredients are constitutive of the interview and are one key to analyzing the social organization of knowledge production in the interview (see also Schaeffer and Maynard, Chapter 11, this volume).

◆ Attention to Accounting

Ethnomethodological approaches to the analysis of interviews are characterized by the treatment of answers (and sometimes questions) as *accounts,* as distinct from reports about matters exterior to the interview or responses to questions. These accounts are best understood as sense-making work through which participants engage in explaining, attributing, justifying, describing, and otherwise finding possible sense or orderliness in the various events, people, places, and courses of action they talk about. In a first important sense, to be developed in the next section of the chapter, interviewees can be seen to account for themselves as competent members of the social category to which the interviewer has assigned them. That is, people are interviewed *as members* of some specific cate-

gory, or population, such as technical support line call takers or, as in the next example, *as* parents, teachers, or students. Accounting for oneself involves invoking a social world in which one's version of competent membership in a category could make sense. Accounting, then, is more than reporting or responding; it is a way of arranging versions of how things are or could be. It turns out that accounting is rife within interviews. As David Silverman (1993) puts it, "In studying accounts, we are studying displays of cultural particulars as well as displays of members' artful practices in assembling those particulars" (p. 114). This leads to the recognition that by "analyzing how people talk to one another, one is directly gaining access to a cultural universe and its content of moral assumptions" (p. 108).

The following transcribed example (see Extract 2), from a study I conducted with Jayne Keogh, comes from a set of interviews between parents and teachers held at a secondary school parents' night in Brisbane, Australia (see Baker and Keogh 1995). The interviews in this set are therefore not research interviews in the sense that they were conducted for research purposes; rather, they were conducted for school purposes and were recorded for research purposes. The interviews took place in a large room at the school that was set up with a number of stations where teachers sat at desks and additional chairs were provided for parents. Parents and, in most cases, the student who was the subject of the interview came to a teacher's desk, engaged in talk with the teacher, and left; then another family would come to the teacher. The following encounter involves the teacher, the student, Barry, and Barry's mother, although Barry does not speak in this exchange.

It can be seen that in turn 1 the teacher begins by addressing Barry ("how did you go?") and asking Barry for a look at (presumably) some report card or document that he holds. In turn 2, Barry's mother answers for him with a negative assessment of

EXTRACT 2

Turn	Speaker	
I	Teacher:	Right now <u>Barry</u>, (2.0) how did you go can I just have a look at that?
2	Mother:	Not real good actually [we're not really happy with it
3	Teacher:	[No
		(3.0)
	Teacher:	I think Barry's he's had a lot of activity
4	Mother:	Mm
5	Teacher:	with his um, er rap dance=
6	Mother:	=Yeah yeah=
7	Teacher:	the rock eisteddfod
8	Mother:	He's had the rock ((festival)) and he's had ((theatre group)), yeah I know, that's all finished now
9	Teacher:	Yeah, but that's good, I mean I don't think there's anything <u>wrong</u> with that and I think it might um perhaps, had something to do, perhaps, with his results
10	Mother:	Yeah

the report, followed by a three-second silence, after which the teacher addresses the mother by referring to Barry as "he," third person, which turns out to make Barry the third person in the interview. This observation led us to discuss the interviews that had this feature as talk designed for an overhearing audience, in this case the silent student (Baker and Keogh 1995; see also Silverman, Baker, and Keogh 1998).

Following this logic, we analyzed the interviews in terms of the accounting that parents and teachers did for the students' achievement (given that the students did not account for themselves) and in terms of their accounting for their competence *as teachers and parents* of the students. In this respect, we treated the interviews not as literal reports about the students, but as accounts about how parents and teachers invoked attributes of their respective categorical responsibilities and thus talked into being a version of how home-school communications should be arranged. Barry is audience to this work done by his mother and teacher.

It can be seen in this illustration how quickly the accounting begins: In turn 3,

the teacher finds a candidate reason for Barry's poor performance; the mother concurs with this account and then, in turn 8, claims responsibility for it ("that's all finished now"), which the teacher hears as a defense of her mothering practice ("Yeah, but that's good, I mean I don't think there's anything <u>wrong</u> with that"). An ethnomethodological approach to such interview data, using notions of membership categorization and accounting, treats the talk as much more than reports about Barry, showing how interinstitutional relations are produced from within the talk itself.

A further demonstration of this last point concerning turn design as context sensitive and context producing, is provided by closer investigation of the design of the first turn by the teacher. The teacher opens the talk; she thus claims to be the host of the interview. This makes sense given that the interview occurs at school, not in Barry's home, where Barry or a parent might be host. "Right now <u>Barry</u>" followed by a within-turn pause can be heard as representing Barry as one in a series of students whose parents the teacher will see that evening. (The converse, an opening along the lines of "Right now Miss X," spoken by Barry or a parent, would turn the relation around, so that Miss X becomes one in a series of teachers that the family will see that evening.) Barry, as *one in a series,* can account for the question that follows: "how did you go can I just have a look at that?" This account gets the teacher off the possible hook that she does not have at her fingertips all the relevant information about Barry, even though she is his teacher. So in this very first turn she is also doing a description of her conditions of work. Turn design, then, is sensitive to the institutional relations within which the talk occurs and that the talk simultaneously achieves. In interviews, then, there is always the display of appreciation of "who, situationally speaking, they are, and what, situationally speaking, they are up to" (Zimmerman 1992: 50). Interviews are definitely not "time out" from the social worlds that the participants are talking about; rather, they are reflexive descriptions of those worlds. Heritage (1984) makes the point that "in designing the accounts which formulate their actions, actors address the unavoidable accountability of their own accounting practices" (p. 177).

◆ *Membership Categorization Work in Interview Talk*

A powerful approach to uncovering the reflexive relation of speaker, audience, and topic in research interviews is found in the use of membership categorization work by speakers. Membership categorization analysis originated in the work of Harvey Sacks (1974, 1992) and has been developed by Lena Jayyusi (1984), Stephen Hester and Peter Eglin (1997), and David Silverman (1998). Sacks's (1974) initial writings on membership categorization proposed the idea that membership categories are resources with which people do reasoning.

Membership categories carry with them more or less tightly associated activities, or "predicates" (for example, babies are members who conventionally cry), and further, membership categories come in sets (for example, babies and mothers are two membership categories that are heard to belong to the same set, or "device," such as "family"). Membership categorization analysis turns on the identification of how speakers and hearers generate and use categories and membership categorization devices as ways of describing and making sense of events and situations. It turns out that interviews, as much as any other site of talk-in-interaction, are replete with the use of membership categorization work—reasoning with categories, reasoning from activities to categories, reasoning from categories to activities. Observing how categories are generated and elaborated within interview talk is a sensitive way of investigating how "particulars" are assembled into a social world and moral universe as described by speakers. I have summarized an approach to this way of examining interview talk in the following terms:

> Interview responses . . . are treated as accounts . . . by a member of a category for activities attached to that category. . . . in this accounting work, we look for the use of membership categorization devices by the interviewer and respondent, and show how both are involved in the generation of versions of social reality built around categories and activities. Further, in the work done with categories and activities, we see the local production in each case of versions of a moral order. (Baker 1997:131)

Researchers implicitly use membership categories to "collect" interviewees within or as representatives of a posited category of social actor. Interviewees are then made accountable members of that particular category in the sense that they then are meant to sound like members of that category and speak from within that particular, research-generated categorical incumbency and not some other. In this sense, they are accountable for speaking as competent members of that category might speak, and, for the most part, interviewees do this. One exception is found where the theory of the category in which incumbency is proposed is not shared, where an individual does not know how to sound like a member of the category. Such a situation arose on one occasion in my earlier studies of "adolescent-adult" interviews, when one interviewee did not produce items (particulars) that matched the cultural concept of "adolescent" in play within the questions (Baker 1984). Most of the people interviewed were able to (re)produce, as I put it, an adult theory of adolescence, and were therefore able to answer the questions in the interviewer's adult terms, and I suggested that "being" an adolescent amounted to displaying exactly that cultural knowledge of adult-adolescent relationships.

Going beyond this first matter of the categorical incumbency assigned to the interviewee, the use of membership categorization analysis can uncover much more within interview data. Taking as established the category membership from within which the interviewee is asked to speak, we can look further for the array of other, related categories that are generated in the interactive talk. These other categories are produced as a "cast of characters" *surrounding* the interviewee in the interviewee's accounts of membership of the category. These characters are introduced with and through associated predicates or attributes, and those attributes are specific to the interviewee's descriptions of his or her own conditions of work or life and, importantly, his or her own attributes within those descriptions. We read these other characters, then, as incumbents of other categories that connect with the research-relevant category and that are, in effect, elaborations of it.

The following segment of data (see Extract 3), from a study by Kathy Roulston

(2001) of interviews with itinerant primary school music teachers in Queensland, Australia, provides an illustration of this way of analyzing interview data. This extract comes from an interview that Roulston— herself an experienced primary school music teacher now undertaking higher-degree research—conducted with a teacher. In this interview, the teacher has been describing her relations with office staff in the various schools she visits (except for Roulston, pseudonyms are used in the transcript), who are variously "nice as pie," "down to earth," or "a real bitch"—clearly morally laden attributes variously assigned to members of the category. She moves from her discussion of them to identifying some new categories of persons she encounters during the week: groundsmen and cleaners.

This segment of interview talk is nicely "rounded" in that the teacher begins and ends with the same lineup of characters as being the ones who matter in her getting her job done. (At the end, a comparison is drawn with classroom teachers, who are made out *not* to be crucial to her coping with the job.) The office staff, groundsmen, and cleaners are given different degrees of precisely the attribute that the itinerant music teacher needs: helpfulness. In this respect, her remarks are an indirect way of stating what she needs, via description and valorization of those who give it.

Roulston (2001) makes the point that these characters are brought to life within accounts through the use of such devices as reporting their direct speech and other scenic practices, in which the interviewer (herself an experienced music teacher) can hear and appreciate the particulars that represent the pattern (as in turn 114, "Wow"). That the researcher and interviewee in this case share coincumbency of the category that is the focus of the research is of course not incidental to how the interview talk proceeds. The interviewer's "wow" in this (very) active interview (see Holstein and Gubrium 1995) signals coincumbency. After this assessment ("wow") the teacher goes further to imply that the groundsman

EXTRACT 3

Turn	Speaker	
104	Teacher:	but o:::h it's (.) yeah the office people (.) if you can get on with the office and the cleaners
105	Roulston:	I'll tell you what [that counts for a lot doesn't it=
106	Teacher:	[and the groundsman
107	Roulston:	=because they're the ones that you're working with really aren't they heh heh heh=
108	Teacher:	=you know I can go to Frank at um Varsity and say 'Oh Frank (.) 've
109		got a little job for you' he'd say 'Oh OK what is it' and I'll tell him and he said (.) you know one day I wanted a filing cabinet [moved from my block (.) two blocks over
110	Roulston:	[yeah
111	Teacher:	we're exchanging he said (1.0) 'OK when do you want it done' I said 'Whenever you
112		can' [you know 'I'll empty it' (1.0) and within five minutes he was there to do it
113	Roulston:	[yeah
114	Roulston:	Wow
115	Teacher:	you know 'Oh Frank I'd like the piano moved' heh heh ((mock annoyance))
116		I don't upaknow these pe(h)ople that wa(h)nt' heh heh you know but he always (.) he's always friendly about it (.) [the one at Roseview depends on what mood he's in=
117	Roulston:	[yeah
118	Roulston:	=yeah yeah=
119	Teacher:	=Austin don't have one (2.0) and the one at (.) Eldergrove (.) he's pretty good=
120	Roulston:	=yeah=
121	Teacher:	=he's only part-time he works twenty hours a week but if I've asked him to do something (.) he's he's done it he mightn't have been able to do it straight away (.)
122	Teacher:	but (.) he comes in and does things for me so (1.0) yeah but this is it get on with the cleaners the secretary (.) and the groundsman and your'er fine
123		(1.0)

Frank will even move the piano on a moment's notice. Whether or not Frank the groundsman even exists, the force of the teacher's account of his willingness to help is, to the researcher-audience, an effective and telling particular about the moral world of the music teacher's work. As Rod Watson and T. S. Weinberg (1982) put it:

We are not aiming for a truth-functional approach to the content of the interlocutors' accounts. In no way are we attempting to assess the truth-value of these accounts; we are interested in how some aspects of the accounts are put together irrespective of their truth-value. (P. 57)

◆ The Production of Identities

In many studies, the persons interviewed might themselves be the "subjects" of the research. That is, rather than being talked with as witnesses to some scenes or events, or as commentators on some external situation, people might be interviewed about themselves as members of some particular category (see Baker 1997; Antaki and Widdicombe 1998; Widdicombe 1998). This is the case in a recent study of a 15-year-old girl named Hannah, one of several young people who were at the center of Michele Knobel's (1999) case studies of literacy learning at school. This study involved Knobel's observing and videotaping Hannah's classroom and interviewing Hannah, her teacher, and her mother in various locations at home and school. Hannah therefore knew that she was a prime subject of the research, and she knew that classroom observations, home visits, and talks with the researcher would form data for the study.

As I have proposed in a prior analysis of these materials (Honan et al. 2000), Hannah could be seen to be "representing herself" to the researcher throughout all the research activities and documenting for the researcher just who she is, what she is like, how she learns literacy, and so on. She knows that the researcher will eventually assemble bits and pieces of these observations and interviews into the ethnographic text of a case study. Whereas in many such studies researchers seek to draw from their scattered observations coherent portraits of the case study subjects, in this case the researcher was theoretically alert to competing ways in which Hannah might represent herself. However, the case study text is opened with the question "Who is Hannah?" and we might take it that Hannah also understood this to be the main research interest.

In this kind of ethnographic case study we can observe a version of the "documentary method of interpretation" (Garfinkel 1967; Watson and Weinberg 1982), in which "particulars" are interpreted with reference to an "underlying pattern" and in which both the particulars and the underlying pattern are open to revision in light of each other. Each thing that Hannah says and does could count as a "particular" that we might study against other particulars in order to locate some underlying pattern or, in this case, patterns. The ethnographic text is like a "documentary" film, showing us Hannah here and there, and others talking about Hannah. Hannah is a documentary subject, then, in three senses: (a) She is the subject of Knobel's research and later text, which documents the lives of each of several young people; (b) Knobel herself uses "particulars" and assembles them so as to point to "underlying patterns," as shown in the published text; and (c) Hannah can be seen to do the work of "documenting herself" to Knobel throughout the data collection period.

The documentary method of interpretation also can be found *inside* the course of interview talk undertaken as part of the study. Interview talk can be seen as one of many interactive events in which people accomplish a sense of identity. In the study from which these materials are drawn, the interviews can be seen as sites where Hannah, her teacher, and her mother, in talk with the researcher, accomplish the identity of Hannah (which in this research is the very point of the interviews). These others accomplish reflexively their own identities, speaking as teacher and mother. The interviewer is intimately engaged in the construction of these versions of Hannah through the questions she asks and through how she hears what is said.

Using an extract from an interview segment presented in Knobel's (1999) chapter on Hannah, I will show this documentary work undertaken by the interviewer, Michele, and Hannah. The exchange (Extract 4) begins at a point where Michele has asked Hannah how much she knows about the background of her two inter-

EXTRACT 4

Turn	Speaker	
111	Michele:	Right OK OK. uhm, and what about your friends, Phon and Ha, did they come here as refugees, or they just moved over?
112	Hannah:	N:o, I think they were actually born here. I'm not too sure. I think Phon might have actually moved over here, and so did Ha. But I don't know- I don't know much, I just know that they- Ha's come from Vietnam. Phon's come from Cambodia. That's all I know.
113	Michele:	Right. That's all they've ever told you. Yeah yeah. And sometimes it's hard to ask people more
114	Hannah:	Well I've never even really thought about it ((smiles))
115	Michele:	Oh ((laughs)) No, no, I was just interested. Ok, and if you had three wishes in the whole world, what would you wish?
116	Hannah:	Oh I always thought about that. U:hmm, that all the violence goes away, that there were no pollution and that it would never happen again, a:nd that we used, that we did stuff like in the olden days
117	Michele:	Oh what do you mean by that?
118	Hannah:	Horse and cart, so we wouldn't cause pollution and, like, did stuff so it wouldn't cause pollution, or we used- just stuff that didn't cause pollution, we used stuff that didn't cause pollution

national friends. Hannah claims not to know much.

What we see is a brief interaction in which Hannah expresses her lack of knowledge of her friends' histories and in which the interviewer acknowledges that finding. However, there is much identity-production work occurring in this fleeting interaction. A first observation is that by asking the question in turn 111, the interviewer has done a description of Hannah by implying that Hannah could know this information; possibly, that she should know it. It is in this sense that no question is neutral in respect to the way it characterizes the person being interviewed. Hence the identity work that emerges in the interview is a product of the questioning as much as it is a product of the answering. A second observation to be made is that Hannah's "lack of knowledge" is entirely a product of the question's having been asked in the first place. Otherwise, it would never surface as a "particular" about Hannah.

What is most compelling about the identity work in this fleeting segment, however, is the way in which the interviewer works

with Hannah to account for her lack of knowledge and thus to recover her as a person who, on further reflection, might not be expected to know this information. The sequence involved in this "repair" work is quite elegant. Hannah completes her turn 112 with "That's all I know." If this interview were just about gathering information about Hannah from Hannah, this comment could have concluded the topic. That is, the interviewer could have moved on at that point to another question. Instead, the interviewer supplies *two* accounts while expressing agreement ("Yeah yeah"), accounts that effectively present some reasons Hannah might not know this kind of information.

The interviewer, in effect, is doing part of Hannah's identity work for her by supplying these reasons. Hannah is recovered as a competent person by the interviewer's offer of these reasons. These reasons imply that Hannah's lack of knowledge was due to the facts that (a) friends do not always tell you everything and (b) asking such questions—seeking the missing information—is a possibly delicate matter.

This turn (113) is also the interviewer's description of Hannah: She is produced here as a member of a category of people who would appreciate this delicacy.

In documentary method terms, the "particular" that this sequence produced about Hannah—her not knowing the information about her friends—is adjusted from possibly pointing to a "lack" in Hannah to pointing to a different "underlying pattern" that the interviewer has intimated. This different pattern is an underlying competent Hannah in a world where we may not be expected to know such matters (even though the initial question in turn 111 intimated that these are things we should or could know).

But the identity work does not stop there. In turn 114 Hannah offers what could be a counterexplanation for her lack of knowledge and a counterparticular to offset the "particular" that the interviewer has just produced. Hannah says, "Well I've never even really thought about it" and smiles. In this turn she removes herself from the identity attribution that the interviewer has found for her and provides an alternative. The interviewer receives this alternative first as a surprise—"Oh"—and laughs. The second part of turn 115 includes the interviewer's disclaimer *and* an account: "No, no, I was just interested." What is being disclaimed? To what is the "No, no" directed?

The account, however, "I was just interested" (= "this is why I asked") seems to implicate Hannah's identity. We cannot know how Hannah heard it, but it seems the interviewer is characterizing the preceding talk, with its admission by Hannah that she never thought about the matter, as not important, or not consequential, thus resurrecting Hannah's competence once again. It seems that both interviewer and Hannah are engaged in positing and negotiating "particulars" about Hannah. Hannah's correction (turn 114) of Michele's generous offer (turn 113) is especially intriguing in terms of Hannah's position as a documentary subject and of her possibly speaking "for the record." We should note that after the "No, no" disclaimer, the interviewer changes the topic as appears in turns 116-119.

In response to the interviewer's question in turn 115, Hannah initially offers three wishes. The interviewer follows up in turn 119 with a second question, specifying "wishes just for yourself." This signals another order of wishes, "just for yourself," and retrospectively describes Hannah's first three wishes as in a category "not just for yourself." This respecification of the question asks Hannah to draw on her knowledge of this second category "just for yourself."

Hannah shows some difficulty with finding candidate "wishes" to fill this category (see Extract 5). This interview segment reads more like an interrogation, with the interviewer providing a lot of "why" questions. At turn 127, the interviewer appears to change the topic somewhat abruptly. This segment is reminiscent of other interviews with adolescents, in which the interviewer asks for lists of things that belong in particular categories (Baker 1984) and then hears candidate answers as not fitting those categories. This can lead to puzzlement, as might be present in turns 121-25. In such sequences the interviewer can be seen to be working very hard to make sense of what the interviewee is saying and how it can possibly fit into the presumably shared category system.

Within this segment, however, is a sequence that is recoverable in terms of the documentary work both interviewer and interviewee are doing. Hannah has said she would like it if her school and all of her friends and teachers could move to the country. This may or may not be an order of "wish" intended by the interviewer as a wish "just for herself." We could read Hannah's wish as ambiguous on this point. In any case, the interviewer pursues the ideas by seeking explanations in three consecutive turns (121, 123, and 125). These turns that seek explanations produce answers by Hannah in which she offers more

EXTRACT 5

Turn	Speaker	
120	Hannah:	U:hmm. . . . u:hmm . . . that my scho:ol- that all my friends and all the people in my class and friends and stuff, that- and that my school was like in out in the country- we lived out in the country. So we're like based out in the country, and I still have all my friends and the teachers
121	Michele:	Why's that?
122	Hannah:	'Cause I'd like to live out there. Don't like living here
123	Michele:	Why- How come you [do-
124	Hannah:	[Oh I like- I like living here but, I like country better
125	Michele:	Why's that?
126	Hannah:	Well, I haven't actually lived there, and I like- I like to like, have fun and
127	Michele:	Oh is that right? What did you want to be when you leave school?

particulars about herself: turn 122, she does not like living in the city; turn 124, she does like living in the city, but prefers the country; and turn 126, she has not "actually" lived in the country. Hannah produces two self-corrections in this segment, each prompted by a "why" question from the interviewer. It seems the interviewer is after some kind of accounting for Hannah's wish (Why do you not like living here? Why do you like the country better?). Hannah deflects the accounting in each case, once by withdrawing the grounds for the account (I do like living in the city) and once by correcting an implied claim (that she has lived in the country). She is revising the particulars of herself as a documentary subject in these turns.

These revisions are oriented to the possibility of Hannah's being held accountable. Michele has produced Hannah as a "theoretic actor" (McHugh 1970), as one who can be taken to know what she is doing and who can account for her activities in ways understood to be competent. Young children, for example, are not held to be theoretic actors in this sense. So here, Hannah is being held accountable for her "wishes."

In addition to using her status as a theoretic actor to revise her claims, Hannah calls on another membership category altogether as part of the production of herself

at this moment in the interview. First she offers the confession or concession that she has not "actually" lived in the country (which may be hearable as a weakening of the rationality of her wish). She follows this with an appeal to herself as someone who "likes to have fun." This dramatically shifts who she is speaking as, from the "wish + reason producer" organized by the interviewer to something like "just a kid." In turn 127 the interviewer changes course. This is a pragmatic move that works to get Hannah off the other conversational hook.

Turn 127 produces Hannah as someone who has ideas about what to be when she leaves school. And the identity work goes on. The interviewer and Hannah could both take it that the point of having the interviews is to gain a sense of who Hannah is, but the interviews might more usefully be described as work that produces, for the participants and later readers, a sense of who Hannah could be. The turn-by-turn interactive work that has gone into proposing and managing "particulars" about Hannah shows how some items are withdrawn from the interview record whereas others are let stand. Most important, the version of Hannah that anyone could take away from this talk is produced by both participants. Hannah works to assemble a sense of herself at various points in the interview, hearing and dealing with the identity implications in Michele's talk. I would propose further that as Michele interviews Hannah, Hannah uses particulars of what Michele says to achieve a "sense of Michele" (see also Holstein and Gubrium 1995). I have not attempted that analysis here, but would offer the observation that any subject of an ethnographic case study who enters repeatedly into research conversations such as these would reflect back to an interviewer the sense that he or she has of the interviewer's identity and interests.

◆ Versions of Worlds

According to Gubrium and Holstein (1997), ethnomethodological studies focus on "how members accomplish, manage, and reproduce a sense of social structure, and themselves confer privilege on select versions. Research centers on the properties of practical reasoning and the constitutive work that produce the unchallenged appearance of a stable reality" (p. 44). By extension, ethnomethodological studies of interviews do the same thing. Some of the properties of practical reasoning—centrally, the use of membership categorization and of accounting—have been shown in relation to the transcript segments presented above, as has the constitutive work involved in producing identities. Interview participants can be seen to be engaging in a range of practices and procedures that make the interview happen as an accountable event in itself (see Silverman 1973; Watson and Weinberg 1982). They can also be seen to be engaging in a range of practices and procedures that assign structure, sense, rationality, and order to the worlds they describe. Accounts are central to this work. Silverman (1993) has pointed out Garfinkel's (1967) insistence that accounts are part of the worlds they describe and has further stated that interviewees "invoke a sense of social structure in order to assemble recognizably 'sensible' accounts which are adequate for the purposes

at hand" (p. 114). Such assembling of recognizably "sensible" accounts raises the intriguing question of what kind of social world is posited such that the accounts are sensible displays of possible courses of actions within it.

A final transcript excerpt (see Extract 6) demonstrates how finely the work of assembling sensible accounts is organized in interviews and how the interview talk invokes a sense of social structure and order. In the study from which this extract is drawn, Greer Johnson and I invited elderly Italian Australians living in a regional community to tell their courtship and marriage stories to an interviewer for the purpose of a book to be written (see Baker and Johnson 2000). In analyzing conversational interaction in the interviews where the stories were told, we studied orientations that were evident in the opening turns of the storytelling. These included orientations to the written list of possible topics that might be addressed, orientation to the interviewer's indications of what kind of detail was wanted, and orientation to the destiny of the storytelling in a book. The extract shows the beginning of an interview conducted by Greer with Celia. In common with other interviews designed to encourage talk and elicit information, the interviewer provides prompts, checks, and questions.

An orientation to a list is observable in the reading of this extract; the reader can probably infer that the list included such matters as how you met your partner, the courtship, and the marriage. This is inferable because Celia shows her use of a list as an organizing device in her beginning following a six-second silence, and then at turns 14, 16, and 36. It can also be seen that Celia and the interviewer have shared knowledge of people and places. This shared knowledge is formulated at turn 3.

Both Celia and the interviewer know that Celia's brother is named "Marco," and they both know that they both know it. The significance of this turn, as we have de-

EXTRACT 6

Turn	Speaker	
I	Greer:	[This is an interview] with Celia Rosetti (.) on Sunday (.) the sixteenth of March nineteen ninety seven
		(6.0)
2	Celia:	I first met my partner (.) in (0.8) in Caltabellotta where I was born (0.9) my parents (.) had a hotel (0.9) and he worked on the farm (.) which was the closest farm to the (.) to the ↑ town (0.4) he went ↑ past the hotel every time he had to ↑ go to town (.) therefore (.) he called into the hotel often (0.2) he then became friendly with my brother (.) and- ((at this point it sounds as if the recorder was turned off; Celia may have signaled to stop to have a drink))
3	Greer:	So that was (.) Marco
4	Celia:	Mmm mmm mmmm and we began going out together (0.4) [((laughs))
5	Greer:	[Why are (hh) you laughing?
6	Celia:	I'm laughing at it ↑ because our ↑ first date, when he asked to take me out to the pictures (.) we were making ravioli at the hotel that ↑ night and when you make them in the hotel it was about three or four hundred dozen you know (.) and ((laugh)) I put him down so that he spent the evening plac- ((cough/laugh)) placing the ravioli and counting them.
7	Greer:	Oh for the next day?
8	Celia:	((cough/laugh)) Yes for the next day's function.
9	Greer:	So that was the first [time
10	Celia:	[(coughs) That was the first time (.) when he plucked up courage to ask could he take me to the pictures .hhh
11	Greer:	And how old were you (.) when [you first
12	Celia:	[A:h, I was about eighteen=
13	Greer:	=Uh huh=
14	Celia:	=And I was married when I was (0.2) arr nineteen and a half.
15	Greer:	Uh huh
16	Celia:	Um (1.0) we spent our courtship (0.2) by going to pictures (0.9) and to dances (0.8) entertainment was very limited at that time.
17	Greer:	What were the dances like=
18	Celia:	=O:h
19	Greer:	that you went to
20	Celia:	Oh well we went to the (0.2) dance at the (0.7) Italian Club in town (0.1) and went to the dances at Avola
21	Greer:	Uh huh.
22	Celia:	If it was too far out (.) we couldn't go because (0.9) ahh (0.9) we had to do our ↑ work before ↑ going and ah (0.1) Marco my brother (0.9) wouldn't wait sometimes ((laugh))
***		[turns 23-33 omitted]
34	Celia:	But ah (0.2) that's about all we had the opportunity to do.
35	Greer:	So your parents were happy ↑ about

scribed it, is to indicate to Celia how to balance the telling of a story to an insider with the telling of a story to outsider audiences, for the book, "for the record" (Baker and Johnson 2000). We can see that on the next mention of reference to this person, Celia in turn 22 uses the phrase "Marco my brother."

This sensitivity to the story's destiny concerning Marco in this case is equivalent to some of the other opening turns canvassed above (see Extract 1, turn 1; Extract 2, turn 1).

Each opening move by the interviewer contains an implicit description of the local, situated circumstances of the interview, which is a characterization of the world within which the interview is situated and of how the interview fits inside that world. As Watson and Weinberg (1982) put it, "Such interviews and our accounts of them involve many reflexivities; they constitute, in the phenomenological sense, the circumstances they describe" (p. 73).

The participants can also be seen to be engaging in a range of interpretive practices and procedures that assign structure, sense, rationality, and order to the worlds they describe. For example, as shown in turns 4-8, Celia uses laughter *as* an interpretive puzzle for the interviewer. In effect, she is inviting the interviewer to ask for an account of why she is laughing:

What sense of social structure provides for Celia's explanation to be seen as *sensibly* funny? How does Celia invoke that sense? She does this in part by calling on an understanding that first dates in courtship are meant to be private affairs for the couple and not immersion into a family's work. The interviewer, in turn 7, finds and offers a sensible account for why the event turned out as it did: The family needed the ravioli prepared "for the next day." Both interviewee and interviewer are engaged in "putting together a world that is recognizably familiar, orderly and moral" (Baker 1997:143).

◆ Conclusion: Connecting Talk and Topic

Conventional content or thematic reading or coding of interview data is aimed primarily at uncovering what people say about topics. As I have shown in this chapter, ethnomethodological interests extend very deeply into how people talk about those topics in the local, situated event that is the interview. Talk about a topic is understood as a display of practical and moral reasoning, not only about the topic of the interview, but about what a competent or sensible *interview account* of events, people, courses of action, and so on could sound like. In this "roundabout" way, interviews, like any other instances of talk-in-interaction, provide an order of data about how the social world is, or could be, put together *in everyday life.*

From this perspective, social order is not something imposed on interview data by analysts, but something assembled by the participants using their commonsense members' resources. Ethnomethodological analyses of interview talk show the deployment by *both* participants of routine ways of assembling what comes to be seen as rationality, morality, or social order, and by extension displays of "culture in action" (Hester and Eglin 1997).

The five sections I have presented in this chapter are meant to represent related dimensions of an ethnomethodological interest in interview data. The entry point of studying the interview as conversational interaction shows that, to an ethnomethodologist, the interview data *are* the social organization of talk between interviewer and interviewee. From that initial point I have worked through the topics of accounting activities, membership categorization work, and identity work toward two questions: What kind of social world are the speakers making happen in their talk? and What kind of social world must speakers assume such that they speak this way? These are some of the resources that researchers may use in investigating interview talk just like any other talk where members "make sense of, find their way about in, and act on the [interview] circumstances in which they find themselves" (Heritage 1984:4).

Studying the social organization of talk about, or around, a topic does not mean losing sight of what is said in terms of propositional "content" in terms of reports on realities external to the interview—for example, that Barry has been too active in theater events, or that Frank the groundsman moved a filing cabinet, or that Celia's family made hundreds of dozens of ravioli. Nor does it mean losing the "interior to persons" reports, such as that the software help-line call taker doesn't mind long calls or that Hannah has never thought about where her friends were born. However, there is much reason researchers should proceed with caution in treating these kinds of reports as "interview data" without looking closely at the specific local circumstances and conversational interactions that generated these reports.

In a more positive light, however, ethnomethodological analyses of interview data are interesting to generate because they represent a far more reflexive social science research practice than most other approaches. In such analyses it becomes impossible *not* to see the artful practices of interviewer and interviewee in making the interview happen, and consequently it becomes very difficult to unhitch "answers" from their (em)bedding in an actual, local situation of production. The investigation of the reflexivities involved leads to a continuously developing appreciation of how the social world is assembled and accounted for. Although researchers rarely conduct interviews with the intent of performing ethnomethodological analysis, in-

terviews are replete with evidence of how relevant identities and memberships are assembled as part of the talk about the topic and of how the topic can accountably be talked about. Interviews can be opened to this distinctive order of interest with the use of the keys I have described, and fundamental aspects of social organization can be found there.

◆ Notes

1. This work was part of a study titled "The Social Organization of Expert-Lay Communication: A Micro-analytic Investigation of Calls to a Computer Software Help Line," conducted by Carolyn Baker, Mike Emmison, and Alan Firth and funded by an Australian Research Council Large Grant, 1999-2001.

2. Following are explanations of the notation symbols used in the transcript extracts in this chapter:

underlining	emphasis
(0.2)	silence or pause, timed in seconds
(.)	microsecond pause
((click))	transcriber's description of sound, item, or activity
=	no discernible gap between turns
[	talk of speakers overlaps at this point
o:::h	vowel sound extended
↑	rising intonation
(h)/(hh)	laughing sound
.hh	inbreath

■ References

Antaki, C. and S. Widdicombe. 1998. "Identity as an Achievement and as a Tool." Pp. 1-14 in *Identities in Talk*, edited by C. Antaki and S. Widdicombe. London: Sage.

Baker, C. D. 1984. "The 'Search for Adultness': Membership Work in Adolescent-Adult Talk." *Human Studies* 7:301-23.

———. 1997. "Membership Categorization and Interview Accounts." Pp. 130-43 in *Qualitative Research: Theory, Method and Practice,* edited by D. Silverman. London: Sage.

Baker, C. D. and G. Johnson. 2000. "Stories of Courtship and Marriage: Orientations in Openings." *Narrative Inquiry* 10(2):1-25.

Baker, C. D. and J. Keogh. 1995. "Accounting for Achievement in Parent-Teacher Interviews." *Human Studies* 18:263-300.

Button, G., ed. 1991. *Ethnomethodology and the Human Sciences.* Cambridge: Cambridge University Press.

Garfinkel, H. 1967. *Studies in Ethnomethodology.* Englewood Cliffs, NJ: Prentice Hall.

Gubrium, J. F. and J. A. Holstein. 1997. *The New Language of Qualitative Method.* New York: Oxford University Press.

Heritage, J. 1984. *Garfinkel and Ethnomethodology.* Cambridge: Polity.

Hester, S. and P. Eglin, eds. 1997. *Culture in Action: Studies in Membership Categorization Analysis.* Washington, DC: International Institute for Ethnomethodology and Conversation Analysis/ University Press of America.

Holstein, J. A. and J. F. Gubrium. 1995. *The Active Interview.* Thousand Oaks, CA: Sage.

———. 1997. "Active Interviewing." Pp. 113-29 in *Qualitative Research: Theory, Method and Practice,* edited by D. Silverman. London: Sage.

Honan, E., M. Knobel, C. D. Baker, and B. Davies. 2000. "Producing Possible Hannahs: Theory and the Subject of Research." *Qualitative Inquiry* 6:9-32.

Jayyusi, L. 1984. *Categorization and the Moral Order.* London: Routledge & Kegan Paul.

Knobel, M. 1999. *Everyday Literacies: Students, Discourse and Social Practice.* New York: Peter Lang.

McHugh, P. 1970. "A Common-Sense Perception of Deviance." Pp. 151-81 in *Recent Sociology,* Vol. 2, *Patterns of Communicative Behavior,* edited by H. P. Dreitzel. London: Macmillan.

Rapley, M. and C. Antaki. 1998. " 'What do you think about . . . ?': Generating Views in an Interview." *Text* 18:587-608.

Roulston, K. 2001. "Investigating the 'Cast of Characters' in a Cultural World." In *How to Analyse Talk in Institutional Settings: A Casebook of Methods,* edited by A. McHoul and M. Rapley. London: Continuum International.

Sacks, H. 1974. "On the Analysability of Stories by Children." Pp. 216-32 in *Ethnomethodology,* edited by R. Turner. Harmondsworth: Penguin.

———. 1992. *Lectures on Conversation,* Vols. 1-2. Edited by G. Jefferson. Oxford: Blackwell.

Sacks, H., E. A. Schegloff, and G. Jefferson. 1974. "A Simplest Systematics for the Organization of Turn-Taking in Conversation." *Language* 50:696-735.

Silverman, D. 1973. "Interview Talk: Bringing Off a Research Instrument." *Sociology* 7:31-48.

———. 1993. *Interpreting Qualitative Data: Methods for Analysing Talk, Text and Interaction.* London: Sage.

———. 1998. *Harvey Sacks: Social Science and Conversation Analysis.* Cambridge: Polity.

Silverman, D., C. D. Baker, and J. Keogh. 1998. "The Case of the Silent Child: Advice-Giving and Advice-Reception in Parent-Teacher Interviews." Pp. 220-40 in *Children and Social Competence: Arenas of Action,* edited by I. Hutchby and J. Moran-Ellis. London: Falmer.

Turner, R. 1974. "Words, Utterances and Activities." In *Ethnomethodology,* edited by R. Turner. Harmondsworth: Penguin.

Watson, R. and T. S. Weinberg. 1982. "Interviews and the Interactional Construction of Accounts of Homosexual Identity." *Social Analysis* 11:56-78.

Widdicombe, S. 1998. "Identity as an Analysts' and a Participants' Resource." Pp. 191-206 in *Identities in Talk,* edited by C. Antaki and S. Widdicombe. London: Sage.

Zimmerman, D. H. 1992. "Achieving Context: Openings in Emergency Calls." Pp. 35-51 in *Text and Context: Contributions to Ethnomethodology,* edited by G. Watson and R. M. Seiler. Newbury Park, CA: Sage.

Part IV

REPRESENTATIONAL ISSUES

20

REVISITING THE RELATIONSHIP BETWEEN PARTICIPANT OBSERVATION AND INTERVIEWING

◆ Paul Atkinson
   Amanda Coffey

In this chapter we propose a reevaluation of the relationship between participant observation and interviewing in sociological field research. Comparisons between these two methods of data collection have been part of the discourse of qualitative methodologists for more than four decades. The starting point for this reexamination is a paper published by Howard Becker and Blanche Geer in the 1950s in which they outline the relative merits of participant observation and interviewing (Becker and Geer [1957] 1970a). (The paper and its ensuing debate were reprinted in 1970 in a collection edited by William Filstead; page references here are to the version published in that anthology.) That paper was, and has remained, an influential reference point for scholars engaged in

field research. The subject matter and arguments presented in the paper remain valuable in their own right, as well as provide a means of tracing significant changes in how the conduct of field research is conceptualized.

In the first half of this chapter, we reread the paper by Becker and Geer through a contemporary lens, as a step to rethinking relationships between participant observation and interviewing. We consider briefly the use of the notion of triangulation to mediate the relationships between participant observation and interviewing. We then move on to propose a possible approach to ethnographic data that subsumes participant observation and interviewing. Developing our argument initially through a reconsideration of the classic position exemplified by Becker and Geer, we argue that field researchers must not assume that what is done should enjoy primacy over what is said, and that therefore observation and interviewing stand in opposition to one another. Actions, we argue, are understandable because they can be talked about. Equally, accounts—including those derived from interviewing—are actions. Social life is performed and narrated, and we need to recognize the performative qualities of social life and talk. In doing so, we shall not find it necessary to juxtapose talk and events as if they occupied different spheres of meaning. We thus propose an analytic stance that transcends some of the methodological puzzles that have appeared to confront qualitative methods for several decades.

◆ Rereading Becker and Geer

In the 1960s, sociologists in the interactionist tradition in the United States—and, to a lesser extent, elsewhere—were formulating a view of field research that was to become canonical. The authors who represented the "second Chicago school," as identified by Gary Alan Fine (1995), including Howard Becker, Blanche Geer, Everett Hughes, Anselm Strauss, and Leonard Schatzman, did much to promote empirical field research in a variety of institutional and other settings: hospitals, schools, colleges and universities, and other workplaces. Their interest in research methods was firmly grounded in their shared commitment to practical empirical research. They wrote from a blend of interests that reflected a shared intellectual culture: symbolic interactionism, social psychology, pragmatist epistemology, organizational and occupational sociology. Their starting point was normally the practice of social research rather than abstract epistemology. They blended their personal experience of and commitment to field research with the desire to promote system-

atic and coherent research among their students and colleagues. The diaspora from Chicago itself led to the promotion of such methodological perspectives in various centers of excellence in the United States. The publication of various textbooks and edited collections helped to promote and disseminate the new methodological systems in the 1960s and early 1970s (Schatzman and Strauss 1973; Lofland 1971; McCall and Simmons 1969; Filstead 1970). Becker and Geer's paper "Participant Observation and Interviewing: A Comparison" was a key ingredient in this movement. It was anthologized and became part of the codification of research methods, incorporated into the craft knowledge of several generations of graduate students and researchers.

The advice offered by authors such as Becker and Geer, Schatzman, and Strauss was essentially sensible, straightforward, and practical. It bears all the hallmarks of the work of researchers who were thoroughly versed in the practical work of field research and who also appreciated the value of clear and systematic advice for their peers and their advanced students. The development and spread of qualitative research methods owes much to that particular generation of authors. However, with the benefit of hindsight, much of that methodological advice now looks dated, and the common sense of one generation can seem limited to another.

In the original paper, Becker and Geer compare the relative strengths and applications of participant observation and interviewing. The paper deals with both the relationships between these techniques and the possibility of complementarity. Although it would be quite unwarranted to accuse Becker and his colleagues of naïveté, from today's perspectives (and we use the plural here advisedly) one is struck by the extent to which the data collection methods are treated as relatively unproblematic in themselves. A closer reading of Becker and Geer is worthwhile, not merely for historical purposes, but in order to unpack some of the implicit assumptions that informed the original paper and understandings of field research that stemmed from them. It is helpful to reread the paper in conjunction with Martin Trow's ([1957] 1970) reply and the rejoinder by Becker and Geer ([1957] 1970b). We do so not in order to belittle the contributions of Becker and Geer or of their contemporaries. On the contrary, we think that the issues they raised remain worthy of fresh consideration. We would pay them least respect were we merely to treat their ideas as part of a stock of taken-for-granted ideas.

A GOLD STANDARD?

Becker and Geer ([1957] 1970a) claim a specific advantage for participant observation over other kinds of data collection strategy, based in part on their own research on medical students (Becker et al., 1961). They suggest:

> The most complete form of the sociological datum, after all, is the form in which the participant observer gathers it: An observation of some social event, the events which precede and follow it, and explanations of its meaning by participants and spectators, before, during, and after its occurrence. Such a datum gives us more information about the event under study than data gathered by any other sociological method. Participant observation can thus provide us with a yardstick against which to measure the completeness of data gathered in other ways, a model which can serve to let us know what modes of information escape us when we use other methods. (P. 133)

Trow's ([1957] 1970) response challenges this apparent claim for participant observation's status as a gold-standard method for sociological data collection. Trow reiterates the commonplace assumption that the choice of research methods

should be dictated by the research problem, rather than the unchallenged superiority of one kind of strategy:

> It is with this assertion, that a given method of collecting data—any method—has an inherent superiority over others by virtue of its special qualities and divorced from the nature of the problem studied, that I take sharp issue. The authoritative view, and I would have thought this the view most widely accepted by social scientists, is that different kinds of information about man and society are gathered most fully and economically in different ways, and that the problem under investigation properly dictates the methods of investigation. (P. 143)

Here is not the place to divert attention to unpacking the value of this particular topos, except to note that in the world of real research, social scientists do not dream up "problems" to investigate out of thin air, divorced from concerns of theory and methodology, and only then search for precisely the right method. Clearly, problems and methods come as part of packages of ideas—whether or not one chooses to call them "paradigms." The notion that one can simply apply the best method to an independently derived problem is at best unrealistic. However, the rebuttal by Becker and Geer ([1957] 1970b) clarifies their original argument and helps sharpen our own focus. They point out that theirs was not a sweeping claim for the superiority of participant observation over all other methods in all cases. On the contrary, they stress their original emphasis on the observation and understanding of *events:*

> It is possible Trow thought we were arguing the general superiority of participant observation because he misunderstood our use of the word "event." We intended to refer only to specific and limited events which are observable, not to include in the term such large

and complex aggregates of specific events as national political campaigns. (P. 151)

Contrary to some possible, glib readings of their paper, then, Becker and Geer are certainly not advocating the wholesale superiority of participant observation over interviewing, nor are they proposing participant observation as the only valid method for sociological fieldwork.

EVENTS AND COMPLETENESS

Becker and Geer claim that the significance of participant observation and its superiority over interviewing rests on the "completeness" of the data. They propose that observation of events in context yields a more *complete* record and understanding of *events* than reliance on interviewing *about those events* alone. Their comparison between participant observation and interviewing is not wholesale, therefore. Becker and Geer make specific claims. In some ways, the original argument—especially as clarified by Becker and Geer—is unremarkable. Indeed, as formulated it is virtually unassailable. It is hard to quarrel with the assertion that the study of observable events is better accomplished by the observation of those events than by the collection of retrospective and decontextualized descriptions of them. Clearly, Becker and Geer are advocating a holistic approach to data collection and its interpretation. They believe that the sociological understanding of a given social world is optimized by the deployment of participation, observation, and conversation (in the form of field interviews). What is remarkable, however, and what strikes us from a contemporary vantage point, is the extent to which Becker and Geer treat "events" as self-evident and the extent to which they assume that the observation of "events" is a primary goal of participant observation. In turn they also seem to assume that interviews are primarily about events.

Their own illustration of the phenomenon is telling, and it bears reexamination. Their remarks on research methods were informed by their recent fieldwork with medical students at the University of Kansas (Becker et al. 1961). The example they give from their fieldwork is illuminating about the general perspective from which they wrote. Becker and Geer give an extract from their field materials in which they discuss medical students' perceptions of their teachers. Being in a subordinate position, the students, Becker and Geer ([1957] 1970a) argue, are likely to develop a kind of mythology about their teachers, and so to interpret their actions in a particular way: "Any such mythology will distort people's view of events to such a degree that they will report as fact things which have not occurred, but which seem to them to have occurred" (p. 138). In comparing participant observation and interviewing, therefore, Becker and Geer suggest that observation can be a corrective, allowing for adjudication of what "really" happened:

The point is that things can be reported in an interview through such a distorting lens, and the interviewer may have no way of knowing what is fact and what is distortion of this kind; participant observation makes it possible to check such points. (P. 138)

The actual example Becker and Geer use to demonstrate this assertion strikes a false note with the contemporary reader. The medical students had, apparently, formed the view that particular resident physicians on the teaching staff would regularly humiliate the students. The extract of field notes reproduced in the paper shows either Becker or Geer (the author of the data extract is not specified) reflecting on his or her observations of a particular teaching episode and students' reflections on it. Following a particular encounter with one of the residents, a student reported to his fellow students that the resident had "chewed him out." The observer felt able to intervene and say that the resident had actually been "pretty decent." Another student disputed the observer's description and affirmed that such behavior by a resident was always "chewing out," no matter how "God damn nice" the resident might be. In evaluating this episode, Becker and Geer ([1957] 1970a) conclude:

> In short, participant observation makes it possible to check descriptions against fact and, noting discrepancies, become aware of systematic distortions made by the person under study; such distortions are less likely to be discovered by interviewing alone. (P. 139)

They add a caveat to this point, distinguishing between the descriptive content and the process of the interview:

> This point, let us repeat, is only relevant when the interview is used as a source of information about situations and events the researcher himself has not seen. It is not relevant when it is the person's behavior in the interview itself that is under analysis. (P. 139)

Notwithstanding that last proviso—to which we shall return later—Becker and Geer may strike the contemporary reader as naive, schooled as that reader now is in the complexities of accounts, actions, and interpretations, and at home amid the ambiguities of postmodern analysis (Gubrium and Holstein 1997; Silverman 1993; Atkinson 1996). They seem to be operating with a strangely unproblematic view of "events," and thus of the social world. They strongly imply that there are "events" that are amenable to definitive description and evaluation by sociological observers. Consequently, the observer can adjudicate between a true description of events and a distorted one, and can therefore evaluate degrees of "distortion" in such descriptions.

It is, incidentally, instructive to read the data extract used in the paper and to which

we have referred here—a passage from processed field notes in narrative form, incorporating short verbatim quotes. It does not contain a description of the events that are under consideration and that are the subject of the disputed interpretation. The "events" that are described are the students' comments about the resident and the subsequent conversation between the observer and the students. The original interaction between the resident and the student, on which the latter's claim of being "chewed out" is based, is summarized in the most cursory fashion. Strikingly, it is totally impossible to reconstruct the original interaction from the data provided. Any adjudication as to the reasonableness of the student's complaint, the observer's corrective intervention, or the second student's reaffirmation of the students' perspective—their "mythology" as the authors describe it—is not possible.

In principle, this treatment of data is congruent with the general analysis that is enshrined in *Boys in White* (Becker et al. 1961). Becker and his colleagues do not actually base their account on "events" in the sense that they report and analyze much of what medical students or their teachers actually do. Their analysis is concerned with the development of students' perspectives rather than with, say, their embodied skills or their actual encounters with hospital patients. To that extent, Becker and Geer are consistent: The published monograph and their methodological prescriptions are congruent. The problems we raise, by contrast, reflect their treatment of observation, interviewing, accounts, and events as all rather unproblematic.

One might argue in defense of Becker and Geer that they use the data extract only by way of illustration, that the general argument is important rather than the details of a particular example. Yet this is not just an isolated incident or a minor discrepancy. It is thoroughly characteristic of the wider research project from which it is taken, which is in turn representative of a lot of work based on some combination of participant observation and interviewing, of a kind typical among the generation of researchers represented by Becker and Geer. Any reading of *Boys in White* (Becker et al. 1961), other than a most cursory one, will emphasize the problem. Although the Chicago research team spent a considerable amount of time engaged in participant observation with the medical students and their teachers, the book does remarkably little to report what these social actors actually did. We gain few glimpses of, say, the actual work with patients on hospital wards or in clinics. The "data" seem to consist primarily of what the students themselves *said about* their lives and work. The primary data, in practice, therefore seem to be conversations about events and actors' perspectives on events and happenings. At least, it is those data that are reported directly in the monograph.

A reexamination of the original formulation of the problem by Becker and Geer highlights some significant issues and problems. As we have seen, their argument is a very specific one that is extremely plausible. Even within their argument's restricted scope, Becker and Geer seem to establish a strong case for the value of participant observation. On closer inspection, however, the argument seems less straightforward, and raises some potentially intriguing issues that we shall attempt to address afresh in the final section of this chapter. Before that, in the next section we turn to consider another approach to the combination of participant observation and interviewing, through the notion of methodological triangulation.

◆ Triangulation

One of the key areas in which claims have been made for the productive *combination* of participant observation and interviewing is in the methodological discussion of *triangulation*. Although authors such as Norman Denzin (1970) have certainly not

intended to promote a naive or vulgar view of research methods and their proper relationships, the rhetoric of between-method triangulation clearly implies for many enthusiasts the possibility of combining participant observation and interviewing so as to capitalize on the respective strengths of these methods, or to counteract the perceived limitations of each.

Denzin's original formulation of methodological triangulation also conveys the impression that researchers could combine methods such as participant observation and interviewing to draw on the methods' complementary strengths and offset their respective weaknesses. Denzin's (1978) own summary of methodological triangulation captures the essence of this approach:

> In organizational studies, for example, it is extremely difficult to launch large-scale participant-observation studies when the participants are widely distributed by time and place. In such extractions participant observation may be adapted only to certain categories of persons, certain events, certain places, or certain times. The interview method can then be employed to study those events that do not directly come under the eyes of the participant observer. (P. 303)

Here interviewing is treated as a potential proxy for direct observation: It is implied that researchers can glean data about events and actors through indirect means in order to supplement the method of direct observation.

It is clear that Denzin's formulation of the relationships between methods is actually addressed to an issue that is slightly different from the one examined by Becker and Geer. But (in his early writings) Denzin too treats the methods themselves as relatively unproblematic. His early views of triangulation assume that research methods should be determined by research problems and that methods can be combined in terms of their respective strengths and weaknesses: "Methodological triangulation involves a complex process of playing each method off against the other so as to maximize the validity of field efforts" (Denzin 1978:304). Denzin emphasizes the degree to which the combination of methods is a matter of strategic decision making, and that research design and choice of methods are emergent features of concrete projects: "Assessment cannot be solely derived from principles given in research manuals—it is an emergent process, contingent on the investigator, the research setting, and the investigator's theoretical perspective" (p. 304).

Subsequent editions of Denzin's text reflect the changing character of methodological thinking and make explicit reference to potential, and actual, criticisms of this approach to triangulation. Denzin acknowledges that his accounts of the relationships between methods such as interviewing and observation were open to the interpretation, and the accusation, that they were unduly positivistic (for critiques of the early Denzin approach, see Silverman 1985, 1993). Indeed, Denzin did seem to imply that research problems are prior to and independent from methods, and that methods can be brought to bear on research problems in unproblematic ways. Although Denzin himself was clearly no naive positivist in intention, the implications of his text certainly seemed to suggest an easy accommodation between methods, and between methods and problems. The rhetoric of research problems driving the choice of methods too readily implied an independent and prior "list" of researchable topics divorced from the theories and methods that constructed those topics.

The simplest view of triangulation treats the relationships between methods as relatively unproblematic, and those methods themselves as even more straightforward in themselves. More sophisticated versions of triangulation may treat the relationships between methods in a less straightforward fashion—stressing the differences between them rather than complementarity—but

can still be predicated on unproblematic views of the methods themselves. Current perspectives on methodology and epistemology incline toward a quite different view. Treatments of participant observation and interviewing would not try to privilege one over the other, or try to seek out ways simply to integrate them or treat their outcomes in an additive way.

REFLEXIVITY

The underlying problem with the simple or "optimistic" version of triangulation is that it treats the nature of social reality as unduly unproblematic and the relationships between the social world and the methods of investigating it as transparent. But we cannot assume a unitary and stable social world that can simply be viewed from different standpoints or from different perspectives. Rather, we have to pay due attention to the principle of reflexivity. *Reflexivity* is a term that is widely used, with a diverse range of connotations (and sometimes with virtually no meaning at all). Here we use it in a specific way: to acknowledge that the methods we use to describe the world are—to some degree—constitutive of the realities they describe (Hammersley and Atkinson 1995; Gubrium and Holstein 1997). In other words, the research methods we use imply or depend on particular kinds of transactions and engagements with the world. Each kind of transaction therefore generates a distinctive set of descriptions, versions, and understandings of the world. These are not arbitrary or whimsical. They are generated out of our systematic and methodical explorations of a given social world; they are not private fantasies. Equally, they are not purely contingent. There are systematic relationships between methods and representations, but they cannot be washed out or eliminated through simpleminded aggregation. Rather, we have to address what methods do construct and what sense we can make of those constructions. Such a realization does not deprive us of different modes of data collection and analysis. It does, however, require us to address the distinctive and intrinsic attributes of particular methods, to retain some fidelity to those methods and their products.

From this perspective, for instance, the status of interview data is especially problematic. In particular, the precise referential value of interviews is questionable. Interviews are not regarded as intrinsically worthless sources of data. Rather, as Silverman (1993) points out, we cannot approach interview data simply from the point of view of "truth" or "distortion," and we cannot use such data with a view to remedying the incompleteness of observations. By the same token, we cannot rely on our observations to correct presumed inaccuracies in interview accounts. On the contrary, it is argued that interviews generate data that have intrinsic properties of their own. In essence, we need to treat interviews as generating accounts and performances that have their own properties and ought to be analyzed in accordance with such characteristics. We need, therefore, to appreciate that interviews are occasions in which are enacted particular kinds of narratives and in which "informants" construct themselves and others as particular kinds of moral agents. Examples of this kind of approach include Margaret Voysey's (1975) analysis of parents' accounts of life with handicapped children and Nigel Gilbert and Michael Mulkay's (1980) analysis of natural scientists' accounts of scientific discoveries.

These and analyses like them by no means reject the utility of interview data, but they insist on a particular analytic strategy. The data are examined for their properties as accounts. Voysey, for instance, suspended the taken-for-granted view that the presence of a handicapped child disrupts normal family life; she examined, rather, how parents constructed moral accounts of "normal" parenting and family conduct.

Likewise, Gilbert and Mulkay document scientists' often inconsistent and contradictory accounting devices in their descriptions of scientific discovery, which construct science and scientists in distinctive ways. These are coherent and consistent ways of dealing with interview data. They do not, however, lend themselves to aggregation to observational data in order to achieve "triangulation" in any conventional sense.

From such perspectives, then, the analyst does not worry about whether "the informant is telling the truth" (Dean and Whyte 1958), if by that one understands the analyst's task to be that of distinguishing factual accuracy from distortion, bias, or deception. Similarly, ironic contrasts between what people do and what they say they do (see Deutscher 1973) become irrelevant. Rather, attention is paid to the coherence and plausibility of accounts, to their performative qualities, the repertoires of accounts and moral types that they contain, and so on. In the remainder of this chapter we address the implications of this position a little further. In essence, we argue that participant observation and interviewing are themselves distinctive forms of social action, generating distinctive kinds of accounts and giving rise to particular versions of social analysis. Each yields particular sorts of textual representation: There are other kinds of texts and other kinds of representation in and of social fields. If we cannot simply add them together and superimpose them to make a single coherent narrative or picture, what are the proper relations between them?

◆ Talk, Experience, and Action

Radical criticisms of the interview can treat naturally occurring social action as primary and talk about action as but a poor substitute for the observation of action, echoing Becker and Geer's original argument. From that perspective, we cannot take the interview as a proxy for action. Hence we cannot rely on it for information about what people do or what they have done; rather, it serves only as a mechanism for eliciting what people say they do. From this perspective, the interview inhabits a quite different universe from the observation of social action. One can readily move to the position that grants primacy to the recording of naturally occurring social interaction and relegates virtually everything else to the periphery of sociological interest. This particular view is sometimes accompanied by appeals for primary reliance on the analysis of permanent recordings of spoken activity, such as conversation analysis (Atkinson and Heritage 1984; Boden and Zimmerman 1991; Sacks 1992).

This is one possible position, but it is an unnecessary and unhelpful one. It is unduly insensitive to the variety of social action. It is also in danger of endorsing a particular kind of naturalism; the endorsement of one sort of action or activity over another implicitly attributes authenticity to one while denying it to others. It runs the risk of assuming that some sort of actions are "natural" whereas others are "contrived" (Hammersley and Atkinson 1995; Silverman 1985, 1993).

A more productive way of thinking about these relationships is to start from a more symmetrical perspective, rather than trying to privilege one source, or method, over another. This approach is, in one respect at least, more in keeping with contemporary epistemology. It is also antipathetic to the excesses of some recent enthusiasms that have rejected the study of action in situ in favor of an almost exclusive focus on interviews, narratives, and accounts (Atkinson and Silverman 1997). We can fruitfully begin to think of what we observe (and the work of observing) and the contents of interviews (and the work of interviewing) as incorporating social actions of different kinds and yielding data of different forms. We can thus be released from

trying to combine them to produce information from them about something else and concentrate more on the performance of the social actions themselves.

Indeed, we know enough about the performance of everyday social action to be thoroughly suspicious of methodological formulations that even appear to attach particular kinds of authenticity to it. All of Erving Goffman's work, for instance, is—with varying degrees of explicitness—concerned with rendering problematic such a naive view. Admittedly, some of Goffman's key insights might seem to suggest the contrary. His famous essay on role distance, for example, seems to imply a dichotomy, not a continuity, between an ironic distance and a wholehearted commitment (Goffman 1961). Likewise, some accounts that are thoroughly or partially indebted to Goffman, such as Arlie Hochschild's *The Managed Heart* (1983)—an account of the self-conscious management of emotional work among workers such as airline flight attendants—seem to imply a contrast between authentic and insincere social actions. Hochschild distances herself from Goffman's vision of the social self, and her analysis depends on the presence of a deep self that preexists and authors authentic and inauthentic performances. But if we take full and serious account of the performativity of social life (the dramaturgical metaphor), then it clearly makes no more sense to assume any action as inherently authentic, and thus to grant it priority.

Part of the reported comparison between participant observation and interviewing has revolved around the ironic contrast between what people do and what people say (they do). This has also fed into the equally hoary question posed to and by field researchers: How do you know if your informant is telling the truth? These related problems equally reflect the position we have characterized as naive: the contrasts between actions and accounts, and between truth and dissimulation.

INTERVIEWING AS ACTION

This approach to interviewing as action can be illustrated with reference to the topic of memory. One way of thinking about interviews and the data they yield is to think about informants producing descriptions of past events. In part, therefore, the interview is aimed at the elicitation of memories. Viewed from a naive perspective, it also follows that one of the main problems of this kind of data collection concerns the accuracy or reliability of such recollections. Such a perspective certainly presents pressing problems if—to return to the preoccupations of Becker and Geer— one is using the interview to gather information about "events." The same is true of the elicitation of "experiences." It is possible to view the interview as a means for the retrieval of informants' personal experiences—a biographically grounded view of memories and past events.

The analytic problems of memory and experience are equivalent from our point of view. It is possible to address memory and experience sociologically, and it is possible to address them through the interview (and through other "documents of life"). But it is appropriate to do so only if one accepts that memory and experience are social actions in themselves. They are both enacted. Seen from this perspective, memory is not (simply) a matter of individual psychology, and is certainly not only a function of internal mental states. Equally, it is not a private issue. (We are not denying the existence of psychological processes in general, or the personal qualities and significance of memories—ours is a methodological argument about the appropriate way of conducting and conceptualizing social research.) Memory is a cultural phenomenon, and is therefore a collective one. What is "memorable" is a function of the cultural categories that shape what is thinkable and what is not, what is counted as appropriate, what is valued, what is noteworthy, and so on. Memory is far from uniquely (auto)biographical. It can reside in material culture, for instance: The deliberate collection or hoarding of memorabilia and souvenirs— photographs, tourist artifacts, family treasures, or other bric-a-brac—is one enactment of memory, for instance. Equally, memory is grounded in what is tellable. In many ways the past is a narrative enactment.

Memory *and* personal experience are narrated. Narrative is a collective, shared cultural resource (see in this volume Cándida Smith, Chapter 17; Narayan and George, Chapter 22). Authors such as Ken Plummer (1995) have reminded us that even the most intimate and personal of experiences are constructed through shared narrative formats. The "private" does not escape the "public" categories of narrativity. Just as C. Wright Mills (1940) demonstrated that "motive" should be seen as cultural and linguistic in character, and not as a feature of internal mental states or predispositions, we must recognize that memories and experiences are constructed through the resources of narrative and discourse. Narratives and the resources of physical traces, places, and things—these are the constituents of biography, memory, and experience. When we conduct an interview, then, we are not simply collecting information about nonobservable or unobserved actions, or past events, or private experiences. Interviews generate accounts and narratives that are forms of social action in their own right.

EVENTS AND ACCOUNTS AS ENACTMENTS

At this point we return to the original formulation offered by Becker and Geer ([1957] 1970a). They refer to the study of "events," arguing that observation provides access to events in a way that interviews cannot. In one sense, that is self-evidently true. We can observe and we can make permanent recordings of events. On the other hand, we need to ask ourselves what constitutes an "event." Clearly an event is not merely a string of unrelated moments of behavior, nor is it devoid of significance. In order to be observable and reportable, events in themselves must have some degree of coherence and internal structure. An "event" in the social world is not something that just happens: It is made to happen. It has a beginning, a middle, and an end. It is differentiated from the surrounding stream of activity. Its structure and the observer's capacity to recognize it are essentially narrative in form. In that sense, therefore, a radical distinction between "events" that are observed and "accounts" that are narrated starts to become less stark, and the boundary maintenance becomes more difficult to sustain.

Does this mean that we still acknowledge the primacy of particular kinds of social actions? Not necessarily. By acknowledging that accounts, recollections, and experiences are enacted, we can start to avoid the strict dualism between "what people do" and "what people say." This is a recurrent topic in the methodological discourse of social science. It rests on the commonplace observation that there may be differences or discrepancies between observed actions and accounts about action. (This may be proposed as a rather vulgar counterargument against vulgar triangulation.) They are different kinds of enactments, certainly, but we would argue that the specific dualism that implicitly asserts an authenticity for what people (observably) do and the fallibility of accounts of action is both unhelpful and "untrue." By treating both the observed and the narrated as kinds of social action, we move beyond such simple articulations and instead reassert the methodological principle of symmetry.

We therefore bracket the assumption of authenticity, or the "natural" character of "naturally occurring" action, and the contrasts that are founded on that implicit dualism. If we recognize that memories, experiences, motives, and so on are themselves forms of action, and equally recognize that they and mundane routine activi-

ties are enacted, then we can indeed begin to deal with these issues in a symmetrical, but nonreductionist, way. In other words, it is not necessary to assert the primacy of one form of data over another, or to assert the primacy of one form of action over another. Equally, a recognition of the performative action of interview talk removes the temptation to deal with such data as if they give us access to personal or private "experiences." We need, therefore, to divorce the use of the interview from the myth of inferiority: the essentially romantic view of the social actor as a repository of "inner" feelings and intensely personal recollections. Rather, interviews become equally valid ways of capturing shared cultural understandings and enactments of the social world.

THE POSITION OF
THE RESEARCHER

We have thus far said very little about the position of the researcher within these different kinds of research "events." One of the distinctions between participant observation and interviewing has pivoted on the relationship of the researcher to the field of study. In the case of observational work, claims have been made that participant observation enables the researcher to participate firsthand in the happenings of the setting; these claims have been countered, of course, by warnings that the researcher may affect (contaminate) the setting or become too much of a participant, and thereby lose the capacity to observe critically. In contrast, the interview has been perceived as an artificial enactment, with unequal relations and potentially less contamination between participants, and more recently as a site for collaboration and the genuine sharing of experiences.

Here we would wish to stress again the symmetry of the two broad approaches. This does not necessary imply complementarity or sameness, but recognizes the complexity of research experiences and relationships. Through both participant observation and interviewing there is the potential for "contamination," although this is a paralyzing and unhelpful way of characterizing the research process (and can actually render all research inadequate). Rather, through active reflexivity we should recognize that we are part of the social events and processes we observe *and* help to narrate. To overemphasize our potential to change things artificially swells our own importance. To deny our being "there" misunderstands the inherent qualities of both methods—in terms of documenting and making sense of social worlds of which we are a part (either through participant observation or as facilitators of shared accounts and narrative strategies).

The (auto)biographical work that is common to both approaches is also worth noting. Again, in digressing from Becker and Geer's assertion of the primary goal of describing events, we should recognize that the process of undertaking research is suffused with biographical and identity work (Coffey 1999). The complex relationships among field settings, significant social actors, the practical accomplishment of the research, and the researcher-self are increasingly recognized as significant to all those who engage in research of a qualitative nature (whether that be participant observation, interviewing, or some combination of the two).

◆ Conclusion

We began this chapter with a retrospective evaluation of Becker and Geer's ([1957] 1970a) original observations concerning the respective merits and weaknesses of participant observation and interviewing. We did so for two reasons. First, Becker and Geer's paper is a locus classicus in the corpus of methodological writing in qualitative sociology. Second, it helps us to identify a particular constellation of assumptions concerning observation and in-

terviewing characteristic of that period, during which many aspects of qualitative fieldwork were being codified. We repeat our acknowledgment that the scholars of that generation were responsible for the demystification of qualitative methods, providing practical advice manuals for the research community as well as acting as methodological advocates. Their contribution should not be underestimated, and it was never our intention to do so. However, we have reached a point that suggests a position very different from that articulated by Becker and Geer. This difference reflects a good deal of methodological change and development over the intervening years, not least in the burgeoning of qualitative methods texts and the increased acceptance and innovative use of the whole variety of qualitative research strategies.

For a long time, ethnographers and other qualitative researchers have relied on the ironic contrast between "what people do" and "what people say they do." That contrast is—as we have suggested—based on some further differences. It assumes that what people do is unproblematic and is amenable to direct observation and description; what people say, on the other hand, is treated as a much more unstable category. The relationship between action and talk is perceived as problematic because accounts can distort: Accounts can be motivated in various ways, and can function as excuses, legitimations, rationalizations, and so on. However, actors may falsify their accounts. Deliberate deception, wishful thinking, recipient design for difficult audiences—these can all affect the accuracy and reliability of actors' accounts (according to a well-established tradition). As a consequence, discussions of interviewing have often sought to address the question, How do you know if your informant is telling the truth? As we have now seen, however, these issues are radically changed if one abandons the initial presumption of difference. If we accept that interview talk is action—is performative—then ironic contrasts between "doing" and "acting" become increasingly redundant. Taken-for-granted distinctions between talk and action are erroneous and irrelevant when one recognizes that talk is action. In a performative view, interviews, and other accounts, need not be seen as poor surrogates or proxies for unobserved activities. They can be interrogated for their own properties—their narrative structures and functions (see Riessman, Chapter 16, this volume). Accounts are, or are composed of, speech acts and may therefore legitimately be regarded as games or types of action in their own right.

By the same token, actions or events, even observed firsthand, are not inherently endowed with meaning, nor is their meaning unequivocally available for inspection. The kinds of "events" that Becker and Geer ([1957] 1970a) discuss are recognized as such precisely because they are describable and narratable by participants and by onlookers, including ethnographers and other observers. After all, the "data" of participant observation are the events as narrated (written down, often retrospectively) by observers, and hence rely on the same culturally shared categories of memory, account, narrative, and experience. In retro-spect, it seems odd that Becker and Geer felt able to legislate for "what really happened" and to discount the tellings of medical students. From our point of view, they could and should have paid much more attention to several things: how the "events" were performed; how the medical students narrated and evaluated the "events"; how certain events or classes of events were endowed with significance through the medical students' own tellings; and how they themselves, as observers, recorded and described the "events." They might thus have found themselves dealing with classes of performance and rhetoric, in different contexts, in different modes, rather than incommensurable kinds of phenomena. And once articulated in this way, their particular distinction between participant observation and interviewing, and the primacy of the former, becomes untenable. This does not deny the different qualities of these methods as data collection strategies. Rather, in emphasizing their commonalities in terms of social action and performance (and extinguishing the false dichotomy), we may actually be in a better, and certainly a more informed, position to "choose."

■ References

Atkinson, J. M. and J. Heritage, eds. 1984. *Structures of Social Action: Studies in Analysis.* Cambridge: Cambridge University Press.

Atkinson, P. 1996. *Sociological Readings and Re-readings.* Aldershot, England: Ashgate.

Atkinson, P. and D. Silverman. 1997. "Kundera's *Immortality:* The Interview Society and the Invention of Self." *Qualitative Inquiry* 3:304-25.

Becker, H. S. and B. Geer. 1970a. "Participant Observation and Interviewing: A Comparison." Pp. 133-42 in *Qualitative Methodology: Firsthand Involvement with the Social World,* edited by W. J. Filstead. Chicago: Markham. Reprinted from *Human Organization* 16 (1957):28-32.

———. 1970b. "Participant Observation and Interviewing: A Rejoinder." Pp. 150-52 in *Qualitative Methodology: Firsthand Involvement with the Social World,* edited by W. J. Filstead. Chicago: Markham. Reprinted from *Human Organization* 16 (1957):39-40.

Becker, H. S., B. Geer, E. C. Hughes, and A. L. Strauss. 1961. *Boys in White: Student Culture in Medical School.* Chicago: University of Chicago Press.

Boden, D. and D. H. Zimmerman, eds. 1991. *Talk and Social Structure: Studies in Ethnomethodology and Conversation Analysis.* Berkeley: University of California Press.

Coffey, A. 1999. *The Ethnographic Self: Fieldwork and the Representation of Identity.* London: Sage.

Dean, J. P. and W. F. Whyte. 1958. "How Do You Know If the Informant Is Telling the Truth?" *Human Organization* 17:34-38.

Denzin, N. K. 1970. *The Research Act.* Chicago: Aldine.

———. 1978. *The Research Act.* 2d ed. New York: McGraw-Hill.

Deutscher, E. 1973. *What We Say/What We Do: Sentiments and Acts.* Glenview, IL: Scott, Foresman.

Filstead, W. J., ed. 1970. *Qualitative Methodology: Firsthand Involvement with the Social World.* Chicago: Markham.

Fine, G. A., ed. 1995. *A Second Chicago School? The Development of a Postwar American Sociology.* Chicago: University of Chicago Press.

Gilbert, N. and M. Mulkay. 1980. *Opening Pandora's Box: A Sociological Account of Scientists' Discourse.* Cambridge: Cambridge University Press.

Goffman, E. 1961. *Encounters: Two Studies in the Sociology of Interaction.* Indianapolis: Bobbs-Merrill.

Gubrium, J. F. and J. A. Holstein. 1997. *The New Language of Qualitative Method.* New York: Oxford University Press.

Hammersley, M. and P. Atkinson. 1995. *Ethnography: Principles in Practice.* 2d ed. London: Routledge.

Hochschild, A. R. 1983. *The Managed Heart: Commercialization of Human Feeling.* Berkeley: University of California Press.

Lofland, J. 1971. *Analyzing Social Settings.* Belmont, CA: Wadsworth.

McCall, G. J. and J. L. Simmons, eds. 1969. *Issues in Participant Observation: A Text and Reader.* Reading, MA: Addison-Wesley.

Mills, C. W. 1940. "Situated Actions and Vocabularies of Motive." *American Sociological Review* 5:439-52.

Plummer, K. 1995. *Telling Sexual Stories: Power, Change and Social Worlds.* London: Routledge.

Sacks, H. 1992. *Lectures on Conversation,* Vols. 1-2. Edited by G. Jefferson. Oxford: Blackwell.

Schatzman, L. and A. L. Strauss. 1973. *Field Research: Strategies for a Natural Sociology.* Englewood Cliffs, NJ: Prentice Hall.

Silverman, D. 1985. *Qualitative Methodology and Sociology.* Aldershot, England: Gower.

———. 1993. *Interpreting Qualitative Data: Methods for Analysing Talk, Text and Interaction.* London: Sage.

Trow, M. 1970. "Comment on 'Participant Observation and Interviewing': A Comparison." Pp. 143-49 in *Qualitative Methodology: Firsthand Involvement with the Social World,* edited by W. J. Filstead. Chicago: Markham. Reprinted from *Human Organization* 16 (1957):33-35.

Voysey, M. 1975. *A Constant Burden.* London: Routledge & Kegan Paul.

21

CROSS-CULTURAL INTERVIEWING

◆ Anne Ryen

In recent decades there has been vast growth in cross-cultural studies, one indication of which has been the increasing numbers of publications in the area. Close to 40 percent of all cross-cultural studies published to date were published in the 1980s; 75 percent were published in the 1970s and 1980s combined. The trend will undoubtedly continue in the new millennium, propelled by the globalization of capital and business and by huge leaps in cross-cultural communication and negotiations (Tse and Francis 1994; Habib 1987; Shenkar and Zeira 1990; Bilbow 1996). This has resulted in a rapid increase in new research periodicals; topics centered on cross-cultural studies are now covered by close to 80 journals (Ember and Levinson 1991).

Accompanying this growth, researchers have pointed to the methodological difficulties of transporting experiential data across cultures. Field-workers have been faced with such perennial problems as understanding local nuances in the languages and cultures of their respondents (Deutscher 1968; Wax 1960) and the difficulties associated with using interpreters (Freeman 1983; Berreman 1962). Researchers have had constant personal reminders that in the eyes of those they study, the role of researcher is not always the most salient one for them. As a bachelor in India, M. N. Srinivas (1979) found that the Indian villagers he studied went out of their way to look for a bride for him; they were as much concerned for his welfare as he was with understanding their lives. British African researcher Kate Crehan (1991) found that because she was perceived as foreign in Zambian society, the villagers she studied coped with her unmarried status by assign-

AUTHOR'S NOTE: My grateful thanks to David Silverman, department colleagues, the two *Handbook* reviewers, and the editors, who all read and commented on an earlier draft of this chapter. I would also like to thank the Norwegian Research Council for funding.

ing her a "functional male" role. This role was denied her when she was doing field-work among "her own" people in Britain, where she was seen as indigenous and needed to deal with related limited female rights and responsibilities. The "insider-outsider" problem of doing cross-cultural research clearly reverberates in many directions.

Although these challenges are particularly prevalent in participant observation studies, a substantial amount of data collected in such studies come from interviewing in the field (Lofland 1971). It is this particular aspect of cross-cultural research that is the focus of this chapter. Although cross-cultural interviewing is often combined with other methodologies (see Spradley 1979), in this chapter I will focus on the communicative challenges of interviewing as it is mediated by the relation between interviewer and interviewee, who in the case of cross-cultural encounters often inhabit vastly different worlds or engage each other with sharply contrasting aims.

Traditionally, *cross-cultural interviewing* refers to the collection of interview data across cultural and national borders. However, there are many research examples that show this to be too narrow a delimitation. Several fieldwork reports describe insider-outsider challenges faced by researchers conducting ethnic interviews within their own societies (Warren 1977; Montero 1977). Even indigenous researchers studying their own people in societies with class, ethnic, and sectarian divisions have reported challenges arising from the insider-outsider problem, among them Jharna Nath (1991) from her fieldwork in Bangladesh, S. Kamil (1991) in Pakistan, Masliana Bangun (1991) in Indonesia, Anne Abeyewardene (1991) in Sri Lanka and Minako, and M. Kurokawa Maykovich in the United States and Canada (1977). Such challenges have also been found in studies where researchers have conducted interviews with fellow ethnics who constitute minorities within larger societies, such as

Constantinos Phellas's (2000) in-depth interview study of male Anglo-Cypriot residents in London and Kalivant Bhopal's (2000) research involving interviews with South Asian women in East London. In many ways, the insider-outsider problem is generic to all forms of interviewing conducted under the auspices of cultural difference, whether ethnicity or culture writ large mediates the relation between interviewer and interviewee.

Much of the literature dealing with the insider-outsider problem rests on naturalistic assumptions about culture and communication (see Gubrium and Holstein 1997). These assumptions both positively inform the methodological literature in the area, especially as it bears on interviewing, and, in their deconstruction, present the opportunity for research to move in a different direction. The argument here is that the naturalistic assumptions pose insider-outsider challenges because of how culture and communication are viewed as a nexus for interviewing.

The naturalistic view is characterized by a belief that, in principle, social reality is transparent in people's words and actions. Given that the researcher follows certain technical guidelines in the interviewing, he or she is assumed to have access to data reflecting this transparent reality.[1] The data are regarded as preproduced, culturally stored, and independent of the interviewer-interviewee relationship. The challenge, then, is first to get the interviewee to cooperate and then to get hold of the data in the form they are stored in the interviewee's cultural reservoir (see Holstein and Gubrium, Chapter 1, this volume). The large share of literature on cross-cultural interviewing is thus informed, the methodological imperatives of which move in the direction of overcoming the communicative hurdles put in place by cultural differences. This firm belief in a preexisting cultural reality is the epistemological basis for the demand that the researcher catch or grasp that reality as closely as possible to the way the interviewee does.

◆ Communicative Challenges

The naturalistic challenges of cross-cultural interviewing are usually presented as problems of communication. Both nonverbal and verbal challenges have been identified that relate to the problems of maintaining rapport between interviewer and interviewee.

ESTABLISHING AND MAINTAINING RAPPORT

Textbooks on fieldwork and interviews all stress the importance of interviewers' establishing good relations in the field in general and with interviewees in particular. As Steinar Kvale (1996) points out: "In a research setting it is up to the interviewer to create in a short time a contact that allows the interaction to get beyond merely a polite conversation or exchange of ideas. The interviewer must establish an atmosphere in which the subject feels safe enough to talk freely about his or her experiences and feelings" (p. 125). The interviewer's ability to develop trust and rapport and establish relationships with interviewees facilitates valid data collection. The challenge for the researcher is to make staying in the field and keeping the good relations already established acceptable to those being studied. A common recommendation to researchers is that they should "gain the trust of the community by openness and frankness; participate in community activities whilst retaining an independent stance on local controversies and disputes" (Casley and Lury 1987:69).

In traditional studies using in-depth interviews, the research is dependent on the researcher's establishing relationships that allow him or her to get access to the respondents' own perspectives, and this is not necessarily quickly achieved. The problem is exacerbated in cross-cultural studies. Indeed, the researcher is often quickly reminded that confirmed rapport with a group of interviewees or with particular persons is a necessity to valid cultural understanding. Rapport, however, is the outcome of communication and is not established once and forever. Rather, and especially in cross-cultural contexts, it is mediated by the complex external and internal ingredients of day-to-day involvement. In research situations that often entail researchers' staying for extended periods in cultures other than their own, the importance of rapport cannot be overestimated. If researcher and subjects have established good rapport, subjects will be cooperative and will have enough confidence in the researcher to pass on information about themselves ranging from the details of daily life to sensitive matters (Shaffir 1991; Dean, Eichhorn, and Dean 1969; Wax 1971). The cross-cultural researcher will also learn that the roles available or enacted, which are sometimes quite vague at the start, develop as the project unfolds. Especially in "noninterview societies" (see Atkinson and Silverman 1997), researchers often need to work out their roles in the very process of conducting the research, as the work by Srinivas (1979) and Crehan (1991) mentioned above suggests.

Alternatively, field data can be regarded as "constructs of the process by which we acquire them" (Rabinow 1977:xi). In Paul Rabinow's (1977) reflections on the relationship between the informant and the anthropologist, or the insider and the outsider, in his own fieldwork in Morocco, he says:

> This highlighting, identification, and analysis also disturbed Ali's [an informant] usual patterns of experience. He was constantly being forced to reflect on his own activities and objectify them. Because he was a good informant, he seemed to enjoy this process and soon began to develop an art of presenting his world to me. The better he became at it, the more we shared together. But the more we engaged in such activity, the more he experienced

aspects of his own life in new ways. Under my systematic questioning, Ali was taking realms of his own world and interpreting them for an outsider. This meant that he, too, was spending more time in this liminal, self-conscious world between cultures. (P. 38)

Rabinow later adds, "Things become more secure as this liminal world is mutually constructed but, by definition, it never really loses its quality of externality" (p. 153). From this perspective, fieldwork and interviewing are parts of a constantly developing process.

Rapport building is difficult enough between research participants who hail from the same culture; the cross-cultural context adds the complexities and the vicissitudes of relatively enduring research encounters. Cross-cultural researchers frequently refer to the importance of the researcher's relationship with community members. M. N. Panini (1991) notes in this regard: "In a way, the fieldworker's search for the status of an 'insider' is like chasing a mirage. In societies comprising . . . class, ethnic, and factional divisions, a fieldworker cannot be accepted as an insider of every section of society" (p. 8). Hilda Tadria (1991) conveys this in reference to her own fieldwork experiences in Uganda. One woman recommended to Tadria that if she wanted to get unprejudiced data, she needed to stop dressing "like a government employee." However, after she bought and dressed in some secondhand clothes, she notes, "people were saying that I was disguising myself as a peasant because I was a spy" (p. 90), whereupon she decided to go back to wearing her original clothing.

The role of the ostensible insider generates its own problems in the long term, the duration often required in cross-cultural research. Mario Rutten (1995, 1996) recalls that in order to secure prolonged field relations, he had to socialize with his interviewees, who were small-scale entrepreneurs in Malaysia, India, and Indonesia. In Malaysia, he visited a karaoke bar for the first time in his life, and his alcohol consumption was involuntarily raised during his fieldwork among Chinese businessmen, who told him, "If you want to join us in the evening, you have to drink as much as we do." Things became more delicate, however, when he was confronted with their expectations that he join them in "womanizing." [2] (See also Jayaraman 1979:272 on fieldwork in Sri Lanka.)

This relates to the experiences of some women researchers who have faced sexual overtures from male interviewees while doing fieldwork; sexual innuendo can be exaggerated in cross-cultural encounters. Sexual activity, propositions, and actual physical molestation are not infrequent themes in field reports, such as Mary Ellen Conaway's (1986) description of being physically molested and Eva Moreno's (1995) of being raped. Colin Thurnbull (1986) has described his relationship with a local woman during his fieldwork with the Mbuti of Africa, and Ruth Landes (1986) has written about her dilemmas as an unattached woman in the field. In a contrasting turn of events, Dona Davis (1986) found that people in the Newfoundland community she studied seemed friendlier and more at ease after they discovered she was having an affair.

Researchers are sometimes unwilling to write about their erotic experiences in the field (see Kong, Mahoney, and Plummer, Chapter 5, this volume). The reasons for this are varied and include issues of ethics, gendered effects, and potential implications for career chances. Some researchers may also be unwilling to confront the issues of positionality, hierarchy, exploitation, and that racism that such experiences may raise (see Kulick and Willson 1995). For example, Evelyn Blackwood (1995:68) asserts that an erotic attraction between a researcher and a person in the field will not necessarily dissolve differences between them, but may serve instead to highlight those differences. This topic has also been related to the reflexive turn within anthropology and theorizing the self (Probyn 1993; Wengle 1988; Newton 1993).

Researchers doing fieldwork often report attempts by the natives to get them to conform to local norms. For example, the Nahua Indians tried to get Peggy Golde (1986) married. As noted earlier, a landlord and trader in India tried to find a bride for Srinivas (1979). Nancie Gonzalez (1986) has written about the difficulties she encountered as a divorced woman doing fieldwork in Roman Catholic Guatemala. Similarly, Srinivas (1979) comments on the impact of his role as a bachelor on his access to parts of the field. Carol Warren (1988) describes this aspect of fieldwork: "The man or woman entering a strange culture becomes a stranger. . . . Their place in the society . . . is negotiated from the existing cultural stock of knowledge and action available to define and cope with strangers" (p. 189). She also points to the dicey dynamics involved in negotiating roles after one has established a place in a strange culture.

If the insider-outsider dilemma looms large in cross-cultural studies, it can also lead in surprising directions. Jayaraman (1979) found that his belonging to the Brahman caste and the caste system of their home country made his informants reluctant to disclose information. Because of Sunanda Patwardhan's (1979) language, the untouchables in her study saw her as an outsider and not as a Brahman. This fortunately protected her from hostile reactions. Anand Chakravarti (1979), as an urban Indian doing research in rural India, found caste membership to be vital to her interviewees. Because there was no equivalent in the field to her caste, her interviewees related to the caste of her fiancé, who was a Brahman. Veena Dua (1979) notes how she, as an unmarried woman, used local categories to manage the hostility of wives to her spending time with their husbands as interviewees.[3]

Resembling an insider can dissipate the advantage of naïveté, reducing the investigatory advantages of the novice. Regarding

his fieldwork among the Tharu, a tribal community in the Himalaya, Triloki Pandey (1979) states:

> My first fieldwork introduced me to a people who were not much different from the lower caste members I had known in my natal village as a child. Whenever I asked my Tharu friends questions about their religion, their response was: "What sort of a Brahmin are you that you are asking us questions about religion? You should know all this and tell us about them." (P. 260)

Rapport and data collection also relate to power differences and local norms of reciprocity. Not everybody in the field appreciates the curiosity of a field-worker or interviewer.[4] (See the discussion of the institutionalization of the stranger in Holstein and Gubrium, Chapter 1, this volume.) Pandey (1979) recalls that he was asked to help an interviewee by lying. Dua (1979) illustrates the complications of doing fieldwork in castes of different status. Srinivas (1979) remembers how he was trapped due to his naïveté, and A. M. Shah (1979) reports how the research team's field notes were inspected by villagers. The local social elite may try to give advice, actively interfere in research projects, and even monopolize the field-worker's time. (For several examples from India, see Srinivas 1979; on development projects in general, see Uphoff 1991.)

If rapport triggers prolonged relationships and a seemingly open road to "good" data, the expectations concerning reciprocity between the researcher and his or her informants or interviewees can pose their own hazards. For example, Maren Bellwinkel's (1979) impoverished respondents expected her to give them gifts and loans. B. S. Baviskar (1979) was asked to collect systematic data for his informants on productivity in local sugar factories. A researcher's local landlord may be discontented with the rent he or she is paying (Pandey 1979), or the researcher may wind up providing information to interviewees that they would otherwise find difficult to obtain.[5]

Lest we take the insider-outsider problem too far as it relates to rapport building, we should bear in mind that cross-cultural differences are increasingly being homogenized by globalization. There is considerable unevenness in this development, of course, and there are always local particulars to consider, but the vast cultural divides that the traditional methodological literature seemingly cautions about concerning issues of rapport may be gradually disappearing. Indeed, as more and more cultures around the globe are coming to resemble interview societies (Atkinson and Silverman 1997), the problems of cross-cultural interviewing may very well reflect a historical epoch.

Globalization through television and the Internet is arguably dissolving former identities and loyalties based on geography or places. Men and women do business, work, and marry across international borders, and because of television and the Internet, children are raised in the generalized place of nowhere, so to speak (see Denzin 1997 on "hyperreality"). A study of cross-national perspectives on photographs, for example, points to the possible impact of Western mass media on visual perceptions (McIsaac and Ozkalp 1992), which bears on the internationalization of elicitation techniques for interviews.[6]

However, because of the uneven distribution of telecommunication throughout the world, internationally this process will likely also be very uneven. The future prospects and relevance of this development for the rapport needs and related communicative considerations of cross-cultural interviewing are still unclear. A paradox is observed in the comment that "increasing transnational flows of culture seem to be producing, not global homogenization, but the growing assertion of heterogeneity and local distinctivity" (Sibley 1995:183-84; see also Friedman 1994; Harrison 1999). And, as Birgit Meyer and Peter Geschiere

(1999) note, there is also the possibility that one outcome of "global flows" of culture may be reactive attempts at "cultural closure," in which case we might have to continue to keep one foot on square one in considering matters of rapport building for cross-cultural interviewing.

Rapport building also has confronted the varied critiques of poststructuralist commentators, who certainly would not envision the problems of cross-cultural interviewing in chiefly procedural terms. Power and perspective are center stage here. For example, poststructuralist critics have accused studies of communities and groups in Third World countries of Western ethnocentrism, imputing to the researchers a variety of vested interests and underlying motives (Asad 1973; Marcus and Fischer 1986; Szwed 1972). They have accused researchers of undertaking studies on minorities from the perspective of the dominant group. (For critiques of orthodox social science perspectives on representations of African American experiences and feminist critiques of Western social science, see Stanfield 1994.) Poststructuralists have criticized the norms and values of dominant ethnic groups for constructing the very realities researchers figured they were only studying (Stanfield 1993; Hymes 1972; Gubrium and Holstein 1997; Vidich and Lyman 1994). As a result, John Stanfield (1994), for one, has called for alternative ethnic modeling in qualitative research.

Feminist researchers have put forth parallel views (see Olesen 1994). Both Ruth Behar (1993) and Lila Abu-Lughod (1990) have argued that to liberate ethnography from the domination linked to its colonial past, self/other distinctions need to be dissolved, or at the very least critically reappraised. Researcher bias in particular is related to this issue of subjectivity. In her book *Writing Women's Worlds* (1993), Abu-Lughod presents women's stories and conversations as narrative chapters; as a way of critiquing ethnographic typification, she drops the traditional formal conclusion to avoid reestablishing the authority of the expert's voice. (For references to self and othering, reflexivity, co-constructions, and the ethnographic encounter, see Riesman 1977; Crapanzano 1980; Dwyer 1982; Rosaldo 1986; Dumont 1992; Clough 1992; Behar 1993.) The point is to draw critical attention to the scientist claims of traditional ethnographic studies, including data generated from cross-cultural interviews, as they relate to the problem and meaning of rapport building.

NONVERBAL COMMUNICATION

As Walburga von Raffler-Engel (1988) notes, nonverbal communication is an often unarticulated obstacle to cross-cultural interaction: "When two people of different cultures talk with each other in one of the two languages familiar to both of them, they automatically assume that they also share the extra-linguistic features of communication" (p. 74). She asserts that the most extensive disequilibrium in cross-cultural encounters comes from the features that lie below consciousness.

Two common forms of nonverbal communication problems are often noted: lack of comprehension and misunderstanding. In cases of the former, the receiver misses the information evident in the nonverbal signal; in cases of the latter, the receiver misinterprets the signal. In his work on misunderstandings in multicultural Israel, for example, Rafael Schneller (1988) found that different cultural groups use similar gestures, but with different meanings intended. He notes that the problems caused by misinterpreted signals are accentuated by implicit messages, such as gestures dominating explicit messages in the form of words when the two are in conflict. An illustration of a gesture that has different meanings is the head nod; in most parts of Europe, nodding signifies agreement, whereas in certain southern areas, such as in parts of Greece, nodding means no.

Such communicative problems extend to material culture. As Mary Douglas and Baron Isherwood (1996) note, "It is standard ethnographic practice to assume that all material possessions carry social meanings and to concentrate a main part of cultural analysis [and we would presume interviewing] upon their use as communicators" (p. 38). Goods are used to make visible and stable the categories of culture, not just for subsistence and competitive display. Edward E. Evans-Pritchard's (1940) account of the Nuer's cattle shows how rules stated in terms of cattle were basic to the network of kinship and provides a perspective on the cattle's double role. Cattle provided subsistence but also were used to draw the lines of social relationships. It is this approach to goods that Douglas and Isherwood assert is a proper route to cultural understanding. In an important message for cross-cultural interviewers, they advise us that commodities are "good for thinking; treat them as a nonverbal medium for the human creative faculty" (pp. 40-41).

Marcel Mauss's essay The Gift (1990), which centers on the social organization of gift exchange, makes explicit the theme of consumption and especially goods and rituals as maps of social order (see also Appadurai 1986; Bourdieu 1984). According to Don Slater (1997), "As communicators, goods are primarily 'markers' that indicate social relationships and classifications." He continues, "Through the use of goods we can construct and maintain an intelligible social universe, since by classifying, comparing, and ordering the things we have and use we make sense of and organize our social relations, classifying persons and events" (p. 150). Consequently, goods can also be used for exclusion and inclusion.[7] The latter relates to rapport, of course, and is dependent on knowledge of material categories; this virtually demands that an interviewer establish a place in the information network from which to gain knowledge of the meaning of goods.[8] The implication for cross-cultural interviewing is that interviewing must be accompanied by ongoing ethnographic knowledge of material culture, especially as that bears on cultural communication. The rub, of course, is that entering a new field usually implies that the researcher has limited information about the categories that particular goods mark in the community. The implication here is that, to conduct effective cross-cultural interviewing, a researcher must have sufficient time to establish a modicum of community membership (Ryen 2000).

Breaks and silences are another challenging aspect of cross-cultural communication with obvious consequences for interviewing. In some countries, it is regarded as inappropriate to talk during meals (Dahl and Habert 1986); in others, long pauses are an integral part of everyday social interaction, not signals for turn taking, such as invariably occurs in interview exchanges (Ryen 2000). Compared to speech patterns in some cultures in the Third World, the fast pace of Western speech hardly provides room for long breaks during talk. Thus Western interviewers risk interrupting interviewees' accounts by starting to talk in the middle of their sentences or stories. In some Asian cultures, silences and pauses are active parts of communication. These can be differentiated and operate as forms of respect, agreement, or disagreement (Smutkupt and Barna 1976). Helmut Morsbach's (1988a, 1988b) work on silence and bowing in Japan, comparing Japanese with Americans' and Australians' interpretations of silent periods in everyday discourse, is relevant to interviewing. This also has been discussed in the context of marketing research, another field in which cross-cultural communication is important (Tung 1984; Tse et al. 1988; Graham and Gronhaug 1989; Stewart, Hecker, and Graham 1987).

Nonverbal communication constitutes a vital part of intercultural encounters. Indeed, as Kvale (1996) notes, one problem with the analysis of qualitative interviews—the form that cross-cultural interviewing often takes—is researchers' usual tendency to focus on purely verbal communication while ignoring bodily expressions and other unverbalized texts.[9]

CONTEXT AND VERBAL COMMUNICATION

Social reality and how we talk about reality are intertwined. Reality varies according to the context of its articulation, and this by implication presents a challenge especially for cross-cultural, interview research. In low-context languages, for example, the interactional context has little impact upon the meaning of what is said; the message, in effect, is in the words. This is exemplified by Germanic languages; speakers of these languages are viewed as having faces without expressions and make economical use of body language. In the high-context Latin languages, in contrast, messages cannot be interpreted literally, but have to be linked to performances (Hall 1976, 1988).

Moving from a low-context to a high-context language can be interactionally complicated. Acquiring the ability to speak another language for purposes of cross-cultural interviewing thus requires that interviewers learn more than vocabulary and grammar. (Blum-Kulka, House, and Kasper 1989 provide a useful overview of publications on such aspects of "cross-cultural pragmatics"; on the role of affect in cross-cultural negotiations, see George, Jones, and Gonzalez 1998.) As John Gumperz (1982; Gumperz and Cook-Gumperz 1982) explains in his work on the cultural specificity of speech act behavior, "Cross-cultural differences in expectations of linguistic behavior, interpretative strategies, and signaling devices can lead to breakdowns in interethnic communication" (cited in Blum-Kulka et al. 1989:6).

Gumperz's work on the communicative shape of ethnic communication is pioneering and directly pertinent to cross-cultural interviewing. The extract below from his linguistic material illustrates how the inter-

```
 6    A:    I have done my graduate certificate in Education from L. Uni-
 7          versity. I had been teaching after getting that teacher's training in
 8          H., in H.
 9    B:    Oh, so you have done some teaching
10    A:    Some [I have done I have done some [teaching
11    B:         [in H. [                      I see
12    A:    Um . . . I completed two terms . . . uh, unfortunately I had to
13          leave from that place because [uh I was appointed only
14    B:                                [oh
15    A:    for two terms
16    B:    Oh so you did not get to finish your probation, I suppose
17    A:    (sighs) so that is uh [my start was alright but later
18    B:                        [oh
19    A:    on what happened it is a mi-a great chaos, I don't know
20          where I stand or what I can do . . . um, [after
21    B:                                            [and now you find
22          you can't get a job
23    A:    No, this is not actually the situation, [I have not
24    B:                                          [oh
25    A:    completely explained [my position
26    B:                         [yes
```

pretation of speakers' meanings is an interactional and collaborative activity. Linguistic contextualization processes mediate informational and verbal messages.[10] Gumperz's (1977, 1978, 1979) analyses of interactions between British English and Indian English speakers in England show that differences in cues resulted in systematic miscommunication. Gumperz asserts that the problems were the result of differences in systems of conversational inference and cues for signaling speech acts. At the same time, the results are notably embodied in the interactional machinery and style of the speakers' encounter, which constructs cultural data of its own, a point I will take up in the next section of this chapter.

An illustration is drawn from an interview-counseling session recorded in an industrial suburb in London (Gumperz 1982:183). The communication is between English-speaking persons. The client is a male Pakistani teacher of mathematics, born in South Asia but with a university de-

gree from England. The counselor is a female staff member of a center funded by the Department of Employment, which deals with interethnic communication problems in British industry. The participants are said to agree on the general definition of the event but to differ in expectations and on what needs to be done.

The extract above shows how misinterpretation is an interactional and collaborative activity, and how linguistic contextualization processes mediate verbal messages. A, the Pakistani teacher, has been unable to secure permanent employment and has been told that he lacks the necessary communicative skills for high school teaching, for which he has been referred to the center. B is a center counselor. The extract illustrates misunderstandings and a failure to negotiate a common frame of reference despite repeated attempts.

B's focus on "done" (line 9) is an indirect probe for more information about A's working experience.[11] A's (12-15) next remark can be interpreted as intended to lead to a longer narrative, but his contextualization invites problems. His voice drops and the tempo of his account speeds up, followed by what may be assumed to be the main point in his argument. However, here it starts with "unfortunately" (12). In England, new graduates often begin with probationary short-term appointments. B's "oh" (14) and response (16) indicates that she assumes A is talking about such a post, from which he later was dismissed. This is assumed to be justified by his use of the word "unfortunately." But when A says that his "start was alright" (17), B interjects another surprised "oh" (18) that can be viewed as a form of repair or correction. A's words and prosody run counter to the expectations of English speakers. Repairs and corrections imply that new or nonshared information is to be introduced and usually marked by accent or rise in pitch and transitions such as "Oh" or "I mean." He then seems inconsistent and is not responding to B's reply, which explains her second interjection (18). A's "I don't know where I stand or what I can do" (19 and 20) is spoken with a contoured intonation that by Indian English speakers is interpreted as a signal that what is to come is important to the speaker. However, he finds himself being interrupted by B (22). His reply (23) suggests annoyance before he eventually starts his narrative (29, not shown).

Throughout, B seems to be trying to make A concentrate on what she thinks is the point of the interview, which is more training. As Gumperz (1982) notes:

> The interaction is punctuated by long asides, misunderstandings of fact and misreadings of intent. A, on the other hand, finds he is not being listened to and not given a chance to explain his problem. . . . in spite of repeated attempts, both speakers utterly fail in their efforts to negotiate a common frame in terms to decide on what is being focused on and where the argument is going at any one time. (P. 185)

Gumperz summarizes by quoting an Indian English speaker: "They're on parallel tracks which don't meet."

Differences in systems of conversational inferences and cues for signaling speech acts combine into distinctive interactional styles. This is why problems often arise when speakers from different speech communities interact. "Only by looking at the whole range of linguistic phenomena that enter into conversational management can we understand what goes on in an interaction" (Gumperz 1982:186).[12]

Short of becoming community members themselves, some researchers make use of local interpreters. But still issues arise related to the ways in which individuals use language, the connotative meanings of words, pronunciation problems or problems with specific sounds, and challenges associated with linguistic styles in different contexts. The problem may not necessarily be a matter of posing the right questions, but one of the researcher's communicating questions to the interpreter in culturally appropriate ways that invite further communication. It is of vital importance that words and concepts be interpreted in the same ways by interviewers, interpreters, and respondents to avoid violating validity.

For interpreters, English is often their second language, and there is a high probability that people for whom English is a second, or even a third, language will use English in different ways from native speakers. The same applies to local interpreters of any language when the speakers in question belong to different cultures. The further the distance between the cultures, the more an interpreter has to transform language to convey the same content. For example, the word *yes* has often proved to be a problematic response in interviews and other information-seeking contexts. In certain cultures, *yes* is heard as agreement, whereas in others it is simply a response confirming that the question has been heard. Such differences have proved problematic in negotiations of business contracts, for example, where unsavvy interpretations can produce unfortunate results. Agreements that one side understood to be confirmed with a yes may never be implemented, with the result that the partners are seen as unreliable. In Asian cultures, an explicit no to a request is often seen as rude, or as threatening to the opposite party's face when subordinates are present (Dahl and Habert 1986). However, in these cultures closer relationships seem to allow greater tolerance of linguistic directness (Bilbow 1998; Brown and Levinson 1978).

International business is increasingly dependent on cross-cultural interviewing, to which many of the issues noted above apply. In my own work in this area in Tanzania, humor proved to be a way around miscommunication. In interview research focused on fringe benefits, for example, I posed a question to coresearchers about the "cold lunch" as a fringe benefit in Tanzania. My Tanzanian coresearchers laughed in a friendly way and told me that a cold lunch is given only to one's enemies. In another instance, a publishing company that wanted to market its products in India by using the owl as a symbol of wisdom eventually learned that among Indians this bird is associated with "bad fortune." Another company tried to introduce its animal feed products to the Muslim areas of Arab countries, but unfortunately the company's advertising brochure pictured on its cover a well-fed pig, an animal that Muslims consider to be unclean. These are only a few examples of how local symbolic relevancies mediate meaning, any of which can apply in the interview encounter.

Norms also vary among cultures concerning how and when it is appropriate for two parties to begin serious business (Dahl and Habert 1986; Hall 1988). Indeed, gaps may be found between any two cultures, not only between the traditional exotic and nonexotic groups, as A. Bennett (1986) has shown in his work on relatedly specialized training for foreign managers in the United States.[13]

As business and corporate organizational concerns increasingly penetrate cross-cultural communication, seemingly straightforward matters such as questions about quality, quantity, and frequency are increasingly raised in interviews. Poor communication in this regard may erode rapport in the very process of interviewing, with unfortunate economic consequences. The researcher may be cut off from prompting or asking detailed follow-up questions to elaborate or clarify numerical information, for example. The problem probably looms larger in short-term projects than in long-term, traditional participant observation studies. Indeed, Hein Streefkerk (1993) found that in his research he could collect data on quantities, numbers of workers, and wage levels only in indirect ways over long periods of time, because employers avoided giving him exact information on these and other important economic data.[14]

◆ *Cultural Data as Collaborative Accomplishment*

Lest we dwell exclusively on the communicative problems that derive from a naturalistic view of cultural facts, let us briefly consider how a perspective on shared meaning as a locally collaborative accomplishment relates to cross-cultural interviewing. Because little work has focused on collaborative accomplishment in cross-cultural interviewing, I will use my own data from e-mail communication with an Asian businessman in East Africa as an illustration of how this is done (Ryen and Silverman 2000; relatedly, see also in this volume Mann and Stewart, Chapter 12; Baker, Chapter 19). In the following exchanges, AR (the researcher) and Sachin (the Kenyan entrepreneur) work at achieving acceptable forms of "sign-offs" or closings at the ends of their e-mail messages. Taken together, these exchanges illustrate how both parties achieve mutual understanding about the preferred interpersonal relationship on a turn-by-turn basis, which I would argue accomplishes a form of cultural understanding *within* the interview process itself.

Sachin ends his first message as follows:

> tell me more about yourself in your next email. . . .
>   love
>   Sachin (Ending of first message
>   dated October 26, 1998)

AR replies, among other things:

> I am married and have two small children. (October 30, 1998)

Presumably, even if she is married, AR does not necessarily have to mention it. In categorizing herself as "married" with "two small children," she also categorizes the other person, who in the next few exchanges becomes a "friend" or something "more," not a potential lover. Moreover, AR does not use "love" as a closing, but "hilsen" (Norwegian for "greetings"). Sachin has apparently monitored the category-bound implications here, for his next message ends with "regards Sachin" (November 5, 1998).

In later messages, Sachin no longer uses "love," but rather "well regards" (November 17, 1998), "well cheerio" (December 10, 1998), and "cheeeers" (December 26, 1998). In her later correspondence, AR relaxes the interpersonal distance of her preceding closings from her somewhat impersonal "*hilsen*" to "*beste hilsen*" (November 23, 1998) and then "*Kjaere* [dear] Sachin" (December 22, 1998). Despite her self-identification as sexually unavailable, AR responds to Sachin's information that he intends to get married soon by writing, "Lucky woman to marry you,—tell me more!" (November 10, 1998). This recontextualizes Sachin's sexual availability to his future bride. AR intentionally uses such banter to maintain a friendly relationship with a respondent who is, after all, giving his time freely to help her. As we see

above, flattery ("lucky woman") is a verbal reward that researchers can offer their research subjects and that helps to facilitate a continuing exchange. A researcher might use such friendly, noninstrumental framing to preface a whole message. So one of AR's e-mails begins, "Sachin, this time I have no research questions" (November 30, 1998).

Sachin's grandmother died a few days before AR actually visited him. Religious tradition demanded that she cancel parts of her research agenda, and much of their talk referred instead to the family. So one of his next e-mail messages began:

> Dear ANNI,
>   hope you and the entire family is in the best of the health and spirits by the grace of the almighty. . . . How are your kids. . . . I bet they must be giving you a run for your money. . . . and your husband . . . is he ok. (July 11, 1999)

This set of exchanges shows how AR and Sachin negotiate the shared parameters of their relationship, invoking a range of paired identities: researcher-researched, female-male, married woman-single man, friend-friend. They don't simply arrive, in good methodological order, at some preexisting set of culture-bound roles and start the interview process. Their subject positions as interview participants, in other words, are not preset by culture, but emerge in ongoing interaction (see Holstein and Gubrium, Chapter 1, this volume). AR begins by implying her sexual unavailability, and Sachin's recognition of this is evidenced in his modification of his e-mail sign-off. However, conscious of the rewards that research subjects rightly may expect, AR later uses what Harvey Sacks (1992a, 1992b) calls a "category-modifier" to show her respondent that just because she is "unavailable" does not mean that she cannot treat him as a friend or that, indeed, she is unaware of his attractiveness to other women.

These exchanges show that interview researchers must be very careful how they use categories. Sacks (1992a) puts the issue succinctly:

> Suppose you're an anthropologist or sociologist standing somewhere. You see somebody do some action, and you see it to be some activity. How can you go about formulating who is it that did it, for the purposes of your report? Can you use at least what you might take to be the most conservative formulation—his name? Knowing, of course, that any category you choose would have the[se] kinds of systematic problems: how would you go about selecting a given category from the set that would equally well characterise or identify that person at hand? (Pp. 467-68)

In a chapter titled "Pursuing Members' Meaning," Robert Emerson, Rachel Fretz, and Linda Shaw (1995) argue that "deeper, fuller memos and analyses in a final ethnography require examining not simply what terms members use, but when, where, and how they use them and how they actually categorize or classify events and objects in specific situations" (p. 126). This implies that the analysis of cultural particulars should also focus on how meaning is collaboratively produced within the interview. Sacks (1992a) shows how one cannot resolve such problems simply "by taking the best possible notes at the time and making your decisions afterwards" (p. 468). Sacks (1992a) quotes from two linguists who appear to have no problem in characterizing particular (invented) utterances as "simple," "complex," "casual," or "ceremonial" and explains that such rapid characterizations of data assume "that we can know that without an analysis of what it is [they] are doing [with words]" (p. 429), a viewpoint that shortchanges the local accomplishment of the characterization.

Let us try to follow Sacks's argument on this and consider how it might relate to cross-cultural interviewing. First, the conclusion that studying other cultures can open our minds to our own is common-place. Indeed, it can lead in a Durkheimian direction, where differences are simply "explained" as a product of "culture" or "common knowledge" without problematizing the communicative "machinery" involved. Second, a focus on the natural "thereness" of culture deflects our attention from how meaning is locally assembled. For example, Sacks (1992a) points out how, in Evans-Pritchard's work on the Nuer, Evans-Pritchard asserts that "the Nuer tend to define all social processes and relationships in terms of cattle." But, as Sacks goes on to say, "it's one thing to say that every conversation ends up about cattle and another to show how that's so" (p. 389).

The interviewer who is alert to the collaborative accomplishment of culture relates to the life of the interview as storied and managed by and through narratives and participants. The focus is on *how* the interview is narratively constructed. Narrative shifts, for example, produce different contexts, and it is within these different contexts that questions are asked and answered and, most significantly, meaning produced in the process. Interviewers' questions, cues, and prompts are not simply stimuli to empty the interviewee's reservoir of cultural data; rather, they actively contribute to the contexts in which experiences are narrated. Both interviewer and interviewee actively co-construct meaning and, notably, also who and what they represent to each other in the process. This differs from considerations of the communicative challenges of cross-cultural interviewing discussed earlier. The problems seen as the integral role dilemmas of cross-cultural interviews—the insider-outsider issue—are here regarded as *indigenous* parts of meaning construction in ongoing social interaction. The insider-outsider problem is transformed into something research participants themselves accomplish and resolve rather than merely cope with or suffer from.

How far is culture reducible to members' ongoing categorization practices? If collaborative accomplishment constructs cultural understanding, how can related explanatory purchase be obtained for concepts such as "culture," "cultural differences," and "cross-cultural communication"? Sacks again provides direction. Put crudely, for Sacks, if "culture" has any salience, it is not as a source of explanation—as it might be when we approach it as the cause of miscommunication—but as a member's method. In this sense, "culture" is best approached as what Sacks (1992a) calls an "inference-making machine" (p. 119). This refers to a locally employed descriptive apparatus that can be documented for how descriptions are used and administered in specific contexts, such as took place in the "cross-cultural" communication between AR and Sachin described above. Orienting to culture as an interactive resource, both AR and Sachin used categories available to them to position each other within the interview context and, as a result, constructed the interactive and moral contours of their relationship. They did not simply correctly or incorrectly appropriate external categories to organize their relationship as interviewer and interviewee. In skillfully using these categories, they constructed the social organization of the interview process in the course of ongoing social interaction.

In this regard, consider the external reality of ostensible "coincidences," for example. To the layperson, coincidence may be the product of some mysterious external reality. To the social researcher, a focus on coincidence may seem to be a feature of particular cultures or subcultures, as in accounts of cultures of poverty where the poor are seen to stress coincidence or luck rather than rational behavior. However, Sacks (1992b:237-40) shows that it could be that people *package* their accounts in terms of coincidence in order to produce "relevant-at-that-moment tellable stories." This is directly pertinent to Emanuel Schegloff's (1992) comment that Sacks proposes that "much of the observable orderliness of the world may be better understood as the by-products of ambient organizations which are quite unconcerned with those outcomes rather than as products which were the design target of some explanation" (p. xxiv). If we take Schegloff seriously, it is also worth pursuing the "ambient social organization" demonstrably attended by interview participants. The result for cross-cultural interviewing would be that we would begin by bracketing the concept of "culture" in order to build our knowledge of how interviewer and interviewee collaboratively use and assemble accounts of "cultures" in communicative practice. This would serve to reveal the constructive, as much as the procedural, contours of the interviewing in question.

■ Notes

1. According to Gubrium and Holstein (1997; Holstein and Gubrium 1995), traditional approaches portray subjects as rather passive "vessels of answers." It is assumed that the researcher will be able to get access to this store of data by establishing rapport with subjects and by posing questions in what is seen as the correct, neutral way.

2. Rutten conveyed this information to me in a personal communication.

3. By calling the women *bhabi,* Dua (1979) took on the role of their men's sister. By excluding herself from being a sister-in-law, she was protecting herself from local norms that give men sexual liberties with their wives' sisters.

4. Streefkerk (1993) reports about his difficulties in getting access to data on quantitative "facts" from his entrepreneurs: "Many entrepreneurs did not like my efforts to count the number of workers and they gave incomplete information and tried to hinder my attempts to visit shop floors" (p. 18). This kind of problem is accentuated by the low quality of public statistics in many countries, which often rules out triangulation. Respondents can also be skillful at circumventing the informational needs of interviewers. Ahmed (1984; cited in Rutten 1995), for example, discusses how researchers tried to cross-check data on small-scale industries in Bangladesh by repeating certain questions from their

last visit. However, most of the industrialists who were questioned simply asked the researchers to copy down information from their previous visit.

5. This also applies to myself sending Web addresses with information on comparable Western products, brochures, information on production gear when setting up new productions, and so on. Also, in cultures where it is regarded as impolite to oppose a guest, interviewees may accept researchers' requests to find materials or documents for them, but never follow through. This happened in my own experience in communicating with an Asian entrepreneur. In one of his e-mails he wrote, "The questions that you have asked me have been answered in the package i sent you . . . so if you have more please email them to me" (July 11, 1999). That package never arrived, and I never asked him about it.

6. McIsaac and Ozkalp (1992) studied American and Turkish women's perceptions of body positions of male and female models as shown in slides.

7. See Slater (1997:152) for his criticism of Douglas on modern consumption culture, where he comments that Douglas too easily translates her perspective on the relationship between meanings and rituals of consumption and social order. He also points to the impact of vested commercial interests. See also Bourdieu (1984).

8. This also applies to the researcher. During fieldwork with entrepreneurs in East Africa, my African colleagues claimed that the entrepreneurs watching this white, Western person arriving in a LandCruiser were initially more interested in the potential funding than in the interviews.

9. However, the growing interest in the analysis of videotapes does begin to address this problem.

10. The text is an illustration of the "naturally occurring data" traditionally preferred in ethnomethodological studies. For a discussion, see Silverman (1993).

11. All of my comments here are closely based on Gumperz (1982).

12. This makes context-bound interpretive preferences an alternative perspective on attitudes and stereotypes. This is a perspective Gumperz (1982) has employed in teaching sessions to improve relations between staff and supervisors in workplaces that employ members of different ethnic groups (see also Gumperz 1978). However, analyses also show that participants may lose nuances of meaning without communication breaking down, due to a high level of linguistic tolerance in close relationships (Bilbow 1996).

13. In general, representatives from different cultures may respond differently to the same phenomena (Johnson et al. 1996; Mangione, Fowler, and Louis 1992), and the definitions of particular words may vary, such as the definitions of *family* and *sister* in Western compared with African cultures. Further, in some cultures certain phenomena are given special terms, such as *parastatal sector* (Bureau of Statistics and Labour Department 1993), and phenomena that are important in some cultures, such as witchcraft and medicine men, are regarded as nonexistent in others.

14. For discussions of some special problems related to cross-cultural data on quantity, see Claudia Zaslavsky's (1990) work on comparing numbers and on number superstition, P. H. Gulliver's (1958) on age and social organization, and Andreas Fuglesang's (1982:55, 65) on ethnocentrism in Western tests of mental development and on comparing models for assessing quantity by visual perception.

■ *References*

Abeyewardene, A. 1991. "Familial versus Professional Responsibilities: Fieldwork Experiences in Sri Lanka." Pp. 52-58 in *From the Female Eye: Accounts of Women Fieldworkers Studying Their Own Communities,* edited by M. N. Panini. Delhi: Hindustan Publishing.

Abu-Lughod, L. 1990. "Can There Be a Feminist Ethnography?" *Women and Performance* 5:7-27.
———. 1993. *Writing Women's Worlds: Bedouin Stories.* Berkeley: University of California Press.

Ahmed, Q. K. 1984. "Rural Industries Study Project (RISP); An Introduction." *Bangladesh Development Studies* 12(1-2):iii-xi.

Appadurai, A., ed. 1986. *The Social Life of Things: Commodities in Cultural Perspective.* Cambridge: Cambridge University Press.

Asad, T. 1973. *Anthropology and the Colonial Encounter.* New York: Humanities.

Atkinson, P. and D. Silverman. 1997. "Kundera's *Immortality:* The Interview Society and the Invention of Self." *Qualitative Inquiry* 3:304-25.

Bangun, M. 1991. "Sensitive Social Relationships: An Urban Professional Woman in a Village Setting." Pp. 81-87 in *From the Female Eye: Accounts of Women Fieldworkers Studying Their Own Communities,* edited by M. N. Panini. Delhi: Hindustan Publishing.

Baviskar, B. S. 1979. "Walking on the Edge of Factionalism: An Industrial Cooperative in Rural Maharashtra." Pp. 184-201 in *The Fieldworker and the Field: Problems and Challenges in Sociological Investigation,* edited by M. N. Srinivas, A. M. Shah, and E. A. Ramaswamy. Bombay: Oxford University Press.

Behar, R. 1993. *Translated Woman: Crossing the Border with Esperanza's Story.* Boston: Beacon.

Bellwinkel, M. 1979. "Objective Appreciation through Subjective Involvement: A Slum in Kanpur." Pp. 141-52 in *The Fieldworker and the Field: Problems and Challenges in Sociological Investigation,* edited by M. N. Srinivas, A. M. Shah, and E. A. Ramaswamy. Bombay: Oxford University Press.

Bennett, A. 1986. "American Culture Is Often a Puzzle for Foreign Managers in the U.S." *Wall Street Journal,* February 20.

Berreman, G. D. 1962. *Behind Many Masks: Ethnography and Impression Management in a Himalayan Village.* Ithaca, NY: Cornell University Press.

Bhopal, K. 2000. "Gender, 'Race' and Power in the Research Process: South Asian Women in East London." Pp. 67-79 in *Research and Inequality,* edited by C. Truman, D. M. Mertens, and B. Humphries. London: UCL.

Bilbow, G. T. 1996. "Managing Impressions in the Multicultural Workplace: An Impression Management-Based Model for Cross-Cultural Discourse Analysis and Awareness Training for the Workplace." Ph.D. dissertation, City University of Hong Kong.

———. 1998. "Look Who's Talking: An Analysis of 'Chair-Talk' in Business Meetings." *Journal of Business and Technical Communication* 12:157-99.

Blackwood, E. 1995. "Falling in Love with an-Other Lesbian: Reflections on Identity in Fieldwork." Pp. 51-76 in *Taboo: Sex, Identity, and Erotic Subjectivity in Anthropological Fieldwork,* edited by D. Kulick and M. Willson. London: Routledge.

Blum-Kulka, S., J. House, and G. Kasper. 1989. "Investigating Cross-Cultural Pragmatics: An Introductory Overview." Pp. 1-34 in *Cross-Cultural Pragmatics: Requests and Apologies,* edited by S. Blum-Kulka, J. House, and G. Kasper. Norwood, NJ: Ablex.

Bourdieu, P. 1984. *Distinction: A Social Critique of the Judgement of Taste.* Translated by R. Nice. Cambridge, MA: Harvard University Press.

Brown, P. and S. C. Levinson. 1978. "Universals in Language Usage: Politeness Phenomena." Pp. 256-58 in *Questions and Politeness: Strategies in Social Interaction,* edited by E. N. Goody. Cambridge: Cambridge University Press.

Bureau of Statistics and Labour Department. 1993. *Tanzania (Mainland): The Labour Force Survey, 1990/91.* Dar es Salaam: Author.

Casley, D. J. and D. A. Lury. 1987. *Data Collection in Developing Countries.* New York: Oxford University Press.

Chakravarti, A. 1979. "Experiences of an Encapsulated Observer: A Village in Rajasthan." Pp. 38-57 in *The Fieldworker and the Field: Problems and Challenges in Sociological Investigation,* edited by M. N. Srinivas, A. M. Shah, and E. A. Ramaswamy. Bombay: Oxford University Press.

Clough, P. T. 1992. *The End(s) of Ethnography: From Realism to Social Criticism.* Newbury Park, CA: Sage.

Conaway, M. E. 1986. "The Pretense of the Neutral Researcher." Pp. 52-63 in *Self, Sex and Gender in Cross-Cultural Fieldwork,* edited by T. L. Whitehead and M. E. Conaway. Urbana: University of Illinois Press.

Crapanzano, V. 1980. *Tuhami: Portrait of a Moroccan.* Chicago: University of Chicago Press.

Crehan, K. 1991. "Listening to Different Voices." Pp. 99-106 in *From the Female Eye: Accounts of Women Fieldworkers Studying Their Own Communities,* edited by M. N. Panini. Delhi: Hindustan Publishing.

Dahl, Ø. and K. Habert. 1986. *Møte mellom kulturer: Tverrkulturell kommunikasjon.* Stavanger, Norway: Universitetsforlaget.

Davis, D. 1986. "Changing Self-Image: Studying Menopausal Women in a Newfoundland Fishing Village." Pp. 240-61 in *Self, Sex and Gender in Cross-Cultural Fieldwork,* edited by T. L. Whitehead and M. E. Conaway. Urbana: University of Illinois Press.

Dean, J. P., R. L. Eichhorn, and L. R. Dean. 1969. "Establishing Field Relations." Pp. 68-70 in *Issues in Participant Observation: A Text and Reader,* edited by G. J. McCall and J. L. Simmons. Reading, MA: Addison-Wesley.

Denzin, N. K. 1997. *Interpretive Ethnography: Ethnographic Practices for the 21st Century.* Thousands Oaks, CA: Sage.

Deutscher, I. 1968. "Asking Questions Cross-Culturally: Some Problems of Linguistic Comparability." Pp. 318-41 in *Institutions and the Person,* edited by H. S. Becker, B. Geer, D. Riesman, and R. Weiss. Chicago: Aldine.

Douglas, M. and B. Isherwood. 1996. *The World of Goods: Towards an Anthropology of Consumption.* London: Routledge.

Dua, V. 1979. "A Woman's Encounter with Arya Samaj and Untouchables: A Slum in Jullundur." Pp. 115-26 in *The Fieldworker and the Field: Problems and Challenges in Sociological Investigation,* edited by M. N. Srinivas, A. M. Shah, and E. A. Ramaswamy. Bombay: Oxford University Press.

Dumont, J.-P. 1992. *The Headman and I: Ambiguity and Ambivalence in the Fieldworking Experience.* Prospect Heights, IL: Waveland.

Dwyer, K. 1982. *Moroccan Dialogues: Anthropology in Question.* Baltimore: Johns Hopkins University Press.

Ember, C. R. and D. Levinson. 1991. "The Substantive Contributions of Worldwide Cross-Cultural Studies. *Behavior Science Research* 25:79-141.

Emerson, R. M., R. I. Fretz, and L. L. Shaw. 1995. *Writing Ethnographic Fieldnotes.* Chicago: University of Chicago Press.

Evans-Pritchard, E. E. 1940. "The Nuer." Pp. 17-19 in E. E. Evans-Pritchard, *The Political Institutions of a Nilotic People.* Oxford: Clarendon.

Freeman, D. 1983. *Margaret Mead and Samoa: The Making and Unmaking of an Anthropological Myth.* Cambridge, MA: Harvard University Press.

Friedman, J. 1994. *Cultural Identity and Global Process.* London: Sage.

Fuglesang, A. 1982. *About Understanding: Ideas and Observations on Cross-Cultural Communication.* Uppsala: Dag Hammarskjøld Foundation.

George, J. M., G. R. Jones, and J. A. Gonzalez. 1998. "The Role of Affect in Cross-Cultural Negotiations." *Journal of International Business Studies* 29:749-72.

Golde, P. 1986. "Odyssey of Encounter." Pp. 67-93 in *Women in the Field: Anthropological Experiences,* edited by P. Golde. Berkeley: University of California Press.

Gonzalez, N. 1986. "The Anthropologist as Female Head of Household." Pp. 84-100 in *Self, Sex and Gender in Cross-Cultural Fieldwork,* edited by T. L. Whitehead and M. E. Conaway. Urbana: University of Illinois Press.

Graham, J. L. and K. Gronhaug. 1989. "Ned Hall Didn't Have to Get a Haircut, or Why We Haven't Learned Much about International Marketing in the Last 25 Years." *Journal of Higher Education* 60:152-87.

Gubrium, J. F. and J. A. Holstein. 1997. *The New Language of Qualitative Method.* New York: Oxford University Press.

Gulliver, P. H. 1958. "Counting by the Fingers by Two East African Tribes." *African Notes* 51:259-62.

Gumperz, J. J. 1977."Sociocultural Knowledge in Conversational Inferences." In *28th Annual Round Table Monograph Series on Language and Linguistics.* Washington, DC: Georgetown University Press.

———. 1978. "The Conversational Analysis of Interethnic Communication." In *Interethnic Communication,* edited by E. L. Ross. Athens: University of Georgia Press.

———. 1979. "The Sociolinguistic Basis of Speech Act Theory." In *Speech Act: Ten Years After,* edited by J. Boyd and S. Ferra. Milan: Versus.

———. 1982. *Discourse Strategies.* Cambridge: Cambridge University Press.

Gumperz, J. J. and J. Cook-Gumperz. 1982. "Interethnic Communication in Committee Negotiations." Pp. 145-62 in *Language and Social Identity,* edited by J. J. Gumperz. Cambridge: Cambridge University Press.

Habib, G. M. 1987. "Measures of Manifest Conflicts in International Joint Ventures." *Academy of Management Journal* 30:808-16.

Hall, E. T. 1976. *Beyond Culture.* Garden City, NY: Doubleday.

———. 1988. "The Hidden Dimensions of Time and Space in Today's World." Pp. 145-52 in *Cross-Cultural Perspectives in Nonverbal Communication,* edited by F. Poyatos. Toronto: C. J. Hogrefe.

Harrison, S. 1999. "Cultural Boundaries." *Anthropology Today* 15(5):10-13.

Heritage, J. C. 1997. "Conversation Analysis and Institutional Talk: Analysing Data." Pp. 161-82 in *Qualitative Research: Theory, Method and Practice,* edited by D. Silverman. London: Sage.

Holstein, J. A. and J. F. Gubrium. 1995. *The Active Interview.* Thousand Oaks, CA: Sage.

Hymes, D., ed. 1972. *Reinventing Anthropology.* New York: Pantheon.

Jayaraman, R. 1979. "Problems of Entry: Sri Lanka, Zambia and Australia." Pp. 266-75 in *The Fieldworker and the Field: Problems and Challenges in Sociological Investigation,* edited by M. N. Srinivas, A. M. Shah, and E. A. Ramaswamy. Bombay: Oxford University Press.

Johnson, T., D. O'Rourke, S. Sudman, and R. Warnecke. 1996. "Assessing Question Comprehension across Cultures: Evidence from the United States." Presented at the Essex '96 Conference, Essex, England.

Kamil, S. 1991. "Maidenhood, Marriage and Fieldwork: Experiences in India and Pakistan." Pp. 36-40 in *From the Female Eye: Accounts of Women Fieldworkers Studying Their Own Communities,* edited by M. N. Panini. Delhi: Hindustan Publishing.

Kulick, D. and M. Willson, eds. 1995. *Taboo: Sex, Identity, and Erotic Subjectivity in Anthropological Fieldwork.* London: Routledge.

Kvale, S. 1996. *InterViews: An Introduction to Qualitative Research Interviewing.* Thousand Oaks, CA: Sage.

Landes, R. 1986. "A Woman Anthropologist in Brazil." Pp. 119-39 in *Women in the Field: Anthropological Experiences,* edited by P. Golde. Berkeley: University of California Press.

Lofland, J. 1971. *Analyzing Social Settings.* Belmont, CA: Wadsworth.

Mangione, T. W., F. J. Fowler, Jr., and T. A. Louis. 1992. "Question Characteristics and Interviewer Effects." *Journal of Official Statistics* 8:293-307.

Marcus, G. E. and M. M. J. Fischer. 1986. *Anthropology as Cultural Critique: An Experimental Moment in the Human Sciences.* Chicago: University of Chicago Press.

Mauss, M. 1990. *The Gift: The Form and Reason for Exchange in Archaic Societies.* New York: Norton.

Maykovich, M. K. 1977. "The Difficulties of a Minority Researcher in Minority Communities." *Journal of Social Issues* 33(4):108-19.

McIsaac, M. S. and E. Ozkalp. 1992. "Crossnational Perspectives on Gender Differences and Perspectives of Professional Competence in Photographs." *International Journal of Instructional Media* 19:349-66.

Meyer, B. and P. Geschiere. 1999. "Introduction." Pp. 1-15 in *Globalization and Identity: Dialectics of Flow and Closure,* edited by B. Meyer and P. Geschiere. Oxford: Blackwell.

Montero, D. 1977. "Research among Racial and Cultural Minorities: An Overview." *Journal of Social Issues* 33(4):1-10.

Moreno, E. 1995. "Rape in the Field: Reflections from a Survivor." Pp. 219-51 in *Taboo: Sex, Identity, and Erotic Subjectivity in Anthropological Fieldwork,* edited by D. Kulick and M. Willson. London: Routledge.

Morsbach, H. 1988a. "The Importance of Silence and Stillness in Japanese Nonverbal Communication: A Cross-Cultural Approach." Pp. 201-18 in *Cross-Cultural Perspectives in Nonverbal Communication,* edited by F. Poyatos. Toronto: C. J. Hogrefe.

———. 1988b. "Nonverbal Communication and Hierarchical Relationships: The Case of Bowing in Japan." Pp. 189-99 in *Cross-Cultural Perspectives in Nonverbal Communication,* edited by F. Poyatos. Toronto: C. J. Hogrefe.

Nath, J. 1991. "A Bengali Woman in Three Different Field Situations." Pp. 59-65 in *From the Female Eye: Accounts of Women Fieldworkers Studying Their Own Communities,* edited by M. N. Panini. Delhi: Hindustan Publishing.

Newton, E. 1993. "My Best Informant's Dress: The Erotic Equation in Fieldwork." *Cultural Anthropology* 8:3-23.

Olesen, V. 1994. "Feminisms and Models of Qualitative Research." Pp. 158-74 in *Handbook of Qualitative Research,* edited by N. K. Denzin and Y. S. Lincoln. Thousand Oaks, CA: Sage.

Pandey, T. N. 1979. "The Anthropologist-Informant Relationship: The Navajo and Zuni in America and the Tharu in India." Pp. 246-65 in *The Fieldworker and the Field: Problems and Challenges in Sociological Investigation,* edited by M. N. Srinivas, A. M. Shah, and E. A. Ramaswamy. Bombay: Oxford University Press.

Panini, M. N. 1991. "Introduction: Reflections in Feminism and Fieldwork." Pp. 1-10 in *From the Female Eye: Accounts of Women Fieldworkers Studying Their Own Communities,* edited by M. N. Panini. Delhi: Hindustan Publishing.

Patwardhan, S. 1979. "Making My Way through Caste Images: Untouchables in Poona." Pp. 153-60 in *The Fieldworker and the Field: Problems and Challenges in Sociological Investigation,* edited by M. N. Srinivas, A. M. Shah, and E. A. Ramaswamy. Bombay: Oxford University Press.

Phellas, C. N. 2000 "Cultural and Sexual Identities in In-Depth Interviewing." Pp. 52-64 in *Research and Inequality,* edited by C. Truman, D. M. Mertens, and B. Humphries. London: UCL.

Probyn, E. 1993. *Sexing the Self: Gendered Positions in Cultural Studies.* London: Routledge.

Rabinow, P. 1977. *Reflections on Fieldwork in Morocco.* Berkeley: University of California Press.

Riesman, P. 1977. *Freedom in Fulani Social Life.* Chicago: University of Chicago Press.

Rosaldo, R. 1986. "Ilongot Hunting as Story and Experience." Pp. 97-138 in *The Anthropology of Experience,* edited by V. W. Turner and E. M. Bruner. Urbana: University of Illinois Press.

Rutten, M. 1995. *Farms and Factories: Social Profile of Large Farmers and Rural Industrialists in West India.* Delhi: Oxford University Press.

———. 1996. "Business Strategy and Life-Style: Owners of Combine-Harvesters in North Malaysia." *Kajian Malaysia* (Journal of Malaysian Studies) 14(1-2):112-50.

Ryen, A. 2000. "Colonial Methodology? Methodological Challenges to Cross-Cultural Projects Collecting Data by Structured Interviews." Pp. 220-35 in *Research and Inequality,* edited by C. Truman, D. M. Mertens, and B. Humphries. London: UCL.

Ryen, A. and D. Silverman. 2000. "Marking Boundaries: Culture as Category Work." *Qualitative Inquiry* 6:107-27.

Sacks, H. 1992a. *Lectures on Conversation,* Vol. 1. Edited by G. Jefferson. Oxford: Blackwell.

———. 1992b. *Lectures on Conversation,* Vol. 2. Edited by G. Jefferson. Oxford: Blackwell.

Schegloff, E. A. 1992. "Introduction." In H. Sacks, *Lectures on Conversation,* Vol. 2. Edited by G. Jefferson. Oxford: Blackwell.

Schneller, R. 1988. "The Israeli Experience of Cross-Cultural Misunderstanding: Insights and Lessons." Pp. 153-73 in *Cross-Cultural Perspectives in Nonverbal Communication,* edited by F. Poyatos. Toronto: C. J. Hogrefe.

Shaffir, W. B. 1991. "Managing a Convincing Self-Presentation: Some Personal Reflections on Entering the Field." Pp. 72-96 in *Experiencing Fieldwork: An Inside View of Qualitative Research,* edited by W. B. Shaffir and R. A. Stebbins. Newbury Park: Sage.

Shah, A. M. 1979. "Studying the Present and the Past: A Village in Gurajat." Pp. 29-37 in *The Fieldworker and the Field: Problems and Challenges in Sociological Investigation,* edited by M. N. Srinivas, A. M. Shah, and E. A. Ramaswamy. Bombay: Oxford University Press.

Shenkar, O. and Y. Zeira. 1990. "International Joint Ventures: A Tough Test for HR." *Personnel Journal* 67(1):26-31.

Slater, D. 1997. *Consumer Culture and Modernity.* Cambridge: Polity.

Sibley, D. 1995. *Geographies of Exclusion: Society and Difference in the West.* London: Routledge.

Silverman, D. 1993. *Interpreting Qualitative Data: Methods for Analysing Talk, Text and Interaction.* London: Sage.

Smutkupt, S. and L. M. Barna. 1976. "Impact of Non-verbal Communication in an Intercultural Setting: Thailand." *International and Intercultural Annual* 3:130-38.

Spradley, J. P. 1979. *The Ethnographic Interview.* New York: Holt, Rinehart & Winston.

Srinivas, M. N. 1979. "The Fieldworker and the Field: A Village in Karnataka." Pp. 19-28 in *The Fieldworker and the Field: Problems and Challenges in Sociological Investigation,* edited by M. N. Srinivas, A. M. Shah, and E. A. Ramaswamy. Bombay: Oxford University Press.

Stanfield, J. H., II. 1993. "Methodological Reflections: An introduction." Pp. 3-15 in *Race and Ethnicity in Research Methods,* edited by J. H. Stanfield II and R. M. Dennis. Newbury Park, CA: Sage.

———. 1994. "Ethnic Modeling in Qualitative Research." Pp. 175-88 in *Handbook of Qualitative Research,* edited by N. K. Denzin and Y. S. Lincoln. Thousand Oaks, CA: Sage.

Stewart, D. W., S. Hecker, and J. L. Graham. 1987. "It's More Than What You Say: Assessing the Influence of Nonverbal Communication in Marketing." *Psychology and Marketing* 4:303-22.

Streefkerk, H. 1993. *On the Production of Knowledge: Fieldwork in South Gurajat, 1971-1991.* Amsterdam: VU University Press.

Szwed, J. F. 1972. "An American Anthropological Dilemma: The Politics of Afro-American Culture." Pp. 153-81 in *Reinventing Anthropology,* edited by D. Hymes. New York: Pantheon.

Tadria, H. M. K. 1991. "Challenges of Participation and Observation: Fieldwork Experience among Some Peasants of Uganda." Pp. 88-98 in *From the Female Eye: Accounts of Women Fieldworkers Studying Their Own Communities,* edited by M. N. Panini. Delhi: Hindustan Publishing.

Thurnbull, C. M. 1986. "Sex and Gender: The Role of Subjectivity in Field Research." Pp. 17-27 in *Self, Sex and Gender in Cross-Cultural Fieldwork,* edited by T. L. Whitehead and M. E. Conaway. Urbana: University of Illinois Press.

Tse, D. K. and J. Francis. 1994. "Cultural Differences in Conducting Intra- and Intercultural Negotiations: A Sino-Canadian Comparison." *Journal of International Studies* 25:537-56.

Tse, D. K., K. Lee, I. Vertinsky, and D. A. Wehrung. 1988. "Does Culture Matter? A Cross-Cultural Study of Executives' Choice, Decisiveness and Risk Adjustment in International Marketing." *Journal of Marketing* 52(4):81-95.

Tung, R. I. 1984. "How to Negotiate with the Japanese. *California Management Review* 26(4):62-77.

Uphoff, N. 1991. "Fitting Projects to People." Pp. 467-511 in *Putting People First: Sociological Variables in Rural Development,* edited by M. M. Cernea. New York: Oxford University Press.

Vidich, A. J. and S. M. Lyman. 1994. "Qualitative Methods: Their History in Sociology and Anthropology." Pp. 23-59 in *Handbook of Qualitative Research,* edited by N. K. Denzin and Y. S. Lincoln. Thousand Oaks, CA: Sage.

von Raffler-Engel, W. 1988. "The Impact of Covert Factors in Cross-Cultural Communication." Pp. 71-104 in *Cross-Cultural Perspectives in Nonverbal Communication,* edited by F. Poyatos. Toronto: C. J. Hogrefe.

Warren, C. A. B. 1977. "Fieldwork in the Gay World: Issues in Phenomenological Research." *Journal of Social Issues* 33(4):93-107.

———. 1988. *Gender Issues in Field Research.* Newbury Park, CA: Sage.

Wax, R. H. 1960. "Twelve Years Later: An Analysis of Field Experiences." Pp. 166-78 in *Human Organization Research: Field Relations and Techniques,* edited by R. N. Adams and J. J. Preiss. Homewood, IL: Dorsey.

———. 1971. *Doing Fieldwork: Warnings and Advice.* Chicago: University of Chicago Press.

Wengle, J. L. 1988. *Ethnographers in the Field: The Psychology of Research.* Tuscaloosa: University of Alabama Press.

Zaslavsky, C. 1990. *Africa Counts: Number and Pattern in African Culture.* New York: Lawrence Hill.

22

PERSONAL AND FOLK NARRATIVE AS CULTURAL REPRESENTATION

♦ **Kirin Narayan**
Kenneth M. George

There is a thirst among the Paxtun women for autobiography. There is also a correct way to "seek the person out" with questions. One day, when my daughter's nanny had observed me eliciting a life story from someone, she later tried to correct me on the grounds that I did not know how to interrogate properly. "You foreigners don't know how to search [*latawel*] one another," she reproached me. "When we Pakistanis ask a person's story, we don't let a single detail go by. We dig in all the corners, high and low. We seek the person out. That's how we do things. We are storytellers and story seekers. We know how to draw out a person's heart." (Grima 1991:81-82)

As this outspoken Paxtun woman from Northwest Pakistan reminds us, asking people for and about stories is a widespread practice, even though the ways of asking and the kinds of stories told may vary. Indeed, most of us are already old experts at coaxing, inviting, or outright demanding stories in our everyday lives. From a child's wheedling "Tell me" to a friend's bright-eyed prod "And then what happened?" we regularly make and receive such requests.

In pursuing stories within an interview context, however, we create a frame of analytic reflection around storytelling transactions. The delights of a well-told tale may continue to sweep us along, but as interviewers we usually elicit and evaluate stories from the vantage points of particular

AUTHORS' NOTE: We extend our great thanks to Lila Abu-Lughod and Maria Lepowsky for their helpful critiques of this chapter.

professional agendas. Like Benedicte Grima's (1991) Paxtun critic, the people we seek to interview sometimes already have their own ideas about how a person should go about extracting stories. For them too, stories move about in a range of interpersonal and institutional settings, and the presence of a researcher eagerly seeking stories may provide yet another occasion for retellings. In addition to scholars, there are other specialists with their own purposes and methods for eliciting stories—therapists, shamans, lawyers, doctors, talk-show hosts, priests, immigration officers, police detectives, journalists, human rights workers, and so on. This interactive process of extracting and yielding stories plays an ongoing role in the shaping of social life.

Our task in this chapter is to describe interviewing for two sorts of stories: personal narratives and folk narratives. The distinction between these may seem commonsensical at first: Personal narratives are idiosyncratic, whereas folk narratives are collective. However, we will argue that the distinction is actually less clear. Second, we explore the process of eliciting stories in interviews, emphasizing the need for researchers to be aware of the social life of stories that extends beyond the interview. Third, we argue that it is important for researchers to supplement interviews *for* stories with interviews *about* stories in order to comprehend the interpretive frames that surround storytelling transactions. Finally, we point out the usefulness of critically examining interview transcripts in evolving practice.

Many excellent publications offering insights and guidelines for ethnographic interviewing, or folkloristic interviewing more generally, are already available (Atkinson 1998; Briggs 1986; Holstein and Gubrium 1995; Ives 1995; Jackson 1987; Langness and Frank 1981; Spradley 1979). Rather than rehash insights from these other works, we direct interested readers to them. Here we will draw on a selection of memorable examples of prior interviews for stories, working from the larger ethnographic record and also from our own fieldwork experiences.

◆ Folk Narrative and Personal Narrative

For the better part of the 20th century, most anthropologists, folklorists, and literary specialists assumed that personal narratives are uniquely individual, shaped more by the vagaries of experience than by the conventions of collective tradition. From this vantage point, experience appears to dictate the content and form of personal narrative, and so the teller is of central importance. In contrast, folk narratives have been seen as highly conventional, widely shared cultural representations mediated by the narrative community at large. As Franz Boas (1916) asserts, folk narratives, like myths, "present in a way an autobiography of the tribe" (p. 393). Yet, time and again, the people with whom anthropologists work have not made the same distinction between "personal" and "folk" in terms of the significance of stories to individuals' lives.

Personal stories are also shaped through the use of culturally recognized—and, sometimes, transculturally negotiated—narrative and linguistic conventions that are themselves differentially put to use by people positioned by gender, age, or class. As life story research in anthropology has shown, such stories are closely tied to cultural conceptions of personhood (Langness and Frank 1981). So, for example, when Renato Rosaldo (1976) asked his Ilongot "brother" Tukbaw to speak about his own life, he found that Tukbaw chose to build stories around the wise words and advice of his father rather than provide introspective vignettes about feelings or events. Or, when Grima (1991) went to Northwest Pakistan in the hope of researching Paxtun women's romance narratives, she soon learned that the stories the women themselves most liked to tell involved tragic tales of personal suffering—the more tragic the better. A woman who had not suffered was assumed not to have a life story. For example, a 30-year-old unmarried schoolteacher told Grima: "I have no story to tell. I have been through no hardships" (p. 84).

Similarly, in Northwest India, Kirin Narayan was also startled when Vidhya Sharma, an educated Kangra village woman, claimed that she had no life story. "Look, it's only when something different has happened that a woman has a story to tell," Vidhya said, speaking Hindi. "If everything just goes on the way it's supposed to, all you can think of is that you ate, drank, slept, served your husband and brought up your children. What's the story in that?" (Narayan n.d.:1). Building on cultural conceptions, individuals may also elaborate their own tastes and convictions about appropriate life stories. Ruth Behar (1993), for example, found that the Mexican peddler—Esperanza—whose life story she recorded followed a narrative structure that moved from suffering to rage to redemption and appeared to expect other women's narratives to follow this pattern too. When Behar proposed to ask other women for their life stories, Esperanza objected to Behar's choice of a respected schoolteacher, declaring, "But she, what has she suffered? I never heard that her husband beat her or that she suffered from rages" (p. 12).

The genre that anthropologists have developed to write about people's lives is labeled *life history,* but we prefer the term *life story* or even *life stories* because it draws attention to the fragmentary and constructed nature of personal narratives (see Peacock and Holland 1991). Sometimes, asking someone to tell a life story may appear altogether too overwhelming or foreign a request, whereas asking about particular eras or incidents may stimulate retellings. For example, Migdim, an old, semiblind Bedouin woman, waved off Lila Abu-Lughod's (1993) request for her life

story, stating, "I've forgotten all of that. I've got no mind to remember with any more." Migdim then proceeded to add some generalities about the past nomadic experiences of the group: "We used to milk the sheep. We used to pack up and leave here and set up camp out west" (p. 46). As Abu-Lughod points out, for this old woman, like others in the community, "the conventional form of 'a life' as a self-centered passage through time was not familiar. Instead there were memorable events, fixed into dramatic stories with fine details" (p. 46). As Abu-Lughod learned, when Migdim reminisced in the company of family members about particular past events, she was indeed a spirited storyteller with a sharp memory for things that had happened to her.

Whether entire life stories or passing anecdotes, personal narratives emerge within what is culturally "storyworthy." By looking at the subjects that people choose to dwell on in narrating their lives, we are in a position to see what most matters to them, from their point of view. Describing the hunting stories that Ilongot men of the Philippines love to tell, Rosaldo (1986) observes, "Narrative can provide a particularly rich source of knowledge about the significance people find in their workaday lives. Such narratives often reveal more about what can make life worth living than about how it is routinely lived" (p. 98).

In addition to being implicitly encoded in cultural practice, conventions for talking about lives can also be actively inculcated by institutional demands of various kinds (see Holstein and Gubrium 2000; Gubrium and Holstein 2001). As Kenneth George (1978) learned in his fieldwork with pastor John Sherfey, the religious doctrines of evangelical Protestant congregations in the United States require adherents to "testify" to their spiritual salvation through stories about their personal conversion experience (see also Harding 1987; Titon 1988; Titon & George 1977, 1978). Or as Carole Cain (1991) has argued, Alcoholics Anonymous teaches newcomers how to tell stories in which they are not just drinkers, but alcoholics who have hit rock bottom and need help. Through pamphlets, the examples of others' storytelling, and feedback from fellow participants at A.A. meetings, people joining the group learn how to shape personal experience along the lines of this key story form.

Ironically, the presence of conventions for telling the right stories about particular kinds of life experience means that people who have not actually lived through these experiences might nonetheless learn how to recount convincing stories of their own. So, for example, Bruce Jackson (1996) writes about meeting Jim, a "perfect informant" who readily told long, detailed tales about his war experiences in Vietnam. Jim kept not only Jackson but other veterans spellbound. It eventually turned out, however, that Jim had never been in Vietnam at all; he had so steeped himself in widespread accounts of being there that he told the stories as his own. Other veterans had sniffed out the inconsistencies and exaggerations even before Jackson became aware of the hoax. Yet when Jackson asked them, "Why didn't you ever blow the whistle on him?" one of the veterans responded in a classic defense of a mesmerizing storyteller, "Wasn't doing me any harm. And he told such great stories. I loved listening to him tell those goddamned stories. I mean, I was *there* and I couldn't tell stories like that guy" (p. 220).

Even as personal narratives are shaped by shared conventions, folk narratives circulating within and across communities are personalized through retellings. After all, people remember and retell shared stories—myths, legends, folktales, parables, jokes, and so on—because these are personally as well as socially meaningful. Yet folk narratives have tended to be so analytically yoked to communities that many collections and analyses have rarely mentioned tellers, or have alluded to them only by name—as though their existence is important only because they serve as conduits of traditional knowledge. Shifting atten-

tion from traditional stories to the storytellers, it becomes clear that storytellers put their own creative and aesthetic stamp on folk narratives, personalizing them through retellings to fit particular occasions (Azadovskii 1974; Dégh 1969). As Swamiji, a Hindu holy man who delighted in making moral and spiritual points through stories once reflected to Narayan, people tell stories according to their own feelings and the feelings of their audience. As Swamiji said: "When you tell a story, you should look at the situation and tell it. Then it turns out well. If you just tell any story any time, it's not really good. You must consider the time and shape the story so it's right. All stories are told for some purpose" (Narayan 1989:37).

Occasionally, tellers may make explicit links between their folk narratives and their lives. So, for example, Urmilaji, a woman in the Himalayan foothills, once compared hard times she had experienced to the wanderings of an exiled king and queen in one of the folktales she had told Narayan. In making this explicit connection, Urmilaji was shedding light not just on her own life, but on the traditional tale as well. Similarly, when Urmilaji's family priest retold the same story, foregrounding the beleaguered king and downplaying the travails of his loyal wife, it became clear that both tellers were recasting the tale according to their own gendered experiences (Narayan 1997: 121-24; see also Taggart 1990).

Reading life histories, one can occasionally sense the subject straining against an anthropologist's conceptions of appropriate "personal" content in an interview. So, for example, when the energetic !Kung woman Nisa suggested to Marjorie Shostak (1981), "Let's continue our talk about long ago. Let's also talk about the stories that the old people know" (p. 40), it is possible that Nisa was trying to include some of her repertoire of traditional tales within the frame of her life stories. Sometimes, subjects are more emphatic. Julie Cruikshank (1990), for example, found that three Yukon women elders whose life stories she was recording insisted that their myths were *part* of their lives and so should be included along with their more personal reminiscences.

Breaking down the division between personal and folk narratives forces researchers to revise their assumptions about how to conduct interviews and about what they should include in their texts. Rather than suppressing the disjunction between the kinds of stories researchers might seek and the forms of discourse that they receive in interviews, exploring this gap between "analytic categories" and the locally conceived genres that index social power can be a source of creative scholarly insight and creativity (see Ben-Amos [1969] 1976; Bauman and Briggs 1992; Briggs 1986). As Michael Young (1983) admits in his prologue to *Magicians of Manumanua: Living Myth in Kalauna*, the book emerged from his attempt to make sense of the ritual expert Iyahalina's puzzling response to a request for his life history:

> Instead of telling me tales from his childhood, recounting the circumstances of his marriage, or enumerating his mature achievements, he narrated a sequence of myths and legends that described the activities of his ancestors. He concluded with a passionate peroration on the ritual duties they had bequeathed him, the central task of which was to "sit still" in order to anchor the community in prosperity. (Pp. 3-4)

As Young learned, Iyahalina and other hereditary guardians of myths on Goodenough Island identified with the heroes of their myths and drew on mythic themes to construct their own autobiographical narratives. At the same time, possession of these myths was a means of asserting status. Similarly, Maria Lepowsky (1994:126) found that in Vanatinai, New Guinea, women could also own authoritative versions of myths, a fact that she links to women's stature within this more gender-egalitarian society.

Whether folk or personal, narratives are not just a means of cultural representation; they are also potent tools in social interaction, a form of cultural work. By *cultural work*, we mean the ways that narrators and audiences use narrative resources for political and social ends. Although stories of different kinds certainly contain representations of cultural values, concerns, and patterns, we cannot forget that stories are also practices intended to get things done: to entertain, edify, shock, terrorize, intimidate, heal, comfort, persuade, testify, divulge, and so on. Narrative form, then, not only conjures up other worlds, whether imagined or remembered; it is also a way of artfully arranging words for social and political consequences in the immediacies of this world.

◆ Getting Stories

Alert researchers should ideally try to be present when stories are narrated as part of ongoing social life, and so be in a position to overhear spontaneously evoked commentaries, debates, revisions, and retellings. Yet researchers are not always so lucky as to be in the right place at the right time, to participate in the many varied moments when people tell or comment upon stories that circulate in everyday life. When researchers do have a chance to listen in, their very presence cannot help but shape different aspects of the storytelling occasion. Further, being present for a single narrative performance is usually not enough for a researcher to gain insight into the larger ongoing life of stories and storytelling encounters. Interviews, then, are a useful supplement to the ethnographer's taking part in social life in an engaged, observant way (see Atkinson and Coffey, Chapter 20, this volume).

Because all storytelling events are situationally unique, narratives heard or exchanged in interviews should not be carelessly confused with or substituted for narratives that take place outside of the interview context. All stories emerging from an interview will bear the mark of an interviewer's presence and the hierarchical dynamics of the interview situation. Yet we should not dismiss interview narratives as contrived or worthless. Like so many other social encounters, interviews are culturally negotiated events worthy of analysis (see Briggs 1986). Because the interview can be an invitation to narrate, it is a wonderful opportunity for the researcher to grasp—or at least begin to think about—the complexity of stories exchanged elsewhere in a community.

The word *interview* has roots in Old French, and at one time meant something like "to see one another." Although we cannot ignore the social hierarchies of inquiry, we want to underscore how "seeing one another" in interviews requires close attentiveness and an openness to the surprises of dialogue and exchange. How an interview runs its course depends very much on all participants involved. It is important for the interviewer to be flexible and ready to follow unexpected paths that emerge in the course of talking together with interviewees. In fact, in our experience, interviews often end up having less to do with structured questions or answers than with the animated exchange of stories. The interviewer's willingness to reveal his or her own stories can also add to the depth of an interview, inspiring the person being interviewed to open up, knowing that the interviewer is willing to be vulnerable too.

The ethnographic interview is a bid on the part of a researcher to get an interviewee to converse openly about a set of issues of concern to the researcher. The political conditions surrounding the consent and participation of interviewees in ethnographic interviews—and in the negotiated elicitation of stories—have been anticipated in human subjects protocols designed to hold in check the potentially coercive impulses of social scientific and humanistic inquiry. Setting up an interview becomes an invitation to narrate, albeit one that can be refused, subverted, or turned back on the interviewer.

Most basically, when looking for stories in interviews, researchers should keep in mind that all people are not equally skilled storytellers. Some people are energetic raconteurs who will use the interview as a welcome occasion to spin stories. Stories may pour toward the researcher in such dizzying numbers that all he or she need do is show engagement with nods or murmurs while the recording equipment rolls. In the presence of such practiced storytellers, an interviewer may have to struggle to direct the stories toward subjects suited to his or her specific interests. Sometimes, the interviewer may need to clarify details. But mostly, when a storyteller takes charge, an interviewer's work is to listen with attentive care so as to be able to formulate necessary questions when the retelling is over.

In other cases, the interviewer has to work harder. With some respondents, it may take a while for the interviewer to formulate the right questions that will inspire the telling of stories. Questions that can be answered with a simple yes or no are particular hazards, and can give an interviewer a sense of getting nowhere at all. Sometimes, a person is more willing to tell stories outside the formal context of an interview, without recording devices or notebooks at hand. Occasionally, a person being interviewed is willing to tell stories about some things, but not others. Here, for example, is a moment from Narayan's fieldwork in the Northwest Himalayan foothills: Suman Kumari (SK), a woman who had been animatedly telling stories about her grandmother's and mother's difficult lives, comes to a place in her narrative for which there no longer appears to be a clear prior story. Narayan had already been struggling to keep the stories flowing by asking what Suman's mother's brothers had made of Suman's father's not working. Finally, giving up on questions that received brief answers, Narayan (KN) asked as broad a question as possible.

KN: And after that?

SK: After that what can I say? What can I say, Bahenji? [Turns to her half sister, who, along with the mother, is listening in] After that—that's all: sons and all that, and daughters-in-law.

KN: [Seeing that SK is still speaking from the perspective of her mother, tries to turn the interview to SK's own life] And your earliest memories were of this place? What was your childhood like?

SK: [Looking at her sister again] What should I tell her about my childhood, Bahenji?

Sister: That you went to school in your childhood—that's just fine. [Both sisters laugh]

SK: What happened is that we went to school, we ate food. Sometimes there would be mangoes on the trees and we'd eat a lot. In the house, she [indicating her mother] would say, "Go to sleep." But as soon as she was asleep, then all three of us would run out!

In a cursory way, Suman Kumari spoke about collecting mangoes, of going to school, of knitting, yet her own life clearly did not have as much interest to her as did the lives of her mother and grandmother. Although Narayan tried to refuel the narrative with questions, these reminiscences soon sputtered to a halt.

Asking people to be more specific can sometimes be a good way of getting them to expand on stories. For example, if someone says, "Life was hard," the interviewer might ask in what ways life was hard, or if there are any particular moments that stand out as being especially hard; such probes can result in the unpacking of stories. However, the more an interviewer works at extracting a story, the less sure he or she can be that it is a story already present in the person's repertoire rather than one created only by the interview. This is one of the reasons it has been suggested that researchers

should include the questions they asked interview respondents in their final published works; this information can be crucial to showing how the materials emerged as part of a dialogic process (Dwyer 1982).

Folklorists make the distinction between "active bearers" and "passive bearers" (von Sydow 1948:12-15). Active bearers are those who are actively engaged in transmitting folk knowledge; passive bearers are those who may know folklore, but who may not think of themselves as competent tellers to pass the folklore on. The distinction is fluid: Sometimes an active bearer may slip into a passive role, for example, with age and failing memory. Equally, a passive bearer might assume a more active role through various circumstances, such as growing seniority, migration, or the death of an active bearer. In some contexts, a perfectly competent active bearer of stories may be forced to defer to the authority of a storyteller who is socially recognized. In Kangra, for example, when Narayan worked with women's ritual tales, she found that many women were passive bearers of ritual tales. Yet it was the senior women in patrilineages, considered "very wise," who were called on to tell stories in the context of ritual worship. In cases where related, less senior women interrupted, telling their own versions, there were enormous tensions around these transgressions, with relatives of the older women sometimes advising Narayan to erase her tapes.

It is important, then, for researchers to ascertain where individual storytellers stand in relation to wider social conventions around narrative practices and how a storyteller might be evaluated within his or her own community. Also, researchers will find it valuable to reflect on the structural relations between interviewers and interviewees, and what motives may be built into the transmission of stories from the interviewees' side. For example, in Barbara Myerhoff's (1978) memorable ethnography about elderly American Jews, the retired tailor, Shmuel, seemed to hint at how vital transmitting his memories to the safe-keeping of an ethnographer was for his own peace of mind. After recounting incidents from his childhood in Eastern Europe, he mused:

> For myself, growing old would be altogether a different thing if that little town was there still. . . . But when I come back from these stories and remember the way they lived is gone forever, wiped out like you would erase a line of writing, then it means another thing altogether for me to accept leaving this life. If my life goes now, it means nothing. But if my life goes, with my memories, and all that is lost, that is something else to bear. (P. 74)

Shmuel sent Myerhoff home with what he called "all this package of stories"; a day later, he died in his sleep. Shmuel's frank words remind us that sometimes interviews are of value not just to scholars. Transmitting memories to an eager audience, ensuring the survival of stories beyond a limited lifetime, an interviewee may also have a stake in the process.

The elicitation of stories in interviews may be subject to wider constraints around narrative practice. Examples abound in many Native American communities, where storytelling is often intimately linked to seasons, especially winter. Telling or eliciting stories at other times can be complicated. So, for example, if a storyteller among the Anishanaabe (Ojibwa) wishes to tell myths outside the winter months, he or she can put on a white weasel pelt, as though simulating snow. Exploring indigenous sacred traditions in highland Sulawesi, George (1996) found he had to adjust his interview work to take into account taboos that regulated the time and place for narrative activity. During the long months that stretched from the time of preparing rice fields to the time of harvest, communitywide prohibitions against storytelling and singing were in place and effectively prevented George from gathering

and discussing narrative materials. Once the postharvest ritual season began, a period that extended for about two months, he was at liberty to record and discuss traditional songs and stories. Even then, certain taboos remained in effect, such as those that allowed *sumengo*—a genre of ritual song associated with head-hunting narratives—to be performed and discussed for only one week out of the year in any given community. As a result, George had to adjust his research, moving from community to community as sets of taboos came into effect in one and relaxed in another.

The kinds of stories appropriate to tell may vary not just with calendrical cycles, but with social location. Gender and age are particularly important factors to consider. For example, among Southeast Asia's Ilongot (Rosaldo 1986), Karo Batak (Steedly 1993), Meratus Dayak (Tsing 1993), and Pitu Ulunna Salu (George 1996) communities, personal stories about the experience of going on journeys figure as an especially prominent genre for adult males in both everyday and ritual life. Interestingly, many of the mythic and historical narratives in these regions feature male "culture heroes" whose journeys led to the foundation of the communities in question. Thus men's contemporary tales of personal journeys resonate well with the foundational narratives of any specific locale. Women in these same communities have less to say about personal journeys but comparatively more when it comes to talking about trance experience (George 1996; Steedly 1993; Tsing 1993). Although both men and women in these communities go on journeys and go into trance, in an important sense it is more relevantly male to make a story of personal travel and more relevantly female to talk about trance experience. The very familiarity and pervasiveness of this pattern makes it all the more striking when, for example, a woman recounts the dangers of a journey she has made. Her move into a typically "male" narrative terrain, then, is an exceptionally revealing and socially salient example of gender play and transgression.

Storytelling forms are not static. Like other genres, kinds of stories evolve within the play of power in ongoing social life and in dialogue with other genres (Bauman and Briggs 1992). This means that there may be shifts in the kinds of stories that are appropriate for different social groups to tell. In his long-term research among the Kwaio of the Solomon Islands, Roger Keesing (1985) at first found men ready to talk about their lives, whereas women "were fragmented and brief, distancing themselves from serious autobiography with reciprocal jests" (p. 29). On return visits, he found that men's efforts to codify cultural rules and conventions or *kastom* as a form of postcolonial resistance to outside influences had also inspired women to think of culture as an objectifiable "thing" and to lay claim to their own accounts of *kastom* in which women's importance was given its due. When Kwaio women finally spoke out, they did so in counterpoint to the men, who had previously been working with Keesing to codify *kastom*. Also, senior women recounted their lives "*as moral texts,* as exemplifications of the trials, responsibilities, virtues and tragedies of A Woman's Life" (p. 33). Speaking out, for Kwaio women, was a bid to power. While acknowledging the wider historical shifts that made women perceive their life stories as valuable texts to transact, Keesing also mentions the importance of what he terms "the politics of the elicitation situation" (p. 37)—that is, the particular interpersonal circumstances of the interview. That he was joined by a female field-worker during the time that he was finally able to record women's stories was also a key factor in his coaxing Kwaio women who had previously been silent about their lives to become animated speaking subjects.

Anthropologists have typically addressed the self-revelatory content of one life story at a time. However, moving beyond one life story to compare several related life stories brings expected narrative forms and their transgressions into clearer focus. Oscar Lewis (1961) pioneered this method of juxtaposing life stories in his work with a poor Mexican family, where each family member recounted his or her own stories, revealing multifaceted, crosscutting, and even diverging perspectives on the same episodes. Other researchers have also used this method to show how positioned perspectives and gendered conventions pervade the shaping of life stories (see Mintz [1960] 1974; Viramma, Racine, and Racine 1997).

For folklorists, there is an implicit understanding that any retelling is a version rather than *the* story. To track the wider lives of entire stories and their constituent parts beyond particular iterations, folklorists have developed such tools as taletype indexes and motif indexes. At the same time, attention to performance has revealed how stories emerge within the parameters of particular contexts rather than as perfect forms that float above social life. The same attention to the surfacing of versions in performance can be applied to life histories. So, for example, Laurel Kendall (1988) was able to record multiple versions of the stories that Yongsu's Mother, a Korean shaman, dramatically retold to Kendall, neighbors, and clients to make varied points about gender, about the power of gods, about dangers of ritual lapses, and so on.

We would like to emphasize how valuable it is for researchers to elicit several versions of folktales and life stories—from the same persons through time and from different individuals—so that they can see how the uniqueness of particular tellings emerges within larger patterns. Collecting multiple versions of folk narratives and life stories, and talking to different storytellers, is vital to researchers' understanding of how narrative traditions are creatively reworked by particular tellers for particular social ends. Also, situating the performance of different versions within social interactions reveals the role of storytelling in the exercise of power, authority, and identity.

◆ Interviews about Stories

Getting a story during an interview still leaves unfinished the intellectual work of making sense of the story. Many researchers have found that there are great rewards in engaging the subjects of their research in the interpretive process, through asking for their opinions on meaning and through dialogues exposing the interpretive biases of both the storytellers and the scholars.

For folklore scholarship, Alan Dundes (1966) has coined the term *oral literary criticism* to characterize the move beyond eliciting texts to also comprehending indigenous meanings. In Dundes's classic formulation, oral literary criticism involves the collection of (a) metafolklore, that is, folklore about folklore (for example, folktales about folktales) that gives a sense of how a genre is locally conceived; (b) asides and explanations during folklore performances; (c) systematic exegeses of texts by storytellers and their audiences; and (d) analysts' attempts to comprehend possibly unconscious symbols by also looking at other texts in which the same symbols are used (p. 507). In an article affirming the theoretical and methodological value of this method, Narayan (1995) also adds the elicitation of generalized testimonies about a genre of folklore, supplementing talk about particular texts. Thus if an interviewee finds it too revealing to explain *why* he or she tells a particular story, the interviewer can elicit valuable insights by asking about why people more generally tell stories, and what kinds of meanings certain sorts of stories might carry.

Narayan sought to put this method to work through a collaboration with Urmila Devi Sood, or "Urmilaji," the wise woman we met earlier. After hearing Urmilaji's tales, Narayan transcribed them, thought about them, and came back to talk more about texts in particular and what meanings they held, and about storytelling in general. Sometimes her questions mystified Urmilaji, and at other times Urmilaji expounded implicit meanings in the tales, self-evident to most Kangra people but perplexing to Narayan. Speaking with Urmilaji about her stories, Narayan also came to understand how stories can be associated with particular prior tellers, keeping their wisdom and influence alive. Urmilaji, for example, loved many of these tales because they had been gifts, lovingly imparted, by her father and ancient aunt-in-law.

In addition to interviewing storytellers, it is also valuable for researchers to interview a range of people about what particular stories mean to them. Kay Stone (1985), for example, interviewed Americans of all ages about their memories of and reactions to popular fairy tales, in particular the story of Cinderella. She found that the males tended not to remember fairy tales, whereas the females worked out their self-images partly in dialogue with fairytale characters. Girls and women sometimes chafed at the messages in fairy tales, and some also reworked the stories to carry alternate endings. So, for example, a 9-year-old girl who preferred the character of Jack in "Jack and the Beanstalk" to Cinderella suggested that perhaps Cinderella could recover her slipper from the prince, and then "maybe she doesn't marry him, but she gets a lot of money anyway, and she gets a job" (p. 144).

Talking to people about stories gives researchers a chance to learn how the stories work interpersonally and psychologically. Keith Basso (1996) has explored how, among the Western Apache, historical tales bearing moral points are associated with various sites in the landscape. A place called "Trail Goes Down between Two Hills" for example, is associated with a story about lascivious Old Man Owl and how he is tricked by two beautiful girls; one might tell this story to comment on how someone's behavior involves uncurbed appetites and so is laughable and offensive (pp. 113-20). By telling a story instead of speaking directly, an individual can imply criticism rather than state it directly. The moral points carried within stories become embodied within the geographic landscape, reminding people of occasions when places have been pointed out to them. As Nick Thompson, a spirited elderly Apache, explained to Basso, stories "go to work on your mind and make you think about your life" (p. 58). Using the metaphor of hunting to characterize how stories are aimed at appropriate quarry, Thompson went on to describe how, when a person acts inappropriately, someone goes hunting for that person:

> So someone stalks you and tells a story about what happened long ago. It doesn't matter if other people are around—you're going to know that he's aiming that story at you. All of a sudden it *hits* you! It's like an arrow, they say. Sometimes it just bounces off—it's too soft and you don't think about anything. But when it's strong it goes in deep and starts working on your mind right away. No one says anything to you, only that story is all, but now you know that people have been watching you and talking about you. They don't like how you've been acting. So you have to think about your life. (Pp. 58-59)

The messages, then, are reinforced by place: "You're going to see the place where it happened, maybe every day if it's nearby. . . . If you don't see it, you're going to hear its name and see it in your mind" (p. 59). Even when the original storyteller dies, the place will continue to stalk the person, reminding him or her how to live right. In this conception of storytelling, then, a good story pierces deep and transforms a person from inside even while its effects are continually reinforced by the outer landscape.

In some societies, much of the power of stories lies in the ways they are internalized and embodied—"living myth," as Young (1983) memorably puts it. Thus an interviewer's inviting someone to stand aside so that he or she can extract explicit meaning may have no cultural frame of reference and, indeed, may be annoying. As Elsie Mather, a Yup'ik teacher, forcefully wrote to Phyllis Morrow (1995) when the question of explication came up in the course of their collaboration in documenting Yup'ik oral traditions:

> Why do people want to reduce traditional stories to information, to some function? Isn't it enough that we hear and read them? They cause us to wonder about things, and sometimes they touch us briefly along the way, or we connect the information or idea into something we are doing at the moment. This is what the old people say a lot. They tell us to listen even when we don't understand, that later on we will make some meaning or that something that we had listened to before will touch us in some way. Understanding and knowing occur over one's lifetime. . . .
>
> Why would I want to spoil the repetition and telling of stories with questions? Why would I want to know what they mean? (P. 33)

Like Nick Thompson, Morrow reminds us how stories live in ongoing reverberations through lived practices, not just in analytic reflection. Asking people for meaning isolated from particular contexts of retelling or remembering is to fix meaning in inappropriate ways. As Margaret Mills (1991) found in her research in Afghanistan, storytellers may actually thrive on the ambiguity of storytelling and the intertextual relations among stories, as this allows them to make sly commentaries on the sociopolitical world beyond the stories.

The analytic stance that breaks up stories may be perceived as dangerous for other reasons, too. In a dramatic example of the dangers of a researcher's blithely asking about stories without being cognizant of their social role or power, Barre Toelken (1996) has traced different moments of "enlightenment" in his long-term research on Navajo Coyote tales. With growing understanding of these Coyote tales, he was told that the tales were not just entertainment for winter months, but were also used in Navajo healing ceremonies. As Toelken was discussing the use of these tales with an elderly Navajo singer one night, the singer asked him, "Are you ready to lose someone in your family?" Baffled, Toelken asked him to explain. That is the cost of taking up witchcraft, the singer told him. Without being aware of it, Toelken had gained a reputation among the Navajo as someone with an interest in witchcraft because of the sorts of questions he had asked, and this had potentially malevolent repercussions for the Navajo people around him. As Toelken (1996) writes:

> For just as the tales themselves in their narration are normally used to create a harmonious world in which to live, and just as elliptical references to the tales can be used within rituals to clarify and enhance the healing processes, so the tales can be dismembered and used outside the proper ritual arena by witches to promote disharmony and to thwart the healing processes. In discussing parts and motifs separately, by dealing with them as interesting ideas which might lead me to discoveries of my own, I had been doing something like taking all the powerful medicines to be found in all the doctors' offices in the land and dumping them by the bucketload out of a low-flying chopper over downtown Los Angeles. (P. 11)

For researchers, then, asking for help with interpretations is like walking a razor's edge: On one hand, in asking, researchers run the danger of making severe cultural faux pas, as Toelken did; on the other hand, in not asking, they risk attributing their own interpretive frames to their subjects. The same dangers hold for both folk narratives and personal narratives, although with personal narratives people may be even more sensitive to interpreta-

tions that researchers make without consulting them.

A powerful example of the conflict that can arise when informants do not share the interpretations with their interviewers is described in an essay by Katherine Borland (1991). Borland interviewed her grandmother, Beatrice Hanson, about events that had taken place in 1944 when Beatrice attended a horse race and bet against the wishes of her father. Borland then wrote a student essay in which she interpreted her grandmother's actions as enacting a female struggle for autonomy and, thus, as being feminist. Her grandmother, however, after reading the essay, wrote back a 14-page letter in which she pointedly objected to being theorized in her feminist granddaughter's framework and asked questions that all scholars would do well to heed:

> So your interpretation of the story as a female struggle for autonomy within a hostile male environment is entirely YOUR interpretation. You've read into the story what you wished to—what pleases YOU. That it was never—by any wildest stretch of the imagination—the concern of the originator of the story makes such an interpretation a definite and complete distortion, and in this respect I question its authenticity. The story is no longer MY story at all. The skeleton remains, but it has become your story. Right? How far is it permissible to go in the name of folklore [or scholarship generally] and still be honest in respect to the original narrative? (P. 70)

This disagreement resulted in a dialogue in which both grandmother and granddaughter explained the assumptions they were working from and the different associations they brought to the term *feminist*. In the process of this conflict and the ensuing discussion, each woman stretched to understand the other's position, and each was educated in the process.

Indeed, feminist work on life stories has been at the forefront of the exploration of issues of possible reciprocity amid the hierarchical imbalances of interviews and their outcomes (see Personal Narratives Group 1989; Gluck and Patai 1991). Sociologist Ann Oakley (1981), for example, long ago advocated replacing a distanced interviewing technique that seeks to deflect questions aimed at the interviewer with a "different role, that could be termed 'no intimacy without reciprocity,'" especially for in-depth interviewing through time. As she writes: "This involves being sensitive not only to those questions that are asked (by either party) but to those that are not asked. The interviewee's definition of the interview is important" (p. 49). Elaine Lawless (1991) has worked out a system of "reciprocal ethnography" that she used in eliciting the life stories of Pentecostal women ministers; even as she sought to interpret their personal narratives, she allowed the women to critique and reflect on her ethnographic practices. Such an openness to the perspectives of the people interviewed can radically reframe the scholarly project, enhancing accountability to the contradictions and inequalities of the real world.

◆ *Reflecting on Interviews*

We have found that researchers can learn much not just from looking to the work of others, but from looking back at their own interview practices, whether this involves listening again to tapes or studying transcripts. Most immediately, such a review can help a researcher to frame questions about stories already recorded, and so more self-consciously engage interviewees in an unfolding interpretive process. More generally, encountering one's own shortcomings can be very instructive for future practice. For example, interviewers may discover moments where they have asked questions that elicited yes or no responses instead of stories, moments where they

have interrupted, or moments where they have radically misunderstood what someone was trying to say and taken an interview off on a new tangent. Bruce Jackson (1987) summarizes what many interviewers likely feel as they transcribe their own tapes: "The most important thing I learned was that I talked too much" (p. 81).

We now turn to a segment from an interview conducted by Narayan, who will reflect critically on her own practices. This interview was conducted in the fall of 1995, with a second-generation South Asian American called Zeynab (Z). At the time, Narayan (KN) was interviewing partly to comprehend second-generation South Asian American experience as an anthropologist and partly to construct a character for a novel she was writing. In her questions, she was striving to enter experience from within. In this segment, Zeynab has been talking about growing up in Southern California, and how her father's brother and his wife had come to live with the family, creating conflict and even urging Zeynab's father to divorce. Narayan's commentary appears in italics.

Z: And my mother didn't have anyone to talk to about these things.

KN: So she would talk to you? *[This query is based on Zeynab's having earlier told me that she was very close to her mother.]*

Z: Yeah. I still remember. I didn't understand exactly what was going on at the time. All I remember was my mother in the kitchen. Like I'll be doing the dishes and she'll be cleaning the floor and she'll be crying. And it wasn't ever that she told me, she never said that my sister-in-law was saying this and that, it was like, "I'm very alone, I have no one to talk to, I miss home." She did not have any intention of turning my father against his brother. So she just kept quiet. She took all of that in.

KN: When she said "home," what images came into your mind? *[Here my own agenda of understanding how second-*

generation South Asian Americans construct "home" is breaking in, redirecting the narrative flow. Ideally, I would have waited until a break in the larger narrative of growing up to ask this question.]

Z: I guess for me, I had very strong images of when I was there as a child. Because my Nana [maternal grandfather] was still alive at that time.

KN: How old were you? Cause you were born here . . . *[Again, looking back, I am breaking in to ask for specification and possibly redirecting the story. I should have just kept my mouth shut, making affirmative sounds, then later asked her about her visits back to Pakistan.]*

Z: I was born in Los Angeles and maybe after a year or two we went back, and then every maybe year or two we would go back. My mother would take us. Some of my earliest memories are from there. My fondest memories too. We used to go to my Nana's house. It was a very nice house. One of the women who worked in the house, her husband was breeding pigeons on the roof. So we used to go up on the roof. Some of my NICEST memories are from that time. So . . .

KN: What did you see from the roof? *[In retrospect, I wish I could clap my hand over my mouth. With my desire to imaginatively participate in her experience, and my own strong visual sense, I am interrupting Zeynab from her own story. Zeynab, however, found her way back to what she was trying to say].*

Zeynab responded, "I think it's more the air I remember. The color of the sky. You know, seeing the other rooftops from the distance." In her own construction of the story, what she saw from the roof was less key than her going up there to play with pigeons, and then returning to playing games with cousins, or going out to be treated to ice cream by her uncles. With time, Narayan hopes to have become more attentive to allowing stories to take shape

without her intervention, learning to keep questions in her head until the teller has finished speaking. Narayan is also puzzling over whether her practice of turning off the tape recorder when an interviewee asks her questions (that is, when she tells stories about her own South Asian American experience) is appropriate or misleading. On the one hand, she is not interested in recording her own stories; on the other hand, might the inclusion of her own storytelling input in interview situations lessen the hierarchical imbalance?

Yet, as Narayan looks back at this exchange with Zeynab, she sees that there is something grand and lovely about the spaciousness she evoked with her hasty question about the views from that rooftop. Perhaps one of the most important lessons interviewers can learn from the mortifying process of looking back at their own interviews is to forgive themselves, make the best of what they have done, and look ahead to the next interview. In querying their own interview practices, researchers would do well to recall the poet Rainer Maria Rilke's (1984:34) stricture to "live the questions" rather than look for fixed and certain answers.

◆ Conclusions

The interest in "getting stories" has an institutional backdrop and a place within broader fields of everyday inquiry. As we stated at the opening of this chapter, it is not just scholars who want to obtain stories; police officers, medical and psychiatric diagnosticians, journalists, refugee agents, shamans, social workers, state and corporate bureaucrats, courts, and human rights workers want stories too. Interview narratives have been put to use not just by anthropologists and folklorists, but also by colonizers seeking to comprehend "the native mind," by nationalists wanting to mobilize support around an imagined "spirit of the people," and by those promoting regional and state articulations of identity.

The distinction between "personal" and "folk" narrative, we have argued, is often blurred in practice, and so cross-fertilizing methodologies and theories usually associated with one body of stories or the other may be sources of creative insight. We have emphasized the need for researchers to follow other people's own conceptions of stories, as speech genres and as interpersonal, politically charged transactions with lives outside an interview context. Paying attention to the kinds of people who are storytellers, the kinds of stories appropriate to tell within social locations, transformations in the kinds of stories told, and the shifting multiplicity of versions enhances researchers' appreciation for the specificity of stories that emerge within interviews.

We have underscored the value for researchers of talking about stories with both storytellers and listeners, in addition to gathering stories in interviews. Researchers' sensitivity to indigenous conceptions of the meanings and psychological impacts of stories can bring the researchers' own interpretive biases to light, where they can be transformed in constructive dialogues.

Sometimes, cultural sensitivity may require that interviewers hold back on analytic questions that carve up stories into constituent elements, cutting them away from the ongoing flow of lived experience.

Finally, we have noted the fruits that researchers may glean by critically examining their own interview tapes or transcripts, learning to ask and to listen with greater skill. Often, being a good interviewer for stories involves not just asking the right questions, but sympathetically listening and holding back questions so the person being interviewed can shape stories in his or her own way. Equally, being a good interviewer may involve responding to questions from an interviewee, and so entering into a reciprocal exchange.

Telling and listening to stories is at the heart of social and cultural life. Much of what we understand as personhood, identity, intimacy, secrecy, experience, belief, history, and common sense turns on the exchange of stories between people. In receiving stories, we are often receiving gifts of self; it is incumbent on us as researchers to handle these gifts with respect as we pass them onward in our scholarly productions.

■ *References*

Abu-Lughod, L. 1993. *Writing Women's Worlds: Bedouin Stories.* Berkeley: University of California Press.

Atkinson, R. 1998. *The Life Story Interview.* Thousand Oaks, CA: Sage.

Azadovskii, M. 1974. *A Siberian Tale Teller.* Translated by J. Dow. Austin: University of Texas Press.

Basso, K. 1996. *Wisdom Sits in Places: Landscape and Language among the Western Apache.* Albuquerque: University of New Mexico Press.

Bauman, R. and C. L. Briggs. 1992. "Genre, Intertextuality and Social Power." *Journal of Linguistic Anthropology* 2:131-72.

Behar, R. 1993. *Translated Woman: Crossing the Border with Esperanza's Story.* Boston: Beacon.

Ben-Amos, D. [1969] 1976. "Analytical Categories and Ethnic Genres." Pp. 215-42 in *Folklore Genres,* edited by D. Ben-Amos. Austin: University of Texas Press.

Boas, F. 1916. *Tsimshian Mythology* (31st Annual Report of the Bureau of American Ethnology). Washington, DC: Smithsonian Institution.

Borland, K. 1991. " 'That's Not What I Said': Interpretive Conflict in Oral Narrative Research." Pp. 63-76 in *Women's Words: The Feminist Practice of Oral History,* edited by S. B. Gluck and D. Patai. New York: Routledge.

Briggs, C. L. 1986. *Learning How to Ask: A Sociolinguistic Appraisal of the Role of the Interview in Social Science Research.* Cambridge: Cambridge University Press.

Cain, C. 1991. "Personal Stories, Identity Acquisition and Self-Understanding in Alcoholics Anonymous." *Ethos* 19:210-53.

Cruikshank, J. with A. Sidney, K. Smith, and A. Ned. 1990. *Life Lived Like a Story: Life Stories of Three Yukon Native Elders.* Lincoln: University of Nebraska Press.

Dégh, L. 1969. *Folktales and Society: Story Telling in a Hungarian Peasant Community.* Translated by E. M. Schossberger. Bloomington: Indiana University Press.

Dundes, A. 1966. "Metafolklore and Oral Literary Criticism." *Monist* 60:505-16.

Dwyer, K. 1982. *Moroccan Dialogues: Anthropology in Question.* Baltimore: Johns Hopkins University Press.

George, K. M. 1978. " 'I Still Got It': The Conversion Narrative of John C. Sherfey." M.A. thesis, University of North Carolina, Chapel Hill.

———. 1996. *Showing Signs of Violence: The Cultural Politics of a Twentieth-Century Headhunting Ritual.* Berkeley: University of California Press.

Gluck, S. B. and D. Patai, eds. 1991. *Women's Words: The Feminist Practice of Oral History.* New York: Routledge.

Grima, B. 1991. "Suffering in Women's Performance of *Paxto*." Pp. 78-101 in *Gender, Genre and Power in South Asian Expressive Traditions,* edited by A. Appadurai, F. J. Korom, and M. Mills. Philadelphia: University of Pennsylvania Press.

Gubrium, J. F. and J. A. Holstein, eds. 2001. *Institutional Selves: Troubled Identities in a Postmodern World.* New York: Oxford University Press.

Harding, S. 1987. "Convicted by the Holy Spirit: The Rhetoric of Fundamental Baptist Conversion." *American Ethnologist* 14:167-81.

Holstein, J. A. and J. F. Gubrium. 1995. *The Active Interview.* Thousand Oaks, CA: Sage.

———. 2000. *The Self We Live By: Narrative Identity in a Postmodern World.* New York: Oxford University Press.

Ives, E. D. 1995. *The Tape Recorded Interview: A Manual for Fieldworkers in Folklore and Oral History.* 2d ed. Knoxville: University of Tennessee Press.

Jackson, B. 1987. *Fieldwork.* Urbana: University of Illinois Press.

———. 1996. "The Perfect Informant." Pp. 206-26 in *The Word Observed: Reflections on the Fieldwork Process,* edited by B. Jackson and E. D. Ives. Bloomington: Indiana University Press.

Keesing, R. 1985. "Kwaio Women Speak." *American Anthropologist* 87:27-39.

Kendall, L. 1988. *The Life and Hard Times of a Korean Shaman: Of Tales and the Telling of Tales.* Honolulu: University of Hawaii Press.

Langness, L. L. and G. Frank. 1981. *Lives: An Anthropological Approach to Biography.* Novato, CA: Chandler & Sharp.

Lawless, E. 1991. "Women's Life Stories and Reciprocal Ethnography as Feminist and Emergent." *Journal of Folklore Research* 29:35-60.

Lepowsky, M. 1994. *Fruit of the Motherland: Gender in an Egalitarian Society.* New York: Columbia University Press.

Lewis, O. 1961. *The Children of Sánchez: Autobiography of a Mexican Family.* New York: Random House.

Mills, M. 1991. *Rhetorics and Politics in Afghan Traditional Storytelling.* Philadelphia: University of Pennsylvania Press.

Mintz, S. [1960] 1974. *Worker in the Cane.* New York: Norton.

Morrow, P. 1995. "On Shaky Ground." Pp. 27-51 in *When Our Words Return: Writing, Hearing and Remembering Oral Traditions of Alaska and the Yukon.* Logan: Utah State University Press.

Myerhoff, B. 1978. *Number Our Days.* New York: Simon & Schuster.

Narayan, K. 1989. *Storytellers, Saints and Scoundrels: Folk Narrative in Hindu Religious Teaching.* Philadelphia: University of Pennsylvania Press.

———. 1995. "The Practice of Oral Literary Criticism: Women's Songs in Kangra, India." *Journal of American Folklore* 108:243-64.

———. 1997. *Mondays on the Dark Night of the Moon: Himalayan Foothill Folktales* (assembled in collaboration with U. D. Sood). New York: Oxford University Press.

———. n.d. "Unspeakable Lives: Silences in the Life Stories of Women in Kangra, Northwest India." Unpublished manuscript.

Oakley, A. 1981. "Interviewing Women: A Contradiction in Terms?" Pp. 30-61 in *Doing Feminist Research,* edited by H. Roberts. London: Routledge & Kegan Paul.

Peacock, J. L. and D. C. Holland. 1993. "The Narrated Self: Life Stories in Process." *Ethos* 21:367-83.

Personal Narratives Group, ed. 1989. *Interpreting Women's Lives: Feminist Theory and Personal Narratives.* Bloomington: Indiana University Press.

Rilke, R. M. 1984. *Letters to a Young Poet.* Translated by S. Mitchell. New York: Random House.

Rosaldo, R. 1976. "The Story of Tukbaw: 'They Listen as He Orates.' " Pp. 121-51 in *The Biographical Process,* edited by F. Reynolds and D. Capps. The Hague: Mouton.

———. 1986. "Ilongot Hunting as Story and Experience." Pp. 97-138 in *The Anthropology of Experience,* edited by V. W. Turner and E. M. Bruner. Urbana: University of Illinois Press.

Shostak, M. 1981. *Nisa: The Life and Words of a !Kung Woman.* Cambridge, MA: Harvard University Press.

Spradley, J. P. 1979. *The Ethnographic Interview.* New York: Holt, Rinehart & Winston.

Steedly, M. M. 1993. *Hanging without a Rope: Narrative Experience in Colonial and Postcolonial Karoland.* Princeton, NJ: Princeton University Press.

Stone, K. 1985. "The Misuses of Enchantment: Controversies on the Significance of Fairy Tales." Pp. 125-45 in *Women's Folklore, Women's Culture,* edited by R. A. Jordan and S. J. Kalcik. Philadelphia: University of Pennsylvania Press.

Taggart, J. M. 1990. *Enchanted Maidens: Gender Relations in Spanish Folktales of Courtship and Marriage.* Princeton, NJ: Princeton University Press.

Titon, J. T. 1988. *Powerhouse for God: Speech, Chant, and Song in an Appalachian Baptist Church.* Austin: University of Texas Press.

Titon, J. T. and K. M. George. 1977. "Dressed in the Armor of God." *Alcheringa: Ethnopoetics* 3(2):10-31.

———. 1978. "Testimonies." *Alcheringa: Ethnopoetics* 4(1):69-83.

Toelken, B. 1996. "From Entertainment to Realization in Navajo Fieldwork." Pp. 1-17 in *The Word Observed: Reflections on the Fieldwork Process,* edited by B. Jackson and E. D. Ives. Bloomington: Indiana University Press.

Tsing, A. 1993. *In the Realm of the Diamond Queen: Marginality in an Out-of-the-Way Place.* Princeton, NJ: Princeton University Press.

Viramma, J. Racine, and J.-L. Racine. 1997. *Viramma: Life of an Untouchable.* London: Verso.

von Sydow, C. 1948. *Selected Papers in Folklore.* Copenhagen: Rosenhilde & Bagger.

Young, M. 1983. *Magicians of Manumanua: Living Myth in Kalauna.* Berkeley: University of California Press.

23

THEIR STORY/MY STORY/OUR STORY

Including the Researcher's Experience in Interview Research

◆ Carolyn Ellis
Leigh Berger

I cull books on interviewing from my bookcases and arrange them alphabetically on an empty shelf, the product of the last few days of cleaning my office. Even the floor, my favorite storage area, is empty of the usual stacks of manuscripts and books. I feel free, excited to begin the chapter I'm writing with Leigh on including the researcher's experience in interview research. The task shouldn't be too difficult. The chapter is a continuation of what I've spent the last 15 years doing, which is using autoethnographic stories—stories written in an autobiographical genre about the relationship of self, other, and culture—in social science research. Since researchers now commonly discuss their own experience in their research, this project seems

timely. I smile contentedly as I think about the growing recognition and acceptance of autoethnography among interpretive ethnographers.

As I muse about autoethnography, I hear Leigh's car pull in to the driveway. I herd our four barking dogs into the bedroom, then open the front door. Once Leigh is seated in my office and has admired how tidy and organized it is, I let the dogs out of the bedroom. Without pausing, they fly up the stairs. By the time I get to my office, three of them surround Leigh, sniffing her clothes, while the fourth sits on her lap, licking her face. Leigh greets them warmly. They quickly settle down and claim their usual sleeping spots in my office.

AUTHORS' NOTE: We thank Arthur P. Bochner, Jim Holstein, Jay Gubrium, and two anonymous reviewers for their helpful reading and editing of the manuscript for this chapter.

Leigh sits beside me as I type notes from our conversation into the computer. "Okay, now let's think about what we have to do here," *I start.* "The paper isn't due for six months, so we have plenty of time."

"Oh, yes, plenty," *Leigh agrees.* "What exactly is our goal?"

"The idea is to look at the inclusion of the researcher's experience in interview research," *I respond.* "Not so much how we do it, but the different forms it can take and how this inclusion deepens and enriches what we know about our subjects of research. Maybe we'll try to move from lesser to greater degrees of involvement of the researcher and provide exemplars of the variety."

"So you mean a typology then?" *Leigh inquires, laughing because I usually argue for stories and against typologies.* "So what would we include?"

I too chuckle at the irony and continue, "I thought we'd select an excerpt from my piece with Lisa and Christine [Ellis, Kiesinger, and Tillmann-Healy 1997] on interactive interviewing where we talk about bulimia. And one from my chapter with Art [Ellis and Bochner 1992] on co-constructed narratives, where we discuss our decision to have an abortion early in our relationship."

"They both show the researcher as full participant," *Leigh says thoughtfully, breaking through the emotions that arise as I think about including a selection from the abortion story. It's hard emotionally for me to confront that piece, but I want to include it because it provides an instructive exemplar of co-constructed narratives.* "What will we do for exemplars that show inclusion to a lesser degree?" *Leigh continues.*

"That's where you come in," *I respond.* "Remember that interview you did with Karen, your informant at the Messianic Judaism congregation? The one where you reflect on what the interview makes you think about in terms of your own spiritual beliefs? How about an excerpt from that interview story?"

"I thought you didn't like the Karen I presented there," *Leigh says.*

"I don't. It always seemed to me that you needed to write in more of your reflections on spirituality as you wrote that story. More reflection would have deepened readers' understanding of Karen's beliefs and made her a more complex character. This is your chance to add more reflection, although the focus should remain on Karen."

"So we'll have three types then—interactive interviews, co-constructed narratives, and reflexive dyadic interviews?" *Leigh asks, returning the focus to the paper rather than thinking more deeply about the difficulties of revealing her thoughts about her own spirituality, especially to an academic audience.*

"No, there are four. Your interview with Karen parallels the interactive interview I did with Lisa and Christine. They're both interactive and emergent in that we're concerned with the stories created and evolving in each interview context. But while the three authors act as researchers and participants alike in the bulimia study, you as researcher stay focused on the experience of your participant, Karen."

"Okay, I see where you're going. And what's the parallel case to co-constructed narrative?"

"In our co-constructed narrative about abortion, Art and I focused exclusively on our story. We wrote our experiences separately and then came together to co-construct them into a collective story we could agree on. The parallel case would be one in which a researcher carries out the same process with another couple, staying focused on them but adding her reflections. I know you've wanted to interview a family member of someone who converted to Messianic Judaism. I'd like you to do a co-constructed interview with the convert and family member, if you're willing."

"I'd love to," *Leigh says hesitantly.* "But after thinking about it, I'm not sure it's a good idea to interview family members of Messianic Jews. Families seem to have so much animosity toward those who convert. I don't want to cause my participants any problems."

"But I have planned to interview the rabbi of the Messianic congregation and his wife about their roles in marriage," she continues, more enthusiastically. "I could conduct this as a co-constructed interview and include questions about how their families reacted to their conversion."

"That would work," I respond.

"Though I'm not sure the couple would be willing to write anything," Leigh cautions.

"You could interview them separately and tape record their individual stories and then work with them to co-construct their collective story."

"I can do that," Leigh responds. "I'll set up the interview. What needs to be done now?"

"Before turning to the cases, let's work on the literature review to show how some of the trends in the literature have guided us to where we are. This will set the stage for the reader."

◆ Literature Review

Many researchers, particularly feminists, have debunked the myth of value-free scientific inquiry (Cook and Fonow 1986; Reinharz 1992; Roberts 1981), calling for researchers to acknowledge their personal, political, and professional interests. Instead of insisting on a rigid separation of researcher and respondent, they have construed the interview as an active relationship occurring in a context permeated by issues of power, emotionality, and interpersonal process (Holstein and Gubrium 1995).

Interviews now are commonly understood as collaborative, communicative events that evolve their own norms and rules (Briggs 1986; Kvale 1996). As a result, researchers who use interviews should not focus solely on the outcomes—the words spoken by interviewees—but should examine the collaborative activities of interviewees from which these outcomes are produced (Chase and Bell 1994; Futrell and Willard 1994; Hertz 1995; Jorgenson 1995; Langellier and Hall 1989; Miller 1996; Mishler 1986; Suchman and Jordan 1992).

The literature is replete with examples of writers who draw attention to the relational aspects of the interview and the interactional construction of meaning in the interview context (Holstein and Gubrium 1995; Langellier and Hall 1989; Oakley 1981). This interaction is situated in the context of an ongoing relationship where the personal and social identities of both interviewers and interviewees are important factors (Collins 1986; DeVault 1990; Riessman 1987), and the relationship continually changes as each responds to the other (Jorgenson 1991, 1995). Thus interpretive scholars note the "double subjectivity" (Lewis and Meredith 1988) that abounds in interviewing: how each participant's attitudes, feelings, and thoughts affect and are affected by the emerging reciprocity between the participants.

Moving away from the orthodox model of distance and separation, interactive interviewers often encourage self-disclosure and emotionality on the part of the researcher. Researcher involvement can help subjects feel more comfortable sharing information and close the hierarchical gap between researchers and respondents that traditional interviewing encourages (Bergen 1993; Cook and Fonow 1986; Douglas 1985; Hertz 1995; Oakley 1981), thus promoting dialogue rather than interrogation (Bristow and Esper 1988). In this interactive context, respondents become narrators who improvise stories in response to the questions, probes, and personal stories of the interviewers (Bruner 1986; Chase and Bell 1994; Holstein and Gubrium 1995; Mishler 1986; Myerhoff 1992; Riessman 1993).

The interactive interviewing context requires an interviewer who listens empathically (Mies 1983; Stanley and Wise 1983), identifies with participants, and shows respect for participants' emotionality (Mies 1983). Unlike traditional research, where feelings and private realms of experience often are avoided, interactive interviews assume that emotions and personal meanings are legitimate topics of research (Anderson et al. 1987). As a result, interactive interviewers explore sensitive topics that are intimate, may be personally discrediting, and normally are shrouded in secrecy (Renzetti and Lee 1993). When doing so, they pay close attention to ethical issues of privacy and confidentiality as they try to listen "around" and "beyond" the words (DeVault 1990), exploring the unsaid as much as the said (Ochberg 1996).

Research on sensitive and emotional topics has raised questions about the boundary between research interviewing and psychotherapy (Lieblich 1996; Miller 1996; see also Gale 1992; Maione and Chenail 1999). Writers ponder how a researcher should respond if a subject asks for help (Lieblich 1996; Miller 1996), and they question the morality of withholding information and assistance (Cook and Fonow 1986; Oakley 1981; Reinharz 1992; Webb 1984). Some researchers have voiced concern about the emotional harm that can be done to participants with whom they develop personal relationships (Stacey 1988) and about the emotional load such relationships can place on researchers who are not trained as psychotherapists (Brannen 1988; Edwards 1993). On the other hand, some writers emphasize the positive therapeutic benefits that can accrue to respondents and interviewers who participate in interactive interviews (Bloom 1996; Gale 1992; Hutchinson, Wilson, and Wilson 1994; Langellier and Hall 1989; Romanoff 2001; Rosenwald 1996).

Increasingly, research monographs are concerned with subjects' responses to what is written about them (see Agronick and Helson 1996; Apter 1996; Chase 1996; Josselson 1996). After spending time as an interviewee, Colleen Larson (1997) laments that she did not feel she was able to tell in the interview setting the complex

and authentic stories she needed and wanted to tell (see also Tillmann-Healy and Kiesinger 2000). Along with other researchers, especially those doing participatory and action research (e.g., Stringer 1996), Larson (1997) suggests a more collaborative and longitudinal approach that gives interviewees opportunities to reflect on, elaborate, and build on the stories they have told before, as well as to respond to and change what gets reported (see also Belenky et al. 1981-82; Duelli Klein 1983; Tripp 1983). Many interactive researchers have heeded the call for research that gives something useful back to respondents and their communities, rather than research that is pointed exclusively toward restricted academic audiences (Bochner and Ellis 1996; Finch 1984; Oakley 1981). Consequently, interviewers must now face their ethical responsibility to their respondents on both personal and policy levels (Bergen 1993).

Interactive interviews offer opportunities for self-conscious reflection by researchers as well as respondents. Some interviewers now discuss how they feel during interviews (Bar-On 1996; Berger 1997b; Kiesinger 1998; Markham 1998; Miller 1996) and how they use their feelings, experiences, and self-analysis to understand and interpret the experiences of others (DeVault 1999; Douglas 1985; Ellis 1998; Griffith and Smith 1987). Barbara Rothman (1986), for example, writes poignantly about the pain she suffered as she took on the feelings of women who had undergone amniocentesis. By immersing herself in the women's emotional worlds, she felt able to understand and to write about their experiences in a more powerful and empathic way than she could have by keeping herself emotionally distanced. Other researchers discuss how they gained insight into themselves and were changed in the process of interviewing others (Miller 1996). For example, Janet Yerby and Bill Gourd (1994) show how their interviews with members of a nontraditional family had a therapeutic effect on their own marital relationship. Kristin Langellier and Deanna Hall (1989), moreover, report that their research on mother-daughter story-telling strengthened their relationships with their own mothers.

Some writers now advocate that researchers interview peers with whom they have already established relationships (Platt 1981; Segura 1989) and that researchers make use of the everyday situations in which they are involved (Stanley and Wise 1983). Qualitative researchers have co-constructed narratives with family members and friends (Austin 1996; Berger 1997b; Bochner and Ellis 1992; Ellis and Bochner 1992; Fox 1996; Kiesinger 1992; Yerby and Gourd 1994). They have studied themselves reflexively in the process of observing, communicating with, and writing about others (Abu-Lughod 1995; Adler and Adler 1997; Angrosino 1998; Behar 1995; Blee 1998; Crapanzano 1980; Dumont 1978; Ellingson 1998; Goodall 1991, 1999; Jones 1998; Karp 1996; Kondo 1990; Lagerwey 1998; Lather and Smithies 1997; Linden 1993; Markham 1998; Myerhoff 1978; Mykhalovskiy 1997; Ponticelli 1996; Rabinow 1977; Richardson 1992, 1997; Rosaldo 1989; Tillmann-Healy 1996; Zola 1982b). They have conducted interactive interviews about emotional and personal topics (Ellis et al. 1997; Kiesinger 1998; Macleod 1999). And they have introspectively written about their own experiences and their own families as the focus of research (Behar 1996; Berger 1997a, 1997b, 1998; Bochner 1997; Clough 1999; Coyle 1998; Denzin 1999; Eisenberg 1998; Ellis 1993, 1995, 1996; Ellis and Bochner 1996, 2000; Jago 1996; Kolker 1996; Kulick and Willson 1995; Krieger 1991, 1996; Lewin and Leap 1996; Murphy 1987; Pacanowsky 1988; Paget 1993; Payne 1996; Perry 1996; Quinney 1996; Richardson 1997, 1998; Robillard 1997, 1999; Ronai 1992, 1995; Ross and Geist 1997; Shostak 1996; Tillmann-Healy 1996; Trujillo 1998; Williams 1991; Zola 1982a).

Following the trajectory suggested here, interviewing then changes in function as well as form (J. A. Holstein and J. F. Gubrium, personal communication). The interviewing process becomes less a conduit of information from informants to researchers that represents how things are, and more a sea swell of meaning making in which researchers connect their own experiences to those of others and provide stories that open up conversations about how we live and cope.

◆ Types of Collaborative Interviewing

The stories interviewers write about themselves range from descriptions of the researcher's positioning and experience with the subject at hand to reflections on the research process and the researcher's feelings about the subject being explored, to including the researcher as a central character in the story, to making the personal experience of the researcher the focus of the study. In this section, we organize these variations into several categories, which we call reflexive dyadic interviews, interactive interviews, mediated co-constructed narratives, and unmediated co-constructed narratives. We present an exemplar for each of these categories to illustrate how the different types of interviews unfold. After this discussion, we return to our introductory narrative and conclude with a co-constructed story that reflects on the methodological issues involved in the writing of this chapter and on how including the researcher's self in interviews deepens and enriches our understanding of our own research interests.

REFLEXIVE DYADIC INTERVIEWING: ACTS OF FAITH

Reflexive dyadic interviews follow the typical protocol of the interviewer asking questions and the interviewee answering them, but the interviewer typically shares personal experience with the topic at hand or reflects on the communicative process of the interview. In this case, the researcher's disclosures are more than tactics to encourage the respondent to open up; rather, the researcher often feels a reciprocal desire to disclose, given the intimacy of the details being shared by the interviewee. The interview is conducted more as a conversation between two equals than as a distinctly hierarchical, question-and-answer exchange, and the interviewer tries to tune in to the interactively produced meanings and emotional dynamics within the interview itself (Gubrium and Holstein 1997). When telling the story of the research, the interviewers might reflect deeply on the personal experience that brought them to the topic, what they learned about and from themselves and their emotional responses in the course of the interview, and/or how they used knowledge of the self or the topic at hand to understand what the interviewee was saying. Thus the final product includes the cognitive and emotional reflections of the researcher, which add context and layers to the story being told about participants, such as in the exemplar discussed below.

* * *

Since January 1998, I (Leigh) have been conducting ethnographic fieldwork for my dissertation at Dalet Shalom Messianic Jewish Congregation. Messianic Jews believe that they can retain their cultural and ethnic ties to Judaism while recognizing Jesus (whom they refer to by the Hebrew name "Yeshua") as the Messiah. My dissertation research traces my own spiritual journey throughout the ethnographic process, showing how my stories and feelings about religion interact with the stories told by my participants.

The congregation's secretary, Karen, immediately became my main "informant," guiding me through the world of Messianic Judaism. Although I brought some questions to my first interview with Karen, I let the conversation evolve as naturally as possible. Karen spoke at length about her spiritual experiences over the course of her life and also asked me several questions about my own experiences, such as how often I had thought about Jesus and what my religious experiences were like as I was growing up. As we became more comfortable with each other, I began volunteering information, for example, pointing out similarities between our relationships with our grandparents. Although our taped interviews focused mainly on Karen, what she expressed during the interviews undoubtedly was dependent on "the particularities of the subject/researcher relationship" (Angrosino 1989:315-16). For example, my identity as a Jewish woman gave us several points of connection. Several times, Karen said, "Well, you understand what it's like to be Jewish," or "There are all these Jewish cultural things, but I know I don't have to explain all that to you."

An added dimension to our research relationship was that Karen wanted me to accept Yeshua as the Messiah. I felt uncomfortable about her desire for me to convert, while I simultaneously felt that my resistance disappointed her. These relational and emotional dynamics shaped our interview process. Kathleen Blee (1998) explains that the interaction between interviewer and respondent is intensely complex, shaped by positive and negative emotions, and that "just as researchers may try to invoke rapport to facilitate data collection in interviewing situations, so too respondents may attempt to create emotional dynamics to serve their strategic interests" (p. 395).

Karen's stories led me to reflect on my own experiences with and feelings about religion and spirituality. At times, I related to the story Karen told, able because of our similarities to appreciate her attachment to Jewish ritual. Other times, it was difficult for me to understand her transformation from a fairly liberal, secular Jew to an evangelical Messianic Jewish believer. I reflect on these many complexities within the story that follows.

I sip my herbal tea and place the cup back down on the small Formica café table. Karen and I have been in the Barnes and Noble coffee shop for about 15 minutes. "So, how did you find Dalet Shalom?" I ask her.

Karen adjusts her glasses and smiles, "A woman I know heard about it. I was telling her that I had been thinking a lot about Yeshua, but that I also knew I loved being Jewish. I could never change from being Jewish because that is so much a part of who I am. After this woman told me about it, I found the phone number in the phone book and called. I remember the rabbi spoke to me for about an hour. He was so warm and understanding! He told me to come to services on Saturday to see how I felt." She laughs at the memory. "I remember that I arrived late and the place was packed! I couldn't find a seat. Finally, I noticed there was one right up front—right under the rabbi's nose! So there I am, right up front, and . . ." Her eyes fill with tears in the pause before she continues, "I can't even name one of the songs I heard that day. I can't even tell you what the sermon was about. All I know is I was filled with emotion, and I couldn't stop crying. Finally, the rabbi asked if there was anyone who wanted to come know Yeshua, so I raised my hand. I was still crying, and as I moved to go up to the rabbi, I saw a male figure next to me wearing white. I felt this sense of comfort, as if I could just rest my head on his shoulder."

She picks up a napkin to wipe her eyes. "I felt the presence of his arm around me, and I knew it was Yeshua, welcoming me."

"Wow," I respond. I wonder what I would have done if I had ever felt a spiritual presence during a religious service. I wonder if I will ever experience during fieldwork the kind of visions of which Dalet Shalom congregants often speak.

"So were services at Dalet Shalom very different from what you were used to grow-

ing up?" I continue, seeking a point of contact.

She nods, "Yes. At home we basically celebrated Passover and Hanukkah."

I smile in recognition. "Yes, me too. At least in my parents' house. I mostly learned about religion from my grandparents because they were more observant. They kept kosher and my grandfather walked to synagogue."

Her eyes light up with familiarity. "Yes! Exactly! We have pictures of my grandfather saying the morning service prayers."

"So would you say your perspective on life has changed a lot since your conversion?"

"Oh, definitely! I can't even express how much happier I am, Leigh. One day you'll get to feel that too. I know that Yeshua is calling to you. Just don't be afraid of what the Lord has to offer you. Just ask Him what He wants. Have you had questions— questions you've wanted to ask God?"

I contemplate what she is asking me, feeling awkward about having to answer questions about my own beliefs. I know I shouldn't feel this uncomfortable. After all, she's been open to answering my questions. I decide that I owe her an honest response. "Yes, I suppose I have. Sometimes I wonder why certain things happen, like why my sister is deaf and diabetic, or why my father is mentally ill. And I wonder about why good things happen too, like what causes things to go extremely well."

She is quiet for a moment. "So, what do you think about Dalet Shalom?"

"Oh, there are many things I like about Dalet Shalom. I like the dancing and the praise and worship. I think the people are warm and inviting." I remain silent about the things that I do not feel comfortable with or agree with, such as their fundamental belief in the Bible, and their stance against homosexuality and abortion.

"Where do you think the Lord is taking you?" Karen pushes some strands of hair behind one ear.

"I don't know. That's not really a question I ever ask," I confess.

"Do you think about Yeshua a lot?"

I smile because doing this research has caused me to think of Yeshua almost daily. "Of course. But thinking about Yeshua has always been scary for me." The image of Jesus I held in my mind prior to my excursions into the Messianic world was one of dangerous attraction. Salvation extends its hands of allure and promise, a sense of safety blanketed with acceptance. I have always been afraid of Jesus, a fact I hesitate to admit. After all, how can I fear the epitome of peace and kindness? But for me, Jesus was too complicated to face. I didn't know what to do with the concept of Him, and of salvation. I was fascinated by the ease with which some people seemed to believe— really believe—in their religion. Not only fascinated, but envious. Why couldn't it be that easy for me? Why was I constantly questioning, debating, doubting?

"Intellectualizing it makes it harder. I think that is where the fear comes from. But I've also seen a big change in you since you've been coming to services."

Surprised by this observation, I inquire, "What change?"

"You seem more peaceful. I think the Lord is trying to talk to you." She watches as some people order pastries and coffee. "I just can't imagine how I lived my life without Yeshua in it. I just . . . I am a completely different person now. I look at these people, and ask myself how they all do it." As she says this, I wonder if her real question is how I do it. "How do they live their lives without Him? Not having that belief . . ." Her voice breaks and tears slip from her eyes. "The thought of it just makes me so sad."

Witnessing her deep emotional reaction, I think about my own emotional discomfort when the conversation turned to me and my beliefs. Am I being dishonest by not telling her the things that trouble me? I know that I cannot convert to Messianic Judaism, so am I unfairly deceiving her by not directly telling her this?

In listening to and writing Karen's stories about faith and conversion, I come to understand more fully the complicated array of emotions that accompanies religious belief. By revealing her stories, Karen presents me with an opportunity to witness her religious experiences and try them on for size. When Karen begins to ask me questions about my beliefs, she opens a window into how she sees me and allows me to reflect upon how it feels to be an interviewee. This leaves me better able to understand Karen's emotions as a participant in my research. Rather than Karen's merely reporting information to me, the researcher, our emotions are produced in an unfolding conversation (Holstein and Gubrium 1995). Here, readers can connect to the story either through my perceptions or through Karen's, interpreting our experiences for themselves.

As a researcher, I do not dismiss Karen's beliefs as mere social constructions, but allow that she actually experienced something spiritually transcendent during her conversion. Although I am unable to relate fully to Karen's religious beliefs, I remain open to her descriptions and gain new insights into my own beliefs by questioning my faith and comparing it to her spiritual beliefs. Her descriptions of visions, in fact, cause me to reflect on whether or not I may someday experience something similar.

Although qualitative researchers often focus on how positive and empathic feelings shape their interactions in the field, my not being able to identify completely with Karen illuminates how negative or differing emotions can shape ethnographic relationships as well (Blee 1998). Both participant and researcher negotiate the emotional dynamics of any situation, positive or negative. Narrative's openness to multiple perspectives can successfully communicate the difficulties and dilemmas of studying those with whom we do not connect as well as those we do.

INTERACTIVE INTERVIEWS: EXPERIENCING BULIMIA

Sometimes interviewers desire to position themselves in a more self-consciously collaborative way than occurs in reflexive one-on-one interviews. The prototype of this approach is the interactive interview, which usually takes place in a collaborative, small group setting (Ellis et al. 1997). The goal of an interactive interview is for all those participating, usually two to four people, including the primary researcher, to act both as researchers and as research participants. Each is given space to share his or her story in the context of the developing relationships among all participants. Interactive interviewing works especially well when all participants also are trained as researchers (see, e.g., Ellis et al. 1997; Tillmann-Healy and Kiesinger 2000). Even if that is not the case, however, participants can be given an important role in determining the research process and its content, as well as in interpreting the meanings of the interviews (see, e.g., Macleod 1999). Likewise, the feelings, insights, and stories that the primary researcher brings to the interactive session are as important as those of other participants; the understandings that emerge among all parties during interaction—what they learn together—are as compelling as the stories each brings to the session. Ideally, all participants should have some history together or be willing to work to develop a strong affiliation. It is helpful for the researcher as well as coparticipants to have personal experience with the topic under investigation; if that is not the case, the researcher should be willing to take on the role and lived experience of other participants in this regard. This strategy is particularly useful when the researcher is examining personal and/or emotional topics that require reciprocity and the building of trust, such as eating disorders, as in the case elaborated below.

*　*　*

The article "Interactive Interviewing: Talking about Emotional Experience" (Ellis et al. 1997) describes a project about the embodiment and meanings of bulimia. The research was conducted by three researchers: Lisa, at the time a Ph.D. candidate; Christine, a recent Ph.D.; and Carolyn, a

professor. Lisa and Christine have had direct personal experience with bulimia; I (Carolyn) have not. But we all share concerns about food and bodies that arise from women's immersion in cultural contradictions of thinness of bodies and abundance of food and commodities. Also, we share a desire to work within a methodological and theoretical orientation that privileges emotional and concrete details of everyday life and that critically interrogates traditional social science interviewing practices.

In this project, we were interested in learning more about bulimia and how we might methodologically access important bodily, emotional, and interactive details of the experience. Our final paper consisted of four stories, two written from transcripts of dyadic interviews between Christine and Lisa (Kiesinger 1995; Tillmann-Healy 1996), one from the numerous interactive sessions in which all three of us participated, and the last from a dinner at a restaurant written as a narrative ethnography. These accounts tell the story of the development of our interactive interviewing project, with each story adding another textured layer to the approach.

The excerpts below come from the story I wrote about our group discussions. I reflect from the position of a participant who did not engage in the bulimic behaviors we sought to understand. As an "outsider," I show how I consider the problems and risks in this kind of interview situation, how I attempt to get inside a world I know little about, and how Christine and Lisa move me to consider my own relationship to my body and food and to see the similarities between their world and mine.

Initially I do not understand that I am fashioning my story as well (Parry 1991). I hesitantly add my thoughts about food—how I too love to eat and am a "sugar junky," how I try to remember to pause after one helping to wait for fullness cues. I also speak of our differences—how my generation enjoyed adventure and being out of control, while theirs seems to want to have it all—adventure and control, fullness and thinness. . . .

They say that going out to dinner is their favorite activity. I admit it is one of mine too. They say they obsess about food. I deny that I do, but then think about how much food enters my consciousness on any given day. As Christine and Lisa say, working on this project makes me think more about food and my body. Is it healthy to concentrate so much on these details? "There's too much to accomplish to become consumed by these issues," I think. For me, perhaps, but not for young women like Christine and Lisa whose lives are intertwined so intricately with the subject. I wonder how our research can help us to refashion personal and cultural scripts about women's bodies.

Sometimes I think I understand their world so well, it frightens me. I imagine being them and purging, and then admiring my thin body. Then I recoil, knowing I won't engage in such an unhealthy activity. At age 45, health is more important than appearance. What about when I was 20? What if someone had suggested purging to me then? Were the diet pills I occasionally took so different?

I understand the desire to be physically attractive. In my sophomore year in college I lost 47 pounds by eating 500 calories a day. I wore contact lenses, even when I had to take Excedrin each time I inserted the lenses into my watery, itchy, red eyes. What really separates me from Lisa and Christine? Twenty years? Growing up in an earlier decade where those in my cohort rebelled against gender stereotypes and were less inclined to take on cultural labels? Coming of age in a decade where the thrill of "getting away with something" involved drugs and sex, not bingeing and purging? We all have our temptations.

Being thin is less important to me now than ever. Is that because other issues have my attention now, and I have a career I enjoy and a mate who loves and accepts me? Or is it only because a "beautiful" body is less attainable now? I remember a scene that I've never told anyone about. At a con-

ference a few years ago, I wore a bathing suit to the hotel pool and ran into Christine and her sister; their perfection moved me to wrap my body in a towel.

All these thoughts abound as I try to enter their worlds, become their bodies with their concerns. I neither can nor want to distance myself from this intimate, interactive situation. I try to normalize what they do, to take away some of the stigma of shit and vomit. That doesn't mean I support their self-destructive behaviors; it means I am willing to consider that they are not so different from the rest of us. All women are affected by cultural messages of abundance and thinness.

Prior to this study, I had some contact with women who were bulimic. Although I voiced concerns about the role that cultural expectations played in their behavior, I saw them as "other," as strange, different from me. The more they told me about themselves, in some ways the more other they became. It was only when I put myself in an interview situation with them and we talked in depth about our relationship to food that I started to see the similarities between them and me. It is only since then that I can admit how much food and the desire to be physically attractive have affected my life. As we share stories, we create deeper understandings in interaction with each other. I am no longer healthy and they sick; I am not their professor and they my students. We are three women together trying to understand an intimate part of our lives. We have taken different routes, but even those become more understandable as we trace our histories, think about the messages and values of the different eras in which we grew up, and discuss where we are in our lives now. By seeing myself as a subject as well as a researcher, I am able to move from the distanced observer to the feeling participant and learn things I could not learn before, both about them and about me.

Eating dinner together also provides another occasion for learning about eating disorders. The short excerpt below shows the co-construction from our three independent accounts of our collective story of eating together.

When Carolyn sits down across from her, Christine instantly is aware that they have never eaten together. Because she tends to synchronize her eating pattern with others, she panics. Will Carolyn eat quickly or slowly? Does she talk while eating? Is she a sharer? Will Carolyn, a seasoned ethnographer, be watching her every move?

Lisa's stomach growls continuously as they sit talking without picking up their menus. Why don't they order? When finally the waitress stops to ask if they want an appetizer, Carolyn looks questioningly at Lisa and Christine. Lisa can almost taste the salty-greasy choices—oozing processed-cheese nachos, fried mozzarella sticks, and hot chicken wings. But she's not feeling particularly "bad," and she knows Christine almost never eats appetizers. They shake their heads "no" simultaneously. Carolyn had considered ordering some for the table, but after their response, she thinks that she really shouldn't have them either.

Carolyn takes one of the menus tucked behind the salt and pepper shakers. Immediately Christine and Lisa reach for menus as well. It seems they have been waiting for Carolyn to make the first move. Right away, Carolyn knows what she wants. But Christine and Lisa grasp their menus tightly, immersed, reading line by line. For what seems like minutes to Carolyn, they say nothing. Carolyn continues holding her menu in front of her face so they don't feel rushed. She'd like to know what they're thinking. Minutes go by.

This excerpt portrays the impact of bulimia on how we thought, felt, and related as we ate a meal. These stories reveal our concerns about sharing food, our rules for eating with others, the inner dialogues that occupy us during dinner, our obsession with the food in front of us, our concerns about how we were being perceived by oth-

ers, and the similarities and differences in the eating experiences of women who do and do not have bulimia.

MEDIATED AND UNMEDIATED CO-CONSTRUCTED NARRATIVES

Researchers also may share their stories through co-constructed narratives, or tales jointly constructed by relational partners about epiphanies in their lives (see Bochner and Ellis 1996; Ellis and Bochner 1996). This approach may be *mediated,* meaning a researcher may monitor the conversation of two relational partners, or *unmediated,* meaning a researcher might study his or her own relationship with a partner or two researchers might study their relationship with each other. In either case, these stories show dyads engaged in the specific, concrete, and unique details of daily living. They cope with the untidy ambiguities, ambivalences, and contradictions of relationship life and try to make sense of their local situations. This type of research focuses on the interactional sequences by which interpretations of lived experiences are constructed, coordinated, and solidified into stories. The local narratives that are jointly produced thus display couples in the process of "doing" their relationships as they try to turn fragmented, vague, or disjointed events into intelligible, coherent accounts.

MEDIATED CO-CONSTRUCTED NARRATIVES: ONE FLESH

Mediated co-constructed narrative research is similar to conjoint marital therapy (Satir 1983), where couples participate together in therapy after providing their different perspectives on the same events. It also is related to interpersonal process recall (Elliott 1986; Gale 1992), where an interviewer asks two participants to watch a tape of their therapy session and rate and comment on meaningful moments. In mediated co-constructed narratives, a researcher serves as coordinator and moderator as a couple engages in a joint construction of an epiphany in their relationship. The researcher asks them to reflect on the event and to write, talk into a tape recorder, or be interviewed separately about the experience. Then, in the presence of the researcher, the participants hold a discussion about the event. Sometimes the participants are asked to exchange transcripts or stories written independently and read each other's constructions before the discussion, although this may not always be feasible. Nevertheless, the goal is to produce or co-construct a version of the event that takes into account each individual's perspective.

The researcher stays in the role of researcher as he or she take notes on (and/or tapes) the interaction. The researcher then writes the participants' story from the materials they provide as well as from his or her own observation of and participation in their co-construction. While writing their story, the researcher reflects on how he or she, as the researcher, views the participants and analyzes their conversational style and their negotiation of the co-construction of their separate stories. The researcher might describe events leading up to the interview, the physical and emotional environment of the interview, and his or her role in the interview (for example, what the researcher asked the participants, how he or she responded to them, and how the researcher possibly influenced the conversation). The account of the interview process becomes part of the story told. The researcher also might include his or her views on and experience with the topic at hand and discussion of how his or her views and feelings have developed and changed as a result of observation of and interaction with the participants. Including the researcher's experience helps readers understand more about the researcher's interest in the topic and provides background for how he or she interprets what is going on. Although the researcher becomes a charac-

ter in the story, his or her identity remains one of researcher rather than researcher-participant as in interactive interviewing. As shown below, the focus stays on the experience of the other research participants rather than on the interviewer.

* * *

As my (Leigh's) dissertation research continued, I wanted to interview a couple about the role of Messianic belief in married life. Every congregant I asked referred me to Rabbi Aaron Levinson and his wife, Rebecca. I was repeatedly told that they "really live up to biblical guidelines for marriage." Both Aaron and Rebecca had Messianic conversion experiences in the early 1970s. Aaron became very involved at the organizational level of the Messianic movement and opened Dalet Shalom in 1980. A few years later, he and Rebecca met and married. When I approached Aaron and Rebecca, they were happy to be interviewed, and I set up an appointment with them in June 1999.

Originally, I conducted two-hour taped interviews separately with Aaron and Rebecca about their marriage and Messianic expectations for marriage roles. I then conducted a follow-up joint interview once the initial interviews were transcribed. Ideally, I would have preferred that Aaron and Rebecca had had a chance to read and comment on one another's transcripts, but because of their schedules, we were not able to arrange for this. In addition, once I read the original transcripts, I realized that Aaron and Rebecca agreed with one another about every topic we had discussed. Asking them to comment on each other's individual stories most likely would not have produced stories any different from the ones they had already told me. I thought that I might be able to show the collaborative nature of their relationship by writing a story of our interview that included details about how they interacted.

In writing a story based on our follow-up joint interview session, I used what I already knew about Aaron and Rebecca, shaping their mannerisms and voices. I recalled the way Aaron had cried when he described first meeting Rebecca. I remembered Rebecca's blush at detailing their first telephone conversation, and how nervous she had been. Many times while volunteering in the Dalet Shalom office, I witnessed Aaron's romantic gestures toward Rebecca, such as unexpectedly buying her flowers. All of these elements filtered my understanding of their relationship prior to our interviews.

In this excerpt, I interview Aaron and Rebecca together, reflecting on their interaction with one another and the emotions present in the interview. In addition, I show how Rebecca's reflections on her family's reaction to her conversion cause me to reflect on my own family relationships. Unlike Karen, Aaron and Rebecca do not ask me questions about my own experiences; they remain focused on the questions I have for them.

I shuffle my transcripts and smile at Rabbi Aaron Levinson and his wife, Rebecca. "Well, I have the transcripts from the last interview here." I pat the papers beneath my hand. A few weeks earlier, I had interviewed Aaron about the role of men in Messianic theology, following that with a separate interview with Rebecca about women's roles. "And I must say that even though I interviewed you separately, there is no disagreement between the two of you."

They both smile, and Aaron takes Rebecca's hand in his own. "We're always together. We have to be, as it says in the Bible, one flesh." *I notice the intimacy and genuine caring for one another that their gestures communicate.*

"Well, I did have some questions about some things we didn't get to cover in our previous interviews."

"Yes?" *Aaron runs his hand over his white beard and adjusts his glasses. The sparkling brown eyes behind them inquisitively meet my own.*

"How do you advise congregants about handling nonbelieving family members?" *In the Messianic world, non-Messianic followers (especially Jewish ones) are referred to as "nonbelievers."*

"Well, I'll let Rebecca handle that. She's dealt a lot with that issue." *Aaron willingly gives the floor to Rebecca, showing a trust and respect for her experience with this topic. This give-and-take, primarily orchestrated by Aaron, seems characteristic of much of their communication with one another.*

Pushing some of her curly brown hair behind her shoulders, Rebecca takes the floor without missing a beat. "How do you handle nonbelieving family members? First of all, you do so with love because love really does conquer all. I'll give you an example. I have a family member who lives in Israel, and who is an observant and religious Jew—not Messianic. When he addresses less observant family members, he pounds ideas into them: 'You have to do this, you have to do that.' The more he does that, the more the rest of the family resists worshiping the Lord. They see him as forcing beliefs on them. Now when Aaron and I go visit my family in Israel, we love them. We don't force any ideas on them, and because of that, they're more willing to be open to our ideas."

She pauses, contemplating her next words, and I wonder if she is considering whether or not to say anything else. I wait, allowing the silence to encourage further information. "I will say that when I first came to know the Messiah, I was very anxious about how this would be received in my family. I had all these questions about how to deal with my loyalty to my family, our rabbi, my friends . . ." *Her voice trails off, and I perceive that her eyes are focused somewhere on the past. Her gold bracelets quietly clink together as she adjusts her hair once again, and her expression is sad as she finds her voice.* "My family sat shivah [a Jewish mourning practice for the dead] when I came to accept the Messiah. I was no longer a part of the family, and we didn't speak for a long time." Aaron reaches out to touch her shoulder, offering emotional support. She touches his hand and smiles, reassuring him that she is okay.

Sitting in my seat, I feel my chest tighten, and I wonder at the power of a newfound faith that allowed her to face this pain in exchange for her belief. I try to imagine my own family cutting me off for choosing an alternative belief system. If that were the fate that awaited me, how many of my choices in life would be different? Biting my lip, I think about how much my grandparents were opposed to family members' dating and marrying anyone outside of the Jewish faith. If they were still alive, would I be in a long-term relationship with a Christian man? I wonder if I would have crossed that line anyway, and what the results would have been. Although I cannot imagine my grandparents completely cutting me off, I cannot say for sure. I ponder whether anticipation of their deep disappointment might have been enough to dissuade me from dating men outside of Judaism.

I realize Rebecca has continued to talk, and I snap back to attention. "Eventually, someone in the Jewish community spoke to my parents. To this day, I have no idea what this person said to them, but whatever it was, I know she is resting in peace with the Lord because my family decided to ask me for forgiveness, and I was accepted back into the family again." She says this quickly, as if to brush aside the emotions this story makes her recall. "But I never ever push any of my beliefs on them. All I do is act with love, and show them through my loving actions and attitude how strong my dedication to the Lord is. And although at this time they do not know the Messiah as we know the Messiah, they see that Aaron and I are very observant. Their acceptance comes through our love and through us letting the fruit of our belief show." She turns to Aaron for confirmation, and he smiles and nods at her words.

I hesitate, wanting to probe further into this experience. Rebecca has tied things up a little too nicely, and I know that her feelings regarding her family's sudden "forgiveness" were probably not as simple as she describes. Certainly, she must have felt some residual anger for their rejection. Did she really "forgive and forget" that easily? But I don't want to force her into areas she may not be emotionally ready or willing to enter. I decide to let it go for now. Maybe there will be a better time or place for such questions later.

In the scene above, I am open with readers about my own thoughts and feelings during my conversation with Aaron and Rebecca. Letting readers know what I think and how I emotionally react to Aaron and Rebecca brings them into the interview context with me, allowing them to watch as the interview progresses and to imagine how they might respond in a similar situation. Some readers may draw conclusions that are different from mine, or may interpret Aaron's and Rebecca's words and actions in a different light.

Throughout our interview, Aaron and Rebecca enact marriage roles through actions rather than words. Although they hold more traditional views about marriage than I do, I am able to see and understand how and why these roles work for them. Their silent exchanges reinforce Messianic views on how spouses should interact: The man is considered the head of the household and the person who, after discussions with the wife, has the final say on all decisions. For example, even though Rebecca holds the floor when answering my question about non-Messianic family members, she does so only after Aaron has directed her to do so. Rebecca seeks Aaron's confirmation and support of what she says through nonverbal behaviors such as exchanging glances and touching. Aaron reassures her through actions such as nodding and placing a hand on her shoulder. Allowing their interaction to evolve more naturally reveals how Aaron and Rebecca's co-construction is beneath the surface of their words, in a conversational dance so skillfully performed that their give-and-take appears almost flawless.

UNMEDIATED: CO-CONSTRUCTED NARRATIVES: DECIDING ABOUT ABORTION

In unmediated co-constructed narratives, the focus turns directly to the self, as researchers examine their own relationships rather than the relationships of others. In such narratives, researchers use the same procedures as described above, except there is no outside researcher mediating the interview process. The two researchers, or a researcher and partner, write their stories separately, exchange them with each other, read them, and then discuss them. Then they attempt to co-construct a collective version. They might present the result in the form of a script, a short story, or an essay; or they might analyze or even perform their narrative for an audience. Other participants in the event might be asked to add their voices as well. Although the result is a collective interpretation, individual voices might be kept separate, as the exemplar below demonstrates.

* * *

"Telling and Performing Personal Stories: The Constraints of Choice in Abortion" (Ellis and Bochner 1992; see also Bochner and Ellis 1992) tells the story of a decision my partner, Art, and I (Carolyn) had to make upon discovering only 10 weeks into our relationship that I was pregnant. After much agonizing, I had an abortion. This experience had a profound impact on our relationship and our personal lives. For the next two months, we were numb, self-protective, and unable to express our thoughts and feelings about the abortion. When we finally broke through our resistance, we realized how much the experience had affected us and how deeply we had ventured into our private and submerged registers of emotion.

With a self-consciously therapeutic motive, we decided to write a story about our experience to try to understand what had happened at a deep emotional level. We wanted to reveal ourselves to ourselves as we revealed ourselves to others. Hoping to provide companionship to others who may have been similarly bruised by the ambivalence and contradictions associated with the constraint of making such a choice, we attempted to share the complex emotions that were part of this experience so that readers might experience our experience—actually feel it—and consider how they might feel or have felt in similar situations. We tried to write in an open, revealing way that would connect us to readers, especially those who had themselves suffered the complexities of abortion. We hoped to tell enough in our story so that readers might, as Jaber Gubrium and James Holstein (1997) point out, connect our emotions to the cultures in which they arise.

In telling our story, we first independently constructed a detailed chronology of the emotions, events, decisions, and coping strategies that had taken place. After completing our individual accounts, we read each other's versions and began to co-construct a single story of what had happened. We took notes on our discussions and asked others with whom we had consulted during the decision making about the abortion to contribute to the narrative, thus producing a multivocal text.

We wrote our final story as a script that presented, in sequence, critical scenes in which we expressed our self-reflections, feelings, and analysis of the main events—the discovery and shock of the pregnancy, pre- and postdecision interactions, and the abortion procedure described side by side in both the female and male voices. Later, we performed this narrative at a professional social science conference, a step that became a vital part of our attempt to cope with and bring closure to this experience. The excerpt below details the abortion procedure in two voices, Ted's as Art's voice and Alice's as Carolyn's voice.

Alice: *The suction machine is turned on. I tighten my grip on Ted's wrists, he tightens his. I feel excruciating pain. I moan and scream. Everything speeds up. The nurse yells, "Deep breaths. Deep breaths." I try to, but the screams get in the way. Ted's face is now right next to mine. I hear his voice, sense his encouragement. I don't know what Ted is saying, but I'm glad he's here. There is confusion. I hear the suctioning noise, and then they're pulling out my whole uterus. I bear down, my nails sink into Ted's wrists. Then I am in the pain, going round and round like in a tangled sheet. I feel it being sucked out of my vagina. My god I can't stand the pain. I hear gut-wrenching screams. Then the doctor's voice, "Five more seconds, just five more seconds, that's all." I am comforted and know that I can stand anything for five seconds. I feel I am with friends. The nurse continues yelling, "Breathe. Breathe." And I try as hard as I can to breathe as I imagine one should when having a baby. Ted is encouraging, gripping. Then I feel another cutting as the doctor does a D&C to make sure nothing was missed. The pain takes over my full consciousness.*

Ted: *Suddenly I hear the rumble of the suction machine and I feel a vibration pass through Alice's body as the machine extracts the last remnants of the fetus. I see the blood and am repulsed by the horror of this crude technological achievement. I want to look away, but I can't. I am face-to-face with the terror of creation and destruction. Alice has a firm hold on my hands. I cannot turn away. She cannot escape the physical pain; I cannot feel it. I cannot evade the horror of what I see in front of me; she cannot witness it. My ears are ringing from the frenzied sound created by the simultaneous talking and screaming and rumbling that is engulfing the room. The action is fast and furious. Alice's ferocious cries submerge the sound of the machine. "Hold on, baby," I say. I clutch her hands as tight as I can. Her*

breathing intensifies, growing louder and louder. "Oh, god," she screams. "Oh, my god." Ironically, her cries and screams echo the sounds of orgasmic pleasure she released the afternoon this fetus was created.

Alice: *Then Quiet. The machine is turned off. "That's all," the doctor says. A nurse puts a pad between my legs and I have visions of blood gushing from my angry uterus. Ted's grip eases. I relax, but the leftover pain continues to reverberate through my body.*

Ted: *Then, abruptly, with no forewarning, the machine is turned off. Alice lies still, out of breath, quiet. The doctor's assistant whisks away the tray of remains covered by a bloody towel.*

In the literature on abortion, details of the emotional and communicative processes of the experience are obscure, leaving readers without a sense of the complexity, confusion, and vacillation often associated with the lived experience of abortion. The emotional trauma seems bleached of its most profound and stirring meanings. Most of the literature bypasses interpersonal and emotional conflicts in favor of political ideology or moral indignation. Because Art and I are both authors and subjects in our story, we have the freedom to explore emotional trauma as we experienced it separately and together. Although our own relationship may be vulnerable, we are not limited by concerns of doing emotional harm to other research participants or our fears about losing control of our words and experiences to another researcher. Thus we are able in our story to explore emotional complexities from both the female and male perspectives and to consider such graphic differences as those between Art's experience of grief and my experience of unworthiness or the meaning of my repeated use of the term *baby* juxtaposed against Art's references to *fetus*. These descriptive revelations lead us to contemplate further the significance of frames: grief versus self-contempt, physical pain juxtaposed against emotional pain, and the experience-near female voice compared to the more distanced male voice. Writing and discussing this story helps us to unify the past (the pregnancy and abortion) with an anticipated and hopeful future—to bring closure to this experience as one we might live with together.

◆ In the Middle of Flexibility and Confusion: Two or Three Things We Know for Sure (Allison 1995)

Books and papers cover my desk and surround my chair. Humming from the computer and printer fills the room. Staring at the screen, I feel walled in; the only way out is to finish this chapter. I pick up the stack of pages in front of me. The ragged edges, unevenly stapled paragraphs, and half sheets refute the order I try to impose by tapping all four sides of the stack on the desk. I read through the draft Leigh and I have written of "Their Story/My Story." It's already November 17th, I remind myself as I squint at the small date on my watch. I look again, just in case I've misread it. Jay Gubrium periodically reminds us of the December 1st deadline, and I don't want to be late. Besides, I need to move to all the other unfinished commitments I have taken on. I sigh. This chapter isn't coming together as we'd hoped.

Leigh and I have constructed a typology of kinds of interview studies that include the researcher's experience and have used four exemplars from our own studies to demonstrate. The chapter works well enough in theory, but I'm not sure it's working in practice. Our interview exemplars don't quite match the ideal types we have described. And the continuum from lesser to greater involvement of the researcher—well, that hasn't worked either. What do we do now?

It's too late to conduct other interviews or select other studies as exemplars.

I should have chosen my excerpts more carefully; Leigh and I should have worked more closely while she was doing her interviews for this chapter, I admonish myself. Now I have to rewrite my description of the types so that our exemplars are really exemplars. Or I will have to choose other excerpts, and Leigh will have to rewrite her interview stories to fit our types.

Choosing the former, I frantically start to edit our text. I glance again at my watch as I type. Leigh will be here in 30 minutes, and this is the only day this week I can work on our chapter. Next week is filled with dissertation defenses, proposal hearings, conference planning, and other deadlines. I type faster.

Suddenly a ray of light makes its way through a crack in the wall and a smile breaks over my face. I stop editing and start to type what I am thinking: In doing this chapter, Leigh and I are engaged in writing what we have called in the text an unmediated co-constructed narrative. She brings her (interview) stories and I bring mine, and we work to put them together in a co-constructed story we both agree on. We have written about how difficult these projects are to accomplish, how they never quite work out as you think they will, how it is important to leave room for improvisation, and how difficult it is for researchers to include their stories without taking over the stories of others. We agree that in our interview studies we're trying to reflect life as lived, not simply follow traditional social science procedures. But until now, we had forgotten to take our own advice in writing this chapter. Given our goals and flexible procedures, should it be a surprise that we are having trouble fitting our work into neat categories and traditional social science sections? Should it be a surprise that I feel compelled to include here our reflexive story of writing this chapter?

As I type this paragraph, Leigh pulls in to my driveway. I open the front door only a crack, so the dogs can't run out. Leigh squeezes through the narrow opening I provide and greets me and the barking dogs. "Quite a doorbell," she says, laughing.

I start to offer apologies for the noise, but instead just shrug, "I know. What can I say?"

As I fix glasses of tea, all four dogs take turns sniffing the smells of Leigh's dog hidden on her clothes. Our Australian shepherd Sunya, wide-eyed and poised in anticipation, drops a ball in front of Leigh, enticing her to play. Ande, our Jack Russell, jumps into her arms when she reaches down to pet Likker and Traf, the two rat terriers. As we move to my office, the dogs run in behind us. They knock the piles of books and papers across the floor, eliminating any possibility of organization, before they jump on Leigh and vie for attention. When I yell at them to be quiet, then squirt them with water from a bottle I keep in my office, they scamper playfully into the hallway, still barking. Apologizing to Leigh for the mess, I quickly close the office door. "There's no room," I yell as they whine and scratch on the wooden door.

I tell Leigh that our interview types and the excerpts we have chosen aren't quite fitting together. She seems disheartened and offers to rewrite her excerpts or to write other stories from her interviews. "Maybe it's okay that they aren't working," I offer. She looks at me quizzically, perhaps thinking that the herbal tea we're drinking has gone to my head. "Well, just think how you did your interviews," I say. "That summer we both were traveling. You also were writing your dissertation proposal and I was working on a book. We didn't have much time to talk about how you'd do the interviews with your participants to fill in our last two 'cells.' "

Smiling at my use of the term cells, she replies, "I knew we were using your articles on co-constructed narratives and interactive interviews as two of our cases. So I reread those and then just let my interviews evolve."

"I know," I reply, "and often that's the best way to do it. Anyway, I didn't want to be too rigid about how you did them. I wasn't in the interview context with you, so there was much I didn't know. You also were using the interviews to gather data for your dissertation, not just this chapter."

"And my participants had their own constraints and agendas," Leigh says.

"As all participants do," I reply and we nod in agreement. "As we do in the writing of this chapter. Think how long it's taken us to find time to get together. That's the nature of research. Why should I have expected this to work exactly as planned? Why did I expect this situation to be any different?"

"So what's not working?" Leigh asks.

"Your dyadic interview. It doesn't really show you reflecting during the interview, like we say happens. Instead, you tell Karen's story and then you tell yours."

"Well, I was trying to show how Karen's story led me to reflect while I transcribed and wrote the interview. As Laurel Richardson [1994] says, writing served as a process of inquiry . . ."

"Just as in this piece we're writing now," I interrupt, "and it's all an evolving process."

Leigh nods and continues, "I also reflected during the interview process. But I was unsure of which reflective moment to focus on for the chapter. What else?"

I am impressed, as always, by her lack of defensiveness. Reminding myself that she is my student and this is the first time we have worked together as coauthors, I choose my words carefully. "Your interview participants in the co-constructed mediated narrative didn't read each others' individual transcripts before you met for a joint interview. I've always thought of that as an important part of the process."

"I asked them to, but when they said they didn't have time to read the transcripts before I came back for a second interview, well, I pushed a little, but I also didn't want to negatively impact my relationship with *them because . . . well mainly because I care what they think. . . ."*

"And it's not your style to be pushy . . . ," I interrupt, thinking about her reticence to push Rebecca on the emotions surrounding her family's sudden forgiveness of her conversion.

"No, it isn't," Leigh laughs. "Besides, Rabbi Aaron and Rebecca are authority figures in the temple. I needed them for my dissertation research. It didn't seem appropriate to push." (Similar to your relationship to me, I think.) "With Karen, it was different. We're peers and the interaction was on a different level."

I think about how different Leigh's interviews were from mine. Although both of us knew our respondents, my participants were close friends, long-term students, and loved ones. Leigh's interviews involved relationships made in the process of fieldwork that probably would not continue after her dissertation was done. My situation provided more latitude and, at the same time, less than hers did. In some ways, my participants and I could ask for more from each other and reveal more in the process because we knew each other so well. But because our lives were so intertwined, we also had a lot to lose if the interviews didn't go well. No matter the circumstances, though, my style was to push more than Leigh. I am reminded that we all have to find a comfortable interactive style in interviews that emphasizes relationship and communication.

"There didn't seem to be much to co-construct anyway," Leigh continues, breaking into my thoughts. "In the individual interviews, both of them said almost the same things and portrayed the same images in their stories about gender roles and religion. It was clear they had talked this over a lot."

"Even in the joint conversation," Leigh continues, "when I probed, they basically agreed. I took notice of the nonverbals, such as hand-holding and how they looked at each other, and they do seem to have a good relationship. But rather than both of them

answering, each took over certain questions. That seemed to be where the agreement took place—they agreed on who should speak on which question. You can see how focused I am on dynamics in the interview."

"That explains, then, why your narrative doesn't have much of a co-constructed feeling," I say. "It's not so much they co-constructed a story as that they took turns telling individual stories . . ."

"Which, of course, is a form of co-construction," Leigh interjects.

I nod, pleased at her insight, and continue. *"I think you might have gotten different stories had you asked them to discuss an epiphany that was yet unresolved, which may be necessary for this kind of interview to work best. What they gave you didn't center on a crisis or turning point that had not yet been processed, which is the idea."*

As I talk, I think about my own unmediated co-constructed story with Art about abortion. *"When Art and I wrote our stories, it was about an unresolved epiphany in our relationship. I couldn't wait to read his transcript and show him mine. The co-construction process we went through was very important. I wonder, then, why I chose an excerpt to present here that kept the two individual stories side by side instead of one that showed the co-construction process."*

"There's also a problem with the portion I chose to demonstrate interactive interviews," I add, thinking that pointing out the problems in my cases will make Leigh feel more comfortable about the problems in hers. "It's all me and doesn't show Christine, Lisa, and me in interaction, and that's the whole point of interactive interviews—that what happens in the interaction is as important as the stories each brings to the interview. Maybe I should show a different excerpt from both of these pieces or add a second."

"And I could always rewrite my story about Karen," Leigh offers, "to show how I reflected during the interview. But with

Rebecca and Aaron . . . well how could I know ahead of time that they might not provide a good example of co-constructed narrative . . ." Her voice trails off. "I guess I should have concentrated more on an unresolved event, as you said, or pushed more in the interviews about their families' responses to their conversion." We stare at each other for a while. Then we simultaneously look at our watches, as though the gun is ready to go off to signify time to run toward the finish line.

"Well, we still have to be careful that we are trying to be truthful about what happened in the interviews, and not intruding too much into their stories," I respond. "At what point are we taking too much control over the stories that get told? Are we manipulating the 'data' to fit the categories and in doing so privileging our categories over the stories and the interview contexts? I'm concerned about that. I don't think I want to second guess the excerpts I initially chose from my published pieces, although I think I'll add an excerpt from my interaction with Christine and Lisa at dinner."

"Good idea," says Leigh. "I don't know how I could rewrite the story of Rebecca and Aaron to fit more with the way you describe co-construction in your article with Art."

"You can't. It's important for readers to see that this process doesn't always go the way you planned. Anyway, both excerpts, yours and mine, demonstrate that co-constructed stories sometimes retain individual voices, or sometimes never had them in the first place. But the co-constructed version presented is still the agreed-upon collective story."

"Good point. I do think, though, that there are good reasons to present another portion of Karen's story to show the reflection that went on during the interview process. I have all that in my notes, so it wouldn't be that difficult."

"I agree. I like that we're concentrating more on making our story work, flexibly dealing with what happened, rather than being too concerned with methodological rules."

"What do you think about using the conversation we're having as the conclusion to our chapter?" I ask suddenly. "Or is it too much of us, the authors, intruding into the research story?"

Leigh laughs, "It is interesting that the issues we deal with in writing this chapter are the same ones we encountered in doing our interview studies in the first place."

"Well, at least now I don't have to worry about our typology and our categories bleeding into each other. Instead we can view our schema as a heuristic device to introduce readers to the variety of ways interviewers can insert themselves into their interviews and the stories they write about others."

"Glad we resolved all that," Leigh says, breathing a sigh of relief.

"Not so fast. We still have the conclusion to write," I remind her, then silently remind myself not to dominate the conversation, as Leigh sometimes seems hesitant to challenge my authority. "What do we want to leave the readers with?"

"Well, the point of all this, other than showing the ways in which researchers can add their experiences to an interview, has been to show how what we learn in and about interviews can be deepened by our participation," Leigh offers.

"I agree. As I see it, the most important thing that happens is that you get a deeper understanding both of self and of others in this process, because you're not only exploring them, you're exploring you."

"Yes, as Jack Douglas [1985] and Michael Jackson [1989] emphasize, 'Understanding ourselves is part of the process of understanding others.' "

"And vice versa."

"That's certainly true for me," Leigh acknowledges. "For example, I understood Karen's background by thinking about my own and how similar they were, and she made me examine my own religious beliefs, especially the possibility of believing in Jesus."

"And working with Christine and Lisa certainly helped me to understand bulimia

on a cultural level and to reframe my own concerns with eating. In doing this," I continue, "I was drawn to how much we can come to understand by concentrating on our similarities with those we study, in addition to our differences. So often we see those we study as different from us but similar to each other. In this research, I was forced to consider how they and I were alike as well. I had to try on their worlds."

Leigh chimes in, "When I first decided to study Messianic Judaism, I was sure I would dislike the congregants and be angry with them for claiming to be both Jewish and believers in Jesus. Now after spending so much time with members and exploring my own feelings that come up in the interviews, I've come to understand the complexity of their beliefs and I connect to their ability to express and be in their emotions."

"So really what we're advocating here is mutual understanding as opposed to advocating that we, as all-knowing researchers, understand the other unidirectionally. It's similar to what happens in our day-to-day lives, where we try to understand others by comparing our experiences to theirs. We ask them, What do you think, do, what are your relationships like? Sometimes we tell stories about ours and wait to hear them compare their lives to ours. The exchange becomes more of a conversation than, as Holstein and Gubrium [1995] describe traditional interviews, information produced for the interviewer."

"I hope our texts also encourage readers to think about and feel their commonalities with our participants and with us," I continue. "As we examine ourselves, we invite readers to do the same, and to enter into their own conversations."

"I think the multiple voices in the text also play a part here."

"Yes, things are revealed and constructed in interaction that might not be accomplished with one voice."

"Well, there's that. But I was still thinking of readers," Leigh responds. "As Laurel Richardson and Ernest Lockridge [1998] remind us, multiple voices in co-constructed pieces give readers multiple places to stand and look. Some readers might relate to Rebecca and Aaron's relationship, where they seemingly agree on everything. Or they might relate to me as an outside observer trying to decipher from nonverbal cues whether something else might be going on."

"In letting them look with you as a researcher, you provide an interview frame for readers to enter, as you did with Rabbi Aaron and Rebecca. This allows readers to understand more fully what went on there or even to come up with alternate interpretations. They also can feel with you as a researcher. Or feel with you as a character in your story. That's what Art and I had in mind in the abortion piece. We wanted to present a version of both the female and male experience of abortion, within the context of our collective confusion, ambivalence, and feelings. These are feelings that other respondents most likely wouldn't reveal. And even if they did, it might not be ethical to ask them to. To be able to invite readers to enter our emotional, physical, and spiritual, as well as cognitive, experience—well, that's what can happen when you include yourself as a character. It opens up other realms of existence."

"As long as you can handle the vulnerability it entails," Leigh says quietly. "Our own emotionality, physicality, spirituality—these realms seem to bring with them a great deal more vulnerability than we're accustomed to in traditional social science."

"That's for sure," I respond. We sit silently, both contemplating the vulnerability in the stories we tell in this chapter. Simultaneously, we shake out of our reverie.

"I think we should retitle our chapter 'Their Story/My Story/Our Story,'" I say, typing the words as I speak them.

■ *References*

Abu-Lughod, L. 1995. "A Tale of Two Pregnancies." Pp. 339-49 in *Women Writing Culture*, edited by R. Behar and D. A. Gordon. Berkeley: University of California Press.

Adler, P. A. and P. Adler. 1997. "Parent-as-Researcher: the Politics of Researching in the Personal Life." Pp. 21-44 in *Reflexivity and Voice*, edited by R. Hertz. Thousand Oaks, CA: Sage.

Agronick, G. and R. Helson. 1996. "Who Benefits from an Examined Life? Correlates of Influence Attributed to Participation in a Longitudinal Study." Pp. 80-93 in *The Narrative Study of Lives*, Vol. 4, *Ethics and Process in the Narrative Study of Lives*, edited by R. Josselson. Thousand Oaks, CA: Sage.

Allison, D. 1995. *Two or Three Things I Know for Sure*. New York: Plume.

Anderson, K., S. Armitage, D. Jack, and J. Wittner. 1987. "Beginning Where We Are: Feminist Methodology in Oral History." *Oral History Review* 15:103-27.

Angrosino, M. V. 1989. "The Two Lives of Rebecca Levengstone: Symbolic Interaction in the Generation of the Life History." *Journal of Anthropological Research* 45:315-26.

———. 1998. *Opportunity House: Ethnographic Stories of Mental Retardation*. Walnut Creek, CA: AltaMira.

Apter, T. 1996. "Expert Witness: Who Controls the Psychologist's Narrative?" Pp. 22-44 in *The Narrative Study of Lives*, Vol. 4, *Ethics and Process in the Narrative Study of Lives*, edited by R. Josselson. Thousand Oaks, CA: Sage.

Austin, D. A. 1996. "Kaleidoscope: The Same and Different." Pp. 206-30 in *Composing Ethnography: Alternative Forms of Qualitative Writing*, edited by C. Ellis and A. P. Bochner. Walnut Creek, CA: AltaMira.

Bar-On, D. 1996. "Ethical Issues in Biographical Interviews and Analysis." Pp. 9-21 in *The Narrative Study of Lives*, Vol. 4, *Ethics and Process in the Narrative Study of Lives*, edited by R. Josselson. Thousand Oaks, CA: Sage.

Behar, R. 1995. "Writing in My Father's Name: A Diary of *Translated Woman*'s First Year." Pp. 65-82 in *Women Writing Culture*, edited by R. Behar and D. A. Gordon. Berkeley: University of California Press.

———. 1996. *The Vulnerable Observer: Anthropology That Breaks Your Heart*. Boston: Beacon.

Belenky, M. F., B. M. Clinchy, N. R. Goldberger, and J. M. Tarule. 1981-82. "Listening to Women's Voices." *Newsletter, Education for Women's Development Project* (Simon's Rock of Bard College, Great Barrington, MA), no. 2.

Bergen, R. K. 1993. "Interviewing Survivors of Marital Rape: Doing Feminist Research on Sensitive Topics." Pp. 197-211 in *Researching Sensitive Topics*, edited by C. M. Renzetti and R. M. Lee. Newbury Park, CA: Sage.

Berger, L. 1997a. "Between the Candy Store and the Mall: The Spiritual Loss of a Father." *Journal of Personal and Interpersonal Loss* 2:397-409.

———. 1997b. "Sister, Sister: Siblings, Deafness, and the Representation of Signed Voice." M.A. thesis, University of South Florida, Tampa.

———. 1998. "Silent Movies: Scenes from a Life." Pp. 137-46 in *Fiction and Social Research: By Ice or Fire*, edited by A. Banks and S. P. Banks. Walnut Creek, CA: AltaMira.

Blee, K. M. 1998. "White-Knuckle Research: Emotional Dynamics in Fieldwork with Racist Activists." *Qualitative Sociology* 21:381-99.

Bloom, L. 1996. "Stories of One's Own: Nonunitary Subjectivity in Narrative Representation." *Qualitative Inquiry* 2:176-97.

Bochner, A. P. 1997. "It's About Time: Narrative and the Divided Self." *Qualitative Inquiry* 3: 418-38.

Bochner, A. P. and C. Ellis. 1992. "Personal Narrative as a Social Approach to Interpersonal Communication." *Communication Theory* 2:165-72.

———. 1996. "Talking over Ethnography." Pp. 13-45 in *Composing Ethnography: Alternative Forms of Qualitative Writing*, edited by C. Ellis and A. P. Bochner. Walnut Creek, CA: AltaMira.

Brannen, J. 1988. "The Study of Sensitive Subjects." *Sociological Review* 36:552-63.

Briggs, C. L. 1986. *Learning How to Ask: A Sociolinguistic Appraisal of the Role of the Interview in Social Science Research.* Cambridge: Cambridge University Press.

Bristow, A. R. and J. A. Esper. 1988. "A Feminist Research Ethos." In *A Feminist Ethic for Social Science Research,* edited by Nebraska Sociological Feminist Collective. New York: Edwin Mellen.

Bruner, J. 1986. *Actual Minds, Possible Worlds.* Cambridge, MA: Harvard University Press.

Chase, S. 1996. "Personal Vulnerability and Interpretive Authority in Narrative Research." Pp. 45-59 in *The Narrative Study of Lives,* Vol. 4, *Ethics and Process in the Narrative Study of Lives,* edited by R. Josselson. Thousand Oaks, CA: Sage.

Chase, S. and C. Bell. 1994. "Interpreting the Complexity of Women's Subjectivity." Pp. 63-81 in *Interactive Oral History Interviewing,* edited by E. McMahon and K. L. Rogers. Hillsdale, NJ: Lawrence Erlbaum.

Clough, P. T. 1999. "And Now Writing." Presented at the annual meeting of the Society for the Study of Symbolic Interaction, August, Chicago.

Collins, P. H. 1986. "Learning from the Outsider Within: The Sociological Significance of Black Feminist Thought." *Social Problems* 33:14-32.

Cook, J. A. and M. M. Fonow. 1986. "Knowledge and Women's Interests: Issues of Epistemology and Methodology in Feminist Sociological Research." *Sociological Inquiry* 56:2-27.

Coyle, S. 1998. "Dancing with the Chameleon." Pp. 147-63 in *Fiction and Social Research: By Ice or Fire,* edited by A. Banks and S. P. Banks. Walnut Creek, CA: AltaMira.

Crapanzano, V. 1980. *Tuhami: Portrait of a Moroccan.* Chicago: University of Chicago Press.

Denzin, N. K. 1999. "Performing Montana: Part II." Presented at the annual meeting of the Society for the Study of Symbolic Interaction, August, Chicago.

DeVault, M. L. 1990. "Talking and Listening from Women's Standpoint: Feminist Strategies for Interviewing and Analysis." *Social Problems* 37:96-116.

———. 1999. *Liberating Method: Feminism and Social Research.* Philadelphia: Temple University Press.

Douglas, J. D. 1985. *Creative Interviewing.* Beverly Hills, CA: Sage.

Duelli Klein, R. 1983. "How to Do What We Want to Do: Thoughts about Feminist Methodology." Pp. 99-121 in *Theories of Women's Studies,* edited by G. Bowles and R. Duelli Klein. New York: Routledge & Kegan Paul.

Dumont, J.-P. 1978. *The Headman and I: Ambiguity and Ambivalence in the Fieldworking Experience.* Austin: University of Texas Press.

Edwards, R. 1993. "An Education in Interviewing: Placing the Researcher and the Research." Pp. 181-96 in *Researching Sensitive Topics,* edited by C. M. Renzetti and R. M. Lee. Newbury Park, CA: Sage.

Eisenberg, E. M. 1998. "From Anxiety to Possibility: Poems 1987-1997." Pp. 195-202 in *Fiction and Social Research: By Ice or Fire,* edited by A. Banks and S. P. Banks. Walnut Creek, CA: AltaMira.

Ellingson, L. 1998. " 'Then You Know How I Feel': Empathy, Identification, and Reflexivity in Fieldwork." *Qualitative Inquiry* 4:492-514.

Elliott, R. 1986. "Interpersonal Process Recall (IPR) as a Psychotherapy Process Research Method." Pp. 503-28 in *The Psychotherapeutic Process: A Research Handbook,* edited by L. Greeneberg and W. Pinsof. New York: Guilford.

Ellis, C. 1993. " 'There Are Survivors': Telling a Story of Sudden Death." *Sociological Quarterly* 34:711-30.

———. 1995. *Final Negotiations: A Story of Love, Loss, and Chronic Illness.* Philadelphia: Temple University Press.

———. 1996. "Maternal Connections." Pp. 240-43 in *Composing Ethnography: Alternative Forms of Qualitative Writing,* edited by C. Ellis and A. P. Bochner. Walnut Creek, CA: AltaMira.

———. 1998. "Exploring Loss through Autoethnographic Inquiry: Autoethnographic Stories, Co-constructed Narratives, and Interactive Interviews." Pp. 49-61 in *Perspectives on Loss: A Sourcebook,* edited by J. H. Harvey. Philadelphia: Taylor & Francis.

Ellis, C. and A. P. Bochner. 1992. "Telling and Performing Personal Stories: The Constraints of Choice in Abortion." Pp. 79-101 in *Investigating Subjectivity: Research on Lived Experience,* edited by C. Ellis and M. G. Flaherty. Newbury Park, CA: Sage.

————, eds. 1996. *Composing Ethnography: Alternative Forms of Qualitative Writing.* Walnut Creek, CA: AltaMira.

————. 2000. "Autoethnography, Personal Narrative, Reflexivity: Researcher as Subject." Pp. 733-68 in *Handbook of Qualitative Research,* 2d ed., edited by N. K. Denzin and Y. S. Lincoln. Thousand Oaks, CA: Sage.

Ellis, C., C. E. Kiesinger, and L. M. Tillmann-Healy. 1997. "Interactive Interviewing: Talking about Emotional Experience." Pp. 119-49 in *Reflexivity and Voice,* edited by R. Hertz. Thousand Oaks, CA: Sage.

Finch, J. 1984. " 'It's Great to Have Someone to Talk To': The Ethics and Politics of Interviewing Women." Pp. 70-87 in *Social Researching: Politics, Problems, Practice,* edited by C. Bell and H. Roberts. London: Routledge & Kegan Paul.

Fox, K. 1996. "Silent Voices: A Subversive Reading of Child Sexual Abuse." Pp. 330-47 in *Composing Ethnography: Alternative Forms of Qualitative Writing,* edited by C. Ellis and A. P. Bochner. Walnut Creek, CA: AltaMira.

Futrell, A. and C. Willard. 1994. "Intersubjectivity and Interviewing." Pp. 83-105 in *Interactive Oral History Interviewing,* edited by E. McMahon and K. L. Rogers. Hillsdale, NJ: Lawrence Erlbaum.

Gale, J. 1992. "When Research Interviews Are More Therapeutic Than Therapy Interviews." *Qualitative Report* 1 [On-line]. Available Internet: http://www.nova.edu/ssss/QR/QR1-4/gale.html

Goodall, H. L., Jr. 1991. *Living in the Rock 'n' Roll Mystery: Reading Context, Self, and Others as Clues.* Carbondale: Southern Illinois University Press.

————. 1999. *Writing the New Ethnography.* Walnut Creek, CA: AltaMira.

Griffith, A. and D. Smith. 1987. "Constructing Cultural Knowledge: Mothering as Discourse." Pp. 87-103 in *Women and Education,* edited by J. Gaskell and A. T. McLaren. Calgary, Alberta: Detselig.

Gubrium, J. F. and J. A. Holstein. 1997. *The New Language of Qualitative Method.* New York: Oxford University Press.

Hertz, R. 1995. "Separate but Simultaneous Interviewing of Husbands and Wives: Making Sense of Their Stories." *Qualitative Inquiry* 1:429-51.

Holstein, J. A. and J. F. Gubrium. 1995. *The Active Interview.* Thousand Oaks, CA: Sage.

Hutchinson, S., M. Wilson, and H. S. Wilson. 1994. "Benefits of Participating in Research Interviews." *Image: Journal of Nursing Scholarship* 26:161-64.

Jackson, M. 1989. *Paths toward a Clearing: Radical Empiricism and Ethnographic Inquiry.* Bloomington: Indiana University Press.

Jago, B. 1996. "Postcards, Ghosts, and Fathers: Revising Family Stories." *Qualitative Inquiry* 2:495-516.

Jones, S. H. 1998. *Kaleidoscope Notes: Writing Women's Music and Organizational Culture.* Walnut Creek, CA: AltaMira.

Jorgenson, J. 1991. "Co-constructing the Interviewer/Co-constructing 'Family.' " Pp. 210-25 in *Research and Reflexivity,* edited by F. Steier. London: Sage.

————. 1995. "Relationalizing Rapport in Interpersonal Settings." Pp. 155-70 in *Social Approaches to Communication,* edited by W. Leeds-Hurwitz. New York: Guilford.

Josselson, R. 1996. "On Writing Other People's Lives: Self-Analytic Reflections of a Narrative Researcher." Pp. 60-71 in *The Narrative Study of Lives,* Vol. 4, *Ethics and Process in the Narrative Study of Lives,* edited by R. Josselson. Thousand Oaks, CA: Sage.

Karp, D. A. 1996. *Speaking of Sadness: Depression, Disconnection, and the Meanings of Illness.* New York: Oxford University Press.

Kiesinger, C. 1992. "Writing It Down: Sisters, Food, Eating, and Body Image." Unpublished manuscript, University of South Florida, Tampa.

————. 1995. "Anorexic and Bulimic Lives: Making Sense of Food and Eating." Ph.D. dissertation, University of South Florida, Tampa.

————. 1998. "Portrait of an Anorexic Life." Pp. 115-36 in *Fiction and Social Research: By Ice or Fire,* edited by A. Banks and S. P. Banks. Walnut Creek, CA: AltaMira.

Kolker, A. 1996. "Thrown Overboard: The Human Costs of Health Care Rationing." Pp. 133-59 in *Composing Ethnography: Alternative Forms of Qualitative Writing,* edited by C. Ellis and A. P. Bochner. Walnut Creek, CA: AltaMira.

Kondo, D. K. 1990. *Crafting Selves: Power, Gender, and Discourses of Identity in a Japanese Workplace.* Chicago: University of Chicago Press,

Krieger, S. 1991. *Social Science and the Self: Personal Essays on an Art Form.* New Brunswick, NJ: Rutgers University Press.

———. 1996. *The Family Silver: Essays on Relationships among Women.* Berkeley: University of California Press.

Kulick, D. and M. Willson, eds. 1995. *Taboo: Sex, Identity, and Erotic Subjectivity in Anthropological Fieldwork.* London: Routledge.

Kvale, S. 1996. *InterViews: An Introduction to Qualitative Research Interviewing.* Thousand Oaks, CA: Sage.

Lagerwey, M. 1998. *Reading Auschwitz.* Walnut Creek, CA: AltaMira.

Langellier, K. and D. Hall. 1989. "Interviewing Women: A Phenomenological Approach to Feminist Communication Research." Pp. 193-220 in *Doing Research on Women's Communication,* edited by K. Carter and C. Spitzack. Norwood, NJ: Ablex.

Larson, C. L. 1997. "Re-presenting the Subject: Problems in Personal Narrative Inquiry." *International Journal of Qualitative Studies in Education* 10:455-70.

Lather, P. and C. Smithies. 1997. *Troubling the Angels: Women Living with HIV/AIDS.* Boulder, CO: Westview.

Lewin, E. and W. L. Leap. 1996. *Out in the Field: Reflections of Lesbian and Gay Anthropologists.* Urbana: University of Illinois Press.

Lewis, J. and B. Meredith. 1988. *Daughters Who Care: Daughters Caring for Mothers at Home.* London: Routledge & Kegan Paul.

Lieblich, A. 1996. "Some Unforeseen Outcomes of Conducting Narrative Research with People of One's Own Culture." Pp. 151-84 in *The Narrative Study of Lives,* Vol. 4, *Ethics and Process in the Narrative Study of Lives,* edited by R. Josselson. Thousand Oaks, CA: Sage.

Linden, R. R. 1993. *Making Stories, Making Selves: Feminist Reflections on the Holocaust.* Columbus: Ohio State University Press.

Macleod, V. A. 1999. " 'Getting It Off Our Chests': Living with Breast Cancer Survival." Ph.D. dissertation. Department of Interdisciplinary Education, University of South Florida, Tampa.

Maione, P. V. and R. J. Chenail. 1999. "Qualitative Inquiry in Psychotherapy: Research on the Common Factors." Pp. 57-88 in *The Heart and Soul of Change: The Role of Common Factors in Psychotherapy,* edited by M. A. Hubble, B. L. Duncan, and S. D. Miller. Washington, DC: American Psychological Association.

Markham, A. M. 1998. *Life Online: Researching Real Experience in Virtual Space.* Walnut Creek, CA: AltaMira.

Mies, M. 1983. "Toward a Methodology for Feminist Research." Pp. 117-39 in *Theories of Women's Studies,* edited by G. Bowles and R. Duelli Klein. New York: Routledge & Kegan Paul.

Miller, M. 1996. "Ethics and Understanding through Interrelationship: I and Thou in Dialogue." Pp. 129-47 in *The Narrative Study of Lives,* Vol. 4, *Ethics and Process in the Narrative Study of Lives,* edited by R. Josselson. Thousand Oaks, CA: Sage.

Mishler, E. G. 1986. *Research Interviewing: Context and Narrative.* Cambridge, MA: Harvard University Press.

Murphy, R. F. 1987. *The Body Silent.* New York: Holt.

Myerhoff, B. 1978. *Number Our Days.* New York: Simon & Schuster.

———. 1992. *Remembered Lives: The Work of Rituals, Storytelling, and Growing Older.* Ann Arbor: University of Michigan Press.

Mykhalovskiy, E. 1997. "Reconsidering Table Talk: Critical Thoughts on the Relationship between Sociology, Autobiography and Self-Indulgence." Pp. 229-51 in *Reflexivity and Voice,* edited by R. Hertz. Thousand Oaks, CA: Sage.

Oakley, A. 1981. "Interviewing Women: A Contradiction in Terms?" Pp. 30-61 in *Doing Feminist Research,* edited by H. Roberts. London: Routledge & Kegan Paul.

Ochberg, R. L. 1996. "Interpreting Life Stories." Pp. 97-113 in *The Narrative Study of Lives*, Vol. 4, *Ethics and Process in the Narrative Study of Lives*, edited by R. Josselson. Thousand Oaks, CA: Sage.

Pacanowsky, M. 1988. "Slouching towards Chicago: Fiction as Scholarly Writing." *Quarterly Journal of Speech* 74:453-68.

Paget, M. 1993. *A Complex Sorrow: Reflections on Cancer and an Abbreviated Life*. Philadelphia: Temple University Press.

Parry, A. 1991. "A Universe of Stories." *Family Process* 30:37-54.

Payne, D. 1996. "Autobiology." Pp. 49-75 in *Composing Ethnography: Alternative Forms of Qualitative Writing*, edited by C. Ellis and A. P. Bochner. Walnut Creek, CA: AltaMira.

Perry, J. 1996. "Writing the Self: Exploring the Stigma of Hearing Impairment." *Sociological Spectrum* 16:239-61.

Platt, J. 1981. "On Interviewing One's Peers." *British Journal of Sociology* 32:75-91.

Ponticelli, C. 1996. "The Spiritual Warfare of Exodus: A Postpositivist Research Adventure." *Qualitative Inquiry* 2:198-219.

Quinney, R. 1996. "Once My Father Traveled West to California." Pp. 349-74 in *Composing Ethnography: Alternative Forms of Qualitative Writing*, edited by C. Ellis and A. P. Bochner. Walnut Creek, CA: AltaMira.

Rabinow, P. 1977. *Reflections on Fieldwork in Morocco*. Berkeley: University of California Press.

Reinharz, S. 1992. *Feminist Methods in Social Research*. New York: Oxford University Press.

Renzetti, C. M. and R. M. Lee, eds. 1993. *Researching Sensitive Topics*. Newbury Park, CA: Sage.

Richardson, L. 1992. "The Consequences of Poetic Representation: Writing the Other, Rewriting the Self." Pp. 125-37 in *Investigating Subjectivity: Research on Lived Experience*, edited by C. Ellis and M. G. Flaherty. Newbury Park, CA: Sage.

———. 1994. "Writing: A Method of Inquiry." Pp. 516-29 in *Handbook of Qualitative Research*, edited by N. K. Denzin and Y. S. Lincoln. Thousand Oaks, CA: Sage.

———. 1997. *Fields of Play: Constructing an Academic Life*. New Brunswick, NJ: Rutgers University Press.

———. 1998 "Meta-Jeopardy." *Qualitative Inquiry* 4:464-68.

Richardson, L. and E. Lockridge. 1998. "Fiction and Ethnography: A Conversation." *Qualitative Inquiry* 4:328-37.

Riessman, C. K. 1987. "When Gender Is Not Enough: Women Interviewing Women." *Gender & Society* 1:172-207.

———. 1993. *Narrative Analysis*. Newbury Park, CA: Sage.

Roberts, H., ed. 1981. *Doing Feminist Research*. London: Routledge & Kegan Paul.

Robillard, A. B. 1997. "Communication Problems in the Intensive Care Unit." Pp. 252-64 in *Reflexivity and Voice*, edited by R. Hertz. Thousand Oaks, CA: Sage.

———. 1999. *Meaning of Disability: The Lived Experience of Paralysis*. Philadelphia: Temple University Press.

Romanoff, B. D. 2001. "Reclaiming Voice: Ethnographic Inquiry and Qualitative Research in a Postmodern Age." In *Meaning Reconstruction and the Experience of Loss*, edited by R. A. Neimeyer. Washington, DC: American Psychological Association.

Ronai, C. R. 1992. "The Reflexive Self through Narrative: A Night in the Life of an Erotic Dancer/Researcher." Pp. 102-24 in *Investigating Subjectivity: Research on Lived Experience*, edited by C. Ellis and M. G. Flaherty. Newbury Park, CA: Sage.

———. 1995. "Multiple Reflections of Child Sex Abuse: An Argument for a Layered Account." *Journal of Contemporary Ethnography* 23:395-426.

Rosaldo, R. 1989. *Culture and Truth: The Remaking of Social Analysis*. Boston: Beacon.

Rosenwald, G. 1996. "Making Whole: Method and Ethics in Mainstream and Narrative Psychology." Pp. 245-74 in *The Narrative Study of Lives*, Vol. 4, *Ethics and Process in the Narrative Study of Lives*, edited by R. Josselson. Thousand Oaks, CA: Sage.

Ross, J. L. and P. Geist. 1997. "Elation and Devastation: Women's Journeys through Pregnancy and Miscarriage." Pp. 167-84 in *Courage of Conviction: Women's Words, Women's Wisdom*, edited by L. A. M. Perry and P. Geist. Mountain View, CA: Mayfield.

Rothman, B. K. 1986. "Reflections: On Hard Work." *Qualitative Sociology* 9:48-53.

Satir, V. 1983. *Conjoint Family Therapy*. 3d ed. Palo Alto, CA: Science & Behavior.

Segura, D. 1989. "Chicana and Mexican Immigrant Women at Work: The Impact of Class, Race and Gender on Occupational Mobility." *Gender & Society* 3:37-52.

Shostak, A., ed. 1996. *Private Sociology: Unsparing Reflections, Uncommon Gains*. Dix Hills, NY: General Hall.

Stacey, J. 1988. "Can There Be a Feminist Ethnography?" *Women's Studies International Forum* 11:21-27.

Stanley, L. and S. Wise. 1983. " 'Back into the Personal'; or, Our Attempt to Construct 'Feminist Research.' " Pp. 20-62 in *Theories of Women's Studies*, edited by G. Bowles and R. Duelli Klein. London: Routledge & Kegan Paul.

Stringer, E. 1996. *Action Research: A Handbook for Practitioners*. Thousand Oaks, CA: Sage.

Suchman, L. and B. Jordan. 1992. "Validity and the Collaborative Construction of Meaning in Face-to-Face Surveys." Pp. 241-67 in *Questions about Questions: Inquiries into the Cognitive Bases of Surveys*, edited by J. M. Tanur. New York: Russell Sage Foundation.

Tillmann-Healy, L. M. 1996. "A Secret Life in a Culture of Thinness: Reflections on Body, Food, and Bulimia." Pp. 77-109 in *Composing Ethnography: Alternative Forms of Qualitative Writing*, edited by C. Ellis and A. P. Bochner. Walnut Creek, CA: AltaMira.

Tillmann-Healy, L. M. and C. Kiesinger. 2000. "Mirrors: Seeing Each Other and Ourselves Through Fieldwork." Pp. 81-108 in *The Emotional Nature of Qualitative Research*, edited by K. R. Gilbert. Boca Raton, FL: CRC.

Tripp, D. 1983. "Co-authorship and Negotiation: The Interview as Act of Creation." *Interchange* 14:32-45.

Trujillo, N. 1998. "In Search of Naunny's Grave." *Text and Performance Quarterly* 18:344-68.

Webb, C. 1984. "Feminist Methodology in Nursing Research." *Journal of Advanced Nursing* 9:249-56.

Williams, P. 1991. *The Alchemy of Race and Rights: Diary of a Law Professor*. Cambridge, MA: Harvard University Press.

Yerby, J. and W. Gourd. 1994. "Our Marriage/Their Marriage: Performing Reflexive Fieldwork." Presented at the annual Couch and Stone Symposium of the Society for the Study of Symbolic Interaction, University of Illinois, Urbana-Champagne.

Zola, I. K. 1982a. *Missing Pieces: A Chronicle of Living with a Disability*. Philadelphia: Temple University Press.

——. 1982b. *Ordinary Lives: Voices of Disability*. Watertown, MA: Applewood.

24

INTERVIEWING, POWER/KNOWLEDGE, AND SOCIAL INEQUALITY

◆ Charles L. Briggs

Back in 1986, I published a book titled *Learning How to Ask: A Sociolinguistic Appraisal of the Role of the Interview in Social Science Research*. Analyzing interviews that I had conducted during more than a decade's research in New Mexico, I argued that the interview is fairly unique and rather poorly understood as a communicative event. I was particularly interested in the asymmetries of power that emerge in interview situations and how they are embodied in what I referred to as "metacommunicative norms," principles that invest interviewers with control over the referential content of what is said (by posing questions), the length and scope of answers (by deciding when to probe or ask a new question), and the way that all participants construct their positionality with respect to the interview and the information it produces. Interview data have multiple

footings, to use Erving Goffman's (1981) term, being simultaneously rooted in the dynamics of the interview, the social spheres constructed by the responses, and the academic or other domains (theoretical and empirical) that give rise to the project and to which it contributes.

I argued that differences between contrasting sets of such norms often lead to problems that range from misunderstandings to resistance and conflict between interviewers and respondents. I suggested that interviewing deploys discourse that is highly adapted to producing the precise types of information that will be recontextualized in the books, articles, reports, media productions, and the like that are envisioned as the final product. When interviews provide the nation-state and its institutions with representations of marginalized populations, the possibilities for constructing a "minority voice" that confirms the hegemonic status quo is thus acute.

My goal was not to suggest that researchers should abandon interviews, a position that would be as counterproductive as it would be unrealistic. Rather, I sought to bring into focus the discrepancy between the complex character of interview data as discursive phenomena and the way they are reified as reflections of the social phenomena depicted in questions and answers. I also attempted to demonstrate how deeply the power relations that emerge in interviews are embedded in the data they produce. Drawing on work in a number of fields, I suggested that this discursive mediation should not be viewed as a source of contamination but rather as a crucial source of insights into both interviewing processes and the social worlds they seek to document.

The present juncture provides an excellent moment to return to these questions. A great deal of work—inspired by poststructuralism; postmodernism; ethnic, cultural, and women's studies; subaltern studies; research on globalization; and other perspectives—has explored the way that discourses of difference lie at the center of producing and resisting structures of social inequality. At the same time, the social and political importance of interviews of many sorts has expanded greatly in the decade and a half since I published my study; we now live, as Paul Atkinson and David Silverman (1997) put it, in the interview society. In many countries, a populist aura attempts simultaneously to project the voice of the "average citizen" into the middle of electoral politics and to place the voices of candidates and officials as those of concerned citizens or political outsiders; this political agenda is closely tied to new communications technologies. Television and radio programs that specialize in interviews with persons who have special stories to tell, candidates, politicians, specialists, and celebrities have flourished. Political candidates use question-and-answer-based media events as central features of electoral campaigns, and polling increasingly guides who runs, what candidates say, and whom they address.

My goal in this chapter is to extend the discursive analysis of power relations in the interview that I began in *Learning How to Ask* in such a way as to connect it with approaches to discourse that emerge from these perspectives and historical developments. I hope to be able to provide some insight into why interviewing is playing such a profound role in shaping forms of knowledge and practices in contemporary society and how interviews are being used in legitimating the growing social inequality that characterizes a globalizing world. I argue that research on interviewing can deeply inform contemporary concerns with knowledge, power, and difference.

◆ Modernity, Knowledge, and Power

Zygmunt Bauman (1987) argues that modernity created pervasive asymmetries of knowledge and power and used them in recasting growing social inequality, which was being exacerbated by the emergent capitalist economy, as the product of individual differences. John Locke ([1690] 1959) played a key role in creating a new cartography of language, knowledge, and discourse that mapped social inequality. In his *Essay Concerning Human Understanding*, Locke sharply separated rational reflections on individual experience and the articulation of thought in "plain," serious speech from imprecise, shifting, ambiguous uses of words, which he associated with rhetoric, poetry, and the like. This linguistic cartography was projected onto a social one. Gentlemen, who had the leisure and training to reflect rationally on their use of language, exemplified ideal speech. Women, the poor, laborers, merchants, cooks, lovers, and rural folk, on the other hand, spoke in the imprecise ways that Locke condemned; such persons were largely incapable of developing greater rationality and linguistic precision by virtue of their lives. Inhabitants of the Americas provided Locke with an image of the linguistic baseline, the sort of knowledge of language that humans possess before their speech is shaped by civilization. Locke's discursive model of the modern subject—autonomous, disinterested, and rational—became the model of the scientist (see Shapin 1994), the citizen (see MacPherson 1962), and the public sphere (see Habermas [1962] 1989). At the same time, another fellow of the Royal Society, John Aubrey, was interviewing the traditional people of the countryside in constructing a portrait of the customs and language that defined modernity vis-à-vis its premodern opposite (see Aubrey 1972; Bauman and Briggs in press).

The productiveness of Locke's program seems to revolve around a central contradiction. His ideology projected an overtly egalitarian tone in that it constructed language as an essential part of the makeup of all human beings. At the same time, Locke authorized a set of standardizing practices and a powerful means of assessing the rationality of each individual and instituting gatekeeping mechanisms. Locke's ideology of language and politics naturalized both the emergent social and political structures of modernity and the idea that the degree to which individuals approximate the ideal of the modern subject naturally locates them within relations of inequality.

Zygmunt Bauman (1987) goes on to argue that this knowledge-inequality connection prompted the rise of "legislators" who exercise surveillance and control over the projected transformation of their social inferiors from premodern to modern ways of knowing. Arguing that we must examine how "effects of power circulate among scientific statements, what constitutes, as it were, their internal régime of power,"

Michel Foucault (1980:112) has pointed to the role of legislators in medical, legal, criminological, academic, and other institutions in producing discourses that create the objects they regulate.

The power invested in interviews to construct discourses that are then legitimated as the words of others points to their effectiveness as technologies that can be used in naturalizing the role of specialists in creating systems of difference. But we can also take a larger lesson from Foucault's work. Ian Hacking (1990) suggests that the systematic collection and publication of statistics by the nation-state regarding the lives of its citizens produced a revolution in the 19th century in terms of the way in which society was conceptualized and structured, one that centered on statistical definitions of the "normal" subject and its "abnormal" counterparts. We might suggest, following Foucault, that the growing ubiquity and visibility of interviewing in the 20th century has created a widely disseminated idea that both social similarity and difference can best be explained through the use of interviews to reveal individual social and intrapsychic worlds and to compare them, thereby identifying patterns of consensus and disagreement. Interviewing is thus a "technology" that invents both notions of individual subjectivities and collective social and political patterns and then obscures the operation of this process beneath notions of objectivity and science—or, in the case of journalistic and television interviews, of insight and art.

Although Foucault draws our attention to institutions as epistemological regimes, he does little to elucidate the social dynamics that render them such powerful sites for producing discourse. Drawing on sociolinguistic research (see Hymes 1974), Pierre Bourdieu (1991) argues that forms of communicative competence constitute symbolic capital, the acquisition of which is constrained by such gatekeeping institutions as schools and professional societies (see also Erickson and Shultz 1982). Members of dominant sectors use interviews in furthering institutionalized agendas, such as the compilation of census information and the use of surveying for purposes of enhancing consumption or devising political rhetoric. Bourdieu ([1972] 1979, 1990) suggests that polling creates the illusion of a "public opinion," creating images of national conversations that serve the interests of institutions whose legitimacy derives from the relations of class-based inequality that are reproduced in the supposedly inclusive nature of this "public." Drawing on Bourdieu, we can suggest that interviews create and sustain the power relations of modern society in a variety of ways, by producing representations of social life that are deeply and invisibly informed by class relations and by providing modes of screening individuals, through employment, counseling, social service, and other interviews, for the forms of competence that will position them in relation to institutions. Dominated communities are common targets for interview projects, providing both models of difference and objects of surveillance and regulation.

Having reflected more deeply on the work of Foucault and Bourdieu during the past 15 years, I would criticize my earlier study for rooting its analysis of power too directly in interview settings themselves. Applying these writers' perspectives suggests that it is the *circulation* of discourse among a range of institutional contexts that imbues interviews with the power to shape contemporary life. Nevertheless, neither Foucault nor Bourdieu is very helpful when it comes to identifying concretely the discursive and institutional means by which this circulation takes place and how we can trace it in particular instances. Here the totalizing thrust of viewing discourse as political technology or symbolic capital can be suitably complemented by a discourse-analytic perspective that explores textual and contextual dimensions of the production, circulation, and interpretation of interviews as grounded social practice.

◆ Heteroglossia and Recontextualization in Interviews

Hayden White (1978) argues that the power of historical narratives derives from the way their rhetoric achieves two contradictory effects. First, historians imagine past events, thereby creating schemes of social classification and forms of agency and causation. Interview researchers similarly imagine the social worlds depicted in the content of responses, creating images of political participation, family life, work experience, and so forth. But interview materials simultaneously imagine an intra-psychic world for the interviewee, a space inhabited by opinions, memories, emotions, plans, preferences, and desires. As I argued in *Learning How to Ask,* interviews are saturated by images of the social dynamics of the interview itself, projections of the social context in which it takes place, the roles and power dynamics of interviewer and respondent, and their respective agendas. But a fourth sphere is being constructed, that of the imagined texts that will be created through the use of interview data. This realm becomes explicit in statements on consent forms regarding the textual rights that participants are granting researchers. The disclaimers that interviewees frequently insert, such as "I don't want the people who read your book to get the impression that . . . ," suggest that respondents often shape their responses in keeping with imaginings of future texts and audiences. Not only are these four realms constructed simultaneously, but interviews are punctuated by the distinct and often competing imaginations of researchers and respondents.

Second, historical rhetoric converts the arbitrary into the real, casting imaginations as reflections of what actually took place, thereby hiding the imaginary and arbitrary character of such constructions. Although a variety of strategies for converting imaginations into reality are used in the wealth of different sorts of projects that rely on interviews, erasing the third and fourth realms constructed in interviews in favor of the first two is key. In other words, some researchers highlight opinions, memories, and other reflections of the mental worlds of the respondents; others foreground the social worlds that are represented. Both of these strategies revolve around obscuring the role of constructions of the social dynamics of the interview and the way projected uses of the data are embedded in responses.

The richest rhetorical resource for the erasure of these domains consists of techniques for eliminating "distortion" and "bias"—explicit signs of the effects of the interaction and perceptions of research agendas on interview content. Suggesting that interview data (including surveys) can be obtained in such a way that their contextual grounding can be factored out (through sampling, question wording, training of interviewers, and the like) constitutes simultaneously a claim to the epistemological marginality of these realms and a prohibition on allowing any explicit evidence of their presence to appear in texts that report interview data.

Feminist interviewing has often made the position of the interviewer in relationship to the respondent a central object of description and analysis (see DeVault 1990; Harding 1987; Reinharz 1992; see also in this volume Reinharz and Chase, Chapter 4; DeVault and McCoy, Chapter 18). A great deal of attention has focused on the use of narratives that emerge in interviews as means of drawing attention to the complex processes that shape the construction of identities in interviews (see, e.g., Bruner 1990; Chase 1995; Mishler 1986, 2000; Riessman 1993). Postmodern scholars have sometimes violated this prohibition systematically and explicitly, highlighting the interaction between the participants and their visions of how the materials will be used; Ruth Behar's (1993) *Translated Woman* provides a notable example. Norman Denzin (1989) and others have brought postmodern perspectives to bear on the issue of interviewing in general, questioning the privileged authority of the interviewer or researcher and urging a decentering of subject positions.

Such notions as bias, distortion, reliability, and validity reveal a great deal about the assumptions that commonly underlie interview-based research. Elliot Mishler (1986) argues that researchers commonly see interview data as behavior that can be analyzed using stimulus-response models associated with scientific experimentation. The information obtained in this manner is seen as a set of stable "social facts" that have an objective existence independent of the linguistic and contextual settings in which they are "expressed" (see Karp and Kendall 1982). Jaber Gubrium and James Holstein (1997) suggest that this epistemological stance of naturalism, the notion that the task of researchers is to richly and accurately document the "natural" environment of the social world without disrupting it, lies at the center of much qualitative research and inspires related concerns. The reductionism of received interview practices also springs from Western ideologies of language (see Joseph and Taylor 1990; Schieffelin, Woolard, and Kroskrity 1998; Kroskrity 2000) that treat verbal interaction in Lockean fashion as a transfer of referential content from one party to another, as if participants had no interests or communicative foci that interfere with their playing the roles of interviewer and respondent (see Back and Cross 1982; Clark and Schober 1992; Dijkstra and van der Zouwen 1977, 1982: 3-4; Foddy 1993: 13-14). Interviewing thus provides a valuable source of data on the ideologies of language that underlie social scientific research, particularly in that conceptions that have been banished from the realm of explicit theory are often preserved implicitly in "purely methodological" spheres.

The complexity of interviews does not emerge simply from the manner in which connections with distinct realms are imagined in the course of interviews. Rather, the process involves practices for extracting discourse from one social setting and inserting it in a range of other settings. In my work with Richard Bauman, we have argued that a vital part of the process of rendering discourse socially powerful involves gaining control over its recontextualization—rights to determine when, where, how, and by whom it will be used in other settings (Bauman and Briggs 1990; Briggs and Bauman 1992; see also Silverstein and Urban 1996). Interview discourse is maximally configured in terms of both form and content for recontextualization into the sorts of texts that the researcher anticipates creating—interviewees are granted very few rights over this process. Survey instruments and techniques for implementing them maximize the social control of interviewers by the researchers who direct the study as well of interviewees by interviewers, creating hierarchies of discursive authority that also include individuals responsible for coding data.

The recontextualization process provides another angle on the complexity of interview data. A statement that emerges in an interview is tied explicitly to the question that precedes it and generally indirectly to previous questions and responses, the broad range of texts, agendas, and contexts that shape questions and interviewing practices, and the anticipated uses of the data. Quotations or summaries taken from interviews used in publications are, of course, deeply entwined in this broad range of recontextualizations. As the work of Mikhail Bakhtin (1981) would suggest, this recontextualization process informs each word that is spoken, such that the different contexts, vocabularies, styles, subject positions, and the like are built into what is said and how it is uttered. Responses are like crossroads at which multiple paths converge, with signs pointing in all directions.

The power of researchers thus lies not only in their control over what takes place in the interview itself but particularly in their ability to use that setting as a site that is geared toward creating a broad field for the circulation of discourse.

At the same time that researchers attempt to control how material will move between different sites, they seek to render all save a few dimensions of this process invisible. In order to seem "unbiased" and to be suitable for recontextualization in a range of future settings, interview materials must be systematically decontextualized in various ways, leaving only minimal road signs that point in the direction of social or intrapsychic worlds. Otherwise, data and analyses are likely to be rejected by positivistic researchers either as biased or as being too complex and contextually specific to permit abstraction and generalization. Atkinson and Silverman (1997) observe that even many critical, revisionist approaches to interviewing attempt to empower individuals to create biographical, authentic voices, thereby reifying an individual and confessional approach to discourse that is also promoted by corporate media. The indexical signs that point, as it were, to the embedding of this process in larger social and material structures are thus largely erased.

One advantage in viewing interviews not as unified political technologies but as politically situated and interested practices for producing and recontextualizing discourse is that this perspective enables us to see that respondents often attempt to resist discursive relations that are stacked against them. The literature on interviewing abounds with advice regarding "uncooperative" respondents (see Adler and Adler, Chapter 8, this volume). Scholars seldom seem to recognize that individuals who decline to participate or to answer particular questions, or who plead ignorance, "mislead" the interviewer, and the like, may be pursuing strategies designed to disrupt the recontextualization process (see

Dunbar, Rodriguez, and Parker, Chapter 7, this volume).

I suggested in *Learning How to Ask* that the apparent failure of interviews I conducted early in my research on "Mexicanos" or Mexican Americans in New Mexico reflected precisely this type of contestation. The fact that I had a research project in hand and was asking reasonable questions of individuals who had detailed knowledge of the issues in question led me to believe that extensive answers would be forthcoming. My elderly respondents saw things differently. As the most authoritative sources of information on Mexicano cultural politics, they found it difficult to accept the idea that a young gringo should structure such discussions. Most of my initial questions were thus met with a jolting "¡Pues, quién sabe! [Well, who knows!]." By learning to respect these individuals' right to control the recontextualization of discourse about the past, I was able to gain insight not only into Mexican cultural politics but into the politics of memory and strategies of resistance to cultural and political-economic domination.

◆ Three Contradictions of Power and Knowledge in Contemporary Society

I alluded above to the way that differences in the distribution of knowledge came to be viewed as explaining social inequality in modern society. Locke clearly articulated a fundamental modernist contradiction as he simultaneously advanced the idea that common possession of capacities for language, rationality, and reflection render us all part of humanity and condemn most people to subordinate social categories on the basis of their purported failure to develop this potential. Two basic contradictions similarly seem to structure the relationship between knowledge and social inequality in late-capitalist societies, and I suggest that interviewing plays a key role in mediating them.

Lisa Lowe (1996) argues that economic and political structures place people of color in a contradictory position in the United States. On the one hand, the need to maintain a pool of cheap laborers who enjoy few legal and occupational protections prompts the racialization of populations and their placement in subordinate social categories. Immanuel Wallerstein makes a similar argument for the economic underpinnings of the construction of racial categories worldwide (see Balibar and Wallerstein 1991). Nonetheless, U.S. political ideologies are based on the imagination of a shared cultural and political community; ascriptive barriers of race, gender, and class that create hierarchies of types of citizenship thus render it difficult to conceive of U.S. society as actually reflecting this privileged political ideology, at least when these obstacles become visible. The work of critical discourse analysts suggests that similar processes are at work in European nation-states (see Blommaert 1997; Blommaert and Verschueren 1998; van Dijk 1984; Wodak 1999).

By conducting interviews among, say, African Americans, or asserting that X percentage of survey respondents are Latinos, researchers can project the sense that "minorities" are included in national conversations about politics, economics, medicine, education, or whatnot—even when significant (and currently growing) barriers limit the participation of people of color in the institutions that regulate these domains. By the same token, by classifying respondents as members of racialized groups, researchers can create a synecdochic logic that suggests that an Asian American, for example, is speaking *as* an Asian American and is representing all Asian Americans, thereby confirming a sense of people of color as one-sided subjects. These practices also project interviews as capable of including racialized, subordinated voices in a seemingly equal position within national conversations. Whereas native-born, middle-class whites just naturally seem to be part of the dialogue, people of color and working-class persons can be portrayed as needing the mediation of researchers, journalists, or other professionals to make their voices heard on public stages. Here interviewing has assumed a crucial part of the role of the legislator identified by Bauman (1987).

Second, as globalization is augmenting social inequality, both within and between countries, a number of observers have sought to characterize its effects on the participation of populations on the so-called periphery. Arjun Appadurai (1996) argues that globalization is producing new modes of inclusion, suggesting that deterritorialization and denationalization disrupt centralization of control over global flows of capital, people, goods, culture, and information. He thus suggests that the United States no longer dominates "a world system of images but is only one node of a complex transnational construction of imaginary landscapes" (p. 31). Appadurai's vision of globalization is thus one of a global egalitarianism, in that even the poor and powerless can participate actively in shaping widely distributed practices of the imagination.

Other writers view globalization as largely *exclusionary,* as exacerbating social differences based on access to capital, commodities, information, and culture. Michel-Rolph Trouillot (1991) has pinpointed a key issue here in a brief but highly suggestive passage. Insofar as a universal transition is postulated from "modern" to "postmodern" or from "national" to "deterritorialized" ideologies and social forms, what are the implications for social segments that were deemed to have failed to be incorporated into *modern* social, cultural, and economic patterns? If this supposedly universal stage of globalized, postmodern culture is tied to a questioning of the "metanarratives" and cultural premises of modernization, it would seem to exclude people who never gained access to progress and modernity. Zygmunt Bauman (1998)

suggests that the production of social fragmentation, differentiation, and inequality so fundamental to globalization fixes some people in space and restricts access to the globally circulating capital and culture that others increasingly enjoy; getting localized while others get globalized "is a sign of social deprivation and degradation" (p. 2).

CNN provides a striking illustration of the power of interviewing in mediating this contradiction between the inclusive and exclusive effects of globalization. The cable television news network's broadcasts take the voices and images of East Timorese refugees or victims of Venezuelan floods and project them to audiences worldwide, creating the sense of a global conversation. Nevertheless, whereas experts, particularly those living in industrialized countries, can make broad pronouncements on global phenomena, poor victims of wars, epidemics, and disasters are called upon to speak about the most immediate and concrete dimensions of their own experience. Different segments of the same broadcast can present interviews with the president or prime minister of a rich and powerful nation-state, the CEO of a transnational corporation that has just completed a huge merger, and survivors of genocidal campaigns. The sense that the faces, songs, and stories of all people are included in these global flows is thus projected without attention being drawn to the increasingly monopolistic formations of capital and power that determine who gets to speak and when as well as what counts as a local voice.

The illusion of equality goes hand in hand with quite different constructions of historical agency as we view leaders and CEOs speaking about their roles as globalizing agents, as catalysts of changes that produce structural changes that lead to more globalized markets, transnational intervention into affairs of seemingly sovereign nation-states, and greater social inequality. Individuals constructed as localizing agents, on the other hand, are portrayed as experiencing the effects of such policies. Interviews animate the role of the legislator, who controls the production and circulation of public voices on a global basis while creating the illusion that he or she is simply a witness to conversations and events that shape history. Interviewing thus aids the large transnational corporations that own the global media in projecting images of a worldwide community of producers and consumers, and of the very different positions that they occoupy in relation to capital.

◆ *Conclusion*

David Harvey (1989) has argued that new technologies of transport and communication have effected a victory of time over space, producing time-space compression and continual fragmentations of time-space patterns that lead to the postmodern feeling of dislocation. The notion that global capital is undermining the power of nation-states and destroying our sense of place, identity, and authenticity has moved from scholarly discourse, where it has become increasingly criticized and qualified, into popular and corporate discourses. Such influential observers as Robert Putnam (1993) have argued that this process is undermining the foundations of democracy, which are described as resting in the face-to-face interactions that characterized civil society—as epitomized by small-town society. This postmodern nostalgia for a supposedly authentic and interactional past does not, of course, lead Putnam or the governments (including the U.S. government) that have taken up his cry to call for an end to global political intervention or corporate expansion. Rather, it creates a vast need to project what appear to be forms of face-to-face communication and decision making as forming the center of social and political processes.

Enter the interview, that archetype of dyadic communication. Whether interviews take place in interviewees' homes, on *The Oprah Winfrey Show,* or on *CNN Headline News,* or even when interlocutors are connected only by telephone lines, these encounters create vox populi that seemingly provide an interpersonal—rather than purely private or purely public and depersonalized—space for the articulation of individual perspectives. I argued in *Learning How to Ask* that this image is largely illusory, in that interviews are structured by power asymmetries and by conventions that produce discursively complex material that is geared toward the institutional ends for which it was created. I have argued here that construing the interview itself as the locus of knowledge production places audiences and analysts alike in the grip of a powerful illusion. I have suggested, rather, that the power of interviewing lies in the status of the interpersonal interaction as one site in a complex process of controlling the decontextualization and recontextualization of discourse, one that links broader scholarly, corporate, and political agendas; previously circulating messages (be they scholarly literatures or campaign slogans); forms of disciplinary authority or celebrity stature; and the creation of texts, media programs, Web sites, and the like that serve the interests of interviewers and their employers. The sense that the people have spoken through such venues is sustained by the heteroglossic nature of what is said, being shot through with the echo of the words and contexts that shaped its production and that guide its recontextualization.

We are now more thoroughly modern than ever, in the sense that the illusion of shared participation in discourse and the production of knowledge legitimates practices for creating social inequality and modes of exclusion that seem to spring naturally from differences in what individuals know and can project into the public sphere. Ironically, new technologies are reinvigorating desire for the sense that it is interpersonal interaction and self-expression that shape our identities and lives; Internet chat rooms have taken a quite visible place alongside radio and television talk shows, call-ins by listeners and viewers, electronic "town meetings," and interviews by journalists in satisfying this longing. Corporations are increasingly requiring their employees to end service encounters with the briefest of interviews: "How was everything?"

Interviews played key roles in the political technologies of the modern era, being central to the power of the state to enumerate and imagine its citizens, of physicians to medicalize their patients' ills, of psychiatrists to illuminate madness and define sanity, of lawyers and courts to construct criminals and invent crimes, and so forth. As Foucault and many others have argued, these are powers of abstraction, disembodiment, and objectification. As postmodern angst and global insecurity create resistance to master narratives and faceless, bureaucratic control, the productive power of the illusion of social interaction and self-expression that fuels both scholarly and popular senses of interviews positions them even more crucially within the technologies and social relations of a globalized world. As tools are required for inventing new forms of social inequality and the practices

needed to construe them as products of passivity in the face of global forces and/or as individual failings, uses of interviewing are sure to expand.

I called in 1986 for systematic inquiry into the discursive and political underpinnings of interviews and the need to dispense with the illusion that we know what they are and what functions they serve. This call was echoed in the same year by Mishler (1986). The scholarly debates and social, political-economic, and technological transformations that have emerged since that time suggest to me that the failure to devote substantive critical attention to interviews would place scholars as passive onlookers—or willing participants—in creating new practices of imagination for producing and legitimating social inequality in the 21st century. It thus seems clearer than ever that we must establish anew that systematic inquiry into interviewing is of far more than "merely methodological" significance. Just as a political economy of the production and circulation of interview materials and their role in shaping social representations and relations can fundamentally illuminate the dynamics of the historical moment in which we live, such critical perspectives are needed to help us avoid taking on the task of providing a key discursive machinery to be used in extending and naturalizing social inequality.

■ *References*

Appadurai, A. 1996. *Modernity at Large: Cultural Dimensions of Globalization.* Minneapolis: University of Minnesota Press.

Atkinson, P. and D. Silverman. 1997. "Kundera's *Immortality:* The Interview Society and the Invention of Self." *Qualitative Inquiry* 3:304-25.

Aubrey, J. 1972. *Three Prose Works.* Edited by J. Buchanan-Brown. Carbondale: Southern Illinois University Press.

Back, K. W. and T. S. Cross. 1982. "Response Effects of Role Restricted Respondent Characteristics." Pp. 189-207 in *Response Behaviour in the Survey-Interview,* edited by W. Dijkstra and J. van der Zouwen. London: Academic Press.

Bakhtin, M. M. 1981. *The Dialogic Imagination: Four Essays.* Edited by M. Holquist; translated by C. Emerson and M. Holquist. Austin: University of Texas Press.

Balibar, E. and I. Wallerstein. 1991. *Race, Nation, Class: Ambiguous Identities.* London: Verso.

Bauman, R. and C. L. Briggs. 1990. "Poetics and Performance as Critical Perspectives on Language and Social Life." *Annual Review of Anthropology* 19:59-88.

———. in press. *Modernizing Discourse: Language Ideologies and the Politics of Inequality.* Cambridge, UK: Cambridge University Press.

Bauman, Z. 1987. *Legislators and Interpreters: On Modernity, Postmodernity, and Intellectuals.* Ithaca, NY: Cornell University Press.

———. 1998. *Globalization: The Human Consequences.* New York: Columbia University Press.

Behar, R. 1993. *Translated Woman: Crossing the Border with Esperanza's Story.* Boston: Beacon.

Blommaert, J. 1997. "The Slow Shift in Orthodoxy: (Re)formulations of 'Integration' in Belgium." *Pragmatics* 7:499-518.

Blommaert, J. and J. Verschueren. 1998. *Debating Diversity: Analysing the Discourse of Tolerance.* London: Routledge.

Bourdieu, P. [1972] 1979. "Public Opinion Does Not Exist." Pp. 124-30 in P. Bourdieu, *Communication and Class Struggle,* Vol. 1. New York: International General.

———. 1990. "Opinion Polls: A 'Science' without a Scientist." Pp. 168-74 in P. Bourdieu, *In Other Words: Essays Towards a Reflexive Sociology.* Translated by M. Adamson. Cambridge: Polity.

———. 1991. *Language and Symbolic Power.* Translated by G. Raymond and M. Adamson. Cambridge, MA: Harvard University Press.

Briggs, C. L. 1986. *Learning How to Ask: A Sociolinguistic Appraisal of the Role of the Interview in Social Science Research.* Cambridge: Cambridge University Press.

Briggs, C. L. and R. Bauman. 1992. "Genre, Intertextuality, and Social Power." *Journal of Linguistic Anthropology* 2:131-72.

Bruner, J. S. 1990. *Acts of Meaning.* Cambridge, MA: Harvard University Press.

Chase, S. E. 1995. *Ambiguous Empowerment: The Work of Narratives of Women School Superintendents.* Amherst: University of Massachusetts Press.

Clark, H. H. and M. F. Schober. 1992. "Asking Questions and Influencing Answers." Pp. 15-48 in *Questions about Questions: Inquiries into the Cognitive Bases of Surveys,* edited by J. M. Tanur. New York: Russell Sage Foundation.

Denzin, N. K. 1989. *Interpretive Interactionism.* Newbury Park, CA: Sage.

DeVault, M. L. 1990. "Talking and Listening from Women's Standpoint: Feminist Strategies for Interviewing and Analysis." *Social Problems* 37:96-116.

Dijkstra, W. and J. van der Zouwen. 1977. "Testing Auxiliary Hypotheses behind the Interview." *Annals of Systems Research* 6:49-63.

———, eds. 1982. *Response Behaviour in the Survey-Interview.* London: Academic Press.

Erickson, F. and J. Shultz. 1982. *The Counselor as Gatekeeper: Social Interaction in Interviews.* New York: Academic Press.

Foddy, W. 1993. *Constructing Questions for Interviews and Questionnaires: Theory and Practice in Social Research.* Cambridge: Cambridge University Press.

Foucault, M. 1980. *Power/Knowledge: Selected Interviews and Other Writings, 1972-1977.* Edited by C. Gordon; translated by L. Marshall, J. Mepham, and K. Soper. New York: Pantheon.

Goffman, E. 1981. *Forms of Talk.* Philadelphia: University of Pennsylvania Press.

Gubrium, J. F. and J. A. Holstein. 1997. *The New Language of Qualitative Method.* New York: Oxford University Press.

Habermas, J. [1962] 1989. *The Structural Transformation of the Public Sphere: An Inquiry into a Category of Bourgeois Society.* Translated by T. Burger. Cambridge: MIT Press.

Hacking, I. 1990. *The Taming of Chance.* Cambridge: Cambridge University Press.

Harding, S., ed. 1987. *Feminism and Methodology: Social Science Issues.* Bloomington: Indiana University Press.

Harvey, D. 1989. *The Condition of Postmodernity.* Cambridge, MA: Blackwell.

Hymes, D. 1974. *Foundations in Sociolinguistics: An Ethnographic Perspective.* Philadelphia: University of Pennsylvania Press.

Joseph, J. E. and T. J. Taylor, eds. 1990. *Ideologies of Language.* London: Routledge.

Karp, I. and M. B. Kendall. 1982. "Reflexivity in Fieldwork." Pp. 249-73 in *Explaining Social Behavior: Consciousness, Human Action, and Social Structure,* edited by P. F. Secord. Beverly Hills, CA: Sage.

Kroskrity, P. V., ed. 2000. *Regimes of Language: Ideologies, Polities, and Identities.* Santa Fe, NM: School of American Research Press.

Locke, J. [1690] 1959. *An Essay Concerning Human Understanding,* 2 vols. New York: Dover.

Lowe, L. 1996. *Immigrant Acts: On Asian American Cultural Politics.* Durham, NC: Duke University Press.

MacPherson, C. B. 1962. *The Political Theory of Possessive Individualism: Hobbes to Locke.* Oxford: Oxford University Press.

Mishler, E. G. 1986. *Research Interviewing: Context and Narrative.* Cambridge, MA: Harvard University Press.

———. 2000. *Storylines: Craftartists' Narratives of Identity.* Cambridge, MA: Harvard University Press.

Putnam, R. D. 2000. *Bowling Alone: The Collapse and Revival of American Community.* New York: Simon & Schuster.

Reinharz, S. 1992. *Feminist Methods in Social Research.* New York: Oxford University Press.

Riessman, C. K. 1993. *Narrative Analysis.* Newbury Park, CA: Sage.

Schieffelin, B. B., K. A. Woolard, and P. V. Kroskrity, eds. 1998. *Language Ideologies: Practice and Theory.* New York: Oxford University Press.

Shapin, S. 1994. *A Social History of Truth: Civility and Science in Seventeenth-Century England.* Chicago: University of Chicago Press.

Silverstein, M. and G. Urban, eds. 1996. *Natural Histories of Discourse.* Chicago: University of Chicago Press.

Trouillot, M.-R. 1991. "Anthropology and the Savage Slot: The Poetics and Politics of Otherness." Pp. 17-44 in *Recapturing Anthropology: Working in the Present,* edited by R. G. Fox. Santa Fe, NM: School of American Research Press.

van Dijk, T. A. 1984. *Prejudice in Discourse: An Analysis of Ethnic Prejudice in Cognition and Conversation.* Amsterdam: J. Benjamins.

White, H. 1978. *Tropics of Discourse: Essays in Cultural Criticism.* Baltimore: Johns Hopkins University Press.

Wodak, R. 1999. "Discourse and Racism: European Perspectives." *Annual Review of Anthropology* 28:175-99.

AUTHOR INDEX

Abelove, H., 91
Abeyewardene, A., 430
Abu-Lughod, L., 434-435, 451, 471
Acker, J., 49
Ackermann, F., 301
Adam, B., 94
Adams, J. M., 163
Adler, P., 35, 45, 154, 158, 159, 162, 163, 165, 471
Adler, P. A., 35, 45, 154, 157, 158, 159, 160, 162, 163, 165, 471
Agar, M., 187, 294, 301
Agronick, G., 470
Aguilar, N., 296, 297
Ahmed, Q. K., 422-423
Aisenberg, N., 77
Alanko, T., 260
Alasuutari, P., 7
Albrecht, T. L., 35
Albright, L., 126
Allen, B., 358
Allison, D., 483
Altheide, D. L., 274
Altork, K., 81
Amoss, P. T., 113
Anders, E., 242
Andersen, M. L., 85, 134
Anderson, E., 136, 163-164
Anderson, K., 85, 361-362, 470
Anderson, L., 159
Anderson, T., 267, 275

Andre Bechely, L. N., 370
Aneshensel, C. S., 181
Angrosino, M. V., 471, 472
Anspach, R. R., 156-157, 159
Antaki, C., 284, 398, 404
Aoki, K., 252
Appadurai, A., 435, 502
Appleby, J., 364
Apter, T., 470
Aquilino, W. S., 178, 181, 182
Arbinger, P., 242
Archibald, C., 116
Arendell, T., 59, 60, 64, 86
Aristotle, 365
Armitage, S., 470
Armstrong, D., 303
Aron, R., 364
Asad, T., 434
Asher, R., 160
Ashplant, T., 358
Atkinson, J. M., 224, 275, 278, 423
Atkinson, P., 18, 303, 304, 342, 419, 421, 423, 431, 434, 496, 500
Atkinson, R., 450
Attanucci, J., 334
Aubrey, J., 497
Ault, A., 77
Austin, D. A., 471
Aycock, A., 253
Azadovskii, M., 452

SUBJECT INDEX

Accountability, 221-222

Accounts:
  ethnomethodological analysis, 399-401, 410-411
  participant observation, 422, 424-425, 426
  transcription quality, 268, 269-270, 273-275

Adolescents. *See* Child/adolescent interviews

Africa:
  cross-cultural interviewing, 429-430, 432
  secret societies, 156-157

African Americans. *See* Race/ethnicity

Agency:
  child/adolescent interviews, 39
  historical development, 7-8, 9
  narrative analysis, 334, 338
  participant observation, 422
  race/ethnicity, 132
  social inequality, 502-503
  subjects, 13

Alcoholics Anonymous, 84, 451-452

American Occupational Structure, The (Blau/ Duncan), 74

An Invitation to Reflexive Sociology (Bourdieu), 101

Asian Law Journal, 134

Asian/Pacific Islanders. *See* Race/ethnicity

Asymmetrical model:
  empowerment, 16, 17, 19
  interviews, 4, 12
  social inequality, 495, 496

Australia, 42, 436
  ethnomethodology, 396-397, 399-401, 402-403, 408-410

Authenticity:
  empowerment, 17-19, 20
  gays/lesbians, 98, 99-100
  participant observation, 423, 425
  personal narratives, 17-19
  race/ethnicity, 136-137

Authority:
  child/adolescent interviews, 34
  cross-cultural interviewing, 434-435
  gays/lesbians, 97-98, 99
  grounded theory analysis, 313
  historical development, 5, 6
  personal/folk narratives, 450, 453, 455, 457
  race/ethnicity, 134
  women, 86

Autoethnography, 467

Baltimore Sun, 131

Bangladesh, 430

Between Women: Domestics and Their Employers (Rollins), 75

Bias. *See* Research bias

Bisexual Center (San Francisco), 166

Boys in White (Becker et al.), 290, 419-420

Brazil, 36

British Columbia, 372

ABOUT THE EDITORS

Jaber F. Gubrium is Chair and Professor of Sociology at the University of Missouri, Columbia. His research focuses on the descriptive organization of personal identity, family, the life course, aging, and adaptations to illness. He is the editor of the *Journal of Aging Studies* and author or editor of more than 20 books, including *Living and Dying at Murray Manor, Caretakers, Describing Care, Oldtimers and Alzheimer's, Out of Control,* and *Speaking of Life.*

James A. Holstein is Professor of Sociology in the Department of Social and Cultural Sciences at Marquette University. He has studied diverse people-processing and social control settings, including courts, schools, and mental health agencies. He is the author or editor of numerous books, including *Court-Ordered Insanity, Dispute Domains and Welfare Claims, Reconsidering Social Constructionism,* and *Social Problems in Everyday Life.* He is also editor of the journal *Social Problems.*

As collaborators for more than a decade, Gubrium and Holstein have developed their distinctive constructionist approach to everyday life in a variety of texts, including *What Is Family? Constructing the Life Course, Aging and Everyday Life, The Active Interview,* and *The New Language of Qualitative Method.* They continue to explore the theoretical and methodological implications of interpretive practice as it unfolds at the intersection of narrative, culture, and social interaction. Their most recent works—companion volumes *The Self We Live By: Narrative Identity in a Postmodern World* and *Institutional Selves: Troubled Identities in a Postmodern World*—consider the impact on self-construction of a postmodern world of increasingly diverse institutional identities. They also have edited the *Handbook of Interview Research* and *Postmodern Interviewing.*

ABOUT THE CONTRIBUTORS

Patricia A. Adler and **Peter Adler** have written and worked together for more than 25 years. Patricia is Professor of Sociology at the University of Colorado. Peter is Professor of Sociology at the University of Denver, where he served as chair from 1987 to 1993. Their interests include qualitative methods, deviant behavior, drugs and society, sociology of sport, sociology of children, social theory, and work, occupations, and leisure. Together, they have published numerous articles and books, including *Momentum* (1981), *Wheeling and Dealing* (1985; second edition 1993), *Membership Roles in Field Research* (1987), *Backboards and Blackboards* (1991), and *Peer Power* (1998). They have served as editors of the *Journal of Contemporary Ethnography* (1986-94) and as the founding editors of *Sociological Studies of Child Development* (1985-92). Their coedited anthologies include *Constructions of Deviance,* now in its third edition, and *Sociological Odyssey.*

Paul Atkinson is Professor of Sociology at Cardiff University in Wales. He is currently directing two research projects on the social consequences of new genetic technologies and is completing an ethnographic study of an international opera company. His publications include the second edition of *Ethnography: Principles in Practice* (with Martyn Hammersley; 1995), *Sociological Readings and Rereadings* (1996), *Making Sense of Qualitative Data* (with Amanda Coffey; 1996), *Supervising the PhD* (with Sara Delamont and Odette Parry; 1997), and *The Doctoral Experience* (with Sara Delamont and Odette Parry; 2000). He is coeditor of the *Handbook of Ethnography* (2001) and of the journal *Qualitative Research.*

Carolyn D. Baker is a Reader in the Graduate School of Education at the University of Queensland, where she specializes in qualitative methodology, including ethnomethodology and conversation analysis. She has published widely on talk and interaction in institutional settings and in interviews. Her current research projects include studies of telephone calls to a computer software technical support line (with Mike Emmison, Queensland, and Alan Firth, Aalborg), studies of talk in interview narratives, and studies of talk at work in preschool and primary school classrooms. Her recent publications include "Membership Categorization and Interview Accounts" (in *Qualitative Research: Theory, Method and Practice,* edited by David Silverman, 1997); "Courtship and Marriage Stories: Orientations in Openings" (with G. Johnson; in *Narrative Inquiry,* 2000), and "A Child's Say in Parent-Teacher Talk at the Preschool: Doing Conversation Analytic Research in Early Childhood Settings" (with

M. Leiminer; in *Contemporary Issues in Early Childhood,* 2000). She is currently preparing for publication a book titled *Conducting and Analyzing Interviews.*

Leigh Berger received her M.A. in sociology and is pursuing her Ph.D. in the Department of Communication at the University of South Florida in Tampa. Her dissertation research is a narrative ethnography of a Messianic Jewish congregation that explores how its spirituality is experienced and also illuminates the personal journey of the ethnographer. She hopes her writing invites the reader to observe ethnographic encounters, to participate in them, and to come away with a better understanding of both their social worlds and themselves.

Charles L. Briggs is Professor and Chair of the Department of Ethnic Studies at the University of California, San Diego. He has been awarded fellowships by the Andrew W. Mellon Foundation, the National Endowment for the Humanities, the John Simon Guggenheim Memorial Foundation, the Woodrow Wilson International Center for Scholars, and the Center for Advanced Studies in the Behavioral Sciences. His books include *Learning How to Ask: A Sociolinguistic Appraisal of the Role of the Interview in Social Science Research, The Wood Carvers of Córdova, New Mexico: Social Dimensions of an Artistic "Revival," Competence in Performance: The Creativity of Tradition in Mexicano Verbal Art, The Lost Gold Mine of Juan Mondragón* (with Julián Josué Vigil), and *Stories in Times of Cholera: The Transnational Circulation of Bacteria and Racial Stigmata in a Venezuelan Epidemic* (forthcoming).

Richard Cándida Smith is Professor of History at the University of California at Berkeley. He is the author of *Utopia and Dissent: Art, Poetry, and Politics in California* (1995) and *Mallarmé's Children: Symbolism and the Renewal of Experience* (1999). He is currently working on a biography of the painter Jay DeFeo.

Kathy Charmaz is Professor of Sociology and Coordinator of the Faculty Writing Program at Sonoma State University. She assists faculty in writing for publication and teaches in the areas of sociological theory, social psychology, qualitative methods, health and illness, and aging and dying. Her books include two recent coedited volumes, *The Unknown Country: Death in Australia, Britain and the USA* and *Health, Illness, and Healing: Society, Social Context, and Self.* In addition, she has written *Good Days, Bad Days: The Self in Chronic Illness and Time,* which won awards from the Society for the Study of Symbolic Interaction and the Pacific Sociological Association. She currently serves as editor of *Symbolic Interaction.*

Susan E. Chase is Chair and Associate Professor of Sociology at the University of Tulsa. She also is a cofounder of the Women's Studies Program at the University of Tulsa. Her publications include *Mothers and Children: Feminist Analyses and Personal Narratives* (with Mary Rogers; 2001) and *Ambiguous Empowerment: The Work Narratives of Women School Superintendents* (1995).

Amanda Coffey lectures in sociology and research methods at Cardiff University in Wales. Her research interests focus on young people and citizenship, gender and education, and ethnographic representations. Her publications include *The Ethnographic Self* (1999), *Feminism and the Classroom Teacher* (with Sara Delamont; 2000), and *Education and Social Change* (2001). She is coeditor of the *Handbook of Ethnography* (2001).

Mick P. Couper is Senior Associate Research Scientist in the Survey Research Center and Adjunct Associate Professor in the Department of Sociology, both at the University of Michigan. He is also a Research Associate Professor in the Joint Program in Survey Methodology. He holds a Ph.D. in sociology from Rhodes University, an M.A. in applied social research from the University of Michigan, and an M.Soc.Sc. from the University of Cape Town. He is coauthor, with Robert Groves, of *Nonresponse in*

Household Interview Surveys (1998) and chief editor of *Computer Assisted Survey Information Collection* (1999). His current research focuses on nonresponse, the role of the interviewer, and computer-assisted survey data collection (including CATI, CAPI, audio-CASI, and Web surveys).

Marjorie L. DeVault is Associate Professor of Sociology and a member of the Women's Studies Program at Syracuse University. She received her Ph.D. from Northwestern University and writes on women's work, household life, and qualitative and feminist research methodologies. She is the author of *Feeding the Family: The Social Organization of Caring as Gendered Work* and *Liberating Method: Feminism and Social Research.*

Christopher Dunbar, Jr., is Assistant Professor in the Department of Educational Administration at Michigan State University. He received his Ph.D. in educational policy studies from the University of Illinois. His research interests include urban school leadership, ethnographic studies, alternative education, charter schools, and African American males and education. His work has been published in *Qualitative Inquiry, Cultural Studies,* and *Theory into Practice.* He teaches courses on schools, families and communities, organizational theory, and qualitative research.

Donna Eder is Professor of Sociology at Indiana University. She has written numerous journal articles and book chapters in the areas of gender, schooling, and women's culture. Her book *School Talk: Gender and Adolescent Culture* is an in-depth study of middle school peer cultures and the ways in which gender stereotypes are maintained and resisted. In her current research, she is conducting in-depth interviews with storytellers from different cultures to understand more fully the role of storytelling in teaching about social differences and social dynamics. She has also done group interviews with elementary students to identify how stories teach them to view differences across groups of people and cultures.

Carolyn Ellis is Professor of Communication and Sociology and Co-Director of the Institute for Interpretive Human Studies at the University of South Florida. She is the author of *Final Negotiations: A Story of Love, Loss, and Chronic Illness* and *Fisher Folk: Two Communities on Chesapeake Bay.* She is coeditor of *Composing Ethnography, Investigating Subjectivity, Social Perspectives on Emotion* (Volume 3), and the book series Ethnographic Alternatives. Her current research focuses on illness narratives, autoethnography, and emotional sociology.

Laura Fingerson is Assistant Professor in Sociology at the University of Wisconsin–Milwaukee. Her research interests include the sociology of children and adolescents; gender, race, and class; and qualitative and quantitative methods. Her current research explores adolescent girls' and boys' discourses on the body and menstruation. Through individual and single-sex group interviews, she uncovers what boys and girls are saying about the body and menstruation; how they use language to construct their discourses; how they socially construct the body, masculinity, and femininity; and how they use their bodies as sites of power and agency. Her recent work also includes an analysis of girls' collective and collaborative talk about family television programs and a quantitative look at parents' influences on their children's sexual decision making.

Kenneth M. George is Professor of Anthropology at the University of Wisconsin–Madison and specializes in the cultural politics of religion, art, and violence in Indonesia. He is the author of *Showing Signs of Violence* (1996), which was awarded the 1998 Harry J. Benda Prize by the Association for Asian Studies. His current research centers on contemporary Islamic art in Southeast Asia and the Indonesian artist A. D. Pirous. His recent articles include "Signature Work: Bandung, 1994" (in *Ethnos*) and "Some Things That Have Happened to 'The Sun after September 1965': Politics and the Interpretation of an Indonesian Painting" (in *Comparative Studies in Society and History*).

Sue Ellen Hansen is a Research Investigator in the Survey Research Center at the University of Michigan. She holds an M.A. in applied social research and a Ph.D. in sociology from the University of Michigan. She has extensive knowledge of computer-assisted interviewing systems and has worked closely with users of such systems. Her primary research interests concern the design and evaluation of computer-assisted data collection systems, interviewer-respondent interaction in the computer-assisted interview, and interviewer training and performance evaluation.

Travis S. K. Kong completed his doctoral dissertation, titled "The Voices in Between . . . : The Body Politics of Hong Kong Gay Men," at the University of Essex. His article "The Seduction of the Golden Boy: The Body Politics of Hong Kong Gay Men" is forthcoming in *Body and Society*. His research interests include sexuality and gender studies, media studies, cultural studies, and postcolonial studies. He currently lectures in the Department of Applied Social Studies at the Hong Kong Polytechnic University.

Dan Mahoney is a doctoral candidate in the Department of Sociology at the University of Essex in the United Kingdom. His dissertation is an investigation of how gay men construct notions of intimacy and belonging with friends, partners, or family members through the narrative practice of storytelling. His research interests are in the areas of intimacy, identity construction, sexuality, family relations, and qualitative research methods. He lectures at the Ryerson Polytechnic University in Toronto.

Chris Mann is employed by the University of Cambridge to conduct several innovative research studies that focus on equal opportunities issues in higher education. She is based in the Faculty of Social and Political Sciences and is a member of the Centre for Family Research. She is coauthor, with Fiona Stewart, of *Internet Communication and Qualitative Research: A Handbook for Researching Online* (2000).

Douglas W. Maynard is Professor of Sociology at the University of Wisconsin–Madison. He does research in the areas of ethnomethodology and conversation analysis, has interests in science and technology studies, and is particularly concerned with survey research as a set of technologies for the scientific study of society. With Hanneke Houtkoop-Steenstra, Nora Cate Schaeffer, and Hans van der Zouwen, he is coediting a book titled *Standardization and Tacit Knowledge: Interaction and Practice in the Survey Interview*. He also is coeditor (with John Heritage) of the forthcoming *Practicing Medicine: Talk and Action in Primary Care Encounters*. He has published extensively on "bad news" and "good news" in conversational and professional interaction and is the author of the forthcoming *Bad News, Good News, and the Benign Order of Everyday Life*.

Liza McCoy is Assistant Professor of Sociology at the University of Calgary in Alberta, Canada. Her research has looked at knowledge practices in the areas of health, education, management, and photographic representation.

Kirin Narayan is Professor of Anthropology and of the Languages and Cultures of Asia at the University of Wisconsin–Madison. Much of her work has addressed the place of stories in people's lives, whether in the form of folktales, oral histories, ballads, ethnographic narratives, or fiction. She is the author of *Storytellers, Saints, and Scoundrels: Folk Narrative in Hindu Religious Teaching* (1989), which won the 1990 Victor Turner Prize for Ethnographic Writing and was cowinner of the Elsie Clews Parsons Prize for Folklore. Working in collaboration with Urmila Devi Sood, a village woman in Northwest India, she is also author of *Mondays on the Dark Night of the Moon: Himalayan Foothill Folktales* (1997). She has published a novel, *Love Stars and All That* (1994), and has recently completed a second novel, *Becoming a Foreigner,* that builds from her fieldwork in the Himalayan foothills and interviews among second-generation South Asian Americans.

Laurence Parker is Associate Professor in the Department of Educational Policy Studies at the University of Illinois. His areas of specialization are urban educational policy, critical race theory and education, and higher-education desegregation. His most recent publication is a coedited book titled *Race Is . . . Race Isn't . . . : Critical Race Theory and Qualitative Studies in Education.*

Ken Plummer is Professor of Sociology at the University of Essex. He is author or editor of several books, including *The Making of the Modern Homosexual* (1982), *Telling Sexual Stories* (1995), and *Documents of Life* (second edition, 2000). Currently, he is writing a book titled *Intimate Citizenship* and is the editor of the journal *Sexualities.*

Blake D. Poland is Associate Professor in the Department of Public Health Sciences at the University of Toronto. His research focuses primarily on community development as an arena of practice for health professionals and on lay perceptions of tobacco control. His work is informed by a critical-interpretive perspective and social justice orientation. He also has published on the methodological and epistemological aspects of qualitative research in *Qualitative Inquiry, Health Promotion International, Canadian Journal of Public Health,* and the *Operational Geographer,* as well as in several book chapters. He is lead editor of *Settings for Health Promotion: Linking Theory and Practice* (2000).

Shulamit Reinharz has been Professor of Sociology at Brandeis University since 1991, the first and only woman to hold that rank at the university. In 1992, she became Director of the Women's Studies Program and developed a graduate degree component along with a National Board, a program on domestic violence, and a program on women's health. Her publications include four books, *Feminist Methods in Social Research* (1992), *Qualitative Gerontology* (1987), *On Becoming a Social Scientist* (1979/84), and *Psychology and Community Change* (1984). She serves on the editorial boards of many sociology journals. In the field of Jewish women's studies, she has created an academic journal and is the editor of a book series.

Catherine Kohler Riessman is Research Professor, Department of Sociology, Boston College. Her research has been in medical sociology, especially women's health, and in the narrative study of lives. Using narrative methods of interviewing and analysis, she has examined accounts of a variety of life events that disrupt individuals' assumptions about biographical order, specifically divorce, chronic illness, and infertility. She has conducted fieldwork in South India on childless women, supported by an Indo-American Fellowship (CIES). Her books include *Divorce Talk* (1990) and *Narrative Analysis* (1993). She has published articles in *Gender & Society, Narrative Inquiry, Women and Health,* and the *American Journal of Public Health.* She also has contributed chapters to edited books on narrative approaches in the social sciences.

Dalia Rodriguez is a graduate student in the Department of Educational Policy Studies at the University of Illinois. Her main research interests focus on the social context of education, with an emphasis in educational policy, including racial/ethnic inequality in the legal and educational contexts.

Anne Ryen is Associate Professor at Agder University College and a Senior Researcher at Agder Research Foundation, Kristiansand, Norway. Her main interests are qualitative methodology, fringe benefits, and social security. She has conducted research in South Africa, Kenya, Tanzania, and Indonesia. She is currently leading three research clusters, on gender-related issues in Tanzania, on local government in developing countries, and on local government in Norway. She is also conducting research on social security in Indonesia and on fringe benefits in Norway. Her most recent publication is "Marking Boundaries: Culture as Category Work" (with David Silverman, in *Qualitative Inquiry,* 2000). She is in the process of coediting a book titled *Child Care, Ethics, and Methodology* and of writing another titled *The Interview* (both to be published in Norway).

Nora Cate Schaeffer is Professor of Sociology at the University of Wisconsin–Madison, where she teaches courses in survey research methods and conducts research on issues in survey design and questionnaire development. Before receiving her doctorate from the University of Chicago, she worked at the National Opinion Research Center. She has taught questionnaire design at the Summer Institute of the Survey Research Center at the University of Michigan and through the University of Michigan–University of Maryland Joint Program in Survey Methodology. She has served on the Panel to Evaluate Alternative Census Methodology for the National Research Council of the National Academy of Science; on the National Science Foundation Advisory Committee for the Social, Behavioral and Economic Sciences; and on the governing Council of the American Association for Public Opinion Research. She has been a member of the editorial boards for *Public Opinion Quarterly, Sociological Methods & Research,* and *Sociological Methodology.*

Michael L. Schwalbe is Associate Professor of Sociology at North Carolina State University. He is the author of *Unlocking the Iron Cage: The Men's Movement, Gender Politics, and American Culture* (1996) and *The Sociologically Examined Life* (1998). Currently, he is writing a biography based on the life histories of two working-class black men in the American South.

Clive F. Seale is a Reader in Medical Sociology at the Department of Sociology, Goldsmiths College, University of London. His books include *Researching Society and Culture* (1998), *Constructing Death: The Sociology of Dying and Bereavement* (1998), and *The Quality of Qualitative Research* (1999). He is currently engaged in a study of media representations of dying and grief.

Roger W. Shuy is Distinguished Research Professor of Linguistics at Georgetown University, where he founded and then directed the Sociolinguistics Program for 30 years, interrupted only by a term as Chair of the Linguistics Department. One of the founders of the American Association of Applied Linguistics, he has also served as its President. He has conducted research on regional and social dialects, literacy, medical discourse, classroom language, and, for the past 20 years, the intersection of language and law. Of his 27 books, the most recent are *Language Crimes: The Use and Abuse of Language Evidence in the Courtroom* (1996), *The Language of Confession, Interrogation, and Deception* (1998), and *Bureaucratic Language in Government and Business* (1998). Forthcoming is *A Few Months to Live,* an ethnographic study of terminally ill patients. Since his retirement from teaching in 1996, he continues to consult with attorneys on law cases and to carry out research from his Montana home.

Fiona Stewart is Chief Knowledge Officer at Brands Online Ltd, an Australian on-line research company, and Director of Realworld Research & Communications. Her interests are currently focused upon the use of WAP technologies for consumer polling and on-line market research. She is coauthor, with Chris Mann, of *Internet Communication and Qualitative Research: A Handbook for Researching Online* (2000).

G. Clare Wenger is Professor of Gerontology, Director of CSPRD, Associate Director of IMSCAR, and Director of Postgraduate Studies in Gerontology at the University of Wales, Bangor. She has been involved in research in the aging field since 1978, including a 20-year study of the aging process in rural Wales. She contributes regularly to the doctoral program in gerontology of the Sanders-Brown Center for Aging at the University of Kentucky and is International Adviser to the Centre for Gerontology and Geriatric Medicine at the Medical Institute of Baharati Vidyapeeth Deemed University, India. She is on the editorial board of the *Journal of Cross-Cultural Gerontology* and has published widely in the field of aging. Her main areas of interest are the family sociology of older people, social networks, comparative transnational research, and the use of social research findings in social policy development.

Michelle Wolkomir is Assistant Professor of Sociology at Centenary College of Louisiana. Her current research project examines the lives of gay and ex-gay Christian men, focusing on how these men resolve the identity dilemmas that arise from the conflict between Christian doctrine and gay sexuality.